MW01596864

PAPERS OF THE
LEEDS INTERNATIONAL LATIN SEMINAR

ISSN 1362-3818

TENTH VOLUME
1998

ARCA
Classical and Medieval Texts, Papers and Monographs

38

General Editors
Neil Adkin (University of Nebraska – Lincoln)
Francis Cairns (University of Leeds)
Robin Seager (University of Liverpool)
Frederick Williams (Queen's University, Belfast)
Assistant Editor: Sandra Cairns

ISSN 0309–5541

PAPERS OF THE LEEDS INTERNATIONAL LATIN SEMINAR

TENTH VOLUME 1998

**Greek Poetry, Drama, Prose
Roman Poetry**

Edited by
Francis Cairns and Malcolm Heath

FRANCIS CAIRNS

Published by Francis Cairns (Publications) Ltd
c/o The University, Leeds, LS2 9JT, Great Britain

First published 1998

Copyright © Francis Cairns (Publications) 1998

All rights reserved. No part of this publication may be reproduced,
stored in a retrieval system, or transmitted in any form or by any
means, electronic, mechanical, photocopying, recording, or
otherwise, without the prior written permission of the Publisher.

British Library Cataloguing in Publication
A catalogue record for this book is available from the British
Library

ISBN 0 905205 95 2

Printed in Great Britain by
Antony Rowe Limited, Chippenham, Wiltshire

CONTENTS

MICHAEL REICHEL (Universität Freiburg i.Br.)
How oral is Homer's narrative?   1

MALCOLM HEATH (University of Leeds)
Was Homer a Roman?   23

DOUGLAS L. CAIRNS (University of Leeds)
῎Αωτος, ῎Ανθος, and the death of Archemorus in Bacchylides'
ninth Ode   57

J.G. HOWIE (University of Edinburgh)
Thucydides and Pindar: the *Archaeology* and *Nemean* 7   75

IAN RUTHERFORD (University of Reading)
Theoria as theatre: pilgrimage in Greek drama   131

C. ANNE WILSON (University of Leeds)
Wine rituals, Maenads and Dionysian fire   157

A.S. HOLLIS (Keble College, Oxford)
Nicander and Lucretius   169

ERNST A. SCHMIDT (Eberhard-Karls-Universität Tübingen)
Freedom and ownership: a contribution to the discussion of
Vergil's first *Eclogue*   185

FRANCIS CAIRNS (University of Leeds)
Tibullus 2.2   203

ANDREAS MICHALOPOULOS (University of Leeds)
Some cases of Propertian etymologising   235

ALEX HARDIE (Royal Holloway College, London / FCO)
Horace, the Paean and Roman *Choreia* (*Odes* 4.6)   251

R.K. GIBSON (University of Manchester)
Meretrix or matrona? Stereotypes in *Ars Amatoria* 3   295

KARL GALINSKY (University of Texas at Austin)
The speech of Pythagoras at Ovid *Metamorphoses* 15.75–478   313

K.M. COLEMAN (Harvard University)
Martial Book 8 and the politics of AD 93   337

LINDSAY WATSON (University of Sydney)
Martial 8.21, literary *lusus*, and imperial panegyric   359

ALAIN M. GOWING (University of Washington)
Greek advice for a Roman senator: Cassius Dio and
the Dialogue between Philiscus and Cicero (38.18–29)   373

Postscript   391
Meetings of the Leeds International Latin Seminar, 1988–1998   393
PLLS: Contents of volumes 1–10   401
PLLS: Author-index of volumes 1–10   406

PAPERS OF THE LEEDS INTERNATIONAL LATIN SEMINAR   TENTH VOLUME (1998) 1–22
Published by Francis Cairns (Publications) Ltd (Leeds 1998). ARCA 38. ISBN 0 905205 95 2

HOW ORAL IS HOMER'S NARRATIVE?

MICHAEL REICHEL
Universität Freiburg i.Br.

I. Orality vs. literacy in Homer: the search for criteria

Among followers of the Parry/Lord school the nature of Homeric composition seems no longer to be considered an open question. The orality of the Homeric epics is taken as a point of departure for individual studies, not as a theory which still has to be proved or, at least, weighed against other theories. So scholars who support the notion that writing played an important role in the composition of the *Iliad* and the *Odyssey* find themselves in an almost apologetic position. In the present paper I shall attempt to challenge the oralist view of Homer, which has become almost the new orthodoxy in Homeric scholarship.

The often-heard argument that technical difficulties alone would have made it impossible to write down a poem of approximately 15,000 lines in the eighth or seventh century is unconvincing. The Akkadian *Gilgamesh Epic* in the Ninivite recension, a well-structured epic of about 3,600 lines, was written in a cuneiform script on clay tablets. The alphabetic script as a writing system and papyrus or parchment as writing materials were incomparably easier to handle. Thus, by an *argumentum a fortiori*, we should not for purely technical reasons exclude the notion of written Homeric epics.[1] Besides, writing techniques did not change substantially between the ages of Homer and Herodotus, who committed an even longer narrative to writing.

---

[1]   It is not of primary importance for my approach whether Homer wrote himself or dictated to a scribe. In the latter case, however, my picture of Homer would be rather different from Lord's 'oral dictating poet' since, in my view, writing helped not only to preserve the poems but also in their composition.

The issue of oral vs. written composition of the Homeric epics cannot be settled by focusing attention on metre, enjambement, formulas, themes, type-scenes, ring-composition and the like. These elements of epic style and of what might be called the 'narrative microstructure' of the poems are not likely to be affected to any great extent by the introduction of writing, at least not at a very early stage of written epic poetry. More valuable criteria for distinguishing between oral and written epic are the poet's capacity for innovation in subject-matter, for plot-construction and generally for what can be subsumed under 'macrostructure'. This aspect of Homer's art has largely been ignored in recent decades as a consequence (perhaps unintentional) of the findings of Parry and Lord. In order to establish points of comparison between Greek epic and living oral traditions of heroic epic, many scholars concentrated on those elements of the poems which exhibited similar features, i.e. the stylistic and microstructural elements already mentioned. Oralist approaches to Homeric macrostructure have been confined to establishing 'narrative patterns' and 'narrative sequences' in a rather narrow sense. Paradoxically, the comparative method in the field of oral studies has served to broaden our understanding of epic poetry only to a limited extent. In many ways it has led rather to a neglect of those features which reveal an individual poet's style and which are not traceable in other poems or poetic traditions. As a consequence, contemporary Homeric scholarship has lost sight of some important discoveries about Homeric poetry made many years ago. It is enough to mention here two books, both coincidentally published in 1938: Samuel Bassett's *The Poetry of Homer*[2] and Wolfgang Schadewaldt's *Iliasstudien*.[3] Both works are more often referred to than used, although many of their observations on Homeric structure have immediate relevance to the issue of oral vs. written composition in Homer.[4] A typical example of current oralist argumentation is the following quotation from Minna Skafte Jensen:[5]

---

[2] S.E. Bassett *The Poetry of Homer* (Sather Classical Lectures 15, Berkeley 1938).

[3] W. Schadewaldt *Iliasstudien* (Leipzig [1]1938, [2]1943, repr. Darmstadt [3]1966).

[4] Schadewaldt wanted to uphold the unity of the *Iliad* against proponents of the older analytic theories which dominated Homeric studies till the early 20th century. At that time he was not concerned with the then evolving oralist approaches to Homer, but he summed up his earlier research in the light of the oralist theory in his last book: *Der Aufbau der Ilias: Strukturen und Konzeptionen* (Frankfurt a.M. 1975). K. Reinhardt *Die Ilias und ihr Dichter* ed. by U. Hölscher (Göttingen 1961) is also important for our understanding of the large-scale structure of the *Iliad*.

[5] M. Skafte Jensen *The Homeric Question and the Oral-Formulaic Theory* (Copenhagen 1980) 29.

Matters such as formulas, type scenes, lack of enjambement, etc., can be measured; ... nobody can deny that they are there. They may be considered details as compared to the visions of a Schadewaldt, but in an argumentation concerning compositorial technique they must carry much more weight.

After so much work on formulas, themes and other traces of oral tradition in the Homeric poems, it is time once more to pay close attention to macrostructure, as was done before the paradigm-shift in Homeric studies brought about by the Parry/Lord school. One of the more recent areas of Homeric research, narratology, as exemplified in the monographs by Irene de Jong,[6] Scott Richardson[7], James Morrison,[8] and Lillian Doherty,[9] is supportive of this enterprise.[10] It should however be noted that, long before the term 'narratology' was coined by Tzvetan Todorov in his *Grammaire du Décaméron* in 1969, many studies of the Homeric poems, especially those of unitarian provenance, had applied methods and generated observations that might justly be called 'narratological'.[11]

In the following sections (II–V) I shall discuss briefly four different yet interconnected aspects of Homeric macrostructure, in particular in

---

[6] I.J.F. de Jong *Narrators and Focalizers: The Presentation of the Story in the Iliad* (Amsterdam 1987).

[7] S. Richardson *The Homeric Narrator* (Nashville 1990).

[8] J.V. Morrison *Homeric Misdirection: False Predictions in the Iliad* (Ann Arbor 1992).

[9] L.E. Doherty *Siren Songs: Gender, Audiences, and Narrators in the Odyssey* (Ann Arbor 1995).

[10] For narratological investigations of Homer see also: B. Hellwig *Raum und Zeit im homerischen Epos* (Spudasmata 2, Hildesheim 1964); W. Suerbaum 'Die Ich-Erzählungen des Odysseus. Überlegungen zur epischen Technik der Odyssee' *Poetica* 2 (1968) 150-77; B. Effe 'Entstehung und Funktion 'personaler' Erzählweisen in der Erzählliteratur der Antike' *Poetica* 7 (1975) 135-57 (on Homer: 141-4); *id.* 'Epische Objektivität und auktoriales Erzählen' *Gymn.* 90 (1983) 171-86 (on Homer: 174-8). J. Latacz 'Zeus' Reise zu den Aithiopen (Zu Ilias 1,304-495)' in G. Kurz / D. Müller / W. Nicolai (eds.) *Gnomosyne: Menschliches Denken und Handeln in der frühgriechischen Literatur (Festschrift W. Marg)* (München 1981) 53-80; repr. in J. Latacz *Erschließung der Antike: Kleine Schriften zur Literatur der Griechen und Römer* (Stuttgart and Leipzig 1994) 175-203; M.W. Edwards *Homer: Poet of the Iliad* (Baltimore and London 1987) 29-41; M. Lynn-George *Epos: Word, Narrative and the Iliad* (Basingstoke and London 1988). For a survey of scholarship in this area see E.-R. Schwinge 'Homerische Epen und Erzählforschung' in J. Latacz (ed.) *Zweihundert Jahre Homer-Forschung: Rückblick und Ausblick* (Stuttgart and Leipzig 1991) 482-512; I.J.F. de Jong 'Homer and narratology' in J. Morris / B. Powell (eds.) *A New Companion to Homer* (Mnemos. suppl. 163, Leiden – New York – Köln 1997) 305-25. Extensive bibliographies are included in the monographs by de Jong (above, n.6) and Richardson (above, n.7).

[11] This is already true of studies from the 19th century such as C. Kraut *Die epische Prolepsis, nachgewiesen in der Ilias* (Gymn.-Progr. Tübingen 1863), and Zielinski's investigation (below n 13), discussed in section II of this paper.

the *Iliad*.[12] I would stress that my approach is not narratological *stricto sensu*, i.e. it is not a systematic analysis of narrative differences such as that offered by de Jong. Section VI will compare Homer's narrative techniques with those used in a South Slavic oral epic on which oralists have focused attention and which has often been considered as the best illustration for oral composition of the Homeric epics.

II. Parallel action

Almost a hundred years ago Thaddaeus Zielinski published a study of parallel action in Homer which has become one of the milestones of classical scholarship.[13] Zielinski discovered certain regularities in the way Homer handles different threads of plot. He explained these regularities by a 'law of chronological incompatibility', which has been referred to since then as 'Zielinski's law'. As it happens, it is the only instance in our discipline where a purely literary phenomenon, rather than a linguistic or metrical regularity, has been raised to the status of a 'law' named after its πρῶτος εὑρετής. Many scholars have tried to modify or even to refute 'Zielinski's law' with discussions being concentrated on very intricate details of Homer's poetical usage of time. The debate has focused mainly on two issues: first, to what extent and how does Homer's narration present simultaneous events? Second, how valid is Zielinski's distinction between 'real action' ('wirkliche Handlung') and 'imaginary action' ('scheinbare Handlung') in terms of chronological sequence? This distinction mainly overlaps the now universally acknowledged concepts of 'narrated time' and 'narrative time' (although it is by no means identical with them). A thorough treatment of the entire subject has recently been published by Antonios Rengakos.[14]

---

[12] Within the scope of this article I must restrict myself to a few examples, although cumulative evidence plays an important role in my argument. The points made here I have discussed in detail in my book *Fernbeziehungen in der Ilias* (ScriptOralia 62, Tübingen 1994), and in some articles: 'Retardationstechniken in der Ilias' in W. Kullmann / M. Reichel (eds.) *Der Übergang von der Mündlichkeit zur Literatur bei den Griechen* (ScriptOralia 30, Tübingen 1990) 125-51; 'Gräzistische Bemerkungen zur Struktur des Gilgamesch-Epos' in B. Brogyanyi / R. Lipp (eds.) *Historical Philology: Greek, Latin, and Romance. Papers in Honor of Oswald Szemerény* vol. II (Amsterdam–Philadelphia 1992) 187-208; 'Narratologische Methoden in der Homerforschung' in H. Tristram (ed.) *Neue Methoden der Epenforschung — New Methods in the Research of Epic* (forthcoming).

[13] Th. Zielinski 'Die Behandlung gleichzeitiger Ereignisse im antiken Epos. Erster Theil' (Philologus Suppl. 8, Leipzig 1899–1901) 405–49.

[14] A. Rengakos 'Zeit und Gleichzeitigkeit in den homerischen Epen' *A&A* 41 (1995) 1–33, which includes an almost complete account of scholarly literature on this question,

Homeric use of parallel action represents an advanced stage in a historical morphology of narrative techniques. In the most primitive epic the narrator follows only one thread of plot, without diverting his attention to actions happening at different places at the same time, as was already observed by Axel Olrik in 1909:[15]

> Moderne dichtung [...] liebt die verschiedenen fäden der handlung in einander zu verwickeln. die volkspoesie hält den einzelnen strang fest, sie ist immer e i n s t r ä n g i g. sie geht nicht zurück, um fehlende voraussetzungen nachzuholen. ist eine vorgeschichte notwendig, dann wird sie im gespräche gegeben.

An example confirming this statement will be discussed in section VI below. This simple method of story-telling can be hypothesised for some of the oral epic that preceded Homer. But other pre-Homeric epic almost certainly contained a simple form of parallel action; only thus can the highly developed use of different threads of plot in Homeric epos be explained. In any case Homer's ability to control the actions on the many different planes of his narrative is one of the strongest arguments in support of written composition, though it has rarely been used as such. In the *Iliad* the narrator constantly moves between different scenes: the Achaean camp, the city of Troy, Olympus, Mount Ida, and the battlefield; the battlefield too is divided into the Achaean and the Trojan sides and subdivided into many different places of action.[16] Bassett counted in the *Iliad* 76 changes of scene without movement of a character and 149 changes with such a movement.[17] On the first count a change of scene occurs about every 200 lines, and on the second about every 70 lines. Whenever the poet shifts between different scenes, he painstakingly calculates the time that passes along

---

shows that 'Zielinski's law' has been understood in three different ways by other scholars (1ff.). He emphasises that Homer does indeed narrate simultaneous events (17ff.). Furthermore, he tries to prove that those actions that are narrated as successive events by Homer, but are supposed by Zielinski and his followers to happen 'in reality' simultaneously, must for purely logical reasons be taken to happen one after another (20ff.).

[15] A. Olrik 'Epische Gesetze der Volksdichtung' *Zs. für dt. Altertum u. dt. Lit.* 51 (1909) 1–12, here 8 (the conventions of the original are preserved in the quotation).

[16] Not only Homer's poetic use of time but also his use of space demonstrates his overall control of the narrative and his careful planning. Cf. J. Cuillandre *La droite et la gauche dans les poèmes homériques* ... (Rennes 1943) 15–110. See also A. Thornton *Homer's Iliad: its Composition and the Motif of Supplication* (Hypomnemata 81, Göttingen 1984) 150–63; M.M. Willcock *The Iliad of Homer, ed. with Introd. and Comm., vol. II* (Basingstoke and London 1984) 225.

[17] Bassett *The Poetry of Homer* (above n.2) 55. Battle scenes are disregarded in this calculation.

one or more diverse lines of action. This is well exemplified by *Iliad* 6, where the story-line alternates between the battlefield and the city of Troy and, within Troy, between the actions centred around different characters (Hector, Hecabe, Paris). Homer pays scrupulous attention to the chronological ordering of parallel events by segmenting them into smaller parts and by coordinating these segments. Zielinski has given many instances of this technique, which he described as 'analysirend-desultorische Methode'. Even more impressive are those cases where a very long time-span (i.e. of narrative time) elapses before the narrator resumes a particular thread of plot. In 11.806–48 Patroclus, returning from Nestor, meets the wounded Eurypylus and takes care of him; in 15.390–405 Patroclus leaves Eurypylus' tent and returns to Achilles. The two passages are separated by more than 2,000 verses — about twice the average length of an entire heroic epic in the South Slavic tradition. A similar case is Nestor attending the wounded Machaon. In 11.516ff./618ff. he accompanies him to his tent; in 14.1–8 — about 1,500 verses later — Nestor leaves Machaon. In both instances the poet connects the latter scene with the former by explicit back-references. In 3.421–48 we have the bedroom scene between Paris and Helen; this thread of plot is taken up again in 6.313–69, approximately 1,800 verses later, when Hector meets with Paris and Helen in their house. Tilman Krischer sees in Homer's use of parallel action a natural result of an oral poet's technique;[18] but, to my knowledge, no corroborative evidence from oral poetry has ever been adduced to support this claim. Homer's ability to develop several threads of action simultaneously and to 'synchronise' them presupposes a written mode of composition.

III. Cross-references

Frequent references to earlier or later sections of the narrative are one of the most characteristic features of Homeric epic.[19] Forward-references were already recognised by the ancient commentators on

---

[18] T. Krischer *Formale Konventionen der homerischen Epik* (Zetemata 56, München 1971) 120.

[19] The standard works on this subject are G.E. Duckworth *Foreshadowing and Suspense in the Epics of Homer, Apollonius, and Vergil* (Diss. Princeton 1933) and Schadewaldt *Iliasstudien* (above n.3). Cf. also Hellwig *Raum und Zeit* (above n.10) 46–58; Thornton *Homer's Iliad* (above n.16) 59–72; de Jong *Narrators and Focalizers* (above n.6) 81–90; Richardson *Homeric Narrator* (above n.7) 132–9 *et passim*; Morrison *Homeric Misdirection* (above n.8); O. Taplin *Homeric Soundings: The Shaping of the Iliad* (Oxford 1992) 8f. *et passim*. For a survey of earlier research and further literature see my *Fernbeziehungen in der Ilias* (above n.12) 12–33.

Homer, who described them under labels such as προαναφώνησις, πρόληψις, or προοικονομία.[20] The epic narrator himself can tell his audience about the future course of action as he does in the proems of the *Iliad* and the *Odyssey*. Homer also likes to foreshadow future events by commenting on actions or speeches of his characters (e.g. *Il*. 2.419–20; 11.604). The authorial forecasts almost always give reliable information about the future. The same is true of announcements made by Zeus, who not only prophesies future events, but can also influence them. Speeches by Zeus often include a lengthy and detailed anticipation of things to come (e.g. *Il*. 8.470–77; 15.49–77; *Od*. 1.64–79; 5.29–42). In contrast, speeches by mortal characters tend to be much less certain and definite. They can be divided into several partly overlapping categories: oath (e.g. *Il*. 1.239–44); promise (e.g. *Il*. 18.333–7); declaration of intention (e.g. *Il*. 22.416–20); threat (e.g. *Il*. 20.452–3); wish (e.g. *Od*. 4.333–46); request (e.g. *Od*. 7.151–2); expectation (e.g. *Il*. 9.654–5); aspiration (e.g. *Il*. 16.83–6); declaration of fear (e.g. *Il*. 18.261–83); worry (e.g. *Od*. 20.37–43); order (e.g. *Od*. 16.267–307); prohibition (e.g. *Od*. 2.373–6); recommendation (e.g. *Il*. 11.794–803); admonition (e.g. *Il*. 9.247ff.); prayer (e.g. *Il*. 16.233–48); allusion (e.g. *Od*. 16.99–104) etc. The distinction between certain and uncertain announcements, which is determined by the narrative perspective and by the internal logic of the narration, is strictly observed in Homeric epic. Homer also frequently makes back-references to earlier parts of the story, sometimes with a curious but striking observance of detail (e.g. *Il*. 17.24–8; 19.51–3; 21.396–9). At certain points too the poet likes to sum up what has happened so far. Recapitulations of this type (Gr. ἀνακεφαλαίωσις) are more frequent in the *Odyssey* than in the *Iliad* (*Il*. 18.429–61; *Od*. 7.241–97; 17.108–49; 23.310–43; 24.121–90).

Foreshadowing of future events is also a characteristic of heroic epics from other traditions. It is very much in evidence in the Germanic epics of the middle ages,[21] e.g. in the OE. *Beowulf*,[22] or in the MHG.

---

[20] See G.E. Duckworth 'προαναφώνησις in the scholia to Homer' *AJP* 52 (1931) 320–38.

[21] Cf. A. Gerz *Rolle und Funktion der epischen Vorausdeutung im Mhd. Epos* (Germanische Studien 97, Berlin 1930), who adduces examples from more than 40 epic poems. See also H. Burger 'Vorausdeutung und Erzählstruktur in mittelalterlichen Texten' in S. Sonderegger / A.M. Haas / H. Burger (eds.) *Typologia Litterarum: Festschrift für M. Wehrli* (Zürich 1969) 125–53; repr. in A. Ritter (ed.) *Zeitgestaltung in der Erzählkunst* (WdF 447, Darmstadt 1978) 247–77.

Nibelungenlied.[23] In the latter poem these announcements usually, although not exclusively, appear in the fourth line of the 'Nibelungenstrophe'. Foreshadowing by allegorical dreams is a device used regularly in the OF. *Chanson de Roland*[24] and in the Akk. *Gilgamesh Epic*.[25] It also appears in the *Nibelungenlied* and in the Homeric *Odyssey* (e.g. 4.795–841; 19.535–69).[26]

The internal reference system of the Homeric epics is the clearest mark of 'textuality' in A.B. Lord's definition: "By textuality I mean that awareness, on the part of the composer, of the words he is using, of a text as such — as against content".[27] The large number of cross-references, their richness in detail, their correctness and their balanced distribution can only be explained by the existence of a fixed text, which, in turn, is hardly conceivable without the aid of writing.[28] While the written mode of composition is the *causa efficiens* of Homer's elaborate technique of cross-referencing, its *causa finalis* is to be seen in the oral performance of the poems.[29] Cross-references help the

---

[22] Cf. A. Bonjour 'The use of anticipation in Beowulf' in *Twelve Beowulf Papers 1940–1960 with Additional Comments* (Neuchâtel – Genève 1962) 11–28; Ch. Moorman 'Suspense and foreknowledge in 'Beowulf'' *College English* 15 (1953/54) 379–83; A.G. Brodeur *The Art of Beowulf* (Berkeley – Los Angeles 1959) esp. 220ff.

[23] Cf. A. Bonjour 'Anticipations et prophéties dans le 'Nibelungenlied'' *Et. Germ.* 7 (1952) 241–51; S. Beyschlag 'Die Funktion der epischen Vorausdeutung im Aufbau des Nibelungenliedes' *Beitr. z. Gesch. d. dt. Spr. u. Lit.* (Halle) 76 (1954) 38–55 (including a list of more than 100 foreshadowings); B. Wachinger *Studien zum Nibelungenlied: Vorausdeutungen — Aufbau — Motivierung* (Tübingen 1960) 4–55.

[24] Cf. K.-J. Steinmeyer *Untersuchungen zur allegorischen Bedeutung der Träume im altfranzösischen Rolandslied* (Langue et Parole 5, München 1963).

[25] On narrative devices in the *Gilgamesh Epic*, cf. K. Hecker *Untersuchungen zur akkadischen Epik* (Alter Orient und Altes Testament, Sonderreihe Bd. 8, Kevelaer / Neukirchen-Vluyn 1974) *passim*; J.H. Tigay *The Evolution of the Gilgamesh Epic* (Philadelphia 1982) esp. 3–10; Reichel 'Gräzistische Bemerkungen zur Struktur des Gilgamesch-Epos' (above n.12).

[26] On dreams in the Homeric epics, cf. J. Hundt *Der Traumglaube bei Homer* (Greifswald 1935); A.R. Amory 'The Gates of Horn and Ivory' *YCS* 20 (1966) 1–57; A.H.M. Kessels *Studies on the Dream in Greek Literature* (Utrecht 1978); J.F. Morris ''Dream scenes' in Homer, a study in variation' *TAPA* 113 (1983) 39–54.

[27] A.B. Lord *The Singer Resumes the Tale* ed. by Mary Louise Lord (Ithaca and London 1995) 21.

[28] It is not necessary here to repeat the arguments of the controversial debate about the fixing of the text of the Homeric epics by C.M. Bowra, A.B. Lord, G.S. Kirk, Adam Parry, and many others. For recent contributions to this discussion see M.L. West 'Archaische Heldendichtung: Singen und Schreiben', in Kullmann/Reichel (eds.) *Übergang* (above n.12) 33–50; B.P. Powell *Homer and the Origin of the Greek Alphabet* (Cambridge 1991) esp. 221–37; G. Nagy *Homeric Questions* (Austin 1996).

[29] Cf. Schadewaldt *Iliasstudien* (above n.3) 114; J.A. Notopoulos 'Continuity and interconnexion in Homeric oral composition' *TAPA* 82 (1951) 81–101.

audience to follow the story-line of a large-scale epic.[30] In this con-
nection it should be stressed that the core plot of the *Iliad* is probably
Homer's own invention, as the neoanalytic method has demonstrated.[31]
Many motifs of the epic will have originated in earlier tradition, par-
ticularly in the oral antecedents of the *Epic Cycle*. But the structure of
the main plot and two of the main characters, Hector and Patroclus,
cannot be traced back to pre-Homeric poetry and mythology. So Homer
could not expect his listeners to be familiar with the essentials of his
tale. For that reason cross-references became much more important in
the *Iliad* than in epics narrating often-heard stories.

Although statistics have not always had healthy effects on Homeric
scholarship, I venture to offer some mathematical support for my
argument. Within certain limitations, it is possible to quantify the
internal reference system and to project it onto a diagram. I restrict
myself to explicit and self-evident cross-references between the 24
books of the *Iliad*. Although the book-division in its present form is not
likely to be due to Homer himself,[32] the average length of these
sections of the epic may well have corresponded to that of the units of
recitation by rhapsodes.[33] For our present purpose, this partition can
serve as a useful basis. Between two given books,[34] for example books
1 and 9, only one forward-reference and one backward-reference will
be included in the calculations to be offered (i.e. 1→9 and 9→1),

---

[30] Another important feature of the *Iliad* is that about two dozen human and divine
characters are depicted as clearly differentiated individuals: Achilles, Hector,
Patroclus, Agamemnon, Nestor, Odysseus, Diomedes, Ajax, Menelaus, Paris, Aeneas,
Sarpedon, Polydamas, Helen, Andromache, Priam, Hecabe, Zeus, Hera, Athene,
Apollo, Poseidon, Thetis. The poet introduces many of these characters at regular
intervals and very often he connects their several appearances through forward- and
back-references. Cf. my *Fernbeziehungen in der Ilias* (above n.12) 99–324, where I
tried to follow up all the cross-references through the different threads of plot centred
around individual characters.

[31] Cf. W. Kullmann 'Oral poetry theory and neoanalysis in Homeric research' *GRBS* 25
(1984) 307–23, esp. 316, 319; repr. in *Homerische Motive: Beiträge zur Entstehung,
Eigenart und Wirkung von Ilias und Odyssee* ed. R.J. Müller (Stuttgart 1992) 140–55,
esp. 148, 151. For details, see *id. Die Quellen der Ilias (Troischer Sagenkreis)*
(Hermes Einzelschriften 14, Wiesbaden 1960).

[32] For different views on the origin of Homeric book-division see e.g. C.H. Whitman
Homer and the Heroic Tradition (Cambridge/Mass. 1958) 283; G.P. Goold 'The
nature of Homeric composition' *ICS* 2 (1977) 1–34, here 26–30; Taplin *Homeric
Soundings* (above n.19) 285–93; K. Stanley *The Shield of Homer: Narrative Structure
in the Iliad* (Princeton 1993) 249–61 *et passim*; N. Richardson *The Iliad: a com-
mentary. Volume VI: books 21–24* (Cambridge 1993) 20–21.

[33] Cf. J.A. Notopoulos 'Studies in early Greek oral poetry' *HSCP* 68 (1964) 1–77, esp.
1–18, here 10–11.

[34] Cross-references within one and the same book are here disregarded.

although the actual number of connecting links between two books may be much larger. In these terms, we might theoretically expect to find as many as 552 cross-references within the *Iliad*: $24 \times 23 = 552$. In fact 149 cross-references can be identified. On this calculation, the 'degree of interlocking' is 27%. If cross-references between adjacent books of the *Iliad* are excluded, the maximum number of potential long-distance connections ('Fernbeziehungen') would be 506 — since the first and last books of the epic may each be linked to 22 other books, and the remaining 22 books to 21 books each. Therefore: $(2 \times 22) + (22 \times 21) = 506$. On this basis, there are 122 actual cross-references in the text, a quotient of 24.1%. The 149 cross-references identified on the first calculation can be divided into 49 forward-references and 100 back-references. On the second calculation the respective numbers are 40 and 82. Thus the ratio between forward-references and back-references is approximately 1:2. It must be added, however, that the forward-references tend to be longer than the back-references in average number of lines.[35]

The diagram opposite should be read from top to bottom.[36] The books in the upper line are those in which the references occur, while the books in the lower line are those which are referred to. Lines pointing to the right are forward-references, and those pointing to the left back-references. It goes without saying that the diagram gives only an outline concept of the complexity and the density of the internal reference system of the *Iliad*.

One of the additional results emerging from this diagram is that book 10 of the *Iliad* refers to other sections of the epic, but is never referred to.[37] This confirms the theory that the *Doloneia* was neither an original part of Homer's epic nor a separate poem ('Einzellied'), but a later addition. It is also noticeable that books 2–7, which encompass the day of the first battle in the *Iliad*, contain a number of internal references, but are rarely referred to in later books. Obviously this section of the poem is not as well integrated into the thematic structure

---

[35] Cf. E. Balensiefen *Die Zeitgestaltung in Homers Ilias* (unpubl. diss. Tübingen 1955) 19–20. Starting from different premises, Balensiefen counts 72 forward-references in the *Iliad* with a total number of 221 lines, and 122 back-references totalling 281 lines. If we take the factor of length into account, the ratio between both types of cross-reference approximates 1 : 1.3.

[36] For the computer creation of this diagram I am obliged to Mrs. Julia Sonntag. It is based on the one in my *Fernbeziehungen in der Ilias* (above n.12), following p.328. References can be found *ibid.* 329–40. For the sake of symmetry, the Iliadic books are here designated by Greek letters.

[37] This was already observed by W. Leaf in his commentary on the *Iliad*, vol. I, 423.

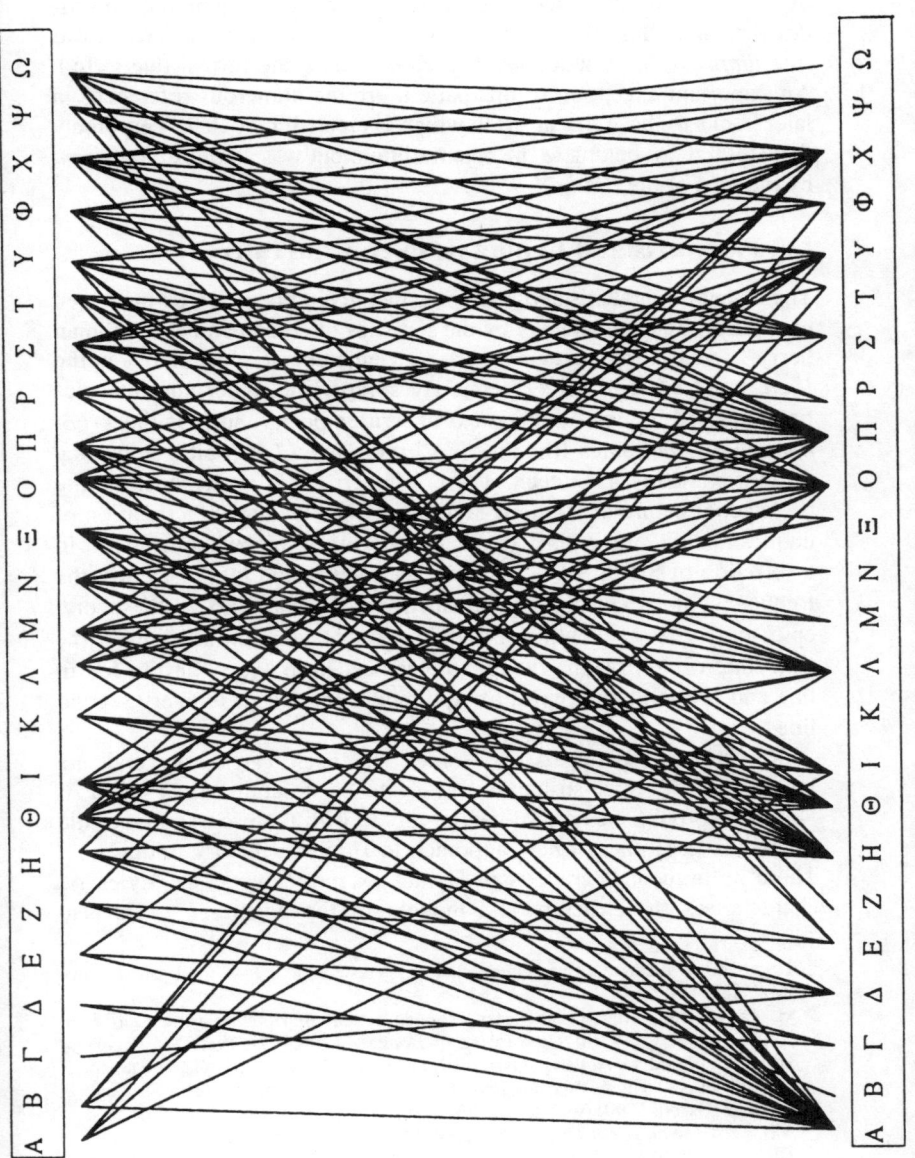

of the *Iliad* as other sections. Instead, it contains numerous motif-doublets and allusions to events in the earlier history of the Trojan war (the *diapeira*, the Catalogues, the *teichoskopia*, the formal duels etc.). An important exception to this pattern are the numerous references in later books to the Achaean wall, which is erected in book 7. Very likely the wall did not belong to the epic tradition, but was an *autoschediasma* by the poet of the *Iliad*.

IV. Parataxis and hypotaxis in epic narrative

The extent of parataxis and hypotaxis in a given poem can be measured on a purely syntactical level by the statistics of enjambement.[38] Milman Parry[39] found a frequency of 'necessary enjambement' of 26.6% in the *Iliad*, and 28.5% in the *Odyssey*. By comparison, other ancient epics firmly rooted in a cultural context of written poetry, such as the *Argonautica* of Apollonius Rhodius or Virgil's *Aeneid*, exhibit a frequency of approximately 49% each. These numbers seem to demonstrate the 'paratactic' nature of Homeric style. But when we turn to a tradition of unquestionably oral poetry, the picture becomes somewhat different. In a selection of South Slavic epic poetry investigated by A.B. Lord, the frequency of 'necessary enjambement' is 14.9%.[40] So in these oral epics only every seventh line requires a syntactic continuation in the next line, while in Homeric epic this is needed in every third to fourth line and in the literary epics of Apollonius and Virgil in every second line.

Research on parataxis in Homer has been carried beyond the boundaries of verse-structure and sentence-structure. In 1949 J.A. Notopoulos published an influential article with the programmatic title 'Parataxis in Homer: a new approach to Homeric literary criticism'.[41] There he argued: "Parataxis in Homer extends beyond the style and characterises the structure and thought of the poems" (7). He also

---

[38] To be more precise, enjambement includes verse structure as well as sentence structure.

[39] M. Parry 'The distinctive character of enjambement in Homeric verse' *TAPA* 60 (1929) 200–220; repr. in *The Making of Homeric Verse: The Collected Papers of Milman Parry* ed. by A. Parry (Oxford 1971) 251–65. The most complete treatment of this subject is C. Higbie *Measure and Music: Enjambement and Sentence Structure in the Iliad* (Oxford 1990) (with further literature).

[40] A.B. Lord *The Singer of Tales* (Cambridge, Mass. [1]1960, [2]1964) 54.

[41] *TAPA* 80 (1949) 1–23. Earlier studies in this direction are B.A. van Groningen *Paratactische compositie in de oudste grieksche literatuur* (Amsterdam 1937); B.E. Perry 'The early Greek capacity for viewing things separately' *TAPA* 68 (1937) 403–27.

offered an explanation for this: "The paratactic type of composition is ... the result of oral composition and certain conditions which accompany oral composition" (9).[42] The same approach to Homeric composition can be found in the works of other leading oralists.[43] Bernard Fenik in his study of Homeric battle scenes adhered to similar principles of interpretation — to the point of atomising the Iliadic narrative.[44] In a general reflection on his method he wrote:

> Where we might tend to spy an elaborate system of cross-reference and selective repetition the poet is simply proceeding step by step, developing one or at most two patterns at a time. One pattern or one typical scene is juxtaposed to another. At most he will interrupt a larger pattern to develop a smaller one, and then continue in the original direction once the smaller is finished.

E.R. Dodds also voiced the warning: "we should ... remember that in poems designed for piecemeal oral recitation there is a limit to the amount of deliberate cross-reference ('Fernverbindung') which it is reasonable to postulate".[45] Oralists tend to forget that certain narrative features like Homer's technique of parallel action and his use of cross-references have an objective basis in the text. It is not a question of hypothesising this: they can be positively shown to be there. Taken together they create an effect of what might be called 'narrative hypotaxis', by analogy with Notopoulos' extension of the term 'parataxis'.[46] This will be further exemplified in the following section.

V. Retardation

Apart from parallel action and the internal reference system another

---

[42] Cf. W.J. Ong *Orality and Literacy: The Technologizing of the Word* (London – New York 1982, repr. 1988) 36–8, who includes among the "characteristics of orally based thought and expression" in the first place "additive rather than subordinative".

[43] See for instance Lord *The Singer of Tales* (above n.40) 148.

[44] B. Fenik *Typical Battle Scenes in the Iliad: Studies in the Narrative Techniques of Homeric Battle Description* (Hermes Einzelschriften 21, Wiesbaden 1968) here 44. In his later book *Homer and the Nibelungenlied: Comparative Studies in Epic Style* (Cambridge, Mass. – London 1986) 1–43 Fenik put more emphasis on the artistic design of the *Iliad*.

[45] E.R. Dodds 'Homer' in M. Platnauer (ed.) *Fifty Years (and Twelve) of Classical Scholarship* (Oxford ²1968, ¹1954) 1–49, here 13. This remark seems to be directed against Schadewaldt's *Iliasstudien*.

[46] For more refined concepts of 'parataxis' in Homeric epic see J.B. Hainsworth 'The criticism of an oral Homer' *JHS* 90 (1970) 90–98; R. Friedrich *Stilwandel im homerischen Epos: Studien zur Poetik und Theorie der epischen Gattung* (Heidelberg 1975) 23ff., 110–25; W.G. Thalmann *Conventions of Form and Thought in Early Greek Epic Poetry* (Baltimore – London 1984) 4–6, 33–4.

characteristic of Homer's art contributes to the narrative design of the epics, i.e. Homer's technique of retardation. Contrary to the oralist view, the smaller sections of Homeric narrative are not in fact more or less self-contained units, but are almost always subordinated to a pre-conceived plan. Again an extensive demonstration lies outside the scope of this paper.[47] But, if the battle narrative of the *Iliad* is taken as an example its general tendency is towards an Achaean supremacy. This reaches its culmination in book 22, where Achilles kills Hector, thereby destroying any Trojan hope of salvation and, at the same time, anticipating the outcome of the Trojan war after the close of the Homeric *Iliad*. Ancient scholiasts understood this and regarded the monomachy between the two protagonists as the τέλος of the poem.[48] In these terms, long stretches of the *Iliad*, particularly books 8–18, must be classified as retardation, since the action moves in the opposite direction, i.e. towards a Trojan supremacy. This in turn is motivated by Thetis' request to Zeus in book 1 to restore the honour of her son Achilles by giving κράτος to the Trojans (1.503–10). The defeat of the Achaeans is the main goal of the action on the days of the second and third great battle of the *Iliad* (books 8–9 and 11–18 respectively). Again, the poet does not move in a straightforward manner to this goal, but inserts small-scale retardations, the most significant of which is effected by Hera and Poseidon's support for the Achaeans in books 13–14. Within this part of the narrative the movement towards the intended goal of Achaean supremacy is in turn interrupted by temporary Trojan successes. Whenever the poet sets a goal of the action for himself (and for his audience), we expect a movement of the action towards this goal. Any delay, interruption or reversal of this movement constitutes a retardational phase, which, at the same time, defines a new goal, though one of a lesser degree. The following scheme is an over-simplification,[49] but illustrates what is going on; the arrows show the movements of the action:

---

[47] In my article 'Retardationstechniken in der Ilias' (above n.12) I offered a typological classification of different types of retardation and discussed their function in the epic narrative. Morrison *Homeric Misdirection* (above n.8) 36–7 has independently arrived at a similar classification. On retardation, see also Thornton *Homer's Iliad* (above n.16) 59–72.

[48] Schol. Ab *ad* 20.443 (*Scholia Graeca in Homeri Iliadem. Scholia vetera*, rec. H. Erbse, 7 vols., Berlin 1969–88).

[49] For a good characterisation of Homeric battle narrative see J. Latacz *Kampfparänese, Kampfdarstellung und Kampfwirklichkeit in der Ilias, bei Kallinos und Tyrtaios* (Zetemata 66, München 1977) 96–113 (with detailed diagrams on pp.101–110, 112).

goal (1st degree), reached in books 19–22:
→ Achaean supremacy
goal (2nd degree), motivated by Thetis' request in book 1:
← Trojan supremacy = retardation (1st degree)
temporary suspension of this goal in books 2–7
→ Achaean supremacy = retardation (2nd degree)
goal (2nd degree), reached in books 8–18:
← Trojan supremacy = retardation (1st degree)
goal (3rd degree) in books 13–14 (Poseidon's support):
→ Achaean supremacy = retardation (2nd degree)
goal (4th degree) in brief passages of books 13–14:
← Trojan supremacy = retardation (3rd degree).

These sections are not autonomous appended units, but organic parts of a hierarchical system.[50] The poet never simply narrates events as they come to his mind; he announces and foreshadows virtually every single goal of the action. Within a retardational phase he often reminds his listeners of the temporary character of the immediate movement of the story. To give just one example: after Achilles has withdrawn from the battle in book 1, Homer reminds his audience at regular intervals that Achilles is still there although he has no part in the action (e.g. 2.688–94; 4.509–13; 5.787–91; 6.99–100; 7.226–30). In such ways each retardation is subordinated to a superior goal on a higher narrative level. This may justifiably be called 'narrative hypotaxis'; it might even be compared to a Ciceronian period, in which each subordinate clause has a clearly defined place and fulfils a pre-planned function within the syntactic pattern. Homer avoids what might be termed a 'narrative anacolouthon': there are hardly any loose ends in the narrative; and even with minor characters, who appear only two or three times, the poet takes care to connect their appearances by cross-references.[51] 'Parataxis', as understood by Notopoulos and other oralists, may be an appropriate description of the narrative structure of orally composed epics. But this concept is manifestly inadequate as a characterisation of the *Iliad* and *Odyssey*. It comes very close to a *petitio principii* if one describes Homeric narrative as 'paratactic' in order to prove its orality.

---

[50] Scholars who prefer to interpret this scheme in terms of ring-composition must accept that ring-composition of this type is irreconcilable with any definition of Homeric narrative as 'paratactic'.

[51] Many examples are cited in my *Fernbeziehungen in der Ilias* (above n.12) 279–300.

VI. Homer and Avdo Međedović

From 5–12 July, 1935, the guslar Avdo Međedović dictated an heroic epic of 12,311 verses, *The Wedding of Smailagić Meho*, to Milman Parry and his assistant.[52] It is one of the peculiarities of modern Homeric scholarship that this single South Slavic epic poem has been called on time and again as proof of the oral composition of Homeric epos: John Miles Foley claimed it as "the most convincing argument yet made for the oral composition of the *Iliad* and *Odyssey*",[53] in a recent article, W. Merritt Sale has again emphasised the 'analogy' between Homer and Avdo.[54] The comparisons made between this oral epic — an impressive poem in its own right — and the Homeric poems do justice neither to Homer nor to Avdo, who composed in an entirely different socio-cultural environment.

Some reservations against stretching the alleged parallels too far were voiced in 1977 by Dorothea Wender, who pointed out some of the deficiencies of Avdo's narrative.[55] Criticism of this sort has always provoked the same reaction from oralists: instead of refuting it they reject it outright as coming from Homerists ignorant of the Serbo-Croatian language and so unable to access the original text. This is of course a methodologically invalid way of proceeding; and in any case it should be stressed that, for purely logical reasons, inferences can be, but are not automatically, invalidated by the use of a secondary source. We may also note that Zdeslav Dukat, a native speaker himself and an expert in the poetic tradition of South Slavic heroic poetry, passed a devastating judgement on *The Wedding of Smailagić Meho*, concluding that its only remarkable feature is its length.[56]

[52] *Serbo-Croatian Heroic Songs, coll. by M. Parry, vol. 3: The Wedding of Smailagić Meho (Avdo Međedović)* trl. with intr., notes, and comm. by A.B. Lord (Cambridge, Mass. 1974); *vol. 4: Ženidba Smailagina sina, kazivao je Avdo Međedović* ed. by D.E. Bynum with A.B. Lord (Cambridge, Mass. 1974). On the singer's background, cf. Lord's introduction. See also A.B. Lord 'Avdo Međedović, Guslar' in *Epic Singers and Oral Tradition* (Ithaca and London 1991) 57–71.

[53] J.M. Foley *The Theory of Oral Composition: History and Methodology* (Bloomington and Indianapolis 1988) 98.

[54] W.M. Sale 'Homer and Avdo: Investigating orality through external consistency' in I. Worthington (ed.) *Voice into Text: Orality and Literacy in Ancient Greece* (Mnemosyne Suppl. 157, Leiden – New York – Köln 1996) 21–42.

[55] D. Wender 'Homer, Avdo Međedović and The Elephant's Child' *AJP* 98 (1977) 327–47.

[56] Z. Dukat "Die Hochzeit von Smailagić Meho': Das erste serbokroatische mündliche Grossepos' *ZA* 36 (1986) 5–12. Dukat states: "wenn man Lords begeisterte Äusserungen über Avdos Originalität und Genialität liest, drängt sich der Verdacht auf, dass der einzige wirkliche Grund dieser Begeisterung in dem Umfang des

In the following I shall briefly address some of the points raised by Sale. One of the most conspicuous traits of *The Wedding of Smailagić Meho* is its clear-cut distinction between good and bad characters, which overlaps in large part with that between friend and foe, i.e. Moslem and Christian.[57] Black-and-white characterisation is typical of many heroic poems, e.g. the OF. *Chanson de Roland* (where the roles of Christians and Moslems are reversed) or the MHG. *Kudrun*. The situation is completely different in the *Iliad*, where the poet's sympathies are clearly not one-sided: nowhere is there a denigration of the Trojan side.[58] This even-handedness is one of the essentials of Homer's 'narrative ethos', and it is absent from the *Smailagić Meho*. The *Iliad*'s main opponents Achilles and Hector are both depicted as mainly positive, if psychologically complex, characters. While Sale admits that Meho is a rather simple character compared to Hector, he regards Tale of Orašac, the protagonist of the second half of Avdo's poem, as "a highly complicated man" (34). Although Avdo's colourful depiction of Tale creates a credible image of a warrior, the alleged 'complexity' of Tale's personality is not explored by the singer for ethical purposes, as Homer exploits the personalities of Achilles, Hector and Helen.

Since my starting point was the relevance of macrostructure as a criterion for oral vs. literary composition, further remarks will be restricted to this aspect of Avdo's art. First, the use of parallel action: as was pointed out by Wender (331–2) and Dukat (10), Avdo's attention is almost completely focused on one line of action for very long stretches of his narrative, i.e. hundreds or even thousands of verses. In contrast to Homer, Avdo is either unwilling or unable to follow different threads of plot simultaneously. A change of scene normally occurs when a character moves to a different place and the narrator, so to speak, accompanies him.[59] In the first half of the epic Avdo con-

---

Gedichtes gesucht werden muss" (11). He also notices that Wender's assessment is basically correct (6–7). See also *id.* 'Einige kritische Bemerkungen zur Oral-Poetry Theorie' *ZA* 36 (1986) 13–20.

[57] Cf. Dukat "Die Hochzeit von Smailagić Meho" (above n.56) 11: "Die Parteilichkeit des Sängers überschreitet die Grenze der Erträglichkeit".

[58] Cf. J.T. Kakridis *Homer Revisited* (Lund 1971) 54–67; see now also S. Schmal *Feind–bilder bei den frühen Griechen* (Frankfurt a.M. 1995) 25–66.

[59] This mode of narration may be compared to the film narrative of *Rope* (1948), directed by Alfred Hitchcock. In this picture the camera followed the actors like a human observer, without a single break or a sudden change of scene. Richardson *The Homeric Narrator* (above n.7) 118–20 considers the narrative structure of this film an analogy to that of the *Iliad*, but this comparison completely misses the point. If a director wanted to put the *Iliad* on the screen, closely adhering to Homer's principles of narration, he would have to make many 'cuts', which is the normal way of shooting a film.

centrates on the adventures of his young hero Mehmed. In the second
half, in order to advance the action, Avdo needs to describe the military
measures undertaken by Tale of Orašac. So he shifts the focus of his
narration to Tale. Consequently, he almost 'forgets' Mehmed. Only at
the end of the epic, after the great battle is over, does Mehmed re-
appear, with the enemy general Peter as his captive. Avdo does not tell
us how Mehmed captured the general or how he overcame other
enemies in battle. He thus misses the opportunity to narrate the first
heroic trial of a young warrior who is his main hero — in a decisive
battle.[60] In heroic poetry of any kind this would definitely be a blunder
on the part of the poet. Avdo could have avoided it by dividing his
attention between different characters and scenes of action — which is
the normal procedure in the battle narratives of the *Iliad*. No matter
how complex the situation in the different locations where fighting
takes place, Homer never loses track even of his minor characters, let
alone of his main heroes. Another awkward omission in the *Smailagić
Meho* is that we do not learn about the proceedings inside the city of
Buda after Mehmed's departure until Tale's army finally arrives on the
scene. Then, and only then, Avdo briefly switches his attention to
Fatima's mother, who is staying in Buda, and, a little later, to the
vizier.[61] As regards the use of parallel action, the difference between
Avdo and Homer could hardly be more pronounced. Although there are
some initial steps towards a shift of scene without a person moving
from one place to another in the *Smailagić Meho*, the narrative tech-
niques used by Avdo and by Homer are different not in degree, but in
principle.[62]

Second, cross-references: long and frequent retrospections are a
marked characteristic of the *Smailagić Meho*. When Mehmed and
Osman tell Mehmed's father and his uncle what they experienced on

---

[60] It is true that the course of the battle does not depend on Mehmed's deeds, as Sale
'Homer and Avdo' (above n.54) 28 points out. But Avdo composed an heroic epic, not
a military history. See also Wender 'Homer, Avdo Međedović and The Elephant's
Child' (above n.55) 332.

[61] See pp. 204–5 and 210 of Lord's translation. In the second instance, the change of
scene is clearly marked by the narrator: "Now let me tell you about the vizier". At the
end of the epic an embassy carrying a letter is sent to the sultan in Stambol. The
'movement' is narrated within a single verse, which comes very close to an
'unconnected' change of scene.

[62] In that respect Avdo's poem is perhaps not a true representative of Slavic epic from
the Krajina. As Dukat "Die Hochzeit von Smailagić Meho" (above n.56) points out,
many poems of this tradition show a marked tendency to include both sides of the
action, thereby displaying a double-sided structure (9: "Verdoppelungsstruktur der
Handlung"; cf. 16). See also M. Braun *Das serbokroatische Heldenlied* (Göttingen
1961) 258.

their journey, the recapitulation of events already narrated occupies more than 600 verses. The detailed letter to the sultan at the end of the epic is another example of lengthy re-narration. In both cases the retrospections serve a clearly definable function: positioned at turning points in the narrative, they remind the listener of what has happened so far, and what causes have created the situation of the moment. Homer achieves the same result more economically, as can be seen from the much briefer recapitulations in the *Iliad* and the *Odyssey*.[63] Odysseus' words to Alcinous in *Od.* 12.452–3 ἐχθρὸν δέ μοί ἐστιν/ αὖτις ἀριζήλως εἰρημένα μυθολογεύειν do not apply to Avdo's practice. A tiresome example of his multiple retrospection comes in the twenty or so letters dictated by the pasha, to summon troops and their commanders.[64] They all include a brief summary of earlier events, and they all serve the same function. Obviously this mechanistic use of retrospection, which is governed by a catalogue-like structure, lengthens the poem without really enriching its content or advancing its action. Lord himself acknowledged this fact; in his translation he used a smaller type for this section.

Forward-references are much less in evidence in the *Smailagić Meho* than back-references. There are of course a number of foreshadowings of future events. For instance, Mehmed tries to cheer up his bride Fatima by promising her that Tale will have the vizier killed, as will happen at the end of the poem. Lord has drawn attention to some examples of Avdo's technique of preparation and of flash-back, his use of suspense and irony and other features of his narrative.[65] But it would be misleading to over-emphasise isolated examples or to base an evaluation of Avdo's art of narration on a comparatively small number of cases. Taken together, they do not come even close to the cumulative evidence adduced for the Homeric epics. Admittedly generalisations of this kind remain suspect as long as we have no systematic investigation of the internal reference system in the *Smailagić*

---

[63] See above. The closest parallel that I can find in the genre of heroic epic is the report that Beowulf gives to king Hygelac in *Beowulf* vv. 2000–2151.

[64] Is it possible that the frequent use made of letters in this poem reflects the illiterate poet's respect for the medium of writing, which is known, but not accessible, to him?

[65] See Lord's introduction, esp. 19–20. Cf. also 'An example of Homeric qualities of repetition in Međedović's 'Smailagić Meho'', in W. Gesemann et al. (eds.) *Serta Slavica: Gedenkschrift für A. Schmaus* (München 1971) 458–64; 'Avdo Međedović, Guslar' in *Epic Singers* (above n.52) 57–71, here 65–6; 'Homer as an oral-traditional poet' *ibid.* 72–103, here 94–101; 'Words heard and words seen' *ibid.* 15–37, here 30–32; 'The merging of two worlds: oral and written poetry as carriers of ancient values' in J.M. Foley (ed.) *Oral Tradition in Literature: Interpretation in Context* (Columbia 1986) 19–64, here 53–64; *The Singer Resumes the Tale* (above n.27) 203–11.

Meho or in other oral epics. But it can be safely said that a specific form of foreshadowing, frequent in Homer, namely authorial announcements of the future, is entirely missing in Avdo's poem. The same applies to all other types of explicit and definite forecasts of oncoming events. The explanation for this may be the performance situation of the oral bard, who strongly depends on the attentiveness and responsiveness of his audience. An improvising epic singer cannot know in advance how he can extend his narrative, or even if he will finish it at all. An uninterested audience can cause him to end his tale sooner than he had hoped. Or an audience which expresses particular interest in a certain motif or description can cause him to linger over that subject. By making definite announcements of events that are to take place much later in the narrative an improvising oral poet would impose unnecessary restrictions upon his narrative, and would set goals for himself and his audience that he might be unable to reach. It is interesting to note that, even in this very unusual hotel-room situation, and faced with a most interested and most enthusiastic listener, Avdo apparently did not make use of this possibility. With a literate poet, who composes at will and at a slow pace, things are of course different.

Third, narrative parataxis: the overall impression created by the *Smailagić Meho* is that it can indeed be characterised as 'paratactic' in Notopoulos' sense of the term. Sale admits that in respect of structure Avdo's poem is not comparable to Homeric epos. Nonetheless, he denies that the actual differences can be explained by the use of writing on the part of Homer.[66] Regrettably, however, Sale refers only to one recent study, by Keith Stanley, for the structure of the *Iliad*.[67] Stanley's approach is based upon the premise that the structuring device of ring-composition, which is evident in many smaller sections of Homeric epic, also dominates the large-scale structure of the *Iliad*. Similar approaches have been taken by many scholars in the past,[68] mostly with dubious results. To a large extent, this guiding principle has tempted scholars to find 'analogies' and 'parallels' between sections of the epic which are in fact dissimilar in content, function, and wording. So, to be fair to Avdo, it should not be regarded as a sign of inferior structural quality if these alleged "larger annular and interlocking forms", that

---

[66] Sale 'Homer and Avdo' (above n.54) 35–40, 42.

[67] Stanley *The Shield of Homer* (above n.32).

[68] E.g. Sheppard, Stürmer, Peters, Stählin, Myres, Pfister, Whitman, Webster, Turolla, Beck, Jackson-Knight, Andreae/Flashar, Gordesiani, Balthes. Often this approach appears in combination with the attempt to establish structural parallels between early Greek poetry and contemporary vase-painting. M.L. West *CR* 17 (1967) 268 has ironically referred to this method as the " 'geometric pot' school of criticism".

"pose a genuine challenge to oralists" (Sale, 38–9), cannot be identified in his or, for that matter, other oral poetry. Lord, on the other hand, is convinced that the entire narrative of Avdo's poem can be analysed "in terms of rings or chiastic constructions resembling Cedric Whitman's analysis of Homer's *Iliad*."[69] His examples, however, being confined to single scenes, fall far short of corroborating this claim. But in any case I should be much less surprised if ring-composition on a large scale could be revealed in strictly oral poetry than in Homer's epic, which has proceeded far beyond this rather archaic ordering principle.

VII. Conclusion

In 1958 C.H. Whitman wrote: "The developed form of Homeric epic differs radically ... not only from the primitive saga, but even from the most sophisticated evolvements of oral poetry found anywhere".[70] In spite of all the research done in the last decades (and in spite of Lord's above-quoted claim to the contrary), this statement has still not been conclusively disproved. Homer's sophisticated use of parallel action, of cross-referencing and of retardation differentiates the *Iliad* and the *Odyssey* widely from other heroic epics where oral composition can be demonstrated by external evidence. Yet this kind of argument has been entirely dismissed by oralists. Agathe Thornton[71] writes on this point:

> It might still be objected that the 'quality' of Homer's Iliad is likely to be far superior to any such oral epic from other parts of the world, a superiority which would be supposed to imply writing, and that its superiority has in fact been demonstrated in relation to Serbo-Croat oral poetry. This kind of objection must be radically rejected ... Inferences from 'quality' to composition by writing are not justified.

Minna Skafte Jensen also rejects any argument from 'quality' as

---

[69] Lord *Epic Singers* (above n.52) 32. Lord continues: "Some would doubt that oral-traditional poets would have the ability to construct their scenes, and perhaps even an entire poem of some length, in this manner. Here is proof that they not only *can* do but actually *do* just that". Cf. his response to Lesky (and, by implication, to Schadewaldt), *ibid*. 94–8. See also *id*. 'The merging of two worlds' (above n.65) 53–64.

[70] Whitman *Homer and the Heroic Tradition* (above n.32) 154. See also H. Lloyd-Jones 'Remarks on the Homeric Question', in *Greek Epic, Lyric, and Tragedy: The Academic Papers of Sir Hugh Lloyd-Jones* (Oxford 1990) 3–20, here 17: "The human memory is capable of amazing feats, and in theory the poems, with all the links between their various parts [!], could have been composed without the aid of writing. Only so far no example of anything comparable having been achieved has been adduced; and no one able and willing to perceive the unity of the epics is likely to believe it possible".

[71] Thornton *Homer's Iliad* (above n.16) 16–17.

being of a purely subjective nature.[72] As long as we base our evaluation on a vague feeling of the 'poetic superiority' of the Homeric poems, this is correct. On the other hand, if we define 'quality' clearly in terms of narratological categories, it should be possible to reach a more objective basis of comparison. The purpose of my paper has been to point out some of these categories. They offer the prospect of studying large-scale structures no less 'scientifically' than formulas or enjambement.

---

[72] M. Skafte Jensen *The Homeric Question* (above n.5) 28–45, here 29. See also G.S. Kirk *The Iliad: a commentary, vol 1: books 1–4* (Cambridge 1985) 13–14.

PAPERS OF THE LEEDS INTERNATIONAL LATIN SEMINAR   TENTH VOLUME (1998) 23–56
Published by Francis Cairns (Publications) Ltd (Leeds 1998). ARCA 38. ISBN 0 905205 95 2

WAS HOMER A ROMAN?

MALCOLM HEATH
University of Leeds

Homer was not a Roman. That is obvious; indeed, it is so obvious that one has to wonder how anyone in the ancient world could have supposed that he was or might have been a Roman — yet we know that the possibility was considered. This paper seeks to understand to what extent the theory that Homer was a Roman was a reasonable one in its own cultural milieu.[1] It falls into three main parts. The first identifies the theory's source, a Greek grammarian of the first century BC who spent part of his career in Rome. The second looks at some aspects of the theory's intellectual background; I shall argue that the convergence of certain well-attested strands in Hellenistic Homer scholarship and ethnography made the notion of a Roman Homer thinkable in its first-century context. But not everything that is thinkable is actually thought; the third part of the paper therefore looks at some of the evidence that was, or could have been, cited in support of the theory.

1. The source: Aristodemus of Nysa

Our point of departure is one of the ancient *Lives* of Homer. In reality, of course, the text in question is not a 'life' in the sense of a connected biographical narrative. It is one of a number of mainly short texts, serving as prefaces to Homer's poems,[2] and covering a limited range of topics: Homer's homeland (*patris*),[3] parentage, name, date and so on.

---

[1] An earlier version of the paper was read to the departmental research seminar of the School of Classics at Leeds in March 1997; I am grateful to the participants, and also to Maria Broggiato, Tim Cornell, Michael Reeve and Peter Wiseman, for valuable suggestions.

[2] Leo (1901) 17–34.

[3] This is not necessarily his birthplace: more than one theory, having established Homer's roots in one place, transported him in the womb to another.

The text with which we are concerned (the *Vita Romana*) begins by pointing out the impossibility of making any definite statement about Homer's 'birth or city'. There is then a list of nine theories (a small proportion of the total number proposed in antiquity), of which the eighth is that he was Roman. This view is attributed to Aristodemus of Nysa.[4]

Aristodemus of Nysa is more than just a name to us. Strabo studied with someone of that name, and in the section on Nysa (a city on the river Maeander, in Caria)[5] he tells us something about his teacher's family and career (14.1.48). Aristodemus' father was Menecrates, a *grammatikos* and a pupil of Aristarchus. He may be the Menecrates cited in a scholion on the end of the *Iliad* (ΣbT *Iliad* 24.804), but that is not certain; the hypothesis that a comparison of the *Iliad* and *Odyssey* by Menecrates was the source of a famous passage in the treatise *On Sublimity* (9.11–15) has been accepted by a number of distinguished scholars, but rests (in my view) on a misunderstanding of the scholion.[6] We therefore know almost nothing about Menecrates. Nor do we know much about Aristodemus' brother Sostratus, also a *grammatikos*. It has recently been argued that he was the Sostratus who wrote a poem (summarised by Eustathius) on the six sex-changes of Tiresias;[7] that is plausible, but inevitably uncertain. Strabo tells us additionally of a cousin, also called Aristodemus and also a *grammatikos*; he was tutor to Pompey the Great. It was presumably on his older cousin's recommendation that Strabo's Aristodemus in turn became tutor to Pompey's sons. Before taking up this post he had taught both rhetoric and *grammatikê* (the combination is unusual) in Rhodes, then a leading intellectual centre. After his stay in Rome he returned to Nysa, where again he taught rhetoric and *grammatikê*; it was here, in his extreme old age, that the young Strabo attended his courses.

Another *grammatikos* named Aristodemus merits a passing mention at this point: Aristodemus of Alexandria, a pupil of Aristarchus whose contribution to Pindaric studies is known from the Pindar scholia and Athenaeus.[8] It is conceivable that he was part of the same family; one

---

[4]   The only extended discussion of which I am aware is Dubuisson (1984a).

[5]   Cf. W. Ruge *RE* 17.2 (1937) 1631–40 *s.v.* Nysa (10); Robert (1940); Magie (1950) 128–9, 989–91.

[6]   Hefermehl (1906); *contra* Heath (1998).

[7]   O'Hara (1996).

[8]   Some aspects are discussed in Heath (1993). On the ethnic 'of Alexandria' see Rabe's comment (*PS* lviii n.1): 'Quot grammaticis ethnicon Ἀλεξανδρεύς tribuit Suidas! Nemo credit eos Alexandriae natos esse omnes.'

might imagine, for example, a brother of Menecrates who had also gone to Alexandria to study with Aristarchus, and who had stayed there to teach. But the name is quite common, so we have no positive grounds for assuming such an identification.[9]

It is, however, possible to extend the family in another direction. The *Suda* (I52) mentions a philosopher called Jason, a pupil of Posidonius, his successor at Rhodes, and his maternal grandson. Jason's father was a Menecrates of Nysa. Some have identified this Menecrates (the son-in-law of Posidonius) with the father of Strabo's Aristodemus. But that is chronologically implausible,[10] and Gercke more convincingly postulated a homonym, who is nevertheless likely to have been a member of the same family.[11] Posidonius' well-known close relations with Pompey fit neatly with the Pompeian connections of the family from Nysa.[12]

We now have two Aristodemi of Nysa. One of them is cited in ΣA *Iliad* 9.453c as the proponent of a (far from persuasive) emendation, designed to minimise Phoenix's offence against his father. Since he is described as both rhetor and *grammatikos*, this is most likely to be the younger cousin, Strabo's teacher. It is sometimes inferred that the younger cousin must also be the author of the theory that Homer was a Roman. The inference is not conclusive (the fact that one Aristodemus wrote about Homer does not prove that the other did not); but in the absence of other evidence, the younger one must be the preferred candidate.[13]

---

[9] There are no good grounds for identifying Aristodemus of Alexandria with Aristodemus of Elis or of Thebes (*contra* Jacoby on *FGrH* 383, 414). Since the Pindar scholia cite Aristodemus of Elis (Σ Pi. *Ol.* 3.21b–22a ~ Harpocration *s.v.* Ἑλλανοδίκαι) without distinguishing him, it must remain uncertain which of the citations concerned with Theban matters are from Aristodemus of Thebes rather than Aristodemus of Alexandria.

[10] Since Aristarchus left Alexandria in 145 and died shortly afterwards, his pupil Menecrates could not have been born much, if at all, after 165; but Posidonius' birth is dated to c. 135.

[11] Gercke (1907).

[12] For Pompey's intellectual entourage see Anderson (1963); Crawford (1978).

[13] The only other specific reference to an Aristodemus of Nysa is in the scholia to Parthenius. Again, it is not certain which of the two is the author of the collection of mythological narratives in question; Loicq-Berger (1984) 49–50 assumes that it is the younger cousin, but without argument. There are other Aristodemus-citations with no ethnic; it is possible that some of these relate to the cousins from Nysa, but we cannot be sure.

2. Intellectual background

2.1 Homeric biography

Traditions about Homer's life can be traced back as far as the sixth century BC. The *Contest of Homer and Hesiod* had a sixth-century antecedent;[14] Heraclitus was familiar with a story that features in later accounts of Homer's death (22B56 DK). The claim that Theagenes of Rhegium (at the end of the sixth century) was the first to write about Homer's life should be viewed with caution.[15] But there must in any event have been oral traditions at an earlier date; the rhapsodes provide a plausible context for their transmission (and, indeed, creation).

These early traditions about Homer's life were not unanimous, and the efforts of historians and philosophers in the fifth and fourth centuries to reconcile, rationalise and extrapolate from them only added to the proliferation of conflicting claims. Hellenistic scholars must therefore have recognised that the material transmitted to them was not reliable: even if it contained truth, it did not indicate which of the conflicting traditional claims expressed that truth. It follows that, if anything was to be known about the poet, it would have to be inferred from internal evidence. Recent work on ancient literary biography has viewed this approach with disfavour: deservedly so, when it involves taking elements in the poems as allusions to events in the poet's life.[16] But to ask 'what kind of person, in what kind of circumstances, must we postulate to account for the composition of these texts?' is a legitimate procedure; modern scholarship has to do precisely this.[17]

In asking this question Hellenistic scholars did not feel that they were restricted to choosing between elements already established in the tradition. It was therefore possible in discussing Homer's homeland to break away from the conventional claimants. A good example is Aristarchus, who believed that Homer was an Athenian (a view in which he was followed by his pupil Dionysius of Thrace, who taught in

---

[14] Richardson (1981) 1–3.

[15] Tatian *Ad Gr.* 31 (= 8A1 DK). For Theagenes as the earliest writer on Homer's poetry cf. Porphyry on *Il.* 20.67 (8A2 DK). But it is not clear that Tatian had specific evidence for the contents of Theagenes' writings; he may simply be generalising about the kind of topic covered by those who write on Homer.

[16] See especially Lefkowitz (1981).

[17] Although not all scholars are as bold as Powell (1991) 231–6, who offers us a Euboean Homer acquainted with Palamedes, or Latacz (1996) 69, who describes an East Ionian Homer's family, education, travels and life-history. Ancient grammarians would surely have felt at home with such approaches.

Rhodes in the latter part of the second century).[18] Aristarchus' reasoning is not recorded. We can be sure that linguistic arguments played a part: ΣA *Iliad* 13.197, from Aristonicus' work on Aristarchus' critical signs, relates Homer's use of the dual (seen as a distinguishing feature of Attic dialect) to the question of Homer's *patris*. Likewise the essay on Homer falsely attributed to Plutarch argues that Attic is the main component in the Homeric mix of dialects, mentioning the dual along with other features of Homeric diction (2.12). Beyond that, one can only speculate; I shall point tentatively to three areas in which speculation might operate.

(i) Aristarchus dated Homer to the time of the Ionian migration.[19] Since this migration makes it possible for a poet who is an Athenian by origin to be an inhabitant of some other city, this dating could have provided a mechanism for integrating an Athenian Homer with more traditional views.[20]

(ii) A second consideration which may be relevant is Aristarchus' apparently conservative treatment of passages in Homer that could be seen as 'pro-Athenian', and textually suspect for that reason.[21] The evidence for his view about Solon's alleged interpolation of *Iliad* 2.558 in support of Athens' claim to Salamis (a line which Zenodotus and Aristophanes seem to have rejected) is unclear;[22] but he seems to have

---

[18] *Vita* 5; [Plut.] 2.2 (= Dionysius Thrax F47 Links). The theory of the 'Pisistratean recension' of the Homeric poems may be seen as a counter to this view: see West (1983) 249–51; Ritoók (1993).

[19] This dating is also in Castor *FGrH* 250F4 (1141.25–9). Aristotle had already placed Homer's birth at this time, for reasons unknown. Jacoby (Suppl.) on 328F209 suggests that the Athenian Homer was already current in Aristotle's time; I am not sure how plausible this is.

[20] *AP* 11.442 (later than Aristarchus, since it assumes a highly developed form of the legend of the Pisistratean recension: see n.18 above) claims Homer as an Athenian citizen on the grounds that Athens colonised Smyrna. This claim rests on the story of an original Ionian foundation of Smyrna, later captured by Aeolians and then retaken by Ionians: see Strabo 14.1.4; Ael. Ar. 17.5, 18.2, 20.20, 21.4, 23.26 (where it is stated that Homer was Athenian (a) because his city was a colony, and (b) because of his dialect); Philostr. *Imag.* 2.8.6; Tac. *Ann.* 4.56. In some versions the Athenian foundation occurs first under Theseus, and is reinforced by the Ionian migration; the Thessalian Theseus of [Hdt.] *Vita* 2 is presumably a counter to this version.

[21] [Hdt.] *Vita* 28 accounts for these passages in another way: the poet himself inserted *Iliad* 2.547–8, 552–4, 557–8, *Odyssey* 7.80–1 in preparation for a visit to Athens (for which see also *Cert.* 16).

[22] From ΣA *Il.* 3.230a, 4.273a, 10.53ab we learn that the monograph περὶ τοῦ ναυστάθμου concluded that Ajax and his contingent were *not* stationed with the Athenians, implying the inauthenticity of *Il.* 2.558; but Σb *Il.* 2.558 says he did include

had no doubts about *Iliad* 2.553–5 (athetised by Zenodotus: ΣA *Iliad* 2.553a) or *Odyssey* 7.80–81 (suspect to some, according Σ *Odyssey* 7.80–81).

(iii) Thirdly, there is the suggestion made by Agallis of Corcyra that the two cities portrayed on the Shield of Achilles (*Iliad* 18.490–540) were Athens and Eleusis; the scholia on these lines show a marked interest in possible links with Athenian tradition, indicating that the theory was worked out in some detail. Agallis (one of only two women whose contribution to Homeric studies is recorded in the scholia)[23] is described as a γνώριμος of Aristophanes of Byzantium (ΣD *Iliad* 18.490); if this has the sense 'pupil' (LSJ *s.v.* I 3b), it would make her roughly contemporary with Aristarchus. Her interpretation of the two cities would obviously fit well with an Athenian Homer, but there is no record of Aristarchus' view of it. Nor do we know whether Agallis was anticipating his theory, or working out its implications: if the former, then Aristarchus' theory developed out of ideas that were 'in the air' at the time; if the latter, then it was at least seen as a fruitful starting-point for further research.

2.2 Homeric ethnography

Hellenistic scholars could not fail to realise that Homer portrayed an unfamiliar world, with a society and culture very different from their own. These differences were the source of some of the problems which readers and critics encountered in Homer, and Aristotle had seen that comparative arguments could provide solutions. Why does Homer speak of spears being stood upright on the butt-end (*Iliad* 10.152–3)? That was the norm then, as it still is among the Illyrians (*Poetics* 1461a2–4); ancient Greek customs often coincide with those of present-day non-Greeks (fr. 160 Rose = 383 Gigon, commenting on the same problem). Why does Achilles drag Hector's body round Patroclus' tomb? It was the custom in Thessaly to drag the bodies of murderers round their victim's tomb (fr. 166 = 389). In proposing such solutions Aristotle, author of a treatise on non-Greek customs (νόμιμα βαρβαρικά), was doubtless drawing on his own ethnographic researches; Homeric scholarship intersects at this point with another

---

it in his revised text (the note is confused, and may indicate that it was absent from his first edition), and this was criticised as irrational.
[23] The other is Demo: cf. *RE* Suppl. 3 (1918) 331–3, *s.v.* Demo (2a). Agallis' fragments: Ath. 1, 14d; ΣT *Il.* 18.483–606, ΣD 18.490; Eust. on *Il.* 18.490; *Suda* A1817 *s.v.* Ἀνάγαλλις.

leading Hellenistic interest.[24] Hellenistic scholars invested much effort in describing the distinctive culture of the Homeric world.[25] Aristarchus was, of course, an important contributor to this project. He does not appear to have cited comparative evidence (adhering to the principle — whether or not he formulated it explicitly himself — of explicating Homer from Homer); but it has been pointed out that ethnographic assumptions about the *kind* of culture and society to be looked for in Homer underlie even his work.[26]

As well as describing the customs of different peoples, ancient ethnographers used parallels between them as evidence in reconstructing the origins of nations and their interrelationships.[27] An excellent and pertinent example is Dionysius of Halicarnassus, who takes this approach when arguing that the Romans are of Greek descent; this is an argument to which we shall return. Here, it is enough to note that the same ethnographic method could be brought into play in connection with the question of Homer's homeland: scholars tried to correlate distinctive customs portrayed in the poems with those of candidate homelands. The underlying assumption is articulated in the pseudo-Herodotean *Life* (37): the customs which a poet chooses to portray in his poems are likely to be either a selection from the finest customs of mankind or those of his own homeland. Since this *Life* makes a false claim about its own authorship, it may not seem a promising source of methodological principle; but the pastiche of scholarly method is part of its apparatus for securing verisimilitude.

Pseudo-Herodotus takes the view that Homer was born in Smyrna, of Cymean descent (1–2, 37: cf. Ephorus *FGrH* 70F1, F99), and he supports this position with an ethnographic argument for an Aeolic Homer based on uniquely Aeolic sacrificial practices. The scholia on the passages he cites (*Iliad* 1.459–61 = 2.422–4; *Iliad* 1.462–3 = *Odyssey* 3.459–60) refer more precisely to the customs of Cyme (ΣbT *Iliad* 1.459, 1.463; for Cyme see also ΣbT *Iliad* 4.259). It could also be argued on linguistic grounds that Homer was Aeolic. Zopyrus (*FGrH* 497F3) and Dicaearchus (F90 Wehrli) are reported as saying that Homer should be read in the Aeolic dialect. Several of the *Lives* claim

---

[24] On Hellenistic ethnography see Dihle (1961); cf. Trüdinger (1918), Mueller (1980).
[25] Schmidt (1976) gives a good account.
[26] Schmidt (1976) 162.
[27] Bickerman (1952) is the classic study.

that ὅμηρος is an Aeolic (or specifically Lesbian) word meaning 'blind'.[28]

2.3 Exotic Homers

In arguing for an Aeolic Homer pseudo-Herodotus agrees with one set of strands in the biographical tradition. But the application of the ethnographic method could also produce more exotic Homers. The eighth of the nine theories about Homer's homeland listed in the *Vita Romana* is that Homer was Roman; the ninth is that he was Egyptian, and an ethnographic argument is supplied in support of this view: "others have said that he was an Egyptian, because he introduces the heroes kissing each other on the mouth, which it is customary for the Egyptians to do." This argument is, in fact, highly problematic. The heroes do *not* kiss each other on the mouth,[29] a fact which was registered by ancient scholars (Σ *Odyssey* 17.35; Eustathius on *Odyssey* 17.29). Nor can I find any evidence that kissing on the mouth was regarded as a distinctively Egyptian custom.[30] The text perhaps is corrupt.[31]

The idea of an Egyptian Homer appears in Heliodorus, who makes the Egyptian priest Calasiris mention in passing that Homer was Egyptian (3.12–15, cf. 2.34), to the surprise of his young Greek companion Theagenes. Calasiris' claim that Homer has a typically Egyptian insight into the nature of the gods, and Theagenes' agreement that Homer's liking for concealed meanings is also an Egyptian trait, connect the tradition of allegorical interpretation of Homer to the image

---

[28] *Vita* 4, 6 (Lesbian); [Hdt.] 13 (Cymean); cf. *Cert.* 3. See further Latte (1925) 148–50.

[29] The only parts of the body explicitly kissed in Homer are hands, head and eyes: *Il.* 24.478; *Od.* 16.15, 17.39, 19.417, 23.87, 23.208, 24.398.

[30] The only statement about Egyptian kissing that I have found is negative: Herodotus says that they do not kiss Greeks on the mouth (2.41); this admittedly need not imply that they do not kiss on the mouth at all. Hdt. 1.134 associates kissing on the mouth with Persians (cf. Xen. *Cyr.* 1.4.27, *Ages.* 5.4). Curiously, kissing on the mouth *could* have been cited as a Roman custom: Plut. *QR* 6 (= Aristotle fr. 609 Rose = 701 Gigon) connects the *ius osculi* to traditions of Greek and Trojan settlement in Italy; cf. Marquardt–Mau (1886) 59, and (on kissing on the mouth as a common greeting) 260; according to *RE* 1A.2 (1920) 2063–4 kissing on the mouth was a customary greeting in Rome under the principate, but was not customary among Greek men. I do not know what bearing, if any, this might have on our main theme.

[31] In Allen's edition: ἄλλοι δ᾽ Αἰγύπτιον αὐτὸν εἶπον διὰ τὸ †η† παράγειν τοὺς ἥρωας ἐκ στόματος ἀλλήλους φιλοῦντας, ὅπερ ἐστὶν ἔθος τοῖς Αἰγυπτίοις ποιεῖν; Wilamowitz deletes the †η†. In view of the absence of kissing on the mouth in Homer, and of the negative statement of Hdt. 2.41 (previous note), one might consider reading μὴ; and yet 'because he does not introduce the heroes kissing each other on the mouth, which it is customary for the Egyptians to do' would be a peculiar way of saying '... which the Egyptians also avoid doing'.

of Egypt as the home of mystical wisdom expressed in symbolic form. But the idea is more than a novelist's fancy. Clement of Alexandria goes so far as to claim that 'most people' say Homer was Egyptian (*Stromateis* 1.66); the claim is exaggerated and tendentious, but is evidence that the theory was current. It was also known to Gellius (3.11.6). It is not clear how early it originated. Diodorus of Sicily (1.97.7–9) records the view that Homer was *familiar* with Egypt (its proponents claiming that the Deception of Zeus was based on an Egyptian religious ceremony); this neither entails nor excludes the currency of a theory making him Egyptian.

Another exotic Homer was the Chaldean one. The author of this theory was Zenodotus of Mallos — not the well-known Zenodotus, but a follower of Crates. Crates found cosmological truths in Homer, and Zenodotus' theory was based on evidence of his astrological expertise (ΣAT *Iliad* 23.79b; see also ΣAbT *Iliad* 1.591c). Since the Chaldeans are Babylonians (Strabo 16.1.5–6), the Babylonian Homer we meet in Lucian is in one sense a close relation. The narrator of the *True History* (2.20) visits the Isles of the Blessed, and there meets (among others) Homer, whom he pesters with questions about the burning issues of Homeric scholarship. Were the athetised lines genuine? Yes, all of them: Aristarchus and the rest had no taste. Why did Homer begin the *Iliad* in the way he did? It was just the first thing that came into his head. What was his homeland? Babylon. A more serious writer had inferred from Homer's silence on the subject (by contrast with his references to Egypt) that he knew nothing about Babylon (Strabo 15.3.23); a Babylonian, then, is what Homer was least likely to be. This is no doubt one reason why Lucian chose it: his Babylonian Homer is, of course, a joke.

It is less easy to assess the seriousness of Meleager of Gadara's claim that Homer was a Syrian (Athenaeus 4, 157b). He provides an ethnographic argument: the Syrians do not eat fish.[32] Plato (*Republic* 4, 404bc; cf. Eubulus fr. 120) had noted that fish does not figure in the diet of Homer's heroes (although subsequent scholarship had found it necessary to qualify that claim, as research into Homeric culture produced a more nuanced account of the heroic diet). Local patriotism played a significant part in discussions of Homer's homeland: Ephorus

---

[32] Syrian religious abstention from fish: cf. Ath. 8, 345cd; Diod. Sic. 4.3.11; Hyginus *Fabulae* 197; Hyginus *Astronomica* 2.30, 41; Lucian *De Dea Syria* 14; Menander fr. 754 = 544 K; Ovid *Fasti* 2.43–4; Plut. *QC* 730de; Porph. *De Abstinentia* 2.61; Xen. *Anab.* 1.4.9.

of Cyme accepted the theory of a Cymean Homer; Antimachus of
Colophon accepted the theory of a Colophonian Homer; and while
there is no record of the conclusions reached in the book on Homer's
homeland by the second century AD doctor Hermogenes of Smyrna
(*ISmyrna* 536), they do not defy conjecture. Meleager was proud of his
Syrian background; the epitaph he wrote for himself greets the reader
in Greek, Syrian and Phoenician (Meleager 4 G–P = *AP* 7.419). So
perhaps Meleager's Syrian Homer was an extension of this tendency
into unfamiliar territory. Or perhaps (since he was an epigrammatist
and a cynic philosopher) it was a parody of this tendency and of the
other exotic Homers that had been proposed.

2.4 Romans as Greeks

Even aside from the parodic Babylonian and the possibly parodic
Syrian Homers, we have an Egyptian and a Chaldean Homer. If these
hypotheses could be entertained, then the suggestion of a Roman
Homer looks comparatively sensible. This claim, at least, did not entail
denying that Homer was Greek: for the Romans themselves were
linguistically and ethnically Greek — or so some in the first century
BC maintained.

The most detailed extant presentation of the theory that the Romans
were Greek is in Dionysius of Halicarnassus. But it has older roots.
Heraclides of Pontus, talking about the capture of Rome by the Gauls,
referred to it as a 'Greek city' (F102 Wehrli = *FGrH* 840F23). Accor-
ding to Aristotle (fr. 609 Rose = 700–702 Gigon = *FGrH* 840F13a+c),
Greeks blown off course on their return from Troy were forced to settle
in Italy when the Trojan women they had with them as captives burnt
the ships (it is not clear whether Aristotle himself referred to Rome
here, but Dionysius cites him in that context; Heraclides Lembos did
refer to Rome: 840F13b).[33]

Dionysius himself gives a somewhat different account. He accepts
the story, favoured by the Romans themselves, that Rome was founded
by descendants of the Trojans who fled to Italy with Aeneas (thus
Greeks with Trojan women captives become Trojans accompanied by
Trojan women). Dionysius can integrate this account with his belief

---

[33] The burning of the ships appears in a number of different versions: D. H. *Ant.*1.72.2 =
Hellanicus 4F84 (840F8), Damastes 5F3 (840F9); Plut. *Virt. Mul.* 243e–4a; Strabo 6,
264; [Ar.] *Ausc. Mir.* 109, 840b1–17 (below). On legends of Roman origins:
Strasburger (1968); Galinsky (1986); Gabba (1991); Gruen (1993) 6–51; Cornell
(1975), (1995) 57–72; Maltby (1991) *s.v.* Roma.

that the Romans were Greeks by setting the Trojan migration in the context of successive waves of Greek settlement in Italy and (more radically) by arguing that the Trojans themselves were Greeks (1.61–2), a view sharply at odds with the normal view of Hellenistic Homer scholarship (in which the Trojans are generally seen as barbarians, portrayed unfavourably by a philhellene poet).

As noted earlier, Dionysius provides a good illustration of the ethnographic method of inferring relations between peoples from parallel customs.[34] At the end of book 1, after narrating the early Greek migrations to Italy and the founding of Rome, he reaffirms his conviction that the Romans were of Greek descent and had, despite an admixture of non-Greek elements, preserved clear signs of that origin (1.89–90). Evidence for this thesis, in the form of Greek customs preserved among the Romans (even when, in some cases, they had died out among the Greeks themselves), is presented in 7.70–73.[35] Dionysius also presents a linguistic argument: despite non-Greek influences, Latin was still discernibly Greek, mainly (but not exclusively) Aeolic (1.90). The theory that Latin was an Aeolic Greek dialect had widespread currency in the first century BC.[36] Its supporters included the Greek grammarians Philoxenus of Alexandria (explicitly making the Romans Aeolian colonists),[37] Hypsicrates of Amisos, and Tyrannio (whether the older or the younger is unclear);[38] Varro discussed the importation of Aeolic Greek into Italy in a treatise dedicated to Aristodemus' patron Pompey (fr. 295 Funaioli = John of Lydia *De Magistratibus* 1.5). At a later date Quintilian too noted the similarity of Latin to Aeolic (1.6.31; cf. 1.5.58).

3. The evidence

3.1 Aristodemus

The use of ethnographic arguments in Homeric scholarship, the willingness to consider non-traditional and exotic homelands for

---

[34] Gabba (1991) esp. 93–151.

[35] See also 1.34.4, 38.4, 39.4; 2.12.2–3, 22.1–2; 4.26.5; 6.1.4.

[36] Collart (1954) 205–28; Gabba (1963); Dubuisson (1984b); Schöpsdau (1992).

[37] Philoxenus F323 Theodoridis: the dual developed later than plural, and so is not found in all dialects; the Aeolians do not have it, nor the Romans ἄποικοι ὄντες τῶν Αἰολέων.

[38] The *Suda* attributes this work to the younger Tyrannio, but it has been argued plausibly that this is an error for Tyrannio of Amisos, another of Strabo's teachers, and a pupil of Dionysius of Thrace. See Haas (1977) 97–8.

Homer, and contemporary theories which made the Romans linguisti-
cally and ethnically Greek — all these factors must have contributed to
an environment in which the hypothesis of a Roman Homer was less
unthinkable than it seems to us. Since Aristodemus had spent time in
Rome, he was in a good position to observe Roman customs and to
deploy ethnographic arguments. If we return to the *Vita Romana* and its
(no doubt highly selective) summary of his case, we see at once that he
was applying the familiar ethnographic method to the problem of
Homer's homeland:

> Ἀριστόδημος δ' ὁ Νυσαεὺς Ῥωμαῖον αὐτὸν ἀποδείκνυσιν ἔκ
> τινων ἐθῶν παρὰ Ῥωμαίοις μόνον γινομένων, τοῦτο μὲν ἐκ τῆς
> τῶν πεσσῶν παιδιᾶς, τοῦτο δὲ ἐκ τοῦ ἐπανίστασθαι τῶν θάκων
> τοὺς ἥσσονας τῶν βελτίστων ἑκόντας, ἃ καὶ νῦν ἔτι
> φυλάσσεται παρὰ Ῥωμαίοις ἔθη.

ἐξανίστασθαι Wilamowitz, ὑπανίστασθαι Haslam (*ad* POxy. 3710 col. ii.31) |
τοῖς βελτίστοις Wilamowitz, τοῖς βελτίοσιν Haslam; e.g. <ἐπιόντων> τῶν
βελτίστων

(Aristodemus of Nysa makes him out to be a Roman, on the basis of
certain customs that exist only among the Romans: (a) the playing of
draughts; and (b) the fact that people of inferior status rise from their
seats for superiors of their own accord; these customs are still even now
preserved among the Romans.)

I shall consider these two pieces of evidence in turn.

A1 πεσσοί, a generic term for board-games using pieces or counters,
appears once in Homer (the suitors are found playing πεσσοί in
Odyssey 1.107).[39] There is no doubt that Romans were enthusiastic
about games of this kind. We may note especially the *ludus latruncu-
lorum*, a combat game played without dice; the fact that the *Laus
Pisonis* devotes 19 lines (190–208) to Piso's skill at *latrunculi* may
serve as an index of the game's popularity in Rome.[40] However, the
Life refers to customs existing 'only' among the Romans, and it is
harder to establish that such games would have been seen as *dis-
tinctively* Roman. For this to be the case, we would have to suppose
that a first-century Greek would not have played these games at home
and yet would still have been sufficiently familiar with the concept to

---

[39] The only evidence for scholarly discussion is Apion's description of the suitors' game
(Athenaeus 1, 16f–17b), for which the alleged source is 'Cteson of Ithaca', concerning
whose existence scepticism is in order.
[40] Cf. Austin (1934/5), (1940); Lamer (1927).

recognise Homer's πεσσοί as a game of this kind. Polybius, in praising Scipio Africanus' strategic skill (1.84.6–7), uses an analogy with πεσσοί which must refer to a positional combat game of pure skill, and which implies that his readers in the second century BC would have been familiar with such games. On the other hand, in the second century AD the lexicographer Pollux is arguably confused about the distinction between games of this kind and those involving dice.[41] One might conjecture a trajectory from the one to the other which would give Aristodemus in the first century BC familiarity with the concept though the practice had fallen into disuse; but this conjecture falls foul of Hesychius' clear understanding of the distinction (*s.v.* πεσσὰ πεντέγραμμα καὶ κύβων βολάς). In the absence of more substantial evidence, therefore, the proposed trajectory remains unduly speculative.

An alternative interpretation should be considered: that Aristodemus cited Greek customs that are *paralleled* only among the Romans.[42] That is, he was arguing from customs known from Homer to have been current in early Greece, which may or may not have been preserved among later Greeks, but which the Romans have preserved.[43] This is, in effect, the structure of Dionysius' argument that the Romans are Greeks, which appeals to contemporary as well as archaic Greek usage;

[41] Austin (1940) 262, citing Pollux 7.203, 9.97.

[42] This would fit in with the fact that Herodotus (1.94) singles out πεσσοί as the one game not invented by the Lydians. It would conflict with Plato's attribution of its invention to an Egyptian (*Phaedrus* 274d; cf. Plut. *Is. et Os.* 12, 355de); but some argued that this did not refer to the game, but to an astronomical device (Suet. περὶ τῶν παρ' Ἕλλησι παιδιῶν fr. 1), thus saving the dominant view that the game was invented by Palamedes (Soph. fr. 479; Gorgias *Pal.* 30, etc.).

[43] Logically, one would want to add 'and which are not current among βάρβαροι', but this kind of ethnographic reasoning in antiquity tended to seize on positive correlations without enquiring very deeply into whether they were unique or distinctive correlations. Especially in cases where one term of the correlation is Greek and the other is not, the hellenocentric nature of Greek ethnography (Bickermann (1952) 70, 77–8) created a strong predisposition to assume that the correlation reflects the derivative (or cognate) status of the non-Greek culture, and thus to attach no significance to possible correlations with other non-Greek cultures. But the same tendency can be observed in cases where neither term of the correlation is Greek, as in Timaeus' attempt (*FGrH* 566F36) to establish a Trojan origin for a Roman practice; the awareness displayed by Polybius' methodological criticism of this suggestion (12.4b–4c οὕτω μὲν γὰρ δεήσει πάντας τοὺς βαρβάρους λέγειν Τρώων ἀπογόνους ὑπάρχειν etc.) seems to have been uncommon (see Bickermann (1952) 74). In that example, Timaeus failed to establish uniqueness on the side of the recipient; for an example of indifference to uniqueness on the side of the supposed source consider Athenaeus' identification of Roman imitation of Aeolians in a practice for which he also gives non-Aeolic parallels (cited under E7 below).

citations of Homer may serve to show that contemporary Greek practices were already current in archaic times, as well as to establish that practices no longer current among Greeks once were so. Aristodemus' position would differ only in respect of the additional claim that Homer himself was one of those Greeks who were (or became) Romans. The question then arises why he thought Homer a Roman Greek rather than some other kind of Greek. There is a logical gap to be filled here, to which we shall return (B3).

A2 In Homer, Achilles rises to greet Odysseus, Phoenix and Ajax (*Iliad* 9.193), and Nestor and Odysseus (11.777); in *Odyssey* 16.12 Eumaeus rises when Telemachus arrives, as does Odysseus (still disguised) at 16.42: Eustathius here comments on rising as a mark of respect (though without any Roman reference). But the most telling passage (as Dubuisson has shown)[44] is *Odyssey* 2.14, where Telemachus takes his father's seat and the elders give way to him; here the normal expectation[45] that the younger gives way to the elder is inverted out of respect for the younger man's status or office. Thus Eustathius *ad loc.* (διὰ τὸ τῆς βασιλείας δηλονότι γεραρὸν πρεσβεῖον. ἄλλως γὰρ οἱ νέοι τοῖς πρεσβυτέροις ὑπανίστανται, ὡς πολλαχοῦ δηλοῦται).

The corresponding Roman norm is well-attested. For example, Julius Caesar gave offence by remaining seated when the senate came to him, but took offence when a tribune failed to rise for him at his triumph (Suetonius *Julius* 78; cf. Plutarch *Caesar* 60.5; Dio Cassius 44.8.1–2; Appian *Civil War* 2.107). Accius declined to rise for another Julius Caesar in the *collegium poetarum*, "not because he was forgetful of his *maiestas*, but because in comparing their respective intellectual achievements [*studia*] he was confident of his own superiority" (Valerius Maximus 3.7.11).

3.2 Extrapolations

The *Vita Romana* offers us a brief and no doubt highly simplified version of Aristodemus' arguments. What else might he have said in support of his theory?

---

[44] Dubuisson (1984a) 23.
[45] Younger rising for elder: Xen. *Mem.* 2.3.16 (a universal practice); Ar. *Clds* 993; cf. LSJ *s.v.* ὑπανίστημι. The practice was current even among the Egyptians, whose customs were usually the reverse of those of the Greeks: Hdt. 2.80 (surprisingly ascribing it to the Spartans alone among the Greeks); Nymphodorus *ap.* Σ Soph. *OC* 337.

B1 There is one obvious ethnographic argument. Writers on Homer emphasise the simplicity of the heroic lifestyle (relevant material is conveniently assembled in book 1 of Athenaeus);[46] the heroic abstinence from fish, mentioned earlier, is one aspect of this austerity. Austerity is also a prominent theme in writing on early Rome;[47] there are even references to abstinence from fish.[48]

B2 The theory that Latin was a form of Greek makes it a mainly Aeolic dialect. This would fit in with the widespread view that Homer was Aeolian, which we have seen in pseudo-Herodotus and others.

B3 The familiarity with the west that could be inferred from the *Odyssey* might be used as an argument for a Roman Homer, or at least an Italian one (the *Suda* reports an Italian and a Lucanian Homer,[49] as well as the Roman one). Pseudo-Herodotus (6–7) builds travels in the west into his account of Homer's life, presumably to explain this familiarity. This argument, if it were used, would go some way to closing the logical gap identified above (A1); that is, it could point to a Homer who was a Roman rather than some other kind of Greek.

B4 In this connection, we may also consider the prophecy about Aeneas and his descendants in *Iliad* 20.307–8 (νῦν δὲ δὴ Αἰνείαο βίη Τρώεσσιν ἀνάξει / καὶ παίδων παῖδες, τοί κεν μετόπισθε γένωνται).

---

[46] Schmidt (1976) 159–73. I would caution against Schmidt's acceptance (in modified form) of the hypothesis of Weber (1888), that much of the material on the heroic lifestyle in Athenaeus derives from a monograph on Homeric customs by one Dioscurides; I plan to pursue this question, and to examine Athenaeus' use of this material, elsewhere.

[47] E.g. Plb. 9.10.5; Diod. Sic. 37.3.1–5 (cf. 33.28b); D. H. *Ant.* 2.23.3 (on Roman frugality as a borrowing from Sparta; for the Spartan connection cf. D. H. *Ant.* 2.13.4, 14.2; Varro too links Roman to Spartan and Cretan customs: *De Gente Populi Romani* fr. 37 Fraccaro = Servius *Aeneid* 7.176), 2.74.1 (εὐτέλεια and σωφροσύνη), 10.17.6 (commenting on the story of Cincinnatus); Athenaeus 6, 274a, 275a (citing Posidonius *FGrH* 87F81 = fr. 265–7 Edelstein–Kidd). On the toughness of the Italians generally: Vergil *Aeneid* 9.603 (*durum a stirpe genus*); Servius *ad loc.* cites Cato (*Origines* fr. 76 Peter); Varro *De Gente Populi Romani* fr. 34 Fraccaro. See Vischer (1965) 88–125 on the theme of simplicity in historiography and ethnography, esp. 92–4 (Homer), 96–7, 115–6 (Rome), and 94–7 on the idealisation of Sparta, Crete and Rome.

[48] Diod. Sic. 37.3.3; Ov. *Fasti* 6.173; Varro *Menipp.* fr. 549 Buecheler; *contra* Cassius Hemina *ap.* Plin. *NH* 32.30 (citing a law of Numa).

[49] Why Lucanian? Perhaps this has something to do with the Sibyl. If Homer was allegedly familiar with the Sybil (see n.50 below) and lived before she brought her books to Rome (under Tarquin: D. H. *Ant.* 4.62 etc.), he must have operated in the region of Cumae (note the connection between Cumae and Cyme, one of the traditional homelands). For awareness of Cumae as Lucanian see [Ar.] *Ausc. Mir.* 838a5–14.

Aristophanes of Byzantium regarded these lines as suspect, inferring
from Euripides *Trojan Women* 47 that Troy was still uninhabited in the
fifth century (Σ Euripides *Troades* 47); it follows that he understood
them as referring to Aeneas' rule in the Troad. Interpreted in this sense,
the lines could be seen as inconsistent with the story of Aeneas' flight
to the west (Strabo 13.1.53). Dionysius of Halicarnassus, who accepts
the tradition that Aeneas fled to Italy (1.45.1–53.3), solves the problem
by pointing out that Aeneas could just as well rule over the Trojans in
Italy (1.53.4–5). Others had a different solution: a variant in which
Aeneas' descendants rule over *all* (Αἰνείαο γένος πάντεσσιν ἀνάξει)
was known to Aristonicus and Strabo, and was imitated by Vergil
(*Aeneid* 3.97–8). Such an emendation might well have been prompted
by the perceived conflict between the transmitted text and the tradition
of Aeneas' migration; and a scholar proposing a Roman Homer is
perhaps as good a candidate as any as the source of the conjecture, and
of the explanation (found in the exegetical scholia) that Homer knew of
the future of Rome from the Sibylline oracles (ΣT *Iliad* 20.307–8a[1]).[50]
If Aristodemus was the emender (or accepted the emendation) it would
follow that he admitted Trojans into the Roman ancestry; that is hardly
surprising in the first century BC.

3.3 Dionysius of Halicarnassus

The suggestions made in the previous section are purely speculative. It
is also worth asking whether any actual traces of Aristodemus' theory
are preserved in later sources. I begin with Dionysius of Halicarnassus.
He is concerned with parallels between Roman and Greek customs in
general; I shall extract those examples for which he cites Homeric
evidence. There is of course no reason to assume that Dionysius is
drawing on Aristodemus in these instances. But it is possible; and, at
the very least, his examples attest to scholarly interest in parallels
between Homeric and Roman customs in the first century BC, and
illustrate the kind of thing that might have occurred to a Greek in
making such comparisons. Since the text of Dionysius is easily
accessible and he explains himself clearly, there is no need to do more
than mention these examples.

---

[50] On Homer and Sibyls see Potter (1990) 119-20, citing Parke (1988) 4–5, 109–10. For
Aristodemus as emender see ΣA *Il.* 9.453c (cited in §1 above). If Aristonicus' note
means that Aristarchus was already familiar with the variant, the emender could not be
Aristodemus: but he says only σημειοῦνταί τινες.

C1 7.72.2–4: Contemporary Romans, like archaic Greeks, do not strip naked to compete. For the archaic Greek practice Dionysius cites *Iliad* 23.685 and *Odyssey* 18.66–9, 75–6; this was a recognised point in Homeric scholarship (ΣΑ (cf. D, bT) *Iliad* 23.683). Thucydides (1.6.6) had noted that it was common among barbarians not to strip; so the force of this example is perhaps to show that the Romans are Greeks *despite* seeming to be barbarians in this respect.[51]

C2 7.72.6–9: Secondly, the dance in armour. The Shield of Achilles (Dionysius cites *Iliad* 18.494–6, 590–4, 597–8, 603–6) shows that this was an archaic Greek practice, although Athenaeus tells us that it had ceased to have general currency in the Greek world (14, 631a). The Roman reference is to the *Salii*. One tradition (known to Varro) traced them back to a Greek companion of Aeneas — an Arcadian according to Polemo, a Samothracian according to Critolaus (Varro *ap.* Isidore *Origines* 18.50; cf. Servius on *Aeneid* 2.325, 8.285, 663; Plutarch *Numa* 13.4; *FGrH* 823F1 = Festus 326).

C3 7.72.15–18: To establish a correspondence between details of Greek and Roman sacrificial ritual Dionysius cites *Iliad* 1.449, *Odyssey* 14.422–8.[52]

C4 7.73.2: Contemporary Romans race three-horse chariot teams; the practice has died out among Greeks, but is shown to have been the archaic Greek custom by Homer, where chariots in battle are provided with a third horse (παρήορος: cf. Janko on *Iliad* 16.152–4).

C5 7.73.3: For an athletics programme (following the chariot race) comprising racing, boxing and wrestling Dionysius cites the parallel of Patroclus' funeral games (*Iliad* 23.650–797).

3.4 An anonymous commentator

Fragments of a commentary on the *Odyssey* preserved on papyrus (POxy. 3710) provide one further piece of evidence.

D1 Discussing the instructions which Eurycleia gives to the servant-women at *Odyssey* 20.149–56 to prepare the palace for the suitors' arrival, the commentator suggests that she is not motivated by concern for the suitors themselves: she wants them to move on to their wool-

---

[51] But cf. n.43 on the lack of care in establishing unique correlations in ancient ethnography.
[52] Schmidt (1976) 257–9, 262.

working without undue delay. He then adds that 'the custom of the service is Roman' (Ῥωμαϊκὸν τὸ ἔθος τῆς διακονίας, col. ii.31). The comment is, as Haslam observes (*ad loc.*), 'rather opaque'. Since the lemma for this note is the first half of line 151, and in 150–1 Eurycleia orders the women to spread purple covers over the chairs (ἔν τε θρόνοισ' εὐποιήτοισι τάπητας | βάλλετε πορφυρέους), the reference may be to the taste among wealthy Romans for purple coverings on couches at dinner (see e.g. Virgil *Aeneid* 1.700; Horace *Odes* 3.29.5; *Satires* 2.6.100–9; Martial 3.82.7; Cassius Dio 62.15.3).[53]

The latest author cited in these fragments is Aristonicus, suggesting a date of composition in the first century AD. We know of several Homeric scholars of the early empire who worked in Rome (for example, Seleucus and Epaphroditus), but the commentator of POxy. 3710 cannot be confidently identified with any of them. It may, however, be possible to learn more about his approach from related material preserved by Eustathius.

3.5 Eustathius

Eustathius claims (on *Iliad* 3.228) that Homer's poetry is dense with Roman customs (πεπύκνωται καὶ Ῥωμαϊκοῖς ἔθεσιν ἡ Ὁμηρικὴ ποίησις). The implications of this claim are discussed in more detail in a note on *Odyssey* 1.121, where he gives a concise catalogue of parallel customs; but other relevant parallels are noted at various places in his commentaries.[54] Eustathius does not suppose that Homer himself was a Roman. He uses these parallels to support the theory that the Latins assimilated customs brought to Italy by early Greek migrants; so in his view the Romans are not ethnically Greek, but they preserve customs which we know from Homer originally to have been Greek customs. It is demonstrable that Eustathius draws his material from more than one source (for example, E6 is taken from the scholia, but E7 is from Athenaeus). One of Eustathius' examples (F9) seems to presuppose the principate, and we saw in the preceding section evidence for an interest in Roman parallels on the part of at least one commentator of this period. It is possible to imagine such a scholar developing his own

---

[53] Lobel's suggestion (reported by Haslam) that the reference is to wool-working might lead us to infer a criticism of the theory of an Egyptian Homer (since among the Egyptians it is the men, not the women, who work wool: Hdt. 2.35; Nymphodorus *ap.* Σ Soph. *OC* 337). But I do not think this interpretation is likely, since the wool-working is supplied speculatively by the commentator, and not mentioned in Homer's text.

[54] Hillscher (1892) 435–9 made the first attempt to collect this material.

interpretation of the parallels between Homeric and Roman customs. He may have added new instances from his own observations; so here, too, it would be wrong to assume that the parallels adduced must derive from Aristodemus. But such a scholar is likely to have made use of the work of his predecessors, recycling their observations in support of a different theory; so traces of Aristodemus' argumentation may be preserved in Eustathius, and (as with Dionysius) they provide evidence of the kind of observation that a Greek interested in such links might have made.

In discussing these parallels, we need to consider how each is anchored in the Homeric text. A second consideration is what was said about the relevant passages in Homeric scholarship; the observation of a Roman parallel is obviously more interesting if it can be seen as throwing light on an existing problem in Homer. It is also necessary to consider what aspect of Roman life provides the other term of the parallel. Since Aristodemus would have known antiquarians like Varro we must take account of the possibility that the Roman parallel is not part of current daily life in Rome, but something fossilised in ritual, or regarded by the Romans as typically Roman, even if obsolete. In some cases I can offer at least a partial answer to these questions; in others, I am at a loss, and merely exhibit this little-known material in the hope that others will be able to throw further light on it. I shall take Eustathius' other examples in order, reserving the list of examples in the note on *Odyssey* 1.121 for the next section.

E1 Eustathius on *Iliad* 2.384 (ἅρματος ἀμφὶς ἰδών)· ὅτι δὲ ἡ τοῦ ἅρματος λέξις καὶ ἐπὶ ὅπλου λέγεται, καὶ ὅτι Ῥωμαϊκὸν τοῦτο, καὶ ὅτι διὰ τοῦτο οὐδὲ ὁμωνυμία ἐντεῦθεν γίνεται, δηλοῦσιν οἱ παλαιοὶ σοφοί.

The first example may not, in fact, be relevant. Eustathius connects the word ἅρμα with the Latin *arma*. Compare Σb *Iliad* 2.384: τοῦτο δὲ καὶ †ὁ Θουκυδίδης† ἐν Πολιτείαις φησὶ τὸ ὅπλισμα.[55] I know of no parallel. But this comment may derive from work on connections between Latin and Greek;[56] it need not have a bearing on either the theory that Homer was Roman or the theory that Romans assimilated early Greek customs.

---

[55] The reference to Thucydides is manifestly corrupt. Erbse suggests Aristotle, but does not put it in his text.

[56] Cf. Eust. on *Od.* 6.115 (σφαῖρα ~ *pila*), *Od.* 7.90 (κορώνη ~ *corona*: cf. Philoxenus fr. 315); *Od.* 1.107 (κύβος and cognates ~ *cubitum*).

E2 Eustathius on *Iliad* 2.192: οὔκουν ἅπαντες οἴδασιν οἱ βασιλεῖς καὶ μέδοντες ὅτι πειρᾶται ὁ βασιλεύς, ἀλλ' οἱ ἑπτὰ ἴσως καὶ μόνοι οὓς γέροντας ἀριστῆας Παναχαιῶν μετ' ὀλίγα ἐρεῖ, τουτέστιν ἐντίμους, ἐξ ὧν καὶ ἡ παρὰ Ῥωμαίοις ὕστερον γερουσία. In *Iliad* 2.404 Agamemnon summons the γέροντας ἀριστῆας Παναχαιῶν: these include Nestor, but also Idomeneus, the two Ajaxes, Diomedes, Odysseus and (though without explicit invitation) Menelaus; so 'elders' (γέροντες) does not refer exclusively to old men. Eustathius' explanation is that the word is being used in the sense 'those held in honour' (ἐντίμοι). Compare ΣΑΤ *Iliad* 2.21b: μάλιστα γερόντων· τῶν †ἐννέα τιμίων†, ἐν οἷς καὶ Διομήδης καὶ Αἴαντες; behind the corruption[57] must be the same interpretation of γέροντες as ἐντίμοι (cf. ΣΑbT *Iliad* 2.53d, A 9.70b, bT 4.259). Eustathius refers to the Roman *senatus* as a parallel for this usage. Dionysius, too, in a discussion of the Roman senate (2.12.3–4), notes that the ancients applied γέροντες both to people of advanced age and to 'the best' (οἱ ἄριστοι), and he refers to Homer to illustrate the proposition that it was a Greek custom for a king to have a council of advisers (as Romulus did).

E3 Eustathius on *Iliad* 3.228: καὶ ὅτι τανύπεπλον τὴν Ἑλένην λέγει οὐ μόνον ὡς τανύουσαν Ῥωμαϊκῶς καὶ ἐπισύρουσαν κάτω τὸν πέπλον, ὅς ἐστιν ἐνταῦθα γυναικεῖον ἱμάτιον, ἀλλὰ καὶ ὡς εὔσαρκον καὶ οὐκ ἰσχνήν, ἀλλὰ τείνουσαν καὶ ἐξαπλοῦσαν καὶ ἐμπιπλῶσαν τὸν πέπλον τῷ εὖ διεστηκέναι αὐτῇ τὴν φυὴν τοῦ σώματος. ὅτι δὲ κατὰ τὴν ἀνωτέρω ἑρμηνείαν τῆς τανυπέπλου πεπύκνωται καὶ Ῥωμαϊκοῖς ἔθεσιν ἡ Ὁμηρικὴ ποίησις, ἐν Ὀδυσσείᾳ δεδήλωται.

Eustathius offers two interpretations of the epithet τανύπεπλος, applied to Helen: it may mean that the garment is long, in the Roman fashion (the reference is to the *stola*),[58] or that her fine physique fills out the garment. These two interpretations can be paralleled from several entries in the Homeric lexicon of the sophist Apollonius: βαθύ-πεπλος is referred either to physique or to the style of the garment, reflecting the wearer's dignified status. Apollonius treats βαθύζωνος, βαθύκολπος and ἑλκεσίπεπλος as equivalent to βαθύπεπλος, and also glosses τανύπεπλος in terms of the garment's length (though he makes

---

[57] ἐννέα is wrong, since there are seven of them; but ΣbT *Il.* 2.96–7 has the same corruption.
[58] Marquardt–Mau (1886) 573–4.

no reference to the Romans). Some other passages in Eustathius bear on the same question:

(i) On *Iliad* 7.297, commenting on ἑλκεσίπεπλος, Eustathius explains that it refers to the length of the garment, and again refers to the Roman custom: ἀντὶ τοῦ μακρόπεπλοι, ὃ δὴ καὶ Ῥωμαίοις ἐπεχωρίασεν.

(ii) On *Odyssey* 3.154 he follows the scholia *ad loc.* in understanding βαθύζωνος as a reference to the trailing garments of the Trojans, identifying this as a non-Greek style of female dress.

(iii) On *Odyssey* 4.305 the two interpretations of τανύπεπλος reappear, and it is noted that Helen has maintained the style of dress which she adopted during her stay in Troy; again it is stressed that this is a non-Greek style.

Accordingly, in his note on *Odyssey* 1.121 (see F14 below) Eustathius traces this parallel between Homeric and Roman customs not to Greek migrants to Italy, but to Trojan migrants. There is a precedent in the pseudo-Aristotelian *De Mirabilium Auscultationibus* (109, 840b1–17), where we read how Trojan women forced their Greek captors to settle in Italy by burning their ships; the Homeric descriptions of Trojan women as ἑλκεσίπεπλοι and βαθύκολποι are cited as corresponding to the style of female dress found in Italy. It has been suggested that the source may be Timaeus.[59]

Eustathius supports his treatment of this parallel by arguing that Homer does not describe Greek women as βαθύπεπλος or ἑλκεσίπεπλος. He (or his source) may have misrecollected a point made by Aristarchus against Zenodotus. In the invocation of the Muses in *Iliad* 2.484 Zenodotus read Ὀλυμπιάδες βαθύκολποι, instead of the vulgate Ὀλύμπια δώματ' ἔχουσαι. Aristarchus objected that Homer does not use βαθύκολπος of Greek women (ΣΑ *Iliad* 2.484; cf. ΣΑ *Iliad* 18.389, 24.215b). However, this does not apply to τανύπεπλος: the word is used not only of Helen (who, as we have seen, could have acquired the habit from the Trojans) but also of Thetis (*Iliad* 18.385), the nymph Lampetie (*Odyssey* 12.375), and Odysseus' sister Ctimene (*Odyssey* 15.363). A scholar who had correctly observed the usage of τανύπεπλος would have had no reason to limit this style of female dress in Homer to the Trojans, as Eustathius does; he could have seen it as something shared by Homer's Greeks and the Romans. On the other hand, if (as suggested under B4) Aristodemus recognised a Trojan

---

[59] K. Ziegler *RE* 18.3 (1949) 1152 (*s.v.* Paradoxographoi); Fraser (1972) 1079 n.383.

element in the Roman descent, accepting the limitation of this style to Trojans would have presented no problem to his theory. Identifying Homeric but specifically Trojan elements in Rome could also have contributed to a case for a Roman Homer, helping to bridge the logical gap noted earlier (A1, cf. B3).

E4   Eustathius on *Iliad* 4.3–4 (τοὶ δὲ χρυσέοις δεπάεσσι/ δειδέχατ' ἀλλήλους)· τὸ δὲ δειδέχατο ... τὴν παρὰ τοῖς ὕστερον πρόποσιν δηλοῖ. προπίνουσι γὰρ ἀλλήλοις κατὰ τὸ καὶ παρὰ Ῥωμαίοις ἔθος οἱ ἀλλήλους δεπάεσσι δεξιούμενοι.
Ancient scholars distinguished two forms of πρόποσις. In the modern practice, the person initiating the pledge drinks and then passes the cup to the recipient of the honour; but in Homer the person initiating the pledge passes the cup full. This was inferred from *Iliad* 9.224 (πλησάμενος δ' οἴνοιο δέπας δείδεκτ' Ἀχιλῆα): thus ΣA *Iliad* 9.224, followed by Athenaeus 5, 193a. Galen (10.3.14–16 Kühn) notes that at Roman parties the guests do not engage in music or conversation, but pledge each other and compete in the amount they can drink (ἀλλὰ προπινόντων μὲν ἀλλήλοις, ἁμιλλωμένων δὲ περὶ μεγέθους ἐκπωμάτων). But what was the Roman practice in pledging? Cicero (*Tusculan Disputations* 1.96) has to explain that the Greeks name the person to whom they pass the cup, implying that Greek and Roman practice was not identical in every respect; but positive evidence for the detail in question is hard to find. Dido (*Aeneid* 1.737–8) merely touches the drink with her lips before passing the cup on, so that the recipient drinks *pleno auro*. But this is not reliable evidence for the Roman practice; it may reflect nothing more than Virgil's familiarity with Homeric scholarship (Servius thinks Dido does this because she is a woman). I have not been able to throw further light on the question.

E5   Eustathius on *Iliad* 11.750: τὸ δὲ Ἀκτορίωνε Μολίονε παῖδε διαφωνεῖται παρὰ τοῖς παλαιοῖς. οἱ μὲν γὰρ καὶ ἄμφω τὰς λέξεις πατρωνυμεῖσθαί φασιν, ἵνα λέγῃ Ἀκτορίωνας μὲν ἀναμφιλέκτως τοὺς Ἀκτορίδας, ὅ ἐστιν υἱοὺς Ἄκτορος, Μολίονας δὲ ἢ πατρωνυμικῶς καὶ αὐτὸ οἷα Μόλου ὄντας πατρὸς τοῦ καὶ Ἄκτορος. διὸ καθὰ Ῥωμαϊκῷ ἔθει Ἄκτωρ Μόλος ἀσυνδέτως ὁ πατὴρ κατὰ διωνυμίαν, οὕτω καὶ οἱ αὐτοῦ παῖδες Ἀκτορίωνε Μολίονε ...
The anomalous double patronymic in *Iliad* 11.750 was a problem for ancient scholars. Eustathius records a number of explanations, of which the first is that the father had a double name: the two are the sons of

Molos ὁ καὶ Actor, and this has been expressed asyndetically in the Roman fashion as Actor Molos.[60]

E6 Eustathius on *Iliad* 15.687: ἐν δὲ παλαιοῖς σχολίοις γέγραπται ὅτι Δημήτριός φησι τεθεωρηκέναι τινὰ μεταβαίνοντα, ὡς ὁ ποιητὴς λέγει, κατέχοντα τοὺς χαλινοὺς καὶ ἀνεμποδίστως τηροῦντα τὸν δρόμον τῶν ἵππων, καὶ ὅτι καὶ νῦν ἐν Ῥώμῃ τοῦτο γίνεται. A simile in *Iliad* 15.679–84 describes a man with four horses harnessed together, leaping from one to another with a large crowd of spectators. Eustathius cites ΣbT *Iliad* 15.683–4 (Δημήτριος δὲ ὁ Γονύπεσός <φησι> τεθεωρηκέναι του μεταβαίνοντος, ἀνεμπόδιστον τηροῦντος τὸν δρόμον τῶν ἵππων, κατέχοντος τοὺς χαλινούς. καὶ νῦν δὲ ἐν Ῥώμῃ ποιοῦσί τινες) for the claim that the practice survived in Rome.[61] The Roman reference is to the kind of equestrian acrobat known in Latin as *desultor*.[62]

E7 Eustathius on *Iliad* 20.234–5: ᾠνοχόουν παρὰ τοῖς παλαιοῖς εὐγενέστατοι παῖδες, ὡς ὁ τοῦ Μενελάου υἱός. καὶ παρὰ Ῥωμαίοις δέ, φασί, τοιοῦτοι παῖδες τὴν λειτουργίαν ταύτην ἐξετέλουν ἐν ταῖς δημοτελέσι θυσίαις.

In a discussion of Ganymede's service on Olympus Eustathius cites as a parallel Menelaus' son serving wine at *Odyssey* 15.141; he adds that it was the Roman custom for well-born children to have this function at public sacrifices. The custom is frequent in Homer (*Iliad* 1.470, 9.175; *Odyssey* 1.148, 3.339, 3.471–2, 21.271), and is discussed in the scholia (ΣAbT *Iliad* 1.470, AbT *Iliad* 20.234d).[63] However, Eustathius' immediate source is Athenaeus 10, 424e (= Theophrastus F119 Wimmer; Hieronymus F28 Wehrli; cf. 18b, 192b) on Menelaus' son, and 425a on the Romans; in the latter passage Athenaeus adds that the Romans are imitating the Aeolians, just as they do in their speech (πάντα τοὺς Αἰολεῖς μιμούμενοι, ὡς καὶ κατὰ τοὺς τόνους τῆς φωνῆς). The Aeolian link is the statement that Sappho's brother Larichus served wine in the prytaneion of Mytilene (= fr. 203 LP),

---

[60] For Greek attempts to understand Roman nomenclature in the first century BC cf. Plut. *Marius* 1, a critique of Posidonius (*FGrH* 87F60 = fr. 266 Edelstein–Kidd). Balsdon (1979) 153–60 discusses Greek difficulties with Roman names.
[61] Eustathius mistakenly attributes the last part of the scholion to the source cited in the preceding sentence; Erbse comments: "ipsius scholiastae (an Epaphroditi?) sunt, non Demetrii".
[62] Pollack *RE* 5 (1903) 255–9; cf. Schmidt (1976) 229–31 (231 for *desultor*). The Greek ἀποβάτης is different: see Arnott (1996) 104–5.
[63] Schmidt (1976) 173–80.

although non-Aeolic examples of the practice are also cited.

The Roman reference is to the *camilli*, well-born young men acting as servitors to certain priests,[64] in whom Dionysius also took an interest (2.22; cf. Livy 37.3.6; Macrobius 3.8.6–7). Varro (*De Lingua Latina* 7.34) inferred a Greek derivation, having seen the word in Callimachus (= fr. 723 Pf., see Pfeiffer *ad loc.*). He is thinking of Cadmilus or Casmilus, an epithet of Hermes, who also sometimes acts as a divine waiter (Hipponax fr. 155b West; Lycophron 162; Σ Apollonius of Rhodes 1.917; Servius on *Aeneid* 11.543, 558). Thus too Juba (*FGrH* 275F88 = Plutarch *Numa* 7.10): καὶ τὸν ὑπηρετοῦντα τῷ ἱερεῖ τοῦ Διὸς ἀμφιθαλῆ παῖδα λέγεσθαι Κάμιλλον, ὡς καὶ τὸν Ἑρμῆν οὕτως ἔνιοι τῶν Ἑλλήνων Κάμιλλον ἀπὸ τῆς διακονίας προσηγόρευον.

E8   Eustathius on *Iliad* 24.471–6: ὅτι ὁ γέρων ἰθὺς ἐλθὼν οἴκου ἔνθ᾽ Ἀχιλλεὺς ἵζεσκε Διῒ φίλος, εὗρέ μιν αὐτόν, ἔταροι δ᾽ ἀπάνευθεν καθείατο· ἔθος δὴ τοῦτο Ῥωμαίοις ἔτι καὶ νῦν ἀρέσκον.

At *Iliad* 24.471–6 Priam finds Achilles, and his companions (except for two of them, who are serving him a meal) sitting apart. I take it that in Eustathius' reference to a Roman custom "even now" is likely to signify the time of his source.[65] But the best Roman parallel I have found is in Seneca: the objection that it would be demeaning at a royal symposium to have to eat with slaves implies that the slaves are eating in the same room, but sit separately (*De Constantia Sapientis* 15.1).[66]

E9   Eustathius on *Odyssey* 7.153: ἀρχαϊσμοῦ δὲ τὸ τοὺς ἐπήλυδας ἅμα εἰσόδῳ χαμαὶ καθῆσθαι· ὃ καὶ αὐτὸ παρὰ Λατίνοις φυλάσσεται.

On entering Alcinous' palace Odysseus takes his seat by the hearth, in the ashes, on the floor (χαμαί 7.160). Eustathius says that for newly-arrived strangers to sit on the floor is an archaism, but remains the practice among the Latins. It is possible that this notion derives from the similar story told about Coriolanus' supplication at the hearth of Tullus (Dionysius of Halicarnassus 8.1.4; Plutarch *Coriolanus* 23.1).[67]

---

[64] *RE* 3 (1989) 1431–2 *s.v.* Camillus (1); Marquardt–Wissowa (1885) III 227–30, 451. Compare the four *pueri ingenui patrimi et matrimi, senatorum filii* who minister at *epulae* of the *arvales*.

[65] Contrast van der Valk *ad loc.*: "significat, opinor, dominos solos sine asseclis accumbere, qui, ut videtur, mos Byz."

[66] Marquardt–Mau (1886) 175.

[67] In the parallel story told about Themistocles (Thuc. 1.136.3; cf. Plut. *Them.* 24.4–5, interpreting it as a Molossian custom) the use of the baby to enhance the supplication is an additional and distinctive element.

3.6 Eustathius on *Odyssey* 1.121

We come finally to the list of parallels given in the note on *Odyssey* 1.121, where the theory of Greek customs mentioned in Homer being transmitted to the Latins by Greek settlers is set out.

F1 ὅτι τὸ τῆς δεξιᾶς χειρὸς ἅπτεσθαι ὅπερ καὶ νῦν πολλοῖς τῶν ἐθνῶν ἐπιχωριάζει, δεῖγμα φιλοφροσύνης ἦν ἀσφαλέστατον ... καὶ ὅτι τῶν δεξιῶν χειρῶν ἡ συμβολή, ἔοικεν ἐξ Ἑλλήνων ἐπιχωριάσαι τοῖς Λατίνοις μετὰ καὶ ἄλλων μυρίων ἐθῶν. πολλοὶ γὰρ τῶν Ἑλλήνων οἱ μὲν ἑκόντες μετοικήσαντες εἴτουν ἀποικήσαντες, οἱ δὲ καὶ μετὰ τὴν τῆς Ἰλίου ἅλωσιν εἰς τὰ κατὰ τὴν Ἰταλίαν διεκπεσόντες χωρία, τήν τε ἄψιν τῶν δεξιῶν ὡς εἰκὸς διέδωκαν τοῖς ἐκεῖ καὶ ἄλλων δὲ ἐθῶν Ἑλληνικῶν ἐκείνοις μετέδωκαν, ὧν Ὅμηρος μέμνηται ὁ Ἕλλην σοφός.

For clasping right hands as a mark of friendship and a pledge see *Iliad* 7.108, 10.542, 14.137; *Odyssey* 1.121, 20.197; there is no discussion in the scholia to these passages. It is well-attested in Roman sources; Varro provided an *aition*, citing Callimachus (fr. 189 Pf. = Servius on *Aeneid* 1.408, cf. 8.467). There is Greek evidence for the practice in the fifth century (e.g. Aristophanes *Clouds* 81, *Frogs* 788), and nothing to suggest that it died out in later times (e.g. Heliodorus 10.24.1).[68]

F2 ἡ τῆς διαίτης ἁπλότης. See B1.

F3 τὸ προπίνειν ἀλλήλοις δεξιουμένους ἐκπώμασι. See E4.

F4 τὸ παγγύμνους νύκτωρ καθεύδειν.

This is presumably based on waking-up scenes in which the character dresses (*Odyssey* 2.2–4 = 4.307–9, 15.56–62) — an admittedly tenuous inference.[69] There is sparse evidence for later Greek nightwear. Pollux 10.123 cites the phrase χιτὼν εὐνητήρ from a comedy (= com. adesp. 920 Kock); cf. Herodian *Philetaerus* 175 (= fr. 76 Dain): ἐνεύναιον ἱμάτιον καὶ ἐπιβόλαιον τὸ ἐν τῇ εὐνῇ. The word ἐνεύναιον is glossed as ἐγκοίμητρον, ἐγκοίτιον in Σ *Odyssey* 14.51, followed by Eustathius *ad loc.* In a bilingual school-text published by Dionisotti, ενκυμετρα (= ἐγκοίμητρα) is rendered by *dormitoria* (5); but the Latin

---

[68] *RE* 1A.2 (1920) 2062–3 (*s.v.* Salutatio).
[69] The shipwrecked Odysseus sleeps naked: *Odyssey* 6.1, 136; but that is surely a special case. Nor (for obvious reasons) can Odysseus' nakedness when putatively sleeping with Circe (*Odyssey* 10.301, 341) be relevant.

term shows no sign of existing outside glossaries. Dionisotti comments that "it is not clear what, if anything, the Romans wore in bed", concluding from the sparse evidence that "night-clothes as such were not then current, but retaining (a little) underwear probably was".[70] My own researches have not led to any other conclusion.

F5   τὸ ὑπὸ γυναικῶν λούεσθαι.

Telemachus is bathed by Nestor's daughter at *Odyssey* 3.464–5; free women and goddesses perform the same function at *Odyssey* 4.252 (Helen), 5.264 (Calypso), 10.361, 450 (Circe), *Iliad* 5.905 (Hebe), as well as assorted female slaves (*Odyssey* 4.49, 8.454, 17.88, 19.317, 23.154, 24.366). The practice was discussed by ancient scholars (ΣΑ *Iliad* 5.905a, b *Iliad* 9.905b, T *Iliad* 7.722a; Σ *Odyssey* 3.464, 4.252, 11.601; Athenaeus 1, 10d), who were (naturally) surprised by it.[71] The Roman reference is perhaps to mixed bathing (Martial 3.51; Pliny *Natural History* 33.153).[72] This was certainly seen by Greeks as distinctively Roman: Plutarch (*Cato Maior* 20) comments that after adopting nudity from the Greeks, the Romans 'reinfected' (Sansone's apt rendering of ἀναπεπλήκασι) them with mixed nudity.

F6   τὸ τὰς πολλὰς τῶν γυναικῶν μὴ ἐθέλειν προφαίνειν τὰ πρόσωπα, ἄντα παρειάων καὶ αὐτὰς ἐχούσας λιπαρὰ κρήδεμνα.

Eustathius alludes to *Odyssey* 1.334 (ἄντα παρειάων σχομένη λιπαρὰ κρήδεμνα = 16.416, 18.210, 21.65). Elsewhere (e.g. *Iliad* 3.610.17, *Odyssey* 1.64.9) Eustathius follows the scholia in regarding the κρήδεμνον as a covering for the head, not the face; but on *Odyssey* 1.335 he notes that it must also be something that can hang down to cover the face (a καταπέτασμα). Dicaearchus (F92 Wehrli) criticised Penelope for making sexually provocative use of her veil (assuming that she is veiling her face, but leaving her eyes visible); Porphyry (Σ *Odyssey* 1.332) countered by arguing that the κρήδεμνον is not a covering for the face, but the head, so that Penelope is not provocatively leaving her eyes uncovered, but drawing down her head-covering to conceal her tears.

In later times Greek women continued to cover their heads, but covering the face seems not to have been general; at any rate, it is regarded as noteworthy where the practice does exist: Plutarch *Greek*

[70] Dionisotti (1982) 108.
[71] Schmidt (1976) 173–80.
[72] Marquardt–Mau (1886) 282–3; Blümner (1911) 427–8.

Questions 49 (302ef) records that the women of Chalcedon lift their head-covering to cover one cheek when they meet male strangers; Heraclides of Crete (1.18 Pfister) records that Theban women cover the whole face except the eyes. Roman evidence for women covering the head is not hard to find: see (e.g.) Valerius Maximus 6.3.10; Varro *De Lingua Latina* 5.130; Plutarch *Roman Questions* 14, 267a (πένθους μὲν οἰκεῖον τὸ μὴ σύνηθες, συνηθέστερον δὲ ταῖς μὲν γυναιξὶν ἐγκεκαλυμμέναις, τοῖς δ' ἀνδράσιν ἀκαλύπτοις εἰς τὸ δημόσιον προϊέναι). It is harder to find evidence for Roman women covering the face; but note Tacitus *Annals* 13.45 (on Poppaea covering her face in public: *rarus in publicum egressus, idque velata parte oris, ne satiaret aspectum, vel quia sic decebat*).

F7 τὸ τοὺς ἄνδρας χλαίνας ἀμπέχεσθαι, τουτέστι μανδοειδῆ περιβλήματα ῥάω πρὸς ἀπέκδυσιν, μᾶλλον δὲ πρὸς ἀπόθεσιν· διὸ φησί που ὅτι ἀπέθετο χλαῖναν φοινικόεσσαν, ὁμοίως τῷ ἀπέθετο δὲ ξίφος ὀξὺ ὤμων.

Eustathius refers to *Odyssey* 14.500 (ἀπὸ δὲ χλαῖναν βάλε φοινικόεσσαν), 21.118–9 (ἀπ' ὤμοιϊν χλαῖναν θέτο φοινικόεσσαν / ὀρθὸς ἀναΐξας, ἀπὸ δὲ ξίφος ὀξὺ θέτ' ὤμων). But *Iliad* 2.183, where Odysseus throws off his χλαῖνα, so he could run more easily (βῆ δὲ θέειν, ἀπὸ δὲ χλαῖναν βάλε), is also relevant: Porphyry's discussion shows that a problem was felt to arise from Odysseus' action, which could be seen as lacking decorum (ἀπρεπές). The nature of the χλαῖνα was a matter of scholarly discussion. Ammonius discusses χλαῖνα and χλανίς, χλαῖνα and χλαμύς (*De Adfinium Vocabulorum Differentia* 512–3 Nickau), reporting that Didymus discussed the question at length in his commentary on *Iliad* 2 (cf. ΣAT *Iliad* 2.183), with reference to the views of Aristotle (fr. 500 Rose = 984 Gigon), Phylarchus (*FGrH* 81F62) and Polemo (fr. 99 Preller).

It would perhaps be beside the point to discuss which of the several kinds of cloak known to the Romans was the easiest to take off: the reference is surely to the cloak known as the *laena*.[73] The etymological connection was inevitably made: Juba derived *laena* from χλαῖνα (*FGrH* 275F88 = Plutarch *Numa* 7.10: καὶ γὰρ ἃς ἐφόρουν οἱ ἱερεῖς λαίνας ὁ Ἰόβας χλαίνας φησὶν εἶναι).

As to the nature of the *laena*, Varro (*De Lingua Latina* 5.133) explains that it was made from a lot of wool (an alternative derivation),

---

[73] Marquardt–Mau (1886) 569–70; on Roman cloaks in general see Wilson (1938) 76–129, and for the *laena* 112–7.

and was the equivalent of two togas; hence is was either very thick, or large, so it could be worn doubled up. Compare Servius on *Aeneid* 4.262–3: *laena genus est vestis. est autem proprie toga duplex, amictus auguralis. alii amictum rotundum: alii togam duplicem, in qua flamines sacrificant infibulati.* The line on which Servius is commenting, in which Aeneas is wearing a *laena* (*Aeneid* 4.262–3: *ensis erat Tyrioque ardebat murice laena / demissa ex umeris*) is an echo of *Odyssey* 21.118–9 (quoted above). Note too *Aeneid* 5.421: *haec fatus duplicem ex umeris reiecit amictum*; although Servius *ad loc.* does not interpret this garment as a *laena*, the phrasing recalls the *duplex toga*. A double χλαῖνα is found in *Iliad* 10.133–4 (ἀμφὶ δ' ἄρα χλαῖναν περονήσατο φοινικόεσσαν / διπλῆν ἐκταδίην) and *Odyssey* 19.225–6 (χλαῖναν πορφυρέην οὔλην ἔχε δῖος Ὀδυσσεύς, διπλῆν). It is possible that a scholar who made a link to the Latin *laena* regarded this parallel to the *toga duplex* as a clue to the nature of the χλαῖνα in general; however, ΣΑΤ *Iliad* 10.134a takes the double χλαῖνα in that passage to be a special kind (suitable for the elderly Nestor at night), and there are ἁπλοΐδας χλαίνας at *Iliad* 24.230.

F8   τὸ γονυπετοῦντας ἱκετεύειν εἴτε καὶ καθημένους, ὡς Ὀδυσσεὺς παρὰ Αἰόλῳ ἐπὶ σταθμοῖς ἐπ' οὐδοῦ ἑζόμενος.

On his arrival at Aeolus' palace Odysseus supplicates from a sitting position (*Odyssey* 10.62–3; cf. 17.339). Compare E9.

F9   τὸ τὸν εὐρυκρείοντα δὲ μιᾶς τινος πόλεως ἄρχειν τοῖς ἄλλοις ἀφιέντα τὰς λοιπὰς προφανῶς Ἑλληνικόν.

The epithet εὐρυκρείων is applied to Agamemnon at *Iliad* 1.102. But while he exercises wide-ranging power, he is king of Mycenae alone: others rule other cities, although they are in some sense sub-ordinated to him.[74] Applied to Rome, this seems to presuppose the principate.

F10   τὸ ἐν δημηγορίαις πάντων καθημένων τῶν συνειλεγμένων ἕνα τινὰ δημηγορεῖν ἱστάμενον.

It is normal in Homer for the speaker to stand: *Iliad* 1.58, 2.278–9, 9.52, 19.55, 19.79.[75] In the Roman senate, speakers stood to address a

---

[74] In another discussion of Agamemnon's position (on *Iliad* 7.180) Eustathius acknowledges that some think he was elected leader, rather than having sovereignty over the other kings.

[75] A detail noted by West (1997) 194, who adduces a different cultural parallel: "In both Greek and Akkadian descriptions of assemblies we note the procedural point that the speaker stands up to speak."

seated audience (Cicero *Ad Atticum* 1.14.3). By contrast, the audience in Roman public assemblies stood,[76] and Cicero (*Pro Flacco* 15–17) regards it as a fault of Greek assemblies that the audience sat and remained seated to vote. However, the fact that in *Iliad* 19.76–7 Agamemnon apparently speaks while sitting provoked discussion in the scholia, and the comment in ΣD *Iliad* 1.58 (τὸ γὰρ παλαιὸν κἂν βασιλεὺς ἦν κἂν ἄλλης οἰασδήποτε τύχης λαμπρός, ἐδημηγόρει δέ, ὀρθὸς ἵστατο) implies that later Greeks would expect a speaker of high status to remain seated while speaking.

F11 τὸ τοῖς δεσπόταις συγκαθῆσθαι τοὺς θεράποντας.

The verb συγκαθῆσθαι can mean 'share quarters' (Herodotus 3.68). But Eustathius uses it to explain μνηστῆρσι μεθήμενος (*Odyssey* 1.118: see 1.33.44), and to describe Penelope sitting with Eurynome (*Odyssey* 18.163: 2.173.23); so probably we should take it here in the sense 'sit with'. I presume that he means 'sit with at meals'. Homer's gods and heroes sat to eat, rather than reclining (Athenaeus 1, 11f, 17f; 5, 192e); and this was the original Roman practice also (Varro *De Vita Populi Romani* fr. 30 Riposati; *De Gente Populi Romani* fr. 37 Fraccaro; Columella *De Re Rustica* 11.1.19; cf. Plutarch *Cato Min.* 56.7). Servius (*Aeneid* 1.79) makes the comparison: *olim sedentes vescebantur ... et apud Homerum sedentes dii epulantur.*

For Romans eating with their slaves see Plutarch *Coriolanus* 24.9, *Cato Maior* 3 (Cato consumes the same food and drink as his servants, ὁμοῦ καθήμενος: admittedly this is found surprising by the man who observes it); Seneca *Letters* 47.2 (criticising those who think it demeaning to dine with their slaves), 47.15 (deserving slaves should be invited to share one's meal). Note that this parallel is complementary to E8: you can only sit apart from your slaves when having a meal if you are having the meal with them.

F12 ἴσως δὲ καὶ τὸ τὰς κεφαλὰς ἀκατακαλύπτους ἔχειν· οὐδαμοῦ γοῦν ὁ ποιητὴς εὕρηται οὔτε πίλου ἀσκητοῦ μεμνημένος τοῦ καθ' Ἡσίοδον, οὔτε καυσίας, ἥτις κατὰ τὸν Παυσανίαν πῖλος ἦν πλατὺς ὃν οἱ Μακεδονικοί φησι βασιλεῖς ἐφόρουν λευκὸν αὐτῷ διάδημα περιειλοῦντες, οὔτε ἄλλου περὶ τὴν κεφαλὴν καλύμματος, ἀλλὰ καὶ τὸν Ὀδυσσέα ἐν τοῖς ἑξῆς εἰς φαλάκρωσιν κωμῳδοῦσιν οἱ μνηστῆρες ὡς ἐκκειμένης τῆς αὐτοῦ φαλάκρας εἰς θέαν διὰ τὸ τῆς κεφαλῆς δηλαδὴ ἀκατακάλυπτον.

---

[76] Taylor (1966) 29–31.

Homer does not mention caps or other (non-military) head-coverings, and ΣΤ *Iliad* 10.265b uses this as an argument against the iconographic tradition which portrays Odysseus wearing a πῖλος.

Plutarch *Roman Questions* 14, 267a (quoted under F6 above) provides evidence that Roman men generally went bare-headed; note too that the general wearing of hats was associated with special occasions, such as the Saturnalia (Martial 11.6, 14.1). But this is another instance of a practice that does not seem to be distinctively Roman; I find no evidence that Greek men generally did cover their head.[77]

F13 οὐ μόνον δὲ ἔθη Ἑλληνικὰ τοῖς ἐκεῖ ἐπεπόλασαν ἀλλὰ καὶ λέξεις Ἑλληνικαὶ πολλαὶ καὶ μάλιστα Δώριοι ἐναπέμειναν, εἰ καὶ χρόνῳ ὕστερον ἀπηχρειώθησαν τὰ Ἑλληνικὰ ὀνόματα παράκοπα γεγονότα καὶ βάρβαρα, ὡς καὶ περὶ τούτου αὐτοῦ πραγματεῖαι ἀκριβεῖς τισὶ τῶν παλαιῶν ἐκπεπόνηνται.

We have met Latin borrowings from Greek before (E1 etc.). It is not clear why Eustathius says Doric (rather than Aeolic); it may be relevant that many of the Greek colonies in southern Italy were Dorian.

F14 τὸ μέντοι τῶν γυναικῶν ἑλκεσίπεπλον, αἷς ὁ πέπλος ἐν τῷ βαδίζειν ἐφέλκεται διὰ τὸ βαθὺ τοῦ ἱματισμοῦ, εἴη ἂν κλῆρος τοῖς Ἰταλοῖς ἐκ τοῦ Τρωϊκοῦ Αἰνείου· Ἑλληνὶς γὰρ γυνὴ οὔτε βαθύπεπλος οὔτε ἑλκεσίπεπλος παρ' Ὁμήρῳ εὕρηται.

See E3.

4. Chronological implications

We do not know if Aristodemus considered the chronological implications of his theory, or (if he did) what conclusions he reached.

One might have expected that a Roman Homer would postdate the foundation of Rome, which was (according to the usual estimates) in the middle of the eighth century (Varro's date was 753 BC, Dionysius' 751/0). Such a date would be at the lowest extreme of the range of dates suggested for Homer in antiquity.[78] Theopompus placed Homer 500 years after the fall of Troy: probably he synchronised Homer with Archilochus, and this was later correlated with the synchronism of Archilochus and the Lydian king Gyges (cf. Herodotus 1.12), to give a *floruit* for Homer of around 708/5 BC. This is approximately 500 years after the fall of Troy if we use the Parian Marble's date for the fall of

---

[77] Hats worn when travelling and military headgear are of course special cases.
[78] On ancient dates for Homer see Mosshammer (1979) 193–7, 211–3.

Troy; but when Eratosthenes' dating becomes standard the 500 year period shifts down to 684 BC. In either case, Homer would live comfortably after the foundation of Rome.

But such a late dating of Homer would be surprising in the first century BC. Most estimates put him much earlier, and the Romans themselves do not seem to have doubted that Homer lived before Romulus. Cicero (*Republic* 2.18–19) asserts confidently that Homer lived many years before Romulus, and gives a calculation that would place him not later than the end of the tenth century; this seems to be close to the date given by the chronographer Apollodorus (placing Homer's death in 914). Cornelius Nepos gives a similar date (160 years before the foundation of Rome), according to Gellius (17.21.3); Gellius also records that the annalist Cassius placed Homer 150 years after the fall of Troy, and thus in the eleventh century. This would be very close to Aristarchus' date (140 years after the fall of Troy).

An alternative possibility is that Aristodemus opted for an earlier date for the foundation of Rome. According to some, Rome was founded shortly after the Trojan war (Dionysius of Halicarnassus 1.72). That would be an inevitable implication of the tradition which made Romulus a grandson of Aeneas, followed by Ennius and accepted by Eratosthenes (Servius *auctus* on *Aeneid* 1.273); and there were many other accounts that would imply an early foundation.[79] It is not easy to believe that the eighth-century foundation would have been denied in the first century, and by a scholar who had worked in Rome. But it would have been possible to resolve this contradiction by adopting a theory in which Rome had been founded twice; Dionysius (1.73.3) attributes this view to some Roman historians, and is apparently willing to entertain the possibility.[80]

It is also possible that by 'Roman' Aristodemus meant simply 'of the stock from which the people who inhabited Rome when it was founded were descended'. For his theory is probably not to be interpreted as saying that Homer was a Roman rather than (as people had supposed) a Greek; he is more likely to have meant that Homer was one of those Greeks from whom the modern Romans are descended. This assertion could have been made without a commitment to any particular date for the founding of the city of Rome itself.

---

[79] See the studies cited in n.33 above.
[80] On multiple foundations see Cairns (1979) 71–3, discussing Tib. 2.5.

5. Conclusion

Aristodemus' theory is, in the light of the background outlined here, more reasonable than at first appears. We should not, perhaps, be too charitable in our judgement. The theory makes more sense in context than appears at first sight, but even in context it was not a success. There is no evidence that it was accepted by anyone other than Aristodemus; and I have conjectured that the evidence on which it rested was soon absorbed into other theories, which could give more plausible explanations of the same data. Nevertheless, the theory cannot be regarded (as it would be today) as simply an absurd eccentricity. It is rooted in kinds of evidence and patterns of argument which, however unsatisfactory they may appear to us, held a central and respectable place in the mainstream of ancient scholarship. Studying this theory and its background may therefore help us to gain a clearer picture of the kinds of speculative construction which ancient scholars regarded as legitimate; and this in turn may open the way to a better understanding both of the intellectual life of antiquity, and of the intellectual context of ancient literature.

Bibliography

Anderson, W.S. (1963). *Pompey, his Friends and the Literature of the First Century BC*. University of California Publications in Classical Philology 19.1

Arnott, W.G. (1996). *Alexis: the Fragments*. Cambridge

Austin, R.G. (1934/5). 'Roman board games' *G&R* 4.24–34, 76–82

— (1940). 'Greek board games' *Antiquity* 14.257–71

Balsdon, J.P.V.D. (1979). *Romans and Aliens*. London

Bickerman, E.J. (1952). 'Origines gentium' *CP* 47.65–81 = *Religion and Politics in the Hellenistic and Roman Periods* (Como 1985) 401–17

Blümner, H. (1911). *Die römischen Privataltertümer*. Munich

Cairns, F. (1979). *Tibullus. A Hellenistic Poet at Rome*. Cambridge

Collart, J. (1954). *Varron: grammairien latin*. Paris

Cornell, T.J. (1975). 'Aeneas and the twins: the development of the Roman foundation legend' *PCPS* 21.1–32

— (1995). *The Beginning of Rome*. London

Crawford, M.H. (1978). 'Greek intellectuals and the Roman aristocracy in the first century BC' in P.D.A. Garnsey & C. R. Whittaker (eds) *Imperialism in the Ancient World* (Cambridge 1978) 193–207

Dihle, A. (1961). 'Zur hellenistischen Ethnographie'. *EH* 8.205–39

Dionisotti, C. (1982). 'From Ausonius' schooldays? A schoolbook and its relatives' *JRS* 72.83–125

Dubuisson, M. (1984a). 'Homérologie et politique: le cas d'Aristodémus de Nysa' in J. Servais (ed.) *Stemmata: Mélanges de philologie ... offerts à Jules Labarbe* (Liège 1984) 15–24

— (1984b). 'Le latin est-il une langue barbare?' *Ktema* 9.55–68

Fraser, P.M. (1972). *Ptolemaic Alexandria*. Oxford

Gabba, E. (1963). 'Il Latino come dialetto greco' in *Miscellanea di Studi Alessandrini in memoria di Augusto Rostagni*. Turin

— (1991). *Dionysius and the History of Archaic Rome*. Berkeley

Galinsky, K. (1969). *Aeneas, Sicily and Rome*. Princeton

Gercke, A. (1907). 'War der Schwiegersohn des Poseidonius ein Schüler Aristarchs?' *RM* 62 116–22

Gruen, E.S. (1993). *Culture and National Identity in Republican Rome*. London

Haas, W. (1977). *Die Fragmente der Grammatiker Tyrannion und Diokles*. SGLG 3, Berlin

Heath, M. (1993). 'Ancient interpretations of Pindar's *Seventh Nemean*' *PLLS* 7.169–99

— (1998). 'Menecrates on the end of the *Iliad*' *RM* 141.204–6

Hefermehl, E. (1906). 'Menekrates von Nysa und die Schrift vom Erhabenen' *RM* 61.282–303

Hillscher, A. (1892). 'Hominum litteratorum Graecorum ante Tiberii mortem in urbe Roma commoratorum historia critica' *Jahrbücher für classische Philologie* Suppl. 18.2, 353–444

Lamer, H. (1927). 'Lusoria tabula' *RE* 13.2, 1900–2029

Latacz, J. (1996). *Homer: His Art and his World*. Ann Arbor

Latte, K. (1925). 'Glossographika' *Philologus* 80. 136–75

Lefkowitz, M. (1981). *The Lives of the Greek Poets*. London

Leo, F. (1901). *Die griechisch-römische Biographie nach ihrer literarischen Form*. Leipzig

Loicq-Berger, M.P. (1984). 'Roman grec et réalités gauloises (Parthénios, *Erotica*, 8)' *LEC* 52.39–52

Magie, D. (1950). *Roman Rule in Asia Minor*. Princeton

Maltby, R. (1991). *A Lexicon of Ancient Latin Etymologies*. Leeds

Marquardt, J. and Mau, A. (1886). *Das Privatleben der Römer*. ed. 2, Leipzig

Marquardt, J. and Wissowa, G. (1885). *Römische Staatsverwaltung*. ed. 2, Leipzig

Mosshammer, A.A. (1979). *The Chronicles of Eusebius and Greek Chronographic Tradition*. Lewisburg

Mueller, K.-E. (1980). *Geschichte der antiken Ethnographie*. Wiesbaden

O'Hara, J.J. (1996). 'Sostratus *Suppl. Hell.* 733: a lost, possibly Catullan-era elegy on the six sex changes of Tiresias' *TAPA* 126.173–219

Potter, D. (1990). *Prophecy and History*. Oxford

Parke, H.W. (1988). *Sibyls and Sibylline Prophecies in Classical Antiquity*. London

Powell, B.B. (1991). *Homer and the Origin of the Greek Alphabet*. Cambridge

Richardson, N.J. (1981). 'The contest of Homer and Hesiod and Alcidamas' *Mouseion*' *CQ* 31.1–10

Ritoók, Z. (1993). 'The Pisistratus tradition and the canonization of Homer' *Acta Antiqua Academiae Scientiarum Hungaricae* 34.39–53

Robert, L. (1940). 'La bibliothèque de Nyse de Carie' *Hellenica* 1.144–8

Schmidt, M. (1976). *Die Erklärungen zum Weltbild Homers und zur Kultur der Heroenzeit in den bT-Scholien zur Ilias*. Zetemata 62, Munich

Schöpsdau, K. (1992). 'Vergleiche zwischen Lateinisch und Griechisch in der antiken Sprachwissenschaft' in C.W. Müller *et al.* (eds) *Zum Umgang mit fremden Sprachen in der griechisch-römischen Antike* (Stuttgart 1992) 115–36

Solmsen, F. (1986). 'Aeneas founded Rome with Odysseus' *HSCP* 90.93–100

Strasburger, H. (1968). 'Zur Sage von der Begründung Roms' *SBHeidelberg* 1968.5 = *Studien zur alten Geschichte* (Hildesheim 1982) II 1017–1055

Taylor, L.R. (1966). *Roman Voting Assemblies*. Ann Arbor

Trüdinger, K. (1918). *Studien zur Geschichte der griechisch-römischen Ethnographie*. diss. Basel

Vischer, R. (1965). *Das einfache Leben*. Göttingen

Weber, R. (1888). 'De Dioscuridis περὶ τῶν παρ' Ὁμήρῳ νόμων libello' *Leipziger Studien zur classischen Philologie* 11.87–197

West, M.L. (1983). *The Orphic Poems*. (Oxford)

— (1997). *The East Face of Helicon. West Asiatic Elements in Greek Poetry and Myth*. Oxford

PAPERS OF THE LEEDS INTERNATIONAL LATIN SEMINAR   TENTH VOLUME (1998) 57–73
Published by Francis Cairns (Publications) Ltd (Leeds 1998). ARCA 38. ISBN 0 905205 95 2

῎ΑΩΤΟΣ, ῎ΑΝΘΟΣ, AND THE DEATH OF ARCHEMORUS IN BACCHYLIDES' NINTH ODE [*]

DOUGLAS L. CAIRNS
University of Leeds

The starting point for this paper is the interpretation of an emendation in the text of Bacchylides' ninth ode, but at its centre lies an examination of the semantics of the rare word, ἄωτος/ἄωτον, in archaic and classical Greek, which in turn requires discussion both of the use and interpretation of obscure Homeric terms in later poets and of some important aspects of Pindar's use of metaphor. The argument as a whole, I hope, will show both that the account of the death of Archemorus in Bacchylides 9 conforms to a recurrent and significant typology in literature and myth and that the passage, correctly emended, should be considered alongside other fifth-century contexts as belonging to a crucial stage in the semantic development of ἄωτος/ἄωτον.

Bacchylides recounts the death of Archemorus thus (9.12–14):

> τὸν [sc. Ἀρχέμορον] ξανθοδερκής
> πέφν᾽ ἀωτεύοντα δράκων ὑπέροπλος,
> σᾶμα μέλλοντος φόνου.

In 13 the papyrus' original ἀσαγέροντα is corrected by a later hand to ἀσαγεύοντα, neither of which yields sense; of the emendations proposed,[1] R.A. Neil's ἀωτεύοντα is now universally accepted.[2] Its

---

[*] I should like to thank Francis Cairns, Roger Brock, and Gordon Howie for helpful discussion and valuable written comments.

[1] A.E. Housman, *CR* 12 (1898) 71 proposed ἄσαγ [i.e. ἄσαν] γεύοντα — palaeographically easy, but inappropriate in sense, anticipating σᾶμα μέλλοντος φόνου in 14

acceptance, however, has brought with it modification of the sense in which it was offered, for it was inspired by Hesychius' ἀωτεύειν· ἀπανθίζεσθαι, and supported by reference to Opheltes/Archemorus' flower-gathering in Euripides' *Hypsipyle* fr. 754 N² (= pp. 34–5 Bond). The sense 'sleeping' for the participle was first suggested by W. Headlam,[3] adducing Statius (*Thebaid* 5.502–4) in support,[4] and accepted by Jebb, comparing Simonides' absolute use of the Homeric verb ἀωτέω (governing ὕπνον at *Iliad* 10.159, *Odyssey* 10.548) to mean 'sleep' at fr. 543.8 *PMG*. This interpretation of the participle is defended at length by Maehler,[5] and reflected in the translations of Duchemin (Budé) and Campbell.

I should like to question this orthodoxy on both literary and lexicographical grounds. First, as noted, the motif of Opheltes' flower-gathering is attested by Euripides, the source closest in time to Bacchylides himself; and although Statius makes the child fall asleep at *Thebaid* 5.502–4, he also has him picking flowers at 4.792. Both sleep and flower-gathering would be appropriate in suggesting the innocence and vulnerability of the child at the moment of his death; but it is the latter which is the more common in the typology of similar scenes. The death of Opheltes/Archemorus takes place at Nemea, a moist and fertile valley, an εὐθαλὲς πέδον in this poem (5), a λειμών according to Euripides (*Hypsipyle* frr. 1.ii.31 and 1.iv.21, pp. 26 and 29 Bond; cf. hyp. [b] Pindar *Nemean Odes* ἔν τινι λειμῶνι; also Pausanias 2.15.2:

---

where what one expects is a reference to the behaviour or attitude of the child as the serpent struck; thus R. Ellis's ἀλατεύοντα (*CR* 12 [1898] 65, coll. *inerrat*, Stat. *Theb.* 4.794; cf. Q. Cataudella 'Cruces Bacchylideae' *Aegyptus* 31 [1951] 231–4 = *Intorno ai lirici greci* [Rome 1972] 169–74, coll. *vagatur*, Ov. *Met.* 10.9) is perhaps worth recording, though it implies not careless straying but the condition of beggary or exile. For other early conjectures, see H. Jurenka *Die neugefundenen Lieder des Bakchylides* (Vienna 1898) *ad loc.*

2   Approved by F.G. Kenyon in his *editio princeps* (*The Poems of Bacchylides* [London 1897]), and by W. Headlam in *CR* 12 (1898) 66–7; printed by R.C. Jebb (*Bacchylides: The Poems and Fragments* [Cambridge 1905]), B. Snell–H. Maehler (Teubner, Leipzig 1970), H. Maehler (*Die Lieder des Bakchylides* [Leiden 1982]), J. Irigoin (Budé, Paris 1993), and D.A. Campbell (*Greek Lyric* IV [London 1992]). Its papyrological plausibility is defended by Kenyon, Jebb, and Maehler.

3   (n.2) 66–7; Kenyon had already suggested that a verb meaning εὕδειν would fit, and made the connexion with *Theb.* 5.502–4.

4   Jebb, *CR* 12 (1898) 125 suggests that *livida fax oculis* in *Theb.* 5.508 (cf. Bacch. 9. 12–13 ξανθοδερκὴς ... δράκων) shows that Bacch. was in Statius' mind in this passage; the similarity stops short of proof, but it is perhaps worth observing that Statius' proximate source for the description of the serpent (Ov. *Met.* 3.31–4) does not have this detail.

5   (n.2) II 153; cf. Bond on *Hyps.* fr. 754 N², pp. 91–2.

an ἄλσος, where Opheltes is placed on the grass);[6] in Greek literature
the meadow is regularly envisaged as an inviolate, taboo space,
frequently inhabited or guarded by monstrous beasts and serpents, entry
to which, especially to pick flowers, often presages disaster.[7] The
ominous note struck by the innocent or unsuspecting flower-gatherer is
most familiar in the myths of Kore and other abducted, deflowered
maidens,[8] but is also exemplified in the case of male victims, such as
the Aegisthus of Euripides' *Electra* (777–8), who, standing in well-
watered gardens, is cutting myrtle for garlands when approached by the
strangers who will make him the sacrificial victim,[9] and Hippolytus
(*Hippolytus* 73–87), whose dedication of a garland of flowers from an
inviolate meadow is an ominous sign of the destruction to come.[10] In
view of this typology, Motte, at any rate, is in no doubt that ἀωτεύοντα
in Bacchylides 9.13 means 'while gathering flowers': "le fait de péné-
trer dans l'aire sacrée de certaines prairies, le geste surtout d'en cueillir

6   See A. Motte *Prairies et jardins de la Grèce antique: de la religion à la philosophie*
    (Brussels 1973) 13. For the Nemean meadow, cf. Pi. *N.* 2.4–5 (Νεμεαίου ἐν
    πολυυμνήτῳ Διὸς ἄλσει), 3.18 (ἐν βαθυπεδίῳ Νεμέᾳ). This is just one of several
    moist and fertile places in which Heracles encounters monstrous opponents (Motte
    234–5 n.8); in this ode Heracles' victory over the beast in the meadow constitutes one
    of the many contrasts between his exploit (the auspicious inauguration of a series of
    ἄεθλα, 6–9) and the episode of the Seven and Archemorus (an inauspicious beginning
    to their expedition, yet the origin of Nemean contests [ἄθλησαν, ἀγώνων], 10–24).
7   See Motte (n.6), esp. 36, 42–8, 92, 105, 113, 162, 223, 234–5, 253, and Index iii, *s.vv.*
    'cueillette', 'monstres', 'serpent'. As Gordon Howie reminds me, κῶμα is a feature of
    the uncanny and eroticized ἄλσος/λειμών described in Sappho fr. 2 L-P/V; but this
    'sleep' does not serve as a prelude to destruction in the way that flower-gathering
    regularly does.
8   E.g. Europa (Hes. fr. 140 Merkelbach–West = Bacch. fr. 10 Snell–Maehler, Moschus,
    Eur. 63–73, 89–112; cf. A. fr. 99 Radt), Oreithyia (Choer. fr. 7 Bernabé = *Supp. Hell.*
    321, ed. Lloyd-Jones–Parsons), Stratonike (and her sisters — Hes. fr. 26.18–23
    Merkelbach-West), Creusa (E. *Ion* 887–96), and Kore (*H. Hom. Cer.* 2–21, 417–32);
    cf. (e.g.) Helen's abduction by Hermes at E. *Hel.* 244–9 (where the flower-gathering
    emphasizes Helen's desirability/innocence in the face of unexpected violence). See H.
    Jeanmaire *Couroi et Courètes* (Lille 1939) 271–2; Motte (n.6) 43–4; C. Sourvinou-
    Inwood '*Reading' Greek Culture* (Oxford 1991) 65; C. Calame 'Prairies intouchées et
    jardins d'Aphrodite: espaces "initiatiques" en Grèce' in A. Moreau (ed.) *L'Initiation:
    actes du colloque international de Montpellier 11–14 Avril 1991* (Montpellier 1992) II
    106–8.
9   Motte (n.6) 234. See also F.I. Zeitlin 'The Argive Festival of Hera and Euripides'
    Electra' *TAPA* 101 (1970) 664–5; H.P. Foley *Ritual Irony* (Ithaca 1985) 43–4.
10 See D.L. Cairns 'The meadow of Artemis and the character of the Euripidean
    Hippolytus' *QUCC* 57 (1997) 51–74. Cf. (e.g.) the sinister associations of the λειμὼν
    ἀνθεμόεις of the Sirens (*Od.* 12.45, 159), and on the general associations of the
    meadow with death, see Motte (n.6) 44–8, 233–47. Cf. (e.g.) E. *El.* 777–843, *Pho.*
    1570–6, *IA* 1463, 1544; Theocr. 26.1–26 (with Gow on 5; cf. E. *Ba.* 1048); *AP* 7.189
    (= Aristodocus 2 Gow–Page).

les fleurs, a pour effet immédiat *de hâter la destinée*".[11]
The matter is not, however, so simply settled. Ancient scholarship is
well-nigh unanimous that the noun ἄωτος/ἄωτον and those verbs
apparently derived from it (ἀωτέω in Homer and ἀωτεύω, attested only
in Hesychius *s.v.* and *Anecdota Graeca* I 476.22 Bekker) are to be
connected with 'flowers' (see Apollonius Sophista 50.15–18, 119.18
Bekker; *Etymologicum Magnum* 53.56, 117.46 Gaisford; Hesychius
s.vv. ἀωτεῖτε, ἀωτεύειν, ἄωτος, ἄωτον, ἀωτοῦσιν, λεπτὸν ἄωτον,
λίνοιο λεπτὸν ἄωτον, οἰὸς ἀώτῳ; *Anecdota Graeca* I 476.21 Bekker
s.v. ἄωτον; *Suda* I 258 Adler, *s.vv.* ἀωτεμεῖν, ἄωτον).[12] Some modern
authorities agree,[13] but Maehler[14] argues that the explanation of
Homeric ἄωτος as ἄνθος is a fiction of ancient Homeric scholarship,
and that the two occur in comparable senses only in the fifth century,
observing that, even then, ἄωτος overlaps only with the metaphorical
sense of ἄνθος.[15] Maehler's views are supported by the full discussion
of the word offered by R.A. Raman, who argues that Homeric ἄωτος
means "the 'nap' that *lies on the surface of cloth*, as well as the fleece
that *grows on the surface* of sheep", and that from this sense of 'that
which is/lies on the surface' develops (on the analogy with other terms,
χνοῦς, πίνος, ἄνθος, ἀκμή) the abstract sense, 'the best'. Raman would
also distinguish in etymology the noun ἄωτος/ἄωτον and the verb
ἀωτεῖν.[16]

---

[11] (n.6) 45 (original emphasis). Motte is, however, wrong to take σᾶμα μέλλοντος φόνου
(14) as referring specifically to ἀωτεύοντα — it is the child's death which is the σῆμα
(and the source of the name Archemorus [12], which Bacch. here etymologizes).
Motte is also wrong to supply the detail of Hypsipyle's failure to heed the oracle
advising her not to place the child on the ground (from Hyg. *Fab.* 74), since her role in
leaving Opheltes/Archemorus unguarded is first attested in E.'s play of 408 or 407 BC
(on the date, see Bond's ed., p. 144).

[12] For Eustathius and the Homeric scholia, see *LfgrE s.vv.* ἀωτέω, ἄωτος. The Pindaric
scholia also regularly gloss or paraphrase ἄωτος with ἄνθος or ἀπάνθισμα; see on *O.*
1.15 (I 25.7–8 Drachmann), 3.4 (I 107.14), 9.16 (I 273.27); *P.* 4.130 (II 129.20), 188
(II 143.4); *I.* 5.12 (III 243.18), 6.4 (III 251.11).

[13] See esp. P. Chantraine, *Dictionnaire étymologique* I, *s.vv.* ἀωτέω, ἄωτος, supporting
Hsch. *re* the former, deriving it from ἄωτος and stressing the sense 'flower' of the
latter. M. Frisk (*Griechisches etymologisches Wörterbuch* I, *s.v.*) originally tended
towards 'sleep' as the meaning of ἀωτεῖν in Hom., but later (III, Heidelberg 1972, p.
46) endorsed Chantraine's preference for Hsch.'s explanation. Cf. also Heubeck on
Od. 10.548. Lat. *carpere somnos* (Virg. *Georg.* 3.435; *Aen.* 4.555; Sil. Ital. 16.119;
Claud. *Bell. Gild.* 1.328; see Pease on *Aen.* 4.522 for similar expressions) is probably
modelled on Homer's ὕπνον ἀωτεῖν.

[14] (n.2) II 153 n.6.

[15] Cf. M.S. Silk *Interaction in Poetic Imagery* (Cambridge 1974) Appendix xi, 239–40.

[16] 'Homeric ἄωτος and Pindaric ἄωτος. A semantic problem' *Glotta* 53 (1975) 195–207

It is certainly true that ἄωτος does not mean 'flower' in Homer; it is used (four times) of wool or fleece and (once) of linen cloth;[17] and similarly, in Pindar, with whom it is a *Lieblingswort*,[18] it is never used of flowers in a literal sense. Before the Hellenistic period, no author other than Homer and Pindar uses the noun more than once; thus if ἄωτος does not mean 'flower' in Homer, and never refers to literal flowers in Pindar, there would seem to be no purchase for the view that Bacchylides used ἀωτεύειν in the sense 'pick flowers'.

The trouble with this line of argument is, first, that even in Homer ἄωτος and ἄνθος cannot be so sharply distinguished. If C.J. Ruijgh is right that *a–wo–ti–jo* in a tablet from Knossos is the proper name of a Mycenean shepherd, Ἀϝώτιος (or Ἀϝωτίων),[19] then the association of the word with sheep might be original.[20] But however that may be, it is impossible to establish a consistent denotation on the basis of the word's Homeric occurrences, and none of the senses suggested by recent studies will fit all instances. *Odyssey* 9.434–5 is probably the most straightforward: Odysseus clings tenaciously to the ἀώτου θεσπεσίοιο of Polyphemus' ram. Here the reference is to the animal's fleece, and one could reasonably say that 'fleece' is the meaning of ἄωτος in this case. But at 1.443 (κεκαλυμμένος οἰὸς ἀώτῳ) is Telemachus wrapped in a fleece or a woollen blanket?[21] In the *Iliad* (13.599, 716) the phrase οἰὸς ἀώτῳ recurs, but here the application is to

---

(quotation p. 198, original emphasis). Raman builds on P. Buttmann's *Lexilogus* (trans. J. R. Fishlake,[5] London 1861) 182–9. Buttmann's account also lies behind A. Sideras *Aeschylus Homericus* (Göttingen 1971) 51–2, and Friis-Johansen and Whittle on A. *Supp.* 666.

[17] *Il.* 13.599, 716; *Od.* 1.443, 9.434 (wool/fleece); *Il.* 9.661 (linen).

[18] 20 occurrences: see W.J. Slater's *Lexicon* (Berlin 1969), *s.v.* and cf. Chantraine *s.v.*, C.M. Bowra *Pindar* (Oxford 1964) 228–9, Silk (n.15) 239–40, Gerber on *O.* 1.15, Braswell on *P.* 4.131(c).

[19] *Études sur la grammaire et le vocabulaire du grec mycénien* (Amsterdam 1967) 158.

[20] This possible pointer to the existence of the term in Mycenean might help substantiate J.L. Melena's suggestion that Homeric ἄωτος (meaning, in his opinion, 'the choicest wool') derives from the Mycenean practice of plucking wool rather than shearing ('On the Linear B ideogrammatic syllabogram *ZE*' *Minos* 20–22 [= *Studies ... J. Chadwick*, Salamanca 1987] 389–457, at 404–5). The notion of the 'plucking of the finest' would not be unwelcome as an adjunct to the argument of this paper, but one wonders how far it is a problem for Melena's theory that, if ἄωτος derives from a Mycenean word for 'wool', then its origins are in a period when plucking was universal and shearing unknown (R.J. Forbes *Studies in Ancient Technology* IV [Leiden 1956] 8); thus it could originally have had no qualitative connotations, and a sense 'choicest wool' in Homer would require the hypothesis that the term preserved a dim memory that Mycenean wool was plucked rather than shorn; cf. also n.22 below.

[21] The latter, according to S. West *ad loc.*

a sling, for which ἐΰστρεφεῖ οἰὸς ἀώτῳ is a periphrasis; although in all
these three applications the word ἄωτος does indeed have something to
do with wool, the sense in which this is true is different in each case,
and if the word is to bear the same meaning in each this will have to be
something other than the specific 'fleece' suggested by Raman.[22] But
the real problem for a unitary (or even focal) meaning for Homeric
ἄωτος is its application to linen cloth at *Iliad* 9.661, where Achilles'
maidservants make a bed for Phoenix, laying out κῶεά τε ῥῆγός τε
λίνοιό τε λεπτὸν ἄωτον. Raman attempts to link this application with
the others through the notion of 'that which lies on the surface', and
thus (of linen) 'nap';[23] Buttmann likewise sought a rapprochement with
the senses 'wool' and 'fleece' by arguing for 'lock of the flax plant';[24]
but a literal sense 'nap' will not suit a passage where what is wanted is
a reference to some form of covering — 'they spread out fleeces,
blankets, and the fine nap of linen' is a hopelessly incongruous synec-
doche; while 'the fine lock of the flax plant' (apart from other ob-
jections raised by Raman)[25] would have to be construed as a rather
elaborate periphrasis or *kenning* which would sit uneasily in such a
matter-of-fact context (and it would in any case be poor method to
make the assumption of such a thing integral to one's argument). The
associations of ἄωτος are clearly with wool or cloth; but its specific
denotation, if it had one, is irrecoverable. M.S. Silk calls it an 'iconym',
an archaic and poetic word which has lost its denotation, and thus is
used with various connotations in a range of applications which defy
classification as discrete but related senses of the same word.[26] While

---

[22] Equally, the sense 'finest, choicest wool', revived by Melena and accepted by Janko
(on *Il.* 13.599), will hardly do of the unplucked or unshorn fleece of the Cyclops' ram;
nor am I convinced that we are supposed to envisage (in *Il.* 13) slings fashioned from a
wool of better than usual quality.

[23] Linen may not appear to have much of a nap, but see Plin. *HN* 19.9, 19.21, 36.153
(*lanugo*), with Forbes (n.20) 34–6.

[24] (n.16) 187.

[25] (n.16) 198, 200.

[26] See M.S. Silk 'LSJ and the problem of poetic archaism: from meanings to iconyms'
CQ 33 (1983) 303–30; definition on pp. 311–12, applied to ἄωτος pp. 316–17. For
scepticism regarding Silk's approach, see M. Clarke 'Aeschylus on mud and dust'
Hermathena 158 (1995) 7–26, esp. 12, 24–5. Clarke's criticism ("the only positive
evidence for the existence of any iconym will be the scholar's inability to fit the
attestations into a comprehensible pattern") would not affect my argument, given that
such 'inability' is the proper response to the Homeric evidence. In interpreting that
evidence, it does not much matter whether we wish to say that ἄωτος in Homer
probably possessed a core meaning which we are no longer able to reconstruct or that
it was already an obscure term used differently in different contexts, for the point is

we cannot be absolutely sure that this, rather than our own ignorance or lack of evidence, is the ultimate explanation of the word's indeterminacy in Homer, that indeterminacy must be respected, and it would be wrong to seek to resolve it by importing data drawn from later uses of the word, given that there is no sign whatever that any of the later connotations (whether of 'excellence' or of 'flowers') is active in the Homeric context.[27] Thus we can isolate the associations of Homeric ἄωτος, and perhaps suspect that behind these lies a common denominator which would unite all its applications, but to say that we know what this common factor of meaning is would be to go beyond the evidence.

In a way, though, it is a pity that Raman's attempt to give Homeric ἄωτος a specific meaning, based on the notion of 'that which lies on the surface', is untenable; for otherwise it would be easy to argue for an affinity of that notion with the connotations of the Homeric ἄνθος. But even if that avenue is closed off to us, there remain signs that ἄωτος and ἄνθος operate in similar semantic fields. Already in Homer ἄνθος has a meaning wider than that of the English 'flower' which we routinely regard as its equivalent.[28] Though there are several passages in which we can be reasonably certain that ἄνθος means 'flower', 'bloom', or 'blossom',[29] it is clear that it also covers the growth of non-flowering forms of vegetation,[30] as well as analogous but non-vegetal

---

that it *is* obscure to us and *was* obscure in antiquity (see n.27), and thus available to later poets as an iconym. The behaviour of the word in post-Homeric poetry, in fact, is a powerful (and positive) argument for Silk's case .

[27] The grammarians' explanations of ἄωτος (above) give every impression that the word was a rarity even for them, since they refer, by and large, to the small body of passages which constitutes our own evidence. Equally, Hellenistic and later uses of the word either (a) imitate the Homeric (A. R. 4.176; Theocr. 2.2; Opp. *Cyn.* 4.154; Orph. *Arg.* 1336); (b) reproduce the Pindaric (Call. *H. Ap.* 112; fr. 399.2 Pf.; Theocr. 13.27–8; *Anacreontea* 60.4); or (c) gloss as equivalent to ἄνθος (Call. fr. 260.57 Pf.).

[28] See W.B. Stanford *Greek Metaphor* (Oxford 1936) 111–14; J.M. Aitchison 'Homeric ἄνθος' *Glotta* 41 (1963) 271–8; cf. Raman (n.16) 203–4, *LfgrE s.v.*; also R. Padel *In and Out of the Mind* (Princeton 1992) 134–7; M. Clarke 'The wisdom of Thales and the problem of the word ἱερός' *CQ* 45 (1995) 296–317, at 308–9. For additions/corrections to LSJ *s.v.* ἄνθος, see R. Renehan *Greek Lexicographical Notes* I (Göttingen 1975) 31–2.

[29] *Il.* 2.89, 468, 17.56; *Od.* 6.231, 7.126, 9.51, 23.158.

[30] Certainly at *Od.* 9.449 (grass), possibly also at *Il.* 9.542 and *Od.* 10.304, where Aitchison ([n.28] 272; contrast *LfgrE s.v.* col. 874, 60–8) argues that the opposition root/ἄνθος suggests that the latter denotes all that part of the plant which appears above the surface (hardly 'the scent of a herb' at *Od.* 10.304, and not necessarily 'fruit' at *Il.* 9.542, as Clarke [n.28] 308–9 n.49 alleges); similarly, the adj. πολυανθής, used of a wood at *Od.* 14.353, *might* denote the flourishing/density of vegetation in

forms of sprouting.[31] These references to objects other than flowers are not metaphorical, but offer primary data on the meaning of the term; thus Aitchison argues that ἄνθος means 'that which grows to/on the surface' (cf. Stanford's 'that which rises to the surface'), covering not only flowering but other forms of growth, sprouting, eruption, or excrescence.

Any exact comparison of the senses of Homeric ἄωτος and ἄνθος is inhibited by the indeterminacy of the former; but even so there are indications that the two may already be applied to similar phenomena. We have already seen (*Odyssey* 11.320) that ἀνθεῖν and εὐανθής can be used of the growth of downy hair, a phenomenon which is perhaps comparable in quality to whatever it might be that unites the ἄωτος of wool and linen. In two passages of the *Odyssey*, moreover, we have a comparison between 'woolly hair' and the flower of the hyacinth (οὔλας ἧκε κόμας, ὑακινθίνῳ ἄνθει ὁμοίας, *Odyssey* 6.231 = 23.158), where it is plausible to see the point of comparison not just in the colour of the flower, but also in the texture and appearance of its petals.[32] And at *Iliad* 10.134, when Nestor puts on his cloak, 'woolly

---

general (Aitchison 273), and ἄνθινον at *Od.* 9.84 *might* categorize the Lotus-Eaters as vegetarians (Aitchison, *ibid.*, Heubeck *ad loc.*), since it is the fruit of the plant that they eat, not its flower (9.94). But the lotus *is* a flowering plant, and ἄνθινον εἶδαρ may just reflect this fact (see further *LfgrE s.v.*). The adj. ἀνθεμόεις (when used of meadows, etc.) may likewise denote more than just the presence of flowers, but it is hard to be sure.

[31] *Od.* 11.317–20: Otus and Ephialtes would have ascended to Olympus, had not Apollo destroyed them πρίν σφωϊν ὑπὸ κροτάφοισιν ἰούλους/ ἀνθῆσαι πυκάσαι τε γένυς εὐανθέϊ λάχνῃ. Here both ἀνθ-words refer to the sprouting of the beard; but (*pace* Aitchison [n.28] 272) this is not the case at *Il.* 13.484: Aeneas ἔχει ἥβης ἄνθος, ὅ τε κράτος ἐστὶ μέγιστον, where the context shows that ἥβης ἄνθος refers to a stage in one's youthful development, and not to the growth of the beard as such (so correctly *LfgrE s.v.* ἄνθος 3a), though the stage in question is no doubt that at which the beard sprouts. This is not to say that the phrase is fundamentally 'metaphorical' — youths and plants ἀνθεῖν because they share the same (or a similar) vital force; see *LfgE s.v.* ἄνθος col. 874, 12–49, col. 876, 36–48; Clarke (n.28) 308 and n.49; on the ἄνθος ἥβης see further Janko on *Il.* 13.484; West on *Theog.* 988; Friis-Johansen and Whittle on A. *Supp.* 663–6; Braswell on Pi. *P.* 4.158b; J. Taillardat *Les Images d'Aristophane* (Paris 1965) 47; H.J. Blumenthal 'Homeric Hymn to Demeter 108: κουρήϊον ἄνθος' *Glotta* 60 (1982) 225–7. In the v.l. at *Il.* 9.212 (ἐπεὶ πυρὸς ἄνθος ἀνέπτατο, παύσατο δὲ φλόξ) the point is surely that fire suddenly 'bursts into bloom', i.e. springs up, not that "it is brightly coloured and spreads its seeds abroad" (H. Lloyd-Jones *Greek Epic, Lyric, and Tragedy* [Oxford 1990] 314 = *HSCP* 73 [1969] 101); equally σπέρμα πυρός in *Od.* 5.490, Pi. *O.* 7.48, *P.* 3.37 (cf. fr. adesp. 85 *TGF*) focuses on fire's potential to burst out from its source.

[32] See Garvie on 6.230–1, Stanford and Hainsworth on 6.231; cf. *h. Cer.* 178, with Blumenthal (n.31) 227. On οὖλος see Buttmann (n.16) 456–8.

down bloomed on it' (οὔλη δ' ἐπενήνοθε λάχνη).[33] Even if the verb ἐπενήνοθε is not in fact related to ἄνθος, such an etymology is clearly likely to suggest itself, especially given the association of λάχνη and ἄνθος in πρίν σφωῖν ὑπὸ κροτάφοισιν ἰούλους/ ἀνθῆσαι πυκάσαι τε γένυς εὐανθέϊ λάχνῃ (Odyssey 11.319–20).[34] These hints of a link between ἄνθος and wool, woolly hair, and the texture of woven cloth suggest a degree of common ground between it and ἄωτος, even in Homer.

None of this might seem like very much; but the point is that, after Homer, there manifests itself a considerable degree of overlap between ἄνθος and other terms felt to have a similar reference (e.g. ἄχνη, χνοῦς, πίνος). ἄνθος shares with ἄχνη a reference to the scum on wine, with ἄχνη, χνοῦς, and πίνος to patina on metal objects, and with ἄχνη and χνοῦς to the foam of the sea, to smoke, fire, etc., to the down on fruit, to human and animal hair, and to chaff;[35] also, as Borthwick shows with copious examples, ἄνθος comes, again like ἄχνη and χνοῦς, to be used of nap or down on the surface of cloth, a phenomenon which may indicate a felt connexion with the Homeric usage of ἄωτος.[36] In view of this general tendency of these terms to overlap in sense and connotation, one might expect that any perceived similarity between ἄωτος and ἄνθος would lead to a comparable degree of overlap in meaning. We shall see in a moment that this is indeed the case.

But first we should remember that the word which we are seeking to

---

[33] Cf. Il. 2.219 φοξὸς ἔην κεφαλήν, ψεδνὴ δ' ἐπενήνοθε λάχνη; more remotely h. Cer. 279 ξανθαὶ δὲ κόμαι κατενήνοθεν ὤμους.

[34] The connexion with ἄνθος is affirmed by schol. D on Il. 2.219, Hesych., Suda s.v. ἐπενήνοθεν, Et. M. 354.41–3 Gaisford, Eustath. on Od. 8.365. See Buttmann's discussion (n.16) 110–41; also Frisk (s.vv. ἄνθος, ἐνθεῖν, sceptical), Chantraine (s.v. ἀνενήνοθεν) and LfgrE (s.v. ἐνήνοθεν), both more positive; correct or not, the etymological link is likely to have been felt; see Aitchison (n.28) 273–4; E.K. Borthwick 'The "Flower of the Argives" and a neglected meaning of ἄνθος' JHS 96 (1976) 1–7, at 1; Clarke (n.28) 308–9.

[35] See Borthwick's table, (n.34) 6; Raman (n.16) 201–4. On the range of meaning of ἄνθος more generally, see the works cited in n.28 above.

[36] Borthwick (n.34) 2–5. The degree to which the connotations and applications of these terms interact and overlap is shown in those passages in which they reinforce each other in conveying the same essential idea: thus the description of Laius' hair at OT 742 (χνοάζων ἄρτι λευκανθὲς κάρα) combines χνοῦς and ἄνθος, and Dionysius' discussion of the need to avoid dissonant clashes of consonants in the use of archaic vocabulary, but instead to impart "a certain patina of antiquity and an unforced charm" (De Demosth. 38) piles χνοῦς upon ἄνθος and πίνος — ἵνα ... ἐπανθῇ τις αὐταῖς χνοῦς ἀρχαιοπινὴς καὶ χάρις ἀβίαστος (both passages in Raman [n.16] 201–3); cf. Ep. Gr. 1028.75–6 Kaibel, [τεύ]χων περιμάρμαρον ἄνθεσιν ἄχνας/ φλ[οῖσβ]ο[ν ἐριβ]ρεμέθοντα (Borthwick [n.34] 6).

restore in Bacchylides' text is the participle ἀωτεύοντα, not the noun, ἄωτος. Maehler argues that Simonides' absolute use of the verb ἀωτέω to mean 'sleep' is sufficient to support the claim that his nephew used ἀωτεύειν in the same sense; and as we have seen, there are those who would deny that ἀωτεῖν is a denominative of ἄωτος. But Chantraine (s.v. ἀωτέω), considering derivation either from ἄωρος, 'sleep' or from ἄωτος, is surely right to say that the latter is "plus naturelle", especially since (as he also notes) in the case of the two occurrences of ἀωτέω in Homer, "le sens de 'dormir' ne s'impose pas";[37] given that the sense of the verb is obscure and disputed, it is surely bad method to assume that, in the phrase ὕπνον ἀωτεῖν, the noun is internal accusative. Only Simonides' absolute use of the verb to mean 'sleep' would support that conclusion, but it is not at all unlikely that this should be either a mis-understanding of an obscure Homeric usage or a deliberate use of the verb in a novel or elliptical sense.[38] But however that may be, if Bacchylides did see ἀωτεύειν as an equivalent of (Homeric or Simonidean) ἀωτεῖν, then he, at any rate, must have regarded the latter as a denominative from ἄωτος, for no speaker of Greek could fail to derive a verb of the form ἀωτεύειν from that noun. And even if he had Simonides' use of ἀωτεῖν in mind, Bacchylides is quite capable of remodelling the sense of the terms he borrows from his uncle.[39] Thus we must consider ἀωτεῖν and ἄωτος together, as ancient scholarship does (and as good method requires in the case of terms of such inde-terminate sense), and so we return to the question of what Bacchylides might have thought ἄωτος meant.

Clear indication that ἄωτος was felt to be interchangeable with ἄνθος comes in the Hellenistic period, for Callimachus' κύματος ἄκρῳ ἀώτῳ (*Hecale* fr. 260.57 Pf.) is at once an imitation of Alcman's κύματος ἄνθος (26.3 *PMG*) and a learned interpretation of the obscure

---

[37] Esp. in the case of *Od.* 10.548, where, in the presence of εὕδοντες and ὕπνον, another word meaning 'sleep' would seem excessive (*pace* Buttmann [n.16] 188, Raman [n.16] 207). Cf. n.13 above, and see *LfgrE s.v.* (On Lat. *carpere somnos*, see n.13 above.)

[38] A 'makeshift solution', according to Raman (n.16) 206, who continues, "If the interpretation of ἄωτος presented above is accepted, the connection of ἀωτέω with ἄωτος as a denominative verb becomes semantically impossible". So much the worse for that interpretation, some might think.

[39] E.g. χλωραύχην at 5.172 (of Deianira) from Simon. 586.2 *PMG* (of the nightingale, probably a misunderstanding of *Od.* 19.518).

Homeric term.[40] We could push this perception of interchangeability further back in time if we could be sure that *AP* 13.28 (= 'Antigenes' 1 Diehl = 1 Page *FGE*) is a genuine fifth-century composition.

πολλάκι δὴ φυλᾶς Ἀκαμαντίδος ἐν χοροῖσιν Ὧραι
  ἀνωλόλυξαν κισσοφόροις ἐπὶ διθυράμβοις
αἱ Διονυσιάδες, μίτραισι δὲ καὶ ῥόδων ἀώτοις
  σοφῶν ἀοιδῶν ἐσκίασαν λιπαρὰν ἔθειραν,
οἳ τόνδε τρίποδα σφίσι μάρτυρα Βακχίων ἀέθλων
  ἔθηκαν   (1–6)

Here ἄωτος comes as close as it ever gets to a reference to literal flowers, though ῥόδων ἀώτοις is perhaps less a simple periphrasis for 'roses' (or 'the finest of roses', as Buttmann would have it)[41] than a reference to petals showered on the heads of victorious singers.[42] But we cannot be sure that this is an early poem; to be sure, τόνδε τρίποδα in 5 is obviously intended to mark it as the accompaniment to a genuine didaskalic dedication, and its ascription to 'Bacchylides or Simonides' in the *Anthology* might suggest that, when collected, it was recognized as a piece of some antiquity and thus attached to these famous names. Wilamowitz placed it between 490 and 480, but this was based on the misconception that the poem records the first dithyrambic victory of the tribe Akamantis, lines 1–3 contrasting this with their many previous failures (rather, as Page observes, "the tone is triumphant, and ἀνωλό-λυξαν means 'shouted for joy'").[43] The style is certainly Bacchylidean enough,[44] but this may be mere pastiche. There are also some oddities

[40] For ἄνθος of the foam of the sea, see Hdt. 2.12; *AP* 6.206; cf. A. *Ag.* 659; Pi. *P.* 4.158 (with Borthwick [n.34] 5–7); also Bacch. 13.124–5, where (*pace* Jebb) κυανανθέϊ ... πόντῳ probably does refer to the swelling and breaking of the waves.
[41] Buttmann (n.16) 183, followed by Friis-Johansen and Whittle on A. *Supp.* 666. Bowra (n.18) 228 also has this abstract sense in mind when he mistranslates, "with the choicest roses of wise singers".
[42] D.L. Page (*Further Greek Epigrams* [Cambridge 1981] 12) insists that the adj. σοφῶν in 4 indicates that the ἀοιδοί are poets, but this is surely too rigid. If we then keep the οἳ of the paradosis in 5 (emended by Page to καί), the singers in 5 become the members of the victorious chorus on the present occasion, and the fulcrum of the contrast between past and present is located in line 3 (as opposed to line 5, Page); see U. von Wilamowitz-Moellendorff (*Sappho und Simonides* [Berlin 1913] 218–19). But Page is right that 3–4 read better as a continuation of 1–2; perhaps two lines have been lost after 4 (A. Hecker *Commentationis Criticae de Anthologia Graeca pars prior* [Leiden 1852] 150).
[43] Wilamowitz (n.42) 219–22, Page (n.42) 12.
[44] B. Zimmermann *Dithyrambos: Geschichte einer Gattung* (Göttingen 1992) 40 notes that the poem's dithyrambic style marks it out as unique among other dedicatory inscriptions celebrating dithyrambic victories (though he accepts an early dating).

— a combination of metrical forms unparalleled elsewhere, and the relationship between (the presumably aristocratic) Hipponicus (9), and his decidedly unaristocratic-sounding father, Struthon (10).[45] It would be unwise to build anything on the assumption that this is a genuine fifth-century composition, and there is reason to suspect later forgery.

These passages, then, do not take us beyond the ancient scholarly explanation of ἄωτος as a synonym of ἄνθος, which, it can be argued, tells us nothing about fifth-century perceptions.[46] But now we turn to the evidence of Pindar, the only author to employ the noun ἄωτος with any frequency. The overall impression one gets from Pindar's twenty uses of the word is of its indeterminacy — ἄωτος clearly conveys strong prescriptive/evaluative force (its quasi-superlative nature indicated by its invariable coupling with a noun in the genitive), but its meaning is otherwise elusive. As Silk argues, in Pindar ἄωτος is not only an iconym but an idiosyncrasy, an element in the poet's highly distinctive idiolect; even the abstract sense 'the pick' will not do justice to each and every application.[47] Even so it is clear that many of Pindar's uses of ἄωτος + genitive as 'the pick of ...' convey a sense which might easily be conveyed by a metaphorical use of ἄνθος. But the rapprochement of ἄνθος and ἄωτος in Pindar goes beyond their sharing this abstract sense. All words take on positive connotations from contexts in which they are at home, but since iconyms have no definite denotation, in their case the connotations, however vague, are all there is, all that any poetic successor has on which to reconstruct what the

---

[45] The names Hipponicus and Callias recur in the aristocratic family to which Callias (son of Hipponicus, of the deme Alopeke, who married Cimon's sister Elpinice) belonged, and Hipponicus is not attested outside that family until the late second century BC (J.K. Davies *Athenian Propertied Families* [Oxford 1971] 256; M.J. Osborne and S.G. Byrne [edd.] *A Lexicon of Greek Personal Names* II [Oxford 1994] 238). The name Struthon is otherwise unattested for Attica, though Struthias occurs in Men. *Kolax* frr. 2–3, and Struthias and Struthion are attested in Alciphron (3.43, 1.9 resp.; n.b. all three of these are fictional, comic contexts); see *Lexicon of Greek Personal Names* II 408; similar names in inscriptions from Euboea and the Cyclades in P.M. Fraser and E. Matthews *A Lexicon of Greek Personal Names* I (Oxford 1987) 415.

[46] On the dangers of combining Hellenistic and Classical sources in the investigation of poetic usage see Silk (n.15) 38–9, (n.26) 313 n.35.

[47] Silk (n.26) 317. Although ἄωτος in Pi. is always used with a gen., a glance at Slater's *Lexicon s.v.* is enough to show that the function of the gen. is far from the same in each case; if ἄνθος would occasionally make an adequate replacement for ἄωτος, at other times one might rather think of a term such as ὄμμα, γέρας, or ἄγαλμα, while often 'the ἄωτος of *x*' seems to be little more than a periphrasis for '*x*' (Silk, *ibid.*).

word meant to his predecessors and to build his own meaning.[48] Thus it is important that Pindar frequently uses ἄωτος in contexts in which its associations are decidedly botanical.

The strongest link between ἄωτος and 'flowers' is to be found in two passages in which it occurs as the object of δρέπειν/δρέπεσθαι (δραπὼν ... ἱερὸν εὐζοίας ἄωτον, Pythian 4.130–1; θαμὰ μὲν Ἰσθμιάδων δρέπεσθαι κάλλιστον ἄωτον, Nemean 2.9). Metaphorically, at least, in these passage ἄωτος 'is' a flower. (ἀπο)δρέπειν is always figurative in Pindar, but in most cases the image includes a figurative ἄνθος or καρπόν as object of the verb;[49] where the verb governs other abstract terms from the semantic field 'excellence' as its object, the botanical association is usually reinforced by other elements in the context. Thus, at Pythian 1.48–50 (τιμάν/ οἵαν οὗτις Ἑλλάνων δρέπει/ πλούτου στεφάνωμ' ἀγέρωχον) the image of τιμή as a flower is reinforced by στεφάνωμα.[50] Similarly, Pythian 6.48–9 ἄδικον οὔθ' ὑπέροπλον ἥβαν δρέπων, σοφίαν δ' ἐν μυχοῖσι Πιερίδων surely involves an allusion to the cliché of the ἄνθος ἥβης. Most comparable to the use of ἄωτος as object of δρέπειν/δρέπεσθαι is Olympian 1's praise of Hieron,

θεμιστεῖον ὃς ἀμφέπει σκᾶπτον ἐν πολυμάλῳ[51]
Σικελίᾳ δρέπων μὲν κορυφὰς ἀρετᾶν ἀπὸ πασᾶν (12–13).

κορυφή (with the particular abstract sense, 'pinnacle' [of achievement]) is another Lieblingswort,[52] and one which clearly bears comparison with ἄωτος; here, however, it seems to be used by simple substitution for ἄνθος or καρπόν, as the preparation through πολυμάλῳ suggests.[53] The vegetation imagery here may then influence the appearance of ἄωτος in the subsequent lines (14–15):

[48] See Silk (n.26) 312, 319–20, and (esp.) 328: "An iconym may not have a meaning, but it does have evocable connotations, and the characteristic pattern of the creative uses is to evoke more than one of these".

[49] P. 9.109–11, frr. 6b (f) (see below), 52m. 4–5, 122. 8, 209.

[50] Which suggests that R. Stoneman's explanation ('Ploughing a garland: metaphor and metonymy in Pindar' Maia 33 [1981] 125–37, at 129: 'plucking' synecdoche for 'acquiring') is forced; this is a case of metaphor, not metonymy.

[51] Snell–Maehler print πολυμήλῳ, but πολυμάλῳ is much better attested, fits well with the almost proverbial fruitfulness of Sicily, and can plausibly be seen as preparation for the metaphorical use of δρέπων in the next line (Silk [n.15] 153 n.2; Gerber ad loc.).

[52] See Slater s.v. and Silk (n.15) 35.

[53] On the phenomenon of substitution in Pindaric imagery, see the thought-provoking though over-stated article of Stoneman (n.50).

ἀγλαΐζεται δὲ καί
μουσικᾶς ἐν ἀώτῳ.

One could argue that the occurrence of ἄωτος as object of δρέπειν/
δρέπεσθαι no more definitely associates that term with 'flowers' than
does the similar use of τιμή, ἥβη, or κορυφή; but the point is that τιμή
and κορυφή, at least, are resistant to such associations because they
possess a clear denotation of their own;[54] ἄωτος has no fixed deno-
tation, and thus in the company of δρέπειν — and the additional
elements of botanical imagery which tend to accompany it — it can be
more profoundly affected by the connotations of its context.

One might compare the profusion of vegetation imagery surround-
ing the use of the term in fr. 6b(f):

]ἄρδοντ᾽ ἀοιδαῖς [
]γενναίων ἄωτος νεκταρ,έας αι . [
] . καρπὸν δρέποντες

Despite the fragmentary context, we cannot but be impressed by the
cluster of terms whose primary reference is botanical. In other passages
the botanical associations hang more loosely in the context. At *Isth-
mian* 5.12–13 εὐανθεῖ σὺν ὄλβῳ specifies one of the two things which
'shepherd the ἄλπνιστον ἄωτον of life'.[55] In *Olympian* 8.74–6 we find:

ἀλλ᾽ ἐμὲ χρὴ μναμοσύναν ἀνεγείροντα φράσαι
χειρῶν ἄωτον Βλεψιάδαις ἐπίνικον,
ἕκτος οἷς ἤδη στέφανος περίκειται
φυλλοφόρων ἀπ᾽ ἀγώνων.

Here the best policy is probably to observe that the phrase χειρῶν
ἄωτον ... ἐπίνικον is little more than a paraphrase for νίκαν, and leave
it at that; but one notes the typical association of 'victory' and 'gar-
land'. Three times Pindar (or his imitator, in the case of *Olympian* 5)
uses the phrase στεφάνων ἄωτος/ἄωτοι (*Olympian* 5.1, 9.19; *Isthmian*
6.4). For Buttmann,[56] this collocation is proof "that in Pindar's times no
one hearing the word ἄωτος thought of *a blossom* or *flower*"; but in two
of these cases there is vegetation imagery in the immediate context

---

[54] While with ἥβη we have seen that an association with ἄνθος is an established
connotation.

[55] J. Duchemin *Pindare: poète et prophète* (Paris 1955) 234, tentatively followed by Silk
(n.26) 317 n.49, finds a trace of the 'original force' of ἄωτος in its association with
ποιμαίνοντι here; but Raman (n.16) 199 n.13 argues that the literal significance of the
verb is buried, and that ἄωτος has its regular abstract Pindaric sense (cf. Stoneman
[n.50] 130); see below.

[56] (n.16) 183–4 (quotation 184, original emphasis).

(*Olympian* 9.16 θάλλει, *Isthmian* 6.1 θάλλοντος), and while it is true
that the sense of these phrases is unlikely literally to be 'the flower(s)
of garlands', it is by no means inevitable, given the often tortuous
complexity, even incongruity of Pindar's imagery, that a felt asso-
ciation between ἄωτος and flowers should be incompatible with a
combination such as ἄωτος στεφάνων.

Clearly, one's assessment of the force of ἄωτος in such passages de-
pends, at least to some extent, on one's view of Pindar's use of meta-
phor in general. Stoneman argues forcefully that the poet's practice of
metonymic replacement of one term for another and considerable use
of dead metaphor entails "the illegitimacy of seeking to make complex
or composite pictures out of Pindar's imagery";[57] thus ἄωτος, like
κορυφή, would be a typical replacement for 'excellence' and would
remain entirely unaffected by the connotations thrown up by the con-
texts in which it is used, especially in the case of στεφάνων ἄωτος,
since "'Garland' for 'victory' is automatized".[58] Stoneman's account of
Pindaric practice is persuasive in many cases, but less so in others,
especially where it involves stretching the definition of metonymy to
breaking point.[59] He does not discuss *Pythian* 4.158 (Pelias' obser-
vation σὸν δ᾽ ἄνθος ἥβας ἄρτι κυμαίνει), but one can readily construct
a Stonemanesque interpretation in terms of simple juxtaposition of
cliché or dead metaphor with a standard Pindaric substitution, one form
of 'increase' for another. But how is one to decide that this sort of
explanation is to be preferred to one which recognizes the common use
of ἄνθος of waves or foam, and which is thus prepared to see ex-
ploitation of multiple senses of a dead or clichéd metaphor?[60] If we
grant (as I think we should) that such a thing is possible in Pindar, we
might compare *Isthmian* 5.12–13:

---

[57] (n.50); quotation p. 129.
[58] Stoneman (n.50) 136.
[59] In particular, he is fond of 'species' for 'genus' substitution, where the terms of the
genus in question are so abstract as to allow the recasting of virtually any metaphor in
terms of a species-genus relationship (i.e. the point of comparison is expressed as a
species-genus relationship).
[60] See Borthwick (n.34) 7. As Silk (n.15) 46 points out, κυμαίνειν occurs as 'live'
metaphor for the swelling of human passions in Pi. (fr. 123.4), A. (*Sept.* 443), and Pl.
(*Phd.* 112b, *Leg.* 930a); its use in *P.* 4.158 thus also alludes to the fundamental point
of contact between human and vegetal ἄνθος, the possession of the same (or a similar)
source of energy (see n.31 above).

δύο δέ τοι ζωᾶς ἄωτον μοῦνα ποιμαί-
νοντι τὸν ἄλπνιστον, εὐανθεῖ σὺν ὄλβῳ
εἴ τις εὖ πάσχων λόγον ἐσλὸν ἀκούῃ.

Here (I would argue) ἄωτον not only has its (typically Pindaric) vague, superlative sense, but is glossed in the context by two metaphorical terms which exploit its multiple connotations, ποιμαίνοντι alluding to the Homeric association with wool, and εὐανθεῖ to Pindar's own use of the term as a metaphorical equivalent for ἄνθος. Pindar, it seems to me, is here exemplifying Silk's "characteristic pattern" for the creative use of an iconym, i.e. evoking more than one of its available connotations.[61]

Confirmation that connotations of 'flower' (perhaps already entailing interpretation of a Homeric obscurity) had begun to cluster around ἄωτος in the early fifth century is provided by its occurrence in Aeschylus' *Supplices* 663–6:

ἥβας δ' ἄνθος ἄδρεπτον
ἔστω, μηδ' Ἀφροδίτας
εὐνάτωρ βροτολοιγὸς Ἄ-
ρης κέρσειεν ἄωτον.

Here ἄνθος and ἄωτος are parallel; ἄδρεπτον activates the botanical reference of the cliché ἥβας ἄνθος,[62] and κέρσειεν functions similarly with regard to ἄωτον;[63] just possibly, I suppose, the botanical associations imparted by the verb may be an *ad hoc* expedient in this particular passage, but more likely Aeschylus has interpreted the obscure Homeric *glossa* (already a Pindaric favourite) as an equivalent of ἄνθος.

To sum up: first (given the association between ἄωτος and wool/cloth in Homer), the perceived similarity between wooliness and flowers, the notion of the nap of cloth blooming on its surface, and the possibility of a link between ἄωτος and the various forms of bloom or excrescence which ἄνθος denotes all demand that we should not posit too sharp a disjunction between ἄωτος and ἄνθος in Homer. Next,

---

[61] Silk (n.26) 328 (cf. n.48 above). Something similar might just be happening at *P.* 10.53–4 ἐγκωμίων γὰρ ἄωτος ὕμνων/ ἐπ' ἄλλοτ' ἄλλον ὥτε μέλισσα θύνει λόγον (*pace* Silk [n.15] 97 and 101 n.1).

[62] See Silk (n.15) 100, ἄνθος as 'glide'.

[63] Silk (n.15) 240: "κέρσειεν, 'shear', which *prima facie* implies hair or fleece"; but κείρω is regularly used of grass and other plants (LSJ *s.v.* II), often bears the figurative sense 'cut/mow down' (A. *Pers.* 920–1, etc.), and governs ἄνθος at Anac. 414 *PMG*, E. *Her.* 875–6; see Friis-Johansen and Whittle on 666; cf. Fishlake's n. to Buttmann (n.16) 184, Borthwick (n.34) 3 n.16.

regardless of Pindar's own personal sense of the word's meaning and his intentions in using it, ἄωτος does acquire pronounced botanical overtones in the Pindaric corpus, overtones which are presupposed in its single use in Aeschylus. And finally, we know that the interpretation ἄωτος = ἄνθος which becomes scholarly orthodoxy in later antiquity was established by the time of Callimachus. If the view that ἄωτος is in some sense equivalent to ἄνθος is a mistake, it is a mistake that one can be forgiven for making.

The question, moreover, is not what ἄωτος and ἀωτέω actually meant, but what Bacchylides, in the light of his experience as a poet, thought they meant, and thus what he might reasonably have wanted his coinage, ἀωτεύοντα, to mean. We may conclude that the coining of a verb, ἀωτεύειν, to mean 'pick flowers' involves misinterpretation of previous (and contemporary) uses of ἄωτος and ἀωτεῖν, but there are examples enough of poets interpreting and using (especially obscure) Homeric words in senses which appear to be eccentric or erroneous.[64] Given the semantic affinity of ἄωτος and ἄνθος from the beginning, and the increasing overlap between them in Bacchylides' own day, especially in the work of his great contemporary and rival,[65] he is surely much more likely to have thought that ἄωτος meant 'flower' than that it meant 'sleep'. If, therefore, we continue to believe that Neil's emendation is the best one, we should be prepared to accept that the evidence for its reference to sleep is pretty exiguous, and that there is much more to be said for the alternative interpretation,[66] which can be supported both by fifth-century usage of ἄωτος and by the common motif of the fate of the innocent flower-gatherer; in adapting a Pindaric *Lieblingswort* to convey the latter motif, Bacchylides may himself have contributed to the closer convergence of meaning between ἄωτος and ἄνθος.[67]

---

[64] See M. Leumann *Homerische Wörter* (Basel 1950) 231–3; A.E. Harvey 'Homeric epithets in Greek lyric poetry' *CQ* 7(1957) 206–23, at 213; H. Fränkel *Early Greek Poetry and Philosophy* (Oxford 1975) 28; Silk (n.26) 305; cf. (once more: n.39 above) the case of χλωραύχην, involving a misunderstanding of the χλωρῆϊς ἀηδών of *Od.* 19.518, at Simon. 586.2 *PMG*, and re- (or mis-)interpreted by Bacch. at 5.172.

[65] Bacch. uses ἄωτον in its 'Pindaric' sense at 23.1 (context very fragmentary).

[66] At the very least there is room for the doubt reflected in Snell's (1934) app. crit. Some might wish to argue that Bacch. evokes *both* the sense 'sleep' in Simonides' use of ἀωτεῖν in fr. 543 *and* the botanical associations of ἄωτος in Pindar; but as one cannot both sleep and pluck flowers, one or the other sense must be primary. Bacch. is not the type to prefer the artistic effect of multivalent evocation over narrative determinacy.

[67] Thus Maehler (n.2) II 153 n.6 may be right to suspect that Archemorus' flower-gathering in E. *Hyps.* fr. 754 N² goes back to Bacch., though not necessarily as a 'Mißverständnis'.

PAPERS OF THE LEEDS INTERNATIONAL LATIN SEMINAR   TENTH VOLUME (1998) 75–130
Published by Francis Cairns (Publications) Ltd (Leeds 1998). ARCA 38. ISBN 0 905205 95 2

THUCYDIDES AND PINDAR: THE *ARCHAEOLOGY* AND *NEMEAN* 7

J.G. HOWIE
University of Edinburgh

The following paper, a revised translation of Howie (1984),[1] is an attempt to hear the *Archaeology* in some of the ways in which Thucydides intended it to be heard by his target audience, the cultured and ambitious classes throughout the Greek-speaking world. Such people seem to have been concerned to stress their claims to family privileges and land and to national territory through myths embodying common patterns[2] and featuring heroes and gods linked with the whole of the Greek world through genealogy and through *Lokomotionssagen* that sent them off to different parts of the world. For these figures to have that value they had also to feature in stories which afforded entertainment and edification. The early use of such figures as exempla made adaptation to a variety of purposes a common practice, and already the *Iliad* had some concern for maintaining a degree of realism

---

[1]   The German version, written for a conference held in 1983 by the Academy of Sciences of the GDR was published, with other papers delivered, in *Klio* in the following year; earlier versions had been delivered at Liverpool and at the Institute of Classical Studies in London. I wish to thank Prof. H.-J. Gehrke (Freiburg im Breisgau) and his colleagues on the Editorial Board of *Klio* for permission to publish a new version of my paper. The hospitality, advice and support enjoyed by the writer are gratefully acknowledged in the earlier paper. The writer feels compelled, however, to refer to years of informal instruction in German by Malcolm Burnett (Edinburgh), who has supervised all the writer's ventures in the language. In preparing the present revision help and encouragement have come from Dr E. Bispham (Edinburgh), Prof. F. Cairns (Leeds), Prof. M.W. Dickie (University of Illinois, Chicago), Dr M. Heath (Leeds), Dr Ian Rutherford (Reading) and Prof. A.M. Snodgrass (Cambridge). In gratefully acknowledging their help the writer emphasises that he has sole responsibility for everything finally appearing here.

[2]   In addition to the discussion below see Howie (1991) 66–9.

in the main narrative.[3]

Later rationalistic approaches endangered the impressiveness of heroic myth, but also added an intellectual interest to its narrative interest.[4] The resulting tension between claim and sceptical response is the mainspring of *Nemean* 7, in which the conventional motif of a hindrance to poetic praise takes the form of a challenge[5] issued by the poet's own scepticism about Homer's account of the trials and tribulations of Odysseus.[6] It is argued in this paper that Thucydides' approach to Greek myth and history before the Peloponnesian War is founded on an acquaintance with this kind of argumentation, and that his audience was able to follow him because of their own familiarity with earlier examples, including poetical ones such as Pindar's poem. In this respect the *Archaeology* is like Herodotus' rehearsal of the Persian and Phoenician accounts of the starting-point of the conflict with Greece, which owes its interest and intelligibility for the original audience to epic prooemia, with their stress on the starting-point of the story proper, and to priamels setting others' views beside the poet's own, such as that in Sappho fr. 16 L–P.

Subsequent discoveries and discussions have tended to underline the significance of several aspects of Thucydides discussed in the original version of this paper. One is the continuing presence of Homer in the minds of author and audience. It has since been argued that Thucydides assimilates Cleon and Pericles to Thersites and Achilles;[7] Thucydides' picture of Brasidas has been compared with Homeric champions such as Ajax and Achilles;[8] and in a fragmentary poem of Simonides[9] Achilles appears to have served, in his excellence, as a mythical forerunner of Pausanias,[10] the Spartan leader and supreme commander,

---

[3]   Strasburger (1972) 36; cf. Howie (1995) 167.
[4]   See, for example, Howie (1983) and (1991) on the fascination of Pelops and the range of narrative, moral and intellectual interest that Pindar found in him.
[5]   See Race (1987) 133–7.
[6]   For a translation and analysis of a comparable passage in *O.* 1 (28–36) see Howie (1991) 117–18.
[7]   Cairns (1982).
[8]   Howie (1992) 438–48; see further Hornblower (1996) 38–61. On the Homeric *aristeia* in general see Howie (1996), following Krischer (1971) ch. 1.
[9]   Simonides frr. 10–18 West, esp. fr. 11.1–34.
[10] Parsons (1992) 32; Lloyd-Jones (1994) 1; Hornblower (1996) 39–40; *pace* West (1993) 6 n.15; Pavese (1995) 21. When Simonides introduces Pausanias with the exalted terms 'god-like (θείοιο) Cleombrotus' most excellent (ἄριστος) son' (fr. 11.33), it would have been hard for an audience not to remember Achilles. For a hymn to a hero followed by praise of a mortal laudandus, cf. Pind. *I.* 1.14-35 (combined hymn to Castor and Iolaus). For the term ὁπλότεροι (fr. 11.17), referring to later

and, in his death, as a consolatory exemplum for all the Greeks killed at Plataea.[11] Secondly, Thucydides' acquaintance with discussions of myth and literary criticism offered in poems such as Pindar's *Nemean* 7 may now be compared with Isocrates' conscious use of Pindar in comparing historical and mythical figures and in setting himself a similar challenge, notably in the *Evagoras*.[12] Thirdly, there has been exhaustive discussion of the relationship between *Nemean* 7 and Pindar's *Paean* 6: both poems acknowledge Neoptolemus' arrival in Molossia, differing only in the cause (chance in the epinician and Apollo's vengeance in the *Paean* — composed in praise of that god).[13] One value which Neoptolemus had for the Greek audience remains

---

generations and their knowledge of the heroes (Parsons (1992) 31; Rutherford (1996) 181), cf. Pindar's transition from the exemplum of the epic hero Antilochus to praise of the laudandus, Thrasybulus of Acragas, in *P*. 6.40–45.

[11] Aloni (1994) 20 n.34. Compare Pindar's use of Achilles *à propos* the Aeginetan victor Cleander's kinsman Nicocles in *I*. 8.59–65. For the double function of the section on Achilles with its hymnic conclusion compare the way Pindar can introduce as a theme of praise a myth that has an implicit but clear value as an exemplum and can also, conversely, introduce as an exemplum a myth that has a similarly implicit value as a theme of praise. For the former see *O*. 1, in which the story of Pelops, introduced in grateful praise of the place of the contest, contains the negative exemplum of Tantalus and the positive exemplum of his son Pelops (see Young (1971) 37–8; cf. Howie (1995) 170 n.49, comparing *P*. 1, with its parallel between Zeus, conqueror of Typhos, in the hymnic opening, and Hieron, conqueror of Carthaginian and Etruscan enemies). For the latter see *P*. 10, where unattainable felicity exemplified by Hyperboreans leads to the adventures of Perseus, ancestor of Hercules and hence of the Heracleid rulers of Sparta and Thessaly. The relevance of Pindar is acknowledged in general terms by Aloni (1994) 15.

[12] Race (1987).

[13] The case for an explicit link between Pindar's two poems is pleaded, for example, in Gentili (1988) 143–4. Most (1984) 209 argues that there is no part of *N*. 7 that does not make perfect sense with reference solely to the poem itself and that the reference to maltreatment could refer simply to earlier treatments of Neoptolemus' actions at the fall of Troy, though if the *Paean* was known to the audience they would doubtless think of it as well. Most (1984) 203–4 is certainly right in seeing the claim not to have maltreated Neoptolemus as being in place in an intercessory prayer to another hero and descendant of Zeus, Hercules, on his patrons' behalf; cf. Howie (1989b) 69. However, this would not be the only epinician in which Pindar referred to a commission other than the one being executed. In *I*. 1 he refers to another commission still to be completed, a paean in praise of Apollo and Delos (presumably *Paean* 4); his work for his fellow-Theban, the charioteer Herodotus, must take precedence, and he calls on Apollo's own island to yield and offers assurances that both commissions will be completed (1–10). This lively confidence and obvious self-advertisement is comparable with the implied claims of adaptability to different audiences' needs, inventiveness and freedom from self-repetition made in the conclusion to *N*. 7, for which see, e.g., Most (1984) 203–9; Howie (1989b) 68–9. For a jaunty conclusion to an epinician compare the conclusion of *O*. 13 (114–15). For *Pae*. 6 and the last triad of *N*. 7 see Howie (1989b) 62–70.

constant: as founder of a contemporary monarchy in a less developed region he serves as a link with the heroic past. The Macedonian kings' claims to be Heracleids doubtless had a similar interest for other Greeks and contributed similar support for their own claims. In composing the original version of this paper I tried to identify those aspects of Pindar's poem relevant to the discussion, and offered in an Excursus a demonstration that my interpretation is compatible with any reasonable view of the vexed transition to the story of Neoptolemus. In revising that Excursus I have benefited from a recent discussion of ancient interpretations of the poem.[14] However, my principal intention here is to provide a clear and accessible English version of my earlier contribution, rather than to integrate into it everything that has appeared since. I have therefore not attempted to incorporate into this account observations on many significant aspects of the *Archaeology* and *Nemean* 7 to be found in the important contributions of Hornblower and Most.[15]

§1 Introduction

Thucydides' statement that the Peloponnesian War was the greatest up-heaval ever experienced by Greece (1.1.2) indicates at the very outset of his prooemium an intention to compete wth Homer's *Iliad* and Hero-dotus' *Histories*,[16] and to seek a Panhellenic audience. For Thucydides' contemporaries the *Iliad*, with its picture of a great war full of suffering,[17] offered moral, rhetorical and military instruction,[18] and

---

[14] Heath (1993).

[15] Hornblower (1991); Most (1985).

[16] Lloyd-Jones (1971) 141: "In depreciating the importance of the Persian War ... he is anouncing himself as the rival of Herodotus; in depreciating the importance of the Trojan War he is announcing himself as the rival of Homer."

[17] Magnitude of the Trojan War: *Il.* 2.488–92. In the prooemium to his epic on the Persian War Choerilus of Samos promises to recount how a great war (πόλεμος μέγας) came out of Asia to Europe (fr. 1 Kinkel; cf. Bizer (1937) 7); Choerilus appears to have supported his contention with a catalogue of the Persian forces (frr. 2–4 Kinkel). Suffering as a theme of epic: *Il.* 1.2–5; *Od.* 8.489–90; *Little Iliad* fr. 2 Allen; Pl. *Ion* 535b–e; Dem. 19.148 (referring to the proverbial expression, κακῶν Ἰλιάς); in general see Fränkel (1962) 15–16; Griffin (1976), (1980) 103–43; Macleod (1982) 4–8, offering a good formulation (7) of the consolatory value of suffering in the *Iliad*.

[18] Moral: Xen. *Symp.* 3.5. Rhetorical: Pl. *Ion* 540b–d; Xen. *Symp.* 3.5; cf. [Longin.] *Subl.* 9. Military: Pl. *Ion* 540e–541a (how to wage war), 540d (appropriate speeches of exhortation for leaders).

served to illustrate important general principles.[19] Herodotus' work is comparable in all these respects.[20] Towards the end of the prooemium Thucydides lays claim (in some cases implicitly) to the same instructive elements, ending the list with the most striking aspect of both the *Iliad* and his own work:

i)   speeches appropriate to the circumstances (and hence rhetorically instructive), 1.22.1;[21]

ii) a trustworthy account of events which, given human nature, are likely to be repeated at some time (and hence a reliable source of useful lessons and illustrations of important general principles), 1.22.2–4;[22]

---

[19] General principles are stated in the speeches, especially in speeches of warning or consolation; cf. esp. *Il.* 9.496–512 (Phoenix), 16.440–57 (Hera to Zeus), 24.425–8 (Priam to Hermes, self-consolation), 24.525–33 (Achilles to Priam). For the paradigmatic function of the main narrative of the *Iliad* see Howie (1995).

[20] (i) Magnitude of the Persian War: 7.20.2–21 (size of the Persian army in comparison with earlier hosts in both the mythical and the historical period), 7.59–100 (catalogue of the contingents in the Persian land and sea forces; cf. Choerilus in n.17). (ii) Suffering: 6.98.2; cf. Erbse (1970) 67. (iii) Moral instruction: partly in implicit form, as in Solon's stories of Tellos and Cleobis and Biton (1.30.3–31). (iv) Rhetorical interest: see Jacoby (1913a) 492–6; bibliography in Hunter (1982) 293–4 n.105. (v) Military instruction: e.g. 6.10–14 (Dionysius of Phocaea and the soft indisciplined Ionians, a story which includes the *paraenesis* in 6.11.2–3 praised by [Longin.] *Subl.* 22.1–2). (vi) General principles: like Homer, Herodotus sets general principles within warning speeches; see 1.32 (Solon), 1.71.2 (Sandanis), 1.207.1–2 (Croesus, who claims to have learnt from his own sufferings), 7.10.1–2 (Artabanus), 7.104.1–5 (Demaratus). One of Herodotus' most important principles, that human happiness is impermanent, is placed programmatically at the end of his prooemium (1.5.4). See in general Hunter (1982) chs. 5–6.

[21] Thucydides makes it clear that he had no transcripts of speeches as they were actually delivered; all he offers is their general thrust or gist (ξύμπασα γνώμη, 1.22.1). He also says that the speakers in the speeches he presents will say what was necessary at the time. By these two assertions Thucydides wins for his *speeches* the licence disclaimed in the case of his narrative of *events*, to compose them according to his own best judgement. Moreover, the appropriateness of the speeches he presents implies a rhetorical value, as representing what a speaker ought to say in that sort of situation. Hence he is able to lay claim to whatever rhetorical value they have, and so in this respect to compete with Homer and Herodotus. For an interpretation of the concept ξύμπασα γνώμη see Grosskinsky (1936) 24–7, 74, 87, who argues that Thucydides may sometimes include within one of his speeches points taken from several speeches in the actual debate. For other, more deeply significant functions of certain speeches in Homer and Herodotus which Thucydides' self-authorised licence also allows him to extend to some of those in his own work, see Grosskinsky (1936) 83–101; Strasburger (1932) 38–9, (1958) 31; Hunter (1982) 290–91.

[22] On the paradigmatic significance of Thucydides' work see Grosskinsky (1936) 62–82; Erbse (1969); Hunter (1973), (1980), (1982) 228–30. Hunter (1973) 123–48 points out the general value of the warning speeches, and further suggests that ancient readers were able to draw on Thucydides' account of events for *exempla* in their own

iii) many great sufferings,[23] in the broadest sense of the word (and
   hence abundant material for all the types of instruction in
   question), 1.23.1–4.
Between his opening general claim about the magnitude of the
Peloponnesian War and these detailed claims Thucydides places, by
way of justification, the *Archaeology*.

   A reading of the *Archaeology* in the light of other literature, anterior
and contemporary, suggests that objective proof of the most likely
hypothesis about the general pattern or details of earlier Greek history
was not Thucydides' sole concern; he also took account of certain
claims based on the past. As a working hypothesis, I suggest that he
had two approaches to the past, one external and one internal. By an
external approach I mean the construction of hypotheses speculating
about the past in realistic terms, and the use of proofs drawn from the
real world. By an *internal approach* I mean the author's concern with
the information, concepts or beliefs commonly accepted by all or part
of his Panhellenic audience which might help to win acceptance for his
case (or which had at any rate to be taken into account in presenting it),
and with how his contentions could best be made to fit into established
frames of reference. This article is mainly concerned with Thucydides'
internal approach.[24]

   Scholars have recognised that Greek myths and other stories of the
past embody claims by communities or families to land, inherited
privileges,[25] and other matters of national or family pride, and are often
provided with conventional proofs, such as dedications in temples or
cults.[26] Such stories were fitted into two frames of reference. First,
there was a distinction between a mythical or heroic period (*spatium*

---

speeches. Strasburger (1958) 35–9 thinks that in Thucydides the Spartans generally
provide positive exempla and the Athenians negative ones; see also Edmunds (1975),
offering an illuminating comparison with Hesiod's picture of the end of the Iron Race;
Macleod (1979) 52–60; Cairns (1982), suggesting deliberate allusions to the Homeric
figures Thersites and Achilles in Thucydides' treatment of Cleon and Pericles.

[23] On sufferings in Thucydides see Erbse (1970) 67.

[24] For some remarks on the reconstruction of the complete intellectual background of an
ancient author see Hunter (1982) 277–85.

[25] See Nilsson (1951), Parker (1996) 33–41, esp. 38 (heroes in territorial claims).

[26] Dedications: e.g. Hdt. 5.59–61. Cults: e.g. Hdt. 1.171; Charon of Lampsacus *FGrHist*.
262F67. The Athenian festival of the Apaturia has a key role in Athens' claim to be
Mother City of the Ionians in Asia Minor; see Hdt. 1.147.2; Hellanicus of Lesbos
FGrHist. 4F125; Prinz (1979) 336, 351. Linguistic usage can serve as a conventional
proof: e.g. Aristot. *Poet.* 1448a29–b1. On Herodotus' general use of such proofs see
Fehling (1989) 128–43.

mythicum) and a historical period (*spatium historicum*).[27] Secondly, there was a system of co-ordination in time and place to which myths set in the heroic age were subject,[28] and which served as the basis for chronology within the historical period.[29] The importance of such myths and other stories as a support for national or family claims is evident in the work of the encomiastic poets Pindar and Bacchylides and in the Attic tragedians. It is significant that the rationalisations of heroic myth offered by Hecataeus of Miletus still presented Hercules as a worthy ancestor or founder.[30] Also significant is Herodotus' inconsistency in the standards of criticism he applies to myth: stricter standards are applied to the myth used by the Scythians to support their claim to autochthony than to many a tale told by Greeks.[31]

One question arising from these considerations is what sort of people the external and internal approaches might have appealed to. We might distinguish *a priori* between laymen and people with some relevant expertise (such as military men and merchants engaged in foreign trade), and between persons enjoying a lesser or a greater degree of hereditary privilege under the various forms of state existing then.[32] It might be supposed that those with more privileges would be

---

[27] The principal distinction lies in a difference of strength and size between the heroes, who were sons or close descendants of the gods and also differed in some degree from their ordinary contemporaries in this respect (*Il.* 24.454–6), and the men of the historical period; see *Il.* 5.304, 12.383, 449, 20.285–7. The heroes were the figures with the strength to slay the monsters then at large; cf. Pi. *N.* 2.62–9a, 3.23b–4a (Hercules); Bacch. 18.19–30a (Theseus). The uncertainty regarding such a remote time permitted the poets, appealing to the Muses for their authority, to enjoy a corresponding freedom in fleshing out their versions of myths; cf. Pi. *Parth.* 2.31–2a; *Pae.* 6.51–8a. This fundamental difference is attested for the fifth century by Pindar (*P.* 6.40–45) and Herodotus (1.5.3, 68.3). As for the dividing line between the two periods, Ephorus, writing in the fourth century, began the historical period with the Return of the Heraclidae (*FGrHist.* 70T8, 10; cf. F9). The same dividing line is evidently assumed in the *Archaeology* in 1.12. But for Herodotus a period of comparative certainty only begins around 700 BC; see von Leyden (1952). In fact Thucydides' transitional chapter includes *both* divisions; see below §3 on Thuc. 1.12.

[28] Kirk (1970) 247–9, (1974) 268; Kakridis (1972); Willcock (1978) x–xii.

[29] The genealogy of the Philaids is traced from the historical period back to Ajax in Pherecydes of Athens *FGrHist.* 3F2 and Hellanicus of Lesbos *FGrHist.* 4F22. According to von Fritz (1967) I 364–406 the genealogy of the Spartan kings was the foundation for Herodotus' chronology. On the basis of such family trees see Wade-Gery (1952) 119–29, 88–92; Snodgrass (1971) 10–16.

[30] *FGrHist.* 1F26 (Geryon), F27b (Cerberus); see Jacoby (1912) 2738–40.

[31] Hdt. 4.5–12; cf. Bickermann (1952). For proofs no more credible calmly accepted by Herodotus see 1.82.7–8 and 5.87.3.

[32] For the poetical *cum* rhetorical advantage of acknowledging such varying forms of state, see Pindar's assurance that the straight-speaking man is effective in tyrannies,

jealous of their traditions by comparison with the less privileged, and that experts would be more critical. But it is reasonable to assume that the target audience consisted mainly of free citizens of Greek cities. The most important myths serve as the basis for the territorial rights of whole communities;[33] some even provide all citizens of a community with an origin to be proud of.[34] So it may also be assumed that (like Herodotus as a Greek *vis à vis* Scythian claims) the experts' critical faculties might be more or less acute depending on how their own communities or families were affected by the claim supported by any given myth. It is likely, therefore, that in the *Archaeology* Thucydides had to take care at every point not to overlook the subjective viewpoints of the different social and national groups he sought to include in his audience.

The interplay of the two approaches can be illustrated from another Thucydidean prooemium, the introduction to the Sicilian Expedition. Thucydides' use of toponymy to refute the Sicans' claim to be autochthonous (6.2.2)[35] may have been regarded as scientifically effective by author and audience; but it was also no doubt gratifying to all Greek colonists in the island. By contrast, he treats with respect the claims of the Greek cities, together with that of the Elymians, a non-Greek people allied to the Athenians:

i)   The mention of the sacrifices made by sacred ambassadors at the altar of Apollo Archegetes outside Naxos (6.3.1) is primarily a proof of this city's priority; at the same time, it inevitably reminds

---

democracies and oligarchies (*P*. 2.86–88a). Thucydides' own tastes seem to have lain in the direction of the rule of the Five Thousand established by the constitution of 411 BC, as Prof. H. Kuch pointed out to me in 1983.

[33] E.g. the autochthony of the Athenians and the return of the Heraclidae.

[34] In Tyrtaeus fr. 11 all the Spartans are addressed as descendants of Hercules. In Pi. *P*. 4 the king of Cyrene is descended from Euphamus, to whom a god, Triton, gave a piece of earth, symbolising possession of the land, while the original settlers descend from the other Argonauts. In *N*. 7 the kings of Molossia are said to descend from Neoptolemus, while it is left open for others to claim descent from the Achaeans accompanying him when he was blown off course to Epirus; see n.124 below.

[35] Cf. Herodotus' refutation of the Scythian claim to autochthony, again by toponymy (4.12; cf. n.31). Compare too the ethnography of another island in Herodotus, Cyprus (7.90), in which the element in the population which is of neither Phoenician nor Greek origin is called Ethiopian; i.e. they cannot be called autochthonous. With regard to Thucydides' source for the Sicans' claim, Dover (1953) 12 is surely right to reject Jacoby's idea (*ad* Hellanicus *FGrHist*. 4F79) that Antiochus of Syracuse took this claim at face value. Dover himself considers it more likely that he committed both the Sican and the Greek view to writing and appraised them with the aid of τεκμήρια. Cf. Herodotus' procedure in 4.5–12. If Antiochus is Thucydides' source for the argument then the former must also have been supporting the Greek point of view.

readers of the divine sanction for the colony, and associates all subsequent Greek colonies with that sanction.

ii) When Thucydides mentions the Corinthian Heraclid Archias as founder of Syracuse, he touches on the hero Hercules' importance as a mythical basis for Greek claims to Sicily.[36]

iii) Thucydides tells how Megara Hyblaea, the mother city of Selinus, was founded on land to which the king had brought the colonists and which he had betrayed to them (6.4.1). The implication is presumably that the king was in exile, and, more importantly, that he was thereby transferring his right of ownership to them. Betrayal appears to be a typical motif in such stories.[37]

iv) Thucydides tells how the Elymians were the descendants of Trojan refugees, with whom certain Phocians united after being blown off course on their way back from Troy (6.2.3). There seems to have been a practice of conferring Trojan status upon certain non-Greek peoples.[38] One consideration is surely that strong or advanced peoples are thus denied autochthony. The tradition of the involvement of returning Phocians seems to be intended to justify particularly close relations with the Elymians, such as the *conubium* between Selinus and Segesta (6.62).[39]

From the point of view of the *Archaeology* it is also interesting that the mythical chronology provides a framework for a plausible account of the growth of population and general development of the island of

---

[36] On the role of Hercules and his alleged descendants see Dunbabin (1948) 328–30, 348–54.

[37] Compare the seizure of Same by Andrians and Chalcidians "through treason" (Plut. *Greek Questions* 30) and the Heraclid Aletes' seizure of power in Corinth with the help of the reigning king's youngest daughter, who betrayed the city to him (Σ Pi. *N.* 7.155a, 138–9 Dr.).

[38] See Galinsky (1969) 91–102; Burkert (1979) 25.

[39] On the Elymians see Galinsky (1969) 63–102; Dunbabin (1948) 366–7; Kahrstedt (1953). On Thucydides' sources here see Dover (1953), and Gomme, Andrewes and Dover (1970) 197–210. Asheri (1996) 98 argues that the conferment of a Trojan origin upon the Elymians itself exemplifies a general concern to place intermarriage with native populations on a more acceptable footing. He would explain the identification of Libyans of northern Cyrenaica as Trojan Antenorids in the same way, and also identification of the inhabitants of the Lipari Islands as descendants of Aeolus, of the Iapygians and the Bottiaeans as Cretans, and of the Oenotrians as Arcadians. Certainly Telesicrates of Cyrene, Pindar's patron in *P.* 9, claimed descent from a Libyan princess and a Greek suitor (103–23), and Callimachus, himself a Cyrenaean aristocrat, glorifies early intermarriage in his *Hymn to Apollo*, as approved by the god, with a picture of Greek men and Libyan women dancing together at their (presumably first) celebration of the Carneia at Azilis (85–7). All these identifications, however, exclude the possibility of autochthony.

Sicily up to the time of the Expedition.

Thucydides' opening and principal contention in the *Archaeology* is that there had been nothing of any magnitude in the military or any other sphere, either in the heroic age or in the historical period (cf. 1.15.1).[40] This statement in effect announces the author's intention to undertake a reductive revision of earlier achievements, especially those of the heroic age, in the manner of Hecataeus of Miletus.[41] But Thucydides had the more delicate task. In reducing earlier Greek achievements and exploits so as to justify his choice of a different theme, he ran the risk of offending those members of his prospective Panhellenic audience who considered themselves in any way the heirs of the heroes of the past celebrated in epic and prose.

Thucydides bases his demonstration on an assumption already familiar to his audience: that since the beginning of its history the Greek nation has been growing.[42] With this he combines another familiar assumption, and one that is rhetorically effective in addressing a Greek audience: that it is characteristic of the Greeks always to have been more intelligent than non-Greek peoples.[43] Thucydides refers to these peoples indiscriminately as 'barbarians', and in the *Archaeology* the Greeks seem to have had little to learn from them (cf. 1.8.1).[44]

Thucydides' demonstration falls into three parts. The *first* (1.2) is a broad-brush theoretical picture of the earliest times, presupposing continuous general instability. The less fertile lands, especially Attica, constitute an exception (1.2.3–5), but one that proves the rule. The mention of Attica leads to a brief account of its growth up to the colonisation of Ionia (1.2.5–6). The *second* part (1.3–12) deals with the economic and power-political development of Greece up to the Trojan

---

[40] On the interpretation of the phrase τὰ πρὸ αὐτῶν καὶ τὰ ἔτι παλαίτερα see Bizer (1937) 33–5.

[41] Compare Hecataeus' arbitrary reduction of the number of Aegyptus' sons (*FGrHist.* 1F19). For his more complex revision of Cerberus, also involving reduction (F27, 27b), see §6 below.

[42] Cf. Hdt. 1.58: "I am satisfied that since its very origin the Greek nation has used the same language unaltered. However, from the time when it broke away from the Pelasgians it has developed from weak and puny beginnings into a mass of peoples, because the Pelasgians, especially, and other non-Greek tribes attached themselves to it in large numbers. Before that, the Pelasgian tribe, which was non-Greek, had certainly not attained any great population-numbers."

[43] Cf. Hdt. 1.60: "From long ago the Greeks had distinguished themselves from non-Greeks in being cleverer and less prone to silly notions."

[44] Cf. De Romilly (1956) 269 n.63. Unlike Thucydides, Herodotus acknowledges Greek indebtedness for many inventions to the Egyptians; see Hunter (1982) 273.

War, to which the subsequent upheavals and new foundations up to the colonisation of Italy and Sicily in the historical period are appended (1.12). The *third* part describes the power-political development of Greece in the historical period, and in it Thucydides attempts to show why there was no great Panhellenic military undertaking before the Peloponnesian War (1.13–19). All three parts contain proofs and theoretical insights of a genuinely scientific character. At the same time they exhibit a remarkable interplay between these elements and Thucydides' internal approach, since within that theoretical framework mythical figures and events serve as milestones and the claims of families and communities as proofs.

§2 The argument of Thucydides' prooemium (i): 1.2

The interplay between Thucydides' two approaches is already apparent in the genuinely scientific argument that the fertility of different parts of Greece determines whether or not they have undergone changes of population (1.2.3–6). The Greeks' various myths of national origin serve as evidence for this view, and in turn receive scientific support from it. Both the return of the Heraclidae and the autochthony of the Athenians are given the stamp of historicity. This argument is particularly favourable to the claims of the Arcadians and the Athenians.[45] Significantly, the subsequent explanation of the internal stability of Attica is based on a piece of popular wisdom still preserved in Phocylides and employed by Pindar in praise of an island seen as less than ideally fertile.[46] Moreover, Thucydides' statement that Greeks

---

[45] Thucydides acknowledges the claims to autochthony of both the Athenians and the Arcadians, whereas the Attic tragedians and ceremonial speakers customarily exclusively emphasise the autochthony of the Athenians. According to Strasburger (1972) 23 the Athenian belief that they had not had to drive anyone else out of his land meant that they alone had justice as the basis of their historical existence.

[46] Phocylides fr. 4 D: "A small city that dwells on a rock in a seemly manner (κατὰ κόσμον) is better than the folly of Nineveh." Compare Pi. *Pae.* 4 (fr. 36 S–M), commissioned by the city of Carthaea for the island of Ceos. Pindar's praise of Carthaea is, in outline: Carthaea is a mere narrow-backed breast of land, but not to be exchanged for Babylon (14–15). Even if Ceos is only a rock (21a), it is famed for achievements in Panhellenic contests and poetry (21b–24). Ceos has wine, even if she cannot raise horses or cattle (25–7). The mythical king Euxantius, son of Minos (cf. n.68), refused a seventh share of his father's kingdom on Crete (35–9a), out of fear of the gods because Posidon had destroyed the whole populace of Ceos except for his mother Dexithea (for whom see n.73; 39b–51) and also because of his high esteem of Ceos: "I was given a little: the foliage of the oak tree (52). No suffering, no civil strife was I allotted" (53: οὐ πενθέων δ' ἔλαχον, οὐ στασίων). On *Pae.* 4 see Kienzle (1936) 61–2. On the cultural, intellectual and commercial advantages of a less fertile

uprooted by war or internal upheaval sought refuge in Attica because it was safe there (1.2.6) is based on claims important both to the Athenian state and to certain influential families.

For the Athenian state, Thucydides' account provides comprehensive scientific support for a number of claims, especially that of being the Mother City of all Ionia (explicitly acknowledged at 1.3.2).[47] This claim has recently been examined by F. Prinz.[48] According to Prinz the various Ionian cities each had its own foundation-story;[49] these were probably older than two other general versions of the colonisation of the whole region, which were fundamentally compatible with each other. According to one the inhabitants of Pylos in Messene were forced to leave their homeland, emigrated to Asia Minor under the leadership of the sons of Codrus, and founded twelve cities there. Codrus was supposed to be a descendant of Posidon's son Neleus through Periclymenus, son of Neleus and brother of the Homeric hero Nestor.[50] According to the other general version the Ionians once inhabited the part of the Peloponnese later called Achaea and had been forced to yield to Orestes' son Tisamenus and his followers when the latter were driven out of Sparta and Argos by the returning Heraclidae. Twelve, the number of cities forming the Panionion, was in this version supposed to reflect the twelve cities in Achaea.[51]

According to Prinz, the former general version originated in the desire of the Milesians or Ephesians to find mythical justification for the leading role they sought among the Ionians, claiming that a similar leading role had been played by their founder.[52] A unifying tendency is also detectable in the second general version. The Athenians seized upon these two pre-existing general versions and inserted a central role for themselves into both by making the migrating Ionians first find refuge in Athens and only pass on to Ionia two generations later.[53] In

---

country in general see Kienzle (1936) 15–16.

[47] Earliest testimony: Solon fr. 4 D (= 4a West); see Prinz (1979) 373–4.

[48] Prinz (1979) 314–76, to whom I am greatly indebted, not least for the collection of testimonies.

[49] Prinz (1979) 324, 335; cf. 25–6 (Colophon), 107–8 (Miletus).

[50] Prinz (1979) 318–36. Earliest testimony: Mimnermus fr. 12 D (= 9 West).

[51] Prinz (1979) 341–7. Earliest testimony: Hdt. 1.145–6.

[52] Prinz (1979) 331: Androclus in the Ephesian version, Neleus in the Milesian version, which evidently prevailed.

[53] Prinz (1979) 337–40. The earliest testimony for the Athenian modification of the version involving Achaea is Hdt. 7.95.

the case of the Pylos version, the Athenian version said: (i) that the Athenians chose the Ionians' leader Melanthus in place of their own last Theseid king because of the courage and intelligence he showed when helping them against the Boeotians; (ii) that Melanthus' son and successor Codrus sacrificed himself when resisting an attack by the Dorians; and (iii) that Codrus' son Neleus, after quarrelling with his brother Medon over the kingship, led the great migration to Asia Minor,[54] in which (iv) the descendants of both waves of refugees apparently joined.[55]

The same scientific view of the early history of Athens provides support for the Athenian claim to have defended the Heraclidae against Eurystheus, also recognised in the prooemium (1.9.2). The attractions of the safety of the less fertile land of Attica (see 1.2.6) would also give support to the Athenian claim to have the right to possess Salamis on the ground that Ajax's two sons exchanged their title to the island once ruled over by their grandfather Telamon in return for Athenian citizenship;[56] but this is not mentioned in the prooemium.

Linked to the national claims were details of the organisation of the Athenian state and the claims of certain families. There was a phratry called the Medontidae[57] and a genos called the Salaminii which met in the shrine of Eurysaces and received a state subvention for its celebrations.[58] Members of the Salaminii are said to have included Alcibiades,[59] while Solon,[60] Pisistratus and his sons,[61] and perhaps also the Alcmaeonids at some point,[62] claimed descent from the princes from Pylos. The Philaids, whose members included Miltiades and

---

[54] Prinz (1979) 336–40, 347–55. Earliest testimonies: Pherecydes of Athens *FGrHist*. 3F155; Hellanicus of Lesbos *FGrHist*. 4F125.

[55] Prinz (1979) 337–8.

[56] Prinz (1979) 34–56, esp. 54–6. Solon made skilful use of this connection in the dispute between Athens and Megara for possession of Salamis; see Plut. *Solon* 10.3; Prinz (1979) 52; Nilsson (1951) 27–36, esp. 29.

[57] Davies (1971) 271; Crosby (1941) 21–3; Parker (1996) 108 n.24, 326.

[58] Ferguson (1938); Nilsson (1938) 389, (1951) 30–36, Parker (1996) 57–9, 308–16.

[59] Davies (1971) 10–11.

[60] According to Plut. *Solon* 1.2 Solon was a descendant of Codrus. Solon's descendants included Plato, through his mother Perictione. Plato's father was also a descendant of Codrus: D. L. 3.1.

[61] Hdt. 5.65.3; cf. Nilsson (1951) 63.

[62] Pausanias says that the γένη of the Paeonidae and the Alcmaeonidae are descended from the Pylian Neleids (2.18.9). Herodotus either does not know that version or deliberately ignores it; he calls the Alcmaeonidae an Athenian family (5.62), and in his rebuttal of the charge of signalling to the Persians after Marathon he says that they had been known in Athens for ages past; see Davies (1971) 369.

Cimon and, at some point, the Alcmaeonids, and to whom Thucydides himself was related, claimed descent from Philaeus, son of Ajax.[63] Through such mythical links influential families that were not considered autochthonous were able to represent themselves as the descendants of heroes from outside Attica.[64]

Thucydides' account entails the recognition of these claims, retaining what the audience could regard as their likely realistic basis; and in the case of the colonisation of Ionia, an event of Panhellenic significance, the claim is illustrated in the course of a scientific argument. At the same time his references at this early point in the *Archaeology* to the later expansion in the area and population of the Greek world discreetly hint at the limitations of the heroic age. So in the first part of the *Archaeology* the foundation is laid for a scientific demonstration and the right tone is struck for addressing a Greek audience.

§3 The argument of Thucydides' prooemium (ii): 1.3–12

In the second part of his demonstration Thucydides accepts the tradition that the Trojan War was the first large-scale Panhellenic military operation, and infers from this the weakness of earlier Greeks (1.3). The account of Greek history up to that point (3–8) once again offers excellent theoretical speculations and strong proofs. One thinks especially of the observation on the differing locations of cities founded earlier and cities founded later (1.7), the appeal to epic texts for evidence that in the heroic age piracy was a normal thing and brought no shame (1.5.2), the hypothesis that Homer exaggerated the magnitude of the Trojan War for poetical purposes (1.10.3–11), and the bold assertion that right up to the time of the composition of the *Iliad* there was no common Hellenic identity (1.3.3). On the other hand, there is much that is simply accepted from tradition. Thucydides fundamentally accepts the framework of the traditional Greek heroic and tribal myths right back to Deucalion (1.3.2), and in the course of his implicit argument that the same prerequisite factors preceded the Trojan War as

---

[63] See Hdt. 6.35, and n.29. On Thucydides' genealogy see Toepffer (1883) 282–6, esp. 286; Davies (1971) 233–36: Thucydides' father Olorus was apparently the son of an Athenian of the deme Halimus and a daughter of Miltiades and Hegesipyle, the daughter of the Thracian king Olorus.

[64] Cf. Davies (1971) 323: "It is still impossible to evaluate what was meant by the labels Κοδρίδης and Νηλεΐδης except in so far as they imply a contrast with the *autochthonous* nobility of the city cults" (emphasis added).

the Peloponnesian War, although on a smaller scale, he attributes a historical role to mythical figures like Minos and Pelops,[65] and even to Hellen and his sons.[66] In contrast with general Greek opinion he speaks as if it is still possible to know about such matters (1.4, 1.9.2).[67]

Connections with Minos are part of the local traditions of the Cyclades; as early as the fifth century BC he was believed to be founder of the first Greek community on Ceos and was claimed as an ancestor by one of the families there.[68] It appears likely that the general function of such connections was to give Greek settlements on these islands an early foundation-date.[69]

For the Athenians Minos was a mythical precursor both as ruler over the Cyclades and as the founder of a Greek sea power. Theseus' slaying of the Minotaur and consequent ending of the tribute of Seven Youths and Seven Maidens signified a (deferred) transfer of these functions to Athens. That transfer is dramatised in Bacchylides' dithyramb *Theseus* or *The Youths and Maidens* (17 S–M). In this picture of the last tribute-voyage, the sea they traverse is called the Cretan Sea (4) and Minos and Theseus are presented as of equal status as sons of Zeus and Posidon respectively (20–38). Minos attempts to ravish one of the Maidens. Theseus remonstrates and, pointing to his own comparable divine origin, threatens to act against him there and then. Minos proves his own parentage by successfully calling to Zeus for a sign, a thunderbolt.

---

[65] De Romilly (1956) 276–7; Hunter (1980) 202.

[66] We can readily compare the role Thucydides attributes to them with that of Miltiades the Elder among the Dolonci on the Chersonese in Hdt. 6.34–8.

[67] Contrast Hdt. 1.5.3, 3.122.2; von Leyden (1952) 94–5. For the general principle see Pi. *Parth.* 2 (fr. 94b S–M) 31–2: "Many are the things of the past [I could proclaim] embellishing them with words (ἔπεσιν, with an allusion to epic?), but as for the [truth only] Zeus knows."

[68] For the mythical connections between Minos and the Cyclades see Robert (1920) 208–9; Huxley (1966) 15–16. There were cities called Minoia on Amorgos and Siphnos (Steph. Byz. s.v. Μίνωα, 454 Meineke), and a spring with that name on Delos (Robert 351 n.2; Huxley 16 n.17); it was also supposed to have been an earlier name of the island of Paros (Steph. Byz. *loc. cit.*). Minos was on Paros making a sacrifice when he heard of the death of his son Androgeos (Apollod. 3.15.7, providing the *aition* for a sacrificial custom there), and Minos' sons were living on Paros in the days of Hercules (Apollod. 2.5.9). In Bacch. 1, dated to 454 or 452 BC, it is stated that the victor, Argius of Ceos, is descended from Euxantius, the son of Minos and Dexithea, with whom Minos left half his entourage. Pindar knows the same story: see *Pae.* 4 and n.46. On this myth and the dating of Bacchylides' poem see Maehler (1982) II 3–8. For the islanders' positive view of Minos, see Giesekam (1977).

[69] The frequent appearance of Cretans as the first settlers of a place in Greece is explained by Prinz (1979) 22 as owing to what Greeks saw as a dignified antiquity about Cretan history.

He casts a ring he has been wearing into the sea, challenging Theseus to fetch it if his father really is Posidon. Though Minos is a son of Zeus, his behaviour makes it clear that he is no longer fit to rule. The cruelty of the tribute can no longer even be explained by grief for his son Androgeos, slain by the Athenians. Grief has been replaced by lust. When Theseus dives in, Minos orders the ship to sail on at speed, intending to leave him to drown. His intention is to send the younger man off on a fatal mission (in the manner of Polydectes or Aeetes),[70] but he has in fact unwittingly cast away a token of tenure, in this case one for control of the sea, comparable with the clods of earth in some stories exchanged or given away without awareness of their value.[71] When Theseus re-emerges alongside the ship to the accompaniment of divine singing and crowned with a wreath by Posidon's consort Amphitrite, the Athenians' right to send out colonies and to control the sea are presented as having moral, legal and divine authority.

Thucydides' realistic picture of Minos as a king who ejected Carian and Phoenician pirates from the islands in order to increase his own revenues and who installed his sons as governors (1.4)[72] respects the

---

[70] *Pace* Giesekam (1977), the murderous intentions of Minos are clear. The trick with the ring recurs in the mediaeval ballad of the building of the Bridge over the Artas, where it is used to effect murder of the master builder's wife as a sacrifice for the successful completion of the bridge (text with translation in Trypanis (1971) 470–72).

[71] On tokens of tenure see Strosetzky (1958). As Minos is unaware of the value of what he is throwing away, this story is especially comparable with those in which a hero pretends to be a beggar and is scornfully handed a lump of earth, as is Aletes in Corinth (Σ Pi. *N.* 7.155, 137–8 Dr.) and Temon the Aenianian (Plut. *Greek Questions* 13); see Strosetzky 14–15. Also comparable is the Heracleid Perdiccas, who draws a circle with his dagger round the ground covered by the sunshine scornfully offered to him as wages by the king of Macedonia; see Gierth (1971) 33–4. For a ring with this significance compare Gyges' (admittedly magic) ring, found on the finger of a long-dead potentate (Pl. *Rep.* 2. 359c–360b). The ring may also owe some of its value to being cast over the sea, *qua* territory; cf. the taking of possession of Acanthus by a spear-cast (Plut. *Greek Questions* 30). The loss of the ring is advantageous: had Theseus recovered it, proving his achievement would have entailed handing it back to Minos for identification, in effect returning it to him; the cloak and the wreath in a sense substitute for it as well as being proofs of divine parentage. The loss of the ring could also be seen as corresponding to the deferment of the power it signified (the colonisation of Ionia, with the voyaging involved, does not occur until several generations later; and, for Herodotus, the next Greek sea-power only emerges with Polycrates of Samos in the sixth century BC, while Athens' own sea-power is commonly thought to begin with Themistocles' advice on the disposal of the revenues from the silver-mines at Laurium). Compare the loss of the clod of earth given by Triton to Euphamus in Libya, which Medea prophesies will defer the colonisation of Libya under a descendant of the Argonaut Euphamus for many generations (Pi. *P.* 4.43–56).

[72] Kleingünther (1934) 122–5 suggests that Minos already figured in traditions, and

view taken by the islanders themselves and the links they claimed with him, while at the same time offering a prototype for the Athenian Empire. Furthermore, any earlier inhabitants are presented as non-autochthonous and their ejection as morally justified; Thucydides describes them as "evil-doers" (κακοῦργοι, 1.8.2).[73] This is an important point for Thucydides' internal approach, and he attempts to substantiate it by means of alleged discoveries during the clearing of the graves during the second, full, purification of Delos in 426/5 BC (1.8.1). These findings cannot, of course, be checked now.[74] Indeed, even if they were objectively correct, it must be borne in mind that Thucydides' demonstration relies on arguments of a traditional kind: a Carian national claim to have invented the helmet-crest, the shield-grip and the shield-blazon,[75] and a comparison of modes of burial. Gomme correctly notes that Solon had already employed a comparison of burial customs a century before in the dispute with the Megarians over Salamis. As for the Carian inventions, it is significant that this isolated recognition of an invention by non-Greeks is introduced by Thucydides as evidence, in effect, of Greek territorial rights!

The Athenian colonisation of the islands and Ionia is mentioned, along with other Greek colonisations of varying dates, only at the end of the second part of Thucydides' demonstration (1.12.4), although the

---

sophistic speculations based on them, about early law-making and forms of state, citing Hdt. 1.65; Ephorus *FGrHist.* 70F147; Nicolaus of Damascus *FGrHist.* 90F103aa.2.

[73] For the motif of the morally justified expulsion of non-Greeks see Hdt. 6.137 (Athenian version of the expulsion of the Pelasgians from Attica), 6.138 (Athenian justification of the seizure of Lemnos); Charon of Lampsacus *FGrHist.* 262F67 (bad faith of the Bebryces towards the Greeks); Delphic verse oracle supposedly delivered to Neleus asking whether he should found a city (Σ Aristid., p. 78, Parke–Wormell no. 301 = Fontenrose l. 69): "Neleus, see to it that you drive out the unjust (ἀδίκους) Carians and settle Hellenes and Ionians there." According to Xenomedes of Ceos (Call. fr. 75 Pf. = *FGrHist.* 442F1.60–69) the first inhabitants of Ceos were Carians, Leleges and Telchines, and they were destroyed by the gods because of the misdeeds of the Telchines and the godlessness of their king, Demonax. According to Nicander fr. 116 Schn., the Telchines were destroying the crops. See Maehler (1982) 5–8. Dexithea was spared, and united with Minos shortly afterwards. The same cause was given in Bacch. 1; see n.68 and Maehler (1982) 4–5; it also provides the basis for the story in Pi. *Pae.* 4 (see n.46). For the people of Ceos Thucydides' version must have looked like a point-by-point realistic equivalent of their traditional *ktisis.*

[74] See Rhomaios (1929); Cook (1955) 267–9; Long (1958); Snodgrass (1964).

[75] Hdt. 1.171. Cf. Snodgrass (1964), who notes that the vagueness of Thucydides' references points to something familiar to the audience, and in the case of the weapons, to the traditional Carian inventions. A similar brief reference to a typical element of stories in support of claims is found in 6.4.1; see §1.

colonisation of the islands and Ionia was well known to have taken place much earlier than, for example, the foundation of Syracuse. On the other hand, Thucydides' references to Athens in connection with the general development of Greece (1.6.5) have already made it clear how Athens was capable of this at such an early stage. The Athenians had been the first to give up going about armed in their everyday life, and it was in Athens that wealthy people first adopted a more relaxed life-style, for example wearing long linen garments. On Thucydides' account, these changes must have taken place before the colonisation of Ionia, since he makes the custom of wearing such garments something the Ionians had brought with them through their tribal affinity with the Athenians.[76] The early adoption of such a life-style is also assumed by Bacchylides in his dithyramb on the coming of Theseus to Athens (18 S–M), which begins with the young men addressing Aegeus as "king of the delicate-living Ionians" (2). This description implies that the combination of the Athenians' early adoption of a more (internally) peaceable and relaxed life-style, the luxurious ways of the Ionians in Asia Minor and Athens' claim to be mother city of Ionia was already part of the view of the past held by an Athenian audience earlier in the fifth century BC. Thanks to the early achievement of internal peace and freedom of movement Athens had become a strong and populous state capable of colonising the Cyclades and Ionia.[77] The significance of Athens' innovations regarding dress and personal arms for Thucydides' internal approach becomes clear when he immediately cites two corresponding Spartan innovations which still further distinguished Greeks from barbarians, the adoption of a simple style of dress by the rich (1.6.4) and the introduction of nudity for athletes (1.6.5) — despite the fact that these Spartan innovations belong to the historical period. Thucydides probably sees the first of these Spartan innovations as a sign of internal stability (cf. 1.18.4).

The factors which, according to Thucydides, brought the Pelopids to power in the Peloponnese are also of a realistic kind and find clear parallels in the historical period. Pelops came to power through the great wealth he brought with him from Asia (1.9.2). This power was then extended by his son Atreus. While Atreus was living in exile in Mycenae after the murder of his half-brother Chrysippus, Eurystheus

---

[76] It is more likely that the Athenians took this fashion over from Asia Minor and the Ionian colonies there; see Gomme (1945) 103; De Romilly (1956) 285.

[77] Compare Thucydides' account of the development of Athens in 2.15–16.

entrusted him, as his maternal uncle, with the care of his kingdom while he himself was fighting the Heraclidae; and when Eurystheus was slain in Attica, the people of Mycenae chose Atreus as king. The reasons for their choice were that he seemed to be competent, he had made himself popular with the masses (no doubt during his regency),[78] and they were afraid of the victorious Heraclidae. And in this way the descendants of Pelops became greater than those of Perseus (1.9.2).[79] Wealth, fear of a powerful external enemy, and one man's competence as a ruler and astute manipulation of the people, are all realistic factors contributing to the power eventually inherited by Agamemnon. And it was not the fidelity of Helen's suitors to their oath so much as Agamemnon's power, nor friendship so much as fear, that led so many to join him in the war against Troy (1.9.3).

Thucydides attributes this account of the rise of the Pelopids to "the best informed persons in the Peloponnese" (1.9.2). These authorities have the special qualification of living in the part of the world in which the events took place. There are many such authorities in Herodotus, and it is characteristic of them that they reflect an appropriate local bias.[80] Sometimes Herodotus' authorities seem more carefully crafted than earnestly sought out. His learned Persians, with their series of rationalisations of Greek heroic myth (1.1–4), look decidedly fictive, and the intervention of Phoenician spokesmen on a point affecting the Phoenicians' role in the abduction of Io (1.4) makes the whole thing, on examination, even more likely to be contrived. Thucydides' Peloponnesians, like many of Herodotus' authorities, are anonymous, and their account is likewise favourable to the interests of communities in their own part of the world. The historical basis of Peloponnesian traditions is acknowledged, and there is subtle support for the historicity of Pelops in this pragmatic version which makes no mention of the suitor-contest set by Oenomaus and the consequent trickery on the part of Pelops, Myrtilus or Hippodamia, or of divine aid in the form

---

[78] Cf. De Romilly (1956) 277–8; Hunter (1980) 202. There is an example of how this could be done in the story that when Cypselus was serving as polemarch in Corinth he waived his share of any fines he had to impose: see Nicolaus of Damascus *FGrHist*. 90F57.5; Bockisch (1982) 64–5.

[79] What makes this possible, as Thucydides' public would know, was the marriages that Pelops had made for his daughters; see Hes. fr. 190, where three daughters of Pelops marry three sons of Perseus, one marriage being that of Nicippe and Sthenelus, the parents of Eurystheus. For Pelops' numerous progeny of both sexes see Plut. *Thes*. 2 and West (1985) 109–12.

[80] Fehling (1989) 50–57.

of winged horses.[81] As in Thucydides' account of Minos, finance is assigned a decisive role in this account of Pelops. While this Peloponnesian version has no more factual authority than Herodotus' Persian one, it is always possible that Thucydides has (as Herodotus sometimes does)[82] an actual source, such as Hellanicus of Lesbos, who is known to have made pragmatic revisions of heroic mythology.[83] There is no mention of the feast of Thyestes,[84] but the murder of Chrysippus, an important factor in the story for Thucydides, is included. This approach is comparable with that of Pindar, who describes Pelops' six sons as "eager for feats of excellence" (ἀρεταῖσι, *Olympian* 1.89), thus suggesting a possible motive for the feud between two of them, Atreus and Thyestes,[85] and accepts as a fact the exile of Peleus and Telamon from Aegina for the murder of their half-brother Phocus (the same kind of crime as Atreus and Thyestes' murder of *their* half-brother, Chrysippus), shying away from the story yet implying a realistic defensive explanation in his reference to "what fate drove warlike men out of [Aegina]" (*Nemean* 5.15–16); they were warlike and it was destiny that they should follow the paths they did.[86] Thucydides' Peloponnesian informants seem to follow the same principle as Pindar in the latter poem: "not every unperverted truth is profitable when it shows its face, and silence is often the wisest thing for mortals" (*Nemean* 5.16–18).

Thucydides' account of the Trojan War itself also involves a fundamental interplay between the external and internal approaches. His brilliant analysis of the Catalogue of Ships achieves a reductive rationalisation of Agamemnon's forces. The underlying purpose would

---

[81] Pelops' earlier adventure, his death and rebirth, had already been the subject of a virtuoso revision and semi-rationalisation in Pi. *O*. 1: see Howie (1983), (1991) 117–20.

[82] Fehling (1989) 150–54, 247–9.

[83] Gomme (1945) 109 *ad loc.*; Jacoby on Hellanicus *FGrHist.* 4F157; Jacoby (1913b) 119–20.

[84] The motif is realistic enough, however distasteful, and is twice employed by Herodotus in quasi-historical stories set in Iran (1.73, 1.119).

[85] Pindar presents the feud between the two brothers as an example of the negative side of a generally beneficial competitive attitude in political life. For the positive side see Soph. *OT* 897–8 and Jebb *ad loc.* For the negative side see Darius' criticism of oligarchy in Hdt. 3.82: "In an oligarchy powerful personal enmities often arise when many men desire to show their excellence (ἀρετή) to the whole community ... party strifes arise from that, and murder follows." Compare Thuc. 3.82.3 and Gomme *ad loc.*; Xen. *Mem.* 2.6.16–20. I owe these parallels to Prof. Dickie.

[86] On such *Lokomotionssagen*, as Albin Lesky wittily characterises this widespread type, see Lesky (1966) 32; Prinz (1979) 83.

have been immediately apparent to his original audience, and becomes clear to modern readers when he compares the Persian War with the Peloponnesian War (1.23): to get rid of the impression of endless slaughter created in the *Iliad*, and thus to expose the magnitude of the Achaeans' sufferings (*Iliad* 1.2–5; cf. *Odyssey* 8.81–2; *Little Iliad* fr. 2 Allen) as a poetical fiction (1.10.4–5).

Thucydides also argues perceptively that it was lack of finance (1.11) that compelled an army as large as the Greek one was — even after his own revisions[87] — to fight as long as it did. Yet his whole argumentation depends on two arbitrary assumptions: that the Catalogue is basically true; and that the Trojan War did last as long as tradition said. Thus, although Thucydides declares that Homer, as a poet, probably exaggerated in the Catalogue of Ships, in his detailed argumentation he retains Homer's statements as the basis of his own estimates; and he himself has already secured the cities providing contingents against excessive scepticism based on their small size or their subsequent decline (1.10.1–2). Thucydides' unquestioning acceptance of the duration of the war is remarkable; an impartial researcher would surely have wondered whether the ten years were not also an exaggeration. The only things that Thucydides seriously calls into question are the magnitude of the sufferings, and the general instructive value of the war itself and of Homer's account of it for the conduct of war in Thucydides' own time.

By retaining the traditional ten years Thucydides preserves the chronological framework for the traditional deeds of the heroes (the latter albeit in implicitly revised form),[88] together with the individual leaders from the various communities and contingents implicitly big enough for their revised fighting role and for the foundation-stories connected with their attempted return to Greece. In other words, Thucydides' revision leaves the basic framework of heroic myth unscathed.

Thucydides argues that the size of the Greek army was constrained not so much by the limited population at that time as by the limited finances (1.11). Had he not adopted this view, his audience might well have asked how Greece could have withstood such great losses of men as are presupposed by the epic accounts of the war, the tradition of a

---

[87] See Gomme (1945) 114 *ad loc.*

[88] Compare Hellanicus' revised versions of Achilles' fight with the river (*FGrHist.* 4F28) and of Aeneas' flight from Troy (F32; ἔοικεν, l. 20; οἷα εἰκός, l. 25); see Jacoby (1913b) 119–20.

great storm striking the returning ships,[89] and (often bound up with the latter) the foundation stories.[90] Thucydides' hypothesis of a lack of finance offers an elegant solution.[91] Lack of resources restricted the size of the army and compelled the Greeks to conduct raids and even to farm land in the Chersonese, so that the Trojans only faced part of the Greek forces at any given time (1.11). In the case of the former expedient the audience would remember the references in the *Iliad* to the sacking of evidently weaker Trojan cities.[92] The latter expedient, a strikingly realistic touch, also goes back to earlier traditions. According to the scholia on Thucydides 1.12 (15.4–5 Hude), these farm-workers were under the direction of Acamas and Antimachus.[93] This tradition is bound up with Athenian territorial claims on land in that area in justification of the founding of Elaeus and Amphipolis.[94]

What brought this earlier concentration of power to an end, says Thucydides, was the upheavals connected with the returns of the Greek

---

[89] *Od.* 4.499–501; *Nostoi* (*Homeri Opera* V, ed. T.W. Allen, p. 108); Aesch. *Agam.* 648–80; Eur. *Tro.* 88–91.

[90] In Thucydides' time there were other such stories over and above those contained in the *Nostoi*, as emerges from Bacch. 11.119–23 (foundation of Scione) and Thuc. 4.120 (foundation of Metapontum; Thucydides here speaks of "the [i.e. the well-known] storm"), 6.2.3 (Phocians join Elymians in Sicily; see §1). There was also, for example, the story, not connected with the storm, of the colonisation of Pamphylia by Amphilochus (Hdt. 7.91).

[91] Thucydides uses the same terms for financial aspects throughout the Archaeology, and makes no reference to the invention or use of coinage; see Kallet-Marx (1993) 21–36.

[92] Cf. *Il.* 1.366–74, 6.414–28: Achilles' sack of Thebe, yielding cattle, sheep, and nobility worth a high ransom; Achilles himself says they brought "everything" back to their camp (1.367), and speaks of such attacks on Trojan cities as normal occurrences (1.163–71). For Thucydides' view of the general role of such depredations see 1.5.

[93] See Nilsson (1951) 50. Eustathius on *Il.* 5.4 (2.3.7–8 van der Valk): some said that Diomedes had worked on the land during the time of the action of the *Iliad*. There is a historical example of troops being employed as agricultural labourers in Xen. *Hell.* 2.1.1, 6.2.37; for a contemporary example (Russian troops working the land and being paid in kind in the form of two cabbages each during a period of acutely low pay) see *The Independent* of Sat. 25 Oct. 1996, p. 15, with photograph.

[94] See Nilsson (1951) 50. Aeschines claims (*Fals. Leg.* 31) to have delivered a speech before Philip in which he recounted how one of the sons of Theseus received Ennea Hodoi (the site of the later Athenian colony of Amphipolis) as a dowry on his marriage to the daughter of the Thracian king. Cf. [Apollod.] *Epit.* 6.16–17; Tzetzes on Lycophron 495 (pp. 651–2 Müller): after the end of the war Demophon/Acamas puts in with a few ships in the region of the Thracian Bisaltae; he becomes betrothed to the king's daughter Phyllis; the dowry was supposed to be the kingship; he, however, wants to return to Athens; he promises to come back after a stipulated time, and Phyllis accompanies him as far as Ennea Hodoi; he settles down in Cyprus instead; after waiting for the appointed period Phyllis killed herself. Ps.-Scymnus 707: Elaeus was founded by the Athenian hero Euphorbus. See also Jacoby on Hellanicus *FGrHist.* 4F27.

leaders (1.12.2) and the later migrations of the Thessalians, the Boeotians and the Heraclidae (1.12.3). For a long time no comparable concentration of power arose,[95] since many populous communities in the Greek world of Thucydides' time, the colonies in Ionia and Magna Graecia, were not founded until long after the Trojan War, that is, after the cities in Greece had, at different dates, regained stability (1.12.4).[96]

Thucydides' two approaches, the external and the internal, overlap here. His treatment of the Boeotians, who were important adversaries of the Athenians in the Peloponnesian War, underlines his concern for the internal approach and reveals the importance of the Catalogue of Ships from that point of view. The migrations of the Thessalians and the Boeotians into their respective historical territories[97] were connected with families' claims of descent from the leaders of these migrations, from the Heraclidae in Thessaly[98] and from king Opheltas and his prophet Peripoltas in Boeotia.[99] Thucydides places the migrations of these two linguistically-related peoples in a causal relationship, and dates them sixty years (two generations) after the Trojan War. In these respects he is probably following an earlier account, and he is in agreement with the story that Thessalus, the leader of the Thesprotian migration into the historical Thessaly, was descended from Phidippus, a grandson of Hercules. Phidippus and his brother Antiphus were the leaders of a contingent from Cos and some of the Sporades (*Iliad* 2.676–80), and after the war were blown off course to Thesprotia.[100]

---

[95] Cf. Bizer (1937) 35; Hunter (1982) 24–5 with n.12. De Romilly (1956) 289–91 and Snodgrass (1971) 7–8 deny that the notion of a regression is present in the *Archaeology* in view of what the historian himself says in ch. 12. There, however, the author's purpose is to emphasise that even such power as had been accumulated at the time of the Trojan War still had a very limited basis; cf. Thuc. 1.2.6 and §2. For a discussion of the interplay of progress and regression in the *Archaeology* see Hunter (1982) 262–9.

[96] See Erbse (1970) 56 and n.26; Bizer (1937) 34–5.

[97] See Grote (1888) I 450–55; Beloch (1913) 83–4; *RE* and Roscher *s.vv.* 'Antiphos', 'Pheidippos', 'Thessalos'; Jacoby on Charax of Pergamon *FGrHist.* 103F6; Prinz (1979) 86–7 and n.27.

[98] Pi. *P.* 10.1–3.

[99] Plut. *Mor.* 558a; see *RE s.vv.* 'Opheltas', 'Peripoltas'.

[100] [Aristot.] *Peplus* fr. 640 (Rose); Strabo 9.5.23 (444c); Velleius Paterculus 1.1.3; Polyaen. 1.12. The earliest testimony of a migration from Thesprotia to Thessaly is Hdt. 7.176.4, with no mention of the date or the leader. Thessalus was the grandson of Phidippus; see Polyaen. 8.44, who dates the victory over the incumbent Boeotian inhabitants to the time of Thessalus' father Aeatus. [Apollod.] *Epit.* 5.15 mentions only Antiphus as having been blown off course, directly to Thessaly, where he himself defeats the Pelasgian inhabitants and names the land after his father, Thessalus; cf.

In the Catalogue of Ships the Boeotians are the first contingent
mentioned. They already inhabit the historical Boeotia, and their con-
tingent is drawn from their various cities. If, as is only reasonable to
suppose, the later career and posterity of Phidippus was already known
to the author of the Catalogue, then it contains an implicit
contradiction. Had Thucydides simply been examining the Homeric
account of the Trojan War for evidence of the exaggeration he
postulates, he could have subtracted the Boeotian contingent from
Agamemnon's forces. It is easy to conceive the offence this would have
given to the people whose name stood at the head of the list. On the
other hand Thucydides' acceptance of Homer's inclusion of Boeotians
in the Trojan War threatens to contradict his own account of the decline
of the first great concentration of power, to which these migrations
contribute. He attempts to reconcile the two traditions by saying that
one group of Boeotians was already living in the historical Boeotia.[101]
Behind this expedient we can detect the need (rhetorical as well as
theoretical) to give a coherent picture of the great postwar upheaval
and, at the same time, to avoid a conflict between that picture and a
national claim, enshrined in the Catalogue of Ships, of one of the major
belligerents in the Peloponnesian War. In spite of this adjustment for
the sake of the Boeotians, Thucydides presents a scientifically
illuminating picture of a long period of upheaval which incorporates all
sorts of claim stories. At the same time, the traditional belief in a heroic
age is explained in a manner that is reasonable and doubtless was also
welcome to many among his audience: it was a fundamentally correct
memory of a concentration of military power that exceeded anything
achieved earlier and remained without equal for centuries afterwards.

It was important both for the development of Thucydides' theory
and for his internal approach to defend that earlier concentration of
power against excessive *a priori* scepticism (1.10.1). In this respect
archaeological evidence, in the shape of the ruins of Mycenae,
apparently presented some difficulty.[102] Thucydides therefore argues

---

Tzetzes on Lycophron 911 (p. 871 Müller). In D. S. 19.53.7–8 the Pelasgians drive the
Boeotians out of their homeland in Boeotia during the Trojan War while their warriors
are away at Troy, and the Boeotians only return "after a fourth generation".

[101] Cf. Grote (1888) 452; Beloch (1913) 84.

[102] According to Cook (1955) 266–7, followed by Snodgrass (1971) 9, Thucydides
mainly means the ruins of the city destroyed in the fifth century; and Snodgrass argues
that even the remains of Agamemnon's city still visible in Thucydides' time would not
have given an adequate impression of its extent. In any case, Thucydides' principal
concern was to counter a possible impression or objection on the part of his audience.

that even the external appearance of Athens or Sparta would give a misleading impression, albeit of an opposite kind in either case, an argument surely acceptable to both cities (1.10.2).

In the ways outlined above, therefore, Thucydides endeavours to reduce the magnitude of the Trojan War by means of realistic arguments and always with an eye to traditional claims; and, while doing so, he is also able to cast doubt on the general value of the Trojan war as a theme and on Homer's treatment of it. Even those who had reservations about Thucydides' reconstruction will have noticed that Thucydides takes account of a greater range of factors in the *Archaeology* than Homer does in the *Iliad*; that point at least must have commended his account of the Peloponnesian War to them.[103]

§4 The argument of Thucydides' prooemium (iii): 1.13–23

The third part of Thucydides' demonstration assigns important roles to Athens' principal adversaries, Corinth and Sparta. In the development of sea-trade Corinth is given a role comparable with that of Minos in the earliest part of the story (1.13).[104] In the development of navies the *terminus post quem* is regularly supplied by a local claim, often by the Corinthians, to an invention which establishes the earliest date for a given stage of development.[105] Other landmarks of a still limited growth are the Lelantine War (1.15.3), the achievements of the navies of the Ionians, Samos, and Massilia (1.13.6), and the innovations of the Corcyraeans and the tyrants of Sicily (1.14.2). The highest level of military power on land over a long period is set by Sparta (1.18.1). Sparta's constitution had already stood the test of 400 years at the time of writing. Sparta had never had a tyrant, and was for this very reason able to develop a certain amount of military power, whereas all the tyrants in (Old) Greece stayed clear of major military undertakings for the sake of their internal security (1.17). The highest level of military

---

[103] The Corcyreans' pride in a mythological connection with the Phaeacians as earlier inhabitants of their land is mentioned, significantly enough, soon after the *Archaeology* in 1.25, where they are said to link their own naval prowess with those favourites of the sea-god. Here there is no rationalisation. For the claim see Howie (1989a); for the growth of their colony Epidamnus and the link between growth, luxury and *stasis* in a colony as presented by Thuc. 1.24, see the collection of examples of the traditional view of colonies, *ibid.* 26–7.

[104] Cf. Hunter (1980) 214.

[105] For the various local claims to inventions see Kleingünther (1934) esp. 25–6. (on local patriotism in general). For other Corinthian claims to inventions, see Pi. *O.* 13.16–22 and Kleingünther *loc. cit.*

power achieved under tyranny was in Sicily. In Old Greece the power
of Sparta was sufficient to intervene in other cities and have the tyrants
overthrown (1.18.1). So the proofs of the limitations of military power
on sea and land in Greece have a positive value from the point of view
of Thucydides' internal approach.

The interplay of the external and internal approaches is particularly
important in Thucydides' treatment of the Persian War. At first it looks
as if he is quietly bypassing the question of the relative magnitude of
the Persian and Peloponnesian Wars through the simple assumption
that the power available on the Greek side was not as great during the
Persian War as it had become by the time of the Peloponnesian War
(1.18.2–10). However, after recommending his own work for its
accuracy and usefulness (1.20–22), he comes back to the Persian War
(1.23), and uses it as the immediate foil for the re-introduction of his
own theme (1.23).[106]

Thucydides does not compare the two wars in respect of the forces
deployed. Instead he compares their length and the number of major
battles (1.23.1–3). There are good reasons for this from the point of
view of both his external and his internal approaches. In the case of
earlier conflicts there was little certain knowledge, so it was reasonable
to calculate the amount of power likely to have been available as a
factor determining the magnitude of a war. The vast resources at a
Persian King's disposal were well known in general terms; Herodotus
emphasises the enormous size of Xerxes' forces (7.20–21) and
catalogues the land and sea contingents (61–87, 89–96). Although in
objective terms it might have been possible to offer a convincing
downwardly revised estimate of the forces fielded by Xerxes, that
course has little to commend it from the point of view of the internal
approach. It would have meant reducing the vastness of the forces the
Greeks had pitted themselves against and hence the achievements of
the various communities whose members he was now seeking to
attract.[107] We may remember Pindar's careful equation of Salamis,
Plataea and Himera in *Pythian* 1.75–80, where he says that he will win
his reward in Athens, Sparta and at the court of the Dinomenids in
Syracuse with praise of the battle associated with each audience.
However, the duration of the war and the number of decisive

[106] The rhetorical character of this comparison is seen by Patzer (1940) 107. Cf. Erbse
(1970) 67–8 n.44; Focke (1923) 348 n.4.
[107] Cf. Erbse (1970) 59.

engagements were also known,[108] and Thucydides argues from them that the Peloponnesian War actually had far more to offer in the way of sufferings than the Persian War. Surprising though it appears at first, there is much to be said for his argument in objective terms. Moreover, it permits him to launch into a large-scale *synkrisis* of great eloquence, which in the choice of items for inclusion in the second part, dealing with the Peloponnesian War, passes from objectivity to rhetoric. On the one side there are two land battles and two sea-battles leading to a speedy conclusion to the war (1.23.1). On the other side there are unheard of sufferings of every kind (1.23.1–3). After this final mention of the long-awaited theme of suffering, Thucydides does not scruple to throw all sorts of natural catastrophes and portents into the balance (23.3), and even to change his attitude to the past. In the case of the non-human phenomena the events of this war actually make all earlier traditions credible (1.23.2). Has Thucydides become a mere opportunist? Or does he see in this war a religious significance of the kind Herodotus attributed to some events? Not a question to be tackled here.[109]

§5 The analogy of *Nemean* 7

This analysis raises a question about Thucydides' audience: how could he expect his hearers or readers to understand all the arguments and references detected here? One answer comes from encomiastic poetry, which had accustomed Greek audiences to complex and syntactically dense orally delivered discourse composed with an eye to considerations analogous to Thucydides' internal approach. In this

---

[108] The scholia *ad loc.* (25.17–19 Hude) identify the two land battles as Thermopylae and Plataea and the two sea battles as Artemisium and Salamis, and are followed by Gomme (1945) 151. Bizer (1937) 24 would replace Artemisium by Mycale. In the famous Marathon Oath (see [Longin.] *Subl.* 16) Demosthenes names Marathon, Plataea, Salamis and Artemisium (18.208). Marathon is irrelevant, since its inclusion would extend the duration of the war and give no sense of a quick resolution, but Demosthenes may tilt the balance in favour of Artemisium. Thucydides' wording ταχεῖαν τὴν κρίσιν ἔσχεν skilfully concentrates the interest of the Persian War on the decisive phase; see Bizer 23–4.

[109] In the latter case these natural phenomena would be a sign of the sympathy of the cosmos with a great war. See Bühler (1964) 26–7 on Longinus' interpretation (9.6) of *Il.* 20.61–5. On the possibility of a religious aspect in Thucydides' work see Lloyd-Jones (1971) 137–44; Strasburger (1958) 39–40 and 39 nn. 2, 3; Oost (1975). The parallel detected by Edmunds (1975) between Hesiod's account of the Iron Race (*Op.* 174–201) and Thucydides' account of *stasis* on Corcyra is an important contribution to this discussion.

section I shall attempt to show that Pindar's *Nemean* 7 offers significant analogies with Thucydides' *Archaeology*. I shall argue that, in order to counter any doubts about the reliability of his praise of his patrons, Pindar challenges the reliability of poetical discourse generally, and argues that in the case of both heroic poetry and professional praise of contemporaries one decisive criterion is a divinely sanctioned honour of some kind, and another is the acceptance of that praise by the home community. As an example of poetical exaggeration Pindar instances the *Odyssey*, subjecting it to a concise reductive rationalisation in which epic poetry itself is cited in evidence; and as an illustration of the criteria that raise poetical praise above suspicion he offers a treatment of the career of the hero Neoptolemus, supported by traditional types of proof and constructed in such a way as to be acceptable to a number of different Greek communities that could claim to be that hero's home. For the wider public (a Panhellenic public, as emerges from the opening of *Nemean* 5 and the conclusion of *Olympian* 1) the poem must have offered considerable intellectual interest. For potential clients there was an additional interest: Pindar uses the example of a particular patron and a particular hero to justify the poetical praise of wealthy patrons in general, by associating the question of the credibility of poetical praise of contemporary patrons with the credibility of heroic poetry. In both cases the decisive criterion is an honour conferred by the gods. In the case of a contemporary patron that criterion can be a victory won in sacred games (cf. 6b–8) or a hereditary office (γέρας, 101). In the case of an epic hero it can be a cult (44b–47) or a hereditary office passed down through his posterity (γέρας, 40). The hereditary office is the common denominator; and thereby quietly but clearly the position of all persons with long-inherited privileges is justified as a fundamentally (cf. 54–9a) uninterrupted (αἰεί, 39) divine favour.[110]

After a prooemium addressed to the Goddess of Birth and an announcement naming the father, the boy-victor and their city (1–10), Pindar says that anyone who has had success has to keep the fame of that achievement alive by means of poetry (11–16); saving money on that is a false economy (17–20a).[111] But he then raises a possible

---

[110] On the theme of the vicissitude of human fortune see Kirkwood (1975). On the fundamentally healthy nature of such vicissitudes in the destiny of leading persons or families, see esp. Pi. *O*. 2.35–6; *P*. 3.80–88, 7.19–21.

[111] For the interpretation see Bischoff (1938) 18; Gow (1952) on Theocr. 16.63; Lloyd-Jones (1973) 130 and n.118; Carey (1983) 142–3 *ad loc.*; Most (1984) 144–5.

objection, the possibility of exagggeration by the poet, using as his example the *Odyssey*:[112]

> Yet I expect [ἔλπομαι] that the account of Odysseus became more than his sufferings [ever were] through Homer with his sweet words. For there is something awesome about his lies and his winging devices. Skill deceives by leading astray with discourses [μῦθοι, both stories and speeches], and the largest mass of mortals has a blind heart. (20b–24a)

The juxtaposition of the terms 'more' and 'I expect' (πλέον' ἔλπομαι)[113] clearly alludes to reductive revisions of the Hecataean type, and resembles Thucydides' opening statement about early Greece (οὐ μέγαλα νομίζω, 1.1.3).[114] This declaration of scepticism is followed by a supporting argument in two stages.

The first stage of Pindar's argument (21–3b) shows a technical understanding of the art of the *Odyssey*. When he calls Homer ἀδυεπής ('speaking with sweet words'), the term embraces both the narrative art and the style employed by Homer in his account of Odysseus' sufferings in the *Odyssey*. Both offer a sweetness and a pleasure appropriate to deceptive stories of suffering. Fränkel remarked that Odysseus' sufferings afforded Homer's audience great pleasure.[115] According to Dionysius of Halicarnassus, a speaker in a law-court recounting such sufferings needed a sweet style free from any roughness in sound: "When jurors hear the troubles (κακά) of another man ... charm (χάρις), pleasure (ἡδονή), deception (ἀπάτη) and the like are appropriate" (*Demosthenes* 45). For Dionysius, Lysias was an outstanding exponent of this technique. The narrative parts of his speeches were succinct, clear and incomparably sweet (ἡδεῖαι), and exhibited such powers of persuasion, all unnoticed (λεληθότως; cf. *Nemean* 7.23, κλέπτει), that it was difficult to find a whole narrative or even a portion of one that was untrue (ψευδής) or unpersuasive.[116] In this respect he compares Lysias with Odysseus, who, as Homer says

---

[112] Cf. Lloyd-Jones (1973) 130, comparing Hes. *Th.* 27: "the point here is that poetry can confer fame even on those who do not deserve it."

[113] Compare Herodotus' use of the same word in the criticism of myths in 2.43.3 (Hercules), 2.120.3 ἐγώ μὲν ἔλπομαι (Helen and the Trojan War).

[114] Cf. §1 and n.30, and esp. Hecataeus *FGrHist*. 1F26 (rationalisation of the giant Geryon as a king living in the vicinity of Ambracia and Amphilochian Argos); see Prinz (1979) 149–51. For other possible links between Pindaric and Hecataean myth-criticism see Nenci (1964); Howie (1983) 286–9 and n.125.

[115] See the use of τέρπεσθαι ("enjoy") in *Od.* 15.399–400, 23.308; Fränkel (1962) 15–16.

[116] For ancient views of Pindar's own style, see Most (1984) 11–25.

(*Odyssey* 19.23), in one speech told many lies that resembled true things (*Lysias* 18). How appropriate this comparison is and how relevant to the present discussion emerges when we remember that Odysseus' actual adventures (like the relevant narratives in Lysias) are recounted in the first person.[117] This stage of Pindar's argument is comparable with Thucydides' argument that Homer exaggerated in the *Iliad* in order to enhance his work (1.10.3), because he was a poet.[118] Here, too, what is exaggerated is the magnitude of the sufferings depicted in an epic.

The second stage of Pindar's argument (23c–30a) begins in general terms (23c–24a), and then turns the testimony of epic poetry itself against Homer (24b–30a). Pindar argues that the public is to blame, citing the Greeks at Troy as a mythical exemplum:

> For, if it had been possible for them to see the truth, the mighty Ajax would not have stuck his broad sword through his midriff since, Achilles apart, he was the mightiest man in battle that the straight-blowing escort of the West Wind brought for the recovery of yellow-haired Menelaus' wife to Ilus' city. (24b–30a)

The Greeks' verdict on the relative merits of Ajax and Odysseus was told in the *Aethiopis* and the *Little Iliad*,[119] and Pindar's own estimate of Ajax's merits is drawn from the *Iliad*.[120] Like Thucydides, Pindar has prefaced his main narrative (on Neoptolemus) with a reductive revision of an epic theme, and has cited epic texts in support of his revision (see Thucydides 1.10.3).[121] Furthermore, Pindar shows tact in his choice of Ajax as an exemplum: his patron and immediate local audience were proud of their association with the Aeacids, as is clear from the opening of this poem (9–10). This tact sheds light on Thucydides' choice of his fellow-Athenians as an example of people's uncritical attitude towards past events, and on the assassination of the

---

[117] See Suerbaum (1968).

[118] Cf. Hdt. 2.116 on Homer's rejection of what Herodotus considers the true version of the abduction of Helen as less suitable for his epic; see Hunter (1982) 54–6.

[119] As in *N*. 8.26–7, Pindar presents his suicide as if it were the immediate consequence of the verdict, ignoring the detail in the *Little Iliad* that when Ajax went mad over the verdict he first attacked the captured livestock (doubtless imagining they were the Greek leaders, as in Soph. *Ajax* 1–117); see *Homeri Opera* (ed. T.W. Allen) V p. 106, *Epicorum Graecorum Fragmenta* (ed. M. Davies) p.52. For the artistic tradition see Oliver (1995).

[120] Cf. *Il*. 2.768–9, 17.279–80; see Köhnken (1971) 61 n.122.

[121] Cf. Hdt. 2.116; Hunter (1982) 55 n.8. The passages in Pindar and Thucydides suggest that Herodotus feels no embarrassment, as Hunter supposes, but is employing a method already familiar to his audience.

Athenian tyrant's brother as one such event. In his prooemium the story is referred to cursorily, but from Book Six (53.3) we learn what the audience was aware of anyway, that the Athenians did not know (or did not want to know) that it was not Harmodius and Aristogiton but the Spartans who freed Athens, as they did the other Greek states, from tyranny (cf. 1.18.1). Thucydides has, then, chosen an example of popular ignorance from his own countrymen and given the credit due to their Spartan adversaries, thus showing tact towards all Greeks, especially the Spartans.[122] The fact that it was really a matter of ignoring rather than of simply not knowing[123] shows discretion and rhetorical adroitness on Thucydides' part. Similarly, the example of popular ignorance in the heroic age which Pindar chooses would be welcome to his immediate public in Aegina.

After recalling his earlier precepts on the value of encomium for mortals (30b–31a) Pindar identifies a decisive criterion:

> Honour belongs to those for whom a god swells their splendid story after death. (31b–32)

In other words, the criterion for judging the merits of epic heroes and contemporary patrons is an honour conferred by the gods.[124] In the case of the patron and his son Sogenes a victory at sacred games and a hereditary office mentioned towards the end of the poem (101) come into that category, as the original audience will readily have understood. However, Pindar chooses as an explicit illustration the hero Neoptolemus:

---

[122] Jacoby (1949) 152–68, esp. 162; compare the scolia *PMG* 893, 896, which credit Harmodius and Aristogiton with freeing Athens from tyranny. The version attacked by Thucydides was the official Athenian one, and was in Hellanicus' *Atthis*, the first work of that genre; see Jacoby 158–9. As for the relative ages of Hippias and the victim Hipparchus, Davies (1971) 448 accepts Thucydides' view. Strasburger (1958) 23 notes that it was the practice of Athenian orators on ceremonial occasions to pass from the roll-call of mythical exempla straight on to the first decade of the fifth century, omitting the earlier part of the properly historical period and so avoiding all constitutional conflicts and intervals of tyranny.

[123] Thomas (1989) 245–7 has shown from Ar. *Lys.* 1150–56 that the Athenian public was well aware of the Spartans' role.

[124] For the view that a comparison is being drawn between exaggeration by Homer and exaggeration by the encomiastic poet, and that in the case of Neoptolemus the honours enjoyed by him after death constitute a decisive proof, see Crotty (1982) 162–3. The claim of the kings of Molossia to be descended from Neoptolemus was already recognised in the *Nostoi*; see Hammond (1967) 382. For the concept of a god honouring a mortal see Williams (1978) 37, on Call. *h. Ap.* 29, citing West (1966) on Hes. *Th.* 81.

Bringing help, I come [*or*: he, Neoptolemus, came][125] to the great navel of the broad-breasted Earth. In Pytho's grounds Neoptolemus lies after sacking Priam's city, where Greeks suffered too. (33–36a)

Neoptolemus' grave at Delphi is therefore presented as an honour conferred upon a mighty conqueror. By advancing this interpretation of it at the outset Pindar marks his account as a positive one, since the hero's death was often regarded as punishment for his slaying of Priam as the old man sought refuge at the altar of Zeus Herkeios during the sack of Troy.[126] On the other hand, there is a reminder of all the sufferings of the Greeks; and, by way of underlining this vantage-point, Troy is referred to as the city of Priam, with a clear allusion to the king's death as something that happened against a background of the realities of warfare.[127] In fact the original audience may not have been surprised that a revision was being offered on the subject of this particular figure.[128]

---

[125] On the difficulties of text and interpretation in this passage, see the Excursus. The interpretation offered above is compatible with all interpretations that accept the generalising character of lines 31b–32 and are consistent with their applicability both to the poet's patrons and to Neoptolemus.

[126] See Proclus' epitome (p. 107 Allen). This is the common version, as is clear from the collection of vases in Wiencke (1954). See Pi. *Pae.* 6.112–20; Paus. 4.17.4 cites the proverbial phrase "Neoptolemean vengeance", in the sense of poetic justice. Pindar's κτάνεν (*Pae.* 6.119) need not be taken literally, as Radt (1958) 170 does, but can equally well be understood causally and refer to the "far-working" god's instigation of the killing at the hands of mortal Delphians; see Wilamowitz (1908) 153, and compare the causal use of ὄλεσσε of Agamemnon in bringing Cassandra within reach of Clytemnestra in *P.* 11.33.

[127] Compare the realistic views of the negative side of Peleus and Telamon (*N.* 5.16–18) and of Atreus and Thyestes (*O.* 1.89) discussed in §2.

[128] At the heart of the traditional picture of the sack of Troy, too, lies an awareness of the realities of warfare. For this reason no quarter is given and no religious restriction respected; it all serves as a warning to audiences of the consequences of defeat. The warning given to Meleager in *Il.* 9.590–94 in general terms is shown in its fulfilment by epic and tragic representations of the sack of Troy; see Howie (1989b) 63, (1995) 153 and nn. 47 and 48. Neoptolemus' prominent role as victor and as avenging son of Achilles, slaying the suppliant Priam, on Zeus's altar, and Hector's child Astyanax, and sacrificing Priam's daughter Polyxena, seems already to have been the subject of myth-revision in epic and early lyric. Odysseus' report to Achilles, which fills the despairing soul with pride, makes no mention of any of these three famous actions; Anderson (1997) 89–91 is surely right to see this as a suppression of already familiar episodes. The immediate dramatic motive is surely tact, and the moral effect is to show how the fine deeds of the living can be a joy to their dead kinsfolk (as they are represented in Pindar: *O.* 8.77–84, 14.20–24; *P.* 96–103; *N.* 4.79–88). Without a context the motives of other revisions of individual episodes are unknown. The *Little Iliad* said that he did not slay Priam at the altar; Priam had already been dragged away from it (presumably by another Greek) and Neoptolemus killed him by way of a πάρεργον at the doors of the palace (fr. 16 Allen = 17 Davies). The *Cypria* said that

In the further course of the myth the hero's wanderings and later death at Delphi are recounted. The narrative falls into two parts. The first recounts what the hero did from the end of the Trojan War up to his departure for Delphi from his new kingdom in Molossia:

> Sailing back, he missed Scyros, and, carried off their course, they reached Ephyra.[129] In Molossia he was king for a brief time, but his family has held this privilege ever since. He went away to the god, bringing treasure from the plunder-heaps from Troy. (36b–41)

Neoptolemus' wanderings (πλαγχθέντες, 37),[130] in explicit contrast with the fantastic wanderings of Odysseus (πλάγχθη, *Odyssey* 1.2), are furnished with a proof in the form of an inherited kingdom in contemporary Greece. He misses (ἅμαρτε, 37) his intended destination, Scyros, the home of his mother Deidamia, and he and his companions are carried off course to Molossia. Pindar's version involves two typical motifs in foundation stories: missing his destination, a species of chance,[131] and being carried off course (by a storm).[132] Again there is not a word about divine retribution.

Moreover, the hero later departs from his new kingdom for Delphi with pious intentions. This eliminates several less favourable versions already known to the audience. While as early as the *Little Iliad* (fr. 21

Polyxena had been mortally wounded by Odysseus and Diomedes during the capture of the city and Neoptolemus gave her burial (fr. 26 Allen = 27 Davies). The *Sack of Troy* said that Odysseus killed Astyanax (Proclus' summary, p.108 Allen, p.62 Davies). According to Stesichorus Astyanax was already dead, and therefore not slain by Neoptolemus (fr. 202 PMG). For a clear and convenient account of early accounts of Neoptolemus' actions, see Most (1984) 160–62.

[129] Cichyrus in Thesprotia; see Strabo 7.7.5 (324c); Hammond (1967) 478, 490; cf. Σ *N.* 7.53 (125–6 Dr.).

[130] See Köhnken (1971) 68–9. A hero's sufferings may contribute to his status as a hero, to judge from Hdt. 1.52, where Croesus is said to have made a dedication to Amphiaraus after hearing of his virtue and his suffering (τήν τε ἀρετὴν καὶ τὴν πάθην).

[131] Cf. *h. Ap.* 391–404; Pi. *P.* 4.24–56 (how Euphamus came to be given a clod of earth, a token of tenure); Strabo 6.2.4 (270c) (Croton and Syracuse); Pi. *O.* 7.24–80 (Rhodes); Aristot. fr. 549 Rose = Ath. 13.576a–b (Marseilles), possibly from Hecataeus' Γῆς Περίοδος; see *FGrHist.* 1F55 and Keaney (1980).

[132] *h. Ap.* 405–39 (Cretans carried off course to Delphi); Bacch. 1.119–23; cf. Strabo 5.2.5 (222c) (Metapontum, Nostoi foundation; Pylian followers of Nestor carried off course to Italy while trying to return from Troy); see Maehler (1982) II 241–2 *ad* Bacch. 11.126; Thuc. 4.120 (Scione, Nostoi foundation: Achaeans from Pellene [see *Il.* 2.574] carried off course to Pallene), 6.2.3 (Nostoi foundation: Phocians coming from Troy blown off course first to Libya and then to Sicily join Trojan refugees, in the foundation of the Elymian cities of Eryx and Egesta); see §1, and §3 on the story of Antiphus and Phidippus, blown off course to Thesprotia during the Nostoi.

Allen) there was a story that Neoptolemus was murdered at Delphi by Orestes, to whom Hermione was originally betrothed, there were also, according to the scholia (Σ 58, 124 Dr.) versions in which the visit itself was hostile in intent, and that (a) he planned to conquer the whole of the Peloponnese and with this in mind began with an attack on the shrine at Delphi; or (b) he came to demand compensation from Apollo for compassing his father Achilles' death. The scholia also record a version in which (c) he came to enquire of the god how he should beget children, as his wife Hermione had not borne him any. In this third version Neoptolemus comes to Delphi with no hostile intent.[133] In the fifth-century Pherecydes of Athens (*FGrHist*. 3F64a) this visit of simple enquiry leads to his death when he attempts to stop the Delphians enforcing their customary perquisite of snatching the meat from visitors' sacrifices, and a fight breaks out with them. It also emerges from the scholia to *Paean* 6 that version (b) and the sacrifice incident were mooted as explanations for the reference to the circumstances of his death through Apollo in *Paean* 6 (ἀμφιπόλοις δὲ μυριᾶν περὶ τιμᾶν δηριαζόμενον κτάνεν). Σ 118b identifies the matter in dispute as: "either the meat which the Delphians were carrying off in the customary manner [at which] [Neoptolemus] became enraged and sought to prevent them and for that reason was killed, or the possessions which he was carrying off in compensation for his father when he was killed."

All these versions may confidently be assumed to have been established in Pindar's time, since Euripides' *Andromache* accounts for all four elements in Neoptolemus' death: Hermione is childless, and blames Andromache; Neoptolemus goes to Delphi to ask for Apollo's forgiveness for an earlier visit in which he demanded compensation for the killing of his father; Orestes comes to Delphi and incites the Delphians by alleging that Neoptolemus has come to sack the temple; when Neoptolemus comes to make sacrifice he explains his desire for forgiveness, but Orestes' untruth has had its effect; Neoptolemus is attacked by men lying in wait behind the laurel at the altar; the god apparently joins in the attack, when a frightful call issues from the

---

[133] It should incidentally be noted that Pindar implicitly eliminates any notion that might leach from this version to the effect that Neoptolemus was afflicted by general infertility (which would have been anathema to the Molossian royal house), even before mentioning Neoptolemus' journey to Delphi. He declares that Neoptolemus' family has ruled in Molossia ever since, thereby implying that he left children behind in Molossia when he went to Delphi.

innermost sanctum, inciting the Delphians to fight on; and Neoptolemus dies beside the altar. Thus in the *Andromache* (1090–96) the raid is made to be a contemporary lie with a source and a motive, and the visit is divided into two visits, one to demand compensation and the other to beg forgiveness; both alterations are established techniques of myth-revision.[134]

Pindar's version in *Nemean 7* eliminates any element of hostile intention in Neoptolemus' visit. He then accounts for the hero's death:

And there [at Delphi] he chanced upon a fight over meat, and a man ran him through with a meat-knife. Heavily they grieved, the guides for foreign guests at Delphi. But he had paid the fated due. It was destined that one of the lordly Aeacidae should henceforth be within the ancient grove beside the god's well-walled house and have his home there as a rightful watcher over processions for [him as] a hero with many sacrifices. (42–7)

The death of this pious visitor is recounted in a way that avoids the impression that he was the mere victim of Delphian greed. It is attributed to a combination of chance[135] and the details of a well-known religious rite.[136] Herodotus invokes ritual requirements in this way in

[134] See Howie (1983) 293–4, 297 and n.50.
[135] Already Dissen (1821) 428 saw that chance was being used as an excuse here; cf. Wüst (1967) 155; Hammond (1967) 385.
[136] The Delphians' land was not fertile; for their dependence on the animal sacrifices of visiting worshippers see *h. Ap.* 528–37. The Delphians were proverbial for their rapacity at sacrifices: *Corpus Paroemiographorum* I 393: Δελφοῖσι θύσας αὐτὸς οὐ φαγῇ κρέας; Burkert (1972) 134–7, (1983) 117–20; Roux (1976) 88–9; Nagy (1979) 123–7. When a worshipper sacrificed the altar was surrounded by Delphians grasping meat-knives; when the beast had been skinned and gutted, each of them cut off as much meat as he could manage and ran off with it, often leaving the worshipper without any share for himself; cf. *Aesopica Testimonia* 25 Perry; Burkert (1972) 135, (1983) 118–9; Nagy (1979) 125. Pindar's revision of Neoptolemus' death in *N.* 7 is discussed by Wilamowitz (1908) 154; Hammond (1967) 383, 385–6; Burkert (1972) 136–7, (1983) 119–20; Nagy (1979); Woodbury (1979) 99–100; Carey (1981) 153; Kirkwood (1982) 270. The ancient expositors were already aware that a correction was involved. They understood this part of Pindar's account as describing a dispute between Neoptolemus and the Delphians over their behaviour at the sacrifice (cf. Pherecydes F64a). This version, they said, was replacing the one in *Pae.* 6, which they believed had offended the Aeginetans and which they themselves understood as referring either to a demand for compensation for the death of Achilles (Σ 94a, 129 Dr.; cf. Σ 58, 124 Dr.) or to attempted temple-robbery (Σ 150a, 136–7 Dr.; cf. Σ 58, 125 Dr.). Regardless of whether the ancient expositors' view of the relationship between the two poems is correct, *N.* 7 would on their understanding be most unfavourable to the Delphians, especially as in it Neoptolemus comes simply as a pious and munificent worshipper. In fact the sense of Pindar's lines here seems to waver between the version appearing in Pherecydes, in which the hero is angered by the Delphians' practice and attempts to stop them, and another version, implied by

his account of Marathon, when he explains the Spartans' late arrival by saying that they decided to help on the ninth day of the month but could not take the field until full moon (6.106). The absence of any reinforcement for Leonidas at Thermopylae, either from the Spartans or from the Greeks generally, is similarly explained: because of the festival of the Carneia the Spartans only sent an advance party to the pass, intending to follow in full force with all speed, and the other Greeks were going to do the same; but the Olympic festival happened to coincide with these events (7.206).[137] The combination of ritual and chance (in the form of coincidence) evident in this latter example is also invoked in extenuation of the Ephesians' slaughter of the Chian survivors of the Battle of Lade: they took an overland route and came into Ephesian territory at night at a time when the women were celebrating the Thesmophoria; the Ephesians thought they were marauders bent on seizing the women. The story owes what persuasiveness it has to the fact that the Thesmophoria was the most widespread of all Greek festivals[138] and that the women were separated from their menfolk and lived and slept together.[139] "Such," concludes the historian, "were the (mis)chances the Chians fell upon" (6.16).[140] In Pindar's account Neoptolemus' mischance is then interpreted in oracular-sounding language as fulfilling a destiny that confirms through the establishment of the hero's cult the merits of all the Aeacid heroes,

---

Pindar here, in which the hero is entirely innocent. There are several cases in Pindar where "offensive" mythical events are mentioned in a compressed and ambiguous wording, so that the traditional "offensive" version can be seen as having arisen from a misunderstanding *more Palaephateo*; see Howie (1983) 288–92 and n.89. In this instance, however, modern interpreters are not agreed as to the precise sense of the "original" version being suggested. There are two basic possibilities. One is that the fight breaks out over Neoptolemus' own sacrifice, as in Pherecydes, but is not triggered off by the hero himself (so, apparently, Burkert, in what he considers to be the unchanging central act in all versions: (1972) 137: "da umringen ihn die Delpher, und im Handgemenge, inmitten des Wirrwarrs um zerstückeltes und geraubtes Opfer-fleisch, wird Neoptolemos selbst mit einem der delphischen Messer getötet"; (1983) 119: "there he was surrounded by Delphians, and in the confusion of carving and snatching up the sacrificial meat he was killed with a Delphic knife", where the English version makes no mention of any fighting). The other possibility is that there was a fight over another worshipper's sacrifice (Wilamowitz, Hammond, Woodbury): either Neoptolemus tried to end it (Woodbury) or, preferably, he was uninvolved but in the confused fighting one of the men involved stabbed him (Wilamowitz, Hammond).

[137] See Hignett (1963) 120–27.
[138] Nilsson (1906) 313.
[139] Deubner (1966) 54–5.
[140] The defensive character of this account is noted by How and Wells (1928) 70 *ad loc.*

thus including Ajax as well as Neoptolemus. This is clear from the eloquent peroration rounding off the section:[141]

> For a case with a good name three words will suffice: No liar is the witness standing over the actions of your offspring by Zeus, [o] Aegina. (48–50)

Clearly the witness concerned is no mortal poet but divine authority,[142] reflected in the wording of the explanation of the hero's death and manifested in the institution of his cultic role at Delphi. This version satisfies both communities. The claim of the Molossian royal house to heroic and hence divine ancestry is proclaimed and indeed used as a proof for the poet's own contention about the extent of Neoptolemus' wanderings. Moreover, the shift from singular to plural in Pindar's reference to the hero's coming to Epirus (37b) leaves open the possibility of descent from Neoptolemus' companions for other families there.[143] The hero's arrival is to be attributed to fate in its common guise of chance (cf. 44).[144] The second part of the narrative protects the Delphians from any charge over the killing of what is in this version a pious visitor through their greed for the meat.

The value of a mythical narrative satisfying several different communities, as Pindar's does here, is first touched upon implicitly in connection with the notion of the importance of individual versions originating from local communities themselves or respecting their interests:

> It is a matter of confidence for me to say this: that the authoritative

---

[141] "His words could easily lead someone to believe that he was speaking in a law suit as defender of Neoptolemus", as Smith (1984) 12 observes. For asyndeta in the peroration cf. Aristot. *Rhet.* 3.19.6, 1420a6–7: τελευτὴ τῆς λέξεως ἁρμόττει ἡ ἀσύνδετος; Aristotle concludes with an asyndetic passage deliberately echoing Lysias' peroration in *Against Eratosthenes*. For Pindar's interest in oratory see the exchanges between Pelias and Jason in *P.* 4; Pelias' second speech concludes with three sentences in asyndeton (165–8). For Bacchylides' interest in oratory see his version of Menelaus' speech to the Trojans (15.50–63) in just the style described by Antenor in *Il.* 3.213–5.

[142] See Carey (1983) 155 *ad loc.*

[143] Cf. Σ *N.* 7 94a, 95a (128–9 Dr.).

[144] For the use of ἁμαρτάνειν as an expression appropriate to such fateful chances, cf. Hdt. 1.43.2 (death of Croesus' son Atys through a spear-throw missing its proper target and hitting him), 4.164.4 (Arcesilaus of Cyrene misses the sense of an oracle, and so fulfils his destiny). For this combination of chance and destiny or divine will cf. *Il.* 11.74 (cf. 11.2); Pi. *P.* 4.24–37 (n.131); Aristot. fr. 549 Rose (n.131); Eur. *Ion* 67. Compare Ogilvie (1965) 48–9 on Livy 1.1.4; Immerwahr (1966) 252. This view of chance lies at the root of the drawing of lots, the oldest form of divination at Delphi; see Dietrich (1978) 4.

road for stories of shining feats of prowess is from home [οἴκοθεν, i.e., from the doers' own homes]. (50b–52a)[145]

This statement is applicable to the praise of contemporary patrons no less than to heroic poetry. Praise is authoritative when it is delivered for the hearing of the home community of the hero or patron to be praised; that is the group of people with the greatest interest in it and, notionally, the best knowledge of the matter. This generalisation articulates a principle fundamental to Greek views of the past, that of citing the source recommended by geographical proximity to the scene of the events, or by family or national connection, often with an understandable partisan bias. This principle has been identified in Herodotus,[146] and is also articulated in Pindaric epinician.[147] That it is meant as a recommendation of Pindar's own version is clear from Pindar's later description of his success as he sees it. Significantly, it follows praise of his patron, Thearion:

> I am your guest, trying to keep dark slander [ψόγος] away from you; and, like someone leading water-courses to a friend's land, I shall praise fame [that is] true. That is the fitting wage for good men. If there is an Achaean nearby, one whose home is inland from the Ionian Sea,[148] he will not find fault with me. I [confidently] trust in protection as a foreign guest, and among my fellow-citizens I look [around me] with a bright eye. (61–66a)

The poet claims that a number of parties will be satisfied with his account of Neoptolemus and the praise of Thearion and Sogenes in which it is set. First, the Molossians, not only the royal house claiming descent from Neoptolemus, but also (as noted above) others who could claim descent from Neoptolemus' companions. The Molossian claim to be Achaean is parallel to that made by Cleomenes, the Spartan king, as a descendant of Hercules: "I am not a Dorian, but an Achaean".[149] Secondly, he can rely on official hospitality and protection (προξενία) anywhere in the Greek world, especially at Delphi,[150] and he can move

---

[145] For the nominal sentence in indirect speech cf. Xen. *Hell.* 1.1.15.

[146] Fehling (1989) 1–95.

[147] See esp. *I.* 2.28–9: "The way is not uphill or steep when one brings the praise of the Heliconian maidens to the homes of famous men"; see Race (1987) 134, 151–3.

[148] ὑπέρ = 'inland of'; cf. Carey (1983) 162 *ad loc.*; Hdt. 2.34.2, 148.1; 4.199.1; 7.115.2.

[149] Hdt. 5.72.3; the parallel is seen by Hammond (1967) 382, 490 with n.4. We may also compare the claim of rulers of Macedonia, avowed Heraclids (Hdt. 5.20, 8.137) to inclusion in the Greek fold. The crown prince, Alexander, describes himself as ἀνὴρ Ἕλλην, Μακεδόνων ὕπαρχος; see Hammond and Griffith (1979) 3–14.

[150] The visitor at Delphi had a Delphian responsible for him who had the title πρόξενος;

about confidently among his fellow-citizens in Thebes, a city linked
with Aegina by Herodotus as well as by Pindar because of the mythical
connection of Aegina and Thebe, both daughters of the River
Asopus.[151] The grounds of this confidence are stated in terms that
would be applicable both to his account of the hero and to his praise of
his patrons:

> For I have not exaggerated and have cleared all things violent from
> my path. May the time ahead come kindly to me. Anyone may say,
> once he has learnt [my song], whether I come to utter against the tune
> a murmur [that is] aslant [ψάγιον]. (68a–69)

On the one hand, he has not exaggerated, as Homer did in the *Odyssey*
and as an audience might suspect a professional poet would do for his
contemporary patrons. As for "everything violent", at first sight this
would seem to apply only to Neoptolemus. However, in the language
of Pindar and Bacchylides envy is said to be violent,[152] its violence
taking the form of disparagement or slander.[153] And, in putting forward
this true praise of hero and patrons (48, 61–2), he is prepared to swear
by his hopes of good fortune in the rest of his life. His words are
comparable with an oath by Bacchylides in support of his praise of
Hieron and with Herodotus' pious conclusion of his revisionist view of
Hercules.[154] Pindar's concluding words in this section challenge the

---

see Parke and Wormell (1956) 1.32 with n.63; Stevens (1971) on Eur. *Andr.* 1103;
Monceaux (1886) 49–50. With his expression Δελφῶν ξεναγέται (43) the poet has
already alluded to both the title and the responsibilities of the role. The application of
πέποιθα to the poet receiving hospitality and help is indicated by the similar
expression in *P.* 10, where the poet is speaking of his relations with a patron: πέποιθα
ξενίᾳ προσανέϊ Θώρακος, "I trust (confidently) in the hospitality of Thorax" (64).
The allusion to the Delphians' responsibilities as πρόξενοι, institutional guest-friends
substituting for guest-friends acquired through a personal relationship, the personal
relationship of guest-friend between patron and poet asserted in line 61, and the polar
expression suggested by the juxtaposition of the references to προξενία and δαμόται,
"fellow-citizens", encourage a natural assumption that Pindar's expression here
reflects the poet's dependence on help when abroad. Σ 95b (129–30 Dr.) takes the
expression to refer to an official office as πρόξενος of the Molossians granted to
Pindar, so that he would be relying on his tenure of it as a kind of proof of the
acceptability of his presentation of the story of Neoptolemus here. The role I assume
for Pindar would naturally extend to his coming to other parts of Greece where he
claims he would find a reception none the less friendly because of what he had said
about any of the parties in this poem.
[151] Hdt. 5.89–90; Pi. *I.* 8.16–13.
[152] Bacch. 16.31.
[153] Bacch. 13.199–209; cf. Pi. *N.* 8.32b–34. I owe much to Prof. Dickie for enlightenment
on what is meant by "violent" here.
[154] Bacch. 5.42: "laying my hand on the ground, I declare ... ", thus calling the earth to

hearer to say if there is any surreptitious malice in his poem up to this point.[155] In view of the poet's earlier assurances these words are readily applicable to his patron, but their generalising character raises the question of whether they are also applicable to his account of Neoptolemus. If so, then it is a nod towards the view that myths sometimes arise from a lie whose originator and motives can still be deduced. That view is adopted by the poet himself in his revision of the story of Pelops' death and revival;[156] and, as we have seen, it is applied to one unfavourable version of Neoptolemus' motives in coming to Delphi in Euripides' *Andromache*.

If the words "from [the doers' own] home" (52) are to be understood in the sense suggested above, then the poet has pointed to three such sources or satisfied interested parties. Aegina, Molossia and Delphi are each affected by a particular part of the story. The original home of the Aeacid Neoptolemus is Aegina (9–10). His family retains his kingship in Molossia (38–40a). His final home is Delphi (44b–47; οἰκεῖν, 47). Moreover, Pindar combines in compatible form the potentially conflicting interests of the Delphians and Molossians by making his story consist of two parts each favourable to the party in whose territory it is set; the hero's intentions on leaving for Delphi, evidenced in his bringing offerings with him, and in the accidental character of his death at Delphi, is crucial in this respect. Here, too, he is comparable with Herodotus, as analysed by Fehling, in the way his story combines the interests of at least two communities and makes it appear to be constructed from parts best known to those communities and at the same time favourable to them. From this point of view he differs from Herodotus in only one respect: he does not cite them as sources, but rather presents them as likely to be well satisfied with what he has done in connection with them. The combination of satisfied parties is underlined in his assertions in lines 64–6a, where, in addition to

---

witness; see Maehler (1982) II 99–100. Hdt. 2.45.3: "and to us, now that we have said this much, may there be good will (εὐμένεια) both from the gods and from the heroes".

[155] μαθὼν δέ τις ἂν ἐρεῖ, εἰ παρ' μέλος ἔρχομαι ψάγιον ὄαρον ἐννέπων. For παρ' μέλος as alluding to πλημμελεῖν, 'play off tune', see Dissen (1821) 433; Carey (1983) *ad loc.* For its frequent metaphorical applications as 'offend, wrong' see *LSJ s.v.*, and esp. Pl. *Phdr.* 275e. The adjective ψάγιος, 'aslant', in addition to giving another metaphorical dimension to the notion of offence and injury, also surely echoes in sound ψόγος, 'slander' (61).

[156] In *O*. 1.47–51 the story of Pelops' death and revival has its roots in an interpretation of events motivated by jealousy; cf. n.153 on βίαια (67).

Molossia and Delphi, his own city of Thebes is mentioned. The connection between Thebes and Aegina, an alliance against Athens sealed by the dispatch of the Aeacidae, well known in Aegina, is alluded to later in a transition to the prayers for the patrons towards the end of the poem.[157]

In *Nemean* 7, then, Pindar has anticipated Thucydides' *Archaeology* in three ways. First, he has offered a reductive revision of a Homeric epic as a foil to his own theme, and in that revision he has cited the evidence of epic itself as evidence and has identified the poetical considerations underlying Homer's exaggeration. Secondly, in his treatment of his own theme he has reconciled the interests of the two main communities affected, and has also satisfied the interests of the third community principally interested, the Aeginetans. Thirdly, the respect in which the Homeric epic and the poet's chosen theme are compared is one fundamental to epic, the degree of suffering involved in either.

§6 Shared techniques (i): scepticism and reductive rationalisation

Did Thucydides himself know *Nemean* 7? Even if he did, he could not assume that all the readers he hoped to attract would know it. His own prooemium and Pindar's poem both depend for their effectiveness on the prior existence of a wider body of such work.

Thucydides' concern to present the power accumulated by the Pelopidae in such a way as to protect it against an all too sweeping scepticism among his audience is evidence for widespread familiarity with the technique of reductive rationalisation.[158] His language at that point resembles Pindar's:

> The fact that Mycenae was small or that any of the cities of that time now looks insignificant cannot be taken as conclusive evidence for anyone to doubt that the expeditionary force was as great as the poets have declared and its widespread fame makes it (οὐκ ἀκριβεῖ ἄν τις σημείῳ χρώμενος ἀπιστοίη μὴ γενέσθαι τὸν στόλον τοσοῦτον ὅσον

---

[157] For Pindar's reference there to Aeacus "city-ruler of my nation of good name", Wüst (1967) 147 rightly refers to this alliance with its dimension of mythical genealogy and the dispatch of the images of the Aeacidae to Thebes (Hdt. 5.89–90). Compare, too, [Eur.] *Rh.* 381, where the newly-arrived ally from Thrace is hailed by the Trojans with the same title of πολίαρχος. This link between Thebes and Aegina is explicitly evoked by Pindar in *I.* 8.15–23.

[158] See §1 and n.41.

οἵ τε ποιηταὶ εἰρήκασι καὶ ὁ λόγος κατέχει, 1.10.1; cf. *Nemean*
7.20–21: ἐγὼ δὲ πλέον' ἔλπομαι λόγον 'Οδυσσέος ἢ πάθαν διὰ τὸν
ἀδυεπῆ γενέσθ' "Ομηρον).

Pindar could afford unqualified scepticism about the *Odyssey*. He was
employing it as a foil for his own account of another hero's merits and
sufferings, in the course of which he explicitly protects several of the
heroes of the *Iliad* against scepticism by a defence that could be
adapted to other such figures. Thucydides, on the other hand, strikes a
compromise, and in the course of his discussion of the Trojan War he
twice returns explicitly to this theme.

After his argument in defence of the importance of Mycenae by
appeal to the relative sizes of Athens and Sparta (1.10.2), he offers a
reformulation of his view of the expeditionary force:

> On the basis of likelihood [εἰκός] one ought not to doubt [the size of
> the expeditionary force *a priori*] or take more account of cities'
> external appearance than their power. Rather, one ought to suppose
> that this expeditonary force was the greatest of any there had been up
> to that time but was smaller than those of today. (1.10.3)

In this formulation the relative size of Agamemnon's host is accepted
and a real basis is acknowledged for the Trojan War. This formulation
can be seen as a compromise. It is closely comparable with one of
Hecataeus' revisions (interpreted as defensive by Jacoby),[159] the
rationalisation of Cerberus as a huge snake living around Taenarum
with a bite so deadly that it was known (in a metaphorical sense) as
Hades' Hound:

> I do not think that the snake was so big or so enormous, only more
> frightful than other snakes, and that this was why Eurystheus thought
> it was invincible. (*FGrHist*. 1F27b)

In this way Thucydides lays, as it were, the diplomatic foundations for
his discussion of the Trojan War itself; and after his discussion he
explicitly returns to the question of scepticism towards an exaggerated
public belief about the size of Agamemnon's forces, and by
implication, of the war itself:

> So it was lack of financial resources that caused undertakings prior to
> the Trojan War to be weak; and, while that undertaking itself was the
> most famous of all undertakings up to that time, the actions [taken in
> it] show that it was less than the fame or the reputation now pre-
> vailing because of the poets (1.11.2; καὶ αὐτά γε δὴ ταῦτα,

---

[159] Jacoby (1912) 2738–40; cf. Wipprecht (1902) 24–6; Gitti (1952).

ὀνομαστότατα τῶν πρὶν γενόμενα, δηλοῦται τοῖς ἔργοις ὑποδεέστερα ὄντα τῆς φήμης καὶ τοῦ νῦν περὶ αὐτῶν διὰ τοὺς ποιητὰς λόγου κατεσχηκότος).

This final formulation on the Trojan War returns to the reputation caused by the poets, and its phrasing again resembles Pindar's; compare *Nemean* 7.21: λόγον ... διὰ τὸν ἁδυεπῆ γενέσθ' "Ομηρον.

The theme of artistic exaggeration returns at the end of the detailed treatment of the heroic and historic ages. Taken in isolation, the tone might appear dismissive of the past:

> That is how little effort goes into the search for the truth in the case of most people, and that is the way they turn to what is ready-made. From the evidence cited, however, anyone who considered that the matters I have discussed were such as I have described them would not go wrong, that is, anyone who did not prefer to believe these matters to have been either as the poets have sung of them in praise, ornamenting them for enhanced grandeur, or as prose-writers have composed works on them, more with an eye to enticing an audience than to truth. For these matters cannot be verified, and in most cases have achieved a mythical character, and have thus become incredible. One would thus not go wrong if one considered them to have been as they have been discovered here by the use of the most conspicuous evidence, given that these matters are very old. (1.21.1)

Thucydides displays an awareness of his audience's familiarity with such reductive views of the heroic age and of poetical accounts and common beliefs about events in those times. This scepticism is also reflected in Pindar's daphnephorikon for Agasicles (fr. 94b S–M), in which the uncertainty of events of those days and the ease with which they can be embellished poetically is contrasted with the well-attested achievements of his patron's family (31–45).[160] Indeed Herodotus' story of the discovery of the bones of Orestes assumes a natural scepticism and interest in evidence among ordinary Greeks of the mid-sixth century. The Arcadian blacksmith who discovered the hero's grave in his courtyard explains his decision to open the eight-foot coffin in terms very similar to Thucydides' initial formulation of *a priori* scepticism (1.10.1): "out of disbelief that there were ever men bigger than those today, I opened it up" (1.68.3). His scepticism is refuted in this pious tale with its wonder (θαῦμα) of the greater size of

---

[160] This scepticism is comparable with the impatience with Homeric themes and Homeric modes of heroic narrative affected by Pindar in *Paean* 7b and *P.* 4.27 in promoting his own work.

the heroes.[161] Herodotus' story assumes that ordinary Greeks of the archaic period were already capable of a reductively sceptical view of heroic myth. This scepticism is disavowed by Pindar in his earliest poem: "To me nothing appears incredible so that I should treat it as a [mere] wonder (θαυμάσαι), if the gods have accomplished it" (*Pythian* 10.48–50). This is a statement of the principle which according to Strasburger underlies the *Iliad*, making the heroes more credible by attributing astounding feats to the help they have from the gods.[162] Thucydides may therefore be seen in this respect, too, as closely related to the poets; he, too, carefully rejects mere dismissive scepticism and proposes a reduction that assumes a real basis and an authentic memory of the heroic age and the Trojan War.

§7 Shared techniques (ii): reconciling multiple interests

In general, Pindar's *Nemean* 7 indicates the availability of a whole repertoire of established devices and established approaches which Thucydides could avail himself of in defining the development of Greece and the character of the heroic age, and shows that their very familiarity among his audience made them all the more effective.

One device shared by Thucydides' *Archaeology* and Pindar's *Nemean* 7 is the construction of a narrative from parts agreeable to different groups, such as families or communities, who could be said to be well-placed to testify; and I have compared this with a narrative technique extensively employed by Herodotus in which such groups are explicitly cited as witnesses. Another similarity between the approaches of Thucydides and Pindar is that their accounts of events in the heroic age combine the interests of several Greek communities. This may well have been the form of narrative combining interests which Herodotus identified and modified to include formally identified sources, sometimes combining different Greek communities,[163] but at

---

[161] See §1 and n.27, §3 and n.67.

[162] See Strasburger (1972) 22 and n.72; cf. Pi. *O*. 13.83 and Howie (1995) 167.

[163] Examples are the stories of the foiling of Alyattes' campaigns against Miletus, combining testimonies of the Delphians and the Milesians (1.17–22; see 1.20), and of the miraculous rescue of Arion of Methymna, on which the Corinthians and the Lesbians are entirely agreed; see Fehling (1989) 91, 21–24 respectively. For the foundation of Cyrene Hdt. 4.145–56 offers dovetailing testimonies of the Spartans, Theraeans and Cyrenaeans. Yet Pindar offers an integral account in *P*. 4, and it looks as if Herodotus has divided up an integral *ktisis* in order to produce this effect; see Fehling 91–2.

other times combining Greek and non-Greek sources,[164] or non-Greek sources only.[165]

This way of presenting a story as agreeable to more than one interested party is exhibited in two early Greek religious poems, and the interested parties are Greek communities. In Hesiod's *Theogony* the first two stages of his Greek version of the Succession Myth are recounted in this way.[166] The castration of Uranus by Cronus leads to the birth of Aphrodite, when the severed members are cast into the sea and come close to Cythera before fetching up in Cyprus, where Aphrodite emerges from them (188–200). Thus two old-established cult-places in the Greek world are associated with the birth of the goddess, and brought into a mutually supportive relationship of aition and proof with this stage of the Succession Myth. Cronus' own overthrow is ultimately brought about by Earth and Uranus, who advise Rhea to give birth to her youngest child, Zeus, in Lyctus in Crete. The stone which she dresses up as the newly-born child and gives her jealous consort to swallow and which he subsequently vomits up along with his other children is later laid up by Zeus at Delphi as a "wonder" (453–500). Thus the second stage, too, is associated with different shrines and communities in the Greek world, and is furnished with a conventional proof.[167] Similarly, Nagy has argued that the *Homeric Hymn to Apollo* is constructed so as to serve the interests of Apollo's cults at Delphi and on Delos.[168]

Nagy sees this approach as fundamental to the *Iliad* and the *Odyssey* and, in particular, to the Catalogue of Ships.[169] On this last point Nagy refers to the work of Giovannini, who has argued in detail that the list of participating warriors and communities on the Greek side derives not from the Mycenaean age but from the archaic period, perhaps to the seventh century BC, and is constructed in line with interests of a Panhellenic audience of the *Iliad*.[170] Nagy himself sees the Catalogue

---

[164] E.g. the story of the foundation of the oracles of Zeus at Dodona and of Ammon in Libya, as recounted in rational and mythical form by his Egyptian and Greek informants respectively; see Fehling (1989) 65–70.

[165] Thus the story of the origins of Greco-Persian enmity is told by the Persians and amended by the Phoenicians in a matter of national honour in 1.1–5.2; see Fehling (1989) 50–57.

[166] See Howie (1989b) 60–61. For the Near Eastern background and analogues see West (1966) 18–31.

[167] For such conventional proofs see Fehling (1989) 18–143.

[168] Nagy (1979) 6–7.

[169] Nagy (1979) 6–7, 120, 140–41.

[170] Giovannini (1969) 69.

as a roll-call of the Homeric heroes on a Panhellenic scale, the heroes
being assigned to homelands in line with the site of their primary
cults.[171] To this one must surely add the importance of such a list (and
of the *Iliad* in general) for other Greek communities tracing their
origins or territorial claims to heroes and their followers carried off
course by the storm that struck the Greeks heading for home, such as
Neoptolemus. To these interests may also be added the various families
and communities claiming inherited family privileges or territorial
rights through Hercules, such as the two royal houses of Sparta and
princes in Thessaly. Though the *Iliad* is set a generation later than
Hercules, that hero features prominently. The supreme hero of the
poem, Achilles, cites him as an exemplum in a consolation addressed to
his divine mother (18.117–19). Three of his descendants fight at Troy:
his son, Tlepolemus, leader of the Rhodians (2.653–70), who fights a
hard battle with Sarpedon, another son of Zeus (5.628–62), and
Phidippus and Antiphus from Cos (2.676–9; see §3 above). The origin
of his subjection to Eurystheus is recounted (19.96–133), and the
courageous death at Troy of Periphetes of Mycenae, the son of
Eurystheus' henchman Copreus, is mentioned (15.638–52). Hercules'
own victorious war against Troy and its causes are mentioned (5.640–
42, 14.266, 15.25, 20.145), as is his achievement in killing all Nestor's
elder brothers (11.690–93). This formidable figure leaves sons and
grandsons who are also formidable, at least collectively, driving
Tlepolemus into exile for the slaying of his maternal uncle Licymnius
(2.661–6). Apart from establishing Hercules' own prior claim to have
sacked Troy, these references to Hercules and the Heraclidae have the
same realistic air as Thucydides' reference to the fear inspired in the
Mycenaeans by the Heraclidae after the defeat and death of Eurystheus
(1.9.2). Such indications within the poem may strengthen Nagy's case
that the Catalogue serves to engage the entire Panhellenic audience of
the *Iliad*. At the same time it gives an impression of the magnitude of
the war about to be described, comparable with Thucydides' accounts
of the growth of Greece and Sicily at the beginning of Books One and
Six.

   Thucydides' way of combining the mythistorical bases of the claims
of different communities and families in his account of the growth of
Greece must, then, be set against the background of a general concern
to co-ordinate heroic and divine myths important to the various

---

[171] Nagy (1979) 120, last footnote.

segments of a Panhellenic religious and cultural community within a commonly accepted network consistent in time and place which is fundamental to Greek divine and heroic myth generally. The same principle underlies his account of the growth of Sicily, a prelude to an account of another theatre of war in which he has much suffering to describe.

It is clear from the conscious exploitation of the principle within a Greek context by Pindar in *Nemean* 7 and its extension to partly Greek or wholly non-Greek sets of witnesses by Herodotus that Thucydides and his audience were wholly aware of the principle and of his application of it to both the heroic and the historical periods in his prefaces to Books One and Six. In the case of Book One, the practice of the poets in their praise of cities and countries shows how other aspects of the *Archaeology* would be pleasing to sectors of the Panhellenic audience. The Thessalians have the most fertile land; compare Pindar and Bacchylides' praise of Sicily (*Olympian* 1.12; Bacchylides 5.1).[172] The Corinthians, thanks to their position on the Isthmus, have long been been wealthy; compare Pindar's encomium for Xenophon of Corinth (fr. 122 S–M), in which he describes Corinth as wealthy (2) and refers to the Corinthians as "the masters of the Isthmus" (13).[173] These references should be added to the acceptance of the Boeotians' own view of their role in the Trojan War and the Corinthians' innovations in seafaring. Within this category may also belong the heroic parallels for the piracy of the contemporary Locrians, Acarnanians and Aetolians. In that case further points in Thucydides' demonstration could be seen as having value for both his external and his internal approaches.

It is arguable, therefore, that in his preface Thucydides was operating at more than one level in the way he recommended his work as an account of the greatest war ever experienced by the Greek world and himself as a competent and fair witness who could be trusted to show diligence, accuracy, and avoidance of arbitrary judgements.[174]

---

[172] For fertility as a theme of praise, see Kienzle (1936) 39–40.
[173] For wealth as a theme of praise, see Kienzle (1936) 38–9.
[174] On Thucydides' fairness (by comparison with later Attic orators) in his account of the Pentekontaetia and the Peloponnesian War see Strasburger (1958) 24–31.

Excursus: Pindar *Nemean* 7.31–4

τιμὰ δὲ γίνεται
ὦν θεὸς ἁβρὸν αὔξει λόγον τεθνακότων.
βοαθοῶν τοι παρὰ μέγαν ὀμφαλὸν εὐρυκόλπου
μόλον χθονός.

βοαθόων codd.: βοαθόον Hermann, βοαθοῶν Farnell | ἔμολεν codd.,
ἔμολον Σ*ᵀᴾ*: μόλεν E. Schmid, μόλον Hermann

Honour belongs to those for whom a god swells their splendid story
after death. Bringing help, I come [*or*: he, Neoptolemus, came] to the
great navel of the broad-breasted Earth.

The interpretation of these lines offered in this paper is compatible with
any view of the text or its sense[175] that takes the participle τεθνακότων
(32) with the words preceding it and ascribes to lines 31b–32 a
generalising, gnomic sense, applicable both to Thearion and Sogenes
and to the hero whose story is about to be told. My interpretation is also
compatible with any interpretation of the word βοαθοῶν (or of the
emendation βοαθόον) consistent with that view of lines 31b–32. Some
ancient interpreters understood lines 31b–32 in this way.[176] However,
my interpretation is not compatible with the understanding of Didymus
(and Aristarchus), who took τεθνακότων βοαθόων together as a
genitive absolute, "after the death of the defenders", referring to Hector
and his followers (Aristarchus) or Eurypylus (who was actually slain by
Neoptolemus) and his followers (Didymus).[177]

On the view taken here, the role of helper may belong: (1) to the god
Apollo;[178] or (2) to an account vouchsafed by the god;[179] or (3) to
Pindar, either in the supposedly earlier *Paean* 6 or in the present
poem;[180] or (4) to Neoptolemus, either as worshipper intending to
honour the god or as the future tutelary hero of the god's shrine.[181] All

---

[175] On the problem see Farnell (1932) 291–5, Wüst (1967) 144–5, 154–5, Woodbury
    (1979), who review the interpretations and emendations advanced since G. Hermann;
    Bischoff (1938) 18–20; the general survey of emendations in Gerber (1976); Carey
    (1983); Heath (1993), whose study of ancient interpretations of the poem includes an
    exposition of the views of Aristarchus and Didymus on the basis of Σ 47 (123 Dr.).
[176] Σ 46b (122 Dr.); Heath (1993) 173–4.
[177] Σ 47 (123.1–18 Dr.); Heath (1993) 173–4.
[178] H.J. Rose *ap.* Farnell (1932) 293; Wüst (1967) 145; Most (1984) 157–9.
[179] Wilamowitz: see Wüst (1967) 144, Woodbury (1979) 104.
[180] In *Pae.* 6: Wüst (1967) 145, Lloyd-Jones. In *N.* 7: Segal, Bundy. See Wüst (1967) 145, Woodbury
    (1979) 105–6 and n.42.
[181] As worshipper: Farnell (1932) 294–5, Bischoff (1938) 19 n.32, who compares Aesch.
    Cho. 261 βωμοῖς ἀρήγειν ("come to the altars' aid"), which he suggests was a
    customary expression; see Wüst (1967) 45, Woodbury (1979) 105, Carey (1983) 150.

four identifications of the helper are compatible with a generalising or gnomic reading of lines 31b–32, as promising or being compatible with the favourable treatment accorded to the hero in his relationship with the god in what follows. It is fortunate that the interpretation of this passage does not depend on only one or two of these identifications, as there are arguments and evidence for all of them. I subjoin some salient points in favour of each.

(1) The god Apollo: Apollo appears as helper in both myth and cult. In connection with Delos, Callimachus in *Hymn* 4.27 calls Apollo a mighty helper, βοηθόος; in 2.69 he tells us that in many places the god bears the synonymous and etymologically related cult title βοηδρόμιος. In *Nemean* 7 the whole value of the account is that it has divine sanction, represented both by use of the cult as proof and by the interpretation of the hero's fate that is stated in such confident terms (44–7), which must imply that the Delphians were so distressed by the hero's death (43) that they consulted the god through his oracle. The god returns as witness in the allusive language of 49–50. The witness's identity is clear. The same point is being made as in 31–2, and is further supported by an allusion to the belief that Apollo cannot lie (see *Pythian* 3.29–30, 9.42).

(2) The word vouchsafed by the god: the same considerations apply.

(3a) The poet as helper of the hero: compare Plato *Phaedrus* 275e, a passage offering several possible parallels with this poem. According to Socrates a work of literature in written form is exposed to the same danger as a painting: the public may saddle it with many misinterpretations; when the work is then slandered (πλημμελούμενος; cf. *Nemean* 7.69 παρ' μέλος and n.155) and abused unjustly (οὐκ ἐν δίκῃ; cf. *Nemean* 7.48 εὐώνυμον ἐς δίκαν), it needs its father (i.e. the author) as a helper (βοηθοῦ), as it is not able to help (βοηθῆσαι) or defend itself. Plato's sustained metaphor is apparently drawn from the consequences of misrepresentation in life and in court. βοηθεῖν is common in the Attic orators in legal contexts. Mostly it is used of the jurors when they are called upon by the speaker to help the party concerned in defending his rights (βοηθεῖν or βοηθεῖν τὰ δίκαια: Isaeus 7.4, 8.5, 8.45; Demosthenes 35.5, 40.61, 54.2, 54.42). It is also used in appeals to a possible eyewitness among the jurors to help the

---

As tutelary hero: Woodbury (1979) 107–8, with evidence for a well-established use of βοηθεῖν for the defence of Apollo's shrine by the Amphictyonic League.

party concerned by informing his fellow-jurors (Isaeus 5.20); and it is used by Lysias in his speech *Against Eratosthenes* both of persons apparently desirous of helping Eratosthenes and his associates (βοηθήσοντες) by pleading for him (85) and of the jurors, whom the speaker reminds of Eratosthenes' victims: "since you could not defend them when they were alive, help them now they are dead" (ἀποθανοῦσι βοηθήσατε, 99), i.e. by condemning him. This line of interpretation would result in a close connection between the introduction (31b–34) and the conclusion (48–51a) of this account of the hero and one of the poet's comments on his efforts on behalf of patrons and hero alike (69), the connection taking the form of a sustained metaphor, comparing the poet with an orator defending the hero (βοαθοῶν, 33, εὐώνυμον ἐς δίκαν, 48) against slanders (69), in a case in which divine authority (θεός, 32) served as a witness above all suspicion of falsehood (οὐ ψεῦδις ὁ μάρτυς, 49).

(3b) The poet as helper of the god: there is the evidence of the defensive posture of the version offered, comparable with, for example, the defensive accounts of the relationship between Croesus of Lydia and Apollo and Delphi in Bacchylides 3 and Herodotus 1.

The vagueness of the language at the opening of the account and the reference to both the hero and his grave at Delphi might mean that the poet's words were intended to combine the two applications (3a) and (3b). The echoing of the opening of the account by its close could be adduced as evidence for identifying the helper either as the word (2) or the poet (3a, 3b).

(4) The hero: support comes from the interpretation offered by Σ 58 *ad fin.* (125 Dr.): the poet does not join in such accusations (for which see n.136); he says that Neoptolemus "came to honour the god" (τιμήσων τὸν θεόν).[182]

The two possible interpretations of Neoptolemus' role as helper are not mutually exclusive; the hero would come to the temple with one kind of help in mind (as a prospective worshipper) and remain there to provide help of another kind (as tutelary hero).

However, there is another interpretation of Neoptolemus' role as helper which may not be compatible with the interpretation offered in

---

[182] See Kirkwood (1982), 269. Köhnken (1971) 67 n.143, sees the echo that would result from ᾤχετο δὲ πρὸς θεόν, said of Neoptolemus in line 40, as a strong indication that the original reading was μόλεν, "[Neoptolemus] went".

this paper. This interpretation, advanced most recently by Woodbury,[183] accepts the punctuation of the manuscripts and Σ 47 (123 Dr.) and reads βοαθόων (gen. pl.) in agreement with τεθνακότων, so that the statement that "honour belongs to those for whom a god swells their splendid story after death" (31b–32) would be restricted to those heroes or mortals who had in some way "helped" the god of Delphi or his temple. In support of this view Woodbury offers a most valuable collection of passages as evidence of this special Delphic application of the word.[184] However, such a narrowing-down of the applicability of the criterion after such a very broad opening consideration (11–20a) tells against this interpretation, especially as nothing is said to make it appear applicable to Sogenes himself,[185] or indeed to his father, let alone other potential patrons. The only other possibility with that accentuation and punctuation would be to see the poet as expecting the audience to understand that such helpers exemplified a more general truth. How likely that is I do not know.[186] The desirability of a broader application for the generalisation as a true gnome can be seen from Woodbury's own interpretation of the myth: "What has been established by the god and fate, the poet seems to say, cannot be affected either by the vagaries of poetry or by the blindness of human hearts." The vagueness which Woodbury (rightly) sees in the poet's unspecific references to a god in 31–2 (generalising), and 40 and 46 (narrative) and to a witness in 49 instead of Apollo is not, as Woodbury himself thinks, a sign of the poet's embarrassment about his treatment

---

[183] Woodbury (1979) 107–10, following Sandys, Schroeder, and others: see Woodbury (1979) 103–4, Farnell (1932) 292, Wüst (1967) 144. Woodbury's interpretation appears to be incorporated in the text of Maehler (1984), who has that punctuation and prints Βοαθόων, with the capital suggesting a title for such a category of "Helpers of Delphi".

[184] Woodbury (1979) 107–8; cf. Köhnken (1971) 67 n.44.

[185] See Carey (1983) 149.

[186] Fränkel (1960) 79 sees the mss' punctuation as an example of an archaic Greek tendency to begin with a generalising plural with a specific individual figure in mind and to continue to use the plural when one has already reached a point at which the content is only applicable to that individual. Fränkel renders the passage thus: "We must all die, but honour is received by all those whose fame the god causes to grow after their death, helpers who came to the Earth-Navel — that already applies solely to Neoptolemus, in spite of the plural form, and now the singular comes in: and in Pythian ground he lies, Neoptolemus — and at that point the name is mentioned" (my translation). Fränkel does not include any discussion of the context of the sentence. As with Woodbury's interpretation, my own interpretation is only compatible with this view if the dead are a broader category of which the "helpers" form a part (perhaps in the grammatical relationship of apposition of a single part mentioned to a preceding whole: for this concept see Bühler (1964) 124–5, citing Kühner-Gerth (1898) 1.288–9).

of the same hero in *Paean* 6, but a reflection of the same concern for general validity as in lines 31–2 and earlier in lines 11–20a. Woodbury's valuable evidence for a special Delphic sense of βοηθεῖν is compatible with the interpretations taking the poet or the hero as the helper of the god, as outlined above; see (3b) and (4).

Bibliography

Aloni, A. (1994). 'L'elegia di Simonide dedicata alla battaglia di Platea (Sim. frr. 10–18 W^2' *ZPE* 102.9–22

Anderson, M.J. (1997). *The Fall of Troy in Early Poetry and Art*. Oxford

Beloch, K.J. (1913). *Griechische Geschichte*. 2nd ed. Strassburg

Bickermann, E.J. (1952). 'Origines Gentium' *CP* 47.65–81

Bischoff, H. (1938). *Gnomen Pindars*. Diss. Würzburg

Bizer, F. (1937). *Untersuchungen zur Archäologie des Thukydides*. Diss. Tübingen (repr. Darmstadt 1968)

Bockisch, G. (1982). 'Kypselos und die Bakchiaden' *Klio* 64.51–66

Boeckh, A. (1821). *Pindari Epiniciorum Interpretatio Latina*. Leipzig (repr. Hildesheim 1963)

Boedeker, D. (1995). 'Simonides on Plataea: narrative, elegy, mythodic history' *ZPE* 107.217–29

Bühler, W. (1964). *Beiträge zur Erklärung der Schrift vom Erhabenen*. Göttingen

Burkert, W. (1972). *Homo Necans: Interpretation altgriechischer Opferriten und Mythen*. Berlin

—— (1979). *Structure and History in Greek Mythology and Ritual*. Berkeley

—— (1983). *Homo Necans: The Anthropology of Ancient Greek Sacrificial Ritual and Myth*, tr. P. Bing. Berkeley, Los Angeles, London

Cairns, F. (1982). 'Cleon and Pericles: a suggestion' *JHS* 107.203–4

Carey, C. (1983). *A Commentary on Five Odes of Pindar*. Warminster

Cooke, R.M. (1955). 'Thucydides as archaeologist' *ABSA* 50.266–70

Crosby, M. (1941). 'Greek inscriptions' *Hesperia* 10.15–27

Crotty, K. (1982). *Song and Action*. Baltimore and London

Davies, J.K. (1971). *Athenian Propertied Families 600–300 BC*. Oxford

Davies, M. (1988) (ed.). *Epicorum Graecorum Fragmenta*. Oxford

Deubner, L. (1966). *Attische Feste*. 2nd ed. Darmstadt

Dietrich, B.C. (1978). 'Reflections on the origins of the oracular Apollo' *BICS* 25.1–18

Dönt, E. (1985). 'Pindars siebente Nemeische Ode' *Wiener Studien* 19.105–14

Dover, K.J. (1953). 'La colonizzatione della Sicilia in Tucidide' *Maia* 6.1–20

Dunbabin, T.J. (1948). *The Westen Greeks*. Oxford

Edmunds, L.W. (1975). 'Thucydides' ethics as reflected in the description of stasis (3.82–83)' *HSCP* 79.73–92

Erbse, H. (1969). 'Die politische Lehre des Thukydides' *Gymnasium* 76.395–416

— (1970). 'Über das Prooimion des thukydideischen Geschichtswerkes (I.1–23)' *RM* 113.43–69

Farnell, L.R. (1932). *The Works of Pindar* II. London

Fehling, D. (1989). *Herodotus and his 'Sources': Citation, Invention, and Narrative Art*, tr. J.G. Howie. (ARCA 21) Leeds

Focke, F. (1923). 'Synkrisis' *Hermes* 58.327–68

Fontenrose, J. (1960). *The Cult and Myth of Pyrros at Delphi*. University of California Publications in Classical Philology 4.3.191–266, Berkeley and Los Angeles

Fränkel, H. (1960). 'Eine Stileigenheit der frühgriechischen Literatur' in H. Fränkel (ed. F. Tietze) *Wege und Formen frühgriechischen Denkens*, Munich, 40–96

— (1962). *Dichtung und Philosophie des frühen Griechentums*. Munich

Fritz, K. von (1967). *Die griechische Geschichtsschreibung*. Berlin

Galinsky, G.K. (1969). *Aeneas, Sicily, and Rome*. Princeton

Gentili, B. (1988). *Poetry and its Public in Ancient Greece: From Homer to the Fifth Century*. Baltimore and London

Gerber, D.E. (1976). *Emendations in Pindar*. Amsterdam

Gierth, L. (1971). *Griechische Gründungsgeschichten als Zeugnisse historischen Denkens vor dem Einsetzen der Geschichtsschreibung*. Diss. Freiburg im Breisgau

Giesekam, G. (1977). 'The Portrayal of Minos in Bacchylides 17' *PLLS* 1.237–52

Giovannini, A. (1969). *Étude historique sur les origines du Catalogue des Vaisseaux*. Bern

Gitti, A. (1952). 'Sul proemio delle «Genealogie» di Ecateo' *Rendiconti Lincei* Ser. 8, 7.389–98

Gomme, A.W. (1945). *A Historical Commentary on Thucydides* I. Oxford

Gow, A.S.F. (1952). *Theocritus, edited with a Translation and Commentary*. 2 vols., 2nd ed., Cambridge

Griffin, J. (1976). 'Homeric pathos and objectivity' *CQ* 26.161–87

— (1980). *Homer on Life and Death*. Oxford

Grosskinsky, A. (1936). *Das Programm des Thukydides*. Berlin

Grote, G. (1888). *A History of Greece*. London

Hammond, N.G.L. (1967). *Epirus*. Oxford

Hammond, N.G.L. and Griffith, G.T. (1979). *A History of Macedonia* II. Oxford

Heath, M. (1993). 'Ancient Interpretations of Pindar's *Nemean* 7' *PLLS* 7.169–99

Hignett, C. (1963). *Xerxes' Invasion of Greece*. Oxford

Hornblower, S. (1991). *A Commentary on Thucydides. I: Books I–III*. Oxford

— (1996). *A Commentary on Thucydides. II: Books IV–V.24*. Oxford

How, W.W. and Wells, J. (1928). *A Commentary on Herodotus* vol. 2. Oxford

Howie, J.G. (1983). 'The revision of myth in Pindar *Olympian* 1: The death and revival of Pelops (25–27; 36–66)' *PLLS* 4.277–313

— (1984). 'Thukydides' Einstellung zur Vergangenheit' *Klio* 66.502–32

— (1989a). 'The Phaeacians in the *Odyssey*: fable and territorial claim' *Shadow* 6.23–34

— (1989b). 'Greek Polytheism', in G. Davies (ed.) *Polytheistic Systems* (Edinburgh 1989) 51–76

— (1991). 'Pindar's account of Pelops' contest with Oenomaus (with a translation of *Olympian* 1)' *Nikephoros* 4.55–120

— (1992). 'Η αριστεια απο τον Ομηρο εως τον Ξενοφωντα' *Parnassos* 34.425–48

— (1995). 'The *Iliad* as exemplum', in Ø. Andersen and M. Dickie (edd.) *Homer's World*, Bergen, 141–73

— (1996). 'The major *aristeia* in Homer and Xenophon' *PLLS* 9.197–217

Hunter, V. (1973). *Thucydides the Artful Reporter*. Toronto

— (1980). 'Thucydides on the uses of the past' *Klio* 62.191–218

— (1982). *Past and Process in Herodotus and Thucydides*. Princeton

Huxley, G. (1966). *The Early Ionians*. London

Immerwahr, H.R. (1966). *Form and Thought in Herodotus*. Cleveland

Jacoby, F. (1912). 'Hekataios von Milet' *RE* VII 2667–769

— (1913a). 'Herodotos' R-E Suppl. II 205–520

— (1913b). 'Hellanikos von Lesbos' *RE* VIII 104–53

— (1949). *Atthis*. Oxford

Kahrstedt, U. (1953). 'Die Geschichte der Elymer' *Würzburger Jahrbücher* 6.1–20

Kallet-Marx, L. (1993). *Money, Expense, and Naval Power in Thucydides' History 1–5.24*. Berkeley, Los Angeles, Oxford

Keaney, J.H. (1980). 'Hecataeus as a source of Aristotle' *LCM* 5.87

Kienzle, E. (1936). *Der Lobpreis von Städten und Ländern in der älteren griechischen Dichtung*. Diss. Basel

Kirkwood, G.M. (1975). '*Nemean* 7 and the theme of vicissitude in Pindar', in G.M. Kirkwood (ed.) *Poetry and Poetics from Ancient Greece to the Renaissance: Studies in Honor of James Hutton*, Ithaca, 57–90

— (1982). *Selections from Pindar. Edited with an Introduction and Commentary*. Chico

Kleingünther, A. (1934). Πρῶτος Εὑρετής. *Philologus* Suppl. 26

Köhnken, A. (1971). *Die Funktion des Mythos bei Pindar: Interpretationen zu sechs Pindargedichten*. Berlin

Krischer, T. (1971). *Formale Konventionen der homerischen Epik* (Zetemata 56) Munich

Lesky, A. (1966). 'Der Mythos im Verständnis der Antike I' *Gymnasium* 73.27–44

Leyden, W. von (1952). 'Spatium historicum' *Durham University Journal* 13.89–104

Lloyd-Jones, H. (1971). *The Justice of Zeus*. Berkeley, Los Angeles, London
— (1994). 'Notes on the New Simonides' *ZPE* 101.1–3

Long, C.R. (1958). 'Greeks, Carians, and the purification of Delos' *AJA* 62.297–306

Macleod, C.W. (1979). 'Thucydides on faction (3.82–83)' *PCPS* 205.52–68
— (1982). *Homer: Iliad Book XXIV*. Cambridge

Maehler, H. (1982). *Die Lieder des Bakchylides. Erster Teil*. 2 vols., Leiden
— (1984) (ed.). *Pindari Carmina cum Fragmentis. Pars I: Epinicia*. Leipzig

Monceux, P. (1886). *Les proxénies grecques*. Paris

Most, G.L. (1985). *The Measures of Praise: Structure and Function in Pindar's Second Pythian and Seventh Nemean Odes*. Göttingen

Nagy, G. (1979). *The Best of the Achaeans*. Baltimore and London

Nenci, G. (1964). 'Una risposta delfica alla metodologia ecataica' *Critica storica* 3.269–86

Nilsson, M.P. (1906). *Griechische Feste*. Leipzig
— (1951). *Cults, Myths, Oracles, and Politics in Ancient Greece*. Lund

Ogilvie, R.M. (1965). *A Commentary on Livy, Books 1–5*. Oxford

Oliver, D. Buitron (1995). 'Stories in the Trojan Cycle from the work of Douris', in J.B. Carter and S.P. Morris (edd.) *The Ages of Homer: A Tribute to Emily Townsend Vermeule*, Austin, 437–47

Oost, S.I. (1975). 'Thucydides and the irrational: sundry passages' *CP* 70.186–96

Parke, H.W. and Wormell, D.W. (1956). *A History of the Delphic Oracle*. 2 vols., Oxford

Parker, R. (1996). *Athenian Religion: a history*. Oxford

Parsons, P.J. (ed.) (1992). *POxy*. 59.3965

Patzer, H. (1940). Review of Bizer (1937). *Gnomon* 16 (1940) 347–65, repr. in H. Herter (ed.) *Thukydides*, Darmstadt, 90–113

Pavese, C.O. (1995). 'Elegia di Simonide agli Spartiati per Platea' *ZPE* 107.1–26

Prinz, F. (1979). *Gründungsmythen und Sagenchronologie*. Munich

Race, W.H. (1987). 'Pindaric encomium and Isocrates' *Evagoras*' *TAPA* 117.131–55
— (1996). *Pindar II: Nemean Odes, Isthmian Odes, Fragments*. Loeb Classical Library, Harvard and London

Rhomaios, K.A. (1929). 'Ἡ Κάθαρσις τῆς Δήλου καὶ τὸ εὕρημα τοῦ Σταυροπούλου' *Deltion* 12.181–219

Robert, C. (1920). *Die griechische Heldensage* I. Berlin

Romilly, J. de (1956). *Histoire et raison chez Thucydide*. Paris

Roux, G. (1976). *Delphes: son oracle et ses dieux.* Paris

Rutherford, I. (1996). 'The New Simonides: towards a commentary' *Arethusa* 29.167–92

Smith, O.L. (1984). 'Pindar's Seventh Nemean Ode' *Classica et Mediaevalia* 35.5–17

Snodgrass, A.M. (1964). 'Carian armourers — the growth of a tradition' *JHS* 84.107–18

— (1971). *The Dark Age of Greece.* Edinburgh

Strasburger, H. (1958). 'Die politische Selbstdarstellung der Athener' *Hermes* 86.17–40

— (1972). *Homer und die Geschichtsschreibung.* Heidelberg

Strosetzky, N. (1958). 'Antike Rechtssymbole' *Hermes* 86.1–17

Suerbaum, W. (1968). 'Die Ich-Erzählungen des Odysseus' *Poetica* 2.150–77

Thomas, R. (1989). *Oral Tradition and Written Record in Classical Athens.* Cambridge

Toepffer, J. (1883). *Attische Genealogie.* Berlin

Trypanis, C.A. (1971). *The Penguin Book of Greek Verse.* Harmondsworth

Wade-Gery, H.T. (1952). *The Poet of the Iliad.* Cambridge

West, M.L. (1966). *Hesiod, Theogony, edited with Prolegomena and Commentary.* Oxford

— (1985). *The Hesiodic Catalogue of Women: Its Nature, Structure, and Origins.* Oxford

— (1992) (ed.). *Iambi et Elegi Graeci* II. 2nd ed. Oxford

— (1993). 'Simonides Redivivus' *ZPE* 98.1–14

Wiencke, M. (1954). 'An epic theme in Greek art' *AJA* 58.285–306

Wilamowitz-Moellendorff, U. von (1908). 'Pindars siebentes nemeisches Gedicht' *SPAW* 15 (1908) 328–52, repr. in W.M. Calder III and J. Stern (edd.) *Pindaros und Bakchylides*, Darmstadt 1970, 127–58

Williams, F. (1978). *Callimachus. Hymn to Apollo.* Oxford

Wipprecht, F. (1902). *Zur Entwicklung der rationalistischen Mythendeutung bei den Griechen* I. Prog. Donaueschingen 1901/2, Tübingen 1902

Woodbury, L. (1979). 'Neoptolemus at Delphi: Pindar, Nem.7.30ff.' *Phoenix* 33.95–133

Wüst, E. (1967). *Pindar als geschichtsschreibender Dichter.* Diss. Tübingen

— (1968). 'Der Ring des Minos' *Hermes* 96.527–38

Young, D.C. (1971). *Pindar Isthmian 7, Myth and Exempla.* Leiden

PAPERS OF THE LEEDS INTERNATIONAL LATIN SEMINAR   TENTH VOLUME (1998) 131–56
Published by Francis Cairns (Publications) Ltd (Leeds 1998). ARCA 38. ISBN 0 905205 95 2

THEORIA AS THEATRE: PILGRIMAGE IN GREEK DRAMA[*]

IAN RUTHERFORD
University of Reading

1. Introduction

The purpose of this paper is to survey the use of the theme of pilgrimage or sacred tourism (*theoria*) in Greek dramatic poetry. Its scope is both tragedy and comedy, and also minor dramatic genres. It is not meant to be an exhaustive catalogue, nor to provide exhaustive analyses of the passages it deals with. But I try to touch on the most prominent examples, many of them from Euripides, and to articulate the major aspects of the theme of pilgrimage in Greek drama.

Though pilgrimage is a central subject in the culture of classical Greece, little attention has been paid to it.[1] Part of the reason for the neglect might be that people tend to think of 'pilgrimage' in terms of

---

[*] This paper is part of an ongoing project on pilgrimage. A paper on similar lines was presented at the Leeds International Latin Seminar colloquium in May 1992, and I thank all who contributed on that occasion. More recently, Dr. Christiane Sourvinou-Inwood gave me much assistance. And I thank Prof. Albert Henrichs for a profitable discussion of Euripides' *Erechtheus*; also J.-G. Bodard, for a penetrating discussion of the *Andromache*.

[1] Some of the main treatments are the following: C.P. Bill 'Notes on the Greek θεωρός and θεωρία' *TAPA* 32 (1901) 196–204; H. Koller 'Theoros und Theoria' *Glotta* 36 (1957–8) 273–85; H. Rausch *Theoria: von ihrer sakralen zur philosophischen Bedeutung* (Munich 1982); G. Siebart 'Réflexions sur la notion de pèlerinages dans la Grèce antique' in F. Raphael *et al.* (eds.) *Les Pèlerinages de l'antiquité biblique et classique à l'occident médiéval* (Strassburg 1983) 33–53; D. Wachsmuth *Der Kleine Pauly* 5.730–31, *s.v.* 'Theoria, -oi'; L. Ziehen *RE* 5A.2 (1934) 2228–33 *s.v.* θεωρία, 2239–44 *s.v.* θεωροί. M. Dillon *Pilgrims and Pilgrimage in Ancient Greece* (London 1997) appeared too late for me to take more than cursory notice of it in this paper.

the penitent, ascetic, even self-punishing pilgrims of medieval or modern Europe, undertaking pilgrimages to major Christian centres for the sake of healing or to fulfill vows. It is true there is little sign of this sort of ascetic, penitential pilgrimage in the ancient world. However, as anthropologists and historians of religion are beginning to understand, pilgrimage is a much broader social category than that, and, in one form or another, it is found throughout the world, and in almost all religions.[2]

At its most general, a pilgrimage can be defined in terms of three components: 1) it is a journey to a sanctuary or sacred place; 2) it is undertaken for some religious reason; and 3) it is a journey of a certain length, a longer journey than one would usually make, and often a difficult one. In the ancient Greek world, as in most ancient societies, pilgrimage in this broader sense was a common activity. The landscape was criss-crossed by a network of sanctuaries ranging from the great national ones to the more modest regional and local ones. Some were in remote places, like Dodona, inconveniently situated in the North West of Greece, far from the major centres of civilisation, or the oracle of Zeus Ammon at Siwa in Libya. Others were positioned at cross-roads where different groups of people would tend to meet, like the sanctuary of Poseidon at the Isthmus. Many people, women as well as men,[3] probably went on pilgrimages to some of these centres at some time in their lives; Socrates was considered abnormal for never having gone on any pilgrimage except once to the Isthmus.

The first task in working on pilgrimage in a culture ought to be to produce a typology of where the sanctuaries were, and some idea of where they drew pilgrims from. This is comparatively easy to do for living traditions, where it is possible to observe directly where pilgrims come from and to ask them about their motives.[4] For ancient Greece the picture we can build up of pilgrimage is by contrast fragmentary, but we can see that some sanctuaries drew pilgrims evenly from all over Greece. These included Delphi, Olympia, Dodona, Nemea, the

---

[2] General studies of pilgrimage include: J. Chelini and H. Branthomme *Histoire des pèlerinages non chrétiens. Entre magique et sacré: le chemin des dieux* (Paris 1987); E.A. Morinis *Sacred Journeys: the Anthropology of Pilgrimage* (New York 1992); V. Turner 'The centre out there: pilgrim's goal' *History of Religions* 12 (1972) 191–230 = 'Pilgrimages as social processes' in *Dramas, Fields and Metaphors: Symbolic Action in Human Society* (Cornell 1974) 166–230; J. Eade & M.J. Sallnow *Contesting the Sacred: the Anthropology of Christian Pilgrimage* (London 1991); J.Z. Smith *To Take Place: Toward a Theory of Ritual* (Chicago 1987).

[3] For the role of women, see below, p.139 n.23.

[4] A good example of such a study for Hindu India is S.M. Bhardwaj *Hindu Places of Pilgrimage in India. A Study in Cultural Geography* (Berkeley 1973).

sanctuary of Poseidon at the Isthmus, and that of Zeus Ammon at Siwa. But most sanctuaries drew them from a limited 'catchment area'. In some cases, the catchment area will have been roughly identical to a given geo-political or ethnic entity; for example, there were Boeotian festivals that drew on all the Boeotians, and pilgrimage to the island of Delos was principally confined to Ionians. Sometimes the catchment area might vary depending on the nature of the event. To take one example, in the case of the sanctuary on the island of Samothrace in the north-eastern Aegean, pilgrims to the festival there came mostly from Thrace and Asia Minor, but initiants into the celebrated Mysteries of Samothrace came from all over the Greek world.[5]

Pilgrimage in ancient Greece was partly an individual affair and partly took place under the auspices of the city-state. A *polis* would send regular sacred delegations to the major sanctuaries. The more local sanctuaries might be visited every year, more distant ones more rarely. In some cases these delegations might have contained only a single individual, or a handful, but on other occasions they could have been very large; some attested from the Hellenistic period run into hundreds. Such sacred delegations had three parts. They were led by magistrates and priests, who for the purposes of the pilgrimage were known as *arkhitheoroi*; they would probably have comprised an official escort of people who would take part in a procession at the sanctuary; and, thirdly, they probably also contained an entourage of interested citizens. The second section, the escort, was often a group of young people, adolescent men or women. One thinks for example of the story in Herodotus that the Chians sent a *khoros* of one hundred young men or *neaniai* to Delphi; he mentions this because all but two of them died of plague. In such cases, we may like to think of the pilgrimage as enacting a sort of symbolic *rite de passage*, effecting a transition between two levels of age-status.

Being a *theoros* was a semi-sacred condition: they wore crowns, they were regarded as under divine protection. Sacred truces (*ekekheiriai*) were proclaimed during the period immediately before and after national festivals to protect both *theoroi* and delegates who announced the festivals round Greece.[6] They broke the journey at set way-stations, where they offered sacrifice. The mood seems to have been one of celebration, another striking difference between ancient

---

[5] I do not provide sources for all this data here; but for Samothrace, see S.G. Cole *Theoi Megaloi: the Cult of the Great Gods at Samothrace* (Leiden 1984).

[6] The best account of truces is in G. Rougemont 'La hiéroménie des Pythia et les «trèves sacrées» d'Éleusis, de Delphes et d'Olympie' *BCH* 97 (1973) 75–106, 89–93.

pilgrimage and the modern image of the penitential pilgrim.[7]

The functions of state-pilgrimages varied greatly. They could bring offerings of animals to be sacrificed; they could take expensive dedications, which they dedicated to the gods; they could consult oracles; or their business could be with the great festivals, merely to attend them, or to take part in them by staging processions or artistic performances. If the festival involved an athletic competition, a delegation might include local athletes who would take part.

Not all pilgrimage was state-run. From the end of the fifth century (at the latest) we have evidence for pilgrimage to sanctuaries for the sake of healing. The most popular such sanctuaries were associated with Asclepius, particularly the one at Epidaurus. Healing pilgrimage was wholly a private matter.[8] Private pilgrimage probably took place for the sake of consulting oracles also, and for other reasons, such as making personal dedications to deities.[9] A motivation that bridged the private and the public was that of initiation into the mysteries, such as at Eleusis; initiation itself was a private experience, but there was a major city-organisation in the institution, symbolised by the grand procession from Athens to Eleusis. In assessing the relative frequency of state- and private pilgrimage in the classical period, we are at the mercy of the sources available to us (literary, epigraphic and others), which naturally tend to pay more attention to the great state pilgrimages.

Another function beside these is suggested by the most common Greek words for pilgrim and pilgrimage, θεωρός and θεωρία. The primary sense of the word θεωρία is 'viewing' or 'contemplation' (θέα can mean the same thing). This terminology reflects the fact that a common motive for pilgrimage in ancient Greece was simply to view the sacred centres and the artifacts collected there, especially statues of the gods, as well as rituals that might be put on and the spectacles that might be staged (both θεωρία and θέα can also mean objective 'spectacle' as well as subjective 'watching'). Our first instinct might be to think of this as tourism rather than pilgrimage, and it may be that θεωρός can sometimes mean 'tourist', but the evidence for ancient

---

[7]   For celebration see Ar. *Peace* (§4 below); Soph. *OT* 1491; Aelius Aristides *Hieros Logos* 4 (40).2; Achaeus fr. 27.2.

[8]   The best account of this is in A. Krug *Heilkunst und Heilkult: Medizin in der Antike* (Munich 1984).

[9]   Theophrastus *Char.* 21.4 attests that a man might have the ritual shearing of his son carried out at Delphi (the fact that he regards this as characteristic of a father with a particular deviant personality shows that this practice was rare, but that it was not unattested either).

Greece seems to be that viewing of sacred objects is a religious activity in itself, or at least that tourism and pilgrimage are not sharply distinguished. Thus, 'sacred tourism' is perhaps a better translation. There is a good parallel for this in the pilgrimage-tradition of modern India, where one of the main motives for pilgrimage is precisely 'looking', expressed by the Sanskrit or Hindi noun *darśana* or *darśan* (it is cognate with Greek δέρκομαι). There is an excellent study of *darśan* by Diana Eck, who singles it out as the central motive for pilgrimage in Hinduism, and one of the fundamental concepts in the religion as a whole.[10] The objects of *darśan* can be not just statues and temples, but also sacred places, including fords, great mountains or rivers, like the Ganges. *Darśan* can even be of the various types of holy men recognised in Hinduism. Perhaps the main difference between *darśan* and *theoria* is that the former seems to have a deeper religious significance, and to involve a more or less fixed manner of performance, almost like a ritual. *Prima facie*, ancient Greek *theoria* is not a ritual activity in the same way. Still, the parallel is an illuminating one, and helps to explain why the Greek for a pilgrim is a word that primarily means 'watcher'.

2. Theoric Drama

Perhaps the earliest known example of the use of pilgrimage as a theme in Greek drama is the *Thearoi* of Epicharmus (*CGF* fr. 79 = Athenaeus 8, 362b: pilgrims, perhaps a *khoros*, at Delphi inspecting votive offerings). Also from Sicily we know of a mime entitled *Isthmia Thamenoi* (or *Thamenai*) ("Visitors (or "Women Visitors") to the Isthmian Games") by Sophron (*CGF* fr. 9).[11] This presumably described the sacred journey of some Sicilians to the Isthmian Games (would Syracusans have been particularly keen to see Corinth?). One of the attractions of such mimes may have been that they provided information about panhellenic sanctuaries for people unable to go on pilgrimages there.

The comic tradition continued in Athens. The Aeschylean satyr-drama with the alternative titles *Theoroi* or *Isthmiastai* (*TrGF* fr. 78a) was concerned with the adventures of satyrs who visit the Isthmus. They went to compete in the games, but that also counts as a form of *theoria*. In the surviving fragment of this the satyrs admire their own

---

[10] D.L. Eck *Darśav: Seeing the Divine in India* (ed. 2, Chambersburg 1985).

[11] *CGF* fr. 9 = C. Wendel *Scholia Vetera in Theocritum* (Leipzig 1914) 305.8. The scholiast claims that this is the model for Theocritus 15 (*Adoniazousai*), which is I suppose the reason why Kaibel restores the title as a feminine; but the hypothesis is not necessary.

images on the pediment of the temple, which they seem to have placed there as votive offerings (perhaps this scene could be thought of as an artful adaptation of an already existing topos in which a *khoros* of pilgrims admire the artwork of a temple).[12] Another play featuring satyrs who come to compete in a festival is the source for an isolated fragment in which they show off their skills (= *TrGF* Sophocles fr. dub. 1130).[13] The lost *Athla* by the fifth-century tragedian Achaeus of Eretria may have been a satyr-drama along the same lines.

The theme of pilgrimage is also taken up in Old Comedy. The *mise-en-scène* of Aristophanes' *Amphiaraus* was a pilgrimage to the Amphiareion at Oropus in North Attica; the few fragments that survive suggest that the focus of the play was a consultation of the oracle rather than a healing pilgrimage.[14] Similar was the *Trophonius* of Cratinus, which probably described a pilgrimage to the oracle of Trophonius at Lebadeia in Boeotia (cf. *PCG* fr. 235), but again we have no clear idea of what happened. In Aristophanes' *Skenas Katalambanousai* ("Women Trying to Find A Place for Their Tents"), the *khoros* were probably women pilgrims attending a non-local festival.[15] The identity of the festival remains a mystery, but it may have involved a javelin contest (fr. 492). The following fragment survives (fr. 487):

---

[12] See the studies of A. Setti 'Eschilo. Satirico II: I frammenti dei Θεωροὶ Ἰσθμιασταί ...', *ASNP* 21 (Pisa 1952) 205–44, republished in the author's *Eschilo satirico ed altri saggi* (Rome 1981) 69–123; D.F. Sutton 'Aeschylus' *Theoroi* or *Isthmiastae*: a reconsideration' *GRBS* 22 (1981) 335–43; B. Snell 'Aischylos' Isthmiastai' *Hermes* 84 (1956) 1–11; M. Stieber 'Aeschylus' *Theoroi* and realism in Greek art' *TAPA* 124 (1994) 85–119. There are two major fragments, 78a and 78c, which perhaps belong in reasonably close proximity. The only thing that is clear is that the satyrs have given up dancing and have embraced a new career as athletes.

[13] The satyrs show off their skills to Oineus (Schoineus?), and then ask: ἆρ' ἄκαρπος ἡ θεωρία; (fr. 1130.16), the meaning of which is perhaps "is the show here without fruit?", referring to a journey that they have made to games being organised by Oineus to chose a husband for his daughter (Deianeira or Atalanta); competitors in games could be called *theoroi* (see above), *contra* the implication of R. Carden *The Papyrus Fragments of Sophocles* (Berlin 1974) 146, who thinks it has the sense of "contemplation" (i.e. study); and P. Maas 'Zu dem Satyrspiel Oxyrh.-Papyr. VIII 1083' *BPW* 32 (1912) 1426–9, 1428 = *Kleine Schriften* (Munich 1973) 52, who thinks it means *Anblick*. I wonder if there is also a play on the idea that *theoroi* often bring first-fruit offerings to sanctuaries to dedicate them there, so an ἄκαρπος θεωρία might have been proverbial for something which was expected to be profitable, but in fact turned out not to be.

[14] P. Vicaire 'Image d'Amphiaraus dans la Grèce archaïque et classique' *BAGB* (1979) 2–45, 42; C. Faraone 'Aristophanes, *Amphiaraus*, fr. 29 (Kassel–Austin): oracular response or erotic incantation?' *CQ* 42 (1992) 320–27.

[15] The phrase εἰς Ἴσθμια σκηνὴν ... καταλαμβάνω is found in the context of *theoria* at Ar. *Peace* 879.

λήκυθον
τὴν ἑπτακότυλον τὴν χυτρείαν τὴν καλήν,
ἣν ἐφερόμην, ἵν' ἔχοιμι συνθεάτριαν

(... my nice, earthenware, seven-*kotulai* bottle which I brought so that I could have a fellow spectator.)

Apparently the speaker is isolated and has no one to watch the games with.[16] Another fragment (fr. 494) refers to a prostitute, which seems to be appropriate in the context of an international festival. The theme of wine and women's festivals recalls the *Thesmophoriazousai*. Could the theme of the play have been a take-over of one of the panhellenic festivals by women in the interests of achieving peace during the Peloponnesian War? Or could it have been a dispute arising over the seizing of space for a *skene*?

To move to the fourth century, the *Wealth* of Aristophanes begins with Chremylus and his slave Carion returning from a pilgrimage to Delphi, as a result of which they have met the anthropomorphic abstraction Wealth, represented as a blind old man, and the main action describes a second pilgrimage to an *Asklepieion* with the purpose of recovering his sight through incubation. Carion describes what went on. The god carried out the cure in person, as Carion witnesses staring voyeuristically through holes in his cloak (712–25). He cured Wealth, but the Athenian politician Neocleides he punished by putting an acidic ointment in his eyes. The site of the *Asklepieion* is uncertain; it is often thought to be Zea in Attica, but a location outside of Attica might be indicated by the fact that Wealth salutes Attica on his return (771–3).[17]

From slightly later comes a fragment from a comedy by a certain Heniochus (first quarter of the fourth century BC), in which the cities of Greece are represented as pilgrims who came to Olympia to make a thank-offering, but hung around, delayed by disagreements about aristocracy and democracy, represesented as two alluring *hetairai*. We should probably think of the cities as constituting the *khoros* of the play

---

[16] The speaker of *Lys. Or.* 8.5, who is accusing fellow members of a society (συνουσιασταί) of calumny, says that they claimed that it was only against their will that they went with him to a θεωρία at Eleusis (... ἀκόντων ὑμῶν Ἐλευσινάδε ξυνθεωρεῖν), which suggests that it was the practice for members of such societies to go on *theoriai* together.

[17] Zea: S.B. Aleshire *The Athenian Asklepieion* (Amsterdam 1989) 13, assuming that the only options are Athens and Zea; E.J. Edelstein and L. Edelstein *Asclepius: a Collection and Interpretation of the Testimonies* (Baltimore 1945) 2.212, take it as evidence for the Attic cult. There is a good discussion of the scene in A. Bowie *Aristophanes: Myth, Ritual and Comedy* (Cambridge 1992) 278–9.

(though this has recently been doubted).[18]

From the third century, we have a fragment of a *Theoroi* by Euphron (*PCG* fr. 7), which is probably in the tradition of the pilgrimage-mimes of Sophron. It is also worth mentioning Herodas *Mime* 4, set in an *Asklepieion*, probably an imaginary one, like the one in Aristophanes' *Wealth*, but perhaps the famous one in Cos.[19] Theocritus *Idyll* 15 (*Adoniazousai*) is similar in some ways, though it is concerned not with pilgrims, but with Alexandrians visiting a festival of Adonis.

So there was a tradition of dramas involving *theoroi* visiting religious centres. In many of them the *khoros* were probably *theoroi*. That deployment derived dramatic plausibility from the tendency for sacred delegations to sanctuaries to have included *khoroi*, often composed of young men and women who sang songs of praise in honour of the deity visited.[20] The tradition of 'pilgrimage-drama' seems so coherent, I would suggest, that we are justified in speaking in terms of a sub-genre of pilgrimage-drama. In the remainder of this paper, I want to examine a few more complex examples of the portrayal of pilgrimage in drama.

3. The Theoric Chorus in Tragedy: *Antiope* and *Ion*

The chorus can also be pilgrims in tragedy. The best case is the *Ion* of Euripides. In this play Xuthus and Creusa are pilgrims who come to Delphi to consult the oracle about how Xuthus is to get a son, unaware that Ion, the young temple-priest, is a son of Creusa by Apollo. To begin with, Xuthus embraces Ion as his son, having been told by the oracle that his son will be the first person he meets on leaving the temple. Then Creusa tries to poison Ion, jealous at the prospect of having someone else's son in the family and angry at having been deceived for a second time by Apollo (she may even see Ion as a sort of second Apollo). Creusa's ambivalent attitude toward Apollo is thus at the heart of the action of the play. But her plan is found out, and Ion retaliates by trying to kill Creusa. However, the true relationship between Creusa and Ion is revealed just in time. Athena appears and predicts that Ion will become king of Athens, and Xuthus will never

---

[18] R.L. Hunter 'The comic chorus in the fourth century' *ZPE* 36 (1979) 34–5, doubts whether the cities constituted the *khoros*.

[19] S.M. Sherwin-White *Ancient Cos: an Historical Study from the Dorian Settlement to the Imperial Period* (Hypomnemata 51, Göttingen 1978) 350–52 believes in a Coan site; against: I.C. Cunningham 'Herodas 4' *CQ* 16 (1966) 113–25, 115–17 and *Herodas: Mimiamboi* (Oxford 1971) 128.

[20] Numerous poems written to be performed at sanctuaries survive; chief among them are paeans by Pindar and other poets written to be performed at Delphi and Delos.

know that Ion is not his son.

The *khoros* are women attendants of Creusa, and in the *parodos* they are represented as admiring the sculptures on the pediments of the temple, rather like the participants in some of the fragmentary pilgrimage dramas. Their intermediate position as pilgrims comes out in their tendency to compare and contrast what they see with what they have seen in their home city.[21] They begin by saying: "So it was not only at Athens that there were halls of the gods ..." (184–9); they comment that Iolaos is portrayed as he is represented "in my own weavings" (196–7); and they see Athena and call her "my goddess" (211). Their attitude is excited and joyful, and provides a foil for the following scene, where the same sight makes Creusa weep by reminding her of her past (and the troubles she has left at home), when she was raped by Apollo (247–54). In giving the *khoros* the function of *theoroi*, Euripides may have been influenced by simple theoric dramas of the sort we saw evidence of in §2.[22]

In real life it seems likely that the majority of the *theoroi* would have been men, although delegations to sanctuaries certainly included women also.[23] There was literary precedent for having female pilgrims on the stage (Aristophanes' *Skenas Katalambanousai*, depending on the date; Sophron's mime, depending on gender of the title). In this case, the gender of the *khoros* is chosen to suit their role in the play; they side emotionally with Creusa and identify with her position as a woman maltreated by powerful males, divine and human. The activity of 'sacred gazing' seems to reinforce this schema; it is a passive activity, and significantly it is Creusa and the female *khoros* who engage in it (the ambivalence of Creusa's reaction if anything reinforces her weakness). But Xuthus does not take part in this sacred viewing; he is off consulting the oracle of Trophonius during the first scene of the play. There and at Delphi his mode of interacting with the sanctuary is to consult the oracle directly. His manner of dealing with the sanctuary is

---

[21] This point is made by F. Zeitlin 'The artful eye: vision, ecphrasis and spectacle in Euripidean theatre' in S. Goldhill and R. Osborne (ed.) *Art and Text in Ancient Greek Culture* (Cambridge 1992) 138–96.

[22] On relation with mime see Zeitlin (n.21) 147 and n.25.

[23] Women would probably have gone principally in two capacities: first, *parthenoi* might form part of the escort of an official delegation, like the *kanephoroi* in the *Puthaides*. Second, they might form part of the unofficial contingent. Thus, in his account of the early *theoria* to Delos Thucydides implies that men went with their families. The hellenistic *Puthais* inscriptions mention *kanephoroi*, who must have been girls. Women who went along in these capacities probably 'watched' events and sacred objects like the men; however, women were in general excluded from watching the games at Olympia: see Dillon (n.1) 194.

perhaps also suggested by the information he recalls when trying to account for who Ion's mother may have been; he remembers that when he came to Delphi on a previous pilgrimage "to the torches of the Bacchic one" (ἐς φανάς γε Βακχίου, 550), he got drunk (in the context of the Bacchic festival, of course) and made love to a local Delphian woman, who may, he thinks, have given birth to Ion. The more respectful activity of sacred contemplation is by contrast confined to women.

The *khoros* are spectators in other tragedies also (as A.W. Schlegel observed, it is the function of the *khoros* to act as a substitute audience).[24] Thus in the *Prometheus Bound* the *khoros* have come from the Ocean stream, as has Oceanus, to contemplate the suffering Prometheus. (Io also plays the role of a *theoros* in that play, and her journey is balanced by the heroic journey that Herakles will make in the *Prometheus Unbound*: 188, 302). Again, to take a celebrated Euripidean example, in the *parodos* of the *Iphigeneia in Aulis* a *khoros* of women from Chalcis arrives and admires the Greek army and its fleet (a sort of lyric τειχοσκοπία).[25] It has been suggested that this arrangement ensures the neutrality of the *khoros* since they are not predisposed in favour of either Agamemnon or Clytemnestra. It would be unreasonable to suppose that all such 'visiting *khoroi*' should be traced back to simple pilgrimage-dramas of the sort I identified earlier. Rather, for the *khoros* to be spectators is in the nature of Greek theatre; it follows naturally from their position in the orkhestra and from the convention that they enter at the end of the prologue. So for a *khoros* to be composed of pilgrims is a device that is synchronically wholly consonant with the make–up of the *khoros*, but simultaneously from the diachronic point of view it seems likely that there was a continuous tradition of pilgrim *khoroi*.

To return to the *Ion*, the portrayal of Creusa and the *khoros* as passive *theoroi* is for the most part confined to the earlier part of the play. As the play progresses Creusa takes an active role, and the *khoros* are one with her in this. Changing roles in this way brings them close to disaster; they fear for their lives when the plan goes wrong (1229–

---

[24] On this, see M. Hose *Studien zum Chor bei Euripides* (Stuttgart 1990) 1.32–7, attributing the idea to A.W. Schlegel *Vorlesungen über dramatische Kunst und Literatur* in *Sämtliche Werke* ed. E. Böcking (Leipzig 1846) 5.76–7.

[25] On this scene, see now Zeitlin (n.21) 157–71. Notice that, as in the *Ion*, the role of the *khoros* changes as the play progresses; in the lyric dialogue with Iphigeneia (1500–31), they have become partakers in the sacrifice of Iphigeneia rather than simply spectators.

43).[26] Although their characterisation as spectators is confined for the most part to the *parodos*, it surfaces in one passage in a choral ode later in the play. They take Creusa's part and call upon Persephone to come and assist her plan, anticipating the shame they will feel if Ion, who they believe to be a foreigner, becomes an adopted son of Xuthus and leads the Athenian pilgrimage to Eleusis, with Iacchus looking on (1074–80):[27]

αἰσχύνομαι τὸν πολύυμνον θεόν, εἰ παρὰ Καλλιχόροισι παγαῖς
λαμπάδα θεωρὸς εἰκάδων
ἐννύχιον ἄυπνος ὄψεται,
ὅτε καὶ Διὸς ἀστερωπὸς
ἀνεχόρευσεν αἰθήρ,
χορεύει δὲ σελάνα ...

(I am ashamed before the much-hymned god if by the Kallikhoroi fountains he sees as a sleepless watcher the nightly torch of the twenties, when too the starry ether of Zeus started to dance, and the moon dances ...)

This is the sort of sentiment that one might expect to come naturally to members of a sacred delegation to Delphi. It is also perhaps because they have recently been engaged in sacred contemplation at Delphi that they analyse the situation in terms of "viewing", even though it is not their own viewing in this case or the viewing of the sanctuary by the pilgrim, but rather the reciprocal imagined viewing of the pilgrim by one of the deities linked to the sanctuary.[28]

4. *Theoria* Reclaimed: Aristophanes' *Peace*

Pilgrimage is also a theme in Aristophanes' *Peace*. Here the theme is not going on a pilgrimage (which is impossible in war), but rather the restoration of pilgrimage, which comes with the establishment of peace. Aristophanes personifies *theoria* as a sexually attractive woman, one of two attendants that accompany the goddess Peace when Trygaeus retrieves her from the distant cave in which War has imprisoned her. On Hermes' instruction, Trygaeus restores Theoria to the

---

[26] See also F. Zeitlin 'Mysteries of identity and designs of the self in Euripides' *Ion*' *PCPS* 35 (1989) 144–97, 162.

[27] θεωρός for MS θεωρόν is Musgrave's emendation, adopted by J. Diggle 'On the 'Heracles' and 'Ion' of Euripides' *PCPS* 20 (1974) 3–36, 25–6, who sees the *theoros* as Ion. Iacchus seems to me more likely because his 'watching' explains the context for the shame anticipated by the *khoros*. The same interpretation seems to be implied in Rausch (n.1) 27.

[28] Pilgrimage in Greece is heavily characterised by reciprocal relationships, as I hope to show in my forthcoming book on the subject.

Athenian *boule* (713–14). In doing this, he recalls the joys of sex, food
and wine of past pilgrimages to Brauron and the Isthmus, and it is
almost as if he is alluding to the tradition of pilgrimage-comedies. On
one level, the restoration of *theoria* represents historical reality. The
peace-treaty of 421 BC reported in Thucydides begins with the stipu-
lation that there is to be free access for sacred delegations visiting
sanctuaries. In so far as Trygaeus symbolises Nicias, it may be appro-
priate that he is linked with *theoria*, since Nicias himself organised a
pilgrimage to Delos.[29]

The associations of *theoria* with panhellenic peace come out as early
as lines 337–45, where Trygaeus and the *khoros* are about to pull Peace
out of the cave in which War has imprisoned her, but Trygaeus re-
proaches the leader of the *khoros* for being too quick to anticipate
success (338–45):

> ἀλλ' ὅταν λάβωμεν αὐτήν, τηνικαῦτα χαίρετε
> καὶ βοᾶτε καὶ γελᾶτ'· ἤ-
> δη γὰρ ἐξέσται τόθ' ὑμῖν
> πλεῖν μένειν βινεῖν καθεύδειν,
> ἐς πανηγύρεις θεωρεῖν,
> ἑστιᾶσθαι κότταβίζειν,
>   †συβαρίζειν†
> ἰοῦ ἰοῦ κεκραγέναι.

But when we've got her, then you can rejoice and shout and laugh,
for then at last you'll be able to travel or stay at home, to screw or
sleep, to attend international festivals, to feast, to play cottabus, to be
a regular Sybarite, and to cry 'hurrah, hurrah!'. (tr. Sommerstein)

Thus *theoria* to international festivals is taken to be one of the primary
signs of peace. It is significant that the *khoros* refer to themselves as
Πανέλληνες a few lines earlier (302). Some time later Trygaeus and
the *khoros* succeed in hauling Peace out of the cave. She is represented
as a statue, a dramatic strategy for which Aristophanes was ridiculed by
other comedians.[30] With her are two attendants, who presumably stand
on either side of her, like *paredroi*. Their names are Opora, who sym-
bolises the autumn harvest, and Theoria, who symbolises religious

---

[29] Thuc. 5.18.2: περὶ μὲν τῶν ἱερῶν τῶν κοινῶν, θύειν καὶ ἰέναι καὶ μαντεύεσθαι καὶ
θεωρεῖν κατὰ τὰ πάτρια τὸν βουλόμενον καὶ κατὰ γῆν καὶ κατὰ θάλασσαν ἀδεῶς
("concerning the common sanctuaries, that anyone who wants to should sacrifice,
travel, consult oracles and send delegations in accordance with ancestral custom by
land and sea in safety"); G. Rougemont (n.6); Plu. *Nic.* 4.4–6.

[30] Eupolis fr. 62 (*Autolycus*); Plato Com. fr. 86 (*Metoikoi*).

delegation and festival.[31] Both roles were probably played by mute female actresses. Trygaeus describes Theoria in great detail, describing her mainly in terms of her smell; there is a certainly irony that the smell is the criterion for what is supposed to be a visual experience (524–6). The scene is almost pastoral in quality (one thinks of the analogous description of peacetime in the *Acharnians*). The focus is mainly on the Athenian countryside, and perhaps local festivals are mainly meant. The word ὑποδοχή (one of the things that Theoria smells of) refers to the practice of putting people up when they travelled to go to festivals.[32]

When Trygaeus is about to leave the house of Zeus, Hermes instructs him to marry Opora, and to restore Theoria to the Athenian *boule*, to whom she used to belong (713–14).[33] These two actions occupy the rest of the play, first the restoration of Theoria, and second the wedding, with the *hidrusis* of Peace coming in between (the statue continues to preside over the stage; it probably did not move between the scene in the house of Zeus and the scene back in Athens). The association of Theoria with the *boule* probably reflects the fact that it was the *boule* in Athens which selected and sent out official *theoroi*, and to which they reported on their return (the idea of a return journey is suggested by the comic conceit that Theoria is being restored to the *boule* after a long absence). Perhaps official *theoriai* from other *poleis* attending Athenian festivals also reported to the *boule*. Certainly *theoriai* who came to announce international festivals to be held in other parts of Greece would have made their announcement there.[34]

The notion of *theoria* that Aristophanes has in mind here seems to be fairly general. The slave makes a joke about a *theoria* to Brauron, but the special point in that case is that that festival was particularly

---

[31] On such figures see B. Zweig 'The mute nude female characters in Aristophanes' plays' in A. Richlin (ed.) *Pornography and Representation in Greece and Rome* (Oxford 1992) 73–89. One of the female figures on the Thorikos calendar was originally identified as Theoria by C. Robert, in a review of the original publication by J.N. Svoronos, *GGA* (1899) 548, and L. Deubner *Attische Feste* (Berlin 1932) 250, supported originally by E. Simon 'Attische Monatsbilder' *JDAI* 80 (1965) 105–24, 119–20; but in *Festivals of Attica: an Archaeolgical Commentary* (Madison 1983) 6 n.14 and 101, she changed her mind and suggests that it represents *Pompe*.

[32] The usual word for this is θεωροδοκία. See n.39 below.

[33] ἀπαγαγεῖν at line 714 could be a reflection of the use of the verb in the context of θεωρία, as in Pl. *Phdr.* 58b.

[34] For the importance of the βουλή see A.C. Cassio *Commedia e partecipazione: La pace di Aristofane* (Naples 1985) 125; Dem. 19.128; P.J. Rhodes *The Athenian Boule* (ed. 2, Oxford 1985) 131; Bill (n.1) 202–3. In the case of *theoroi* going to Delphi, we hear that money was provided by the *kolakretai* from the *naukrarika*: see Androtion *FGrH* 324F36 (probably Solonian: cf. Ar. *Ath. Pol.* 8.3).

associated with young girls; he also makes one about the Isthmian festival, but that may be because he can allude to ἰσθμός in the sense of "waist" (877–80). Another possibility is that we are to think of delegations who have come from abroad to attend a festival associated with the goddess Peace. As Cassio stresses, the fact that the premise of the whole comic scene is that *theoria* is impossible during time of war makes it likely that non-local festivals are meant, particularly panhellenic ones.[35] This hypothesis implies an interesting collapsing of categories: peace is the condition which allows the passage of *theoroi* through Greece, but in this case a cult of Peace would also be the focus of their pilgrimage (in the same way perhaps it could be claimed that Opora stands for the *aparkhai* which are brought to the cult centre).

After the parabasis, Trygaeus presents Theoria to the *boule*. He asks her to disrobe, so that the *boule* can "see" her. He pulls back her clothes, which Trygaeus compares to the ritual drawing-back of an animal's neck before sacrifice (which gave the second day of the Apatouria its name, Anarhusis).[36] This moment plays on the idea of *theoria* as an activity involving looking, and it also suggests the symbolic moment in Greek ritual when a husband looks upon his naked wife for the first time (presents, called θεώρητρα, were given on this occasion).[37] There is much sexual symbolism in this scene, playing on the ideas of wrestling and horse-racing. And it ends with a repeat appeal to the *prutanis* to "receive Theoria" (905–8, tr. Sommerstein):[38]

> ἀλλ᾽, ὦ πρυτάνεις, δέχεσθε τὴν Θεωρίαν.
> θέασ᾽ ὡς προθύμως ὁ πρύτανις παρεδέξατο.
> ἀλλ᾽ οὐκ ἄν, εἴ τι προῖκα προσαγαγεῖν σ᾽ ἔδει,
> ἀλλ᾽ ηὗρον ἄν σ᾽ ὑπέχοντα τὴν ἐκεχειρίαν.

(Now, Prytaneis, take possession of Showtime. [*He gives Showtime to the chairman of the Prytaneis*] Look how eagerly the chairman took her from me! [*To the chairman*] You wouldn't have done that if you'd had to introduce some business for no reward; no; I'd have found you extending your ... armistice.)

---

[35] In that case, one might see the audience of the *Peace* as *theoroi*; and commentators note that the θεαταί (962, 1115) have a particularly close involvement with the celebratory second act of the play.

[36] J. Henderson *Maculate Muse* (ed. 2, New York 1991) 178; Cassio (n.34) 123 n.9.

[37] Eustathius on Homer *Il.* 11.730 (3.315.20 van der Valk); Harpocration *s.v.* ἀνακαλυπτήρια (A115). On the *Anakalupteria* see A. Brückner *Anakalupteria* (Berlin 1914); H.S. Schibli *Pherekydes of Syros* (Oxford 1990) 63–5; J.H. Oakley and R. Sinos *The Wedding in Ancient Athens* (Madison, Wis. 1993) 25–6.

[38] The *prutanis* as head of the council: M.H. Hansen *The Athenian Democracy in the Age of Pericles. Structure, Principles and Ideology* (Oxford 1991) 250.

The final line plays on the association between *ekekheiria* (armistice) and the reception of *theoroi* from other states in peacetime, but it unexpectedly reverses it for comic effect: the *prutanis* is imagined as accepting Theoria only because of the prospect of sex; otherwise, he would have extended *ekekheiria*; in other words, he would have kept his hands to himself.

Theoria is symbolised through the motifs of sex, eating, drinking, smelling good, athletic games. But the climax is her "reception" by the *boule* and the *prutanis*, which is surely meant to reflect the importance of "reception" in the reality of pilgrimage. Sacred delegations have to be "received" by the local *polis*; and the *theoroi* who advertise panhellenic festivals are put up in the cities they visit by special officials called θεωροδόκοι.[39]

This portrayal is all the more conspicuous because it is not shared with Opora.[40] Why should such sexual imagery be singled out for Theoria? Is it just that Aristophanes needed only one sexually explicit scene, and the idea of representing Theoria as a voluptuous woman suggested itself, perhaps partly because relatively free sex was a traditional part of *paneguris*.[41] But I wonder whether the explicit sexual imagery is not simply gratuitous, but also serves the purpose of making a more serious point: *theoria*, in so far as it is an instrument which fosters contact among *poleis*, readily suggests the idea of sexual promiscuity; by contrast, the local harvest, symbolised as a monogamous wife, can be seen as analogous to healthy sex. There is a second contrast between the healthy intercourse between states that Theoria represents and its absence in wartime, which by contrast is linked to masturbation or perverted sex. Henderson notes that the progress of the play represents a movement from imagery based on excrement and perverted sex to imagery based on natural sex, and that this symbolises the movement from war to peace.[42] I would argue that the figure of Theoria in the play encapsulates these movements, representing peaceful political intercourse between Athens and other states through the powerful image of healthy, heterosexual sex.

---

[39] For Olympia, we have a fragment of a list of *thearodokoi*, and an unpublished decree for Elis from the mid-5th century provides that the two honorands τᾶν θε<α>ρίαν δέκεσαι ("will receive the sacred embassy"). IOlympia 36 = *Syll.* 171; IOlympia 3; unpublished decree: P. Perlman *The Theorodokia of the Peloponnese* (diss. Berkeley 1984) 30.

[40] Henderson (n.36) 66; the same point is made by Cassio (n.34) 48.

[41] Cf. the fragments from Aristophanes' *Skenas Katalambanousai* (fr. 494) and Heniochus mentioned above.

[42] Henderson (n.36) 64.

5. Death on a Pilgrimage: *Andromache* 1086–1163

The death of Neoptolemus at Delphi was a major theme in Greek mythology, and it was a theme in at least two Attic tragedies. One was the lost *Hermione* of Sophocles, which we know little about.[43] The other was Euripides' *Andromache*, the climax of which was a confrontation at Delphi between Neoptolemus and Orestes, the former the champion of Andromache, the latter the cousin and protector of Hermione. It is reported by a messenger who is a comrade of Neoptolemus, and is therefore partial to him.[44] The confrontation takes place when Neoptolemus goes to Delphi on a sacred mission in order to apologise to Apollo for an earlier visit in which he demanded reparation for Apollo's having killed Achilles (multiple visits to sanctuaries seem to be quite common; we recall that Xuthus had been to Delphi before in the *Ion*).

Neoptolemus and his friends begin with a little "sacred gazing" — three days of it, in fact (1086–7):

> τρεῖς μὲν φαεννὰς ἡλίου διεξόδους
> θέᾳ διδόντες ὅμματ' ἐξεπίμπλαμεν.

(Devoting three bright journeys of the sun to contemplation, we feasted our eyes.)

It seems remarkable that three whole days could have been spent in this way, but one has to remember the somewhat leisurely pace of Delphic tours as evidenced, for example, in Plutarch's *Delphic Dialogues*. This is sometimes taken to be 'sightseeing', but we do better to think of it as a sacred activity. In normal circumstances, it would be regarded as entirely innocent, but in this case it is a cause of suspicion (καὶ τοῦθ' ὕποπτον ἦν ἄρ', 1088). Rumours begin to circulate, spread by Orestes, that Neoptolemus has come to the sanctuary to sack it again. At this point, Neoptolemus goes to the temple to make sacrifice, offering to "pay the penalty" for his earlier attack. The crowd accuse him of lying. And when he goes up onto the platform of the temple to sacrifice, they erupt against him, among them Orestes. Neoptolemus then prays directly in view of the god (1117):

> χὠ μὲν κατ' ὅμμα στὰς προσεύχεται θεῷ.

(Standing in sight, he prays to the god.)

---

[43] On which see D. Sutton *The Lost Sophocles* (London 1984) 57–61.
[44] The slant of the messenger's speech is well analysed by I. de Jong *Narrative in Drama: the Art of the Euripidean Messenger Speech* (*Mnemosyne* Suppl. 116, Leiden 1991) 106–7.

The force of κατ' ὄμμα is surely that Neoptolemus prays in direct
view of Apollo, the culmination of the process of sacred contemplation
described earlier on.[45] Just at this point, the Delphians attack. Neo-
ptolemus is wounded, but he takes a weapon dedicated in the sanctuary,
and stands on the altar steps, a position which ought to have guaranted
him the protection due to a suppliant (mirroring the supplication of
Andromache at the altar of Thetis at the start of the play). He asks why
they attack him when he has come on a sacred journey (εὐσεβεῖς
ὁδοὺς ἥκοντα, 1125–6), but receives no answer and continues to en-
dure the onslaught of the crowd. Finally, he counterattacks, leaping
from the altar (by defending the altar, Neoptolemus plays the opposite
role to the one he played during his former visit to Delphi, when he was
the attacker, and for a moment he seems to impersonate Apollo). The
Delphians are driven along the "crowded exits" (στενοπόρους κατ'
ἐξόδους, 1143),[46] like doves before a hawk. But a mysterious voice
sounds forth from the temple, motivating the Delphians to regroup
(1147–8). The words that were spoken are not specified, but it is as if
these words represent the epiphany of the deity which is the culmi-
nation of the pilgrimage. Finally Neoptolemus is slain by an
anonymous Delphian, as he was in Pindar's account of the death of
Neoptolemus at Delphi in *Nemean* 7. The messenger speech ends with
a condemnation by the messenger of Apollo.[47]

This is a clever adaptation of the traditional story of the death of
Neoptolemus at Delphi. Other versions of the myth accounted for the
presence of the tomb of Neoptolemus there by asserting that he died at
Delphi for one of a number of reasons: (a) because he came to demand
satisfaction from Apollo for killing Achilles, and was killed by a priest,
or by the Delphians; or (b) because he came to sack the sanctuary for
some other reason, and was again killed by a priest, or by the
Delphians; or (c) that he died having got into a quarrel over sacrificial
meat (i.e. he was innocent, or at least not the only guilty party), either
(i) when he came to the sanctuary to bring Apollo first-fruits of the
victory at Troy, or (ii) when he came to the sanctuary to consult the
oracle about having children; to be distinguished from these is (d) the
story that Apollo killed him in revenge for killing Priam at the altar of

---

[45] It is usually taken as "in sight of the Delphians", as by P.T. Stevens *Euripides:
Andromache* (Oxford 1971) 228 (contrasted with the Delphians, who attack by
stealth); perhaps it means that as well.

[46] Bothersome στενοχωρία during a *paneguris* is also mentioned in Theocritus 15
(*Adoniazousae*); Epict. *Diss*. 1.6.26; Lucian *Herod*. 8.

[47] This seems to echo Thetis' condemnation of Apollo in Aeschylus fr. 350.

Zeus at Troy. This is found in Pindar *Paean* 6, mixed up with (cii).[48]
Pindar's evident embarrassment about the circumstances of the death in
Nemean 7 (whether or not this is an 'apology' for *Paean* 6) suggests
that the myth was the object of some disagreement in the fifth century.

Euripides ignores (b) and (d). He reconciles the other versions by
having two trips to Delphi (three, if one includes the third trip when the
dead body of Neoptolemus is carried back to Delphi).[49] For him,
Neoptolemus' first visit corresponds to (a); his second visit corresponds
roughly to (c), since there was a fight, though it was started by other
people and Neoptolemus had no responsibility for it. Furthermore, the
death is superimposed on the story of a family quarrel between the
Greek wife and the barbarian concubine of Neoptolemus, which seems
to distract attention from Apollo's role in the killing (though Apollo is
not excluded entirely). Euripides (or at least the messenger) seems to
have gone out of his way to represent Neoptolemus as a genuine
pilgrim, engaging for three days in sacred contemplation, and even
persisting in the role of a pious pilgrim after he has been attacked. This
is quite inconsistent with the representations of Neoptolemus found
elsewhere.

6. *Theoria* Perverted: Pentheus and the *Bacchae*

One of the subtlest deployments of the pilgrimage-theme in tragedy is
in Euripides' *Bacchae*. To begin with, the journey of Dionysus and the
Bacchants to Thebes can itself be thought of as a sort of pilgrimage to
inspect the sacred places of Thebes. But the most interesting pilgrimage
in the play is the one that Pentheus makes in the other direction, when
Dionysus leads him out of Thebes to spy on the Bacchants. Pilgrimage
was usually a peaceful and joyful activity (as in the *Peace*), but
Pentheus perverts it into something violent and voyeuristic, with
disastrous consequences for himself.

The second messenger speech begins by describing how Dionysus,
Pentheus and the messenger left Thebes to go and see the Bacchants,
and he describes Dionysus as "the conveyer of the sacred delegation"

---

[48] Version (a) = (1) in J. Fontenrose 'The cult and myth of Pyrrhos at Delphi' *UCPCA*
4.3 (1960) 191–266, 212; Apollodorus *Bibl.* 6.14; version (b) = (2) in Fontenrose;
Pausanias 10.7.1; Aristodemus in Σ Pi. *Nem.*7.103; version (c) = (3–4) in Fontenrose;
(i) = Pi. *Paean* 6.110–21; (ii) = Pherecydes *FGrH* 3F64a; version (d) = Pi. *Paean*
6.110–21. See also L. Woodbury 'Neoptolemus at Delphi: Pindar, *Nem.*7.30ff.'
Phoenix 33 (1979) 95–133; K. Ziegler *RE* 16.2 (1935) 2440–62 *s.v.* 'Neoptolemos
(1)'.

[49] Fontenrose (n.48) 213.

(πομπὸς τῆς θεωρίας, 1047).[50] This *theoria*, led by Dionysus, mirrors the other quasi-*theoria* of Bacchants that Dionysus has led to Thebes;[51] and in the prologue Dionysus presents himself as a sort of *theoros* who has come to view the site of his first birth at Thebes, although there is a twist to this in that for Dionysus his destination is also his point of origin. Relevant too is the idea of the *theoros* as one who announces a new festival (in this case a new religion). This balance is also reflected in language implying reciprocity such as: "the one seeing the other who sees".[52]

When they reach Cithaeron, they sit in strict silence "so that we would see without being seen", and indeed they do successfully observe the Bacchants, but not apparently Pentheus, who fails to see them, despite his desire to. So he asks if it might be possible for him to go up a tree (1058–62):

> Πενθεὺς δ᾽ ὁ τλήμων θῆλυν οὐχ ὁρῶν ὄχλον
> ἔλεξε τοιάδ᾽· ὦ ξέν᾽, οὗ μὲν ἔσταμεν,
> οὐκ ἐξικνοῦμαι μαινάδων ὄσσοις νόθων·
> ὄχθων δ᾽ ἔπ᾽, ἀμβὰς ἐς ἐλάτην ὑψαύχενα,
> ἴδοιμ᾽ ἂν ὀρθῶς μαινάδων αἰσχρουργίαν.

(Poor Pentheus, not seeing the female group, said: Stranger, where we are standing, I do not reach the bastard maenads with my eyes. But on the hills, if I went up a tree with a high neck, I would see rightly the obscene activity of the maenads!)

So Dionysus sets Pentheus on a fir-tree, where he can get a better view. Immediately, there follows a sort of reversal (1075):

> ὤφθη δὲ μᾶλλον ἢ κατεῖδε μαινάδας.

(He was seen rather than seeing the maenads.)

This is a supremely ironic moment: having gone out to a *theoria*,

---

[50] The phrase is well analysed by de Jong (n.44) 36, who suggests that we have to distinguish its meaning to the messenger (innocent 'mission') and its meaning to Euripides and the audience ('ritual procession'). The ritual aspects are dealt with by B. Seidensticker 'Sacrificial ritual in the Bacchae' in *Arktouros. Hellenic Studies Presented to B.M.W. Knox* (Berlin 1979) 181–90. You could say that θεωρία is ambiguous here, since it is not only a delegation to go and see the Bacchants, but in reality a 'show' (i.e. the destruction of Pentheus) which they will witness.

[51] On the parodos of the *Bacchae* see A.J. Festugière 'La signification religieuse de la Parodos des Bacchantes' *Eranos* 54 (1956) 72–86. I note Hesychius: θεωρίδες· αἱ περὶ τὸν Διόνυσον βάκχαι ("*Theorides*: the bacchants surrounding Dionysus").

[52] Compare Ovid *Her.* 21 (the second of a pair of truly theoric *Heroides*), where Cydippe says (103): *forsitan haec spectans a te spectabar, Aconti ...* ("perhaps as I was gazing upon these things [sc. the offerings in the sanctuary] I was gazed on by you, Acontius"), which refers clearly to the idea of theoric reciprocity.

Pentheus becomes an object of the gaze of other people.[53] After this, the mortal Dionysus disappears, and an invisible immortal Dionysus speaks from the sky, encouraging the Bacchants to attack Pentheus. In a sense this epiphany, and not the Bacchants, turns out to be the 'true' subject of the *theoria* (as Charles Segal suggests to me). But it is less than a true epiphany because Pentheus never sees the god Dionysus: he just hears his voice.

To look back on it, the *theoria* of Pentheus qualifies as another instance of 'theoric disaster', of the sort that we observed above *à propos* of the *Ion* and the *Andromache*, and in this case disaster seems to come about precisely by way of a transgression of the usual model of a *theoria*. There are at least three aspects to this transgression: first, Pentheus is viewing what he is not supposed to see; secondly, having come to see, Pentheus ends up being seen himself; and thirdly, whereas *theoriai* are supposed to be peaceful, this one is, as it were, a substitute for a violent attack, and it does indeed end in violence.[54]

Pentheus suffers from scopophilia, and the manner of his death is supposed to reflect this.[55] Pentheus' voyeurism comes out at two earlier points in *Bacchae* as well. When Pentheus has Dionysus in his power, he feasts his eyes on him aggressively (453–9). And in the first messenger speech, in a description of an orgy of violence which the Bacchants inflict on some Boeotian villages, which culminates in a description of the semi-ritual σπαραγμός of cattle, the messenger wants to convey the fact that the σπαραγμός took place very fast, and what he wants to say is "faster than someone could blink", but he expresses this by way of an apostrophe to Pentheus, and says: "faster than you could close the eyelids on your royal pupils" (θᾶσσον ... ἢ σὲ ξυνάψαι βλέφαρα βασιλείοις κόραις, 746–7); the ambiguity of κόραι inevitably suggests the inability of Pentheus to control the young women under his charge. It is as if while the messenger has been describing the

---

[53] The expedition of Pentheus is analysed in a different way (*pompe, agon, komos*) by H.P. Foley 'The masque of Dionysus' *TAPA* 110 (1980) 107–33, referring to R. Winnington-Ingram *Euripides and Dionysus* (Cambridge 1948) 24 n.3 (comparing it to a state mission to the Olympic games) and 128 n.2; see also H.P. Foley *Ritual Irony: Poetry and Sacrifice in Euripides* (Cornell 1985) 208–18.

[54] A good dicussion of some of these aspects can be found in C.P. Segal *Dionysiac Poetics and Euripides' Bacchae* (Princeton 1982) 204.

[55] Voyeurism in antiquity: W. Sale 'The psychoanalysis of Pentheus in the *Bacchae* of Euripides' *YCS* 22 (1972) 63–82, 71; J.P. Sullivan *The Satyricon of Petronius* (Indiana 1968) 238–45; R. Schmied 'The story of Aura (Nonnos, 'Dionysiaca' 48.238–978)' *Hermes* 121 (1993) 470–93, 'Appendix: Signs of Voyeurism in the 'Dionysiaca'' 480–83; modern study: D.M. Allen *The Fear of Looking or Scopophiliac-exhibitionistic Conflicts* (Virginia 1964).

ritual σπαραγμός, Pentheus has been staring with saucer eyes, trying to visualise the scene. Perhaps the eyes on the mask that the actor who played Pentheus wore were painted so as to seem particularly wide and bulging.

Pentheus' fatal gaze has two dimensions. On the one hand, 'looking' is an aggressive weapon in a psychic arsenal that also includes his tendencies to lock people up and to ridicule people, and his insecurity and paranoia. On the other hand, Pentheus' reliance on vision symbolises his exclusion from the 'community' of Dionysiac religion; he is an onlooker and nothing more. There is an intimate and subtle link between his role in the story — the fact that he is doomed to be victimised by Bacchants — and his tendency not to get involved but to observe and objectify. Pentheus' tendency to objectify is his tragedy, since the objectifier is impotent in the face of a challenge inspired by the force of shared ecstasy.

7. A Pilgrimage to the Origin of Tragedy: the *Antiope*

I end with a fragmentary tragedy. Euripides' *Antiope* was set at Eleutherae on the border between Attica and Boeotia, where there was a sanctuary of Dionysus, a sanctuary of great significance in the cult of Dionysus at Athens since it was from there that the cult was supposed to have been introduced by Pegasus, and it was to there and back again that the Athenians conveyed the statue of Dionysus before the Greater Dionysia.[56] No analysis of this play can now avoid Froma Zeitlin's recent suggestion that the play might have ended with the cult of Dionysus being symbolically transferred from Eleutherae to Athens.[57]

The identity of the chorus in this play remains problematic. A scholion on the *Hippolytus* reports that they were Thebans, but on the basis of a fragment of Pacuvius it has been concluded that they were probably men of Attica.[58] From fr. 1 they have been thought to be local visitors from over the border in Oenoe in north-eastern Attica, but they could easily come from Athens itself. Euripides is quite inventive about motivating the arrival of choruses in his later tragedies; in view of the relation between Eleutherae and the Greater Dionysia, perhaps these

---

[56] On the sanctuary A. Schachter *Cults of Boeotia* (*BICS* Suppl. 38.1, 1981) 1.174.

[57] F. Zeitlin 'Staging Dionysus between Thebes and Athens' in T.H. Carpenter & C.A. Faraone (eds.) *Masks of Dionysus* (Princeton 1991) 147–82, 181. In particular she suggests (n.69) that Amphion might go to Athens at the end of the play, providing the model for Eubulus fr.10 (cf. R. Hunter *ad loc.*).

[58] J. Kambitsis *L'Antiope d'Euripide: édition commentée et fragments* (Athens 1972) xiv n.2; Zeitlin (n.57) 180.

are men from Athens who have been instructed by an oracle to visit the shrine of Eleutherae. It is even possible that the context is a festival at Eleutherae, such as the one we hear of in a fragment of the historian Timagenes (*FGrH* 381F1).[59]

Besides the primary chorus of Athenians, it has been suggested on the basis of a summary of the play that survives in Hyginus that there was also a secondary chorus of Maenads who accompanied Dirce when she arrived at Eleutherae in the second half of the play. If they can be compared to pilgrims also (and they surely can), the *Antiope* would seem to be the only tragedy with two theoric choruses.[60]

The arrival of Dirce and her bacchants at the sanctuary is pivotal in the structure of the play: she discovers the fugitive Antiope and carries her off, which provokes the venegeance of Amphion and Zethus. Thus a contrast may be implied between two modes of interaction with the shrine: the peaceful men of Athens, who partake passively, and the violent women of Thebes, who disrupt the situation. A comparison suggests itself with the two pilgrimages of Neoptolemus in the *Andromache* (one violent, the other peaceful), and with the two contrasting pilgrimages in the *Ion* (Creusa's peaceful pilgrimage in the present, and Xuthus' more violent pilgrimage to the rite of Dionysus in the past).[61]

There is also a further point. I have already suggested that in view of the link between Eleutherae and the Athenian Dionysia, a visit there by Athenians provides a sort of aetiology for the ritual side of Athenian tragedy. But in the same way, it could be suggested that the visit there of Dirce and her Maenads and her violent death provides an aetiology for the thematic side of tragedy, with the Athenian chorus as the first audience.[62]

8. Conclusion

To conclude: pilgrimage is an important theme in Greek drama, both in Sicilian mime and Old Comedy, in Attic tragedy, particularly

---

[59] = Σ Eur. *Pho.* 159: the children of Niobe were killed on a pilgrimage to a πατρία θυσία there.

[60] One fragment survives which seems to bear directly on the experience of pilgrimage. In fr. XXXVII they or someone else reports seeing the στύλος of Dionysus there. It is impossible to guess who says it, but it could just as easily be the Athenian chorus as the Maenads. On the relation between Hyginus 8 and the Hellenistic hypothesis of the play, see W. Luppe 'Euripides-Hypotheseis in den Hygin-Fabeln Antiope und Ino?' *Philologus* 128 (1984) 41–59.

[61] The contrast between Athens and Thebes in the play is brought out well by Zeitlin (n.57).

[62] Zeitlin (n.57) 173–82.

Euripides, in satyr-drama, in Middle Comedy, and even in Hellenistic poetry. There is some reason to postulate a definite sub-genre of pilgrimage drama, a principal characteristic of which is that the *khoros* represent pilgrims. Use of the form varies from simple plots reenacting a pilgrimage to more complex adaptations of the sort we find in Aristophanes and Euripides. In the more complex treatments, there are two sides to the portrayal. On the one hand, it is represented as a pious and innocent activity (*Peace, Andromache, Ion*). The exception is the *Bacchae*, where the *theoria* of Pentheus is a perverted form (his repressed voyeurism forms a stark contrast with the healthy sexuality represented by Theoria in *Peace*). *Antiope* may have presented a more complex picture. At the same time, pilgrims are represented as vulnerable, particularly at the hands of the gods whose sanctuaries they visit, so that the pilgrimage culminates not in a vision of the deity but in the ritually framed death of the pilgrim. It is from this stark juxtaposition of innocent intention and god-sent destruction that the pilgrimage-narratives which we have been looking at derive their power.

Appendix:
Theoria and Human Sacrifice: the *Erechtheus*

In the fragmentary *Erechtheus*, when Athens is threatened by the Thracian army led by Eumolpus, King Erechtheus is ordered by the oracle of Delphian Apollo to sacrifice his daughter in order to ensure a military victory. He obeys. Some of her sisters subsequently commit suicide, later to be worshipped as the *Huakinthides* (thus the motif 'life of girl given to ensure military victory' is doubled in this play). According to one testimonium, there was a scene in which Praxithea, the mother of the victim, led her daughter out to the altar to be sacrificed "as if she was sending her to a *theoria*":[63]

λέγεται γὰρ Ἐρεχθεὺς μὲν ἐν τῷ πρὸς Εὔμολπον τούτῳ πολέμῳ τὴν θυγατέρα ὑπὲρ τῆς πόλεως ἐπιδοῦναι, τοῦ θεοῦ χρήσαντος, προσαγαγεῖν δ᾽ αὐτὴν κοσμήσασα ἡ μήτηρ ὥσπερ εἰς θεωρίαν πέμπουσα.

(Erechtheus is said to have given up his daughter for the sake of the city in the war against Eumolpus, following the oracle of a god, and her mother is said to have led her forward, having adorned her, as if

---

[63] Aristides 1.87 = C. Austin *Nova fragmenta Euripidis in papyris reperta* (Berlin 1968) 22. It is test. 3 in P. Carrara *Euripide: Eretteo* (Florence 1977) 38; see also Carrara 33 n.39. The attribution to Euripides is not certain, but it must be likely in view of the celebrity of his version of the myth. The passage is discussed also in A. Martínez Díez 'Reconstrucción del «Erecteo» de Eurípides' *Emerita* 43 (1975) 207–39, 231.

she was sending her to a *theoria*.)

The word *theoria* here seems to mean a spectacle, a festival of the sort to which people would come as pilgrims to watch (*theoroi*). The word can be used for local festivals, but it would more usually mean one happening some distance away. Maybe the site of the purported festival coincided with the place of sacrifice, but it is also possible that the sacrifice took place at the starting point of what was to be a longer journey (*theoroi* in fact seem to have sacrificed upon setting out).[64] If the place of the festival is some distance away, which was it? The most likely candidate might seem to be Eleusis, which is traditionally linked to the conflict between Erechtheus and Eumolpus, although the festival there presumably postdates the conflict.[65] Alternatively, in view of the fact that the pilgrim is a young girl, the sanctuary of Artemis at Brauron might be an appropriate destination. Praxithea presumably arrayed her daughter in some special garb. If it was a general *theoria*, this might have been a wreath;[66] if the context was the Brauronia at Brauron, then maybe the girl wore the saffron dress used in that festival (allusion to that dress has been detected in Aeschylus' description of Iphigeneia's saffron dress which falls away when she is sacrificed, at *Agamemnon* 239).[67]

There is a rich irony here. For one thing, joyful festival contrasts with death (and on another level 'seeing' contrasts with the darkness and blindness that death is naturally linked with). We find a similar semantic contrast in *Suppliants* 97, where Theseus confronts the mourning women relatives of the Seven who have sought supplication at the sanctuary of Demeter at Eleusis and observes their "shorn hair" and their clothes which are "not those of θεωροί" (... πεπλώματ᾽ οὐ

---

[64] Thuc. 6.3.1 tells us that when *theoroi* set out from Sicily they offered sacrifice on the altar of Apollo Archagetes at Naxos in Sicily.

[65] C. Collard, M.J. Cropp, K.H. Lee *Euripides: Selected Fragmentary Plays* vol. 1 (Warminster 1995) 152–3.

[66] Crowns: M. Blech *Studien zum Kranz bei den Griechen* (Berlin 1982) 366, citing Σ Ar. *Wealth* 21; also Eur. *Hipp.* 806–7, *Suppl.* 97 (see below). Other suggestions: M.P.J. Dillon 'The didactic nature of the Epidaurian *Iamata*' *ZPE* 101 (1994) 239–60, 246. The elaborate description of the *theoria* of the Aenianes to Delphi in Heliodorus (2.34) suggests that there might have been a tendency toward the colour white (suggesting ritual purity?).

[67] Argued by C. Sourvinou-Inwood 'Aristophanes, *Lysistrata* 641–7' *CQ* 21 (1971) 339–42, *ead. Studies in Girls' Transitions: Aspects of the Arkteia and Age Representation in Attic Iconography* (Athens 1988) 119–24, on the basis of Ar. *Lys.* 645. For the iconography see L. Kahil 'Autour de l'Artémis Attique' *AK* 8 (1965) 20–33, and 'L'Artémis de Brauron. Rites et Mystère' *AK* 20 (1977) 86–98.

θεωρικά).[68] It is incidentally this parallel which makes it likely that the word θεωρίαν comes from the *Erechtheus*. Another level of irony is that the role of a spectator implied in the word θεωρίαν contrasts with the role of a victim (to put it another way, instead of watching a spectacle, she becomes a spectacle for others). And yet a third level of complexity is implied by the breaking of the convention that *theoria* was a primary sign of peacetime relations between states, and in no way a wartime phenomenon (as we saw above in §4). Finally, another level of meaning may be that for the daughter of Erechtheus to be represented as going to a *theoria* anticipates the fact that she and her suicide-sisters were to be commemorated with a festival, for which the story of the play supplies the aetiology (fr. 65.73–80).[69]

It seems likely from what we know of Praxithea's attitude elsewhere in the play that she knew all along that the daughter was going off to be sacrificed (fr. 50), and sent her off in full knowledge that this was no usual *theoria*. The daughter's attitude is uncertain. Perhaps she was ignorant of her fate (that would make for an effective contrast with the mother's resolution), or maybe she knew as well, or found out as the play progressed. She may have played along with the illusion that she is going on a *theoria*, as some tragic heroines self-consciously re-present their death as a marriage: for example, Sophocles' Antigone (*Antigone* 816), and Euripides' Evadne (*Suppliants* 980–89).[70] She could have talked in figurative language about a pilgrimage to the land of the dead, there being a strong thematic link between 'pilgrimage' and 'death'.[71] At any rate, there would be a parallel with the *Iphigeneia at Aulis*, in which Iphigeneia believes that she is going to Aulis to be married, but ends up a willing participant in a human sacrifice. This pattern is related to the idea of the innocence of pilgrimage, as we see it in the Delphi-scene in the *Andromache*, except that there the contrast is

---

[68] C. Collard *Euripides: Supplices* (Groningen 1975) *ad loc.* is helpful. In one sense, the suppliants in this play are truly *theoroi*, because they are representatives of Argos who have come to a sanctuary (one spatially intermediate between Argos, Thebes and Athens), though with the non-typical purpose of supplication. Another example of a contrast between *theoria* and grief is Soph. *OT* 1491, where Oedipus laments that his daughters will return weeping from festivals ἀντὶ τῆς θεωρίας ("instead of sight-seeing").

[69] The evidence for the cult of the *Huakinthides* is well surveyed by E. Kearns *The Heroes of Attica* (*BICS* Suppl. 57, 1989) 201–2.

[70] The relationship between marriage and death in tragedy is well covered by R. Seaford 'The tragic wedding' *JHS* 107 (1987) 106–30. The dramatic context of the fragment is discussed by J. Schmidt *Freiwilliger Opfertod bei Euripides* (Giessen 1921) 67.

[71] To take one example from many, in the *Septem* Aeschylus describes Charon's bark as a μελάγκροκος θεωρίς (857), implying that it is like a ship used to transport *theoroi*.

between Neoptolemus' motivation and the way the Delphians treat him, whereas in the *Erechtheus* the contrast is between the real nature of the ritual act that is to be performed and the euphemistic representation of it.

PAPERS OF THE LEEDS INTERNATIONAL LATIN SEMINAR   TENTH VOLUME (1998) 157–68
Published by Francis Cairns (Publications) Ltd (Leeds 1998). ARCA 38. ISBN 0 905205 95 2

WINE RITUALS, MAENADS AND DIONYSIAN FIRE

C. ANNE WILSON
University of Leeds

Callimachus and Euphorion both said that the Titans, having torn apart the limbs of Dionysus, threw them into a λέβης and gave it to his brother Apollo who stored it away near the tripod. Euphorion added: ἐν πυρὶ Βάκχον δῖον ὑπὲρ φιάλην ἐβάλοντο (fr. 13 Powell), and I have suggested that the verse could be read: "On the fire they threw a φιάλη over godly Bacchus."[1] Here I shall discuss further the implication of the φιάλη for Dionysus rituals at Delphi, and then consider rituals elsewhere in Greece in classical times which could have relied on a similar usage of wine.

Φιάλη was a name for a stillhead, and if Euphorion's verse implies that Bacchus was 'on the fire', then it hints at distilling as a cultic ritual. Even though the verse itself is not immediately clear,[2] the context nevertheless links the word φιάλην (present in all the manuscripts)

---

[1]   Tzetzes *In Lycophronis Alexandram* 208 = Callimachus fr. 643 Pf.; Euphorion fr. 13 Powell (= 15 Meinecke, 12 Scheidweiler, 13 de Cuenca, 14 van Groningen). Discussed in C.A. Wilson 'Dionysian ritual objects in Euphorion and Nonnus' *PLLS* 7 (1993) 213–19, with evidence for the use of the distillate of wine in initiation rites by some gnostic sects and for φιάλη as a stillhead.

[2]   Wilson (n.1) 216–17. There are variants in some words, but ὑπέρ and φιάλην are in all the mss. I have suggested that by poetic hyperbaton ὑπέρ should govern Βάκχον. B.A. van Groningen *Euphorion* (Amsterdam 1977) 39–40 argued that to throw B. over a φιάλη on the fire made no sense, so he divided the verse between two lines and followed O. Müller in changing ὑπὲρ φιάλην to ὑπερφιάλοι ('overweening', of the Titans). But he admitted that his amended text still did not carry the meaning that the Titans boiled B. on the fire, as other ancient authors hinted, and furthermore there is no known myth in which the Titans threw B. directly into a fire. Van Groningen therefore concluded that we no longer know what Euphorion said here; but I believe my reading can supply a viable solution to the problem.

with Dionysus' limbs, resting in a λέβης near the omphalos at Delphi. There was a tomb of Dionysus at Delphi which was seen by Philochorus;[3] and Plutarch (De Iside et Osiride 365A) confirmed that the Hosioi held a secret sacrifice there "when the Thyiades awaken Dionysus Liknites". The trieteric awakening and its secret ritual took place in early November, when Apollo departed to visit the Hyperboreans, and Dionysus was roused to deputise for him at Delphi during the winter months.

Apollo's departure was annual, and in the November of the intervening year Dionysus came in the guise of Chthonius (Orphei Hymni 53.1–4 Quandt). On Apollo's return in the following March, Dionysus left Delphi to spend some months sleeping in the halls of Persephone; his tomb may have been regarded as his entry-point to the underworld. In March the wine from the previous year's vintage would have been at its best and most alcoholic, and the ideal time to distil it would have been just before the departure of Dionysus, while he was still at Delphi to ensure through his presence and power a good outcome for the operation.[4] If the tomb was a small underground chamber sealed above by a flagstone or βάθρον, it would have been a suitable place in which to store the distillate within a container over the summer months, to await the moment for the rebirth of Dionysus Liknites in the following November.

The two-year cycle of the trieteris recognized the two distinct functions of Dionysus, which he carried out in his two separate guises.

---

[3]   Philochorus, reported by Dinarchus of Delos, F. Jacoby FGrH 328 F7. He said: "The σωρός is believed to be a certain βάθρον on which is written, 'Here lies dead Dionysus, son of Semele'." See ps.-Clement Recog. 10.24 for a tomb of Dionysus at Thebes.

[4]   The object of distilling was to concentrate the fire in the wine, so it was important to operate on wine with a high alcohol content, i.e. wine which had already undergone considerable secondary fermentation. Alcohol boils at a temperature of 78°C, well below the boiling point of water. When wine is heated slowly in a vessel with a stillhead fitted over its mouth, the amount of water vapour coming off in the early stages is quite low in proportion to the amount of alcohol. A.R. Butler and J. Needham 'An experimental comparison of the East Asian, Hellenistic and Indian (Gandhāran) stills in relation to the distillation of ethanol and acetic acid' Ambix 27 (1980) 71–2, found that 50 ml of a weak solution (7.5%) of alcohol (ethanol) in water yielded an eightfold increase in alcohol to 60% in the first 5 ml of distillate; but thereafter the proportion of alcohol fell sharply. For a strong solution (46%) the alcohol content was 83% in the first 5 ml graduating down to 75% in the fifth 5 ml, i.e. after 25 ml had been distilled, but for the seventh 5 ml, it dropped to 24%. In both cases the still was equipped with a modern reconstruction of the 'Hellenistic' (μαστάριον) stillhead comprising a breast-shaped cup with inturned rim to collect the condensed vapour, and an outlet tube extending from the rim to carry the liquid into the receiving flask.

In the first winter after his rebirth as Liknites he brought the life back to the vines, departing only after their flowerbuds had begun to show. The following autumn the grapes had already been harvested, and the wine-must had undergone primary fermentation when Dionysus arrived as Chthonius. This time his role was to bring life or 'fire' into the wine. The winter dancing of the maenads on Mount Parnassus may have been perceived as helping to increase the πνεῦμα containing the fire within the maturing wine. It is likely that the initiations of the Thyiades took place in the Korykian cave (cave of the leather bag or wineskin) towards the end of the winter while Dionysus Chthonius was still present. Maenadic initiation guaranteed a close relationship between the initiate and the god not only in this life but also in the chthonic afterlife.

Grapes ripened and wine was made every year, of course, and it was possible to celebrate appropriate stages of the cycle with a series of annual Dionysus festivals, as happened at Athens. What led to the trieteric celebration of Dionysus in northern Greece was the need to intercalate an extra period of time to allow for the god's 'death' and subsequent return to life. At Delphi his 'death' did not take place in the autumn (at the time of the death of the grapes in the winepress), but in spring after he had brought the new wine to its full maturity,[5] and when his rebirth was celebrated he had already been absent for several months during the reign of Apollo. Euphorion's additional verse about Dionysus and the φιάλη could refer to the moment of the secret ritual at the end of the winter when the wine was heated in a vessel with a φιάλη fixed over its mouth (in fact a succession of such cups would have been necessary in the earliest days of wine-distilling, to be succeeded in due course by the single stillhead with an outlet tube). Thereafter a sealed container holding some of the distillate would have been laid to rest in the tomb near the omphalos to await the trieteric

---

[5] The wine of the previous vintage may have been broached at Delphi only a short time before the departure or death of Dionysus. At Athens it was not drunk before the Anthesteria in late February, and that festival too had connections with death. The day of the first drinking of the wine commemorated either Orestes' arrival at Athens as a suppliant after he had murdered his mother, or, according to another tradition, the slaughter of the group of Aetolians who first brought wine to Attica. On the following day young girls swung on swings in commemoration of Erigone, daughter of the mythical wine-bringer Icarius, who hanged herself from a tree after the drunken recipients of the wine had killed her father; and on this day sacrifices were made to chthonic Hermes. The symbolic marriage of Dionysus and the basilinna, however, on the evening between the two days, looked forward, for the ceremony was intended to ensure fertility for the vines in the coming season. See W. Burkert *Homo Necans* (Berkeley 1985) 216–17.

epiphany of Dionysus (Diodorus 4.3) which would have been achieved by flaming the distillate.

The alcohol-rich distillate may also have had a role in the initiation ceremonies of the Thyiades and of other maenads in northern Greece; the gnostics who took over the practice of ritual wine-distilling initiated neophytes by flaming the distillate on their heads.[6] But at the 'awakening' of Dionysus Liknites at Delphi, the alcohol may have been ignited on the head of an image or mask of the god. Before dismissing this as simple trickery, we should bear in mind that Dionysus was wine itself in the view of the early Greeks (cf. Euripides *Bacchae* 284f., *Cyclops* 519–29); more specifically, he was the life of the wine which was its fire.[7] The distilling operation was not an easy one to bring off, for a number of reasons, so its favourable outcome was proof of both the support and the presence of the god.

While the evidence from Euphorion's φιάλη and Dionysus' tomb at Delphi is suggestive, it certainly falls short of absolute proof. But if it is examined alongside other circumstantial evidence within the Dionysus cult and elsewhere, a scenario begins to emerge in which the distilled spirits of wine could have played a central part in Dionysian cultic practice.

A related phenomenon appears to have taken place each year at the Eleusinian Mysteries when a boy was initiated 'from the hearth'. M.P. Nilsson discussed a relief of a seated female figure with a woman and a man standing nearby while the woman holds a lighted torch close to a child cowering between them; and he thought it referred to a ritual at the Eleusinian Mysteries linked to the myth of Demeter and Demophoon.[8] W. Burkert identified the scene as the child being initiated from the hearth at the Mysteries.[9] If the boy's hair or clothing had

---

[6] C.A. Wilson 'Philosophers, Iosis and Water of Life' *Proceedings of the Leeds Philosophical and Literary Society,* Literary and Historical Section 19.5 (1984) 46-68.

[7] Dionysus was closely associated with fire both in literature and on vase-paintings. He is seen emerging from Zeus' thigh with a torch in either hand, with the inscription above Διὸς φῶς 'Light of Zeus' on a late sixth-century painting, *CV* France 10, Bib. Nat. 2, Cabinet des Médailles 219 pl.75.6–7 and 76.2–3; Beazley *ABV* 509 no.20. Pind. fr. 153 Snell–Maehler calls Dionysus φέγγος ὀπώρας; Soph. *Ant.* 1146–8 calls him leader of the fire-breathing stars. For fire in Euripides' *Bacchae* see n.16.

[8] M.P. Nilsson 'Das eleusinische Relief aus der Sammlung Este', *Opuscula selecta* II (Lund 1952) 624–7.

[9] Burkert (n.5) 281. At 281 n.34 he connects this initiation with the 'fire magic' of the recipe in ps.-Hippolytus *Ref.* 4.31. This recipe was identified as a formula for the distillation of wine by H. Diels *Die Entdeckung des Alkohols* (Abhandlungen preuss. Akad. Wiss.; phil.-hist. Kl. 3, 1913) 21–5, 35.

really been set alight, the result could have been a fatal accident. But distilled spirits of wine will burn away safely and completely on hair or cloth if the alcohol content is reduced to 35%.[10] It is therefore quite possible that the initiation was carried out by means of distilled wine poured on the boy's head and ignited by the torch. The new initiate could have represented Demus or even Iacchus (who would have provided a Bacchic link).

Further hints at the early ritual usage of distilled wine may be discerned where the idea of initiation is associated with the 'boiling' of the initiate. 'To boil' (ἕψειν) was the verb used to indicate distilling in the recipe at ps.-Hippolytus *Refutationes* 4.31, first identified by H. Diels, and it was used with the same meaning in some of the protochemical recipes edited by M. Berthelot.[11] The confusion between the 'boiling' of the initiate and the 'boiling' of the wine stems from the legends of Medea who 'boiled' Aison to make him young again, as recorded in the *Nostoi*.[12]

At Aristophanes *Equites* 1321 Demus is boiled 'to make him young'. But Plato hinted that the boiling motif represented an initiation in his simile of Corybantic initiation for initiation into new knowledge at *Euthydemus* 277D, later followed at 285C by the simile of submitting 'as to the Colchian' to being destroyed and boiled, so as to be reborn as a good man with true knowledge. In recent times A.B. Cook and F.M. Cornford recognized the boiling as "a rite of regeneration or resurrection, which has an established place in the cycle of Dionysiac ritual", though they linked it with the mystic phrase 'A kid I have fallen into the milk' from the gold tablets.[13] But a more direct ancient

[10] H. Degering 'Ein Alkoholrezept aus dem 8. Jahrhundert' *Sitzungsber. Preuss. Akad. Wiss., phil.-hist. Kl.* (1917) 513. This can be achieved by plunging lighted sulphur into the distillate; it will extinguish itself at 35% alcohol. The discovery of this property of sulphur was made at an early but unkown date. Probably sulphur was first added experimentally to a distillate containing a low proportion of alcohol with a view to increasing its fire content; but the sulphur would have been extinguished without affecting the alcohol content. When plunged into a more alcoholic distillate the sulphur would have burned for a time, extinguishing itself when the alcohol content reached 35%; the action may well have been wrongly interpreted as increasing the fire in the distillate. Eventually chance spillage of distillate so treated upon clothing or hair in the vicinity of a naked flame would have revealed the safe-burning fire, and led to its use in Dionysian rituals. The addition of sulphur is recommended in the recipe in ps.-Hippolytus *Ref.* 4.31, to make the distillate 'do better'.
[11] M. Berthelot *Collection des anciens alchimistes grecs* (Paris 1887–8) II.3.47.7 etc.
[12] M. Davies *Epicorum graecorum fragmenta* (Göttingen 1988) 68–9, *Nosti* F6.
[13] F.M. Cornford *The Origin of Attic Comedy* (London 1914) 88–9; A.B. Cook *Zeus* (Cambridge 1914) I.627.

162   C. ANNE WILSON

connection can be found in the hypothesis to Euripides' *Medea*, which
refers to the boiling by Medea of Jason, as well as Aison, and quotes
the Aison passage from the *Nostoi*, then continues: "But Aeschylus in
Trophoi relates that she (Medea) boiled the nurses of Dionysus and
their men, and made them young." It thus associates the boiling not
only with Medea but also with the maenads.

We do not know of any myth on the subject on which Aeschylus
could have based his satyr play (now lost), so we can consider the
possibility that he combined something he had heard about actual cultic
practices of north-eastern maenads with a well-known activity of the
mythical Medea. He may himself have visited Thrace as a member of
the Eion expedition of 476–5;[14] but he could also have picked up the
information that 'boiling' was somehow connected with northern
maenads by hearsay from the Athenian soldiers on their return from the
campaign. So this source, too, carries the suggestion of a northern
maenadic initiation in the fifth century based on the 'boiling', i.e.
distilling of wine.

The dramatist who was certainly able to observe northern maenadic
customs was Euripides, who wrote *Bacchae* about 408–7 BC at the
court of King Archelaus, perhaps with a view to performance in a
theatre at Dion or Pella.[15] In the play fire appears on several occasions
as a sign of Dionysus' imminent presence and power.[16] Only once is it
in direct contact with maenads, when they carry fire on their hair but it
does not burn them at *Bacchae* 757–8.

The interpretation of *Bacchae* 755–8 has caused problems, not least
because of the difficulty of establishing the identity of the bronze and
iron at 757. The passage runs:

> ὅποσα δ' ἐπ' ὤμοις ἔθεσαν, οὐ δεσμῶν ὕπο   755
> προσείχετ', οὐδ' ἔπιπτεν ἐς μέλαν πέδον
> οὐ χαλκός, οὐ σίδηρος· ἐπὶ δὲ βοστρύχοις
> πῦρ ἔφερον, οὐδ' ἔκαιεν.

In the past most scholars have taken the two metals thus coupled to

---

[14] M.L. West *Studies in Aeschylus* (Stuttgart 1990) 49.
[15] E.R. Dodds (ed.) *Euripides, Bacchae*² (Oxford 1960) xxxix for Archelaus building a
new theatre at Dion; E.N. Borza *In the Shadow of Olympus* (Princeton 1990) 168, 170,
173 on Pella as the likely site of a theatre, and on the possibility that Euripides wrote
Ba. at Pella.
[16] Fire in various forms signals Dionysus' imminent presence at *Ba.* 523–4, 596–9, 622–
4, 631, 757–8, 1082–3. He is addressed as 'Greatest Light' at 608. For discussion of
the fire phenomena in the context of the ritual elements in *Ba.* see R. Seaford
'Dionysiac drama and Dionysiac mysteries' *CQ* n.s. 31 (1981) 256–8.

mean weapons, and have assumed a lacuna after 756.[17] J. Jackson in 1955 suggested a more complex reworking of the text, transferring οὐ χαλκός, οὐ σίδηρος to follow 761, and deleting ἐς μέλαν πέδον.[18] His version has become more widely accepted since, and has now been printed as an emendation within the text of the OCT edition by J. Diggle (1994). But Jackson himself admitted that there was "a decided element of speculation" in his solution to the problem, and said that sooner or later an account would have to be rendered for 755–8 as transmitted. Here I would like to make a new suggestion as to the meaning of 'bronze' and 'iron' which would keep the text intact.

It is appropriate to mention first another alternative interpretation, originally put forward by a pupil of Wilamowitz, which identifies bronze and iron as a term for household utensils. It has been rejected by most critics, but was accepted by J. Roux.[19] She went even further and suggested that the flames upon the maenads' curls came from braziers plundered along with the metal pots and pans from the villagers' homes, and carried on the women's shoulders. As an analogy she gave many examples, both ancient and modern, of those who walk on fire without damage to their feet.[20] But firewalking is a totally different experience,[21] and the flames from lighted braziers would have soon burnt up the maenads' hair. The other main objection — that maenads who had escaped from their own domestic pots and pans would not be looking for others as booty — is also valid.[22] The maenads fell upon the two villages as destructive enemies turning everything upside down (752–4), not as plunderers; and their only 'booty' was the children.

My own thesis is that the bronze and iron are objects for ritual use

---

[17] Dodds (n.15) suggested the lacuna was once filled by a line on the theme 'Nothing resisted their assault, not bolted doors, not bronze, not iron'. More complex suggestions were made by some earlier critics.

[18] J. Jackson *Marginalia Scaenica* (OUP, London 1955) 17–20. Rejected by Dodds (n.15) 169 *ad loc.* as "too complicated to be very convincing".

[19] Against: Dodds (n.15) 169; Jackson (n.18) 19; H. Oranje *Euripides' Bacchae: the Play and its Audience* (Mnem. suppl. 78, 1984) 183. Supported by J. Roux 'Pillage en Béotie' *REG* 76 (1963) 34–8, and her edition of *Euripide: Les Bacchantes* 2 vols (Paris 1970–72) 482–3.

[20] *Bacchantes* (n.19) 483–4.

[21] For recent firewalking practices in northern Greece and the United States see L. Danforth *Firewalking and Religious Ritual* (Princeton 1989). A group of British scientists who demonstrated firewalking on the BBC 1 television programme *Q.E.D.* on 2 April 1986 deduced correctly that "each sole could probably take two or three seconds without getting singed", according to a review by J. Barnes in *The Observer*, 6 April 1986, p.30.

[22] Oranje (n.19) 183.

carried by maenads which must not be allowed to fall to the ground. The terminology is unexpected, but it must be remembered that in Orphic cult both things and deities were liable to be named in a riddling fashion by names other than their usual ones, as is clear from the Derveni papyrus.[23]

Against this thesis it may be argued that Nonnus did not interpret Euripides' verses thus. He must have had the same text as ours, at least as far as the middle of 756, and he read ὅποσα at 755 as referring back to the τέκνα in 754, for he expanded this version at *Dionysiaca* 45.294-7. But Nonnus lived at a time when the pagan cults had all but disappeared, and he did not always understand terms in earlier literature which denoted Dionysian ritual objects, as is apparent from *Dionysiaca* 9.125-6.[24] Long before Nonnus two or three vase-painters at Athens may have made the same inference about the children.[25] They too would have lacked the local cultic background and the knowledge of Macedonian maenadic terminology which Euripides could have expected in the audience for whom he wrote *Bacchae*. As for Nonnus, he also knew the second part of *Bacchae* 757 and the beginning of 758, since he introduced a maenad with flaming hair skimming across the water at *Dionysiaca* 43.656-7. My suspicion is that he simply took the images he wanted from *Bacchae* 755-8 and ignored the bronze and iron.

Of the two different metal objects carried by maenads I would identify the 'bronze' as a stillhead, sometimes called 'the bronze' in the protochemical texts, and sometimes φιάλη.[26] Other evidence for its use for the distillation of wine and for the flaming of the distillate as an initiation rite has already been discussed; and Euripides' phrase about maenads carrying flames on their heads which do not burn up their hair follows immediately his mention of the 'bronze' and is highly suggestive, even though at *Bacchae* 755-8 the maenads had already rushed away from their mountain glen and their secret rites. The safely burning flames signal the presence of Dionysus nonetheless, now supporting his maenads in their violent reaction to the spying herdsmen; and the inclusion of the bronze suggests that Euripides could have been aware of

---

[23] Provisional text edited by R. Merkelbach, *ZPE* 47 (1982) following 300.

[24] Wilson (n.1) 215-17.

[25] Dodds (n.15) 168 for a krater in Bologna showing a baby sitting astride a maenad's shoulders, and a pyxis by the Meidias painter in the British Museum showing a maenad with a child slung by the leg over her shoulder.

[26] τὸ χαλκεῖον: Berthelot (n.11) II.3.47.5; 3.50.1. φιάλη (illustration): Berthelot I.132.

some connection between that piece of equipment and the magic fire. Euripides cannot have been totally ignorant of contemporary maenadic cultic customs in Macedonia. The thiasus in the mountains as described in *Bacchae* is an all-female affair, and that could mirror local practice.[27] But Macedonian men must have had some ideas about what went on there, either through the filtering of information from an indiscreet maenadic wife, or through the occasional night-time foray by a curious male who, having spied on the women, escaped unnoticed under cover of darkness. (Euripides' spying herdsman is surely based on such a real-life figure, transferred into the revealing light of dawn.) Thus Euripides could have heard of the connection between maenadic bronze and fire, even though he had little idea as to how the fire was produced.

The iron at *Bacchae* 757 is, I suggest, the short sword carried by some maenads on the oreibasia, so they could begin their rites by sacrificing a small or young animal to Dionysus.[28] That this maenadic activity was one recognized at Athens is shown by an illustration on a late fifth-century pyxis. The painting, which may be based on a lost Pentheus play, shows the king about to leave his palace (he stands between two columns). The maenads bearing various ritual objects are outside, already on their way, and two of them carry a fawn upside down. The maenad who grasps the inner rear leg of the fawn with her left hand has a short sword in her right, ready to use in the forthcoming sacrifice of the animal.[29]

Vase-paintings showing maenads with swords began to be made around 470 BC, probably about the time when dramatists first put sword-bearing maenads into plays. An early example is the painting on a pelike dated by Beazley between 470 and 450 which shows a maenad

---

[27] Cf. Livy 39.13.8: *primo sacrarium id feminarum fuisse, nec quemquam eo virum admitti solitum.*

[28] Aesch. *Eum.* 25–6 said Pentheus had been killed 'in the manner of a hare'. For sacrifice of an animal at the beginning of all religious ceremonies see Burkert (n.5) 35–44, esp. 44.

[29] Heidelberg pyxis: F. Brommer *Vasenlisten zur griechischen Heldensage* (3rd edn, Marburg 1973) 485 B6; H. Philippart 'Iconographie des Bacchantes d'Euripide' *RBPh.* 9 (1930) 51 n.132; L. Curtius 'Pentheus' *88. Winkelmannsprogramm* (Berlin 1929) 2–4 Abb.2–6; J.R. March 'Euripides' Bakchai: a reconsideration in the light of vase-paintings' *BICS* 36 (1989) pl.1A and B. Cf. Munich 3267, Lucanian kalpis of the first half of the fourth century showing an armed male figure crouching between two trees where he waits to ambush the maenads; they dance unawares, and one maenad carries a sword, Brommer 486 D8; Philippart 54 n.137; Curtius 11 Ab.14; March pl.1C and D.

with a short sword in her right hand and the severed hind leg of a kid in her left, dancing to the music of a flute-player. He suggested that it illustrated an activity described in a lost play.[30]

Another lost play, one covering parts of the Lycurgus myth, appears to have inspired a late fifth-century Attic hydria showing Lycurgus holding a double-axe above his son while several maenads dance. One holds the severed head of the son in her right hand and a short sword in her left, and another has a sword in her right hand and a hare in her left.[31] The Lycurgus scene suggests a northern provenance for the sword-bearing maenads; and the date of the earlier painting above makes it possible that motif reached Athens as another piece of cultic information from the Thracian region brought back after the Eion campaign.

Much later Callixeinus in his report of Ptolemy II's Grand Procession at Alexandria wrote (Athenaeus *Deipnosophistae* 195b) of "Macedonian women called Mimallones, Bassarai and Lydai", some of them bearing short swords (ἐγχειρίδια) in their hands and others snakes. This statement would guarantee the cultic nature of sword-carrying by northern maenads if the women were a visiting thiasus from Macedonia, the family homeland of the Ptolemies. But several of the scenes in the Procession contained mythic figures, so although the Macedonian maenads there would be a useful indicator for the carrying of swords as cultic ritual objects, they cannot be accepted beyond doubt.[32]

Before we consider the importance of the bronze and iron at *Bacchae* 757, demonstrated by the fact that they are not permitted to fall 'to the black earth', we should return to the question of cultic swords and sacrifice in some earlier Pentheus plays. Two vase-

[30] Berlin 3223, *ARV²* 586.47. For date, J.D. Beazley 'Hydria-fragments in Corinth' *Hesperia* 24 (1955) 312, 309.

[31] Villa Giulia hydria: *ARV²* 1343; G. Cultrera 'Hydria' *Opera d'Arte* (1938) 5–9 and pl.1–3; K. Deichgräber 'Die Lykurgie des Aischylos' *NGG* 3.8 (1939) Taf. 7, Abb.8a and b.

[32] E.E. Rice *The Grand Procession of Ptolemy Philadelphus* (Oxford 1983) 61–2 claimed that it is "impossible to know if they are true Macedonians" or whether the name Μακέται was used more widely to denote other female worshippers of Dionysus because of the well known connection between D. and maenads in the Macedonian region. They could, of course, be 'literary maenads' based on *Ba.* itself: the snakes (*Ba.* 767–8); the swords (*Ba.* 757). We cannot tell whether bronze φιάλαι appeared in the Procession, as Callixeinus described only those things which were silver or gold (Athen. 201F). For trieteric Dionysus delighting in swords and holy maenads, see *Orph. hymn.* 45.3.

paintings illustrate how the swords may have been used there. Both are on Italiote cups of the very late fifth century, and both display an armed Pentheus surrounded by maenads, one of whom holds a short sword. Pentheus' name appears above his figure in one painting (Naples H.2562), and the sword-bearing maenad who is about to attack him holds a thyrsus in her left hand.[33] J.R. March thought it possible that these and some other paintings of similar date might be based on Xenocles' lost *Bacchae* of 415.[34]

Euripides' treatment of the subject was different, perhaps because he had acquired in Macedonia a different view of the role of the swords. In *Bacchae* 755–8 he appears to suggest that they belong to the world of the initiated, and thus are objects too sacred to be allowed to touch the earth or the earthly. "Many are the thyrsus-bearers; few are the initiates" (Plato *Phaedo* 69C), and when the maenads need weapons to deal with their earthly opponents, they use their thyrsi (*Bacchae* 762–4, 1099). Pentheus' earthly nature is referred to at several points in *Bacchae*, in contrast to the aspects of the heavenly represented by Dionysus and by heavenly fire (light).[35]

'To the black earth' (756) is a significant phrase in this context.[36] It recurs at *Bacchae* 1065 when the heavenly tip of the pine tree is drawn down to earth by Dionysus, and Pentheus with his earthly nature is seated briefly near its crest after it has sprung back heavenwards, until the maenads see him and he is brought back to earth where he belongs. The objects which do not fall to the black earth at *Bacchae* 756 may be contrasted with those carried by the 'nurses' (maenads) as they ranged across the countryside with the infant Dionysus at *Iliad* 6.130–40. Lycurgus chased them, failing to recognize the divinity of the young god who escaped into the sea, and also failing to perceive the sacred nature of the maenads' θύσθλα which should have been carried aloft but were scattered on the ground by the terrified women. Thereupon Zeus punished Lycurgus for his lack of vision by immediate blindness,

---

[33] Naples H.2562: Brommer (n.29) 486 D6; Philippart (n.29) 54 n.138; March (n.29) pl.2A. Rubo, Jatta 1617: Brommer 486 D5; Philippart 52 n.133; March pl.2C.

[34] March (n.29) 37.

[35] C. Segal *Dionysiac Poetics and Euripides' Bacchae* (Princeton 1987) 125–57 discussed the 'vertical axis' and the frequent allusions to the heavenly and the earthly in the course of the play.

[36] There was a strong dualist tendency in the Orphic Dionysus cult expressed, for instance, in the verses "I am a child of earth and starry heaven/ but my race is of heaven ..." on some of the gold tablets in G. Zuntz *Persephone* (Oxford 1971) 358–61; S.G. Cole 'New evidence for the mysteries of Dionysos' *GRBS* 21 (1980) 225.

and by death soon afterwards. Comparable is the passage in the
Theocritean poem *Idyll* 26.14–15 where Antinoe, startled by the spying
Pentheus, scattered "with her feet" ἱερὰ πεπονᾱμένα (holy things that
had been fashioned) already placed on altars freshly built from
branches, with the similar implication that sacred objects are kicked
onto the ground and thus desecrated on account of Pentheus'
earthbound conduct. If the bronze and iron at *Bacchae* 757 are, as I
have suggested, stillheads and short swords with an important part to
play in initiation and epiphany rites in the Dionysus cult, then we are
considering sacred objects which, in contrast to those of Homer and
Theocritus, did not fall to the ground, but were supported safely on the
maenads' shoulders by the power of Dionysus.

The secret rites of the mysteries were presented to initiands in
riddling fashion, as R. Seaford has pointed out.[37] At *Bacchae* 757 we
appear to have ritual objects presented in riddling fashion to both
initiates and the non-initiated in the audience. But the clue given by
Euripides when he added the phenomenon of fire burning safely on the
maenads' curls does suggest that the 'bronze' could have been a still-
head and the fire a veiled allusion to an initiation ritual based upon the
distillate of wine. Rituals are very persistent, and it is quite possible
that this one originated in the Dionysus cult a great many years before
its adoption by the gnostics.

The texts gathered here to support my suggestion that wine-distilling
was practised in classical times are relatively few (unsurprisingly, since
the ritual use of the distillate was 'unspeakable'). But since further
archaeological or textual evidence may emerge in future, this short
survey will provide a background which could assist towards its
identification.[38]

---

[37] Seaford (n.16) 254–5; and his 'Immortality, salvation and the elements' *HSCP* 90
(1986) 19–20 for "the deliberately confusing or riddling manner in which the secrets
were revealed to the initiands" as "a traditional feature of the mysteries".

[38] I would like to thank Dr Richard Seaford, who read an earlier version of this paper, for
his advice and encouragement; and also to thank the editors for their comments and Dr
Roger Brock for comments and discussion.

PAPERS OF THE LEEDS INTERNATIONAL LATIN SEMINAR   TENTH VOLUME (1998) 169–84
Published by Francis Cairns (Publications) Ltd (Leeds 1998). ARCA 38. ISBN 0 905205 95 2

NICANDER AND LUCRETIUS[*]

A.S. HOLLIS
Keble College, Oxford

Nicander of Colophon[1] is one of those Hellenistic poets (Euphorion of Chalcis would be another) who were more highly valued by the Romans than by modern critics. According to Quintilian (10.1.56), to be a follower of Nicander was not an ignoble ambition, and to have succeeded in this aim meant something, even for Virgil: *Nicandrum frustra secuti Macer atque Vergilius?*[2] It is clear from the prose

---

[*]   This article grew out of a paper read in Leeds in March 1996. I am most grateful to members of the School of Classics for their hospitality.

[1]   It seems beyond reasonable doubt that there were two poets named Nicander, perhaps grandfather and grandson. The elder, 'Nicander of Colophon, son of Anaxagoras, hexameter poet', was honoured at Delphi in 254/3 BC (*SIG*³ 452), and thus was a contemporary of Callimachus. The younger calls himself 'son of Damaeus' in fr. 110, and in fr. 104 praised an Attalus who is usually thought to have been Attalus III, the last king of Pergamum (died 133 BC); Alan Cameron, however, argues (*Callimachus and his Critics* (Princeton 1995) 199–202) that the reference is to the first Attalus, which would allow a *floruit* of around 200 BC for the younger Nicander. Cameron (202–5) wishes to attribute the *Theriaca* and *Alexipharmaca* (and probably the other didactic poems from which we have significant verbatim quotations) to the elder Nicander; in *ZPE* 112 (1996) 70 n.9 I very tentatively suggest, on grounds of metre and language (though the evidence is not sufficiently extensive), that the *Georgica* might be given to the younger poet. Throughout this article I have continued to refer to Nicander as a single individual. It seems to me entirely possible that, by the first century BC, the literary world had forgotten that there were two poets called Nicander of Colophon; there only remained disputes about Nicander's date and parentage, nearly all of which disappear once we recognise that the tradition has conflated two separate persons.

[2]   On Aemilius Macer, author of a Latin *Theriaca*, more later. Some influence from Nicander's *Theriaca* can be seen in Virgil's *Georgics*; in particular *G.* 3.428–34 on the Calabrian snake, from Nicander's chersydrus (*Ther.* 366–71) and *G.* 3.435–9 where several passages of the *Theriaca* are effectively combined to produce a strongly Nicandrean atmosphere. But Quintilian's words suggest a more extensive and systematic debt of Virgil to Nicander; their most reasonable explanation is surely that

paraphrase of Antoninus Liberalis that Ovid drew extensively on Nicander's transformation poem, the *Heteroeumena*, and Nicander finds a place in Manilius' gallery of poets (2.44–5):

> ille venenatos anguis aconitaque et herbas
> fata refert vitamque sua radice ferentis.

A general lack of interest in Nicander's poetry may have led modern scholars to overlook examples of his influence upon the Romans, e.g. in the healing of Aeneas by means of a marvellous herb (*Aeneid* 12.411–19), a passage full of Nicandrean motifs.[3] While one may be surprised[4] to find Nicander in a Horatian military panegyric, consider *Odes* 4.4.1–12:

> Qualem ministrum fulminis alitem,
> cui rex deorum regnum in avis vagas
>   permisit expertus fidelem
>   Iuppiter in Ganymede flavo,
>
> olim iuventas et patrius vigor
> nido laborum propulit inscium,
>   vernique iam nimbis remotis
>   insolitos docuere nisus
>
> venti paventem, mox in ovilia
> demisit hostem vividus impetus,   10
>   nunc in reluctantis dracones
>   egit amor dapis atque pugnae.

Virgil owed more than a mere title to Nicander's *Georgica*. Of such a debt hardly a trace remains (with the doubtful exceptions of Nicander frr. 36 and 115). All our certain fragments of the *Georgica* are quoted by Athenaeus — hence their strong concentration on flowers and vegetables. It is possible, I think, that Virgil gracefully acknowledges his predecessor in *G.* 4.116–24 where, after brief mention of some more attractive flowers and vegetables, Virgil declines to treat these subjects at length.

[3] See A.S. Hollis 'Hellenistic colouring in Virgil's *Aeneid*', *HSCP* 94 (1992) 269–85, at 283–5.

[4] Horace was as familiar as everyone else with the prologue to Callimachus' *Aetia* and the ending of the *Hymn to Apollo*; Aratus' *Phaenomena* was also common knowledge (*Phaen.* 123–4 reflected in *Odes* 3.6.46–8). From among signs of Horace's interest in less well known Hellenistic poetry, I single out the imitation of Callimachus' lyric fragment 400 Pf. in *Odes* 1.3.1–8, and of the same poet's striking ὑάλοιο φαάντερος (*Hecale* fr. 18.2 H. = fr. 238.16 Pf.) in *splendidior vitro* (*Odes* 3.13.1). Particularly nice is Horace's latinisation of Euphorion fr. 89 Powell ὑετόμαντις ... κορώνη in *Odes* 3.17.12–13 *aquae ... augur / ... cornix* (this also exemplifies the use of two Latin words to represent a Greek compound, as in *Odes* 1.26.1 *Musis amicus* stands for Philodemus' μουσοφιλής).

together with Nicander's account of the hostility between Eagle and Dracon in *Theriaca* 448–56:

> τῷ μέν τ' ἔκπαγλον κοτέων βασιλήιος ὄρνις
> αἰετὸς ἐκ παλαχῆς ἐπαέξεται, ἀντία δ' ἐχθρήν
> δῆριν ἄγει γενύεσσιν ὅταν βλώσκοντα καθ' ὕλην
> δέρκηται· πάσας γὰρ ὄγ' ἠρήμωσε καλιάς,
> αὔτως ὀρνίθων τε τόκον κτίλα τ' ὤεα βρύκων.
> αὐτὰρ ὁ τοῦ καὶ ῥῆνα καὶ ἠνεμόεντα λαγωόν
> ῥεῖα δράκων ἤμερσε νέον μάρψαντος ὄνυξι
> θάμνου ὑπαΐξας· ὁ δ' ἀλεύεται· ἀμφὶ δὲ δαιτός
> μάρνανθ'.

Reference to the eagle as 'King of Birds' (βασιλήιος ὄρνις, 448), and indeed the struggle between eagle and snake (often a portent or a simile),[5] can be reckoned as commonplace. But Horace appears to derive his notion of describing the eagle growing up from *Theriaca* 449 αἰετὸς ἐκ παλαχῆς[6] ἐπαέξεται ("From his earliest days the King of Birds, the Eagle, grows up cherishing fierce wrath against him ..."); comparison of Horace line 10 *amor dapis atque pugnae* with Nicander 455–6 ἀμφὶ δὲ δαιτός/ μάρνανθ' seems to confirm the dependence.

Before launching into the subject of Nicander and Lucretius I should state my own unfashionable opinion that there is some literary interest, and even merit, to be found in Nicander's formidable didactic poems. As a *captatio benevolentiae* I offer a simile describing the crooked motion of a *cerastes*, which is compared to the irregular course of a dinghy when towed behind a cargo-boat which is tacking against the wind (*Theriaca* 268–70):

> τράμπιος ὁλκαίης ἀκάτῳ ἴσος ἤ τε δι' ἅλμης
> πλευρὸν ὅλον βάπτουσα κακοσταθέοντος ἀήτεω
> εἰς ἄνεμον βεβίηται ἀπόκρουστος λιβὸς οὔρῳ.

(... like the dinghy of a cargo ship dipping the whole of its side in the water when the wind is unfavourable, as it forces its way to windward, beaten off course by the south-westerly gale.)

---

[5]   E.g. *Iliad* 12.200–9, Aeschylus *Choephoroe* 247–9 (with Garvie's note), *Aeneid* 11.751–6 (note *luctantem* in 756, corresponding to *reluctantis* in *Odes* 4.4.11).

[6]   The scholiast on *Ther.* 448–9 (p. 184 ed. Crugnola 1971) explains ἐκ παλαχῆς with ἐξ ἀρχῆς. LSJ's translation of παλαχή, 'anything acquired by lot' (connecting with παλάσσω in the sense of shaking lots), would harmonise with two of Hesychius' glosses (λῆξις and μοῖρα), less obviously with the other two (ἀρχή and γενεά). Hesychius also has an entry παλαχθεν, explained ἐκ γενεᾶς ('from birth'), ἐκ παλαιοῦ; that looks to me like an anonymous snippet of learned Hellenistic poetry (Callimachus?).

Some have held that the simile must have been in Nicander's technical source — could this spring from a subconscious desire to deny credit to the poet? We shall see that close observation of everyday activities, with hints of a technical vocabulary, is a notable feature of Nicander (as of Lucretius). The Nicandrean ὁλκάς is far removed from John Masefield's 'Quinquireme of Nineveh', more like his "Dirty British coaster .../ Butting through the Channel in the mad March days." It seems to me quite possible that Nicander's simile caught the fancy of an unknown minor Latin poet who wanted to describe Scylla daughter of Nisus being dragged behind the ship of king Minos ([Virgil] *Ciris* 478–80):

> fertur et incertis iactatur ad omnia ventis
> cumba velut magnas sequitur cum parvula classis
> Afer et hiberno bacchatur in aequore turbo.

If Nicander is ever mentioned in the same breath as Lucretius, he will probably be cited (perhaps together with Aratus) as an example of what the *De Rerum Natura* is *not*. Lucretius himself pays tribute to the philosopher-poet Empedocles (1.729–33), and modern scholars seem to take for granted that he owed little or nothing to Hellenistic didactic poetry.[7] I believe that such an assumption would be false, and that much the most profitable comparison is with Nicander. But one must be careful not to overstate the case; and of course it would be foolish to deny that Lucretius was by far the greater poet, with the grander themes. There was a Latin poet who could reasonably have been called the Roman Nicander — not Lucretius but Aemilius Macer, who seems to have been intermediate in time between Lucretius and Virgil, and who lived long enough for the young Ovid to hear him reciting his *Theriaca* (*Tristia* 4.10.43–4):[8]

> saepe suas volucres legit mihi grandior aevo,
> quaeque nocet serpens, quae iuvat herba, Macer.

---

[7]   A common way of disparaging the likes of Aratus and Nicander (and distancing them from Lucretius and Virgil) is to describe the former pair as mere 'metaphrasts'. Any didactic poet with technical subject matter is likely to draw on a prose treatise, and this greater or lesser dependence upon such a source need not be an important factor in estimating the value of his final poem.

[8]   Perhaps *Alexipharmaca* as well. In *CR* N.S. 23 (1973) 11 I argued that the wording of *Tristia* 4.10.44 suggested an *Alexipharmaca* as well as *Theriaca*. Subsequently I came to think that the line probably referred only to a *Theriaca*. But R.G.M. Nisbet (*Collected Papers on Latin Literature* ed. S.J. Harrison (Oxford 1995) 398) allows for *Alexipharmaca* and E. Courtney (*The Fragmentary Latin Poets* (Oxford 1993) 292) relates some surviving fragments of Aemilius Macer to Nicander's *Alexipharmaca*.

Macer shows that Nicander was in the Roman literary consciousness a few years after Lucretius' death, and we have the evidence of Cicero that Nicander's *Georgica* was admired by the *docti* in 55 BC, not long before Lucretius disappeared from the scene (*De Oratore* 1.69):

> constat inter doctos ... de rebus rusticis hominem ab agro remotissimum Nicandrum Colophonium poetica quadam facultate, non rustica, scripsisse praeclare.[9]

Although Lucretius was later given the epithet *doctus* by Statius (*Silvae* 2.7.76), there was a general disinclination to think of him in these terms until E.J. Kenney's article 'Doctus Lucretius',[10] which was reinforced by Robert Brown in his 'Lucretius and Callimachus'.[11] *De Rerum Natura* Book 1 contains tributes to Ennius (117) and Empedocles (716) by name, but also an unmistakable allusion to Callimachus (fr. 1.26–8 Pf.) in a programmatic context (926–7 *avia Pieridum peragro loca nullius ante/ trita solo*). This in itself suffices to show that Lucretius was cognisant of the learned Hellenistic poetry which so fired the enthusiasm of his contemporaries such as Catullus and Helvius Cinna.

There is one straightforward overlap between Nicander and Lucretius, but it is perhaps the least interesting. When at the end of Book 6 Lucretius describes the horrific death suffered by victims of the Athenian plague, he can hardly have been unaware that, poetically speaking, he was in Nicandrean territory; Virgil, in his account of the animal plague in *Georgics* 3, seems definitely to combine Lucretius with Nicander.[12] One deduction from such passages, applied to both poets, was that they practised professionally as doctors; that is stated for Nicander in his *Suda* entry,[13] and was suggested for Lucretius by none other than Goethe.[14] Caution is in order on both fronts: Cicero[15] tells us that Nicander wrote excellent *Georgica* though he was *homo ab*

---

[9] The same passage reveals that another object of admiration among the *docti* was the *Phaenomena* of Aratus. The latter point is confirmed by an epigram of Helvius Cinna (fr. 11 Courtney) on the copy of Aratus' *Phaenomena* which he brought back with him from Bithynia.

[10] *Mnemosyne* 4.23 (1970) 366–92.

[11] *ICS* 7 (1982) 77–97. Particularly striking is Lucretius' allusion to Callimachus' *Hecale* (frr. 70–73 H.) in 6.749–55.

[12] As noted by Richard Thomas in his commentary on *Georgics* 3.513.

[13] N374 Adler, reproduced in Gow and Scholfield's edition of Nicander (Cambridge 1953) 3.

[14] With at least qualified approval from Peter Wiseman ('The two worlds of Lucretius', in *Cinna the Poet and Other Roman Essays* (Leicester 1974) 21).

[15] *De Or.* 1.69, quoted above.

agro remotissimus, and, if one had to deduce the poet's professional expertise from the subject matter of his poems, other plausible suggestions could be made for both Nicander and Lucretius (as we shall see). Other points of contact between the subject matter of the two poets include striking passages on the dominating power of the winds (*Alexipharmaca* 171–7, cf. *De Rerum Natura* 1.271–6) and on the frenzied public worship of the Phrygian Great Mother Cybele (*Alexipharmaca* 217–20, cf. *De Rerum Natura* 2.618–28). The Lucretian lines are well known. I quote those of Nicander, first *Alexipharmaca* 171–7:

> ἰόεντα θάλασσαν,
> ἥν τε καὶ ἀτμεύειν ἀνέμοις πόρεν Ἐννοσίγαιος
> σὺν πυρί· καὶ γὰρ δὴ τὸ πνοαῖς συνδάμναται ἐχθραῖς.
> πῦρ μὲν ἀείζωον καὶ ἀχύνετον ἔτρεσεν ὕδωρ
> ἀργέστας· καί ῥ’ ἡ μὲν ἀκοσμήεσσα φιλοργής
> δεσπόζει νηῶν τε καὶ ἐμφθορέων αἰζηῶν,
> ὕλη δ’ ἐχθομένοιο πυρὸς κατὰ θεσμὸν ἀκούει.

(... the violet-hued sea, which, together with fire, the Earth-Shaker has enslaved to the winds. For fire too is vanquished by hostile blasts: the undying fire and the expanse of waters tremble before the northwest winds, though the unruly sea, swift to anger, lords it over ships and over the men who perish in it, while to the rule of the abhorred fire the forest is obedient.)

and *Alexipharmaca* 217–20:

> ἢ ἄτε κερνοφόρος ζάκορος βωμίστρια Ῥείης,
> εἰνάδι λαοφόροισιν ἐνιχρίμπτουσα κελεύθοις,
> μακρὸν ἐπεμβοάᾳ γλώσσῃ θρόον, οἱ δὲ τρέουσιν
> Ἰδαίης ῥιγηλὸν ὅτ’ εἰσαῖωσιν ὑλαγμόν.

(... or as the acolyte with her tray of offerings, Rhea's priestess, appearing in the public highways on the ninth day of the month, raises a great shout with her voice, while the people tremble as they hearken to the horrible yelling of the votary of Ida.)

At this point I would like to consider some more general affinities between the two poets. Both Nicander and Lucretius clearly subscribe to the doctrine[16] that the glory of poetic achievement varies in direct proportion to the difficulty of the task. According to this way of thinking, technical and apparently unpromising material is all the more welcome. One of the reasons for which Lucretius claims his garland

---

[16] Articulated also, for example, by Propertius (4.10.4) *non iuvat e facili lecta corona iugo.*

from the Muses is that *obscura de re tam lucida pango/ carmina* (1.933–4); in his case there was the added obstacle that Epicureans for the most part were held to be uninterested in the poetic medium.[17] From this standpoint Nicander's choice of subject-matter (reptiles and anti-dotes to poison) represented not an appalling error of judgement, but a challenge perhaps even greater than that faced by Aratus in his *Phaenomena*.

Near the beginning of their poems, Nicander and Lucretius speak of their poetic allegiances in ways which I find interestingly similar. *Theriaca* 9–12:

> ἑρπηστὰς ἔχιάς τε καὶ ἄχθεα μυρία γαίης
> Τιτήνων ἐνέπουσιν ἀφ᾽ αἵματος, εἰ ἐτεόν περ
> Ἀσκραῖος μυχάτοιο Μελισσήεντος ἐπ᾽ ὄχθαις
> Ἡσίοδος κατέλεξε παρ᾽ ὕδασι Περμησσοῖο.

(... reptiles and vipers and the earth's countless burdens are, so they say, of the Titans' blood — if indeed he spoke the truth, Ascraean Hesiod on the steeps of secluded Melisseeis by the waters of Permessus.)

and *De Rerum Natura* 1.116–19:

> an pecudes alias divinitus insinuet se,
> Ennius ut noster cecinit qui primus amoeno
> detulit ex Helicone perenni fronde coronam
> per gentis Italas hominum quae clara clueret.

Both passages belong to the Hesiodic/Callimachean tradition of poetic initiation. In each case an old master (Hesiod/Ennius) is cited as asserting a particular point (the birth of reptiles from the blood of the Titans/the transmigration of souls between human beings and animals). The younger poets are apparently sceptical[18] with regard to the doctrine (in Lucretius' case, downright hostile to it). Yet mention of the older

---

[17] Cicero *In Pisonem* 70.

[18] For phrases like εἰ ἐτεόν περ, see T.C.W. Stinton 'Si credere dignum est' *PCPS* 22 (1976) 60–89 = *Collected Papers on Greek Tragedy* (Oxford 1990) 236–64, though he does not mention this passage of Nicander. The scholia say that the derivation of reptiles from the Titans' blood was not to be found in Hesiod, and this reference appears in Merkelbach and West's *Fragmenta Hesiodea* (Oxford 1967) among the Spuria (fr. 367), with an apparent suggestion that Nicander confused Hesiod with Acusilaos (*FGrHist.* 2F14). That I find hard to believe; it seems to me more likely that some such passage ascribed to Hesiod (and mentioning Melisseeis?) was current in Nicander's day but subsequently lost. Is it possible that εἰ ἐτεόν περ contains an allusion to the source's dubious authenticity? That would be in the manner of a *doctus poeta*.

poet is clearly of wider significance than for the particular point at issue. Nicander is claiming a place for himself in the Hesiodic school of didactic poetry.[19] And, although Ennius' scientific opinions about the soul may have been totally unsound, he expressed them in 'immortal verses' (De Rerum Natura 1.121) and Lucretius — as we can see from his practice — must here be acknowledging a degree of stylistic dependence upon the older poet.

We have mentioned above Peter Wiseman's qualified support for the idea that Lucretius may have practised as a doctor. In the same essay[20] Wiseman makes further inferences about the poet's professional expertise: he was intimately familiar with the world of the theatre, e.g. Cilician saffron on the stage (2.416), flapping awnings above (4.75–83, 6.109–15), plaster masks (4.296–7) and gold leaf (4.727) such as a brattiarius might use for theatrical statues. More strikingly, perhaps Lucretius was a member of a gang of workmen who replaced the wooden Pons Sublicius across the Tiber. This notion is based upon 2.196–200, with the first person plural verbs ursimus and pressimus, though I would hesitate to deduce from these that Lucretius was personally involved in the work. But certainly Wiseman has drawn attention to a genuine feature of the De Rerum Natura, even if one does not accept his explanation of it. David West[21] has written of the poem's 'fearful clatter of tools' (e.g. 4.513–19, 5.1264–8, 1351–3). Turn now to Nicander. He too was said to have been a medical doctor.[22] On the basis of apparently close observation or technical knowledge, one might consider other professions for him. For example, might he not have been a tanner? Witness Theriaca 421–3, where Nicander is describing the smell emitted by a chelydrus:

> τὸ δ᾽ ἀπὸ χροὸς ἐχθρὸν ἄηται
> οἶον ὅτε πλαδόωντα περὶ σκύλα καὶ δέρε᾽ ἵππων
> γναπτόμενοι μυδόωσιν ὑπ᾽ ἀρβήλοισι λάθαργοι.

(... and from its skin it exhales a hateful air, as when about the damp horse-skins and hides the scraps of leather ooze beneath the paring of the tanner's knives.)

ἄρβηλος is a specialised semi-circular knife used by leather-workers,

---

[19] Just as Callimachus (Ep. 27 Pf. = 56 G–P = Anth. Pal. 9.507) discerned a Hesiodic quality in the Phaenomena of Aratus.

[20] 'The two worlds of Lucretius' (n.14 above) 21–5.

[21] The Imagery and Poetry of Lucretius (Edinburgh 1969) 64.

[22] In the Suda (n.13 above).

while λάθαργος (a scrap of leather) is an equally rare word. Pungent and distasteful smells are another feature common to the poetry of Nicander and Lucretius (e.g. *De Rerum Natura* 4.123–5):

praeterea quaecumque suo de corpore odorem
exspirant acrem, panaces absinthia taetra
habrotonique graves et tristia centaurea.

To sweeten the atmosphere, I could suggest that Nicander was a perfumer, since in *Theriaca* 103–4 he lists different grades of perfume with the technical terms used in the trade to describe them:

ἥν τε θυωροί
πρώτην μεσσατίην τε πολύτριπτόν τε κλέονται.

(... essence which perfumers style 'prime' and 'medium' and 'well-ground'.)

In *Georgica* fr. 85[23] we find an extraordinary description of the texture of the Cumaean cabbage (5–6):

Κύμη τε κακόχροος ἣ μὲν ἔοικε
πέλμασιν οἷσι πέδιλα παλίμβολα κασσύουσιν.

(... and the ill-coloured Cumaean which is like the soles with which men cobble second-hand sandals.)

Not very appetizing! Other humble occupations which appear in these poems are those of the spearmaker (*Theriaca* 170), the handpicker (*Theriaca* 752), the carver pouring away his dirty water (*Alexipharmaca* 258), the olive-presser (*Alexipharmaca* 494)[24] and the salter (*Alexipharmaca* 519–20).

Such interest in the minutiae of technical professions should not, in my opinion, be taken as evidence that the poet himself had practised them. This is a Hellenistic feature which, as so often, has its roots in Homer. Consider, for instance, the splendid simile (with hints of technical vocabulary) from an irrigation worker (*Iliad* 21.257–9):

ὡς δ' ὅτ' ἀνὴρ ὀχετηγὸς ἀπὸ κρήνης μελανύδρου
ἂμ φυτὰ καὶ κήπους ὕδατι ῥόον ἡγεμονεύῃ
χερσὶ μάκελλαν ἔχων, ἀμάρης ἐξ ἔχματα βάλλων.

Callimachus filled his *Hecale* with details of life in old Attica: items of furniture, cooking utensils, ways of preparing food or conveying loads.

---

[23] Not certainly by the author of *Theriaca* and *Alexipharmaca* (see n.1 above).
[24] Cf. Lucr. 2.391–2.

Some specialised interests smell more of the Library[25] than of the countryside, e.g. the names and nature of work-songs, as in *Hecale* fr. 74.25 H.:

ἀείδει καί πού τις ἀνὴρ ὑδατηγὸς ἱμαῖον

(... and somewhere a water-drawer is singing the rope-song.)

Nicander and Lucretius also share a gift for minute observation of nature — for example, of thistledown floating in the breeze (*Alexipharmaca* 126–7):

οἷά τε δὴ γήρεια νέον τεθρυμμένα κάκτου
ἠέρ᾽ ἐπιπλάζοντα διαψαίρουσι πνοῇσι.

(... like the freshly scattered thistledown which roams the air and is fluttered by every breeze.)

and *De Rerum Natura* 3.386–7:

papposque volantis
qui nimia levitate cadunt plerumque gravatim.

Both can conjure up disturbing fugitive visions, like the sinister outsize moths which dart around the lamplight at supper-time in Egypt (*Theriaca* 759–61):

φράζεο δ᾽ Αἰγύπτοιο τά τε τρέφει οὐλοὸς αἶα
κνώδαλα, φαλλαίνῃ ἐναλίγκια τὴν περὶ λύχνους
ἀκρόνυχος δειπνητὸς ἐπήλασε παιφάσσουσαν.

(Consider now monsters which the grim land of Egypt fosters, like the moth which the evening meal-time brings in to flutter round the lamps.)

or the cobweb which you may get in your face if you go for a walk at night (*De Rerum Natura* 3.383–4):

nec nebulam noctu neque aranei tenuia fila
obvia sentimus, quando obretimur euntes.

For a change, let us start with a description in English of a man who wakes up in the middle of the night and, feeling thirsty, reaches for a jug at the side of his bed, taking care not to spill the liquid:

---

[25] Callimachus probably gathered such material from treatises on Attic expressions and customs, or commentaries and monographs on Old Comedy. See my edition of the *Hecale* (Oxford 1990) 5–10.

When a man's eyes are shrouded beneath dark night, and, without thinking, he drinks from a pitcher, tipping it up and pressing his lips close to its ...

If one were told that these words are a translation from a Greek or Latin hexameter poet, would not Lucretius come first to mind? In fact the author was Nicander (*Alexipharmaca* 501–3):

ἢ ὅθ᾽ ὑπὸ ζοφερῆς νυκτὸς κεκαλυμμένος αὐγάς
ἀφραδέως κρωσσοῖο κατακλίνας ποτὸν ἴσχῃ
χείλεσι πρὸς χείλη πιέσας ...

Similarly with the preceding lines (*Alexipharmaca* 495–7):[26]

But if a man whose throat is constrained by parching thirst fall on his knees and draw water from a stream like a bull, parting with his hand the delicate moss-like plants ...

ἢν δέ τις ἀζαλέῃ πεπιεσμένος αὐχένα δίψῃ
ἐκ ποταμοῦ ταυρηδὸν ἐπιπροπεσὼν ποτὸν ἴσχῃ
λεπτὰ διαστείλας παλάμῃ μνιώδεα θρῖα...

In both cases the minutely-detailed observation (the danger of spilling the water in the dark, and the need to push aside the slender plants at the river's edge) is very much what we associate with Lucretius.[27]

There is one particular area from which both Nicander and Lucretius like to draw their illustrations but which is relatively less patronised by other poets, thus forming a notable link between these two. I have in mind the activities of children, stretching back to infancy. As in the case of technical professions, one can find some precedent in Homeric similes. When Apollo destroys the Achaean wall, he is compared to a boy playing on the beach who demolishes his own sandcastle (*Iliad* 15.362–4):[28]

---

[26] One could compare Lucr. 4.1024–5.

[27] For example in 4.414–17 on the puddle (no deeper than a finger's breadth) lying between paving stones in the street, on which Peter Wiseman (n.14 above) 13–14 comments "Most Romans would not even notice a puddle in the road, much less see the vastness of the sky reflected in it, as Lucretius does."

[28] Homeric similes involving children can be most conveniently gathered together through William C. Scott *The Oral Nature of the Homeric Simile* (*Mnemosyne* Suppl. 28 (1974)) 191–205. The usual function of child-similes in the *Iliad* is to describe a character who is acting strangely or foolishly, or to illustrate the protection given by a strong ally (Scott 74). Later didactic poetry provides a splendid simile from a small girl who is unable to resist the temptation of some sweet food, even though she knows that she will get into trouble when her mother returns to the room (Oppian *Halieutica* 3.512–18).

ὡς ὅτε τις ψάμαθον πάϊς ἄγχι θαλάσσης,
ὅς τ᾽ ἐπεὶ οὖν ποιήσῃ ἀθύρματα νηπιέῃσιν
ἂψ αὖτις συνέχευε ποσὶν καὶ χερσὶν ἀθύρων.

Other Hellenistic poets also show some interest in children; e.g. Calli-
machus' portrayal of the precocious baby Artemis (*Hymn* 3.4–39),
Apollonius' picture of the spoiled brat Eros in *Argonautica* 3.114–53
and the small boy in Theocritus 1.47–54 who fails to guard the vine-
yard because he is totally absorbed in plaiting a cage for his cricket.[29]
But these are isolated examples.

To start from the earliest age, Nicander has the newborn baby
suckling from its mother's breast (*Alexipharmaca* 356–7). By *Alexi-
pharmaca* 542–3 the child is crawling on all fours (τετραποδί), in
Alexipharmaca 417–22 a toddler, standing erect and beginning to
teethe. This last passage is studiedly bizarre in its contrast of language
and subject matter:

ἠὲ νέον σπείρημα καὶ ἀμφίκρηνα κομάων
κοῦροι ἀπειπάμενοι ὀλοήν θ᾽ ἑρπηδόνα γυίων,
ὀρθόποδες βαίνοντες ἄνις σμυγεροῖο τιθήνης
ἠλοσύνῃ βρύκουσι κακανθήεντας ὀράμνους,
οἷα νέον βρωτῆρας ὑπὸ γναθμοῖσιν ὀδόντας
φαίνοντες τότε κνηθμὸς ἐνοιδέα δάμναται οὖλα.

(... or as children who, having lately put aside their swaddling-
clothes and head-bindings, and their perilous crawling on all fours,
and walking now upright with no anxious nurse at hand, chew its
sprays of baleful flowers through witlessness, since they are just
bringing to light the incisor teeth in their jaws, at which time itching
assails their swollen gums.)

The oddness puts me in mind of Lucretius 5.229–30, where the poet
observes that young animals do not need rattles or a nurse's baby-talk:

nec crepitacillis opus est, nec cuiquam adhibendast
almae nutricis blanda atque infracta loquella.

Thereafter Nicander is interested in children's toys and games (*The-
riaca* 880, *Alexipharmaca* 168–70, 233), in the bright colours
(*Georgica* fr. 74.64–5) and, above all, the foods which attract them (frr.
75, 80.2, 81.4). Lucretius' references to children are even more wide-
ranging, and expressed in some of the most famous passages in the
whole poem. He starts with the contractions of labour, and the new-
born infant which fills the whole room with mournful wailing (5.222–

---

[29] A Latin parallel in the same spirit would be Icarus in Ovid *Met.* 8.195–200.

7). Children stagger when they are just learning to walk (3.447–8), point at things of which they do not know the name (5.1031), fear the dark (2.55–8), are persuaded to drink unpleasant medicine (1.936–42), win over their primitive parents (5.1017–18), greet their father as he returns home (3.895–6) and whirl around to make themselves giddy (4.400–3).

Finally I would like to suggest that there are certain affinities between the idiosyncratic vocabulary and style of Nicander and Lucretius. This, of course, is a hazardous argument, depending upon allegedly parallel phenomena in the two languages. Both poets have created a highly individual style. Cyril Bailey[30] characterised that of Lucretius as 'peculiar', while Quintilian (10.1.87) called him 'difficilis'; no one surely would deny either epithet to Nicander. Neither poet lacks stylistic antecedents — in Lucretius' case Ennius, in Nicander's, learned poets such as Antimachus of Colophon, Callimachus and Euphorion.[31] But the final result, in both cases, is quite personal and (even if one disregards the subject matter) can not long be mistaken for the work of any other poet.[32] Frequently the style may seem harsh, and not obviously poetical. Take one of my favourite lines of Lucretius — and one of the oddest — 3.388:

> nec repentis itum cuiusviscunque animantis

> (… neither the path of any creeping creature …)[33]

Supposing that this had been preserved as a single-line anonymous fragment, could one for a moment have ascribed it to any reputable poet other than Lucretius? Note the characteristic *animans* = 'living

---

[30] In his three-volume edition of Lucretius (Oxford 1947) I 72.

[31] Though the chronological relationship between Euphorion and Nicander is now, I think, an open question (see n.1 above). For a specific case in which one might be tempted to argue that Euphorion is correcting Nicander, see A.S. Hollis, *ZPE* 112 (1996) 70.

[32] Hellenistic and Roman poets sometimes write brief passages in the style of their colleagues. Thus Nicander pretends to be Aratus in *Ther.* 19–20 (on the Scorpion) τοῦ δὲ τέρας περίσημον ὑπ' ἀστέρας ἀπλανὲς αὔτως/ οἷα κυνηλατέοντος ἀείδελον ἐστήρικται, as does Apollonius Rhodius in *Arg.* 3.1002–4 μέσῳ δέ οἱ αἰθέρι τέκμωρ/ ἀστερόεις στέφανος, τόν τε κλείουσ' Ἀριάδνης,/ πάννυχος οὐρανίοις ἐνελίσσεται εἰδώλοισιν. For Apollonius in bucolic mode cf. *Arg.* 1.1065–6 τὴν δὲ καὶ αὐταί/ νύμφαι ἀποφθιμένην ἀλσηίδες ὠδύραντο. His apparently 'Nicandrean' passage (*Arg.* 4.1505–31) on the death of Mopsus could be just that (see above, notes 1 and 31, on the chronology).

[33] Incidentally, Nicander's favourite subject matter, snakes and insects, appears quite often in Lucretius.

creature', with a somewhat elaborate circumlocution *repentis* ... *animantis*, the noun *itus* (rare except when combined with *reditus*), the apparently clumsy *cuiusviscunque* which by its size dominates the whole line, and the quadrisyllabic line-ending.

Both poets specialise in particular types of word-formation, not unprecedented but extended far beyond previous practice. To start with the humble adverb: the termination *-im* has some quite normal Latin examples (e.g. *paullatim, praesertim*), but Lucretius seems to have coined a remarkable number of new such adverbs, some of which remained *hapax legomena* (e.g. *adumbratim, filatim, mixtim*). He is almost equally fond of adverbs in *-ter*, e.g. the unique *moderanter, praecipitanter, contractabiliter, vitaliter*.[34] Nicander too has a couple of favourite adverbial terminations, in -δην and -δόν; among his more extravagant creations are συμφύρδην, 'mixedly', ποιφύγδην, 'with hissing', μοσχηδόν, 'in the manner of a calf', ὠρυδόν, 'with howling'. It seems not unreasonable to compare Nicander's συμμιγίδην, μιγάδην and μίγδην[35] with Lucretius' *mixtim*. Lucretius also has favourite substantival formations, most notably neuter nouns in *-men* (usually *-amen*). Some of these are standard Latin words, e.g. *carmen, flumen, nomen*; but among Lucretius' *hapax legomena* are *adaugmen, documen, lateramen, vexamen*. As Cyril Bailey says,[36] these formations are notable, and lend a definite character to Lucretius' verse. A Nicandrean counterpart might be the neuter nouns in -αρ. Again, some are normal Greek (e.g. ἧπαρ), others by no means so: e.g. κάρηαρ = 'head' (earlier in Antimachus of Colophon, fr. 155 Matthews), νῶκαρ, 'lethargy', σκίναρ, 'carcase'. The last two are unique and would perhaps create a bizarre impression. Our two poets both employ compound epithets very freely. On the Latin side these were a feature of old epic and tragedy, but Lucretius has almost certainly coined many new ones,[37] as did Nicander. I will mention just the two most ingenious examples, neither of which falls into a recognisable category: Nicander's δερκευνής, 'he who sleeps with his eyes open' (*Alexipharmaca* 67, of a hare), and Lucretius' *anguimanus* (2.537, 5.1303), applied to an elephant.

One of the most striking features of Nicander's verse is the extraordinary proliferation of epithets in -όεις and -ήεις (Callimachus

---

[34] On Lucretian adverbs, see Bailey (n.30 above) I 136–7.
[35] Nicander, of course, has frequent cause to use these terms when detailing the ingredients of a recipe.
[36] (n.30 above) I 135.
[37] Bailey (n.30 above) I 132–4.

provided some precedent, but on nothing like the same scale). According to A.W. James,[38] Nicander employs 110 epithets in -όεις, of which more than half (58) appear to be his own creation. Together with certain other favoured adjectival endings (-αλέος, -οειδής and -ώδης) these words[39] have a marked effect on the overall texture of Nicander's verse. Many of Lucretius' odder formations are clearly due to metrical exigency;[40] in this respect Nicander differs. Among his more bizarre forms we find άκινήεις, άκοσμήεις, ούρανόεις, σιδηρήεις (all coined by Nicander and mostly reappearing in no other author). In these cases the familiar forms (άκίνητος, άκοσμος, etc.) are not exact metrical equivalents, but could easily enough be accommodated in hexameter verse. So Nicander, to a greater degree than Lucretius, seems to create these novel forms out of a desire to give his verse a distinctive flavour. I started this section with a line of Lucretius (3.388) which, while not obviously 'poetical', bears the very strong imprint of his personal style. Searching for a similar line of Nicander, I came up with *Alexipharmaca* 330:

κα σπέραδος κραμβῆεν ἄδην μεμορυχμένον ὄξει.

(... and seed of cabbage thoroughly soaked in vinegar.)

σπέραδος (for σπέρμα) is confined to Nicander, while the epithet κραμβήεις (of the type discussed above) is unique. μεμορυχμένον (from μορύσσω) is a Homeric *hapax legomenon* (*Odyssey* 13.435).

To sum up, it seems to me that in language, as in general style and (to a certain extent) subject matter, there are quite strong affinities between Nicander and Lucretius, which may not be fortuitous; they suggest to me that Lucretius may have consciously imitated some aspects of Nicander. The Roman does not acknowledge such a debt (as he does to Ennius, Empedocles and Callimachus), and no writer of later antiquity picks it up; the nearest approach is in Quintilian, who twice (10.1.87 and 12.11.27) couples Lucretius with the Nicandrean Aemilius Macer. It is a pity that more has not survived of Macer's *Theriaca*.[41] I will end with just a tiny indirect hint that his version of Nicander may

---

[38] *Studies in the Language of Oppian of Cilicia* (Amsterdam 1970) 220.

[39] As Bailey remarked (I 135) of Lucretius' neuter nouns in -*men*.

[40] E.g. (to take some nominal terminations not yet mentioned), *flexura* for the impossible *flexio*, *variantia* for *varietas*, *differitas* for *differentia* and *pestilitas* for *pestilentia*, *maximitas* for *magnitudo*.

[41] See E. Courtney *The Fragmentary Latin Poets* (Oxford 1993) 292–9. He attempts to establish a closer relationship between Nicander and Macer.

also have had a certain Lucretian quality. We are told[42] that Lucan in his ninth book borrowed some of the names of the snakes from Macer. W. Morel[43] reasonably suspected that Lucan 9.723:

> ossaque dissolvens cum corpore tabificus seps

may reflect Aemilius Macer, since we find the same monosyllabic line-ending in Nicander, *Theriaca* 147:

> καὶ λέπας ὑλῆεν, τόθι δίψιος ἐμβατέει σήψ.[44]

The compound epithet *tabificus* (which Lucan applies to the *seps*) is of a very Lucretian type, and in fact occurs first in *De Rerum Natura* 6.737; Bailey[45] counts it among Lucretius' 'bold formations'. So it is just possible that in this phrase of Lucan we can see a mingling of Nicander and Lucretius in the *Theriaca* of Aemilius Macer, and a recognition by Macer that, in order to be Nicandrean, it was appropriate also to be Lucretian.

A natural first reaction to the title 'Nicander and Lucretius' might have been that they are an ill-assorted couple — perhaps like another pairing which has been tried in the past, Callimachus and Lucilius. I willingly concede that it is a question of matching a lightweight poet with a heavyweight, but hope to have persuaded readers that in certain respects the comparison is both reasonable and fruitful. If, however, I have not succeeded in this, my second hope is to have helped bring back into play a Greek poet who was unquestionably admired by sensitive critics and highly talented poets in Rome but who (so far) has profited little from the increased attention paid to Hellenistic poetry in recent years.[46]

---

[42] Macer fr. 6 Courtney (n.41 above) from Schol. Bern. on Lucan 9.701.

[43] *Philologus* 83 (1927–8) 347.

[44] A monosyllabic hexameter-ending is, of course, quite common in Lucretius. We tend to think of it as an Ennian legacy, but not all the Lucretian instances have an Ennian ring, and it is worth noting that there are about 15 such endings in Nicander. Similar endings in other Hellenistic poets include Euphorion fr. 4.2 Powell ἐχθομένη κρέξ, Simias fr. 11.2 Powell ἡ ἀλυκὴ ζάψ, Dionysius Iambus *Suppl. Hell.* 389.

[45] Bailey (n.30 above) I 134.

[46] Some recent issues of *L'Année Philologique* have contained not a single entry relating to Nicander. One work which does attempt to assess Nicander in literary terms, and even has a good word for him, is Graham Zanker's *Realism in Alexandrian Poetry* (London 1986); see his Index *s.v.* Nicander.

PAPERS OF THE LEEDS INTERNATIONAL LATIN SEMINAR   TENTH VOLUME (1998) 185–201
Published by Francis Cairns (Publications) Ltd (Leeds 1998). ARCA 38. ISBN 0 905205 95 2

FREEDOM AND OWNERSHIP:
A Contribution to the Discussion of
Vergil's First *Eclogue*[*]

ERNST A. SCHMIDT
Eberhard-Karls-Universität Tübingen

Discussion of the opening poem of Vergil's Book of *Bucolics* must go on, even after I. M. Le M. Du Quesnay's penetrating and apparently exhaustive article of 1981[1] (henceforth Du Q). The first aim of the present paper is to show that Du Q's main thesis and its corollaries are equally unfounded — indeed that they cannot be correct since they necessitate doing syntactical violence to the text of Vergil and imposing alien meanings on it. It should be emphasised, however, that I take very seriously Du Q's rebuttal of earlier studies with their elements of undebated consensus; and my attempts to reach solutions are greatly indebted to Du Q's criticisms, courage and independence of mind. Hence the findings of this paper are not just a return to earlier explanations and for this reason should be treated as provisional. The

---

[*]   Dr Günther Heilbrunn, Pittsburgh/Pennsylvania, has toiled to correct and improve my
English and my argument; further thanks are due to Professor Cairns who circumspectly edited this paper.
[1]   I. M. Le M. Du Quesnay 'Vergil's First *Eclogue*' *PLLS* 3 (1981) 29–182. Thereafter (apart from studies of specific passages, viz. A. Traina 'La chiusa della prima egloga virgiliana (vv.82–3)' *Lingua e stile* 3 (1986) 45–53; C. Perkell 'On *Eclogue* 1.79–83' *TAPA* 120 (1990) 171–81), only two general articles have appeared: J.R.G. Wright 'Virgil's pastoral programme: Theocritus, Callimachus and *Eclogue* 1' *PCPS* n.s. 29 (1983) 107–60, a "reading of the poem as a programme for bucolic poetry in the line of Theocritus with debts to Callimachus but a new Roman flavour" (129), and offering as its main thesis that "the encounter with the god" is "a poetic initiation in the tradition of Hesiod and Callimachus" (123); cf. n.1 on its relation to Du Q; and J. Van Sickle 'How do we read ancient texts? Codes & critics in Virgil, *Eclogue* One' *MD* 13 (1984) 107–31 (criticising Du Q's method and attempting a general refutation).

second aim of this paper is brevity — and all the more achievable thanks to Du Q's thoroughness; and for brevity's sake issue will not be taken here with Du Q's adherence to the generic approach of F. Cairns,[2] especially since the main elements of Du Q's new reading of *Eclogue* 1 are independent of it.

Du Q's central interpretive point (115–38) is his thesis that Tityrus had been manumitted only informally. So (Du Q argues), since his endeavours to secure money sufficient to buy his full freedom had failed, the menace to his master's estate was also one to his (informal) freedom. In order to secure that freedom (which nevertheless remained slavery; cf. the address *pueri* = 'slaves' in Du Q's interpretation, on which see below, § I) Tityrus could and did "turn to the *praetor* for protection" (125). The apparent difficulty, obscurity, illogicality, and inconsistency of *Eclogue* 1 are due, Du Q attempts to demonstrate, to past interpreters' failure to recognise the common Roman practice of informal manumission as the key to the poem. Its enigmatic character evaporates, so Du Q claims, and the prologue to the book shines forth in its pristine clarity once this has been recognised and acknowledged. On the contrary, in my own view, the result of Du Q's endeavour is an almost impenetrable jungle. In attempting to refute Du Q's interpretation and detailed explanations, I shall concentrate on *Eclogue* 1.27–45, working my way back from the last to the first line of this most important, most difficult, and most controversial passage.

I The address *'Pueri'* in line 45

Du Q's comment on line 45 (*pascite ut ante boves, pueri; summittite tauros*) is that here *pueri* "can only mean 'slaves' " (135). It is, unusually for Du Q, a dogmatic comment. Du Q n.605, adding "The usage is common in comedy, letters and satire", is not really helpful, since *Eclogue* 1 belongs to none of those categories. Du Q's real reason for excluding other possibilities is his basic thesis that Tityrus was, is, and remains a slave, i.e. one only "informally manumitted".

The context of line 45 needs to be considered. The young god's divine help and rescue (*beneficium*, σωτηρία) meant for Tityrus freedom or retaining possession of his farm (see below) or both (thus Du Q, who, however, limits 'freedom' to 'informal manumission', which legally remains servitude). The answer to the countryman's request was

---

[2] As set out in *Generic Composition in Greek and Roman Poetry* (Edinburgh 1972) and later publications. I confess to having never read a better plea on its behalf.

an oracle-like divine and sovereign utterance. And this god on this occasion is supposed to be saying: 'Graze cattle as before, you slaves', and this final word of a god in the hour of need is the climax of a process (27–9) which began with the phrase: *Libertas ... respexit ...*! That is, if not absurd, at least bizarre.

A more detailed examination pays more dividends. It could be asked if the triumvir Octavian in his function as *praetor* might have had no choice on that occasion (taken for the moment as historically factual) but to use the *mot juste* (i.e. a technical term) for the social status of Tityrus. However, *pueri* is hardly the formal designation of an informally manumitted slave; and in any case there is no evidence about the behaviour of magistrates on such occasions. Furthermore we do not know whether or not there is a real background to *Eclogue* 1, i.e. whether or not the poem is an authentic documentary protocol of an historical event. Its historicity may well be doubted, if only because even in antiquity trees and wells are unlikely to have been able to utter words and to call out audibly for "Tityrus" (38–9). We can be certain, however, that Vergil is conveying the impression made on Tityrus by the encounter in Rome (whether real, i.e. based on a real event or experience, or, a safer hypothesis, fictional). That encounter, which will be represented as possible (probable, *veri simile*) in the eyes of contemporaries, is remembered by a fictional figure who had been the beneficiary of that encounter and who is speaking from a grateful heart in a fictional poem.

How then does Tityrus represent his encounter? Du Q 97–138 usefully refers to the ancient, the Roman and the Augustan language of gratitude and to the categories employed to express the experience of help.[3] The reply of the saviour-god will, therefore, be couched in the same language as lines 6–10 and 40–45. It will scarcely be expressed in the official protocol of an administrative act, even if it evokes such a background, i.e. a possible historical event.

Instead of averring that "'pueri' can only mean 'slaves'" I suggest, then, that *pueri* here means "my children", as Guy Lee translated it.[4] *pueri* would thus refer either to Tityrus and to his (absent) 'wife' Amaryllis or to Tityrus alone; in the latter case the speaker would be following the practice of using the plural instead of the singular in such

---

[3]   Central elements of his comments can also be found in V. Pöschl *Die Hirtendichtung Virgils* (Heidelberg 1964) 15–19.

[4]   *Virgil, The Eclogues. The Latin Text with a Verse Translation and Brief Notes* (Penguin Books 1984).

addresses. The idea of help and salvation is connected with that of the 'father' not only in (later) Augustan times but generally in Greek and Roman thought. Andreas Alföldi, *Der Vater des Vaterlandes im römischen Denken* (Darmstadt 1971) is a fundamental source for this complex of ideas. The entire complex of ideas and associations need not be repeated here; it is enough to quote Sophocles *Oedipus Rex* 58: Ὦ παῖδες οἰκτροί. The king who is bidden to save the city (46 and 51: ἀνόρθωσον πόλιν) and who is regarded as σωτήρ (47–8) and, although not god-like, as best of men (31–3 and 46), so addresses the old priest (cf. 9) who is speaking for the chorus of citizens old and young (15–19).[5]

In the picture that Tityrus' grateful memory has preserved of him (cf. *Eclogue* 1.63) Octavian, the young god, speaks like a fatherly king. This may even be the first vestige of the later Augustan notion of the *princeps* as *pater patriae*. Tityrus (and the poet) refrain from explicit identification of the saviour-god and father (and ruler and king) because of the god's youth; more than a decade later Horace would combine *iuvenis* and 'father' (and *princeps*) in *Odes* 1.2.41–2 and 50. Vergil and Tityrus hide (and reveal) that notion in the paternal address *pueri* to Tityrus, whose request about the farm had been for himself and for his 'wife'. This interpretation fits its context superbly, above all if we pay heed to Clausen's reminder of how Wissowa (anticipated by Buecheler and followed by Jachmann) had shown that Tityrus' monthly sacrifice to his benefactor is taken over from Hellenistic ruler-cult.[6]

It is not claimed here that Du Q's central thesis has been refuted by this suggestion but only that it is not confirmed by line 45. In addition, it has been argued that *pueri* as 'children' fits the language of its context better than *pueri* as 'slaves'.

II   Lines 40–41

Du Q offers (125, 127) as a new interpretation of lines 40–41: "It was not possible for me to escape from being a slave" (the "attempts to free himself altogether from slavery had failed") "and nowhere else could anyone like my benefactor, my *deus*, hear my case." In other words Tityrus opens his explanation with the statement that he was informally free, i.e. legally a slave, before his visit to Rome, and that he remains so after the visit; he follows that up by recounting his expectation that

---

[5]   Cf. also Xen. *Cyrop.* 8.1.1; Aristot. *EN* 1160b 22–7.
[6]   W. Clausen *A Commentary on Virgil, Eclogues* (Oxford 1994) 48–9.

he would find help only in Rome and then telling what he experienced there.

The first argument advanced by Du Q (n.564) in favour of this reading is that "the normal view of the situation ... makes it necessary to supply ... *alibi* ... or *alio modo* ... or the like with this clause" (i.e. line 40). But in fact there is no question of supplying anything here or of having a free choice among *alibi, alio modo* or whatever; according to the rules of Latin syntax and stylistics, *alibi* belongs to both phrases, just as *me* and *licebat* in the first phrase belong (without 'supplying' them) also to the second. This is the figure often called ἀπὸ κοινοῦ, a subspecies of *Versparung*,[7] i.e. the deliberate suppression of a word (or words) at the point where they would naturally come and their postponement to a later position. Examples of *Versparung* of an adverb (such as *alibi*) are Lucretius 2.55–6: *nam veluti pueri trepidant atque omnia caecis/ in tenebris metuunt ...* (where *trepidant* too is qualified by *caecis in tenebris*); Tibullus 2.3.68: *glans alat et prisco more bibantur aquae* (cf. Kühner–Stegmann II.561); Ovid *Fasti* 2.277: *Pan erat armenti, Pan illic numen equarum.* Examples involving other parts of speech are Lucretius 4.774: *tantast mobilitas et rerum copia tanta* (cf. Kühner–Stegmann II.561); Pliny *Panegyricus* 44.3: *nemo est ergo tam tui, tam ignarus sui*; more examples can be found at Kühner–Stegmann I.54–5. Horace *Epode* 7.11–12 *neque hic lupis mos nec fuit leonibus/ umquam ...*, which is more or less contemporaneous, is very similar to *Eclogue* 1.40–41: note especially *neque – nec* Horace and Vergil; *mos ... fuit* Horace – *licebat* Vergil; *alibi* Vergil – *umquam* Horace, with in both cases the adverb postponed from the first phrase into the second. *Eclogue* 1 itself offers a parallel in 57–8: *nec tamen interea raucae, tua cura, palumbes/ nec gemere aëria cessabit turtur ab ulmo.*

Du Q's second argument (126) involves four points:

(a) "the phrase *cognoscere divos* is unique"
(b) "*cognoscere deum/deos* does not appear elsewhere in Classical Latin. Moreover it is less than obvious what the Latin, when so construed, means"
(c) "*cognoscere aliquem* cannot mean 'to find or meet someone' "

---

[7] Cf. G. Kiefner *Die Versparung* (Tübingen 1964); G. Maurach *Lateinische Dichtersprache* (Darmstadt 1995) 94 (§128 Ἀπὸ κοινοῦ II (Spätsetzung) referring to Fraenkel on Aesch. *Ag.* 589); 95 n.89 referring to Kiefner (above) 43ff. on "verteilte Aussparung", i.e. cases like *Ecl.* 1.40–41 (*licebat* and *alibi*).

(d) "It could mean 'to get to know someone'. But the intimate familiarity of *cognoscere* in this sense would combine uneasily with the grandeur and distance of *tam praesentis ... divos.*"

Du Q therefore suggests taking *divos* as subject of the second infinitive and *cognoscere* as "to hear a case".

Point (a) is hardly powerful: unique phrases do occur in ancient literature; poetry (and even rhetoric) is and was, even in antiquity, more than conventionalism and the repetition of ready-made formulae and clichés. The principle 'one instance no instance, two instances the norm' is a product of the *déformation professionelle* of philology: poets are not classical scholars.

Point (b) again lacks weight. Du Q n.572 refers to *cognitio deorum* at Cicero *De Natura Deorum* 1.32 (with Pease *ad loc.*, listing other occurrences of this phrase in the same work). If, for instance, *deorum cognitionem ... capere* (2.140) and *accedere ad cognitionem deorum* (2.153) are possible Latin, it is hard to see the significance of Du Q's statement that *cognoscere deos* does not appear elsewhere. Besides, no Latinist may with impunity forget the fundamental heteroglossia[8] of Roman literary culture. If γιγνώσκειν θεόν/θεούς existed in Greek — cf. Theocritus *Idyll* 3.15: νῦν ἔγνων τὸν Ἔρωτα; Euripides *Bacchae* 859–60: γνώσεται δὲ τὸν Διός/ Διόνυσον ... — then *cognoscere deum/deos* was possible and normal Latin and requires no further support.

Points (c) and (d) are sound. But they do not lead inevitably to Du Q's rendering of *tam praesentis cognoscere divos*. Du Q n.573 cites the clause *hominem gravem et prudentem ... cognovi* (Cicero *Ad Atticum* 2.22.7), translating it "I found him [to be] serious and responsible" and stressing that this sense of 'find' is different from 'find' = 'meet' or 'encounter'. A similar usage appears at Cicero *Tusculans* 1.36: *sed ut deos esse natura opinamur, qualesque sint, ratione cognoscimus ....* What, then, prevents us from understanding *Eclogue* 1.41 (literally) as "nor could I elsewhere experience (find, recognise, realise) the gods [to be] so helpful"? This is how Friedrich Klingner translated it: "noch anderswo die Götter so hilfreich nahe gewahren".[9] And do not the

---

[8] Cf. M. Bakhtin 'From the prehistory of novelistic discourse' (first published in Russian, 1967) in M. Holquist (ed.) *The Dialogic Imagination: Four Essays* (Austin Texas 1981) 61–2.

[9] *Virgil, Bucolica / Hirtengedichte* Übersetzt und erläutert von F. Klingner (München 1977).

word-order and the addition of *tam* to *praesentis* virtually guarantee this rendering? Besides, a close parallel appears elsewhere in *Eclogue* 1: *sic canibus catulos similis, sic matribus haedos/ noram* (22–3) — 'I knew (had come to know, had experienced etc.) cubs to be similar ...'.

On the negative side, Du Q's interpretation of lines 40–41 has a number of flaws:

(i) The structure of lines 40–41 (i.e. *neque ... exire licebat/ nec... cognoscere ...*) suggests that they contain a logical parallelism. But 'neither was A possible nor elsewhere B' is hardly a plausible logical parallelism. Indeed, the rendering "It was not possible ... and nowhere else could ..." offered by Du Q destroys even the linguistic parallelism of *neque ... nec*.

(ii) Du Q connects the second negation specifically with *alibi* instead of with the phrase as a whole.

(iii) Du Q has to supply two items, one in each phrase (my italics): Tityrus could not "free himself *altogether* from slavery", which implies that he was not able to do that on his own, by his own means, and that there are degrees of liberty (not in the text); and "It was not possible elsewhere for such powerful gods ... to hear *my* case" (not in the text).

(iv) Du Q's suggested meaning limits the gods' power and independence strangely: they were not able (it was not permitted to them, not allowed to them, they must not, they had no chance) to hear a supplicant's case elsewhere than in Rome. The converse, i.e. that Tityrus could not recognise how helpful gods are elsewhere than in Rome, is emotionally and theologically different — and acceptable: the supplicant who had hoped to experience gods as helpful in Rome and whose hope had been fulfilled connects that experience with Rome. Only there, he feels, has he been able to recognise gods in their helpful epiphany. He would never have concluded from this that the gods' power and possible presence were restricted to Rome.

(v) "Men like my benefactor" (Du Q 125–6) is a weak and oblique rendering of *tam praesentis* ....

(vi) *exire servitio*, for Du Q equivalent to "freeing oneself from slavery", seems, however, to designate the result of a legal procedure (cf. *OLD s.v.* 6a), here in consequence of the slave's activity. Compare Quintilian *Institutio Oratoria* 11.1.88: *licet* (*sc. oratori*) *his* (*sc. libertinis*) *testimonium reddere industriae, per quam exierint de servitute* (quoted by Du Q n.563).

Du Q's attempt to redefine the meaning of lines 40–41 must therefore be rejected. It is, again, motivated solely by the (incorrect) hypothesis that Tityrus had been manumitted only informally.

III Lines 36–9

Lines 36–9, with their symptoms of Amaryllis' love and with the landscape missing its master (the pathetic fallacy), are strangely misunderstood by Du Q 86ff., who interprets them on the basis of the schetliastic propemptikon. But Amaryllis' attitude was far from schetliastic: she was sad, she longed for her lover, she waited for him and she prepared for his return. In no way can her 'faith' here be contrasted with a "breach of faith" on Tityrus' part. What, it might be asked, is unfaithful in Tityrus' leaving for Rome (an action of which neither Amaryllis nor Meliboeus disapproves) in order to obtain his own freedom plus the possession of his property for himself and Amaryllis?

IV Lines 33–5

In Du Q's interpretation lines 33–5 refer to a recent past, to the time of Amaryllis (122). That is impossible. After lines 31–2: ... *dum me Galatea tenebat,/ nec spes libertatis erat nec cura peculi*, the reader must connect lines 33–5 and their imperfect tenses (*exiret* 33, *premeretur* 34, *redibat* 35) with that time and must take them as an explanation of *nec cura peculi* (32). And indeed Du Q offers no alternative explanation of how the transition from lines 31–2 to 33–5 can be understood.

Du Q's reason for thinking that lines 33–5 refer to the time of Amaryllis is that here Tityrus is a hard-working rustic, a fact that sorts badly with the "account of a *servus iners* who has no *cura peculi*." That is not correct: *inertem* (27) does not designate Tityrus specifically at the time of Galatea, but generally and above all at the time of Freedom's gracious turning of her face to him, i.e. recently (and, therefore, precisely at the time to which Du Q ascribes lines 32–5). It does not mean here 'lazy, indolent' (see below); and line 32 does not say: 'I took no care of the cattle', 'I neglected my flock', being dominated by elegiac love of Galatea, "and so [I] could not even hope for freedom" (Du Q 121), but rather 'When Galatea held me, there was no hope of freedom (*spes libertatis*, placed before *cura peculi*, is left out by Du Q 121) and no care of savings' (= 'because there was no care of savings'). *nec cura peculi* (32) is explained by lines 33–5 which show that *peculium* does not designate here 'farm and cattle' (see below on the two meanings of *peculium*) and that *nec cura* is not laziness as regards work on his part (Tityrus has always taken care of his flock) but their (Galatea's and Tityrus') financial negligence.

But Du Q has a more important motive: Amaryllis is not to be given credit for Tityrus' manumission. Although "the situation improved" after Galatea's departure, that was due not to Amaryllis' qualities as a good housewife, but rather to Tityrus ceasing to be an elegiac love-slave: Tityrus "was still in love, this time with Amaryllis" (Du Q 122), but less so, being now relatively free from *servitium amoris*. Poor Amaryllis: she is not only deprived of her merits as the shepherd's mate who makes freedom financially possible, but, unchivalrously, she is not to be the object of romantic elegiac love, although she is *formosa* (5) and the subject of Tityrus' love-song. Undeserving, as it were, of her lover's unconditional devotion, she becomes a (negative) stimulus to his endeavour to free himself: he now commits himself to working! However, if the time of Galatea is characterised by *nec spes libertatis nec cura peculi* (32), it is obvious from the arrangement of lines 27–35 and from the direction of their argument that *nec spes* etc. also means: 'but at the time of Amaryllis there was hope of freedom and care for savings'.

V Lines 31–2

Du Q rejects the notion of Tityrus purchasing his freedom (n.550): "The conventional view is that Tityrus had at last accumulated sufficient *peculium* to buy his freedom and goes to Rome to do so. But he is obviously still in possession of his *peculium*, so he cannot have used it to purchase his freedom. In this respect, the traditional view is once more illogical and confused." This attempt at refutation will not wash. Note as a preliminary that *peculium* which in Latin usage has two different senses, 'savings from the produce' and 'possession of land and livestock', is here taken as if it had only a single meaning.

(i) The existence of a *peculium* (i.e. Tityrus' farm — land and cattle) both before[10] and after his manumission, is taken for granted by Du Q, as by others. Tityrus is "still in possession of his *peculium*". On Du Q's view, as on the conventional view, this situation is unexplained by Vergil. Du Q advances an additional hypothesis: "This new freedom was apparently accompanied by the gift of a small farm as well as

---

[10] Du Q n.553 remarks that "land would not normally be part of the *peculium* of a *pastor*." Cf. n.555 about "the exceptional position of Tityrus as a landowner".

livestock. These would be, technically, Tityrus' *peculium*" (123); "Tityrus' position is thus unusual: though a rustic slave he has been manumitted, apparently at the will of his master, and at no cost to himself. In addition he has been given as his *peculium* not only quite a large number of cattle and sheep, but also land" (123). Thus, in the very heart of a reconstruction that claims both to be an analysis of the text and to demonstrate that it was perfectly clear to contemporary readers because it mirrored conventional notions and general practice, we find an unwarranted assumption ("apparently") and an exception, a unique and unparalleled event ("unusual"). The additional assumption could also be made, and has been made,[11] with equal justification by the partisans of the conventional reading.

(ii)   The *peculium* in line 32 is not "his flock", which he "neglected" (Du Q's paraphrase, 121) in the time of Galatea when he was a slave (here Du Q presumes a *peculium* before Tityrus' manumission and before the additional gift of the *peculium*, cf. also Du Q 123); nor is it only the land and livestock possessed by the informal *libertus*. It is also the earnings from that rural possession, i.e. what Tityrus was able to save after Galatea had left him, when the conditions described in lines 33–5 no longer held good. In all this one thing is certain: a slave could never buy his freedom by selling his land and livestock. The simple reason (apart from the fact that freedom without the means of subsistence would be pointless) is that a slave was legally unable to do so.

If a *dominus* could "manumit any slave and bestow whatever property on him he wished" (Du Q 123), he could surely also manumit a slave able to purchase his freedom with the earnings of his hard work. But if Tityrus already had a *peculium* (land and livestock) before manumission (as Du Q agrees), why should he need a specific additional present at the moment of manumission? Again, Du Q contends that for Tityrus to achieve complete freedom, i.e. to transform the gift of informal freedom into formal freedom, money was needed, which Tityrus failed to supply in sufficient amount; if this were correct, that money would also have to be called *peculium*. In fact the (informally) manumitting master who, in Du Q's reconstruction, replaces Amaryllis (the so-called conventional view) can be dismissed. Introducing him amounts to augmenting the problems of *peculium*, dragging in more gratuitous assumptions alien to the text and rendering the whole

---

[11]   Cf. the quotation from Friedrich Leo's article (below p.198).

explanation even more confused and illogical.

VI Lines 27–30

In Du Q's analysis lines 27–30 are not a single period, but two independent parallel phrases. His argument is that the *geminatio* in subordinate and main clause, *tamen respexit* and *respexit tamen*, is "stylistically inelegant" (119). I cannot see why. What is inelegant about *Pan etiam, Arcadia mecum si iudice certet,/ Pan etiam Arcadia dicat se iudice victum* (*Eclogue* 4.58–9)? Or, if it is inelegant, how is it to be explained away? Is Isaiah 53.7 clumsy: *non aperuit os suum ... quasi agnus coram tondente obmutescet et non aperiet os suum*? With Vergil's variation *tamen respexit — respexit tamen* compare *Eclogue* 1.1 and 4: *Tityre, tu — tu, Tityre*.

Du Q's real motive for transforming the single period into two parallel phrases is to render analogous the two temporal clauses (*candidior postquam tondenti barba cadebat* and *postquam nos Amaryllis habet, Galatea reliquit*) and thereby to deprive the second temporal clause of its causal character. "Tityrus presents the connection between his manumission and his relationship with Amaryllis as temporal, not causal (*postquam*)" (Du Q 122). In fact in the second *postquam* clause Tityrus is giving an explanation of the first, as is also shown by *namque ... dum me Galatea tenebat,/ nec spes ...* (31–2), lines that become meaningless on any other explanation. Du Q states (120) "*quae sera* is an elliptical relative clause with concessive force (*tamen*), a type of expression frequent with this adjective." This statement blurs the fact that *sera tamen* is frequent, but the elliptical relative clause *quae sera tamen* is not.[12] Du Q provides no parallels, and they are, indeed, very rare (cf. Leumann–Hofmann–Szantyr II.421). There is no need to hypothesise the presence of *quae sera tamen* here; on the contrary, it is hard to see why a reader should not have connected *quae* with *respexit*. Du Q takes *inertem* (27) as causal: Tityrus "had been manumitted only late in life because of his laziness" (120); "the *inertia* of Tityrus was that of the lover" (121), i.e. of the (elegiac) lover — but only of Galatea. We have seen that line 32 does not mean that Tityrus was lazy when in love with Galatea, and it is evident that he cannot have been lazy in the time of Amaryllis. *inertia* is not the quality of a lazy slave, but the condition of this old man who realises that it has

---

[12] Elliptical relative clauses in general are not infrequent. Cf. *Ecl.* 1.53; 2.23. Different: *Ecl.* 3.8–9 (aposiopesis).

taken him so long to reach freedom and that he has not much strength or force and therefore feels powerless, feeble, ineffectual.[13] The adjective (which is given additional colour in line 28) stresses the grace and the power of the goddess Freedom; her looking graciously on the *iners* does not mean: 'she made me free in spite of my (earlier) sloth' or 'she could not come earlier because of my being (Du Q: having been in the past) a sluggard' (cf. Du Q 120), or 'she looked upon me only now when I was industrious, after I had finished being lazy', but 'she looked at me in my weakness'. Why must Amaryllis, as in Du Q's reconstruction of the story, lose her credit for Tityrus' freedom? This does not become clear. Du Q stresses the divine character of freedom. That, however, does not speak against Amaryllis' help any more than it would speak against Tityrus' own merit. If we do not acknowledge that Amaryllis is to Tityrus' freedom what the *iuvenis* is to his possessions, then the form and meaning of the whole poem escape us. The song for Amaryllis (5) and the immediately succeeding expression of gratitude to the god (6–10) are connected with each other in the same way as the question why Tityrus went to Rome (26) and the immediately succeeding *Libertas* ... (27–35). Amaryllis and *Libertas* are analogous to the *iuvenis* in Rome and to the salvation of Tityrus' possessions in that they are their prerequisites (see below), the pastoral substructure and mirror of the poem's political and Roman strand. Du Q is right in recognising "that Tityrus [in lines 27–35] does not answer Meliboeus directly ... and that *Libertas* is no more the *causa* than *Roma* was the *deus*" (120). *Libertas* is, indeed, not Tityrus' desire/intention/purpose in travelling to Rome. But before he can explain what his purpose in going to Rome was, he must tell Meliboeus that he had become a free man beforehand or, to put it more cautiously, that 'Freedom had already turned her face upon him': therefore the necessity of going to Rome must have had for its background and very condition that freedom or (again more reservedly) the favourable smile of the goddess.

On Du Q 118–19 we read:

> If Tityrus had been a slave, then he would not have been evicted, but confiscated along with the farm as part of the *instrumentum*. That is how slaves were normally considered and Dio is quite explicit that Octavian confiscated both slaves and equipment along with the land for distribution to the veterans. This is a point of considerable

---

[13] Cf. *TLL s.v.* 1309.67–9; *OLD s.v.* 5a; Hor. *AP* 172; Sen. *Herc.* 696: *iners Senectus.*

importance. Meliboeus assumed (11f.), so the reader must also be expected to assume, that Tityrus was a free man.

That is correct, nothing in the poem contradicts it,[14] and it will also form an integral part of my own interpretation (below). Tityrus is a free man in the dialogue presented by the poem. Meliboeus' surprise at seeing him not evicted is due to his assumption that Tityrus is free (Du Q 118). Meliboeus and Tityrus, who address each other by name, appear to know each other. But they do not seem to be mutually well-informed about biographical details (cf. lines 36–9: although knowing Amaryllis and knowing that she is Tityrus' wife, Meliboeus did not ask about her grief, realising only now that it was for Tityrus' absence and, therefore, only now extrapolating from the girl's longing to that of her landscape). We learn too from Tityrus himself that he is free: *Libertas ... respexit inertem* (27). But what of *servitio me exire (alibi non) licebat* (40), a statement referring to Tityrus' condition after Freedom's favourable glance? I repeat my own suggestion of 1987.[15] The advent of divine Freedom and her smiling face mean that Tityrus, with the help of Amaryllis, had come near to freedom, i.e. had acquired sufficient *peculium* to be able to obtain his (full) freedom. He travelled to Rome in order to have that smile of the goddess (symbolic of an event which he had nearly despaired of) transformed into a legal act, to have it sealed and formally confirmed in an administrative procedure (*exire servitio non nisi Romae licebat*). Formal manumission appears to have required the presence of a magistrate with *imperium*, and for that reason it seems to have been more or less restricted to Rome, where it was easier to find a magistrate. In any case the agreement of a praetor was needed to confirm an informal manumission and to render it formal. Freedom's smile was the prerequisite and the reason for going to Rome; the purpose of the journey was *exire servitio*. But then and only then was Tityrus threatened. The menace did not arise because for Tityrus, as for an informally manumitted slave, confiscation of his land

[14] I find it, then, very odd that Du Q 118 takes *en quo discordia civis/ produxit miseros!* (71–2) to imply that "in fact Meliboeus excludes" Tityrus from the status of a *civis*. Du Q surely cannot be suggesting that free citizens are miserable because of their discord, whereas slaves are happy because of their *concordia*. Neither can this bewildering comment be explained as referring to the fact that Tityrus as a slave would not have been evicted (see above), because that is excluded by the poem itself — even in Du Q's reading: its essential meaning is that Tityrus' happiness is due not to his status but to a god's gracious gift.

[15] E.A. Schmidt *Bukolische Leidenschaft oder Über antike Hirtenpoesie* (Studien zur klassischen Philologie 22, Frankfurt am Main–Bern–New York 1987) 129–38.

would mean that he would be "treated as a slave and confiscated". That is not how Meliboeus understands the rescue — *ergo tua rura manebunt* (46) — but because, as a free man, he would be evicted and lose his estate (see Du Q 118–19 as quoted above). Then and only then the god saved him, not saving his freedom, which was not menaced, but his farm: *ergo tua rura manebunt*.[16]

Specialists will recognise that this interpretation is similar to that of Friedrich Leo in 1903.[17] I repeat Leo's view here in order to underscore my own point. Leo wrote:

> After manumission, Tityrus continued to be in possession of his farm, as was the rule; there was no need for a specific donation, and Tityrus did not have to mention it. However, in consequence of the division of land in Italy, from which Meliboeus and the neighbours had to suffer, this possession was menaced precisely at the moment when Tityrus should have begun to enjoy his freedom. It was this menace from which the 'god' had saved him. That was the goal of the whole dialogue: Tityrus is to relate how it had come to happen; and indeed his story is directed toward that point. Beginning with line 20, he answers Meliboeus' question: he must talk of Rome, because it was there that he saw the god; of his buying his freedom, because that was what had taken him to Rome, ... There was no reason for him to mention explicitly that he obtained freedom, having once come to Rome; it is not a motif begun only to be cut off arbitrarily, it is of secondary significance and has by now done its duty.

On my interpretation, derived, of course, from Leo's, Tityrus' purchase of his freedom is not a secondary motif serving only to bring him to Rome; nor are the two motifs independent of each other. They are interrelated, the first, freedom, being the very condition and pre-requisite for the god's salvation. Without it, Tityrus would not have been in need of the god's help, because it was only as a free person and as the legal owner of his estate that his existence was threatened.[18] The

---

[16] *tua* in this position is hardly predicative — as Coleman and Clausen *ad loc.* take it. The sense 'so the lands will remain yours' is implied equally by the phrase if it is taken in a more natural way: 'so your lands will remain', where the absolute *manere* has in itself, along with the denotation 'to continue to be' (cf. Ov. *AA* 3.439), the connotation 'remain with': cf. Stat. *Silv.* 2.5.17: *manere animi*; Ov. *Met.* 1.17: *nulli sua forma manebat*; Verg. *Ecl.* 5.78: *semper honos nomenque tuum laudesque manebunt* ('... your name ... will endure', not '... the name will remain yours ...'), but implying, of course, that honour will remain with him and praise will remain for him.

[17] 'Vergils erste und neunte Ekloge' *Hermes* 38 (1903) 1–18, (translated) quotation at 7–8.

[18] Cf. Du Q 118–19 (quoted above p.196).

apparent detour of verses 19–40 was necessary not because Tityrus had to explain why he had been in Rome (where he saw the young god), and that he had gone there in order to buy his freedom; rather it was that, in order to tell of the god and to make his gift intelligible, he had to demonstrate in advance that he had become a free man and that his new freedom had made him vulnerable at the moment of the evictions and in need of a miracle, one that came as the help from the god about whom Meliboeus wants to learn in line 18. It is only on this reading, which may appear to be insignificantly different from Leo's, that the eclogue begins to reveal its wonderful and significant structural fabric. Amaryllis mirrors the *iuvenis*; her help inside the pastoral world reflects the god's salvation of the pastoral world from without. Tityrus' bucolic song about Amaryllis (1–5) is the poetic reflection[19] of the bucolic poem as a whole, the poet Vergil's song of gratitude to Octavian.[20]

VII Du Q's thesis and its self-contradictions

I shall now briefly sum up the intrinsic difficulties of Du Q's thesis as based on his analysis of the central part of *Eclogue* 1. According to Du Q, Tityrus "has been manumitted" (116) in the recent past and he "had been manumitted before going to Rome" (119); "he had been a free man for a relatively short time" (121). His manumission was, however, only informal and "he was legally a *servus*" (119). That is, the paragraph which begins with the words *Libertas ... respexit* (27–29), the gracious smile of the goddess Freedom, is taken to designate the informal manumission of a person who legally remains a slave. The difference between informal and formal manumission is understood to be one between incomplete/partial and complete/full freedom: Tityrus "had not been able to acquire sufficient money to buy his full freedom" (Du Q 116); "He was eager to acquire enough money to obtain his full, formal manumission" (123).

There is no evidence in our sources for Du Q's assumption of the proportional relationship 'as sufficient money corresponds to full (i.e. formal) manumission and freedom, so insufficient money corresponds to incomplete (i.e. informal) manumission and freedom'. Moreover the concept is intrinsically flawed: you cannot buy part of freedom for part of the sum required for complete freedom. And even though Du Q too

---

[19] Cf. E.A. Schmidt *Poetische Reflexion. Vergils Bukolik* (München 1972).
[20] Cf. Schmidt (n.15) esp. 134.

seems to have been aware of this flaw (123) — because he suggests that Tityrus had been informally manumitted "unexpectedly and without paying for it" (albeit late because of his elegiac love and neglect of his flock, so that he could not even hope for freedom) — nevertheless Du Q regards money as the means of transforming informal into formal and full freedom. In fact, as argued below, there is evidence that the difference between informal and formal freedom was one of legal procedure, not of money and degrees of freedom.

In Du Q's reconstruction the threat to Tityrus is the confiscation; for the informally free rustic this would amount not to eviction, but to degrading him again to the status of a slave. Du Q offers this hypothesis even though he acknowledges that Meliboeus takes Tityrus' freedom for granted and is amazed at his not having been evicted. This hypothesis is launched in the face of *ergo tua rura manebunt* (46)! Tityrus went to Rome — still on Du Q's interpretation — to secure protection for his freedom, a request that, as conditions were, was aimed primarily at the protection of the farm and only thus entailed also his freedom. Whose farm? In the context of Du Q's argument it must be that of his master, since only in that case would Tityrus, when the land changed its owner, not be "evicted, but confiscated along with the farm as part of the *instrumentum*" (Du Q 118). The "threat of confiscation [of his [master's] farm] ... posed a threat to his [informal] *libertas*" (125). However, in connection with Tityrus' freedom and *peculium* Du Q 123 assumes that Tityrus the slave was also given at the moment of his informal manumission "a small farm as well as livestock". In that case he "would be immune from confiscation" (124). This is rather illogical: whereas the legal background adduced by Du Q has the *auxilium praetoris* granting formal freedom — this and only this can be meant when a person looks for help in Rome in connection with threats to his freedom — Tityrus in Rome, on Du Q's account, secures for "his [?] farm" (127) exemption from confiscation (*ergo tua rura manebunt*, 46) and remains a slave (*pueri*, 45), i.e. informally free.

VIII   A constructive alternative

My own interpretation involves the following principal elements. Like Du Q I take Tityrus' answer to Meliboeus' question (i.e. *Libertas* etc.) to be indirect. Freedom had already smiled on the old rustic, because Amaryllis and he had saved enough money to buy freedom. The formal act in Rome is not the graceful look of the goddess. It is only the legal procedure of *exire servitio*, which has for its prerequisite the accumulation of money. In his gratitude to Amaryllis, the final attainment by Tityrus of the requirements for freedom is represented as the grace of divine Freedom; it is as if, for example, a poet who has worked hard to make his poems worthy and pleasant were to speak of Charis having wiped her perfumed hands upon his verses, or as if a hard-working cattle-breeder were to thank Faunus for his blessings. It is simply a fundamental aspect of ancient thought.

Before and while Tityrus went to Rome, he was neither formally nor informally free; he was a man who knew that he had already secured his freedom and that he needed to ratify it with the seal of an administrative act.[21] Freedom, however, had made him vulnerable, since only as a free man would he be threatened by eviction. Therefore, he addressed the young god in Rome with his petition. And the paternal answer of the saviour god was: 'my children, graze cattle as before'.

The moment of freedom's advent represented both the fulfillment of Tityrus' lifelong dream and his deepest crisis, because it coincided with the time when veterans were being settled. But was it intelligent of Tityrus to purchase his freedom just at that moment? Why did he not wait until the turmoil was over, if as a slave he had nothing to fear from evictions? Perhaps indeed it was not clever of Tityrus to act in this way — although the overall disorder might also have meant a menace to his savings if he had not. But it is deeply understandable that Tityrus reached out for his freedom at the very moment when it finally drew near after so long; and I think that it was Vergil's conscious decision to present an unexpected salvation, and to combine that salvation — in a personal crisis — with the reason for that crisis — a general disturbance.

In this way *Eclogue* 1 could reflect the world of Vergil as well as the world of Tityrus. Poetry is 'free'; and poets can and have been able to vindicate their freedom. But it is precisely because of that freedom that they are in need of subsistence, of the generous and uncompromising gift of the means of an independent life. Is gratitude to the source of that subsistence necessarily a spoiling factor?

---

[21] The problem of whether a slave could of his own volition leave his work and go to Rome scarcely arises. Once the master had accepted the purchase-money from his slave, it made no sense for him to prevent the slave from having the transaction legally confirmed in Rome.

PAPERS OF THE LEEDS INTERNATIONAL LATIN SEMINAR   TENTH VOLUME (1998) 203–34
Published by Francis Cairns (Publications) Ltd (Leeds 1998). ARCA 38. ISBN 0 905205 95 2

TIBULLUS 2.2*

FRANCIS CAIRNS
University of Leeds

Since some of this paper's suggestions are fairly radical, it may be useful to preface it with what, despite subsequent editions, is still perhaps the most frequently consulted text of Tibullus 2.2 available, that of J.P. Postgate's Oxford Classical Text (3rd edition) of 1924.[1]

> Dicamus bona verba: venit Natalis ad aras:
>> quisquis ades, lingua, vir mulierque, fave.
> urantur pia tura focis, urantur odores
>> quos tener e terra divite mittit Arabs.
> ipse suos Genius adsit visurus honores,   5
>> cui decorent sanctas mollia serta comas.
> illius puro destillent tempora nardo,
>> atque satur libo sit madeatque mero,
> adnuat et, Cornute, tibi, quodcumque rogabis.
>> en age (quid cessas? adnuit ille) roga.   10
> auguror, uxoris fidos optabis amores:
>> iam reor hoc ipsos edidicisse deos.
> nec tibi malueris, totum quaecumque per orbem
>> fortis arat valido rusticus arva bove,
> nec tibi, gemmarum quicquid felicibus Indis   15
>> nascitur, Eoi qua maris unda rubet.
> vota cadunt: utinam strepitantibus advolet alis
>> flavaque coniugio vincula portet Amor,
> vincula quae maneant semper dum tarda senectus
>> inducat rugas inficiatque comas.   20
> haec veniat, Natalis, avis prolemque ministret,
>> ludat et ante tuos turba novella pedes.

---

*   I am grateful for advice on this paper to Prof. T.J. Cornell, Dr M. Heath, Dr R. Maltby and Prof. P. Murgatroyd. Their assent to its conclusions should not be assumed.
[1]   Postgate himself writes of the 1924 edition as his third (*Praefatio* xiv), although the press continued to describe it as the second edition (of 1915). Semi-consonantal *v* is retained here although Postgate printed it as *u*.

I. Genre(s) and Speaker

Tibullus 2.2 is a genethliakon celebrating the birthday of Tibullus'
addressee Cornutus.[2] It also 'includes'[3] an example of another genre:
lines 11–22 celebrate Cornutus' marriage and contain a concentration
of epithalamic topoi (the wife's fidelity; a comparison of wealth and
virtue; a marriage god, in this case *Amor*; the colour orange/yellow
(*flava ...vincula*, 18); and hopes for offspring).[4] Thus they constitute an
(included) epithalamium. This 'generic inclusion' suggests an eco-
nomic answer to commentators' questions about Cornutus' marriage (is
it recent or forthcoming, and how does its timing relate to Cornutus'
wish that his wife will be faithful to him?),[5] i.e. that Cornutus was
marrying on his birthday. Birthdays were regarded as good days for
lovemaking in antiquity,[6] doubtless because of the prominence of the
Genius, the generative force, in birthday celebrations. Hence, pre-
sumably, if a man's birthday was convenient and not formally excluded
for religious reasons,[7] it would have been suitable as his wedding day.
An interesting similarity between Tibullus 2.2 and Tibullus 1.7
emerges if 2.2 is viewed in this way: 1.7 also celebrates a birthday, that
of Messalla; its genethliac portion is 'included' in a triumph-poem,[8] a
plausible explanation being that, like Pompey in 61 BC and Caligula in

---

[2]   On the genethliakon, cf. Schmidt (1908); Cesareo (1929); *RE s.vv.* Genethlios,
      Γενέθλιος ἡμέρα; Genius; *RAC s.v.* Geburtstag; *GC* General Index *s.v.* genethliakon;
      Van Dam (1984) 450–506. On Tib. 2.2 as a genethliakon, cf. *GC* 113; Murgatroyd 70.
      A 'generic formula' for the genethliakon will appear in Cairns (forthcoming).
[3]   *Pace* Murgatroyd 70 (on 2.2): "there is no generic admixture". For generic 'inclusion',
      cf. *GC* Ch.7.
[4]   No 'generic formula' as yet exists for the epithalamium. For the genre, cf. *RE s.v.*
      Epithalamium; *RAC s.v.* Epithalamium. For the specific topoi listed, cf.: *fidelity of the
      wife*: Wheeler (1930) 211, 212, 215; *comparison of wealth and love*: Call. *Aet.* fr.
      75.44–9 Pf.; *a marriage god*: Sappho fr. 112 L–P (Eros and Aphrodite); Philoxenos
      ap. Athen. *Deip.* 6A–B (the deified Gamos); Cat. 61; 62 (Hymen, Hymenaeus); *the
      colour orange/yellow*: Cat. 61.8, 115; Murgatroyd on Tib. 2.2.17–18, citing Cat.
      61.10; Ov. *Her.* 21.162; *Met.* 10.1; Lucan 2.361; Pliny *NH* 21.46; Treggiari (1991)
      163 — the bride wore *lutei socci* and *flammeum*; *hopes for offspring*: Wheeler (1930)
      211–12, 215; Cat. 61.204–5.
[5]   Cf., most recently, Murgatroyd 69–70.
[6]   Cf. Virg. *Ecl.* 3.76, with Serv. *ad loc.*: "PHYLLIDA MITTE MIHI amicam communem
      causa natalis diei, in cuius tantum sacrificio licebat voluptatibus operam dare; nam in
      aliis sacrificiis erat castitatis observatio ..."; Prop. 3.10, discussed below, § II.
[7]   For the "taboo times", cf. Treggiari (1991) 162. The prominence given to Lucan's
      marriage in Statius' posthumous genethliakon for him (*Silv.* 2.7.81–8) could reflect a
      similar coincidence between birthday and marriage.
[8]   The inclusion in Tib. 1.7 was erroneously formulated at *GC* 167; for a correction, cf.
      Tibullus 171–2.

AD 40, Messalla triumphed on his birthday.[9]

The speaker of Tibullus 2.2 is universally held to be the poet who "assumes the character of the officiating priest at the regular sacrifice to the Genius ... and pretends to interpret his will" — so Smith 411, echoed more or less closely by subsequent commentators.[10] This approach must to some extent be along the right lines: by beginning 2.2 with a set of ritual prescriptions and commands (1–10) and by continuing to employ language with a religious ring throughout, the speaker — let us for the moment simply call him 'Tibullus', although in fact the elegy contains nothing personal to the poet — is clearly adopting a priestly role. Thus 2.2 joins other Augustan poems where the poet has a discernible additional (and sacral) role — as a *vates* addressing a public assembly (Horace *Epode* 16),[11] as a priest (Propertius 3.1),[12] or as an *augur* (Propertius 3.4, Horace *Odes* 3.27).[13] But precisely what sort of "officiating priest" is Tibullus in 2.2? I propose that he is characterising himself specifically as an *augur/auspex*[14] (I do not distinguish between these terms in what follows)[15] like Horace in *Odes* 3.27 and Propertius in 3.4.[16] This self-characterisation is made in

[9] Cf. Weinstock (1971) 207–9.

[10] E.g. Della Corte (1980) 248 on line 1; Putnam (1973) 165; Newman (1967) 179; Ball (1983) 164; Murgatroyd 69.

[11] Cf. Fraenkel (1957) 42–53 (public assembly); *GC* 183–5 (*vates*).

[12] Cf. Fedeli (1985) 38–40.

[13] On Prop. 3.4, cf. *GC* 185–9; Fedeli (1985) 156–72, and below, § V. On Hor. *Od.* 3.27, cf. *GC* 189–92 (and 66–9); Clay (1993), with intermediate bibliography and further useful remarks on augural matters. I remain, however, unconvinced both by her detailed deductions about Horace's intentions and by her generic conclusions.

[14] The only indications of past scholarly awareness of this seem to be: 1) Two casual remarks of Della Corte (1980) 248 on line 1 *bona verba*: "sono le parole di augurio, etc."; and 249 on line 11: "l'augurio (*auguror* parentetico) andrebbe bene in un carme epitalamico". Since they were not followed up, Della Corte's position remains uncertain. 2) The comment of Putnam (1973) 165 on line 11: "Tibullus is first celebrant, now augur", again not followed up. On the alleged distinction between *auspex* and *augur*, cf. below, nn. 15, 16.

[15] Although much ink has been spilt on trying to discriminate them, success has not been achieved: cf. Catalano (1960) Indice delle materie *s.v. augurium* e *auspicium* (differenze); *TLL s.v. augurium* col. 1371.30–44. Plut. *Mor.* 281A regarded *auspex* as the old word for *augur*!

[16] It goes without saying (see also below § VII) that the role of the speaker here is that of *augur/auspex privatus*, since the circumstances, i.e. marriage and a birthday, are not public. On private augurs, cf. Pease (1920–3) index *s.v. auspicia; TLL s.vv. augur* III, *auspex;* Clay (1993) 172 n.20 reports Prof. J. Linderski as estimating "that, in 80% of its occurrences, *auspex* is the equivalent of *auspex nuptiarum*". But her own statement "Now, an *auspex*, as opposed to an *augur*, took private rather than public omens." (171–2) is an over-simplification: cf. *TLL s.v. augur* III. Technical treatises were written on private as well as public augury, cf. Grandazzi (1993b) 266, referring to

the opening word of the central couplet, *auguror* (11). If *auguror* were
the only indication of an augural context it could of course mean
merely 'I conjecture', since the word has a wide range of reference,[17]
— from the technical (augury *stricto sensu*) to the semi-technical
(prophecy in a sacral context) to the non-vatic but still sacred to secular
surmise or even observation. But the poem contains a web of allusion
to other augural terms, and these, together with the strong positioning
of *auguror*, are the determining factor:[18]

   11: *optabis* (in combination with *auguror*). Various passages of
Servius and Servius auctus[19] deriving ultimately from earlier treatises
on augury handle the distinction between 'sought' and 'unsought'
auguries. Cf., e.g., Servius *ad Aen.* 12.259: "QUOD SAEPE PETIVI quasi
inpetrativum hoc augurium vult videri. ACCIPIO AGNOSCOQUE DEOS
modo quasi de oblativo loquitur: nam in oblativis auguriis in potestate
videntis est, utrum id ad se pertinere velit, an refutet et abominetur."
Tibullus' allusion to this distinction emerges most clearly from another
Servian comment: "auguria aut oblativa sunt, quae non poscuntur, aut
inpetrativa, quae optata veniunt" (Servius *ad Aen.* 6.190). There was
even an attempt to differentiate *augurium* ('sought' signs given by

---

Nigidius Figulus as quoted by Aulus Gellius (*NA* 7.6.10) *in libro primo augurii
privati*.

[17] Cf. further *TLL s.vv. auguro(r), auspicor* and their cognates. The archaic *auguro* and
its later deponent *auguror* are not distinguished in sense: cf. *TLL s.v. auguro(r)*.
Rough sampling of the form *auguror* (*a.*) in Roman elegy and the non-elegiac works
of Ovid revealed the following (ascending) range: *Devoid of sacral context*: Ov. *Tr.*
4.6.40 (unless O.'s claim in ll.39–42 that he 'augurs' from his own (deteriorating)
body is a macabre evocation of one or more of the five augural categories, i.e. *ex diris*
or/and *ex quadrupedibus*); *Non-vatic 'sacral'*: Ov. *Her.* 2.126 (where Barchiesi (1992)
169 *ad loc.* interprets *a.* as "immagino, suppongo"), *Fast.* 4.62 (O. 'conjectures' the
derivation of Venus' name), *Tr.* 2.570 (O. refers to his poetry as *mea Calliope* (568)
before *a.* means only 'I anticipate'), *EP* 3.4.80 (*contentos a. esse deos*, followed by the
sacrificial scene of 81–2), *EP* 4.9.133 (about the now dead and deified Augustus);
Vatic and sacral: Prop. 3.1.36 (he 'prophesies' his posthumous fame, having described
himself (3) as *sacerdos*), Ov. *Met.* 10.27 (Orpheus — a *vates*, 12 — speaks and *a.* is
preceded (26) by *Amor* as *deus*), *EP* 3.1.133 (*a.*, although in itself meaning little more
than 'I suppose', appears between a couplet about oracles (131–2) and one (135–6)
referring to the house of Augustus as a temple).

[18] The accuracy of the ancient sources on augury is sometimes open to question, but not
their derivation from earlier technical treatises; hence they remain good witnesses to
Augustan augural thinking: cf. Catalano (1960) Indice delle materie *s.v.* Servio
Onorato etc. Although Tibullus exploits augural language, he was probably no expert;
poets in general do not appear to have had real expertise (cf. Catalano (1960) 73–4,
extending also (75) to some prose authors too), although Ovid may be the exception:
cf. below and nn.30, 32.

[19] For discussion of these passages, cf. Catalano (1960) Indice delle fonti citate.

certain birds) from *auspicium* (signs given 'unsought' and by any bird) on this basis: cf. Servius auct. *ad Aen.* 1.398: *augurium et petitur et certis avibus ostenditur, auspicium qualibet avi demonstratur et non petitur.*[20] Tibullus' conjunction of *auguror* and *optabis* signals his interest in the question and may indicate that he regarded the distinction as valid.[21] His earlier emphasis on wishing in *rogabis* (9) and *roga* (10), which anticipate *optabis*, initiates the theme, as *malueris* etc. in lines 13–16 continues it. In these passages it is the *auguria* which are 'wished for', while Cornutus is to wish for something which *auguria* might, or might not, give hope of. Tibullus may be blurring the boundaries here, perhaps because birthday wishes were a standard topos of the genethliakon,[22] as of real-life birthdays. But even in strictly augural contexts the wish for something and the wish for a confirmatory augury could be conflated: cf. Servius auct. *ad Aen.* 3.89: *augurium enim est exquisita deorum voluntas per consultationem avium aut signorum, quod tunc peti debet, cum id quod animo agitamus per augurium a diis volumus impetratum.*[23]

15: *felicibus*. A duty of the wedding *auspex* (on this topic, cf. below) was to be the first to say *feliciter* during the ceremony: cf. *'auspex' dicitur paranimphus qui interest nuptiis eo quod ab eo nuptiae auspicentur et quod primus 'feliciter' dicat.* (Schol. Bern. *ad* Lucan *Bellum Civile* 2.371). Cf. also *felix* at Ovid *Metamorphoses* 3.517 (below).

17: *vota cadunt*. A link between *auguria* and *vota* is found, albeit in different circumstances, at Servius *ad Aen.* 9.24: "ONERAVITQUE AETHERA VOTIS … locus autem iste dictus est secundum augurum morem, apud quos fuerat consuetudo, ut si post acceptum augurium ad aquam venissent, inclinati *aquas* haurirent exinde *et* manibus et fusis precibus vota promitterent, ut visum perseveraret augurium, quod

---

[20] Cf. also Servius auct. *ad Aen.* 4.340: *in iure augurali auspicium dicitur quod non petentibus nobis ad ea, quae in animo habemus, vice ominis offertur*; Servius *ad Aen.* 12.246: "namque hoc augurium nec oblativum est nec inpetrativum". It looks as though the near-synonym *peto* was the more frequently used technical term.

[21] Tibullus evinces similar interest in a technicality of haruspicy at 1.10.26, doubtless because of his patron Messalla's status as *augur* and consequent interest in all forms of divination: cf. Cairns (1996) 45, to which add that the appearance of the lemma *hariuga* at Paul. Fest. 100 — albeit with a different haruspical explanation — testifies to a discussion of the term in Verrius Flaccus, on whom cf. below, § VI.

[22] Cf. *GC* 113, 136, 169.

[23] Cf. the subsequent account of *legum dictio* at Servius auct. *ad Aen.* 3.89 and Servius auct. *ad Aen.* 4.340: *vult enim ostendere Aeneam semper animo volutasse, ut quae mente agitaret, offerentur auspicio et augurio firmarentur*, with the preceding section, quoted above, n.20.

aquae intercessu disrumpitur."[24]

17: *strepitantibus advolet alis*. Cf. Festus 197: *oscines aves Ap.
Claudius esse ait, quae ore canentes faciunt auspicium ...; alites quae
alis et volatu*.[25] Tibullus introduces an implicit etymology of *ales*,
indeed one deriving from augural writings; cf. also Servius auct. *ad
Aen*. 3.246: *alites enim certa genera avium ab auguribus appellantur,
quae pinnis vel volatu omina possunt facere*. This conclusion is further
assured by Servius' comment (*ad Aen*. 1.397) on Virgil's *stridentibus
alis*, i.e. "signum augurii est".

17–18: *alis .../ ... Amor*. There were five standard classes of omen in
augury. Through his emphasis on the winged nature of *Amor* Tibullus
alludes to the second (*ex avibus*), the sole class linked pseudo-
etymologically to *augurium* (cf. *LALE s.vv. augur, augurium*).[26]

1: *venit* and 21: *veniat ... avis. venire* in an augural context has
already been illustrated in a passage quoted above (on 11), i.e. Servius
ad Aen. 6.190. Another pertinent etymology is *aves ab adventu earum
dicuntur, quod inde veniant, unde non quis suspicetur* (Paulus Festus
29).[27] Lee–Maltby on 2.2.11: *auguror* comment: "By its etymology (*au*
from *aui*) the word looks forward to *auis* in 21", although on 2.2.21–22
they seemingly interpret *avis* as "dative plural of *auus*". Despite this
implied contradiction their comment may be valid: cf. below, § IV.

Finally, even line 1: *dicamus bona verba* could, in the augural
context of 2.2, reflect a deeper interest in omens than other such
phrases elsewhere. Cicero *De Divinatione* 1.102 (with Pease (1920–3)
ad loc.) stresses that such calls for 'holy silence' imply more than this:
the point also emerges from Paulus Festus 88, although some confusion
is evident: *Faventia bonam ominationem significat. Nam praecones
clamantes populum sacrificiis favere iubebant. Favere enim est bona
fari, at veteres poetae pro silere usi sunt favere*. Hence Tibullus'
injunction in effect to 'speak words of good omen' might also relate in
a general way to ominology/augury.[28]

---

[24] The conjunction of *vota* and *auspicia* at Censorinus *De Die Natali* 2.1: *nunc quoniam
liber de die natali inscribitur, a votis auspicia sumantur* is not really useful in this
context since *auspicia sumere* may mean no more than *exordium sumere*: cf.
Rapisarda (1991) 115 *ad loc.*; *TLL s.v. auspicium* III. Nor is the lemma *Caduca
auspicia* at Paul. Fest. 64 relevant.

[25] This definition reflects the strong interest of Roman etymologists in augury; cf. below,
§ VI.

[26] Cf. also Prop. 3.10.11: *felicibus edita pennis*, discussed below, § V.

[27] This definition derives from Verrius Flaccus, on whom cf. below, § VI.

[28] *dicere* is a technical term of augury when it occurs within certain phrases: cf.

The conclusion that *auguror* has its technical sense at Tibullus
2.2.11 because of its context of augural allusions is reinforced by the
two Ovidian passages where *auguror* is also used technically. One is
Ovid *Metamorphoses* 3.511–27:

> cognita res meritam <u>vati</u> per Achaidas urbes
> attulerat famam, nomenque erat <u>auguris</u> ingens;
> spernit Echionides tamen hunc ex omnibus unus
> contemptor superum Pentheus <u>praesagaque</u> ridet
> verba senis tenebrasque et cladem lucis ademptae   515
> obicit. ille movens albentia tempora canis
> 'quam <u>felix</u> esses, si tu quoque luminis huius
> orbus' ait 'fieres, ne Bacchica sacra videres!
> namque dies aderit, quam non procul <u>auguror</u> esse,
> qua novus huc <u>veniat</u>, proles[29] Semeleia, Liber;   520
> quem nisi templorum fueris dignatus honore,
> mille lacer spargere locis et sanguine silvas
> foedabis matremque tuam matrisque sorores.
> <u>eveniet</u>! neque enim dignabere numen honore,
> meque sub his tenebris nimium vidisse quereris.'   525
> talia dicentem proturbat Echione natus;
> dicta fides sequitur, <u>responsaque vatis</u> aguntur.

auguror is placed here in the mouth of Tiresias, who is warning
Pentheus of the imminent arrival of Bacchus in Thebes. The sacral and
vatic references underlined above in the text are focused by the naming
of Tiresias as *augur* (512). The phrasing of *eveniet* (524) and of
Tibullus 1.5.57: *eveniet; dat signa deus; sunt numina amanti* may have
inspired Housman's emendation *eveniet* in Tibullus 2.2.21. It is perhaps
more useful to note that in both texts the augury is followed by a con-
firmation that the event portended will occur; with *eveniet* (524) com-
pare Tibullus 2.2.17: *vota cadunt*. Another passage (*Tristia* 1.9.49–52),
where neither *auguror* nor *augur* appears but where virtually every
word derives from the technical terminology of augury (and haru-
spicy),[30] confirms Ovid's familiarity with divinatory practice:

Linderski (1986) 2173 n.94, 2199 n.189, 2210–11 and n.241. But those phrases do not
resemble Tibullus' opening words; so it is unlikely that *dicamus* (1) is intended to
evoke them.

[29] With *novus ... veniat, proles* cf. Tib. 2.2.21–2 *veniat ... prolem .../ ... novella*; a
coincidence?

[30] Cf. Linderski (1986) 2226–35, who (2236–7 n.355) questions the technical accuracy
of this Ovidian passage, although he admits that it is "of some interest for the study of
Roman augural doctrine". Ovid's competence should not be underestimated, since no
Roman poet, even one perfectly aware of the technicalities of augury, would have
wanted to reproduce them exactly in his verse. Cf. also above, n.18.

> haec mihi non ovium fibrae tonitrusve sinistri,
>   linguave servatae pennave dixit avis:
> augurium ratio est et coniectura futuri:
>   hac divinavi notitiamque tuli.

Following the haruspical *fibrae* (cf. *TLL s.v.* C) the *tonitrus* (equally
haruspical and augural) lead through *sinistri* into augury proper, the left
being traditionally the favourable side in that discipline.[31] Then Ovid
distinguishes between omens from sounds made by birds, i.e. by
oscines alites, and omens from their flight, i.e. *pinnis vel volatu* (cf.
TLL s.v. ales coll. 1526.84–1527.21). *ratio* and *coniectura* are related
technical terms integral to augural theory,[32] while *notitiam* (used in
conunction with *divinavi*, applicable to augury and haruspicy alike)
exploits the technical usage of *notare* to cover observing signs and
relating them to the events portended.[33] The other Ovidian passage
where *auguror* is used specifically of augury is *Ars Amatoria* 1.203–6,
on which cf. below, § V.

II. Augur, Epithalamium, and Genethliakon

Tibullus' augural voice is certainly appropriate to Cornutus' marriage.
Cicero's contemporaries believed that in early Rome all significant
activities, both private and public, had been preceded by the taking of
auspices.[34] But by Cicero's time the *auspex* functioned virtually only at
weddings and before journeys; on the latter, cf. below, § V. Even the
wedding *auspex*'s role had been reduced to a shell, leaving him an
etiolated 'best man'.[35] However, to judge from remarks both in Cicero
and in writers later than Tibullus, the *auspex* was an essential, albeit
formal, element of a normal and valid Roman marriage-ceremony in
Tibullus' day.[36] Cicero *Pro Cluentio* 14 slurs a marriage with the words

---

[31] Cf. Pease (1920–3) Index *s.v.* right and left.

[32] Cf. Linderski (1986) 2232–3. Luck (1967–77) II.78–9 *ad loc.* notes that Ovid is
drawing a distinction between rational and irrational methods of predicting the future.
The sly subtlety of Ovid's argumentation relies on the fact that *ratio, coniectura*, and
notare are technical terms of divination. By hijacking the terminology of augurs and
thus rationalising their 'art', Ovid doubly undermines the claims of augury and
haruspicy.

[33] E.g. Cic. *De Div.* 1.12, 25, 34, 72, 94, 131; 2.91, 146; *DND* 2.166; 3.14; *Ad Fam.*
6.6.8.

[34] Cf. Cic. *De Div.* 1.28 (*nihil fere* etc.), with the later testimonies collected by Pease
(1920–3) *ad loc.*

[35] Cf. Cic. *De Div.* 1.28 (*nuptiarum auspices*), with Pease (1920–3) *ad loc.*; Treggiari
(1991) 164. Cic. *Ad Att.* 8.3.3 implies that an *augur* also functioned at adoptions.

[36] Other hints of the importance of *auspicia* for weddings are: Fest. 242 (cf. Paul. Fest.

nubit genero socrus nullis auspicibus nullis auctoribus,[37] while Lucan stresses that Brutus was the sole *auspex* at the (second) marriage of Cato to Marcia (*Bellum Civile* 2.371, cf. Fantham (1992) on lines 326–91). Again, Tacitus observes that, when Messallina went through a wedding ceremony with C. Silius, even though she was already married to the emperor Claudius, its scandalousness was compounded by the presence of *auspices* (*Annals* 11.27, cf. also Suetonius *Claudius* 26.2); and Tacitus also notes ironically the presence of *auspices* at the 'marriage' of Nero to (the male) Pythagoras (*Annals* 15.37). Tibullus' voice as *auspex/augur* is thus fully appropriate to the content of the latter half of 2.2, in which the explicit *auguror* (11) appears, since it concerns the marriage of Cornutus.

Including and included genres often have features in common. Is, then, Tibullus' augural role equally appropriate to Cornutus' birthday? There are obstacles to establishing a link between birthdays and augury: little help can be expected from Greek genethliaka since they are few and diverge sharply from Roman examples in topical content;[38] augury was a characteristically Roman practice;[39] and, a birthday not being a movable feast, augury/auspices, if involved at all, must have been less crucial than in weddings, where some flexibility of timing was possible. But despite these obstacles, a cautiously positive answer can be given. In Latin genethliaka and other poems concerned with the day of birth[40] there are enough remarks about the 'felicity' of the birthday/day of birth, enough emphases on the avoidance of evil omens and the presence of good omens, and enough mentions of the beneficent operations of the Fates to allow the conclusion that observation of omens and hence the voice of the *augur/auspex* is germane to Roman

---

244) *s.v. Pronuba* — the 'matron of honour' should have been married once only for 'auspicious' reasons; Fest. 182 (cf. Paul. Fest. 172; Virg. *Ecl.* 8.29 and Iunius Philargyrius on 8.30) — the throwing of nuts to children at weddings provided a *secundum ... auspicium* when the bride entered her new house; Plin. *NH* 10.21 — *aegithum ... prosperrimi augurii nuptialibus negotiis*. Further on omens connected with marriage, cf. Treggiari (1991) 164 n.31.

[37] For an earlier comment on a similar absence, cf. Plaut. *Cas.* 86.

[38] This topic will be discussed in Cairns (forthcoming).

[39] Although the Greeks also practised divination of various types, I have not found it used in connection with Greek birthdays.

[40] Discussions of birthday poems sometimes fail to classify them correctly: thus, e.g., poems accompanying birthday gifts (although containing some genethliac topoi) are anathematika, not genethliaka; and those inviting others to a birthday celebration (e.g. Hor. *Od.* 4.11) are kletika/*vocationes*. But Stat. *Silv.* 2.7, where the birthday of the dead Lucan is celebrated, is a genethliakon.

birthdays. The highest concentration of relevant material comes in
Propertius 3.10, a genethliakon for Cynthia. I have analysed that elegy
generically in detail elsewhere;[41] hence the present discussion can be
summary. Propertius 3.10 is obsessed with good omens and with the
'holy silence' which avoids evil omens. It begins (1–2) with the
appearance of the Muses at the foot of Propertius' bed and the *signum*
they gave (1, 3):[42] by clapping their hands, the Muses provided a good
omen for Cynthia's birthday.

> mirabar, quidnam misissent mane Camenae,
> ante meum stantes sole rubente torum.
> natalis nostrae signum misere puellae
> et manibus faustos ter crepuere sonos. (1–4)

Propertius then proclaims that he does not want to see *dolentis*
('mourners', 7) whose link with death made them ill-omened, espe-
cially on a birthday. His surrounding aspirations (5–6, 8–10) — for a
calm day and for no laments to be heard — indicate, especially when
taken together with their Callimachean model (*Hymn* 2.18–24), his
wish for "holy silence and absence of ill omens".[43] At line 11, Pro-
pertius addresses Cynthia as *felicibus edita pennis* ("born under good
auspices" — literally 'wings'); cf. Sulpicia's genethliac remarks about
the *Parcae* and their gifts at birth to Cerinthus at [Tibullus] 4.5.3–4.[44]
Next, at line 20, Propertius speaks of the "well-omened flame" which
fills the house: *luxerit et tota flamma secunda domo.* Later again, the
pair are to dice — to reveal which of them is (more) deeply in love:

> sit sors et nobis talorum interprete iactu,
> quem gravius pennis verberet ille puer. (27–8)

The appearance here of "the boy" (i.e. *Amor*) and of his "wings", again
in a context of omens and divination which involves the technical term
interprete,[45] is worth stressing, especially in view of the rendering of
Tibullus 2.2.21–2 which will be offered below, § IV. Another Proper-
tian passage linking omens and the birth (not the birthday) of Cynthia is
2.3.23–4, where *Amor* again functions as the giver of omens: *non tibi*

---

[41] In Cairns (1971) 149–52. Cf. now also Fedeli (1985) 335–353, incorporating most of
     the material of Cairns (1971) and accepting most of its conclusions.
[42] Cf. *OLD s.v. signum* 5b ("supernatural sign, omen, portent"). I retain *N*'s *misissent* in
     line 1, whereas Fedeli (1985) *ad loc.* accepts Guyet's emendation *visissent*; the choice
     of reading does not affect the argument.
[43] Cairns (1971) 151.
[44] Cf. Fedeli (1985) on Prop. 3.10.11 for further useful parallels for *pennis*.
[45] Cf. *TLL s.v. interpres* IA2a; Linderski (1986) 2226–9.

*nascenti primis, mea vita, diebus/ candidus argutum sternuit omen
Amor?*
Ovid too seems to have felt a close link between omens and birth-
days. *Tristia* 3.13, an inverse genethliakon for his own birthday,[46]
challenges a standard topos when Ovid protests against the idea that he
should utter words of good omen (*concipiamque bonas ore favente
preces?*, 18). The convention is later denied outright: *in tantis subeunt
nec bona verba malis*, 24. Even more interestingly *Tristia* 5.5, a
genethliakon for Ovid's wife's birthday,[47] first expresses the topos in
its standard form: *lingua favens adsit, nostrorum oblita malorum,/
quae, puto, dedidicit iam bona verba loqui* (5–6) and then follows it at
lines 29–30 with a more specifically augural reference of the same
import: *aspice ut aura tamen fumos e ture coortos/ in partes Italas et
loca dextra ferat* — where the implied etymology of *auspex* from
aspicere[48] confirms the technicality of *loca dextra*. Again Martial
celebrates his friend Restitutus' birthday thus at 10.87.3–4: *linguis
omnibus et favete votis;/ natalem colimus ...*; and at 9.52 he speaks of
his own and Q. Ovidius' birthdays as *felix utraque lux diesque nobis*
(4). A late genethliakon of Iulianus retreads these and other familiar
concepts.[49]
    The conclusion that augury/auspices are not alien to birthdays has so
far been underpinned by undisputed genethliaka and other birthday
poems. Horace *Odes* 3.17 should also be mentioned. It honours Aelius
Lamia, and enjoins a feast for the next day. Lamia is told: *Genium
mero/ curabis* (14–15). Horace had earlier predicted wet and windy
weather for that day in the words *aquae nisi fallit augur/ annosa cornix*
(12–13), where *aquae ... augur cornix* not only renders ὑετόμαντις ...
κορώνη[50] but also alludes to a technicality of Roman augury: cf., in an

---

[46] Cf. *GC* 135–7; Luck (1967–77) II.225–6.
[47] Cf. Luck (1967–77) II.298–302.
[48] Cf. Eutych. gramm. 5.455.10: *ab aspicio auspex*, cited (along with similar passages)
    by *LALE* s.vv. *auspex, auspicium*; *TLL* s.v. *auspicium* col. 1542.36–40.
[49] *PML* 4 (*AL* 2) p.155 no. 154; cf. esp.: *vosque simul iuvenes animis et voce faventes/
    concelebrate diem votis felicibus almum* (3–4). Other scraps of support for the
    auspicia/birthdays link may come via *TLL* s.v. *auspicor* col. 1552.4–15 (i.e. perf. part.
    auspicatus) where the applications appear to be reasonably 'technical' and include
    Plin. *Ep.* 10.17.2 (to Trajan): *cum mihi contigerit, quod erat auspicatissimum, natalem
    tuum in provincia celebrare* and Solinus 1.68, drawing on Pliny *NH* 7.47, from a
    context where various birth circumstances are listed along with comments about their
    predictive value for the later lives of those born.
[50] I.e. Euphorion fr. 30 Cuenca = fr. 93 van Groningen; cf. Kiessling–Heinze (1930) on
    Hor. *Od.* 3.17.9.

augural context, *huius* [sc. *cornicis*] *inter multa auspicia tribuunt etiam
pluvias portendere vocibus* (Isidore *Origines* 12.7.44). *Odes* 3.17
would offer a piquant, and indeed, decisive parallel for Tibullus' au-
gural interest in 2.2 if its genethliac character was universally agreed.
Unfortunately, however, this has been disputed, with powerful voices
both against[51] and in favour.[52] My own view, for which I shall argue
elsewhere,[53] is that the occasion for the feast in *Odes* 3.17 can only be
Lamia's birthday and that *Odes* 3.17 is indeed a genethliakon, although
perhaps of a type unique in Latin literature. If that approach is correct,
then Horace could be added to Propertius and Ovid as fellow-
Augustans who shared Tibullus' interest in the augural/ominological
aspect of birthdays. But, even without *Odes* 3.17, the case is strong.

III. 'Genius-Natalis'/'Natalis': lines 1–2

The modern consensus on 2.2's subject-matter and conceptual develop-
ment goes somewhat as follows: 2.2 begins by declaring that the
'Genius-Natalis' is coming to the altar, possibly in statue form. The
'Genius-Natalis' is again prominent in lines 5–10, where he is told to
"be here in person to see His honours and grant whatever Cornutus
requests" (Murgatroyd 284). Then he reappears in the final couplet
(21–22), where his activities have been interpreted variously, de-
pending on the interpreters' choices of readings. Murgatroyd's views
(based on his own choice) lead him to the paraphrase: "May Natalis
come to them [i.e. Cornutus and his wife] when they are grandparents
and bring them great-grandchildren". There is, however, a serious
obstacle to acceptance of this account of 2.2 (even leaving aside
Murgatroyd's contorted application of 'grandparents' to the bride and
groom and 'children' to their future grandchildren). It is that the entities
beloved of recent commentators ('Genius-Natalis' — Murgatroyd 72
on lines 1–2, *'Genius Natalis'* — Della Corte (1980) 248, 'Birthday-
Spirit' — *GC* 265;[54] Ball (1983) 164–7, or "Natalis, the Birthday Spirit,
<who> was probably identical with the Genius" — Lee–Maltby on
1.7.63) belong entirely to the realm of fantasy. There is not a trace of

---

[51] E.g. Kiessling–Heinze (1930) on line 13; Syndikus (1973) 170 n.18.
[52] E.g. Quinn (1980) 275; Connor (1987) 147–9; Santirocco (1986) 133.
[53] I.e. in Cairns (forthcoming).
[54] With lower case 'spirit'. Two further errors should be noted: the text of Tib. 2.2.21
printed at *GC* 112 is out of kilter with the translation at 266, which appears to render
Housman's emendation *eveniat*; and at 273 *natalis* of Tib. 1.7.63 is misrendered as
'Genius'!

them in the standard handbooks on Roman festivals and religion, i.e.
Warde-Fowler (1899), Wissowa (1912), and Latte (1967), for the
simple reason that there is no ancient evidence for their existence. The
same goes for the vaguer being referred to by earlier commentators as
'Natalis'.[55] Carter (1902) asterisks every instance of the adjective
natalis listed by him *s.v.* Genius. Carter explains his asterisking thus:
"Stellula nomen dei eo loco omissum significat" (viii). Where, then,
did 'Genius-Natalis', 'Natalis', and so forth originate? Apparently they
spring from nothing more than Tibullan editors' practice of capitalising
Natalis in his text at 2.2.1 and 2.2.21, as at 1.7.63 and at [Tibullus] 3.11
(= 4.5) 19 and (?) 3.12 (= 4.6) 1. These capitalisations and the resulting
imaginary entities are superfluous: all the relevant *loci* can and should
be interpreted (as in the literal renderings below) without reference to
them. In two passages (i and v below) *natalis* is apostrophised; but it is
questionable how far apostrophe entails genuine personification. Again,
it should be emphasised that in the classical period *natalis* alone (i.e.
without *dies*) could mean 'birthday' (although *natalis dies* was also
used): Servius on *Eclogues* 3.76 comments explicitly on this usage in
Virgil and Horace, contrasting it with later writers' regular *natalis dies*:
"sane 'natalis' apud maiores plenum fuit, licet posteritas 'natalis dies'
coeperit" (with references to Horace *Epistles* 2.2.210 and Juvenal
12.1). The *loci* involving *natalis* relevant to Tibullus 2.2.21–2 are:

i)   at tu, natalis multos celebrande per annos,
      candidior semper candidiorque veni. (Tibullus 1.7.63–4)

'But, you, [Messalla's] birthday that should be celebrated through
many years, come always more and more well-omened.'

ii) at tu, natalis quoniam deus omnia sentis,
      adnue: quid refert, clamne palamne roget?
                                          ([Tibullus] 3.11 (= 4.5) 19–20)

'But you [addressing not the birthday but the Genius, as earlier at
lines 9–12], since as the birthday god you are aware of everything,
nod assent: what does it matter whether she asks covertly or openly?'

Here *natalis* is adjectival and qualifies *deus*, i.e. the *Genius*.[56]

---

[55] Apart from the manifestations in Smith noted below, he appears in Cesareo (1929) 99.

[56] *at* (19) indicates that the address is once again to the Genius, after an aside to Venus at
ll.13–14. Tränkle (1990) 284–5 on [Tib.] 3.11 (= 4.5) 19 accepts the presence of a
personified *Natalis* here and in passages iv) and v). He also refers for support to
passage iii).

iii)   natalis Iuno, sanctos cape turis acervos,
        quos tibi dat tenera docta puella manu.
                            ([Tibullus] 3.12 (= 4.6) 1–2)

'Juno of the birthday, accept these holy piles of incense which a
learned girl offers you with youthful hand.'

This passage is included because it is sometimes (cf., e.g., Lee–Maltby
on 1.7.63) misused to support the alleged identity of 'Natalis' with the
Genius. But Juno, not *'Natalis'*, is being invoked and, to make the
situation clear, i.e. that Juno is Sulpicia's equivalent of a Genius, she
being female, the adjective *natalis* is applied to Juno. Presumably
natalis was never used to qualify *Genius* because his connections with
birthdays were too obvious to need stating.[57]

iv)   ecce supervacuus — quid enim fuit utile gigni? —
        ad sua natalis tempora noster adest. (Ovid *Tristia* 3.13.1–2)

'Look! At the right time my useless birthday — for what good was it
being born? — is at hand.'

v)   optime natalis! quamvis procul absumus, opto
        candidus huc venias dissimilisque meo (Ovid *Tristia* 5.5.13–14)

'Best [i.e. my wife's] birthday! Although I am far away, I wish you
may come here well-omened and unlike my own birthday.'

The foisting of Genius-Natalis etc. upon Tibullus 2.2 introduces
glaring illogicalities into its conceptual development. With such an
entity involved, the latter half of line 1 would mean "Genius-Natalis is
coming to the altars" (the tense and the mood of *venit* are guaranteed
by the metre). However, in line 5 the Genius is wished, or asked, or
ordered, to present himself — in the subjunctive *adsit*, with the pro-
nominal adjective *ipse* attached to underline this request. Genius-
Natalis would again (on the most popular view) be asked "to come" a
third time (*veniat*) in line 21 — after an invocation of *Amor* in the
intervening lines. The sheer inconsequentiality of saying in line 1 that
"Genius-Natalis is coming", and then saying in line 5 "may he himself
be present" and then again "may he come" in line 21 is patent; and it
suggests that the verb *venit* (1) cannot apply to the Genius or to any
syncretism of the Genius. Otherwise, we might well ask what has
happened between the announcement that the "Genius-Natalis is
coming" (1) and the one, or two, subsequent requests to him to "be

---

[57] The only alleged examples of *Natalis* qualifying *Genius* listed at *TLL s.v.* Genius col.
1838.7 are Tib. 1.7.63 and 2.2.1!

present" and to "come". Of course, we might suppose that Genius-Natalis is deaf or obtuse, or that, through absent-mindedness or boredom, he has wandered off somewhere else between lines 1 and 5 and between lines 5 and 21. Alternatively we might wish to resuscitate the outmoded picture of Tibullus as a rambling and disorderly writer following no particular lines of thought. But, if these explanations seem unattractive, then we need to rethink the events and personalities of 2.2.

One compromise is initially tempting: to accept the existence of a personified *Natalis* but to regard him as separate from the Genius and to confine him to the first and last couplets. But this will not work either. We still have an illogicality if *Natalis* is regarded as the subject of *veniat* in line 21 – although not if *Natalis* there is understood as a vocative. In the latter case, however, apostrophe (as noted) need not entail personification; besides, and more importantly, lines 1–2 have been incorrectly punctuated by editors.[58] By printing lower-case *natalis* in line 1, placing an interpunct after *natalis* and removing the interpunct after *aras*, we achieve:

> dicamus bona verba; venit natalis; ad aras
> quisquis ades, lingua, vir mulierque, fave. (1–2)

The couplet then means (literally):

> 'Let us utter words of good omen. The (i.e. his) birthday is coming. Anyone who is present at the altars, man and woman, keep holy silence.'

The phrase *venit natalis* (1) is now fully parallel to Tibullus 1.7.63 (above, i)), where *natalis* is told "to come", i.e. the two passages present someone's birthday as "coming" (Cornutus) or "to come" (Messalla); cf. also passages iv) and v).[59] The newly emerged clause *ad aras/ quisquis ades* is good Latin;[60] the enjambement is typically Tibullan;[61] and the new, staccato, syntax of line 1 is paralleled by the

---

[58] The capitalisation and punctuation of Tibullus' elegies, both in MSS and editions, are, of course, post-authorial. Conventions differ in different European countries; hence my use of 'interpunct' rather than comma, dash, colon or semi-colon. Luck (1988) punctuates line 1 (following Gronovius and Broukhusius) thus: *Dicamus bona verba, venit Natalis, ad aras:*, presumably taking *ad aras* with *dicamus bona verba.*

[59] There remains a problem at Tib. 1.7.53, where the addressee of *sic venias, hodierne* is disputed.

[60] Cf. *TLL s.v. assum* col. 917.6–23, including (16–17) an example of *ad aras.*

[61] Cf. Veremans (1996) esp. 526, presenting statistics showing that 54.3% of Tibullus' couplets are enjambed, as against only 24.4% in Propertius and 23.2% in Ovid's *Amores.*

even jerkier syntax of line 10: *en age; quid cessas? adnuit ille. roga.*
Finally the personified *Natalis* etc. has been eliminated. The first
couplet, then, announces the birthday of Cornutus, whose name is, by
the common ancient poetic technique of 'delayed naming',[62] mentioned
first only in line 9; and it urges avoidance of ill-omened words on those
who are present at the altar on which birthday offerings are to be made.

At line 5 *adsit* ("may he present himself") is said of the Genius.
There is now no illogicality in this command (or wish) since this is the
first appearance of the Genius in the elegy. Moreover it is (now)
possible to understand why the Genius is first introduced here. With the
repunctuated, retranslated version of lines 1–2, the words of good
omen, holy silence and burning of incense, which are virtually the
entire content of lines 1–4, can be seen as the first instalment of the
honores which the Genius is to come to spectate (*visurus*, 5). Thus *ipse*
(5) is fully appropriate since the *honores* belong by right to the Genius;
and similarly *suos* (5) has its full force. The Genius, then, is the only
deity who appears in the first half of the elegy; and, as Lee–Maltby on
line 5 have suggested, he may well be the statue of the Genius carried
from the Lararium to the altar on this (for him) most holy of days, so
that his "nodding" (10) is more than fanciful.

IV. Lines 21–2

There remains the most intransigent textual and interpretational
problem of 2.2, located in its final couplet (21–2), which contains the
last alleged appearance of *Natalis* etc. The main manuscript tradition
offers the following text, printed here without punctuation or capitali-
sation (the sigla of the apparatus are those of Lenz–Galinsky):

> hic veniat natalis avis prolemque ministret
> ludat et ante tuos turba novella pedes

21 hic veniat *A B Ber. H P Q e*: hic veniet *d*: hec veniat *G*: hec veniet
V²: huc veniat *c*: haec veniat *Postgate*: eveniat *Housman* (reported by
Postgate)

The ambivalence of the written forms *avis* (i.e. nom./voc. sing. of *avis*
-is f. 'bird' or dat./abl. pl. of *avus* m. 'grandfather/ancestor') and *avi*
(i.e. dat. sing of *avis -is* f. 'bird' or nom./voc. pl. of *avus* m. 'grand-
father/ancestor') is patent. Roman poets seem usually to have taken

---

[62] Cf. *Tibullus* 156.

pains to counter it.[63] Their normal means (alone or in combination) were:
  1) Metrical and prosodic (with *avis*): e.g. at Horace *Odes* 3.27.10 and 4.12.6 the final syllable must be short, so *avis* must mean 'bird'; contrariwise, e.g., at Virgil *Aeneid* 7.56 (*avis atavis*) and 7.412 (*avis et*) the final syllable must be long, hence *avis* must mean 'ancestors'.
  2) Grammatical: e.g. employing a feminine adjective in agreement with *avis* (often before it)[64] to guarantee the meaning 'bird'; and juxtaposing with *avi* the noun on which it depends,[65] or combining with *avis* a plural adjective/participle in agreement (which usually precedes) so as to assure the meaning 'grandfathers/ancestors'.[66]
  3) Contextual: providing accompanying concepts like 'nest', 'wings', 'flying', 'singing' or 'feathers' to signal 'bird';[67] and other appropriate accompanying concepts to signal 'grandfathers/ancestors'.[68]
  As a result there appears to be no other case in Roman poetry where scholarship has been at odds over the meaning of one of these forms; and only in one other case does a poet seem to have exploited the potential ambiguity (see n.63). It should also be emphasised that, even though *avis* and *avus* are close in sound, no surviving evidence points to any attempt by ancient etymologists to link the pair.[69] This is the background against which the meaning of *avis* at Tibullus 2.2.21 must be recovered, with the proviso, however, that Tibullus gives us no metrical help and that the context of *avis* is also ambivalent, with *Amor*'s 'wings' (17) being counterbalanced by *prolem* (21), which suggests 'grandfathers/ancestors'.[70]
  The most recent discussion (Maltby (1996) 93–5), before evaluating a number of previously proposed solutions and advancing his own, first

---

[63] Dyson (1997) draws attention to the potential, but instantly resolved, ambivalence of *avi* at Virg. *Aen.* 4.254 and to the more complex (but equally quickly resolved) situation at *Aen.* 7.412, where *avis* means 'ancestors' but where Virgil is also alluding to the etymology of *Ardea* from '*ardea*' (heron).

[64] E.g. Lucr. 6.1219–20; Virg. *Aen.* 6.193; Hor. *Sat.* 2.2.26; Prop. 1.18.30.

[65] E.g. Virg. *Aen.* 5.564; 12.164.

[66] E.g. Tib. 2.1.34; [Tib.] 3.1.2; Prop. 4.6.38; 4.11.102.

[67] E.g. Hor. *Ep.* 1.19; Tib. 1.8.4; Virg. *Aen.* 12.248; Prop. 2.30.30; Ov. *Am.* 1.13.8.

[68] E.g. Virg. *Georg.* 4.209; *Aen.* 10.201; Hor. *Od.* 3.6.46; *Sat.* 1.2.7; Tib. 1.10.18; Prop. 2.34.56.

[69] Cf. *LALE s.vv.*

[70] Cf., e.g., Val. Flacc. *Arg.* 6.125–6; Claudian *Carm.* 1.15–16; Dracont. *Satisfactio* 51–2. In Ov. *Met.* 15.640, which also associates birds of omen and *proles* (*ite bonis avibus prolemque accersite nostram*) the form *avibus* is unambiguous.

summarised the problems as follows (94) — note that for Maltby
Natalis is capitalised and personified:

1. What is the meaning of *hic*?
2. Is *Natalis* nominative, vocative, or used adjectivally with *auis*?
3. Is *auis* fem. sing. nom. "a bird" or "omen", or dat. pl. "ancestors,
   grandparents"?
4. To whom does *tuos* refer in 22?

Given that the new interpretation of 21–2 to be offered here relies on
the two new hypotheses offered above (Tibullus speaks as *augur/
auspex* and 2.2 contains no personified *Natalis* etc.) it would be in-
appropriate to take issue in detail with all earlier approaches. Two
points relevant to my own position can suffice:

1) Mutschler (1985)'s attempt (221–2) to take *hic* as referring to
Amor, with *Natalis* as a vocative, was rejected by Maltby (95) on the
ground that "to make *Amor* the subject of the last couplet is not without
its difficulties". These, for Maltby, are i) that the last couplet then
duplicates the fuller appeal for *Amor*'s epiphany in 17–18 and ii) that
Tibullus 1.7 "ends with an address to *Natalis*". Neither of these ob-
jections is compelling: i) *Amor* never ceases to be in the foreground
after line 17: so, if *hic veniat* (21) refers to *Amor*, it is resuming in
simplified form, not duplicating, *utinam ... advolet .../ ... Amor* (17–
18); ii) If *natalis* is apostrophised in line 21, then sufficient parallelism
with 1.7.63–4 exists, should it be felt essential. But the supposition that
it is essential is founded on the unstated assumption that Tibullus must
end all his genethliaka by addressing '*Natalis*'/*natalis*. This is surely
gratuitous, particularly since the two addressees' personal situations
were so different: the birthday/triumph of Messalla was that of a man
married for some time and already possessed of children, while
Cornutus is childless to date, and probably married only on this his
birthday. All this is not to say that Mutschler's proposals are entirely
acceptable, only that they (and my own suggestions, with which to
some extent they coincide) are not vulnerable to Maltby's objections.

2) Maltby's own solution, i.e. (following others) to read *huc* for *hic*
(21), and to take *Natalis* (21) as subject of *veniat* (21) and *ministret*
(21), *avis* (21) as dative plural (of the bridal pair in their old age —
with Murgatroyd 78 and 273–4), and *tuos* (22) of Cornutus, claims
support from the fact that ring-composition is a well-recognised
Tibullan structural feature,[71] and that verbal parallelisms are frequently

---

[71] Cf. *Tibullus* Ch.8; Murgatroyd Structural Appendix (283–91).

found at the beginnings and ends of Tibullan elegies. The new inter-
pretation to be offered here posits the same degree of verbal parallelism
— and more (see below).

Certain elements of Maltby's solution would be attractive if the
problems of the last couplet were confined to the initial *hic*; e.g. the
emendation *huc* is both palaeographically easy and obvious. However,
line 21 contains the equally difficult, ambivalent *avis*, which cannot
mean both 'bird' and 'grandparents'. When Tibullus recited 2.2, that
ambiguity would have been resolved by the quantity of the second
syllable of *avis*.[72] Some contemporary readers might also have resolved
the problem if they evaluated the possible meaning 'grandfathers'
(taking *avis* as the fathers of Cornutus and his bride, rather than their
ancestors in general) and decided against it because they knew that
Cornutus' father was already dead (cf. § VII). Other readers would
have perceived the combination of *avis* and *veniat* in the phrase *hic
veniat natalis avis* (21) as the first clue. This verbal complex evokes the
ancient etymology linking *avis* ('bird') with *venio* through *adventus*[73]
and suggests that *avis* should be taken as 'bird' rather than 'grand-
parents'. Tibullus' contemporaries would probably have been pre-
disposed to do so anyhow, given Tibullus' augural voice in 2.2, its high
level of augural language and content, and the fact that one standard
meaning of *avis* is 'omen' (cf. *TLL s.v.* coll. 1436.71–1437.83). As
'bird of omen' *avis* can be the complement of *hic*, which must refer to
Amor, who has featured in the preceding lines. *avis* thus picks up from
four lines earlier the augural evocation of winged *Amor* in flight (*stri-
dentibus advolet alis*, 17). Moreover *Amor* is a most fitting addressee
for the injunction *prolemque ministret* (21), that being one of his
cardinal functions! And the disappearance from line 21 of the 'grand-
parents' or 'ancestors', who have in any case been a thorn in the flesh
of interpreters, cannot be unwelcome.

This solution also accords better with Tibullus' linguistic usage.
Postponed *-que* in Tibullus is rare in the hexameter[74] and in penta-
meters it most often (12 times) involves attaching the postponed *-que* to
a verb. The alternative view of 2.2.21 which would take *avis prolem-
que ministrat* together as meaning something like "supply offspring to
the grandfathers/ancestors", would involve postponed *-que* being

---

[72] The presence of the ambiguity in the text must testify to the importance of recitation in
Tibullus' life and work.
[73] Cf. *LALE s.v. avis.*
[74] Cf. Streifinger (1881) 40–41.

attached to a noun. This is not impossible, although the only two certain Tibullan examples of it (*rusticus e lucoque vehit* ..., 1.10.51, and *ite sub imperium sub titulumque, Lares*, 2.4.54) are dissimilar in that both involve a noun governed by a preposition. A second consideration is that in the only other case of *ministrare* in Tibullus (1.10.57) the subject is *Amor!*[75]

Amor, then, is summoned twice as a good omen, but for different purposes: once to assure the permanency of the marriage (17–20); and once as a 'birthday omen' to generate children of the marriage (21–2). Thus the two genres of 2.2 are compounded in the final quatrain, without the redundancy exposed above in the standard interpretation.

On this basis line 21 could be rendered either:

a) "May he [i.e. *Amor*], birthday, come as a bird of <good> omen" or
b) "May he [i.e. *Amor*] come as a birthday bird of <good> omen".

Both renderings would give the poem an extra ring-compositional feature of the type exemplified in Maltby (1996) since it now begins and ends with an omen: *dicamus bona verba* .../ ... *lingua* ... *fave* (1–2) = *veniat* ... *avis* (21). With both there is no sudden transition to a new agent at the end of the elegy, since *Amor* continues to be the subject of *hic veniat* etc. Which is preferable? An objection to a) is that the apostrophe of *natalis* seems clumsy and without function; another is that it would (probably) have the children of line 22 playing around the feet of the 'birthday' — a strange concept. A point in its favour is the parallel which it would create with 1.7.63–4 (see above). An objection to b) is that there seems to be no exact parallel. A bird 'coming' is unproblematic, since *venire* is the *mot juste* for the arrival of birds, including migrants, both in augural and non-augural contexts.[76] Nor is adjectival *natalis* problematic: cf. *OLD s.v. natalis ~is ~e*. But the combination *natalis avis* is unparalleled; and in the closest part-parallel (*haec a Sardois tibi forsitan exulis oris,/ fratre reversuro, nuntia venit avis*, Martial 8.32.7–8) the bird, although it functions as an omen, is a real bird. Nevertheless on the whole I incline to b).

But, however line 21 is rendered, to whom does *tuos* (22) refer? As noted, if *natalis* (21) is taken as apostrophised, this probably has the odd result of making the children of line 22 play around the birthday's feet. If *natalis* (21) is adjectival in agreement with *avis*, *tuos* might

---

[75] Similarly, *Amor* is subject of *ministret* at [Tib.] 3.12.12.

[76] *Non-augural*: e.g. Verg. *Georg.* 2.320; Plin. *NH* 1.10a (*De avibus peregrinis quae veniunt*); 10.65; Tac. *Ann.* 6.28; Servius *De Centum Metris* p. 460.20; *Augural*: Stat. *Theb.* 3.507–8; *Ach.* 1.374–5.

refer to the Genius: cf. Tibullus' account of how, as a child, he ran around the feet of his family Lares: *cursarem vestros cum tener ante pedes* (1.10.16). The parallelisms are impressive — not only *ante vestros/tuos pedes* but also *cursarem = ludat* and *tener = novella*. But elsewhere in 2.2 Tibullus refers to the Genius, to *Amor*, and indeed to *natalis* (unless *natalis* is apostrophised in line 21) in the third person, while the second person singular is reserved for the people attending the celebration (2) and for Cornutus (9, 10, 11, 13, 15). This consideration is not conclusive, since sudden alterations between third person description and second person apostrophe (and also sudden changes of addressee) are characteristic of Roman elegy.[77] More determinant — if the interpretation of *hic ... avis* (21) offered above is correct — is the fact that the Genius has exited from the elegy either at line 11 or, at the latest, at line 17, when *Amor* enters it. So it is less likely that *tuos* refers to the Genius; hence the *turba novella* of line 22 is (with Maltby (1996) 93–5) more probably playing around the feet of its father, Cornutus. If a parallel is needed, cf. Tibullus 1.7.55–6, where, again in a genethliac context, Tibullus wishes that Messalla's children may grow up and stand (not play) around him when he is an old man: *at tibi succrescat proles quae sacra parentis/ augeat et circa stet veneranda senem*. A last (metrical) point: the new interpretation of line 21 involves the hexameter's main caesura falling in the fourth foot, as it also does (on a natural reading) in lines 3, 5, 9, 15 and 19.

V. The Roman Poetic Tradition of Augural Speakers

The other standard occasion for observance of auspices among the Romans was (as noted in § II) the beginning of a journey.[78] Tibullus alludes to this at 1.3.9–13, where, before his departure, Delia consults a diviner about his return — a bastardised form of 'auspices'. Except in Tibullus 2.2 and Horace *Odes* 3.17 (cf. above, § II), the surviving Roman literary tradition of augural speakers appears to focus exclusively on journeys. A heavily discussed[79] Horatian example is *Odes* 3.27, where Horace, in the role of *providus auspex* (8), starts a propemptikon by meditating ominously on Galatea's forthcoming

---

[77] Cf., e.g., Tränkle (1960) 8–10, 143–9.
[78] Cf., e.g., Plaut. *Aul.* 447; *Epid.* 183–4; *Persa* 606–7; *Pseud.* 761–2; *Stich.* 459; Ov. *Met.* 10.8; Livy 5.21.1–2; 6.12.7–8; 8.30.1–2; 21.63.8–9; Sen. *Dial.* 5.2.5: *sine auspiciis populus ... egressus.*
[79] Cf. above, n.13.

journey. Horace draws on at least two of the five standard classes of auguries — *ex quadrupedibus* (2–4) and *ex avibus* (1–2, 9–12, 15–16).[80] But there are no significant linguistic or conceptual overlaps between Tibullus 2.2 and *Odes* 3.27. So, although Horace certainly knew Tibullus and his work,[81] influence in either direction is unlikely: two Augustan poets have independently adopted a role which must have been more widespread in Roman poetry than we know.

The other extant Roman poems with an augural speaker are, like *Odes* 3.27, propemptic; but interestingly, and unlike *Odes* 3.27 and Tibullus 2.2, they seem to form a chain influenced one by the other. The first fully surviving representative of the tradition is Propertius 3.4, which I have discussed in detail elsewhere.[82] It is brief (22 lines) and highly economic, usually handling single topics within single couplets, and it employs a tight ring-compositional structure: Augustus is placed at its beginning (1) — linked, albeit unobtrusively, with 'Jupiter of Latium' (6); then Mars (11), Vesta (11), and (again) Augustus (13) appear at its centre; and Venus (19) and Aeneas (20) come in the reversed penultimate element. Within this appropriate context for public pronouncements, Propertius initially makes assertions, gives predictions and issues orders in a strongly hieratic and authoritative tone to the Roman army leaving for Parthia. Then his augural voice emerges explicitly in 9–10, where he announces formally in *omina fausta cano* (9) the propitiousness of the omens for the planned expedition and instructs the departing Roman army to expiate (*piate*, 9) the defeat and death of Crassus and his son in 53 BC. The succeeding pentameter (10), with its reminiscence of a line of C. Cornelius Gallus (on which see below), continues the authoritative tone of the hexameter. Propertius returns in 13ff. to a more private *persona* and reasserts his status as a love poet; but this does not prevent him from reiterating formal prayers to the chief gods of Rome and of the Julian family at 19–20, before his private *persona* reappears in line 22.

In imitation of Propertius 3.4 Ovid composed *Ars Amatoria* 1.177–228 as a propemptikon for Gaius Caesar, also departing for a Parthian expedition, this time in 1 BC. Comment on it here must be confined to Ovid's augural voice. Ovid reveals himself as an augural speaker at line

---

[80] If the references to a snake (5) and to stormy weather (17–18) have any 'augural' content, they could allude (inaccurately) to two other classes, *ex diris* (?) and *ex caelo* respectively; cf. also *solis ab ortu* (12)?

[81] Cf. *Od.* 1.33; *Ep.* 1.4.

[82] *GC* 185–9.

191. First he mentions the *auspicia* of Augustus in the phrase *auspiciis animisque* (or *annisque*);[83] then he repeats that phrase reversed in line 192. Next (203) Mars and Augustus are jointly invoked as gods to grant their *numen* to the departing Gaius before (205) Ovid comes out with the explicit *auguror* and promises *votiva carmina*:

> Marsque pater Caesarque pater, date numen eunti:
>   nam deus e vobis alter es, alter eris.
> auguror, en, vinces; votivaque carmina reddam,
>   et magno nobis ore sonandus eris. (*Ars Amatoria* 1.203–6)

Ovid is thus more explicitly augural than Propertius; but he has recognised Propertius' augural voice and he indicates this by using *omen* later (212, cf. Propertius 3.4.9) — but of the *malum omen* of the Parthians. Propertius' *cano* is reflected in Ovid's *votiva carmina* (205).

Ovid's recognition of Propertius' more oblique augural utterances may not have been unaided. The chance find of eight fragmentary lines of C. Cornelius Gallus[84] revealed one of them:

> Fata mihi, Caesar, tum erunt mea dulcia, quom tu
>   maxima Romanae pars eri<s> historiae (col. i.2–3)

as the source of Propertius 3.4.10:

> ite et Romanae consulite historiae.[85]

There is good reason to think that Gallus' line also came from a propemptikon, either for Octavian or, more probably, for Julius Caesar, and one for a planned Parthian expedition at that.[86] Gallus' works were familiar to Ovid and influential upon him.[87] Literary sense would be served if the first in the series, i.e. Gallus' propemptikon, was addressed to the 'grandfather' (Julius Caesar), the second (Propertius 3.4) to the 'son' (Augustus), and the third (Ovid's propemptikon for Gaius Caesar) to the 'grandson'. Gallan influence on Ovid's propemptikon to Gaius may extend further. That there was a tradition of augural speakers in Augustan poetry is clear; and neither *Odes* 3.27 nor

---

[83] On the textual problem, cf. Pianezzola (1991) 211–12 on 191–2.

[84] Anderson, Parsons and Nisbet (1979).

[85] On this point, cf. Anderson, Parsons and Nisbet (1979) 152 (with 141).

[86] For the identification of the addressee as Julius Caesar and for the dating, cf. Anderson, Parsons and Nisbet (1979) 152.

[87] In addition to Ovid's tributes to Gallus (*Am.* 1.15.29–30, 3.9.63–4), cf. Hinds (1984) with numerous Ovidian and other echoes of *carmina digna* etc.; Cairns (1993), arguing for in-depth influence of Gallus on *Am.* 1.3.

Tibullus 2.2 looks like the fountainhead of that tradition.[88] This makes
Gallus' propemptikon a tempting candidate as vector; and it hints that
Gallus too may have spoken with an augural voice. A more detailed
possibility is that Gallus also introduced the form *auguror* into Latin
poetry. It is not found in Lucretius or Catullus or Virgil.[89] But it does
appear in Tibullus, Ovid and Propertius (although not in 3.4); and the
contexts in the last three poets are unrelated. This spread of usage
suggests a (lost) source: and again the most likely candidate is Gallus'
propemptikon. If so, then Propertius will have been less explicitly
augural in his imitation of Gallus, while Ovid will have combined
homage to Propertius[90] with a return to Gallan explicitness.

VI. Augury and Politics

Augustan poets clearly adopted augural voices for specific purposes in
specific poems; but they also did so against a political background in
which augury was highly significant. The status of *augur publicus* had
long been greatly prized and much sought-after at Rome.[91] The dis-
tinction of the augurate was, if anything, enhanced in the triumviral and
Augustan periods, when the membership list shows a high proportion
of patricians and *nobiles* and strong linkages to political power.[92]
Something of the broader public perception and impact of augural
theory and practice in the Augustan period can be seen in the life and
work of the contemporary grammarian and writer Verrius Flaccus,
whose *De Verborum Significatu* survives in part in its abridgement by
Pompeius Festus, and in part in the further digest of Festus by Paulus
Diaconus.[93] Around 10 BC Verrius, who had already established a
prestigious school, was enrolled in the imperial household as tutor to
Augustus' grandsons at the munificent annual salary of 100,000
sesterces.[94] His *De Verborum Significatu* reveals a major interest in
augury and was a seminal source of augural information for later

---

[88] Cic. *Ad. Fam.* 6.6, in which Cicero writes as an *augur publicus* to the Etruscan
  haruspex A. Caecina, uses interestingly similar language to Tib. 2.2, including
  auguror (7) and *augurium meum* (12). But it must be ruled out as a source.
[89] Possibly Gallus had imbued the form with such an elegiac tinge that Virgil eschewed
  it; Ovid, however, did use it in hexameter verse.
[90] For some of the details, cf. Hollis (1977); Pianezzola (1991) on Ov. *AA* 177–228; and
  above.
[91] Cf. Lewis (1955) 8–11, 102, 106–8.
[92] Cf. Lewis (1955) 38–44.
[93] Cf. Kaster (1995) Index *s.v.* Verrius Flaccus, M.
[94] Cf. Kaster (1995) 190, 194; Grandazzi (1991) 105.

writers.[95] Indeed the work was structured so as to give prominence at all points to lemmata with augural content. Thus it began with the lemma *Augustus*, whose name commemorated the *augustum augurium* granted to Romulus at the foundation of Rome;[96] and it ended with the lemma *Vernisera auguria*.[97] The *De Verborum Significatu* was in part organised alphabetically and many (and perhaps most or all) other letters also started with lemmata reflecting good omens.[98] Moreover the treatise contained a large number of other augural lemmata.[99]

Neither the incipit of the *De Verborum Significatu* nor its structure nor its content were fortuitous; nor were they empty compliments to a remote Augustus. They reflected *Realpolitik*: augury was of immense practical and political importance to Augustus,[100] who based his power ultimately on his *auctoritas*, who steadily increased his status as supreme, indeed sole, *auctor* throughout his reign, and under whose *auspicia* most Roman generals and armies fought after 29 BC.[101] The fact that Verrius was personally high in the favour of the *princeps* is reflected not only in his being selected as family tutor and in his salary but also in the initial concession granted to him to transfer his school into the palace and bring his other pupils with him.[102] Longer and closer acquaintance between Augustus and Verrius can surely be presumed. But, for all that Verrius best illustrates the true significance of augury in the Augustan age, he was probably not a source of information about augury for the earlier of the Augustan writers whose augural voices have been identified above. For these Varro will have supplied much of what erudition they possessed, although treatises by other writers were available, notably those of Messalla Augur.[103] On the other hand Ovid's later and comparatively fuller and more technical knowledge of augury may owe something directly to Verrius.

VII. Cornutus, Messalla, and Augury

Of the six elegies in Tibullus Book 2, 2.1 is addressed to M. Valerius

---

[95] Cf. Grandazzi (1991) 101–3.
[96] Cf. Grandazzi (1991) 107–8; (1993a) 58.
[97] Cf. Grandazzi (1993a) 58.
[98] Cf. esp. Grandazzi (1993a) 58–60; also Kaster (1995) 191.
[99] For a list, cf. Grandazzi (1993a) 61–3.
[100] Cf. Grandazzi (1993b) 284.
[101] Cf. Galinsky (1996) Chh.I, VIII.
[102] Cf. Kaster (1995) 193
[103] *PIR* V87; Syme (1986) Index of Persons *s.v.* Valerius Messalla ('Rufus'), M. He died in 26 BC at an advanced age.

Messalla Corvinus, and 2.2 and 2.3 to Cornutus, while 2.5 is concerned
with Messalla's son Messalinus — and again with Messalla.[104] This
dedicatory complex is almost unique in Augustan poetry: its only (part)
parallel is the treatment of Tullus and Gallus in Propertius Book 1. In
both cases a political and social relationship between the two patrons
thus intertwined may be conjectured.[105] In Tibullus Book 2, the social
gap between Messalla — ex-consul and augur — and Cornutus makes
the latter a recognisably junior patron of Tibullus. The linkage will,
then, have been intended to publicise the great man's concern with
Cornutus. It is virtually certain that the honorand of 2.2. and 2.3 is
M. Caecilius Cornutus,[106] a fellow Arval Brother of Messalla; and
Murgatroyd int. xvii has suggested that *arva* at 2.2.14 may just possibly
allude to his arval status. The 'etymology' implied in that line (i.e. *arat
... arva*, the evidence for which appears in *LALE s.v. arvus* etc.) re-
inforces this suggestion. More is known about this probable addressee
of 2.2 and 2.3 and about his background than appears in Tibullan com-
mentaries. He came from an unfortunate, if rich,[107] family of praetorian
rank and of conservative optimate sympathies at least from the time of
Marius and Sulla.[108] The earliest known member is *RE s.v.* Caecilius
No.44 and Suppl. I (M.), an ex-praetor who served as a legate in the
Social War; he is probably to be identified with the Cornutus who
escaped in the massacres of Marius and Cinna in 87 BC; he may be the
father of No.45 and Suppl. III (cf. below). No.43 (C.) was tr. pl. in 61
BC, an optimate who as praetor in 57 BC promoted Cicero's recall
from exile. No.45 (M., perhaps the son of No.44) was *praetor urbanus*
in 43 BC and took over control of Rome when both consuls marched
against Antony. He committed suicide when the troops in Rome sub-
sequently went over to Octavian and was probably the father of the
Augustan *arvalis*. The son of the Augustan *arvalis* (M., *PIR²* C35), an
Arval Brother too and *curator locorum publicorum iudicandorum*
under Tiberius, killed himself in AD 24 when accused falsely of
plotting against Tiberius.

The acquaintance of the Cornutus of Tibullus 2.2 with Messalla
probably went back to their joint service with the Liberators in the

[104] The identification of Macer, addressee of Tib. 2.6, is uncertain.

[105] Cf. Cairns (1983) esp. 88–91.

[106] Cf. Syme (1986) 46–7; *PIR²* C34. For further information and speculations, cf. Scheid
(1975) 34–40.

[107] On the family's wealth, cf. Scheid (1975) 37–8.

[108] Cf. Scheid (1975) 34–6.

aftermath of Julius Caesar's murder;[109] and dedications of a later period
to Messalla and to Cornutus at Pergamum (separate but contemporary
and with similar lettering) hint at Cornutus' presence in the *cohors* of
Messalla when the latter was in Asia (presumably in 30 BC, after Ac-
tium).[110] Shared literary interests will have further rendered the two
men mutually congenial: Cornutus was a historian[111] and he also pub-
lished posthumously a work by his father, seemingly on legendary
catasterisms.[112] Cornutus clearly enjoyed strong support from Messalla:
it is hard to comprehend how a non-consular with a non-Caesarian
background could otherwise have attained the prestigious position of
arvalis under Augustus (as his son also did later). The intertwining of
the two men in Tibullus Book 2 is (as noted) another signal of Mes-
salla's wish to promote Cornutus publicly. This raises two questions:
why was Messalla so eager to do so; and why was Cornutus' marriage
and birthday chosen as the occasion for Tibullus' eulogy of him.[113]
Certainly for Cornutus marriage must have been a matter of con-
siderable importance, since he was relatively old at the time and still
childless.[114] But the conjecture[115] that the wife of Cornutus was a
relative of Messalla remains attractive. If the marriage was to create a
familial relationship between the two men, this would further explain
some parallelisms between them implied by Tibullus. The (reversed)
generic inclusions of Tibullus 1.7 and 2.2 may, for example, hint at

---

[109] So Scheid (1975) 36.
[110] For the epigraphic details, cf. Scheid (1975) 39 and n.1. The episode of Messalla's
suppression of a gladiatorial band at Antioch (Dio 51.7) may date his presence in Asia,
but the details of his activities in the east after Actium are hazy.
[111] This derives from an identification made by Scheid (1975) 37 and n.3. Cf. also below,
n. 114.
[112] Scheid (1975) 37. Scheid's suggestion (40) that Cornutus was also by implication a
"spécialiste de la religion romaine" and that this factor influenced his admission to the
Arval Brotherhood might be thought to stretch the evidence; but the augural interest
revealed in Tib. 2.2 perhaps provides some reinforcement.
[113] From the reign of Tiberius on the Arval Brethren conducted sacrifices and other
ceremonies to honour the birthdays of emperors, other members of the imperial house,
and some dead emperors: cf. Schmidt (1908) 70–72; Weinstock (1971) 210–11 with
nn.; Scheid (1990) 412–17. However, the practice is not attested under Augustus; and
it may simply have been an extension of their duty to pray and sacrifice for the
imperial house. Hence it cannot be used as evidence of an Augustan link between
arvals and birthdays.
[114] Cf. Scheid (1975) 37 and n.5, referring to Aelian fr. 31 Hercher (on the historian
Cornutus) and identifying him with the addressee of Tib. 2.2.
[115] Cf. Syme (1986) 47. The details, however, remain obscure; and the old attempt to
identify Cornutus with the poetess Sulpicia's lover Cerinthus (accepted by Scheid
(1975) 38–9 and 38. n 4) is hard to sustain: cf. Murgatroyd int. xvi–xvii.

such an analogy, with Cornutus following in his private life a com-
binatory precedent set by Messalla in the public sphere (see above, § I).
Again 2.1, describing a rustic Ambarvalia celebrated by Tibullus/a
chorus, gives prominence (31–6) to the 'absent Messalla', who is pre-
sumably helping to celebrate the great urban Ambarvalia of Rome in
his official capacity as Frater Arvalis.[116] Given the juxtaposition of 2.1
and 2.2, this emphasis also indirectly underscores the relationship of
the two men as fellow arvals.

   This brings us back to the question of Tibullus' augural voice in 2.2
and its ultimate purpose. In one dimension it could be seen as providing
Tibullus with a pretext for offering Cornutus a joint genethliakon/
epithalamium in the first place and then for continuing to address
Cornutus in 2.3, where Tibullus' own unhappy love-affair functions
implicitly as a foil to the happiness of the married Cornutus. In another
dimension Tibullus' role as augur could be viewed as giving the poet a
privileged and authoritative entrée into Cornutus' home and private
affairs: Tibullus is very directive in 2.2, taking control of the ceremony
even though he claims no specific connection with Cornutus. In this
respect 2.2 may be contrasted with 1.7, where there is less direction and
where Tibullus proclaims his status as eye-witness of Messalla's
victories (9ff.), or with [Tibullus] 3.12 (= 4.6), where Sulpicia speaks
as Cerinthus' lover but is also less directive. But another factor must
somehow come into the equation: as well as being an arval, Messalla
(as noted) held an even more distinguished priesthood, being an *augur
publicus*. More than this, he had received the signal honour of being

---

[116] Doubts raised by Pascal (1988) about the nature of the festival in Tib. 2.1 need not be
entertained, although the nomenclature '*Ambarvalia*' may well be anachronistic; the
'etymology' of something like 'Ambarvalia' in *fruges lustramus et agros* (Tib. 2.1.1)
is unmistakable; cf. *Tibullus* 126–7. A more serious problem emerges from Scheid
(1990) 26–35, 442–51: the rituals documented for the Arvals are confined to the grove
of the Dea Dia and do not include a lustration of the boundaries of Rome of the sort
implied by certain accounts of the 'Ambarvalia'. On this basis Bremmer (1993)
rejected the identification of the festival of Tib. 2.1 as an Ambarvalia and concluded
that the gods, prohibitions and rituals of 2.2 represent a conflation of various real
rituals and Tibullus' imagination. It has, however, been long known that, like other
Roman descriptions of festivals etc., Tib. 2.2 blends reality and literary reminiscence
(so already, for example, *Tibullus* 133–4); and this fact again in no way shakes the
identification of its festival as an 'Ambarvalia'. But Scheid's findings do give pause.
One relevant consideration may be that we have no information about the Arvals'
activities in the 20s BC other than what is thought to be implied by Tib. 2.2. Is it
possible, then, that the newly (re-)created Brotherhood appropriated to itself in its first
flush of enthusiasm some functions of other priesthoods, e.g. pontifical lustration, and
that it had to relinquish them once Augustus' entire sacral system was up and running?

coopted *supra numerum* into that college by Octavian after the Sicilian War of 36 BC (Dio 49.16). The circumstances are unexplained, but they must have been exceptional — plausibly important services to Octavian in that war, compounded by Messalla's transference of allegiance to Octavian frcm Antony. Messalla's pride in his augurate, and Tibullus' awareness of its significance for his patron, are evidenced in the semi-technical augural reference at 2.5.11–12 (lines addressed to Apollo in an elegy celebrating Messalla and his son): *tu procul eventura vides, tibi deditus augur/ scit bene, quid fati provida cantet avis.* Messalla seems also to have had a personal interest in the technicalities of augury and haruspicy.[117]

What, then, is the relationship between Messalla's augurate and Tibullus' augural voice in 2.2? Is Tibullus simply adopting this role as an oblique compliment to Messalla, parallel in this respect to the compliment of 2.1, where (see above) Tibullus' rustic Ambarvalia with Messalla absent recalls the patron's participation as *Frater Arvalis* in the urban festival? Or is there another possibility — to be advanced with due caution? Might Messalla have blessed and distinguished Cornutus' marriage by acting at it in person as a wedding augur? And might Tibullus 2.2 have been composed originally for Messalla to recite at Cornutus' wedding?

Bibliography

Abbreviations (apart from standard reference works)

GC = F. Cairns *Generic Composition in Greek and Roman poetry* (Edinburgh 1972)

LALE = R. Maltby *A Lexicon of Ancient Latin Etymologies* (ARCA 25, Leeds 1991)

Lenz–Galinsky = F.W. Lenz and G.C. Galinsky (edd.) *Albii Tibulli aliorumque carminum libri tres* (3rd ed., Leiden 1971)

Lee–Maltby = G. Lee with R. Maltby *Tibullus: Elegies. Introduction, Text, Translation and Nctes.* (Latin and Greek Texts 6, 3rd. ed. (including Book 3, Text and Translation), Leeds 1990)

Murgatroyd = P. Murgatroyd *Tibullus, Elegies II: edited with introduction and commentary* (Oxford 1994)

Smith = K.F. Smith *The elegies of Albius Tibullus: the Corpus Tibullianum edited with introduction and notes on books I, II, and IV, 2–14* (New York 1913, repr. Darmstadt 1985)

Tibullus = F. Cairns *Tibullus: a Hellenistic poet at Rome* (Cambridge 1979)

[117] Cf. above, § I and n. 21.

Other works

Anderson, R.D., Parsons, P.J., and Nisbet, R.G.M. (1979). 'Elegiacs by Gallus from Qaṣr Ibrîm' *JRS* 69.125–55

Ball, R.J. (1983). *Tibullus the Elegist: a Critical Survey*. (Hypomnemata 77) Göttingen

Barchiesi, A. (1992) (ed.) P. *Ovidii Nasonis Epistulae Heroidum 1–3*. (Biblioteca nazionale. Serie dei classici greci e latini. Testi con commento filologico. Nuova serie diretta da Gian Biagio Conte 1) Firenze

Bremmer, J. (1993). 'Tibullus' colonus and his 'Ambarvalia'' in *De Agricultura. In Memoriam Pieter Willem de Neeve (1945-1990)*, edd. H. Sancisi-Weerdenburg, R.J. van der Spek, H.C. Teitler and H.T. Wallinga (Dutch monographs on ancient history and archaeology 10) Amsterdam, 177–181

Cairns, F. (1971). 'Propertius 3,10 and Roman birthdays' *Hermes* 99.149–55

—. (1983). 'Propertius 1,4 and 1,5 and the 'Gallus' of the Monobiblos' *PLLS* 4.61–103

—. (1993). 'Imitation and originality in Ovid *Amores* 1.3' *PLLS* 7.101–22

—. (1996). 'Ancient 'etymology' and Tibullus: on the classification of 'etymologies' and on 'etymological markers'' *PCPhS* 42.24–59

—. (forthcoming). 'Horace *Odes* 3.17 and the genre genethliakon'

Carter, J.B. (1902). *Epitheta deorum quae apud poetas latinos leguntur*. (Suppl. to *Ausführliches Lexikon der griechischen und römischen Mythologie* ed. W.H. Roscher) Leipzig

Catalano, P. (1960). *Contributi allo studio del diritto augurale I*. (Università di Torino. Memorie dell' Istituto giuridico. Serie II, Memoria 107) Torino

Cesareo, E. (1929). *Il carme natalizio nella poesia latina*. Palermo

Clay, J.S. (1993). '*Providus auspex*: Horace, Ode 3.27' *CJ* 88.167–77

Connor, P. (1987). *Horace's Lyric Poetry: the Force of Humour*. (Ramus Monographs 2) Berwick, Victoria, Australia

Della Corte, F. (1980). *Tibullo. Le Elegie*. Milan

Dyson, J.T. (1997). 'Birds, grandfathers, and neoteric sorcery in *Aeneid* 4.254 and 7.412' *CQ* n.s. 47.314–15

Fantham, E. (1992). *Lucan: De Bello Civili Book II*. Cambridge

Fedeli, P. (1985) (ed.) *Properzio. Il libro terzo delle elegie. Introduzione, testo e commento*. (Studi e commenti 3) Bari

Fraenkel, E. (1957). *Horace*. Oxford

Galinsky, K. (1996). *Augustan Culture: an Interpretative Introduction*. Princeton, New Jersey

Grandazzi, A. (1991). 'Les mots et les choses. La composition du *De Verborum Significatu* de Verrius Flaccus' *RÉL* 69.101–23

—. (1993a). 'Les mots de la divination chez Verrius Flaccus. Première partie' *RPhil.* 67.57–73

—. (1993b). 'Les mots de la divination chez Verrius Flaccus. Seconde partie' *RPhil.* 67.263–85

Kiessling, A. (1930) and Heinze, R. *Q. Horatius Flaccus. Oden und Epoden*. Berlin (repr. Hildesheim and Zurich 1984)

Hinds, S.J. (1984). 'Carmina digna: Gallus P Qaṣr Ibrîm 6–7 metamorphosed' *PLLS* 4.43–54

Hollis, A.S. (1977). *Ovid: Ars Amatoria Book I: Edited with an introduction and commentary*. Oxford

Kaster, R.A. (1995). *C. Suetonius Tranquillus. De Grammaticis et Rhetoribus. Edited with a translation, introduction and commentary*. Oxford

Knox, P.E. (1995). *Ovid. Heroides, Select Epistles*. Cambridge

Latte, K. (1967). *Römische Religionsgeschichte*. (Handbuch der Altertumswissenschaft 5.4) Munich

Lewis, M.W.H. (1955). *The Official Priests of Rome under the Julio-Claudians: a Study of the Nobility from 44 B.C. to 68 A.D.* (Papers and Monographs of the American Academy at Rome 16) Rome

Linderski, J. (1986). 'The augural law' *ANRW* II.16.3.2146–2312

Luck, G. (1967–77). *P. Ovidius Naso. Tristia: Herausgegeben, übersetzt und erklärt*. 2 vols Heidelberg

—. (1988) (ed.) *Albii Tibulli aliorumque carmina*. Stuttgart

Maltby R. (1996). 'Sense and structure in Tibullus (2.2.21–2, 1.1.78, 2.1.83–90, 1.5.1–8, 1.6.5–8)' *PLLS* 9 (1996) 93–102

Mutschler, F.-H. (1985). *Die poetische Kunst Tibulls. Struktur und Bedeutung der Bücher 1 und 2 des Corpus Tibullianum*. (Studien zur klassischen Philologie 18) Frankfurt am Main/Bern/New York/Nancy

Newman, J.K. (1967). *Augustus and the New Poetry*. (Coll. Latomus 88) Brussels–Berchem

Pascal C.B. (1988). 'Tibullus and the Ambarvalia' *AJPh* 109.523–36

Pease, A.S. (1920–3). *M. Tulli Ciceronis de divinatione*. Urbana

Pianezzola, E. *et al.* (1991). *Ovidio. L'Arte di amare*. Fondazione Lorenzo Valla

Putnam, M.C.J. (1973). *Tibullus: a Commentary*. Oklahoma

Quinn, K. (1980). *Horace. The Odes*. London

Rapisarda, C.A. (1991). *Censorini De die natali liber ad Q. Caerellium. Prefazione, testo critico, traduzione e commento*. Bologna

Santirocco, M.S. (1986). *Unity and Design in Horace's Odes*. Chapel Hill–London

Scheid, J. (1975). *Les frères arvales. Recrutement et origine sociale sous les empereurs julio-claudiens*. (Bibliothèque de l'école des hautes études. Section des sciences religieuses 77) Paris

—. (1990). *Romulus et ses frères. Le collège des frères arvales, modèle du culte public dans la Rome des empereurs* (Bibliothèque des Écoles françaises d'Athènes et de Rome 275) Rome

Schmidt, W. (1908). *Geburtstag im Altertum*. (Religionsgeschichtliche Versuche und Vorarbeiten 7.1) Giessen

Streifinger, J. (1881). *De Syntaxi Tibulliana*. Diss. Würzburg

Syme, R. (1986). *The Augustan Aristocracy*. Oxford

Syndikus, H.P. (1973). *Die Lyrik des Horaz: Eine Interpretation der Oden II. Drittes und viertes Buch*. Darmstadt

Tränkle, H. (1960). *Die Sprachkunst des Properz und die Tradition der lateinischen Dichtersprache*. (Hermes Einzelschriften 15) Wiesbaden

—. (1990). *Appendix Tibulliana: Herausgegeben und kommentiert*. (Texte und Kommentare 16) Berlin–New York

Treggiari, S. (1991). *Roman Marriage: Iusti Coniuges from the Time of Cicero to the Time of Ulpian*. Oxford

Van Dam, H.-J. (1984). *P. Papinius Statius Silvae Book II: a Commentary*. (Mnemosyne Suppl. 82) Leiden

Veremans, J. (1996). 'La structure de l'enjambement chez les poètes élégiaques: Tibulle, Properce, Ovide' *Latomus* 55.525–43

Warde-Fowler, W. (1899). *The Roman Festivals of the Period of the Republic: an Introduction to the Study of the Religion of the Romans*. London

Weinstock, S. (1971). *Divus Julius*. Oxford

Wheeler, A.L. (1930). 'Tradition in the epithalamium' *AJPh* 51.205–23

Wissowa, G. (1912). *Religion und Kultus der Römer*. 2nd ed. Munich

PAPERS OF THE LEEDS INTERNATIONAL LATIN SEMINAR   TENTH VOLUME (1998) 235–50
Published by Francis Cairns (Publications) Ltd (Leeds 1998). ARCA 38. ISBN 0 905205 95 2

SOME CASES OF PROPERTIAN ETYMOLOGISING[*]

ANDREAS MICHALOPOULOS
University of Leeds

The importance of 'etymology' — very often pseudo-etymology — in Roman elegy is by now well-established. Cairns (1979) shed light on Tibullus' etymologising, which displays a profound knowledge of etymological associations artistically elaborated upon; and McKeown (1987) 45–62 demonstrated the significant role of etymology in Ovid's *Amores* by discussing a number of convincing etymological wordplays. But comparatively little has been said about the etymological interests of Propertius, with most attention being given to his explicit aetiological etymologising in Book 4.[1]

The present paper will deal with unobtrusive Propertian etymological wordplays under the following categories:[2]

---

[*] Particular thanks are owed to Prof. Francis Cairns and Dr Robert Maltby for their valuable comments on an earlier draft of this paper.

[1] The following bibliography of Propertian etymology is given by O'Hara (1996) 56 n.304: Bailey (1956) 223 *harenosum* (4.1.103) alludes to Jupiter's cult title Ammon, 260 the ἔτυμον of Alcides at 4.9.38; Courtney (1969) 80–81 bilingual wordplay between *Acanthis* and *spinae* in 4.5; Bramble (1974) 89 wordplay between *Pagasae* and *navalibus* at 1.20.17; Ross (1975) 62 *durae ... Iasidos* (1.1.10) alluding to the etymology of Atalanta; King (1980) 212–14 wordplay on "to know" as a unifying motif in 1.13; Koster (1983) the aetiological elegies of Book 4; Zetzel (1983) 92 *laudatis ... comis* (2.1.8) as a bilingual pun on the Greek ἐγκώμιον; Boyd (1984) 85f. wordplay between *Tarpeia* and *turpis* at 4.4.1–2; Cairns (1983) 84–6 *noscere–nota–nomen* in 1.5, (1984) 211–21, (1993) 114 the 'Gallan' etymological wordplay between *notus–ignotus*, *noscere* and *nosse, nomen, nota* and *nobilitas*, reflected at Ov. *Am.* 1.3.21, 26.

[2] For different classifications see O'Hara (1996) 57–102 and Cairns (1996), both of which appeared after this paper was drafted. Since this paper attempts to initiate the

A. etymologising on common nouns from Latin
B. etymologising on common nouns from Greek
C. etymologising on proper names
D. etymologising *ex contrario*.

A. Etymologising on common nouns from Latin

In this type of etymologising a common noun is collocated with a word constituting, or alluding to, its origin.[3]

i) *cupido–capere* (1.1.1–2)

The theme of Propertius' poetry is announced in his first couplet: *Cynthia prima suis miserum me **cepit** ocellis,/ contactum nullis ante **Cupidinibus**.* Isidore (*Origines* 10.42) declares:[4] *cupidus a capiendo multum, id est accipiendo, vocatus.* The implicit etymology underscores Propertius' submission to love and lends additional emphasis to Cynthia's overwhelming influence upon him: she has managed to capture (*cepit*) him, even though other loves (*cupidinibus*), which by nature and etymology might have done so, had failed to attract his attention. The *cupido–capere* etymological association had already appeared at Ennius *Tragoediae* 222 in the words of Medea's nurse: ***cupido cepit** miseram nunc me proloqui/ caelo atque terrae Medeai miserias*, where it is 'marked' by the juxtaposition of the two words at the beginning of the line.[5]

The opening lines of Propertius 1.1 are largely indebted to an epigram of Meleager (*AP* 12.101):

---

[3] investigation of etymology in a poet in whose work it has hitherto been comparatively neglected, I have retained my original classifications and have not sought to interact with those of others.

Within each section examples are discussed in the order of their appearance in the Propertian corpus.

[4] Isidore of course composed his *Etymologiae sive Origines* several centuries after Propertius. But his work and those of other later grammarians were largely indebted to collections of etymologies antedating Propertius. In particular M. Terentius Varro and Verrius Flaccus exercised a great influence upon etymological thought in Rome. Consequently, the fact that evidence to support the etymological wordplays suggested postdates Propertius should not present any difficulties.

[5] For coupling as an etymological marker see Snyder (1980) 76–84 and Cairns (1996) 33. In the same couplet there is another wordplay, between *miseram* and *miserias*; see Jocelyn (1967) *ad loc*. Of course the Latin poets' fondness for alliteration often raises questions about whether a particular collocation is etymologically motivated or not. In such cases contextual needs, the so-called 'etymological markers', and parallels from other authors may facilitate a decision. See Snyder (1980) ch.4 (alliteration) and Maltby (1993).

Τόν με πόθοις ἄτρωτον ὑπὸ στέρνοισι Μυΐσκος
ὄμμασι τοξεύσας τοῦτ᾽ ἐβόησεν ἔπος·
"Τὸν θρασὺν εἷλον ἐγώ· τὸ δ᾽ ἐπ᾽ ὀφρύσι κεῖνο φρύαγμα
σκηπτροφόρου σοφίας ἠνίδε ποσσὶ πατῶ".

It is interesting that there is also a different etymological play there between ὀφρύσι and φρύαγμα, cf. *Etymologicum Magnum* 801.12: φρύαγμα: Ἡ τῶν ἵππων καὶ ἡμιόνων διὰ μυκτήρων ἠχὴ ἀγρίῳ φυσήματι ἐκπίπτουσα· λέγεται δὲ καὶ ἐπὶ τῆς γελάσεως. ᾽Απὸ τοῦ φρυάσσω· τοῦτο παρὰ τὸ ὀφρῦς ὀφρυάσσω· κατὰ ἀποβολὴν τοῦ ο, φρυάσσω. Καὶ φρυαττόμενος, ἐπαιρόμενος· καὶ φρυάττεσθαι, τὸ καταπλήττεσθαι. Μένανδρος. The presence of this wordplay at the beginning of Propertius' work signals the important role that etymologising will play in his elegies; we are justified in expecting more such wordplays.

ii) *avarus–aurum* (1.8.38–9)

The poverty of the elegiac poet and the avarice of his mistress are standard topoi in Roman elegy. 1.8 is built around these topoi. In its first part Propertius' mistress is about to follow a rich praetor to Illyria, while in the second Propertius celebrates her change of mind and decision not to abandon him. It was not his wealth that kept her with him, but the power of his poetry: *quamvis magna daret, quamvis maiora daturus,/ non tamen illa meos fugit avara sinus./ hanc ego non auro, non Indis flectere conchis,/ sed potui blandi carminis obsequio* (1.8.37–40). *avara* and *auro* are etymologically linked. Isidore considers *avarus* a compound of *avidus* and *aurum* (*Origines* 10.9): *avidus dictus ab avendo; avere enim cupere est. hinc et avarus ...; avarus ex eo dictus, quod sit avidus auri.*[6] Propertius uses the etymology to emphasise the power of his poetry. His poems are superior to gold even in the eyes of a girl 'greedy for gold'. The same wordplay appears earlier at Plautus *Miles* 1063–4: *non mihi avaritia umquam innatast: satis habeo divitiarum,/ plus mi auri mille est modiorum Philippi.* There, however, it works differently: Pyrgopolynices justifies his total lack of greediness by his already enormous wealth.

iii) *vultus–velle* (2.10.9–10)

The opening lines of 2.10 surprise the reader. Propertius announces a dramatic turn in his poetic career: he will now write poetry in praise of

---

[6] Cf. Aug. *Civ.* 15.22, p.107.1D *aurum amatur ab avaris.*

Augustus. Fully aware of the difficulties he is about to encounter, Propertius is quick to produce a disclaimer: *quod si deficiant vires, audacia certe/ laus erit: in magnis et voluisse sat est* (2.10.5–6). His will (*voluisse*) to embark upon this new and perilous enterprise is enough to secure him praise. After restating his intention to sing of wars, not love (*bella canam, quando scripta puella mea est*), Propertius returns to his wish for a different subject: *nunc **volo** subducto gravior procedere **vultu**,/ nunc aliam citharam me mea Musa docet* (2.10.9–10). This is his own wish (*volo*) and his new stance will be reflected on his face (*vultu*). Internal wish and external appearance thus form an inseparable pair to mark the change of subject. Propertius could not have found a better way to emphasise this than through the etymological play between *volo* and *vultu*. Roman grammarians are unanimous about the etymology of *vultus*: *vultus ... quartae est, quod quasi rei est vocabulum a "volo" verbo, quomodo a colo cultus* (Priscian II 261.16).[7]

iv) *fraus–fides* (2.20.3–4)

Propertius' affair with Cynthia is one of happiness and pain, of loyalty and infidelity. 2.20 assures his beloved of his faithfulness and rejects her accusations of betrayal: *quidve mea de **fraude** deos, insana, fatigas?/ quid quereris nostram sic cecidisse **fidem**?* (2.20.3–4). *fides* and *fraus*, two polar opposites, signal one the ideal in a relationship and the other its destruction. The effect is sharpened by the etymological link between the two terms: cf. Cassiodorus (*Expositio in Psalmos* 77.31, l.455A.): *fraus ... dicitur quasi fracta fides*, obviously taking *fraus–fraudis* as a compound of *frangere* and *fides*.[8] The wordplay has added significance here, since this is the only couplet which refers directly to Cynthia and Propertius.

Again Propertius has a precedent: the *fraus–fides* association had already been exploited by Plautus at *Asinaria* 561, where Leonida accuses Libanus of betraying the trust of a friend: *ubi **fidentem fraudaveris**.*

---

[7] Cf. Cassiod. *Anim.* 11 l.78H *vultus ... qui a voluntate nominatur, speculum ... est animae suae*; *In Psalm.* 30.23 l.475A *vultus ... dicitur ab eo quod cordis velle per sua signa demonstret*; Isid. *Orig.* 11.1.34 *vultus ... dictus, eo quod per eum animi voluntas ostenditur*.

[8] In Propertius the presence of *cecidisse* also implies that *fraus* is a corrupted state of *fides*.

v) *quare–quaerere* (2.22a.13–4, 2.24a.9–10)

An easily detectable etymological play appears at 2.22a.13–14, where Propertius states that there can be no logic in love: *quaeris, Demophoon, cur sim tam mollis in omnis?/ quod* **quaeris**, *"quare", non habet ullus amor.* Varro (*De Lingua Latina* 6.79) wrote: *ipsum quaerere ab eo quod quae res ut reciperetur datur opera. quare* was also taken as a compound consisting of *qua* and *res*: *a qua et re quare* (Priscian *Institutiones Grammaticae* II.563.12). The play is facilitated by the similarity in sound between the two words and by their direct collocation. Thus Demophoon's amazement at the reasons behind Propertius' behaviour in love is vividly portrayed.

The wordplay reappears in Propertius' answer to a friend who is startled by the poet's preference for women of a lower status: ***quare** ne tibi sit mirum me **quaerere** vilis:/ parcius infamant: num tibi causa levis?* (2.24a.9–10). Propertius' statement is indisputable: this is underlined by the collocation of *quare* and *quaerere*. A parallel *quare–quaerere* etymology can be found in Lucretius' exploration of the reasons for the mind's subordination to whim (4.779–80): ***Quaeritur** in primis **quare**, quod cuique libido/ venerit, extemplo mens cogitet eius id ipsum.* The combination *quaeritur quare* signals the beginning of a philosophical quest.

vi) *iter–ire* (2.27.15–16)

The etymological association of *iter* and *ire* was sanctioned by Varro (*De Lingua Latina* 5.35): *qua ibant ab itu iter appellarunt.*[9] Propertius was well aware of this link and twice exploits it when using compounds of *ire*. In the final couplet of 2.27: *si modo clamantis revocaverit aura puellae,/ concessum nulla lege* **redibit iter** (15–16), the emphatic juxtaposition of *redibit* and *iter* at the line end 'marks' Propertius' etymological intent and encapsulates the basic idea of the elegy, the lover's return from the dead:[10] love is so powerful it can annul death. Similarly *adimus* and *iter* are juxtaposed at the line end in the opening couplet of 3.7, Propertius' lament for the death of Paetus: *Ergo sollicitae tu causa, pecunia, vitae!/ per te immaturum mortis* **adimus iter.** The notion of man finding his own death in his quest for money is thus underpinned.

---

[9] Much later Isidore attested (*Orig.* 15.16.8) *iter vel itus est via qua iri ab homine ... potest ... ; iter est locus transitu facilis; unde appellamus et itum.*

[10] For coupling as an etymological marker see n.5 above.

vii) *terra–torrere* (2.28.3–4)

2.28 is Propertius' agonised prayer to Jupiter for the recovery of his mistress, who is gravely ill. Right at the beginning the time of the year (the hottest) is vividly depicted: *venit enim tempus, quo **torridus** aestuat aer,/ incipit et sicco fervere **terra** Cane* (2.28.3–4). This couplet contains an etymology of *terra* later attested in Isidore (*Differentiae* 1.552): *terra, quod naturali siccitate torreat*. In Propertius *torridus* modifies *aer* to suggest the 'burning' origin of *terra* and to lead on to fever, Cynthia's main anticipated symptom.

Lucretius had twice exploited this particular etymology of *terra*. At 5.214–15 he refers to the drying up of the crops by the heat of the sun as one of the proofs that the world is not of divine origin: *cum iam per **terras** frondent atque omnia florent,/ aut nimiis **torret** fervoribus aetherius sol*. The placing of both *terras* and *torret* at the same *sedes*, right before the caesura, 'marks' the etymologising.[11] At 5.901–3 Lucretius is trying to prove that monsters cannot possibly have existed. His argument against the existence of a fire-breathing Chimaera is that 'fire' consumes every living creature on 'earth': *flamma quidem vero cum corpora fulva leonum/ tam soleat **torrere** atque urere quam genus omne/ visceris in **terris** quodcumque et sanguinis extet*.

viii) *nomen–noscere* and *notare*[12] (3.16.29–30, 3.11.48)

The belief that the nature of things is revealed by their names formed the basis of some ancient etymological and philosophical thinking.[13] It even influenced the opinion of the Roman grammarians on the etymology of *nomen*; cf. Paulus Festus 172: *nomen dictum quasi novimen, quod notitiam facit* and Cassiodorus (*Expositio in Psalmos* 71.17, l.408A): *nomen ... dictum est, quod notam rem faciat*. Dositheus (*Ars Grammatica* VII 390.1) attests the link with *notare*: *nomen dicitur quod unam quamque rem notat, quasi notamen sublata media syllaba per syncopen, vel a graeca origine* παρὰ τὸ ὄνομα. Propertius is aware of both etymologies. In 3.16 he is preparing for a dangerous night journey to Tibur to visit his mistress. Even though lovers are sacrosanct and protected by the gods, he provides instructions for his burial in the event of his being killed: *post mortem tumuli sic infamantur amantum./*

---

[11] For metrical *sedes* as an etymological marker see Cairns (1996) 33.
[12] For other Propertian plays on this association see n.1 above.
[13] The thesis was mainly held by the Stoics. See Woodhead (1928) 74–89, Collish (1985) 56–60.

*me tegat arborea devia terra coma,/ aut humer **ignotae** cumulis valla-tus harenae:/ non iuvat in media **nomen** habere via* (3.16.27–30). Camps[14] suggests that *ignotae* can either be taken as "nameless" or as "in a remote place", but fails to point out its direct etymological asso-ciation with *nomen*: Propertius does not want his name (*nomen*) published on the highway, but prefers to be buried in an unmarked (*ignotae*) mound of sand. Propertius works on the *nomen–notare* etymological association again at 3.11.47–8 in relation to Tarquinius Superbus: *quid nunc* Tarquinii *fractas iuvat esse securis,/ **nomine** quem simili vita* superba ***notat***. Tarquinius is 'marked' by his 'name', which he got because of his way of life; the fact that *nomine* and *notat* frame the line highlights the etymologising.[15]

The *nomen–noscere* etymological wordplay was extremely popular in Latin literature, and is common in comedy.[16]

ix) *cornu–curvum* (3.22.35)

3.22 is Propertius' praise of Italy in the style of rhetorical school exer-cises, such as *laus locorum* and *comparatio*.[17] In attempting to persuade his friend Tullus to return home to Italy, Propertius first enumerates the ways in which Italy excels the rest of the world, and then refers to prodigies and monsters from which Italy is free. One of them is Io, the girl transformed into a cow by Iuno as a punishment for her affair with Jupiter: ***cornua** nec valuit **curvare** in paelice Iuno/ aut faciem turpi dedecorare bove* (3.22.35–6). *cornua* and *curvare* are etymologically linked, cf. Varro (*De Lingua Latina* 7.25): *cornua a curvore dicta, quod pleraque curva*.[18] Propertius may be adapting Virgil *Georgics*

---

[14] Camps (1966) *ad loc.*

[15] On line framing as an etymological signpost see O'Hara (1996) 82–3 and Cairns (1996).

[16] Plaut. *Men.* 294 *Cylindrus ego sum: non **nosti nomen** meum?*, 296–9 *ego te non **novi**, neque **novisse** adeo volo./ CYL. Est tibi Menaechmo **nomen**, tantum quod sciam./ MEN. Pro sano loqueris quom me appellas **nomine**./ sed ubi **novisti** me?*, 337 *Sed miror qui ille **noverit nomen** meum*, 498–9 MEN. *Responde, adulescens, quaeso, quid **nomen** tibist?/ PEN. Etiam derides, quasi **nomen** non **noveris**?*; *Pseud.* 988–90 SI. *Accipe et **cognosce** signum. BA. Oh, Polymachaeroplagides/ purus putus est ipsus; **novi** heus, Polymachaeroplagides/ **nomen** est; Trin.* 905–6 ***novistin** hominem? SYC. Ridicule rogitas, quicum una cibum/ capere soleo. CHARM. Quid est ei **nomen**?* Cf. also Hor. *Sat.* 1.9.3 *accurrit quidam **notus** mihi **nomine** tantum.*

[17] See Underwood (1971) 78–88.

[18] *cerva* in 3.22.34 (*nec solvit Danaas subdita cerva rates*) may, with *cornua*, constitute yet another etymological wordplay based on the derivation of *cerva* from the Greek κέρας "horn". Cf. Varro *L.L.* 5.101 *cervi, quod magna cornua gerunt, gervi, "g" in "c" mutavit ut in multis*; also Paul. Fest. 54 and Serv. *Aen.* 1.184.

4.299–300: *tum vitulus bima* **curvans** *iam* **cornua** *fronte/ quaeritur*. Lucilius 26.27 (605 M) had already exploited the *cornu–curvus* etymology by modifying *cornu* with *curvum*: *rauco contionem sonitu et* **curvis** *cogant* **cornibus**.[19]

x) *vitta–vincire* (4.11.34)

In 4.11, the 'Cornelia elegy', Cornelia recalls her wedding to Paulus: *mox, ubi iam facibus cessit praetexta maritis,/ **vinxit** et acceptas altera* **vitta** *comas,/ iungor, Paule, tuo sic discessura cubili:/ in lapide hoc uni nupta fuisse legar* (4.11.33–6). Attention is drawn to this key event in her life (involving the change of headband worn by Cornelia first as an unmarried girl and then as a married woman) by an etymological wordplay between *vinxit* and *vitta*. Cf. Isidore *Origines* 19.30.4 *vittae dictae sunt, quod vinciant* and 19.31.6, 19.33.7 *vitta dicta quod ea pectus vincitur instar vitis ligantis*.

B. Etymologising on common nouns from Greek

In this type of etymologising a noun thought to have a Greek derivation is collocated with a word constituting — or alluding to — the Latin translation of its Greek derivation.

i) *scopulus–aspicere* (2.30.27)

At 2.30.27–8 Propertius is describing how Cynthia will see the Muses on Helicon: *illic* **aspicies** **scopulis** *haerere Sorores/ et canere antiqui dulcia furta Iovis*. In the grammatical tradition two different derivations are attested for *scopulus*, both from Greek: *scopulus ... aut a speculando dictus est, aut a tegimento navium, ἀπὸ τοῦ σκεπάζειν* (Servius on *Aeneid* 1.45) and *scopulus a saxo eminenti, quasi ab speculando dictus* [i.e. ἀπὸ τοῦ σκοπεῖν] (Isidore *Origines* 16.3.2). Propertius playfully exploits the association of *scopulus* with σκοπεῖν. Cynthia will see (*aspicies*) the Muses sitting on the rocks (*scopulis*), since the rocks are a place closely associated with vision because of the Greek origin of their name, i.e. from σκοπεῖν, "to see". Such a learned etymological wordplay is particularly apt in the context of the Muses, the patron deities of knowledge and culture. Propertius had a predecessor in this wordplay: at Catullus 64.243–5 king Aegeus anxiously

---

[19] The reference here is of course to horns being blown to call an assembly. Virgil has similar wordplay at *Aen.* 7.497 *Ascanius* **curvo** *derexit spicula* **cornu**, 7.513 *pastorale canit signum* **cornuque recurvo**. See O'Hara (1996) 190.

watches the sea from a rock, i.e. a place for observation, in expectation of Theseus' ship: *cum primum infecti* **conspexit** *lintea veli,/ praecipitem sese* **scopulorum** *e vertice iecit,/ amissum credens immiti Thesea fato.*[20]

ii) palaestra–luctor (3.14.1–4)

3.14, a *laus legis*,[21] is Propertius' praise of the Spartan laws allowing girls to exercise naked among men: *multa tuae, Sparte, miramur iura* **palaestrae***,/ sed mage virginei tot bona gymnasii,/ quod non infamis exercet corpore ludos/ inter* **luctantis** *nuda puella viros* (3.14.1–4). In praising a Greek city in a Graeco-Roman context, Propertius inserts a Greek/Latin etymological wordplay. *palaestrae* (1) transliterates the Greek παλαίστρα "wrestling-school" and *luctantis* (4) is the Latin translation of the Greek παλαίω "to wrestle".[22] The grammatical tradition offers conclusive confirmatory evidence: *Mercurius ... amatam ... suam Palaestram remuneratus omne luctamen, quod corpore conficitur, palaestram vocari fecit* (Servius auctus on *Aeneid* 8.138), and *palaestra ... dicta est ἀπὸ τῆς πάλης, id est a luctatione* (Servius on *Georgics* 2.531).[23]

iii) annus–novare (4.1.19–20)

In his account of Rome's humble origins Propertius mentions the annual festival in honour of Pales: **annuaque** *accenso celebrare Parilia faeno,/ qualia nunc curto lustra* **novantur** *equo* (4.1.19–20). Among other derivations for *annus* attested in the grammatical tradition[24] Servius suggests: *annus ... ἀπὸ τοῦ ἀνανεοῦσθαι, id est ab innovatione*, which is recapitulated by Isidore *Origines* 5.36.2: *alii annum dicunt ἀπὸ τοῦ ἀνανεοῦσθαι, id est ab innovatione; renovatur enim*

---

[20] There is an excellent parallel at Virg. *Aen.* 1.180–81 *Aeneas* **scopulum** *interea conscendit, et omnem/* **prospectum** *late pelago petit.* See O'Hara (1996) 119.

[21] Underwood (1971) 72–8.

[22] *palaestra* and *luctor* can be expected to occur together even without etymological intent. However, the παλαίστρα was not simply a wrestling ground, but a place where all gymnastic activities took place, see Flacelière (1965) 103–9. *luctantis* (line 4) leaves no doubt about which sporting activity Propertius refers to.

[23] Cf. Isid. *Orig.* 18.24: *palaestra ... vel ἀπὸ τῆς πάλης, id est a luctatione.* Both Servius and Isidore further suggest a derivation from πάλλειν: *palaestra ... dicta est ... , vel ἀπὸ τοῦ πάλλειν, hoc est a motu urnae; nam ducti sorte luctantur* (Serv. *Georg.* 2.531) and *palaestra ... vel ἀπὸ τοῦ πάλλειν, id est a motu ruinae fortis, nominatum dicunt, scilicet quod in luctando, cum medios arripiant, fere quatiant; idque apud Graecos πάλλειν vocatur* (Isid. *ibid.*).

[24] See Maltby (1991) *s.v. annus.*

semper. Propertius' collocation of *annua* and *novantur* may therefore have been etymologically motivated, especially since "renovation" and "repetition" are particularly relevant to a festival taking place every year. Propertius is probably carrying further a tradition firmly established by Tibullus, who twice in Book 1 pointedly collocates *novus* with *annus*. At 1.1.13–14 Tibullus mentions his annual offering of the firstfruits to Priapus: *et quodcumque mihi pomum **novus** educat **annus**,/ libatum agricolae ponitur ante deo* (his repetition of this act being a manifestation of his piety); and at 1.4.35–6 he refers to snakes sloughing off their skin and rejuvenating themselves each year: *crudeles divi! serpens **novus** exuit **annos**;/ formae non ullam Fata dedere moram.*

C. Etymologising *ex contrario*

In this type of etymological wordplay a noun is collocated with another word that constitutes — or refers to — the opposite of its derivation.[25]

postis–ante (1.16.42)

In a paraclausithyron, the lover addresses his mistress' locked door that denies him admission: ***ante** tuos quotiens verti me, perfida, **postes**,/ debitaque occultis vota tuli manibus!* (1.16.43–4). This image is typical of love elegy.[26] But Propertius increases its effect through a sharp etymological contrast. *ante* is the direct opposite of *post*, which was thought to be the origin of *postis*: cf. Priscian *Partitiones XII versuum Aeneidos principalium* III 475.7 *postes ... dictae, quod post fores stant*, and Isidore *Origines* 15.7.9 *postes eo quod post ostium stent*. Propertius also presents the contrast between *ante* and *postes* visually, i.e. by placing them at the beginning and the end of the line respectively.[27] Moreover, this is the first occurrence in extant Latin verse of *ante postes* instead of *ante fores*, used previously by Lucilius and Horace.[28] Later Ovid re-employed this wordplay when referring to the lover's exclusion from his mistress' house (*Amores* 2.19.21–2): *et sine me **ante** tuos proiectum in limine **postes**/ longa pruinosa frigora nocte pati.*[29]

---

[25] The most famous example of this type of etymologising is criticised by Quintilian *Inst.* 1.6.34 *etiamne a contrariis aliqua sinemus trahi, ut lucus, quia umbra opacus parum luceat?* See also O'Hara (1996) 66.

[26] Copley (1956).

[27] For this line positioning see n.18 above.

[28] Luc. *Sat. inc.* 1107 *ante fores autem et triclini limina quid<a>m*; Hor. *Carm.* 3.10.3 *porrectum ante foris obicere incolis.*

[29] Cf. also Ov. *Met.* 7.602 *ante sacros vidi proiecta cadavera postes.*

D. Etymologising on proper names

In this type of etymologising proper names are collocated with words that refer to or, in the case of foreign names (mainly Greek), translate their derivation. The belief that the name reveals the nature of its bearer is thus underlined.[30]

i) Venus

'Venus' is a particular object of Propertius' etymological interest. A wide variety of derivations for her name are found in the grammatical tradition: *vincire*,[31] *venia*,[32] *vanus*[33] and *venustas*.[34] Propertius is especially concerned with two further etymologies, from *venire* and from *vis*. Cf. Cicero (*De Natura Deorum* 2.69): *quae ... dea ad res omnes veniret Venerem nostri nominaverunt* (3.62: *Venus quia venit ad omnia*),[35] and Augustine (*De Civitate Dei* 6.9, p.264.26D): *Venus ab hoc ... dicitur nuncupata, quod sine vi femina virgo esse non desinat.*[36]

a) *Venus–vis (1.14.16–17)*

The association with *vis* must have been in Propertius' mind at 1.14.15–18: *nam quis divitiis adverso gaudet Amore?/ nulla mihi tristi praemia sint Venere!/ illa potest magnas heroum infringere vires,/ illa etiam duris mentibus esse dolor.* Nobody should be fool enough to prefer wealth over love, since Venus has the power to destroy the strength (*vires*) of heroes. The juxtaposition of *Venere* and *vires* at the end of two successive lines signposts the etymologising.[37] The *Venus–vis* wordplay was particularly popular in Latin literature before Propertius.[38]

---

[30] For this type of etymologising see O'Hara (1996) 66–73.

[31] Varro *L.L.* 5.61–2 *mas ignis, quod ibi semen, aqua femina, quod fetus ab eius humore, et horum vinctionis vis Venus. hinc comicus* (Com. pall. inc. 13–14): *"huic victrix Venus, videsne haec?". non quod vincere velit Venus, sed vincire.*

[32] Serv. auct. *Aen.* 1.720 *Venerem vocari quidam propter promptam veniam dicunt.*

[33] Fulg. *Myth.* 2.1, p.39.11 *Venerem dici voluerunt aut secundum Epicureos bonam rem aut secundum Stoicos vanam rem.*

[34] Firm. *Err.* 17.3 *venustas hominum Venus dicta est.*

[35] Cf. Arnob. *Nat.* 3.33 *quod ad cunctos veniat, Venerem.*

[36] Cf. Isid. *Orig.* 8.11.76: *Venerem exinde dicunt nuncupatam, quod sine vi femina virgo esse non desinat.*

[37] Maltby (1993) 257–75, 269–71, 272 and O'Hara (1996) 86–8 with n.342.

[38] Plaut. *Rud.* 689–90 *prodesse nobis plus potest quam signum in fano hic intus/ Veneris, quod amplexae modo, unde abreptae per vim miserae?*, 839–40 PLESIDIPPUS *Meamne ille amicam leno vi, violentia/ de ara deripere Veneris voluit?*; *Trin.* 658 *ita vi Veneris vinctus, otio captus in fraudem incidi*; Lucr. 4.1113–14 *usque adeo cupide in Veneris*

b) *Venus–vincere (4.1.137–9)*

In his derivation of Venus (quoted above, n.31), Varro, before asserting
the *vincire* etymology, rejects another etymology from *vincere*, which
shows that such a derivation was also current in his time. Propertius
seems to allude to it at 4.1.137–40, when Horos is advising him to
abandon plans to compose elevated poetry and to stick to love elegy:
*militiam **Veneris** blandis patiere sub armis/ et **Veneris** pueris utilis
hostis eris./ nam tibi **victrices** quascumque labore parasti,/ eludit
palmas una puella tuas.* In this context, where Love/Venus is presented
as warfare — a standard *topos* in Roman elegy[39] — a wordplay
bringing out her association with victory is more than appropriate; it is
also fully consistent with Propertius' presentation of himself through-
out his work as a victim at the hands of conquering Venus.[40]

c) *Venus–venire (4.7.18–19)*

The case is otherwise, however, at 4.7.17–20, where Cynthia's ghost
appears in Propertius' dream and reminds him of their secret love-
making in the night: *per quam [fenestram] demisso quotiens tibi fune
pependi,/ alterna **veniens** in tua colla manu?/ saepe **Venus** trivio com-
missa est, pectore mixto/ fecerunt tepidas pallia nostra vias.* Here the
subject is not the power of love or love's victories, but lovers coming
together to enjoy their love. *venire* is a term frequently used in amatory
contexts to mean 'to come to make love'[41] and here it points to Venus
as the deity that brings lovers together. The *Venus–venire* wordplay
was particularly popular in Latin literature.[42]

---

compagibus haerent,/ membra voluptatis dum **vi** labefacta liquescunt, 4.1172 cui
Veneris membris **vis** omnibus exoriatur.

[39] See Murgatroyd (1975) 59–79.

[40] The concept of Venus Victrix is always there in the background. Her cult was intro-
duced by Pompey, who dedicated a temple to her in 55 BC. See Schilling (1954).

[41] Pichon (1966) *s.v. venire*.

[42] Plaut. *Poen.* 318 *quia non iam dudum ante lucem ad aedem **Veneris venimus**,* 322
*nam vigilante **Venere** si **veniant** eae,* 1181 *quae ad Calydoniam **venerant Venerem**;*
Rud. 94 *nunc huc ad **Veneris** fanum **venio** visere,* 308 *me huc obviam iussit sibi **venire**
ad **Veneris** fanum;* Plaut. *fab. inc.* fr. 27.2 ***Venus ventura est** nostra, nolo hoc
pulveret;* Cat. 61.18 ***venit** ad Phrygium **Venus*** (see Michalopoulos (1996) 77); Hor.
Sat. 2.5.79–80 ***venit** enim magnum donandi parca iuventus/ nec tantum **veneris**
quantum studiosa culinae;* Carm. 4.10.1–2 *O crudelis adhuc et **Veneris** muneribus
potens,/ insperata tuae cum **veniet** pluma superbiae;* Tib. 2.1.12–13 *cui tulit hesterna
gaudia nocte **Venus**./ casta placent superis: pura cum veste **venite**,* 2.3.54 *iam **veniant**
praedae, si **Venus** optat opes;* [Tib.] 3.8.2–3 *spectatum e caelo, si sapis, ipse **veni**./
hoc **Venus** ignoscet,* 3.9.17–18 *tunc **veniat** licet ad casses, inlaesus abibit,/ ne **Veneris**
cupidae gaudia turbet, aper.*

ii) *Bacchus–solvere* (3.17.5–6)

Another god frequently mentioned in Propertius' elegies is Bacchus, referred to also by his other cult titles, Iacchus, Liber and Lyaeus.[43] 3.17 is devoted entirely to Bacchus. Propertius prays to him for delivery from the sufferings of love: *per te iunguntur, per te solvuntur amantes:/ tu vitium ex animo dilue, Bacche, meo* (3.17.5–6). Propertius' hope lies in the liberating power of the god, which is exemplified in his cult titles. Although the god is only called Bacchus in 3.17, Propertius unobtrusively alludes in two ways to his other cult title, Lyaeus. Servius auctus (on *Aeneid* 4.58) gives the etymology of Lyaeus thus: *Bacchus dictus Lyaeus ἀπὸ τοῦ λύειν, quod nimio vino membra solvantur.*[44] Hence *solvuntur* (3.17.5) translates the Greek derivation of Lyaeus, thus calling 'Lyaeus' to the attention of his audience.[45] Propertius simultaneously offers an *ex contrario* etymology of Lyaeus by conjoining *solvuntur* with its opposite *iunguntur*. The double etymologising is signalled in the arrangement of the line where emphatic anaphora of *per te* juxtaposes the two contrary derivations.

Propertius' model for the *Lyaeus–solvere* wordplay may have been Tibullus 1.7.39–40, where wine relieves the tormented rustics: *Bacchus et agricolae magno confecta labore/ pectora tristitiae dissoluenda dedit.*[46] Propertius' *ex contrario* wordplay was reemployed by Ovid at *Metamorphoses* 11.67–70, describing the punishment imposed by Lyaeus on the Thracian women for their killing of Orpheus. The difference there is that Dionysus is actually called Lyaeus and not Bacchus, and *ligare* is used instead of *iungere*: *non inpune tamen scelus hoc sinit esse Lyaeus/ amissoque dolens sacrorum vate suorum/ protinus in silvis matres Edonidas omnes,/ quae videre nefas, torta radice ligavit.*[47] Indeed Lyaeus does not merely fail to justify his 'loosening' name, but he acts in exactly the opposite way by binding

---

[43] *Bacchus* (god) 2.30b.38, 3.17.1, 6, 13, 20, 4.1.62, 4.6.76, (wine) 1.3.9, 3.2.9; *Iacchus* (god) 4.2.31, (wine) 2.3.17; *Liber* (god) 1.3.14; *Lyaeus* (wine) 2.33.35, 3.5.21.

[44] Cf. Isid. *Orig.* 8.11.44 *idem autem et Lyaeus ἀπὸ τοῦ λύειν, quod multo vino membra solvantur*; cf. also Plut. *Adul. et Amic.* 68d ἀντιταττόμενον τῷ Λυαίῳ θεῷ καὶ λύοντι τὸ τῶν δυσφόρων σχοίνιον μεριμνᾶν κατὰ Πίνδαρον.

[45] On suppressed etymologising see O'Hara (1996) 79–82.

[46] This wordplay clarifies the textual problems of the passage. Cairns (1996) notes: "*dissoluenda* alludes to Dionysus/Bacchus' cult-title Λυαῖος — the "Looser", an allusion which supports *A*'s reading *tristitiae* against Muretus' and Housman's *laetitiae*: the god "looses" from misery, not from joy!"

[47] Cf. Hor. *Epod.* 9.37–8 *curam metumque Caesaris rerum iuvat/ dulci Lyaeo solvere*, with Mankin (1995) *ad loc.* and Paschalis (1995) 186. Cf. also Hor. *Carm.* 1.7.21–3 and 3.21.21–4 with Paschalis (1995) 184–6.

the Thracian women. This reversal of his nature is due to his immense anger and pain at the death of his favourite poet.

iii) *Scylla–canis* (4.4.39–40)

At 4.4.39–40, where Tarpeia, ready to yield to love and to betray Rome to Tatius, thinks of Scylla, who had done the same when Megara was besieged by Minos: *quid mirum in patrios Scyllam saevisse capillos,/ candidaque in saevos inguina versa canis?* The name *Scylla* was thought to derive from the Greek σκύλαξ "young dog, puppy" (*Etymologicum Magnum* 720.18: Σκύλλα: Παρὰ τὸ φωνὴν ἔχειν σκύλακος. Ὅμηρος [Homer *Odyssey* 12.86]: Τῆς δ' ἦν φωνὴ μὲν ὅσον σκύλακος νεογιλῆς.[48] *canis,* the Latin equivalent of σκύλαξ, points to the derivation of Σκύλλα. This wordplay was particularly popular in Latin literature.[49]

Conclusions

The discussion of etymological wordplay in the elegies of Propertius has revealed it as extending far beyond the explicit aetiological etymologies of his fourth book. Propertius not only displays a wide knowledge of etymological associations but he exploits them in close relation to their context. They contribute to the formation of a dense poetic texture and help to convey and stress underlying themes and ideas. Etymology is thus a fundamental thematic and formal feature of Propertian elegy. His etymologising is variegated, and some examples require a high level of concentration on the part of his audience. Hence, his proud claim to be 'Callimachus Romanus'[50] doubtless includes his etymologising, which had been a prominent characteristic of

---

[48] Cf. Lycoph. 45 μυχοὺς/ στενοὺς ὀπιπεύουσαν ἀγρίαν κύνα, 669 ποία δ' Ἐρινὺς μιξοπάρθενος κύων;

[49] Cat. 60.1–3 *Num te leaena montibus Libystinis/ aut Scylla latrans infima inguinum parte/ tam mente dura procreavit ac taetra* (see Michalopoulos (1996) 76–7); Lucr. 5.892–3 *aut rabidis canibus succinctas semimarinis/ corporibus Scyllas et cetera de genere horum*; Virg. *Ecl.* 6.74–5 *quid loquar aut Scyllam Nisi, quam fama secuta est/ candida succinctam latrantibus inguina monstris*; *Aen.* 3.432 *Scyllam et caeruleis canibus resonantia saxa*; Ov. *Am.* 3.12.21–2 *per nos Scylla patri caros furata capillos/ pube premit rabidos inguinibusque canes*; *Met.* 13.730–32 *Scylla latus dextrum, laevum inrequieta Charybdis/ infestat; vorat haec raptas revomitque carinas,/ illa feris atram canibus succingitur alvum*; [Tib.] 3.7 (4.1).71–2 *nec Scyllae saevo conterruit impetus ore,/ cum canibus rabidas inter fera serperet undas*.

[50] Prop. 4.1b.63–4 *ut nostris tumefacta superbiat Umbria libris,/ Umbria Romani patria Callimachi!*

Hellenistic poetry.[51] Furthermore, his affiliation with Roman Comedy, clearly demonstrated by Yardley,[52] is again repeatedly manifest in the analogies between his own etymological practice and that of Plautus.

Bibliography

Bailey, S. (1956). *Propertiana*. Cambridge

Barsby, J.A. (1996). 'Ovid's *Amores* and Roman comedy' *PLLS* 9.135–57

Boyd, B.W. (1984). 'Tarpeia's tomb: a note on Propertius 4.4' *AJP* 105.85–6

Bramble, J.C. (1974). '*Cui non dictus Hylas puer?* Propertius 1.20' in *Quality and Pleasure in Latin Poetry*, edd. David West and Tony Woodman (Cambridge) 81–93

Butler, H.E. and Barber, E.A. (1933). *The Elegies of Propertius*. Oxford

Cairns, F. (1979). *Tibullus: A Hellenistic Poet at Rome*. Cambridge

— (1983). 'Propertius 1,4 and 1,5 and the "Gallus" of the Monobiblos' *PLLS* 4.61–103

— (1984). 'The etymology of *militia* in Roman elegy' in *Apophoreta Philologica Emmanueli Fernández-Galiano a Sodalibus Oblata*, edd. Luis Gil and Rosa M. Aguilar (Madrid) 211–21

— (1993). 'Imitation and originality in Ovid *Amores* 1.3' *PLLS* 7.101–22

— (1996). ''Ancient etymology' and Tibullus: on the classification of 'etymologies' and on 'etymological markers'' *PCPhS* 42.24–59

Camps, W.W. (1966). *Propertius: Elegies Book III*. Cambridge

Collish, M.L. (1985). *The Stoic Tradition from Antiquity to the Middle Ages, Vol.1: Stoicism in Classical Literature*. Leiden

Copley, F.O. (1956). *Exclusus Amator. A Study in Latin Love Poetry*. Madison

Courtney, E. (1969). 'Three poems of Propertius' *BICS* 16.70–87

Flacelière, R. (1965). *Daily Life in Greece at the Time of Pericles*, trans. Peter Green. London

Jocelyn, H.D. (1967). *The Tragedies of Ennius*. Cambridge

King, J.K. (1980). 'The two Galluses of Propertius' Monobiblos' *Philologus* 124.212–30

Koster, S. (1983). 'Die Etymologien des Properz' in *Tessera: Sechs Beiträge zur Poesie und poetischen Theorie der Antike*, ed. S. Koster (Erlangen) 47–54

Maltby, R. (1991). *A Lexicon of Ancient Latin Etymologies*. (ARCA 25) Leeds

— (1993). 'The limits of etymologising' *Aevum Antiquum* 6.257–75

Mankin, D. (1995). *Horace: Epodes*. Cambridge

---

[51] O'Hara (1996) 21–42.

[52] Yardley (1972), (1987). Barsby (1996) is sceptical about the influence of Roman comedy on the *Amores*.

McKeown, J.C. (1987). *Ovid: Amores, Vol.1: Text and Prolegomena*. (ARCA 20) Liverpool

Michalopoulos, A.N. (1996). 'Some etymologies of proper names in Catullus' *PLLS* 9.75–81

Murgatroyd, P. (1975). '*Militia amoris* and the Roman elegists' *Latomus* 34.59–79

O'Hara, J.J. (1996). *True Names. Vergil and the Alexandrian Tradition of Etymological Wordplay*. Ann Arbor

Paschalis, M. (1995). 'Names and death in Horace's *Odes*' *CW* 88.181–90

Pichon, R. (1966). *Index Verborum Amatoriorum*. Hildesheim

Ross, D.O., Jr (1975). *Backgrounds to Augustan Poetry: Gallus, Elegy and Rome*. Cambridge

Schilling, R. (1954). *La religion romaine de Vénus*. Paris

Snyder, J. (1980). *Puns and Poetry in Lucretius' De Rerum Natura*. Amsterdam

Underwood, J.T., Jr (1971). *Locus communis, Laus legum and Laus locorum: Rhetorical Exercises as a Model for Propertius Book III*. diss. Ohio State University

Woodhead, W.D. (1928). *Etymologizing in Greek Literature from Homer to Philo Judaeus*. Toronto

Yardley, J.C. (1972). 'Comic influences in Propertius' *Phoenix* 26.134–9

— (1987). 'Propertius 4.5, Ovid *Amores* 1.6 and Roman comedy' *PCPhS* n.s.33.179–89

Zetzel, J.E.G. (1983). 'Recreating the canon: Augustan poetry and the Alexandrian past' *Critical Inquiry* 10.83–105

PAPERS OF THE LEEDS INTERNATIONAL LATIN SEMINAR TENTH VOLUME (1998) 251–93
Published by Francis Cairns (Publications) Ltd (Leeds 1998). ARCA 38. ISBN 0 905205 95 2

HORACE, THE PAEAN AND ROMAN *CHOREIA* (*ODES* 4.6)[*]

ALEX HARDIE
Royal Holloway College, London / FCO

I Introduction

Odes 4.6 comprises an address to Apollo (1–28), followed by a state-
ment about the relationship between Apollo and poet (29–30), a series
of instructions to a mixed chorus (of *pueri* and *virgines*) concerning
praise of Apollo and Artemis (31–40), and a concluding statement
attributed to the female element of the chorus (41–4). The occasion,
identified in the final stanza, is the saecular festival of 17 BC (*saeculo
festas referente luces*, 42).

A prominent structural feature of the poem is the break after the
seventh stanza, between the address to Apollo and the remainder of the
poem. The address can itself be read as a hymn, concluding with an
appeal to the god (27), and articulated through hymnal *Relativ-Stil* and
Du-Stil in ring composition (*quem*, 1; *tibi*, 5; *tuis*, 21; *qui*, 26).[1] The
choric instructions can also be read as a self-contained hymn of a type
represented in the Horatian *corpus* by *Odes* 1.21.[2] The relationship
between the two main parts of the poem and the reasons for their

---

[*]   I am grateful to Professor Francis Cairns and to Dr Stephen Harrison for valuable
      critiques of successive drafts of this paper. I am also indebted to Professor Ian
      Rutherford who showed me the text of his study of Pindar's sixth paean, and to Dr
      Denis Feeney for letting me see his comments on the *Ludi Saeculares*, both prior to
      publication.
[1]   K. Buchholz *De Horatio hymnographo* (Königsberg 1912) 65–70; Fraenkel (1957)
      400–1. For hymnal *Du-Stil* and *Relativstil*, E. Norden *Agnostos Theos* (Leipzig–Berlin
      1913, repr. Stuttgart 1956) 143–63, 168–76.
[2]   Cairns (1971a) 443–4.

sharply defined demarcation have attracted much scholarly attention, but remain problematic.[3] One aim of the following analysis, accordingly, will be to define the structural dynamics of the poem, on the basis of a new reading of the dramatic situation which it presents.

Another prominent feature of *Odes* 4.6 is choric activity. The primary choric reference, determined by the poem's saecular context, is to a double chorus of boys and girls, such as performed the *Carmen Saeculare* (*CS*) at the temples of Palatine Apollo and Jupiter Capitolinus at the end of the saecular festival.[4] At the same time, the poem has literary affinities with Greek choral lyric, and in particular with Pindar (§II). The importance of *choreia* for the understanding of 4.6 is further suggested by reference to ill-timed choric activity in Troy on the eve of its destruction (*choreis*, 15).

This paper will review the choric content of 4.6. It will focus on the ways in which Horace deploys and shapes his Pindaric material, on his understanding of Greek festival *choreia*, and on the adaptation of the latter in the context of a major Roman religious festival. A central feature will be consideration of dramatic techniques deriving from Greek choral lyric, and especially from the conventions of choric speaker variation. This will be relevant to the general question of the *persona loquens* (or poetic 'I') in early Greek lyric. More immediately it will, I hope, contribute to the current debate as to whether any of Horace's public odes can appropriately be considered as being 'choric' in character.[5]

II   *Odes* 4.6 and the Sixth Paean

That *Odes* 4.6 imitates Pindar's sixth paean has long been recognised.[6] Common features include Apollo's slaying of Achilles to forestall his

---

[3]   See below, n.60.

[4]   *CIL* 6.32323.139–48: *A.d. III non. Iun. in Palatio* [*Apollini et Dianae*] *sacrificium fecerunt imp. Caesar Augustus M. A*[*grippa ...*] *sacrificioque perfecto puer.* [*X*]*XVII quibus denuntiatum erat patrimi et matrimi et puellae totidem carmen cecinerunt; eodemque modo in Capitolio.* Fraenkel (1957) 400–407. In what follows, *Carmen Saeculare* with initial capitals denotes Horace's poem; without capitals, it denotes either the poem-type or *carmina* written for other saecular festivals.

[5]   Cairns (1971a) 440–44; (1995) 101–7; I.M. Le M. Du Quesnay 'Horace *Odes* 4.5: *Pro Reditu Imperatoris Caesaris Divi Filii Augusti*' in Harrison (1995) 128–87, at 143–8. I do not deal here with the vexed question of whether this or other Horatian odes actually received choric performance.

[6]   Kiessling–Heinze on 1.1; G.L. Hendrickson 'The so-called prelude to the *Carmen Saeculare*' *CPh.* 48 (1953) 73–9 at 76; Fraenkel (1957) 401, with n.1; Syndikus (1973) 347–8; E. Romano *Q. Orazio Flacco: Le Opere* I.2 (Rome 1991) 878.

destruction of Troy (3–12; cf. *Paean* 6.78–91), possibly with a hint at the god's disguise as Paris in *impar*; an allusion to Neoptolemos' slaying of Priam (13–16; cf. *Paean* 6.113–15); and the fact that both poems include instructions of a metrical nature to a chorus (35–6, *Lesbium servate pedem*; cf. *Paean* 6.121–2 μέτρα παιηόνων ἵητε). These are reinforced by verbal correspondences: thus, *filius* ... *Thetidis marinae* (6) translates παῖδα ποντίας/ Θέτιος (83–4); and *pueros* ... *ureret* [sc. Achilles] *ni* ... (18–21) translates Δαρδανίαν/ ἔπραθεν, εἰ μή ... (90–91), with substitution of Trojan *pueri* for their city. The closing reference to Horace as *vates* (44) echoes Pindar's opening designation of himself as προφάταν (6).

There are, of course, great differences between the two poems. *Odes* 4.6 deals with Diana (and Leto) as well as Apollo. It says nothing about Delphi, where the sixth paean was performed, or about the Castalia fountain (prominent in Pindar's first strophe), but refers to Delos, birthplace of Apollo and Diana (*Deliae* ... *deae*, 33), and to the oracle at Patara beside the river Xanthus in Lycia.[7] A further difference, noted by Pasquali, is that the Pindaric Apollo fails, in killing Achilles, to save Troy, since Zeus is unwilling to overturn the dictates of fate, and Neoptolemos, taking his father's place, destroys Troy.[8] But in *Odes* 4.6, Apollo and Jupiter are in accord: Jupiter is persuaded by Apollo to permit the migration of Trojan survivors, leading to the predestined foundation of Rome; had Apollo not killed Achilles, it is suggested, there would have been no survivors, and no city of Rome.

These divergences in content help reveal an unremarked affinity in structure: Pindar's Olympian Zeus, addressed at the start of the paean (1), reappears, again on Olympus, in the pivotal 'destiny of Troy' scene just beyond the centre point (92–4), and directly after the naming of Apollo at the exact centre (91); Horace's Jupiter appears once only, at the exact centre of the ode (22); there, just as Pindar's Ὀλύμποι-/ο ... / ... Ζεύς (92–4) echoes the opening Ὀλυμπίου Διός (1), *divum pater* (Jupiter) echoes the opening *dive* (Apollo); and *ureret* (sc. Achilles) ...

---

[7] At 26, *Phoebe, qui Xantho lavis amne crines*, Horace may be thinking of Virg. *Aen.* 4.143–5 (comparison of Aeneas to Apollo) *qualis ubi hibernam Lyciam Xanthique fluenta/ deserit ac Delum maternam invisit Apollo/ instauratque choros*. A further point may be the close association between the Lycian Apollo and Troy: cf. Pind. *Ol.* 8.47; the association is still distinct in a late 'Homeromanteion': κλῦθι, ἄναξ, ὅς που Λυκίης ἐν πίονι δήμῳ/ εἷς ἢ ἐνὶ Τροίῃ· (*P. Bon.* 3 and *P. Oxy.* LVI 3831; F. Maltomimi 'P. Lond. 121 (= PGM VII), 1–221: Homeromanteion' *ZPE* 106 (1995) 107–22.
[8] A possible saecular context for the Delian content is suggested below, n.166. Pasquali (1920) 752–5.

ni, leading in from the preceding stanza, imitates Pindar's central ἔπραθεν, εἰ μή.⁹ Horace's sensitive structural balancing of Apollo and Jupiter imitates, with variation, the comparable structural signposting in the sixth paean.¹⁰ The Horatian interplay between 'opening' and 'centre' is further enhanced by the central juxtaposition of Venus and Jupiter (21–5), recalling Pindar's opening juxtaposition of Zeus and Aphrodite. There is also a glance, in *Veneris ... gratae*, towards Pindar's Χάριτες (3; Latin *Gratiae*), and to the close relationship between Aphrodite and Charites.¹¹ Thus while the opening stanza of *Odes* 4.6 provides no clearly defined contact with the sixth paean, its central stanza echoes Pindar's opening strophe, and itself echoes Horace's opening word.

The following stanza (25–8) arguably echoes Pindar's closure. Pindar deploys a series of plural imperatives (177–81), which seem to be addressed to the gods attending the Theoxenia, as a paeanic appeal for favour and protection for the choric speakers' *polis* (i.e. Aegina) and people.¹² The Horatian speaker also seeks protection (*defende*, 27), but from Apollo, in respect of the local, 'Daunian' *Camena* (see below). Then the line endings *Thaliae* (25, Apollo's Greek Muse) and *Camenae* (27, 'local', or 'Italian' Muse) are paralleled at *Paean* 6.181 (ending Μοισᾶν), and 183 (ending either θ[...]ᾶν or ἐ[...]ᾶν). The latter is restored by Snell–Maehler (not without difficulties) as θ[αλί]αν, where Apollo as Μουσαγέτης (cf. *doctor ... Thaliae*) is asked to accept (i.e. favour) a metaphorical festive abundance (θαλία) of tribute (183).¹³ The 'Muses' (181) stand for local, probably Aeginetan, paeans, just as the local, Daunian *Camena* relates to, and is present in, Horace's *carmen* (below, p.261). Pindar's closing θ[αλί]αν, if correct, would perform a further function, connecting with the opening Χαρίτεσσιν in reference to Thalia as one of the Graces, and thus evoking the concepts of 'growth' and 'plenty' with which she was associated in that capacity.¹⁴ This would in turn connect with the function of the Theoxenia

---

⁹ For the significance of the central position for Jupiter, see L.A. Moritz 'Some 'central' thoughts on Horace's *Odes' CQ* 62 (1968) 116–31, at 129.
¹⁰ On the Apollo/Zeus balance in *Pae.* 6, Hardie (1996) 236–7; below, p.291.
¹¹ *RE* III.2154.
¹² For paeanic appeal on behalf of πόλις and λάος, cf. esp. Tim. *PMG* 791.237–40.
¹³ ἐ[νοπ]ᾶν has been proposed by G.B. D'Alessio and F. Ferrari 'Pindaro, *Paeana* 6,175–83: una ricostruzione' *SCO* 38 (1988) 159–79, at 176–9, but this involves paleographical and other difficulties, and θ[αλί]αν still looks attractive. On what follows, see Hardie (1996) 237–9.
¹⁴ *RE* III.2152.

festivities (themselves θαλίαι, cf. 14) in commemorating the *aetion* of the cult of Zeus Panhellanios, i.e. the ending of a legendary panhellenic famine (cf. 64). Arguably, Horace signals this Pindaric background in placing *gratae* and *Thaliae* at the end of the first line of successive stanzas. Certainly, Horace's central stanzas are imbued with the language and ideas of Pindar's opening and centre, and probably also of his closure.

These structural affinities assume greater significance in the light of Rutherford's recent discovery that the sixth paean was almost certainly regarded in antiquity as a composite ode.[15] The papyrus fragments show that the third triad was separately titled as an Aeginetan prosodion, and was transmitted by Pindar's Alexandrian editors both as part of the sixth paean and also in the prosodion book. If, as now seems necessary, we assume that Horace knew the sixth paean in this form, the new information carries important implications for our reading of *Odes* 4.6. In particular, there is a *prima facie* case for connecting the division between the second and third triads of the sixth paean with the division between Horace's first seven, and last five, stanzas, noted earlier (p.251). Further consequences flowing from the re-titling of Pindar's third triad will be considered in later sections.

The points of contact between *Odes* 4.6 and Pindar's paean are unquestionably significant; and if the structural points suggested above are on the right lines, earlier work in this area can evidently be supplemented in an informative way. Yet there has been no recent, searching, assessment of Pindar's presence in the poem; indeed some modern treatments seem actually to downplay that presence.[16] In the wider context of the Horace/Pindar relationship, and given the relative rarity of proven correspondences between the texts of Horace and Pindar (in striking contrast to the abundance of extant Virgilian source material), a fresh analysis seems to be called for.

III   Classification as Paean

When the Alexandrian scholars included the sixth paean in the paean-book, they thereby signalled their judgement that the poem was to be

---

[15] Rutherford (1997).

[16] Thus C. Becker *Das Spätwerk des Horaz* (Göttingen 1963) 114 n.3: "Der pindarische Einfluss ... ist freilich nur in zweiter Linie wichtig." Putnam (1986) 118 n.2 seems not to take Pindaric influence as proven, merely noting Pindar's treatment of the death of Achilles in the sixth paean, "a poem Horace may well have had in mind as he wrote". Barchiesi (1996) 8–11 is a partial corrective.

classified overall as a member of that εἶδος.[17] As regards *Odes* 4.6, the question this editorial judgement raises is whether analysis of a Horatian poem should be informed by Alexandrian categorisation in respect of a Pindaric model. As it happens, Horace wrote two poems which are known to have been identified in antiquity as paeans. One is the *CS* (below, pp.260–61) and the other is *Odes* 1.2. The latter reveals some conceptual similarities with Pindar's ninth paean, but there is no demonstrable direct debt to it. The main grounds for regarding *Odes* 1.2 as a paean lie in a more general correspondence with an authoritative ancient definition of the paean in one of its primary functions, i.e. as a hymn sung to Apollo to secure the termination of disease or war.[18]

Self-evidently, verbal imitation alone is insufficient to establish that Horace consciously identified any given ode with the genre (εἶδος) of a Pindaric original: *Odes* 1.12 and *Odes* 3.4 are not to be classed as epinicians because they imitate some phrasing in *Olympians* 2 and *Pythians* 1. On the other hand, *Odes* 1.37, which contains sustained imitation, conceptual and verbal, of Pindar's second dithyramb, can be seen as a Roman dithyramb.[19] This is because the two poems have comparable sacral functions, associated with the god Dionysus.[20] In addition, *Odes* 1.37 conforms to ancient formulations of the typical content of the dithyramb.[21] Despite some well known problems arising from Alexandrian methods of classification, these two examples suggest that Horace was alert to εἶδος classification within the non-epinician books of the Alexandrian edition.[22] They do not prove that Horace actually categorised his own Pindarising odes as members of these same εἴδη; but it is a reasonable inference that Pindaric imitation within an Alexandrian book-εἶδος may at least suggest the alignment of a Horatian ode with that same εἶδος, and hence also with its

[17] On the 17-book Alexandrian edition, Harvey (1955), (on the paean, 172–3); R. Pfeiffer *History of Classical Scholarship* (Oxford 1968) 181–4; P.M. Fraser *Ptolemaic Alexandria* (Oxford 1972) General Index *s.v.* 'Pindar – Alexandrian editions of'. Influence on Horace: Feeney (1993) 44–5.

[18] F. Cairns 'Horace, Odes 1.2' *Eranos* 69 (1971) 68–88 citing (68 n.4) Botschuyver *Scholia in Horatium* III.10 (p.2 on *Odes* 1.2 as *deprecatoria paean*).

[19] Hardie (1977); on dithyramb and triumph poem, F. Cairns *Generic Composition in Greek and Roman Poetry* (Edinburgh 1972) 95–7.

[20] Hardie (1977) 114, 117–18, 123–6, 135–6.

[21] Hardie (1977) 113–14.

[22] Classification problems: Harvey (1955) 159, 164, 173. For Horace's awareness of the Alexandrian edition, cf. the reflections of the Pindaric book-εἴδη in *Odes* 4.2.10–24, with R. Freis 'The catalogue of Pindaric genres in Horace *Odes* 4.2' *CA* 2 (1983) 27–36.

associated functions and content, as found in ancient scholarly definitions or inferred from other surviving examples of the genre.

Beyond this (relatively uncontroversial) point, much remains uncertain. Particular difficulties surround the fragmentary condition of Pindar's non-epinician books. The *Paean* book is relatively well preserved, but there are still enormous gaps, and in consequence we cannot be certain that *Odes* 4.6 does not imitate more than one Pindaric paean. Obvious possibilities would include paeans which praised Artemis as well as Apollo, and Delos rather than Delphi. Again, Horace certainly works in references to non-Pindaric poetry, including the *Iliad*, Callimachus' *Hymn to Apollo*, and perhaps the Homeric hymn to Apollo.[23]

As a hymn type, the paean itself was heterogeneous, with a long history in cult and literature and with a wide range of content and function, even within the surviving fragments of Pindar's paean-book.[24] One consequence, as was recognised in antiquity, is that the label 'paean' can be controversial and has to be deployed with care.[25] Another is that in the absence of any clear set, or sets, of criteria defining the paean, we cannot be sure how Horace himself thought about the εἶδος and its characteristics, or how he assessed the usefulness and authority of Alexandrian scholarly activity in comparison to the actual text of Pindar (although, as will be argued in later sections, he was directly influenced by the editorial transmission of the third triad as a separate prosodion); nor can we recover with any confidence Horace's

---

[23] *Iliad*: cf. 18–19 with *Il.* 6.58–9. With 1–4, cf. Call. *H.* 2.20–25, alluding to Apollo's killing of Achilles and the Niobids, and relating their cessation of grief to the singing of the paean: some kind of paeanic topic or pattern may underlie these texts; with 21–5, cf. *H.* 2.65–8 (Apollo as leader of migratory city foundation). *H. Apoll.*: below, p.272. Barchiesi (1995) suggests that the death of Achilles (9–12) is influenced by Simonides' elegiac hymn to Achilles, prefacing the 'Platea' elegy (P. Oxy. 2327 fr. 5); but Barchiesi himself (35) notes R.G.M. Nisbet's suggestion that the passage may rather have been influenced by Cat. 64.105–9. For a possible wider 'Simonidean' context, Barchiesi (1996).

[24] The Greek paean's origins and functions have been analysed in a series of monographs, of which the most important are Fairbanks (1900); *RE* XVII.2340–62 (A. von Blumenthal); and Käppel (1992), who studies the evolution of the form (with a general survey of previous work at 22–7); see also M.W. Dickie's review of Käppel in *Bryn Mawr Classical Review* 4 (1993) 100–105.

[25] Harvey (1955) 173, citing [Plut.] *de Mus.* 1134c–d and Athen. 696a–b, rejecting a (contemporary) classification of a poem by Aristotle as 'paean'; Käppel (1992) 38–42, citing *P. Oxy.* 2368B col. 1.9–20 (= Lloyd-Jones and Parsons *SH* 293), on a dispute between Aristarchus and Callimachus over classification of Bacchylides 23 as 'dithyramb' or 'paean'. On Pindar's Alexandrian *Paean*-book, see Rutherford (1995).

understanding of the relationship in this area between Alexandrian scholarship and Hellenistic poetry.

These various factors conspire to obscure the parameters of Horatian alignment with any given Pindaric εἶδος. Further uncertainties surround the question of performance. Pindaric paeans were written for sung performance by dancing choruses, in a very different sacral and musical environment from that of Horace.[26] So, in imitating this poetry, did Horace confine himself to matters of content, phraseology and style, or did he regard the circumstances of performance (as known to him) as integral to the εἶδος and thus desiderating representation, in some form, in his own ode?[27] That performance criteria played some part in Horace's presentation of his *persona* as a Roman successor to the early Greek lyric poets is of course clear from his frequent references to musical accompaniment. Whether or not these references are fictitious is a separate issue: the question they raise here is whether choric characteristics might also be regarded as an integral component of a lyric oeuvre. These issues of εἶδος-identification and choric 'performance' are particularly relevant to *Odes* 4.6, and can usefully be explored in that context, because of the ode's intimate relationship with the saecular festival, and by extension with the *Carmen Saeculare* performed on that occasion.

IV   Paeanic Features

The ancient paean was primarily associated with Apollo, identified with the healing god Paean (hence the characteristic paean refrain, ἰὴ Παιάν, and variants).[28] Artemis features as an occasional paean-addressee (separate, joint or subordinate), as does Leto, in effect as third member of a trinity.[29] The paean has a consistent function in seeking the god's protection, and his help in removing or avoiding a threat, as also in expressing joy following deliverance.[30] Other

---

[26] Fraenkel (1957) 283–4; Syndikus (1972) 3–4; Feeney (1993) 43–4.

[27] Mullen (1982) 3–4, 46–89. Some lyric εἴδη seem to have been defined by their ceremonial circumstances of performance (thus *prosodia*: cf. *RE* XXIII.856.57ff.) or by the character of the choric performers (thus *partheneia* and *paidika*: C. Calame *Les choeurs de jeunes filles en Grèce archaïque* II (Rome 1977) 147–77; Cairns (1995) 105–6.

[28] On the refrain, see Rutherford (1991).

[29] Apollo and Artemis as paean-recipients: Käppel (1992) 56–9, 341–4; Fairbanks (1900) 34–5. Leto: Käppel (1992) 56, 57, 61, 142, 146–7, 228–9. For diversification of paean-addressees from the fifth century onwards, Käppel (1992) 61, 344–6.

[30] Käppel (1992) 44–9, Indices 1. Namen und Sachen, *s.vv.* Bitte, Dank.

recurring paeanic features include narrative of the establishment of Apolline cult, and of his deeds (in particular the Pythoktonia).[31] *Odes* 4.6 praises Apollo, and then Apollo and Diana, naming Leto (37). The hymnic address to Apollo deals with Achilles' threat to Troy, his death, and Apollo's role in obtaining Jupiter's sanction for the Trojan colonising migration to Italy (3–20; 21–4). The concentration on the victim, rather than on the god as the active agent of his death, is noteworthy, and might reflect Pindar's narrative focus on Achilles and Neoptolemos;[32] but Pindar, unlike Horace, states explicitly that Apollo killed Achilles (78–9; 85–6).

The address to Apollo concludes with an appeal for protection (27): *Dauniae defende decus Camenae.* The reference to the *Camena* (i.e. to Horace's poetry: see below) corresponds to programmatic (epilogue) expressions of hope that a god(dess) should take pleasure in his/her hymn: thus Timotheus (*Persae* [*PMG* 791] 202–5) in a closing appeal to 'Paian', asks for support for his "new-wrought Muse" (Μοῦσαν νεοτευχῆ). The request for 'defence' is paralleled in Hellenistic texts having to do with the reputations of poets, and it is likely that Horace will have been aware of this usage.[33] But it is also likely that he was aware of its conventional use in paean-appeals for divine protection.[34] The imperative φύλασσε occurs, in a paeanic context, in an address to Apollo in Theognis (781–2: ἀλλὰ σύ, Φοῖβε,/ ἵλαος ἡμετέρην τήνδε φύλασσε πόλιν; "do you, Phoebus, with favour defend this our city"). It recurs in a parallel 'defend this city' appeal in a Hellenistic cult paean to Dionysus at Delphi;[35] and city 'defence' features in Pindar's praise of Apollo in *Paean* 6 (90–91: Δαρδανίαν/ ἔπραθεν, εἰ μὴ

---

[31] Fairbanks (1900) 26–31, 49–50; Käppel (1992) 54–62.

[32] Rutherford (1995) has suggested that a block of paeans at the end of the book (the present *Paeans* II–VII) were more concerned with the actions of heroes and men than with those of gods: Horace might reflect this in his treatment of Achilles; see also Barchiesi (1995), with the reservations noted in n.23 above.

[33] *A. Pl.* 306.9: πάτερ Διόνυσε, φύλασσε μιν (sc. Anacreon); *A.Pl.* 307.7; also Hermesianax fr. 7.27–8 (Homer): αὐτὸς δ᾿ οὗτος ἀοιδός, ὃν ἐκ Διὸς αἶσα φυλάσσει/ ἥδιστον πάντων δαίμονα μουσοπόλων.

[34] Syndikus (1973) 352 notes parallels with hymnic appeals for protection for people, but does not suggest a paeanic context.

[35] Philodamus *Paian in Dionysum* (Käppel *Pai.* 39, 375–80), 12 (recurring refrain) εὔφρων τάνδε πόλιν φύλασσε. O. Kern *Inschriften von Magnesia am Maeander* (Berlin 1900) n°. 80.68 (decree providing for sacrifices to Zeus Sosipolis, Artemis and Apollo): [ψ]ήφισ[μα τόδε] εἶναι εἰς φυλακὴν [τῆς πόλεως]. Cf. Apollo's appeal to Augustus at Prop. 4.6.41–4: *solve metu patriam ...*/ *.../ quam nisi defendes, murorum Romulus augur/ ire Palatinas non bene vidit avis* (Augustus to represent Apollo's defensive function at Rome).

φύλασσεν Ἀπό[λ]λ[ω]ν; "[Achilles] would have burned Troy had not Apollo defended it"). In focusing on the divine protection of Horace's poetry (see below), the speaker draws a parallel with Apollo's earlier protection of Troy and the Trojan migration and implies that the future security of Rome is now interlinked with the success of the saecular *carmen* and its associated *choreia*.

Another verbal pointer to *Odes* 4.6 being a paean is *icta* (9, in a metaphor for the killing of Achilles), with the echoing *servate ... ictum* (35–6, the instruction to preserve the musical beat). The verbal echo recalls the ancient etymology of 'paean' from παίειν (to strike).[36] This was one aspect of an etymologising complex which highlighted the twin, ambiguous character of Apollo, as both beneficent, succouring god and hostile, violent god. παίειν normally signalled the god's capacity for violence, while paean/παύειν was associated with his curative functions.[37] Horace however suggests two senses of 'strike', one peaceful (the lyre-beat), the other hostile (the axe-fall), thereby using the normally 'hostile' etymology to reflect both benign and violent aspects. Diana's *arcus* (34) underlines this: it is in implicit juxtaposition with Horace's lyre (the Apolline instrument; cf. *fidicen*, 25), but it also recalls Apollo's bow/arrow, which in fact killed Achilles.[38] The juxtaposition of *ictum* with *servate*, itself reminiscent of paean-appeals for 'preservation' (Greek σώζειν), supports the etymological play on παίειν/paean.[39]

Relevant to the generic alignment of *Odes* 4.6 is its relationship to the *CS*. The latter was identified in antiquity as a paean. This is affirmed in two related Greek sources, including the Sibylline text which

---

[36] *RE* XVIII.1.2344.24ff.; Fairbanks (1900) 2–3; Maltby (1991) *s.v. paean* (citing *inter alia* Paul. Fest. 222: *Paeana Apollinem vocaverunt, quod sagittarum ictu eum nocere putabant*). Cf. Ar. *Pax* 454; Eur. *IT* 1391 (sailors 'strike' the sea with their oars, before Iphigeneia's paean to Artemis).

[37] Macr. 1.17.16–17.

[38] Contrast of (violent) bow and (peaceful) lyre: Prop. 4.6.69–70: *citharam iam poscit Apollo/ victor et ad placidos exuit arma choros*; cf. esp. 31–6 (Apollo at Actium): *non ille attulerat crinis in colla solutos/ aut testudineae carmen inerme lyrae,/ sed quali aspexit Pelopeum Agamemnona vultu/ egessitque avidis Dorica castra rogis,/ aut qualis flexos solvit Pythona per orbis /serpentem, imbelles quem timuere lyrae*. Cf. also Tib. 2.5.79–80; *AP* 13.22 (Phaedimus); Call. *Aet.* fr. 114.8–9 (statue of Apollo Delius).

[39] σώζειν in paeans: Eur. *IT* 1399; Aristonoos (Käppel *Pai.* 42) 47; Limenius (Käppel *Pai.* 46) 36; Macedonius (Käppel *Pai.* 41) 28. Cf. also *servetis* in the saecular prayer reproduced in *CIL* 6.32323; and Prop. 4.6.37 (Apollo to Augustus): *o ... mundi servator*.

provided the festival with its sacral basis and legitimacy.[40] The use of the term 'paean' is not a loose one: it reflects the identity of the primary divine addressees, Apollo and Diana, and the correspondence between the function of the paean, with its focus on divine protection of the community, and that of the *CS*, with its focus on the safety, prosperity and continuity of the Roman people. Thus, a festival which was based on a Greek prophecy, and was performed *Achivo ritu*, concluded with a *carmen* deriving from the Greek paean.[41] The Sibylline use of παιᾶνες is significant, confirming the currency of the term in 17 BC, and its authoritative relevance to the saecular festival. It not only supplies a context for the paeanic features of *Odes* 4.6, but suggests that the ode relates to the *CS* in its identity as a paean.

Odes 4.6 and the *CS* have much in common:[42] "Apollo as the enemy of the Greeks and the champion of Troy, the escape of Aeneas from Troy and his foundation of Rome, Apollo's championship of the New Troy, his sister Diana as the moon, her concern with the fruitfulness of the earth, the coming marriages of the girls in the chorus." Yet they are very different poems. The *CS* maintains a strict balance and parallelism between Apollo and Diana, while *Odes* 4.6 focuses at first on Apollo alone (later, at 33–40, there is relatively greater emphasis on Diana, with parallel praise of both at 37–8).[43] Another difference lies in the poet's individuality in *Odes* 4.6 (29–30), taken together with the sense of 'locality' conveyed in the appeal *Dauniae defende decus Camenae* (27): *Dauniae* plainly refers to Horace's birthplace in northern Apulia; and *decus Camenae* can refer to Horace himself "the glory of the Daunian Muse".[44] *Camenae*, however, also relates etymologically to *carmen* (30, 43), as well as to the singing performance referred to in *canentes* (37).[45] The reference at 27 is therefore to Horace, his poetry, and public standing (*decus*), and also to the 'Daunian' inspiration of the

---

[40] Zosimus 2.5.5: ... παιᾶνας, δι᾽ ὧν αἱ ὑπὸ Ῥωμαίους σώζονται πόλεις; Sibylline oracle cited at Zosimus 2.6 (18–22), on the singing of Λατῖνοι παιᾶνες. The identification of the *CS* as a paean is noted by Feeney (1998) 32, 34–5. For the *carmen* of 88, see Hardie (1996a).

[41] Fraenkel (1957) 403–6.

[42] Cairns (1971a) 443–4; cf. Barchiesi (1996) 8–9.

[43] With 31–40 cf. *CS* 75–6 *doctus et Phoebi chorus et Dianae/ dicere laudes*; as a summary of the paeanic *CS*, this alludes to the etymology of παιάν from ἐπαινεῖν: Maltby (1991) *s.v. paean*.

[44] Putnam (1986) 121 takes *decus* to refer to Horace. Cf. Mart. 4.14.1: *Sili, Castalidum decus sororum*; *AP* 7.6.3 (Homer as Μουσῶν φέγγος); cf. *AP* 9.24.4.

[45] Putnam (1986) 121; Maltby (1991) *s.v. Camena*.

carmen, and its performance.[46]

Horace elsewhere expresses pride in his Apulian origins (*Odes* 3.30.10–12). In 4.6, *Dauniae* also reflects a characteristic feature of Greek paeans, namely patriotism. Pindaric paeans were communal poems, in which the chorus identifies closely with its city or island.[47] The Cean chorus in the fourth paean (performed in Delos) expresses pride in its island (21–7). The Abderitan chorus in the second paean (performed at Abdera) is similarly patriotic, but with greater provincialism, appropriate to its domestic audience.[48] An inscribed paean by Isyllus of Epidaurus is deeply Epidaurian in content.[49] In Callimachus' second *Hymn*, which has itself been identified by Williams as a paean, patriotic sentiments are articulated towards Cyrene.[50] And Polybius (4.20.8) speaks of Arcadian "hymns and paeans in which each hymn the heroes and gods of their land, according to ancestral custom". One specialised aspect of this topic is pride in colonial origins, itself related to Apollo's oracular role as colonising god.[51] In festival paeans, local patriotism will have been designed to impress interstate, or 'panhellenic' audiences.[52] However 'local' and 'panhellenic' elements can occur in the same poem, and the sixth paean contains an extended dialogue between Aeginetan elements and the panhellenic interests of the temple of Delphi and the Theoxenia festival.[53]

In the Hellenistic and Roman eras, city state patriotism had to find expression within a wider context. Horace's *Dauniae* juxtaposes local identity with loyalty to Rome. *Dauniae* may also suggest provincialism, representative in that sense of provincial Italy as a whole.[54] This

---

[46] Cf. *Odes* 4.9.6–7, *Ceae ... Camenae* (= Simonides' poetry); Pind. *Pae.* 4.23–4 (Cean chorus), γινώσκομαι δὲ καὶ/ Μοῖσαν παρέχων ἄλις. For *decus* as public repute in this context, cf. *CIL* 6.10096.16 (*laudes* and *decus* of a mime actress).

[47] Lefkowitz (1991) 11–15.

[48] Lefkowitz (1991) 14; Dougherty (1994).

[49] Käppel *Pai.* 40. Cf. the epigrammatic appeal by Phaedimus (*AP* 13.22) to Apollo, the πατρώιον σέβας (9), that, with assistance from Eros, he should fire the youths of Schoenus with courage to defend their country.

[50] *H.* 2 as paean: 21, 25, 80, 97–104, with Williams; patriotism: 71–96.

[51] Dougherty (1994) 207, and *passim* (on Pind. *Pae.* 4); cf. Cairns (1979) 70–71.

[52] Lefkowitz (1991) 11–12 (on Pind. *Pae.* 4).

[53] Hardie (1996) 235–41; Rutherford (1997) 17–19. In this context, I think Barchiesi (1996) 10–11 is wrong to downplay the 'panhellenic' background in Pindar.

[54] Orelli construes *Dauniae* as "Latinae"; Wickham as "the Italian Muse"; Kiessling–Heinze as "= *Italae*"; Plessis as "*Italae*"; Syndikus (1973) 352, as "italische Muse". Commentators compare *Odes* 2.1.34–5: *quod mare Dauniae/ non decoloravere caedes?*, where it is clear that the reference of *Dauniae* cannot be confined to the geographical area known as '*Daunia*': but Nisbet-Hubbard's observation that the

would be consistent with the pan-Italian focus of the festival Sibylline oracle (35–7), conditionally promising eternal Roman rule over πᾶσα χθὼν Ἰταλὴ καὶ πᾶσα Λατίνη. The oracle itself reflects a traditional saecular focus on the hegemony of Rome over Latium, already detectable in a fourth century BC precursor of the Saecular Festival.[55]

To sum up: *Odes* 4.6 includes a hymnic address, and a set of hymnic instructions; both passages concern the gods who were the traditional recipients of paeans; and both contain appeals which derive from a major (precatory) function of the paean and from the terminology in which that function typically found expression. A feature linking the two addresses (*icta/ictum*) derives from an ancient definition of the paean; and other material (patriotism, local/Roman contrast) is topical in paeans. In all these respects, as well as in its specific intertextual relationship to the sixth paean, the ode operates in paeanic territory. It lacks, however, the characteristic Greek paean-refrain ἰὴ Παιάν. The absence of the refrain was regarded by some ancient scholars as grounds for rejecting identification of disputed poems as paeans; but such disputes themselves imply that others took a different view. Moreover, although exceedingly common, the refrain is not universal in surviving paeans: it does not feature in the fragments of Pindar's ninth paean, nor in the sixth paean (though it is reflected at 121, ἰὴ ἰῆτε).[56]

If the conventional view of the choric instructions as referring forward to the actual *Carmen Saeculare* is valid (below, p.266), then it can reasonably be inferred that a main function of the ode as a whole is to ensure the successful performance of the *CS* itself.[57] This is further suggested in the vignette of a choric *puella* as bride (*nupta*, 41: itself a symbol of communal fertility and continuity). The linkage of marriage, communal security and successful paean performance is illuminated by Callimachus *Hymn* 2.14–15, where the choric παῖδες are instructed to

---

name 'Daunia' was Greek rather than Italian may be relevant to our context too; cf., and contrast, Quinn: "Daunian=Apulian ... and hence Italian (as opposed to Greek), but especially Horatian ...".

[55] L.R. Taylor 'New light on the history of the Secular Games' *AJP* 55 (1934) 101–20; MacBain (1982) 34–5.

[56] Disputed paeans: Athen. 696b–697b. Paean refrain: Fairbanks (1900) 48–9; found in a Latin poem at Claud. *In Ruf.* I *praef.* 11 (paean cry at Delphi). The refrain is not deployed in Ariphron's 'paean to Hygieia', reproduced at Athen. 702.

[57] And thus the safety of Rome: cf. Gruen (1990) 86–7, on Livius Andronicus and the public *carmen* of 207 at a critical point in the Punic War and preceding the Roman victory at the Metaurus.

sing and dance "if they think to accomplish marriage ... and if the wall is to stand upon its old foundations" (tr. Mair).[58] Here, as in *Odes* 4.6 (23–4), Apollo is the god of city foundation, as well as of poetry, and his favour towards his city will be determined by the pleasure he takes in the poetry which Cyrene collectively offers through its child-chorus. *Odes* 4.6 relates to the successful and ritually pleasing performance of the *CS* in the same way that the dramatic opening to Callimachus' hymn (1–31) relates to what Williams terms the "hymn proper" (32–96). Of course, Callimachus' opening was not the first of its kind. The sixth paean offers a dramatic situation in which an opening appeal to 'Pytho' seeks acceptance at Delphi for the poet (and the Aeginetan chorus). In Pindar and Callimachus, the preliminary 'drama' is an integral part of the hymn/paean. One facet of the originality of *Odes* 4.6 *qua* paean may lie precisely in the separation of a dramatic 'preamble' from the *Carmen Saeculare* as performed, and in the creation of a separate poem, itself a 'paean'. In the final section (IX) I shall put forward further arguments in support of this view, together with a new interpretation of the ode's dramatic setting.

V   Poet and Chorus

On the traditional view, Horace's odes are monodic statements by the poet.[59] In *Odes* 4.6, Horace is identified in the first person in *mihi*, *poetae* (29–30) and *mei* (35). But there are difficulties in reading 4.6 as the utterance of Horace alone. The poet claims to enjoy Apollo's favour (29–30, *spiritum Phoebus mihi, Phoebus artem/ carminis nomenque dedit poetae*), an assertion which must have present validity, but which comes immediately after an appeal to *Phoebus* seeking favour for Horace and his poetry. If the poet feels he enjoys Apollo's favour, why should he make the appeal?[60] The apparent dislocation of dramatic logic coincides with a stylistic shift from the vocatives which frame the address to Apollo (*dive*, 1; *Phoebe/Agyieu*, 26, 28) to third person statements about him (*Phoebus ... Phoebus*, 29). Although there is no

[58] εἰ τελέειν μέλλουσι γάμον ... / ἑστήξειν δὲ τὸ τεῖχος ἐπ' ἀρχαίοισι θεμέθλοις.

[59] R. Heinze 'Die Horazische Ode' *NJ* 51 (1923) 153–68 at 153–4 (= E. Burck [ed.] *Vom Geist des Römertums* [Darmstadt 1972] 172–89, at 172–3).

[60] The problems have largely been ignored in recent times. An exception is F. Cairns 'Horace's first Roman Ode (3.1)' *PLLS* 8 (1995) 91–142, at 104. For early attempts to obelize 29–44, or to divide the poem in two, see Fraenkel (1957) 400 n.2. Syndikus (1973) notes the heightened tone, but unconvincingly suggests that 29–30 represent the fulfilment of the prayer.

difficulty in principle about a shift from *Du-Stil* to *Er-Stil* in the same hymn (for a striking example, cf. Pindar *Olympian* 14.8, to the Charites), the Horatian shift is particularly bold. Moreover, with its repeated emphasis on Apolline inspiration and patronage, it suggests the possibility of tension with the preceding allusion to the presence in Horace's poetry of the 'Daunian Camena' (contrast also *Odes* 2.16.37–9: *mihi .../ spiritum Graiae tenuem Camenae/ Parca ... dedit*).

Again, the intensely personal tone of the poet's self reference (29–30) contrasts with the impersonal wording of *Dauniae decus Camenae* (27), a phrase which it is difficult to see the poet, speaking in his own person, using of himself. More generally, the self confidence of the poet's deployment of *Ichform* (*mihi*, 29; *mei*, 35), his sphragis-like citation of his own name, and his prediction of the chorus' recollection of their successful performance, contrasts with the anxiety and fearfulness of the preceding hymn to Apollo.[61] All these features reinforce the structural demarcation noted at the outset (p.251); and in the boldness of their tone, and of the claims which are made, they seem to suggest precisely that *magna lingua* so fearfully evoked at the outset. In short, Horace's sharply defined *Phoebe ... Phoebus* movement suggests a fresh departure. A new voice seems to emerge, together with a new perspective on Apollo. This presents a problem for the monodic reading of *Odes* 4.6, with its supposition of a single speaking voice. A new approach is needed, together with a reassessment of speaker identity.

The paean was predominantly a choric εἶδος.[62] This is because cult paeans were typically offered by communities; and communities were typically represented by their chorus (see above on Callimachus *Hymn* 2). Not all paeans are choric;[63] but those of most direct relevance for *Odes* 4.6, the paeans of Pindar, are. Moreover, *choreia* was a central part of the cult of Apollo and Artemis.[64] These facts plainly suggest the possibility that *Odes* 4.6 is in some sense 'choric'. The instructions to

---

[61] On *Ichform* in personal statements about the poet, cf. W. Kranze 'Sphragis, Ichform und Namensiegel als Eingangs- und Schlussmotiv antiker Dichtung' *Rh.M.* 104 (1961) 3–46.

[62] Fairbanks (1900) 52–3; Käppel (1992) 80–2; Dougherty (1994) 215. This remained the case in the Hellenistic era, including paeans sung for men, as is clear from the list given in Cameron (1995) 292–4. For choric hymns to Apollo at Claros, Lane Fox (1986) 178–9.

[63] Strabo 9.3.10; Herodas 4.1–20; Käppel (1992) 80; monodic paeans were naturally sung to Asclepius by individuals who had recovered from illness.

[64] Lonsdale (1993) General Index, *s.vv.* Apollo; Artemis.

the chorus (35–7) provide still further support for a choric interpretation: Greek hymnic parallels, most from cult paeans, are all self-referential (i.e. they refer to the hymn/paean itself, currently being performed), and they suggest that the Horatian instructions can be understood to concern the metre and content of the present ode, and to be uttered by the singing chorus itself.[65] The fact that the sixth paean contains just such a choric self-instruction (again in the metrical sphere) constitutes another powerful pointer to choric self-reference in Horace (121–2: ἰὴ ἰῆτε νῦν, μέτρα παιηόνων/ ἰῆτε, νέοι).[66] On this view, Horace's choric instructions will be the words of the chorus blending its personality with that of its χοροδιδάσκαλος. The conventions are illustrated not only in the hymnic parallels cited earlier, but by an explicit attestation in Lucian. At de Saltatione 11, he records the contents of an ephebic song where, he says, a chorus addresses διδασκαλία to itself: καὶ θάτερον δὲ τῶν ᾀσμάτων ... διδασκαλίαν ἔχει ὡς χρὴ ὀρχεῖσθαι. 'Πόρρω' γάρ, φασίν, 'ὦ παῖδες, πόδα μετάβατε καὶ κωμάξατε βέλτιον', τουτέστιν ἄμεινον ὀρχήσασθε ("and the second song ... even contains instruction on how to dance; "Set your foot before you, lads," it says, "and frolic yet more featly," that is, dance better" tr. Harmon). The ephebic chorus here acts as its own χοροδιδάσκαλος.

There is an obvious complication: the literary conventions suggest that the choric instructions refer to Odes 4.6 itself. Yet the traditional view that carmen (43) contains a reference to the CS cannot, in my opinion, be entirely abandoned: it is difficult to believe that Odes 4.6 is simply and solely self-referential, and that a Roman audience would not have seen in carmen (43) a reference to the CS; and indeed one later Roman reader is on record as having taken that view.[67] I suggest

[65] Proposed by Cairns (1971a) 443–4, citing Slater (1969); cf. Syndikus (1973) 347. For parallel choric self-instructions in Greek cult hymns, Nisbet–Hubbard on Odes 1.21.1, citing Isyllus (Käppel Pai. 40) 37; anon. (Käppel Pai. 37) 1; anon. (Käppel Pai. 38) 1–2; Macedonius (Käppel Pai. 41) 1 (all paeans); cf. Soph. Tr. 207–15 (a paean) and Call. H. 2.8 (hymn to Apollo), also cited by Nisbet–Hubbard.

[66] Fraenkel (1957) 401 rightly saw the Pindaric instruction as a precedent for what Horace does at 35.

[67] Schol. AV ad 4.6.1: Hymnum hic Apollini dicit et commendat carmina sua secularibus ludis ... . Contrast Cairns (1971a) 443–4, who excludes reference to the CS. Cairns states "there are no undisputed parallels in antiquity for a lyric poem referring to the composition or performance of another single lyric"; but cf. Pindar's apparent reference to the fourth paean at Isthm. 1.7–9 (Lefkowitz [1991] 9). The reference of carmen to the CS is still clearer if, as Stephen Harrison and Denis Feeney suggest to me, the self-naming vatis Horati alludes to CIL 6.32323.149 carmen composuit Q. Hor[ati]us

that this is one context in which it is legitimate, indeed necessary, to have things both ways: the choric instruction *Lesbium servate pedem* can refer both to the saecular hymn and to *Odes* 4.6 (like the *CS*, written in Sapphics). Thus Horace presents, in a choric hymn, a dramatic situation in which he is acting as χοροδιδάσκαλος for his own *CS*.

These questions reflect a highly contentious area of enquiry into Greek lyric poetry, that of speaker identity. An influential approach to this issue has involved a hypothesised choric 'I'-figure. Essentially a way of understanding multiple identity in the lyric speaker, this has been defined as a "mobile compound of chorus, chorus-leader and poet", any one element of which may predominate at any given time in a choric ode.[68] So far as concerns Pindar's paeans (as opposed to the *epinicia*), some scholars have taken the view that almost all personal statements are made by the chorus as *persona loquens*.[69] This has been challenged, in my view rightly, by D'Alessio (1994). The suggested 'mobility' of the choric 'I'-figure can in fact be exemplified in surviving paeans. In Pindar's fourth paean, the 'I' speaks as the performing Cean chorus (1–2), closely identified with the island itself at 21–7.[70] In the second paean, the 'I' speaks as the Abderitan chorus in programmatic statements at the beginning and end (4; 102), but, taken literally, as Abdera itself at 28: νεόπολίς εἰμι (I am a new city).[71] In the fifth, a concluding appeal for acceptance at Delos as θεράπων of Apollo and Artemis (45–6) might apply to poet, chorus leader or chorus members (considered as individual members of a collective). In 7b, a first person programmatic contrast with Homer suggests that ἐμοί (21) is spoken in the person of the poet; and the poet's personality seems also to emerge in 9 (see below).[72]

In the sixth paean, the first triad contains a series of first person singulars: λίσσομαι ... με δέξαι ... προφάταν (3–6); ἦλθον (9); ἐμαῖς

Flaccus.

[68] Slater (1969) 86–94; Cairns (1979) 121–2; Lefkowitz (1963); (1988); (1991) 1–71; Heath and Lefkowitz (1991); contrast C. Carey 'The performance of the Victory Ode' *AJP* 110 (1989) 545–65; A.P. Burnett 'Performing Pindar's Odes' *CP* 84 (1989) 283–93. For Pindar's paeans, D'Alessio (1994) is of particular value.

[69] Lefkowitz (1963) 225; (1991) 10–11, 70 n.110; Heath and Lefkowitz (1991) 176 n.10; Rutherford (1988) 67. Contrast D'Alessio (1994) 124–6.

[70] *Paean* 4: Lefkowitz (1991) 9.

[71] R. Hamilton *Epinicion* (The Hague 1974) 113, suggests that Abdera is actually talking (rejected by Rutherford [1988] 67 n.8): the phrase is a striking but logical extension of the identity of chorus with community and πόλις.

[72] 7: D'Alessio (1994) 126; 9: *ibid.* 125–6.

... τιμαῖς (11); κατέβαν (13); μο[ι] ... καταβάντ' (58–60). The second triad contains no first person statements at all; and the surviving lines of the third triad contain only one first person plural (εὐνάξομεν, 128).

In addition, two choric apostrophes are built in: the second triad concludes with instructions to νέοι to sing μέτρα παιηόνων (121–2); and the third, opening with apostrophe to Aegina, states that she will recount her own foundation myths (κατερεῖς, 129). The sixth paean thus presents a range of possible speakers: in grammatical terms, first person singular and plural; second person singular and plural.

Discussion of choric identity in the sixth paean will doubtless be influenced by the re-titling of the third triad, and by differing views as to its implications for the performance scenario. My own view is as follows. At the start of the first triad, the dominant *persona loquens* seems to be the visiting poet.[73] This is suggested by με ... προφάταν (5–6), where the point of comparison is an individual Delphian figure, the προφήτης (who seems to have articulated in metrical form the Pythia's inspired utterances).[74] Yet ἀοίδιμον, in its active sense 'singing', might suggest the singing voice of a chorus, as does 58–9: ἔραται δέ μο[ι]/ γλῶσσα μέλιτος ἄωτον γλυκὺν [καταλείβειν ("my tongue loves to pour forth the sweet essence of honey ..."). Arguably, then, a single phrase could, in its component parts, refer to both poet and chorus.[75] At

---

[73] Rutherford (1988) 67 n.8; Lefkowitz (1963) 251 n.108; S. Fogelmark *Studies in Pindar, with particular reference to Paean VI and Nemean VII* (Lund 1972) 117–23; contrast A. Hoekstra 'The absence of the Aeginetans' *Mnem.* 15 (1962) 1–14, at 10–12.

[74] The role of the προφήτης at Delphi (and the existence of the named office) is disputed: H.W. Parke and D.E. Wormell *The Delphic Oracle* I (Oxford 1956) 33; *RE* XXIII.808.8ff.; W.E. McLeod 'Oral bards at Delphi' *TAPA* 92 (1961) 317–25, at 320; Nagy (1989) 26–7; L. Maurizio 'Anthropology and spirit possession: a reconsideration of the Pythia's role at Delphi' *JHS* 115 (1995) 69–86, whose arguments for a versifying Pythia (by implication at all periods in the long history of the oracle) and denial of any versifying role for the προφήτης I find unpersuasive: Strabo 9.3.5 and Plut. 407b cannot simply be sidelined as "contradictory" and "quite late" (84 n.89). Hardie (1996) 231–5, suggests that *Pae.* 6 supplies evidence for a metrical role: Pindar's allusiveness there may reflect an official fiction, that versified oracles represented Apollo's *ipsissima verba*. The versifying role of the προφήτης may never have been officially acknowledged at Delphi, but was, perhaps, an open secret.

[75] For the deployment of composite phraseology in the blending of different elements of choric personality in a quite different context, cf. K. Dover *Aristophanes: Frogs* (Oxford 1993) 239. D'Alessio (1994) 121 n.13 reacts against the suggestion of Slater (1969) 89–90 that the first person in Pindar is a "*vague* combination of Pindar, chorus and chorus leader" (my italics): the simultaneous presence of two elements is, at least in *Pae.* 6, articulated with precision. C.O. Pavese 'Il coro del sesto Peana di Pindaro' in R. Pretagostini (ed.) *Tradizione e innovazione nella cultura greca da Omero all'età ellenistica: scritti in onore di Bruno Gentili* Vol. II (Rome 1993) 469–78, argues for a

12–13, poet and child-chorus seem to be blended by means of a simile from parental discipline (... παῖς ἅτε ματέρι κεδνᾷ/ πειθόμενος κατ-έβαν; "I have come down like a child obeying his/her dear mother").

It can, furthermore, be inferred from statements made in explanation for the poet/chorus' arrival (9–11) that the chorus is non-Delphian, and since it has come to remedy a Delphian lack of male χόρευσις, that it is male.[76] These hints are only confirmed, however, at the end of the second triad, in choric instructions issued to νέοι (121–2). These 'metrical' instructions are issued in the *persona* of the poet, whose 'metrical' role as Πιερίδων προφάτας has evolved towards that of χοροδιδάσκαλος.[77] The instructions, however, must be self-fulfilling, since the injunction to sing the paean-refrain (ἰὴ ἰῆτε, 121) is not en-acted in explicit articulation of the refrain. That part of the injunctions is therefore to be imagined as being enacted by the νέοι through its own choric utterance. The chorus of νέοι is then identified as Aegin-etan in the address to Aegina which follows.[78] In a further sophisti-cation, the nymph Aegina is herself implicitly identified with choric activity, both before and after her rape by Zeus.[79] I would therefore suggest that the personality of the Aeginetan νέοι, visiting Delphi, is present throughout the paean, but that it is supplemented by that of the poet in the first two triads and by that of Aegina in the third. Such an interplay and blending of poet, chorus and place as *personae loquentes* would certainly be complex; but, as will be argued in section VIII, it would also present a coherent and dramatically consistent choric voice.

Against this suggested Pindaric background of shifting/blended *per-sonae loquentes* I would propose that the 'fresh departure' postulated earlier, and the apparent shift in perspective on Apollo, exemplifies the 'mobility' of the choric 'I'-figure, and points to the emergent personal-ity of the individual poet, this being immediately signalled in *mihi* (29) and *poetae* (30); and it implies the predominance hitherto of a collective choric personality, which recedes at 29 (although the chorus of course still sings). The 'youthful' personality of the chorus would be reflected in its interest in mother/offspring relationships (*proles*

---

choral *persona loquens* in 6; and Lefkowitz (1995), contesting D'Alessio, rightly re-stresses the choric presence: but if my approach is correct, hard and fast choice between the poet and the chorus as speaker is unnecessary.

[76] Hardie (1996) 229–31.
[77] For the continuing 'metrical' role at this point of the προφήτης, Hardie (1996) 240–41.
[78] Wilamowitz (1922) 134–5. Rejected by most recent commentators, including Radt (1958) 89; re-argued by Hardie (1996) 229.
[79] Hardie (1996) 221–2.

Niobea, 1; Achilles/Thetis, 6; the unborn child *matris in alvo*, 19–20; also Aeneas/Venus, 21–3).[80] This 'mother/son' theme itself has a counterpart in Pindar's simile of child/mother choric obedience (12–13), as also in Achilles/Thetis (83–4).

If this is correct, the chorus speaks first in its collective personality, and then in the character of the poet, thereby enabling the latter to 'respond' to what has just been said, in an unfolding dramatic situation. In 'responding', the poet makes an emphatic assertion of Phoebus' present favour towards himself, and thereby reassures the chorus in their concern for Apollo's defence of the *Dauniae decus Camenae*. The *carmen* will indeed be *dis amicum* (42). The Apolline *ictus* with which they should concern themselves is the benign musical (paeanic) beat of the poet's thumb (*meique pollicis ictum*, 35–6, with word-play on **Apollo**), and not the god's hostile *sagittarum ictus*. And the chorus members will assuredly proceed to marriage (*nupta*, 41; cf. above pp.263–4, on Callimachus *Hymn* 2.14–15).

There are intriguing parallels with the choral dynamics at the junction of the second and third triads of the sixth paean. The relevance of this passage, with its abrupt transition, to the transition at *Odes* 4.6.29 was emphasised by Fraenkel.[81] The new discovery that the Aeginetan prosodion started at 123 lends further weight to Fraenkel's insight. At 121–2 (end of the second triad), the poet as *persona loquens* addresses (unidentified) 'boys' and urges them to sing the paean refrain (an appeal which, I have suggested elsewhere, is motivated by anxiety to ensure their acceptability at the Delphian Theoxenia, and their personal safety at the festival, and has in mind the awful fate of the Aeacid Neoptolemos: see below, p.281).[82] The appeal to the boys cues in an encomiastic address to Aegina (123ff., the start of the third triad) which identifies the chorus as Aeginetan (see above). The 'Aeginetan' voice, contrasting with the 'poet's' anxiety, implies confidence in its acceptability at the Theoxenia, and also boldly echoes the opening praise of Pytho in its praise of its own island (ὀνομακλύτα, 123; cf. κλυτόμαντι, 2).[83] In *Odes* 4.6, by contrast, choric allusion to the 'Daunian' poet in *Dauniae ... decus Camenae* (27), in an anxious paean-appeal, cues in

[80] Mother/son relationships: Putnam (1986) 118–20.
[81] Fraenkel (1957) 401.
[82] Hardie (1996) 240.
[83] Acceptability: οὕνεκεν οὔ σε παιηόνων/ ἄδορπον εὐνάξομεν (127–8) alludes to participation in the Theoxenia, and thus to choric acceptance to 'Pytho': Hardie (1996) 229.

the voice of the poet, who expresses confidence in the acceptability to Apollo and the gods of the choric *carmen*, in an encomiastic address identifying the choric speakers as the offspring of the leading families of Rome. In Pindar, then, the voice of an anxious poet-χοροδιδάσκαλος cues in the confident boy chorus, speaking for Aegina. In Horace, an anxious child-chorus cues in the self-confident poet. In a further Pindaric touch, Horace identifies himself by name in a self-confident sphragis (*Horati*, 44) fourteen lines after *nomen poetae*, thereby echoing the naming of Aegina (137) at a similar distance from ὀνομακλύτα (sc. νᾶσος) (123).

The re-titling of Pindar's third triad supplies a plausible model, in a major choric work, for the way in which part of a unitary poem could at the same time be regarded as a separate poem. I would suggest that, with this model in mind, Horace presents 29–44 as being, simultaneously, a separate poem in its own right and part of a unitary poem. In doing so, Horace adapted to his own purposes the device of the choric appeal with which Pindar effected the transition from the second triad to the third/the prosodion, probably drawing in Pindar's concluding appeal for divine protection for Aegina (above, p.254). How, then, are we to read the dynamics of Horace's imitation of Pindar's transitional choric instructions, which he places right at the centre of his (postulated) 'second poem'? In particular, can the Pindaric model help resolve the question of present versus future reference? At one level, as noted earlier, the Pindaric instructions are self-fulfilling. At another level, however, as Rutherford (1997) 18 suggests, the appeal is an "introduction to and sort of speech frame for the whole third triad". This is validated by the echo of παιηό/νων (121–2) in παιηόνων (127), where the chorus is self-evidently reacting to the instructions which they have received. In that sense, then, the choric instructions indubitably look forward to the emergence of the Aeginetan choric voice in the next triad, i.e. in the 'Aeginetan prosodion'. Thus, the dual status of the third triad presents us with a situation in which choric injunctions may also have dual status, simultaneously self-fulfilling and forward looking. The third triad thus helps to illuminate not only the internal structure of *Odes* 4.6, but the relationship between *Odes* 4.6 and the *CS*: it takes us measurably closer to a Pindaric context for dual reference in Horace's choric instructions, simultaneously denoting *Odes* 4.6 and the forthcoming *CS*.

In a final choric sophistication (41–4), Horace predicts a statement which will be made in future by the female element of the chorus about its participation in the performance of his festival *carmen*. This is reminiscent, perhaps deliberately so, of the Homeric sphragis in the *Hymn to Apollo* (172–3), where, in the context of performance at the pan-Ionian festival, the singer praises the *Deliades* and predicts what they will in future say about himself, with stress on his Chian origins. The reminiscence, if such it is, is relevant to the issue of 'split poems', since the singer's envoi to the *Deliades* occurs in the middle of what was transmitted as a unitary hymn, but at the end of the Delian section and before the start of the self-contained hymn to Pythian Apollo.

Horace's speaking chorus would appear to present a contrast with the calmer voice of the poet. I have suggested that this contrast derives from, but reverses, the sixth paean. As a paean-opening, however, it has another analogue in Pindar's ninth paean, where a change of tone is detectable between the opening expressions of concern about the portent of the eclipse, and the following address to Apollo (34–40), probably explicable by the emergence at this point of the poet as *persona loquens*.[84] Further analogues may lie in poems in which successive stages of an unfolding scene are conveyed in dramatic form, again with the deployment of different 'speakers'.[85] An important example is Callimachus' *Hymn to Apollo*. A χορηγός/χοροδιδάσκαλος figure interreacts with a chorus of boys, who are given instructions to sing and dance (8), together with implicit warnings about what may befall them if they do not (12–15); the boys are then congratulated on starting their performance (16).[86] This scene-setting modulates into the 'hymn proper' at 32. In a recent treatment of *Hymn 2*, Bing (1993) notes the different 'voices', individual and choric, which emerge in it; and within Callimachus' range of source material, he suggestively adduces the praise of the choric *Deliades* in the Homeric Hymn to Apollo, and their capability of imitating voices (162–4). If this passage is indeed part of the background to *Hymn 2*, it would be interesting evidence of the 'imitative' choric basis of speaker variation;[87] and Horace's recall of the same passage, suggested above, might be a further, conscious

---

[84] D'Alessio (1994) 125–6.

[85] Fraenkel (1957) 180–82 (on *Odes* 1.27), esp. 181: "the role of the poet is ... that of a principal actor who either talks to his fellow actors or responds to their actions and utterances"; G. Williams *Tradition and Originality in Roman Poetry* (Oxford 1968) 194–202; Cairns (1979) 121–2.

[86] Choregos: *H.* 2.12–16, cf. 28–31; Bundy (1972) 87.

[87] P. Bing 'Impersonation of voice in Callimachus' *Hymn to Apollo*' *TAPA* 123 (1993) 181–98, at 186 n.16 surprisingly (given his point about the 'imitative' chorus) rejects the choric character of the hymn as a whole (and thus the choric 'imitation' of the opening voice of the individual speaker); contrast Cairns (1979) 121–2.

reflection of the literary history of the choric conventions.

Among critics who have difficulty with the idea that any Horatian ode, other than the *CS*, might be read as being 'choric' in character, there might be some feeling that 'choric reading' presupposes actual 'choric performance'. Now, it well may be that some or all of the public odes did indeed receive performance, and a choric element cannot, *a priori*, be excluded from any such performing scenario.[88] But no assumption of choric performance need accompany choric interpretation (just as it need not be assumed that Horatian references to musical instruments must be taken at face value). There is no reason why a Horatian ode should not, quite literally, have been read as choric. A model in this respect might again be Callimachus' second *Hymn*, which is, in my view, wholly 'choric' in character: Bing's stress on the cooperative role of the reader in 'hearing' the different speaking voices provides one approach to modern understanding of how a 'choric' ode, and its choric conventions, could have been received by ancient readers.

VI The Double Chorus: Boys and Girls

The choric arrangements for the *CS* are recorded in the festival *Acta* (*CIL* 6.32323.20–21 [Augustus' instructions to the *XVviri*]):] *pueros virginesque patrimos matrim[osque ad carmen can]endum chorosque habendos frequentes u[t adsint.* The performance comprised both the singing of the *carmen*, and choric dance (*chorosque habendos*).[89] It is not clear at what point the dance took place; but in the *Acta* for AD 204, the *carmen* is stated to have been performed three times, with only one reference to dance (on the Capitoline).[90] In 204 the performance is also stated to have been given "with hands joined" (*conexis manibus*), presumably signifying a closed, circular formation and some form of classical ring dance.[91] The 204 *Acta* additionally specify musical accompaniment by lyres and flutes. On that occasion, then, choric participation certainly represented Roman *choreia* on the Greek model.

---

[88] Cf. O. Murray 'Symposium and genre in the poetry of Horace' *JRS* 75 (1985) 39–50, at 43, and *passim*.

[89] This is argued by Pighi (1941) 294 n.2. *chorosque habendos* represents χορὸν ... ἔχοιεν in the Sibylline oracle (see below).

[90] Pighi (1941) 293–4.

[91] For the relevant text, supplementing *CIL* 6.32326–9, Hülsen (1932) 388–94; Pighi (1941) 165–9, 292–4. On Greek ring dance performed 'hand on wrist', see Lonsdale (1993) 66, 190. Pighi (1941) 294 n.2 well compares Prop. 3.5.19: *me iuvat in prima coluisse Helicona iuventa/ Musarumque choris implicuisse manus.*

The celebration of AD 204 was not identical in all respects to that of 17 BC, but there seems no reason to think that there will have been radical divergences in choric stage management in the intervening period. Detailed choric prescription for 17 BC was set out in the Sibylline Oracle (18–22):

> καὶ ἀειδόμενοί τε Λατῖνοι
> παιᾶνες κούροισι κόρῃσί τε νηὸν ἔχοιεν
> ἀθανάτων. χωρὶς δὲ κόραι χορὸν αὐταὶ ἔχοιεν   20
> καὶ χωρὶς παίδων ἄρσην στάχυς, ἀλλὰ γονήων
> πάντες ζωόντων, οἷς ἀμφιθαλὴς ἔτι φύτλη.

(And let Latin paeans, sung by boys and maidens, fill the temple of the gods. And let the maidens separately, and the male progeny of children separately, hold their choric dance, but all to be of living parents, whose fathers and mothers are still alive.)

The stress on separate male and female choruses is striking and is reiterated in the festival *Acta* (*CIL* 6.32323.3: *bi*]*ni chori...*).[92] It has been suggested that this points to an Augustan innovation in the sung performance of Roman public *carmina*.[93] Where *testimonia* to earlier choric performances at Rome are specific about the sex of the chorus, they all refer to *virgines*. Between 217 and 92 BC, no fewer than ten occasions are recorded in which, in response to *prodigia*, a chorus of virgins (twenty-seven, where the number is specified) sang a *carmen* at Rome.[94] This may in part reflect the prominence of female deities, in particular Juno Regina, in the expiatory ceremonies prescribed by the *libri Sibyllini*. But male gods feature in a few such prescriptions.[95] On the single occasion on which boys are recorded as playing a sacral role alongside a girls' *carmen*, in 217 BC, they chant an *obsecratio* which is

---

[92] There is an etymologising complex in χωρὶς δὲ κόραι χορόν; for Latin etymologising in this area, D. West *The Imagery and Poetry of Lucretius* (Edinburgh 1969) 108–9, on Lucr. 2.635 *pueri circum puerum pernice chorea* (where *chorea* interreacts with *pueri*/κοῦροι); for χορός/χώρα interplay, *EM s.v.* χορός. For the double chorus in Greek *choreia*, Soph. *Tr.* 207–15; *AA* 1894, 81 (twin choirs in the service of Zeus Sosipolis at Magnesia); both cited by Nisbet–Hubbard (1970) 253. In Latin literature, cf. also Cat. 34, 62; Hor. *Od.* 1.21; 3.1.4; 3.14.10–11; Virg. *Aen.* 2.238–9.

[93] Fraenkel (1957) 380 n.3; a position reiterated, without reference to Fraenkel or other secondary literature, in P. White *Promised Verse* (Harvard 1993) 303 (n.21). The whole question is complicated by extreme uncertainty as to the interrelationship of the various choric *carmina* attested for the third century, including the first *carmen saeculare*: Cichorius (1922); *RE* Suppl. 5.600 (Fraenkel); and, with a survey of earlier views, Schmidt (1985) 42–4.

[94] MacBain (1982) 127–35.

[95] Thus, e.g. Jupiter in 217 BC (Livy 22.1.17); Apollo in 125 BC (oracle *ap.* Phlegon *Mirab.* X).

evidently different from the *carmen*.[96] In 190, and again in 108 BC, expiatory rites feature, respectively, a *supplicatio* and a sacrifice involving both *pueri* and *virgines*; but *carmina* were not performed on these occasions.[97] The *testimonia* on the first *carmen saeculare* (249 BC) do not specify the sex of the chorus; but if it is correct to connect it with the *chorus Proserpinae* mentioned at Varro *De Lingua Latina* 6.94, then it too will have been all-female.[98]

The pre-Augustan history of Roman expiatory *carmina* is complex and controversial; but if Gagé is correct in postulating some form of linear relationship between these *carmina* and the *Carmen Saeculare*, it may very well be that the latter was indeed the first public *carmen* to be performed by a double chorus, and that this would have been recognised as an important innovation in Roman *choreia*.[99] It would no doubt reflect the Augustan reform of the *Ludi Saeculares* themselves, so that they were no longer focused on the gods of the underworld (Dis and Proserpina), but gave new prominence to the Olympian gods, including Apollo and Diana.[100]

Early choric *carmina* at Rome had patently looked back to Greek cultic analogues.[101] So if choric innovation was indeed a feature of the Augustan *carmen saeculare*, a clear sacral motivation for Horace's imitation of the sixth paean and for the prominence he gives in *Odes* 4.6 to choric matters may be discerned in Pindar's creative interplay of male and female choruses at a major Greek festival, the Delphian Theoxenia. The sixth paean is sung by a visiting (Aeginetan) male chorus (122), but reference is made to performances by a resident female chorus at Delphi, the *Delphides* (15–18). This chorus can itself reasonably be inferred to perform at the Theoxenia; and Pindar makes

---

[96] Macr. 1.6.14: *acta igitur obsecratio est pueris ingenuis itemque libertinis, sed et virginibus patrimis matrimisque pronuntiantibus carmen*: Fraenkel (1957) 380 n.3.

[97] Iul. Obseq. 1 (190), 40 (108). Gagé (1955) 634 n.2 suggests that a *carmen* was sung; but of this there is no evidence, and the numbers involved (30 boys, 30 girls) is unparalleled for a Roman *carmen*.

[98] Schol. Hor. *CS* 8: [*Verrius*] *Flaccus refert carmen saeculare et sacrificium inter annos centum et decem Diti et Proserpinae constitutum ... ex responso decemvirorum ...*; also *... et carmen caniatum inter sacrificia*. Cf. a separate scholium which appears anachronistically to import procedure from the Augustan and later celebrations: *hoc etiam idem libri* [*sc. Sibyllini*] *iusserunt, ut nobilium liberi in Capitolio hoc carmen decantarent*.

[99] Gagé (1955) 367–9.

[100] Mommsen (1905) 354; Fraenkel (1957) 366, 368.

[101] Wissowa (1912) 426–7; Gruen (1990) 85–7.

play on the sexual tension between males and females.[102] But it is not clear whether the girls performed with the male chorus or entirely separately from it. There is evidence from other sources of paean-performances by singing boys and dancing girls.[103] A variant appears in a Simonidean paean performed at Delos (*PMG* 519 fr. 55), where a visiting male chorus appears to instruct the resident *Deliades* to call out the paean refrain.[104] This implies a double chorus, with the males as dominant singers, and the females as respondent refrain singers (and perhaps also as dancers). Comparable choric practices are attested for Delphi.[105] The *Delphides* may, then, have danced in accompaniment; or else, their role may have been taken over by the visiting Aeginetan males.[106]

It is in the final stanza of *Odes* 4.6, with the girls 'speaking' alone, that we may catch the flavour of the separate identities of the two component parts of the saecular chorus, boys and girls, prescribed in the Sibylline text.[107] The girls anticipate the time when they will be married (and will have lost their virginity); as they do so, we may sense something of the sexual dimension which is present in Pindar's treatment of the Aeginetan boys and the *Delphides*, and at the same time of the crucial importance of sexual purity for the successful performance of the *Carmen Saeculare*.[108] This is explicitly affirmed in the address to

---

[102] Hardie (1996) 221–6; on sexual tension and virginity, *ibid.* 228–31.

[103] *Scutum* 278–80; Call. *H.* 4.304–6 (of paean performances on Delos): οἱ μὲν ὑπαείδουσι νόμον Λυκίοιο γέροντος,/ .../ αἱ δὲ ποδὶ πλήσσουσι χορίτιδες ἀσφαλὲς οὖδας (in a context where there is heavy emphasis on sexual distinctions in rites of passage: cf. esp. 296–9).

[104] *PMG* 519 fr. 55.2–3: ιη[.../ .....]ξατε, Δαλίων θύγατ[ρες (*Deliades*); 8:]ἀείδοντες (male chorus); 6: πλαξιάλοι᾿ ἀπ᾿ ᾿Α[...], where either Aegina or Andros might fit. Cf. I.C. Rutherford '*Paeans* by Simonides' *HSCP* 93 (1990) 169–209, at 177–9; he notes that ιη at 2 "is most likely a small refrain".

[105] Euphor. fr. 80 Powell, where *Delphides* utter an antiphonal paean refrain: ὁπλοτέρου τ᾿ ᾿Αχιλῆος ἀκούομεν Εὐρυλόχοιο,/ Δελφίδες ᾧ ὕπο καλὸν Ἴηον ἀντεβόησαν. Compare Käppel (1992) 81 on a paean as "ein Wechsel zwischen der Ololyge von Frauen und dem Paian von Männern".

[106] The latter is implied in the self-instruction to sing the paean-refrain (121–2), a responsive role normally performed by the *Delphides* or *Deliades*: Hardie (1996) 241.

[107] Attempts have been made to divide the *CS* into passages sung by the boys, by the girls and in unison (see most recently Schmidt [1985] 48–52); while it is just possible that 41–4 reflects such a division, *CS* 74 *spem bonam* ... *domum reporto*/ ... *chorus* seems to me to tell in favour of a united singing chorus, with one voice. B. Arnold 'A reevaluation of the artistry of Horace's *Carmen Saeculare*' in C. Deroux (ed.) *Studies in Latin Literature and Roman History* IV (Brussels 1986) 475–91 at 481–5 plausibly suggests the presence of antiphonal patterns within the choric performance.

[108] The sexual dimension is flagged up in both poems by reference to Aphrodite/Venus (*Pae.* 6.4; *Od.* 4.6.21). For sexual purity, etc., cf. Iambl. *VP* 51 (Pythagoras on child-

the chorus: as virgin girls and boys, its members are under the protection of no less a figure than Apollo's own sister, the virgin Diana, who here makes her first appearance (33 *Deliae tutela deae*). *tutela* carries a legal allusion to minor persons as wards, not capable of conducting their own affairs or of defending their own interests.[109]

Here, and in the area of the sexual purity of Roman youth, embodied in the chorus, there is a socio-sacral resonance with the staging of the saecular festival itself: Suetonius (*Augustus* 31.4) records that Augustus "vetoed the presence of young persons of either sex at any nocturnal manifestation [sc. at the saecular games], unless accompanied by some related person of mature age." A likely Augustan corollary of this 'pure youth' festival ethos, itself shrewdly aimed at the extra-marital promiscuity which, in literature as in life, used to accompany public festivals in the ancient world (one of the few contexts in which males might make personal contact with well-born females) was the probable presence in the saecular *pompa* (below, pp.286–7) of the *praesides* of the individual members of the chorus. This element of personal protection of virgins parading in public seems to be attested for AD 204,[110] and in view of the Augustan edict cited above, the same can reasonably be assumed for the Augustan *pompa*. The *clari patres* praised at 31–2 will probably have been present, as a feature of the saecular ideology, at the performance of the *CS*; and in speaking of Diana's *tutela*, Horace may again reflect Augustus' concern with sexual purity at the *Ludi Saeculares*. Linking present virginity and purity to the future bearing of children, and the next Roman generation, is the virgin Diana *Noctiluca*, she who hastens the passage of the months (sc. of fertility and pregnanacy: 38–40).

---

ren): πρὸς δὲ τούτοις θεοφιλεστάτους αὐτοὺς ὄντας ἀποφῆναι, καὶ διὰ τοῦτο φῆσαι κατὰ τοὺς αὐχμοὺς ὑπὸ τῶν πόλεων ἀποστέλλεσθαι παρὰ τῶν θεῶν ὕδωρ αἰτησομένους, ὡς μάλιστ' ἂν ἐκείνοις ὑπακούσαντος τοῦ δαιμονίου καὶ μόνοις διὰ τέλους ἁγνεύουσιν ἐξουσίας ὑπαρχούσης ἐν τοῖς ἱεροῖς διατρίβειν (the reference to communal paeanic appeal for relief from drought is noteworthy); cf. ps.-Acro on Hor. *Ep.* 2.1.133: *antiquitus enim pueris et puellis praecipiebatur cantare carmen, ut aetas innocentior deos placaret.* Cf. Lane Fox (1986) 208–9. For children in ritual actions, Parker (1983) 79–81. For purification in the context of the saecular festival, Zanker (1988) 168; Frazer on Ov. *Fast.* 1.501.

[109] OLD s.v. *tutela*, 3; Paul. *Dig.* 26.1.1 *praef.* ... *tutela, ut Servius definivit, ius ac potestas in capite libero ad tuendum eum, qui propter aetatem ... se defendere nequit.*

[110] Section Va.74 (Diels' probable restoration, accepted by Pighi).

VII Teaching and Choric Persuasion

The designation *vatis Horati* (44) is consistent with the Augustan use of *vates* of the poet-prophet.[111] But it also resonates with the prophetic context in which the *CS* has its origins, i.e. the *Libri Sybillini* which prescribed the "Latin paean" (and indeed all previous Roman public *carmina*). Directly relevant to this interface of prophecy and poetry is Pindar's ἀοίδιμον Πιερίδων προφάταν (6; the singing [*or* sung of] prophet of the *Pierides*).[112]

Pindar's 'metrical' prophetic role surfaces in the choric instructions (121–2) μέτρα παιηό/νων ἵῆτε, νέοι ("send forth the metres of paeans": above, V). The instruction also cross-refers to the metrical 'foot' (ποδί, 18) of the *Delphides*' dancing.[113] I would suggest that this 'metrical' background has influenced the metrical component of Horace's choric instructions (*Lesbium servate pedem meique/ pollicis ictum*, 35–6), together with *docilis modorum/ vatis Horati* (44).[114] The latter, juxtaposing *modorum* and *vatis*, represents interpretative imitation of Pindar's widely separated μέτρα and προφάταν. *docilis*, suggesting choric obedience to Horace's 'metrical' instruction, helps connect *modorum* with *pedem*, thereby reflecting Pindar's linkage of μέτρα and ποδί. Pindar suggests the integral relationship of prophetic 'metre' and 'paean' in μέτρα παιηόνων; and Horace's 'paeanic' *ictum* (etymologising παιάν from παίειν, above, p.260) stresses the metrical underpinning of his paean-*carmen*. *spiritum* (29), too, carries oracular reference to the Delphian πνεῦμα which inspired the Pythia, and, together with *nomen poetae*, looks forward to *vatis Horati*.[115]

---

[111] H. Dahlmann 'Vates' *Philol.* 97 (1948) 337–53; J.K. Newman *Augustus and the New Poetry* (Brussels 1967) 99ff.; R.O.A.M. Lyne *Horace: Behind the Public Poetry* (Oxford 1995) 184–5.

[112] For suggestions as to the possible influence on *vatis* of the new 'Platea' elegy of Simonides, Barchiesi (1995) 38 n.20: these are open to question, but do not in any case affect the view put forward here. For the ambiguity of ἀοίδιμον, Radt (1958) 105–8.

[113] Hardie (1996) 235–41.

[114] *pollicis ictum* strikes a 'metrical' Apolline note, punning on the god's name: cf. Ov. *Ars* 493–4: *subito manifestus Apollo/ movit inauratae pollice fila lyrae*. The sixth paean contains complex interplay between Muses, flowing water (of Castalia), metrical foot and choric footbeat (Hardie [1996] 221–6); against this background, it is tempting to see etymological interplay between *amne* (26) and *Camenae* (27).

[115] *spiritus*: Val. Max. 1.8.10; Luc. 5.132, 165 (*spiritus ingessit vati*). Cf. J. Fontenrose *The Delphic Oracle* (Berkeley and London 1978) 197–203; Syndikus (1973) 352 n.39. For *spiritus* of poetic inspiration, see Nisbet–Hubbard on Hor. *Od.* 2.16.38. For the combination with *ars*, cf. Democritus fr. B 21 D–K (on Homer): Ὅμηρος φύσεως λαχὼν θεαζούσης ἐπέων κόσμον ἐτεκτήνατο παντοίων. For Delphian procedure, cf. Str. 9.3.5: δεχομένην τὸ πνεῦμα ἀποθεσπίζειν ἔμμετρά τε καὶ ἄμετρα· ἐντείνειν δὲ

In speaking of the 'teacher'/'taught' relationship of poet and chorus, Horace makes a point of wider societal application in the *novum saeculum*, namely the moral receptivity of Roman youth as a guarantee of civic stability.[116] Compare *CS* 45: *di, probos mores docili iuventae ... date*, cross-referenced again to choric teaching/learning at 75–6: *doctus et Phoebi chorus et Dianae/ dicere laudes.*[117] Horace implicitly foreshadows these themes in his opening reflections on mythological relationships between children and parents (Leto/Apollo; Niobe/her offspring; Achilles/Peleus), especially of mothers and sons; and this has a Pindaric background in the mother/son simile at *Paean* 6.12.

Philosophical writing on the civic/educational significance of choric activity is relevant to these concepts.[118] Plato deals with the subject in the second book of the *Laws*. He associates early education with choric training, which takes place "through the Muses and Apollo" (654a). He would deny to poets the freedom to "teach the children of well-ordered parents whatever pleases the poet himself, as regards rhythm or melody or expression" (656c). And in elaborating the theme of choric education, he introduces a series of choruses of different age groups (664b–d): the first will be "the children's chorus of the Muses"; and the second will be an Apolline chorus of young men "calling on Paean to be a witness, with persuasion, as to the truth of what is said, and to be propitious to the youth".[119] The choruses, Plato argues, will be better able to persuade the young of the truth than any other mode of communication. Horace's interest in philosophical material on poetry and education is clear from *Epistles* 2.1.126–37, where statements about the educational function and content of poetry modulate into the didactic process of choric learning (in a passage which, moreover, is well understood to connect with the *CS* and with *Odes* 4.6).[120]

Plato's choric formulations reflect his interest in a mode of education and of civic order which involves appeal to a natural human disposition to harmony and order, rather than compulsion and

---

καὶ ταῦτα εἰς μέτρον ποιητάς τινας ὑπουργοῦντας τῷ ἱερῷ; also Plut. *Mor.* 407b.

[116] For children and the saecular festival Zanker (1988) 167, 177; for 'teaching', cf. Putnam (1986) 129.

[117] On *CS* 75, see Wimmel (1987) 247–8; on its relationship to *docili iuventa*, and to the *doctor/docilis* complex in 4.6, *ibid.*, 249. On the wider context, Putnam (1986) 129.

[118] Lonsdale (1993) 71–3; Mullen (1982) 53–6.

[119] 664c: δεύτερος δὲ ὁ ... τόν τε Παιᾶνα ἐπικαλούμενος μάρτυρα τῶν λεγομένων ἀληθείας πέρι καὶ τοῖς νέοις ἵλεων μετὰ πειθοῦς γίγνεσθαι ἐπευχόμενος.

[120] C.O. Brink *Horace on Poetry* II (Cambridge 1982) 156–7; for connections with *CS* and *Od.* 4.6, *ibid.* 173–4.

coercion.[121] The keynote is "persuasion" (πειθώ). That this is explicitly
invoked in Plato's 'Apollo-Paean' chorus might suggest that this εἶδος
was associated particularly closely with the educative and persuasive
function. One factor may have been the standard ancient etymology of
'Pytho' from πειθώ, hence association of Apollo Pythius with 'per-
suasion'.[122] Pindar's sixth paean (addressed in the first instance to 'Py-
tho') deploys this etymology: at 52, πιθεῖν σοφούς ("persuade poets")
associates the informing function of the Muses with the informing
function of the Pythian oracle; and at 12–13, παῖς ἅτε ματέρι κεδνᾷ/
πειθόμενος relates, as has been seen, to parental discipline (and thus to
education in its broadest sense).[123]

Horace's praise of Diana's violent control of animals (33–4), *fuga-
ces/ lyncas et cervos cohibentis arcu*, derives from the same choric-
educative complex of ideas. The animals are to be distinguished from
the girls and boys who are under Diana's *tutela*: the former lack natural
harmony and order (and require violent constraint); the latter possess a
natural sense of rhythm, and require educative guidance and persuasion
(thus, *Lesbium servate pedem*).[124] As will be seen in the next section,
the distinction is critical to understanding the conceptual relationship
between the choric instructions and the address to Apollo, for it tells
the children that they are not vulnerable to being struck by the bows
(*arcu*, 34) either of Diana or of Apollo.[125] Also relevant to the 'choric
persuasion' is the central action of the poem, the intercession of Apollo
and Venus with Jupiter. The supreme god allowed himself to be per-
suaded (variant reading: either *victus* or *flexus*) to permit the Trojan

---

[121] Lonsdale (1993) 45–6, 54, 87.

[122] Mythogr. Vat. 3.8.1 Bode, on Pythian Apollo: φύτιος [πείθιος, Bode] *id est fidem
afferens ... quod omnis falsa credulitas per tenebras orta radiorum eius fulgore de-
struatur; πειθώ namque credulitas interpretatur*; RE XXIV.575.26ff. The etymology
is ancient: for *fides*/πειθώ cf. Lucan 5.79–85; Stat. *Theb.* 8.175–6; also Ov. *Her.*
15.23; Plut. *Mor.* 37c (a play on Nicander's post at Delphi): ὅπως εἰδῇς τοῦ πείθοντος
ὀρθῶς ἀκούειν. The point at issue is the oracle's ability to persuade its consultants of
the truth of its statements.

[123] Hardie (1996) 236–7. For Πειθώ of poets: *AP* 7.2.1 (Antipater, of Homer); Gow–Page
Hellenistic Epigrams II.40.

[124] For these essential differences between animal young and children cf. Pl. *Laws* 653d–
654a. Girls and fawns: Nisbet–Hubbard on Hor. *Od.* 1.23.1 (including choric parallels
from Sappho 58.16 and Bacchylides 13.84–9).

[125] Underpinning all this, and the interplay of *pueri* (18, 31) and Apollo *puer* (37), may be
a further, bilingual etymologising complex: cf. the Latin derivation of *puer* from
disciplinary blows (Paul. Fest. 191: ... *unde pueri, quod puviendo coercentur, id est
plagis*); and the Greek derivation of ἰὴ παιάν from ἵει παῖ ἰόν ("shoot the arrow,
boy") (cf. Williams on Call. *H.* 2.103).

emigration to Italy. This feature, and its significance for the relationship between Apollo and Jupiter, will be considered in the final section (290–91).

VIII   Choric Anxiety

Apollo is both a terrible and a beneficent god: defender and destroyer; healer and sender of plague; god of the lyre and god of the bow. A recurring feature of hymns to Apollo is the contrast between these benign and fearsome aspects.[126] Greek choruses express consciousness of Apollo's fearful aspect (thus, Callimachus *Hymn* 2.14–15; 21–5). It was the task of a chorus to placate the god, to fend off his destructive characteristics, and to ensure that his beneficent aspects came to the fore: if it failed, Apollo's anger might fall on its members as well as on the community it represented. A chorus therefore had good reason to fear the god whom it was praising and placating. A singer's concern to please a god and avoid his/her displeasure is a topic of hymnal epilogues.[127] In hymns to Apollo it relates to the perceived threat which the κοῦρος-god presents to male choruses: that is, to κοῦροι such as himself. Relevant to this ambivalent κοῦρος/κοῦροι relationship is an important motif of Apolline conquests, namely the near-identity of the god with some of his mythical victims.[128]

Choric anxiety is present in the sixth paean. Pindar and his male chorus are visitors to Delphi and appeal for acceptance (5–6: that is, as part of a 'negotiation' scenario postulated by Rutherford, where visiting delegates seek admission to the sanctuary). He claims defensively to be "warding off helplessness both from your citizens [i.e. the Delphians, who commissioned the paean] and from the privileges (τιμαί) due to me". There is a sequel-scenario, presented in the second triad, in Apollo's slaying of the Aiacid Neoptolemos, an earlier visitor to Delphi: he was engaged in a squabble over τιμαί (118) and was killed at the spot where paeans are now performed.[129] It is for this reason that the poet fears the terrible side of the god in the matter of τιμαί at

---

[126] For the idea that the paean itself can be considered an 'ambiguous' hymn-type, Rutherford (1993) 77–92, esp. 88–9; M. Detienne 'L'Apollon meurtier et les crimes de sang' *QUCC* n.s. 22 (1986) 7–17.

[127] Bundy (1972).

[128] Nagy (1979) 61–2, 142–50; R.J. Rabel 'Apollo as a model for Achilles in the *Iliad*' *AJP* 111 (1990) 429–40.

[129] Hence the verbal correspondence of γᾶς παρ' ὀμφαλὸν εὐρύν (120) with χθονὸς ὀμφαλὸν παρὰ σκιάεντα (17) and ἀγῶνα εὐρύν (60).

Delphi. Thus, the νέοι are bidden by 'Pindar' to sing the customary Delphian paean-refrain and μέτρα παιηόνων (121–2) immediately after the Neoptolemos narrative. 'Pindar' aims to make his choric νέοι conform to Delphian custom and ritual requirements. The choric appeal is thus a dramatic, placatory gesture, prompted by recollection of Apollo's ruthless treatment of Neoptolemos, and an anxious acknowledgment of its relevance to the visiting Aeginetan boys and their performance at the altar.[130] At one level, then, the first two triads of the sixth paean (i.e., its 'Delphian' section) operate as a placatory preamble, uttered by the poet-προφάτας, to the third, 'Aeginetan' triad.[131]

'Choric anxiety' can illuminate what is happening in the address to Apollo at Odes 4.6.1–28. sensit (3) means "felt his presence". The verb represents 'perception' of a deity at the moment of his epiphany. That a chorus may 'perceive' an epiphany is shown by Epistles 2.1.134 (poscit opem chorus et praesentia numina sentit) and Callimachus fr. 227.1–2 Pf.: ἔνεστ' Ἀπόλλων τῷ χορῷ· τῆς λύρης ἀκούω·/ καὶ τῶν Ἐρώτων ἠσθόμην. In invoking Apollo, the chorus knows that he is already, or soon will be, present; and in its anxiety, its thoughts turn to those who had experienced the terrible effects of his presence. They focus on Apollo's attitude to grandiloquence (magnae/ vindicem linguae). In a choric context, linguae suggests secondary reference to the singing voice (thus Paean 6.58–9: ἔραται δέ μο[ι]/ γλῶσσα μέλιτος ἄωτον γλυκὺν [καταλείβειν; "my tongue loves to [pour forth] the sweet essence of honey ..."): the chorus is thinking of Apollo's attitude to themselves and their performance; and Apollo has killed the children of a parent who had incurred his displeasure. He is the κοῦρος god (cf. Latonae puerum, 37) and they are themselves pueri (31; cf. identification with Trojan pueri).

The dynamics of the address to Apollo remain difficult. It begins in conventional hymnal Relativstil (dive quem ..., 1). It evokes the terrible face of the divus, citing three of his mythical victims (Niobe, Tityos and Achilles). We might have expected further praise of Apollo to

---

[130] For such 'spontaneous' reactions to fearful elements in lyric narrative, cf. Schol. Pyth. 1.56a: "After recounting Typhos' punishment, as if affected by fear at the narrative, he prays for Zeus' favour"; Race (1990) 42.

[131] Might there be any relevance in the suggestion of H. Meyer Hymnische Stilelemente in der frühgriechischen Dichtung (Würzburg 1933) 24–32 associating προοίμιον and προφήτης, the latter in the sense 'speaking first'? Meyer took his thesis too far in suggesting that προοίμιον could actually mean 'oracular revelation' (29–30); but that does not necessarily invalidate the basic idea.

follow, perhaps naming him, and picking up the opening *dive*; and indeed line 5 (*ceteris maior, tibi miles impar*: hymnal *Du-Stil*) appears to offer this. But expectations (and syntax) are then dislocated by the continuing choric focus on Achilles. The chorus' reasons for addressing Apollo in the first place are left unexplained, as is the occasion and sacral context. Only at line 21 (*tuis*) is it clear that the chorus is still addressing Apollo; and only in 25–8 are the chorus' reasons for doing so vouchsafed, in the paeanic appeal (again with hymnal *Relativstil*: *qui*, 26). Double invocations in hymns are very much in Pindar's style.[132] But the hymnal structure of *Odes* 4.6.1–28, with its extended digression on Achilles, would nonetheless be hard to parallel.[133] What is Horace driving at?

Comprehensive answers to the problems posed by the Apollo/Achilles episode would probably require access to a greater part of the epic tradition than we now possess.[134] One clear theme is the underlying enmity of Apollo and Achilles, of the κοῦρος god for the κοῦρος mortal most akin to himself, related to Apollo's feud with Athena (cf. *Minervae*, 13) and Hera, and perhaps also to disputes as to whether Troy should fall by main force (i.e. to Achilles) or by deceit. Another feature is the chorus' identification with Troy and its ill-timed *choreia* on the eve of its destruction (15), perhaps a learned allusion to the tradition that the Trojans sang paeans as they pulled the horse through the city walls, and thus an implicit reflection on the civic dangers inherent in their own, saecular, paean.[135] This leads into choric identification with the children of Troy, whom Achilles would have butchered and immolated had he been allowed to live (17–20). The hypothetical scenario in the fifth stanza derives from the Pindaric Apollo's defence of Troy (πρὸ πόνων/ δέ κε μεγάλων Δαρδανίαν/ ἔπραθεν, εἰ μὴ φύλασσεν Ἀπόλλων [90–91]) but goes well beyond it in ascribing to Achilles a brutal desire for the total extirpation of Troy

---

[132] Race (1990) 91, 93, 100–101, 144–6.

[133] Pasquali (1920) 751 summarises with deceptive simplicity (and rearrangement): "Apollo che hai fatto sentire la tua potenza a Tityo e a Niobe, che hai salvato Troia nei suoi discendenti e hai colpito Achille, proteggi l'onore della musa di Orazio."

[134] See Nagy (1979) 59–65 for some stimulating suggestions in this context.

[135] Trojan paean: Suda *s.v.* ἐξάρχοντες (2.303.1 Adler): οἱ δὲ Τρῶες μετὰ θορύβου καὶ ἡδονῆς παιᾶνας ἐξάρχοντες. Celebratory paean preceding a reversal in the action: Rutherford (1993) 89–92. Ill-timed celebrations: Putnam (1986) 124, with n.16. Cf. Virg. *Aen.* 2.238–9: *pueri circum innuptaeque puellae/ sacra canunt funemque manu contingere gaudent* (intriguingly reminiscent of the rope used to unify the choruses of *virgines* in the performance of third century *carmina*: Liv. 27.37.14).

which in the *Iliad* is articulated by Agamemnon (6.57–60). It may be that the chorus is defending Apollo against any idea that, in killing Achilles and prolonging the Trojan war, he brought about greater suffering, for Pindar's πρὸ πόνων/ δέ κε μεγάλων (89–90) is conventionally interpreted as suggesting just such a prolongation of suffering.[136] But πρὸ πόνων ... μεγάλων is a controversial phrase, and it is just possible that Horace took it with ἔπραθεν as part of the hypothetical scenario, signifying the hardships which would have been meted out to the Trojans had Achilles captured the city (something like "he would have burned Troy, as a prelude to great hardships ..."). This would account for Horace's 'transfer' to Achilles of the Homeric Agamemnon's brutality; and the fifth stanza would be an interpretative use of Homer to explain a (supposed) Pindaric allusion. On either reading, the Roman chorus is evidently eager to put the best possible construction on Apollo's actions, and to remind him of his supposed defence of *pueri* at Troy. The persuasive implication is that he should be willing to preserve the *pueri* of modern Rome.

So might the 'Daunian' Horace, and his chorus, be thought guilty of presumptuous grandiloquence?[137] By way of 'response', Horace reassures the chorus (above, p.270) and directs its members away from fears about Apollo and the *ictus* of his bow. A comparable passage in the *CS* appeals thus (33–4): *condito mitis placidusque telo/ supplices audi pueros, Apollo.*[138] Horace directs the chorus towards a proper view of their status, obligations and relationship to the two deities they will be addressing in the *CS*. They must carry out instructions from the Apolline *vates* in a ritually correct manner (*rite*, 37, 38), thereby discharging their debt to the gods on behalf of their community. Apollo himself, we might infer, will still be a *magnae vindex linguae* (cf. 1), but in the positive sense of 'champion' of the choric *lingua*/γλῶσσα.[139]

---

[136] For this interpretation, Radt (1948) 146–7.

[137] The most sensitive commentator on (poet's) fears in 4.6 is Quinn: see esp. his note on 1–4.

[138] Tib. 2.5.105–14 presents a complex interplay of Apollo as archer god (105) / protector of poets (113) and Cupid as wounder of the love poet; Apollo is invoked in support of the plea to Nemesis *vati parce* (114). Cf. esp. Juv. 6.172–3 (a striking parallel): *parce, precor, Paean, et tu, dea, pone sagittas;/ nil pueri faciunt ...* (Amphion, of his/Niobe's children). Cf. Fraenkel (1957) 411 n.1.

[139] Cf. the first line of M. Tullius Laurea's epigram, probably inscribed at Cicero's villa at Puteoli (almost certainly pre-dating *Od.* 4.6): *Romanae vindex clarissime linguae.*

IX The Choric Setting

The identification of the occasion of *Odes* 4.6 is delayed until the final stanza. To the original audience, the saecular occasion will probably have come as no surprise; and indeed *Odes* 4.6 was not the first of Horace's Pindarising odes to identify its occasion at the end.[140] In adopting this mode of exposition, Horace may have been imitating Pindar himself (explicit reference to the Theoxenia is delayed until the end of the first strophe of the sixth paean [61]). A question which will have confronted ancient readers, as well as modern, is whether any further information on the occasion is vouchsafed in earlier stanzas. One influential approach, based on the choric instructions (35–40), would suggest that the ode presents a rehearsal of the *CS*.[141] The instructions are indeed a significant occasional marker, but not the only one; and as an approach to the dramatic relationship between 4.6 and *CS*, the 'rehearsal' scenario underplays another closure, that of the address to Apollo (25–8):

> doctor argutae fidicen Thaliae
> Phoebe, qui Xantho lavis amne crines,
> Dauniae defende decus Camenae,
>   levis Agyieu.

In the immediate context of the paeanic appeal, we might reasonably expect to encounter circumstances directly relevant to the content of that appeal. Three aspects of Apollo are presented: he is the lyre-playing *Mousagetes*, the Lycian god who bathes his hair in the Xanthus, and Apollo Agyieus. The first corresponds to Horace's role as χοροδιδάσκαλος, and thus leads the audience into the choric instructions articulated in the latter part of the ode. The second may also have a bearing on saecular ritual. The chorus is alluding to purificatory lustration, a prominent feature of Apolline cult tradition, particularly at Delphi where it is especially associated with Castalia, and is well

---

[140] In *Od.* 1.37, the identification of the occasion as the *triplex triumphus* of 28 is delayed until the final word (*triumpho*, 32): Hardie (1977) 132–4. Not identified as a closure device by D. Esser *Untersuchungen zu den Odenschlüssen bei Horaz* (Meisenheim am Glan 1976).

[141] The suggestion originated with Porphyrio: *adloquitur pueros puellasque, quos carmen docet saeculare*; but of course *docet* (Greek διδάσκει) need not relate directly to our 'rehearsal'. Page speaks of the "training of the chorus"; Quinn (on 29–40) suggests that the poet speaks to the chorus "as though at a rehearsal"; and the rehearsal scenario is critically reflected in Fraenkel's discussion (1957) 405–6.

reflected in Delphian paeans.[142] Of particular interest is the Pindaric reference to the Castalian fountain, before the choric procession to the temple of Apollo, in terms which imply that, like all participants in the Theoxenia, the boys have undergone lustration.[143] This forms part of the chorus' appeal for acceptance by 'Pytho'. At the *Ludi Saeculares*, we have no direct evidence for the lustration of a chorus before the performance of the *carmen saeculare*; but the *Acta* for AD 204 show that the imperial family underwent lustration by water just before ascending to the temple of Palatine Apollo to witness the performance of the *carmen*;[144] and ritual washing is a standard feature of ancient sacral practice, at Rome as well as in the Greek world.[145] We cannot be certain that the double chorus of AD 204 underwent ritual purification by water, but it may plausibly be hypothesised that it did, and that Horace's chorus was purified in the same way. If this is correct, then the seventh stanza will carry a closer relationship to saecular ritual than has been supposed: the praise of Apollo's lustration may be intended to demonstrate choric awareness of a ritual requirement, as well as to suggest (implicitly, just as in the sixth paean) the chorus' own lustration, and to render itself ritually pleasing and acceptable to Apollo.

Further evidence for ritual allusion may be found in the processional setting of the *CS*. In 17 BC, the *CS* was performed twice, on the Palatine and on the Capitol.[146] The *Acta* for AD 204 give additional information about a *pompa*, of which the saecular chorus was part, made between the two locations. It passed along the Sacra Via and through the Forum Romanum, evidently with the Roman *populus* thronging the way.[147] No such *pompa* is attested for 17 BC, but it can reasonably be assumed that the double chorus of 17 did process from

---

[142] Cf. *Od.* 3.4.61–2: *qui rore puro Castaliae lavit/ crinis solutos*; Stat. *Theb.* 1.697–8: ... *seu rore pudico/ Castaliae flavos amor est tibi mergere crinis*; Eur. *Phoen.* 221–5: Φοίβῳ λάτρις ἐγενόμαν./ ἔτι δὲ Κασταλίας ὕδωρ/ ἐπιμένει με, κόμας ἐμᾶς/ δεῦσαι παρθένιον χλιδάν,/ Φοιβείαισι λατρείαις; Schol. *ad loc.* See further Fairbanks (1900) 122 (on a Delphian paean which associates the *Delphides* with Apolline lustration); Aristonous *Paean* 41–4; Hardie (1996) 223–4.

[143] Hardie (1996) 219–20.

[144] Line 58 as given by Hülsen reads: *erat* (22)]*nt t*[(16) *a*]*quas in* [(26)]*nt aquas p*[(15)] *tunc aliis coronis sumptis in pronao aedis Apollinis adscenderunt ibique clar*[*issimi* .... Pighi's text records *q*]*uas*, and suggests *aqua sp*[as the letter division.

[145] G. Appel *De Romanorum precationibus* (Giessen 1909) 184–6; Parker (1983) 226–7. Cf. Virg. *Aen.* 6.229; Prop. 4.6.4, 7; Livy 5.22.4 for Roman youths chosen to transfer Juno from Veii to Rome: *pure lautis corporibus ... venerabundi templum iniere.*

[146] *CIL* 6.32323.147–8.

[147] Text of *Acta* in Pighi (1941) 140–75; *pompa* described in section Va.71–5.

the Palatine to the Capitol, and by the same route. The procession is highlighted in the Domitianic coinage marking the festival of AD 88.[148] One coin shows three boys processing in line (or possibly two boys, with a girl in the middle), each holding a book roll; they are followed by two togate priests, the first of whom (also holding a book roll) has been identified as Domitian. Support for this identification appears in the *Acta* for 204, which state that the emperor followed the chorus, bringing up the rear of the *pompa*. The chorus was on that occasion preceded by the *praesides* (guardians) of its individual members (above, p.277). Other constituent parts of that *pompa* included *togati*, *asinarii*, gladiators and racing chariots. The *pompa* itself was preceded by a separate *translatus* of *XVviri sacris faciundis, tibicines, fidicines* and *cornicines*.

Processional choric odes were a major feature of Greek religious observance, and indeed 'procession' could itself be regarded as a form of dance.[149] Processional paeans are well attested in different parts of the Greek world.[150] A choric paean could be sung while the chorus was either processing or in static mode (i.e. when the processing chorus paused at appropriate sacral locations).[151] The Roman *Carmen Saeculare* was of this latter type, involving two complete performances at temples which were linked by the *pompa*.[152]

The sixth paean refers to a procession from the fountain of Castalia (7–9) to the temple of Apollo, where the paean will have been performed (thus 13; 60). The opening strophe is in fact an appeal to 'Pytho' by the arriving poet and chorus for acceptance at the Theoxenia festival, and it is composed as a *komos*.[153] Now, there is no suggestion that choric movement forms part of the dramatic scenario at the opening of *Odes* 4.6. But there is a likely processional allusion, again in the seventh stanza, in *levis Agyieu* (smooth Agyieus). Apollo Agyieus was the god of the ἀγυιαί, the streets of the city, a title which was well understood at Rome (Macrobius 1.9.6: *idem Apollo apud illos* [sc. the Greeks] *et Ἀγυιεύς nuncupatur, quasi viis praepositus*

---

[148] Mattingly (1930) nos. 427, 428; Pighi (1941) 87; I.S. Ryberg *Rites of the State Religion in Roman Art* (Rome 1955) 176–7.

[149] Lonsdale (1993) 41.

[150] Käppel (1992) 55, 62, 82; Fairbanks (1900) 36, 53, 60; *RE* XXI.1915–17; Dougherty (1994) 214–17.

[151] While processing: *H. Apoll.* 514–19; during pauses at successive sacral sites: *SIG³* 57.28ff. (Miletus, 479/8 BC).

[152] *CS* as *Prozessionslied*: Mommsen (1905) 358; Schmidt (1985).

[153] For the sixth paean as *komos*, Cairns (1991) 70–77; Hardie (1996) 221, 229.

urbanis). As guardian of the streets, Agyieus would have been an appropriate addressee in connection with choric activity in the ἀγυιαί. This is suggested in an oracle cited by Demosthenes at *In Meidiam* 51–2, giving instructions "to set up winebowls and dances in the streets" (κατ᾽ ἀγυιὰς κρατῆρας ἱστάμεν καὶ χορούς ...) and prescribing sacrifices and prayers for good fortune to Apollo Agyieus, Leto and Artemis. The address at *Odes* 4.6.28 has a comparable context, namely choric activity κατ᾽ ἀγυιάς: the reference is to the public singing of the *CS* and to the *pompa* of the double chorus through the streets of Rome.

Another relevant dimension to the address to Apollo Agyieus is his iconographical associations in Augustan Rome. His symbol, the conical *betylos*, appears in coinage which has been convincingly linked with the naval victory at Actium.[154] And as Putnam has stressed in his extended discussion of *levis Agyieu*, the *betylos* featured on the Palatine, in the decoration of the 'Casa di Augusto', the 'Casa di Livia' and also in the temple of Apollo Palatinus itself, where it appears in a terracotta plaque, associated with the accoutrements of Apollo Citharoedus and Diana the huntress.[155] This contemporary iconography supplements the 'processional' reading offered above: *levis* (smooth) will refer to the smooth surface of the *betylos* itself, and thus to Agyieus' icon. There is no evidence that a *betylos* of Apollo Agyieus physically stood in the vicinity of the temple of Apollo; but the prominence of the device in Palatine iconography, and its 'Actian' symbolism, might suggest some association of Agyieus and his *betylos* with the Palatine temple. Picard-Schmitter's interesting suggestion that a spear leaning against the *betylos* in the 'Casa di Augusto' fresco is the spear of Augustus, connecting with the foundation of the Palatine temple on ground struck by lightning, might point in the same direction.[156]

The main cult statuary of the temple of Apollo Palatinus comprised Apollo Citharoedus (by Scopas), Artemis, probably holding a torch

---

[154] H. Küthmann 'Actiaca' *Jahrbuch des römisch-germanischen Zentralmuseums Mainz* 3 (1956) 73–80; Putnam (1986) 127.

[155] Temple of Apollo: G. Carettoni 'Terracotte 'Campana' dallo scavo del tempio di Apollo Palatino' *Rendiconti Pont. Acc. rom. Arch.* 44 (1971–72) 123–39, at 129–31; E. Simon 'Apollo in Rom' *Jahrb. d. deutschen arch. Inst.* 93 (1978) 202–27, at 219–20; Casa di Augusto: G. Carettoni 'Due nuovi ambienti dipinti sul Palatino' *Boll. d'Arte* 46 (1961) 189–99, at 194–6.

[156] M.-Th. Picard-Schmitter 'Bétyles hellénistiques' *MMAI* 57 (1971) 43–88, at 77–9; accepted by J. Gagé 'Apollon impérial, garant des 'fata romana' ' *ANRW* II.17.2 (1981) 561–630, at 567.

(Timotheos) and Leto (Cephisodotus).[157] The Apollo/Artemis/Leto trio represented "the earliest attested reuse of Classical Greek originals as cult statues in Rome", and was thus a striking statement of Augustan interest in classicising influence.[158] Horace's praise of Apollo, Diana (and Leto) in a classicising paean might be reckoned consistent with all this, as might the address to Apollo as *fidicen* (25), and the reference to Diana's *fax* (38); but it may be no more than that, since the trio was a near-universal feature in ancient art and cult. A more specific and persuasive link with the Palatine is the designation of Diana as *Noctiluca* (38), the title by which, according to Varro, she was known on that hill.[159]

Not everyone will be persuaded of the need to tie *Odes* 4.6 down to a particular location. Fraenkel set his face against attempts "to transplant the ode ... into some Roman hall or courtyard or temple in which something arbitrarily spun out of the poem might be enacted".[160] Yet Horace's closest known Greek model, the sixth paean, was performed at or near the temple of Apollo at Delphi; and another paean with which *Odes* 4.6 has features in common, Callimachus' second hymn, is explicitly located in front of the temple of Apollo at Cyrene. Temples of Apollo were, in fact, a regular, ritual setting for Greek cult paeans of which he was the principal addressee.[161] The topography of such temple settings might be reflected in the paeans themselves, helping to tie them to place and indeed occasion. The sixth paean supplies a good example. Arguably, then, *Odes* 4.6, *qua* paean, will itself have a temple setting for its performance (whether real or imaginary), for (again, arguably) this was the natural setting for a Pindarising paean addressed in the first place to Apollo. There may be some risk, in attempts to extrapolate circumstances of 'performance' in this way, of outstripping our limited knowledge of Horace's generic alignment with any given Pindaric εἶδος (§III), and indeed of making unwarranted assumptions about imagined topography in the case of odes which may not have received any public performance. But with *Odes* 4.6, its generic alignment, the ancient evidence for the location of paean performances, the

---

[157] On the Palatine statuary, and its probable reproduction in a relief in Sorrento, Gagé (1955) 532–4. With Artemis' torch, cf. also the torch-bearing *Luna* depicted on the cuirassed statue of Augustus: Zanker (1988) 191–2 (referring to 4.6.37–40).

[158] Zanker (1988) 240–41.

[159] Varro *LL* 5.68; Wissowa (1912) 316.

[160] Fraenkel (1957) 405.

[161] Käppel (1992) 61–2.

known location of the first *CS* performance, and topographical features
in the ode itself seem plausibly to converge on only one possible per-
formance location, the Palatine Temple of Apollo.

A more specific hypothesis about the setting of *Odes* 4.6 may now
be put forward. I would suggest that it represents the scene in the *pro-
naos* of the temple immediately before the performance and the
procession to the temple of Jupiter Optimus Maximus.[162] To young
chorus members contemplating these performances and the public
procession, some apprehension would be natural. After all, a more
public exposure for a *carmen*, its poet and its chorus could hardly be
imagined. It is for that reason that the chorus turns to Apollo Agyieus
to seek his protection beyond the confines of the Palatine temple, and
in the streets of Rome.

Just as Callimachus' second hymn evokes the preliminaries to the
appearance of Apollo from his temple at Cyrene and the 'hymn proper',
Odes 4.6 can be read as a prelude to the *CS* itself. But it presents the
preliminaries as seen from inside the temple of Apollo, and not from
outside. It presents, in dramatic terms, the emotionally charged
moments before the emergence of the chorus, and its performance of
the processional *carmen* which will secure the future of its city, and the
empire. We are to imagine, then, the *CS* following immediately after
completion of *Odes* 4.6, the one leading to the other. The notional
performing sequence as a whole would then be: (a) the choric hymn to
Apollo (1–28); (b) the poet's response, with choric instructions (29–
44); and (c) the *CS* (also in Sapphics). Here, Horace's imitative strategy
in choosing, as his primary model, a Pindaric paean which was itself
regarded as a composite work, may help in understanding the
progressive dynamics of a three-stage work.

Odes 4.6 has much to say about the context, staging and literary
antecedents of the *CS*. It tells us that Horace's approach to composing
his epochal poem was influenced by a sacral requirement to reach back
into Greek poetry for cult antecedents. In line with a prescription con-
veniently formulated in the Sibylline oracle, Horace found his ante-
cedent in the Greek paean. The sixth paean, among other attractive

---

[162] The *Acta* of AD 204 describe this scene in greater detail than do those of 17 BC (text
in Hülsen [1932] 392; Pighi [1941] 164–5 Va.58–60): *tunc aliis coronis sumptis in
pronao aedis Apollinis adscenderunt* [sc. Severus, Antoninus and Geta] *ibique
clar*[*issimi*] *pueri* [21 letter spaces *et*] *puellae* [8 qu]*ibus de*[*nuntiatum erat, pueri*]
praetex[*tati* 20 *puel*]*lae palliolatae cum discriminalibus, manibus contexis, ca*[*rm*]*en*
[16] *mpo* [9]/ [18] *ibus tibicinibus* [18 (the words of the *carmen* follow).

features, offered a sensitive balance between the Delphian Apollo and
(the visiting) Olympian Zeus.[163] For Horace, this will have served as a
helpful precedent for his own presentation of Palatine Apollo and
Capitoline Jupiter. The *CS* itself, despite its twin performance at the
temples of these two gods, plays up Apollo (and Diana) and plays
down the naming of Jupiter. In this, Horace was reflecting Augustus'
action in drawing Jupiter and Juno into the *Graecus ritus* of the re-
formed *Ludi Saeculares*, and into the religious ambience represented by
the new Apollo Palatinus.[164] In re-presenting the Pindaric opening in
the sixth stanza, Horace also demonstrates his awareness of the Pin-
daric balance between Apollo and Zeus; but he reshapes it into the
intercessionary relationship which we find both in the *CS* and in later
saecular poems.[165]

   Odes 4.6 may truly be said to operate at the interface of literature
and cult. Horace reflects the revolutionary, grecising innovations of
Augustan cult in a detailed re-modelling of a Greek predecessor. And
he invites his audience to see the *CS* as a Roman articulation of Greek
public *choreia*, an Augustan successor to the great festival paeans of
Pindar.[166]

Bibliography

Works referred to more than once in the notes are listed below (works
referred to once only are cited in full in the notes).

Barchiesi, A. (1995). 'Simonide e Orazio sulla morte di Achille' *ZPE* 107.33–8
— (1996). 'Poetry, praise, and patronage: Simonides in Book 4 of Horace's
    Odes' CA 15.5–47
Bundy, E.L. (1972). 'The "Quarrel between Kallimachos and Apollonios", Part
    I: the Epilogue of Kallimachos's *Hymn to Apollo' CSCA* 5.39–94
Cairns, F. (1971a). 'Five 'religious' odes of Horace' *AJP* 92.433–52
— (1979). *Tibullus: a Hellenistic Poet at Rome*. Cambridge

---

[163] Hardie (1996) 236–7, 245.
[164] Feeney (1998) 31, 33–5.
[165] Intercession: Hardie (1996a) 278–9.
[166] If P. Brind'Amour were correct in suggesting that the *saeculum* of 110 years repre-
    sents an attempt to connect the Roman festival with the pan-Ionian festival on Delos
    ('L'origine des jeux séculaires' *ANRW* 16.2 [1978] 1334–1417), additional light would
    be shed on the 'Delian' content of *Odes* 4.6 (i.e. *Deliae ... deae*, 33; and the possible
    echo of the Homeric hymn to Apollo at 40–44).

— (1986). 'Propertius and the Battle of Actium' in Woodman and West (edd.) (1986) 129–68

— (1991). 'Propertius 4.9: "*Hercules Exclusus*" and the dimensions of genre' in Galinsky (ed.) (1991) 65–95

D'Alessio, G.B. (1994). 'First-person problems in Pindar' *BICS* 39.117–39

Delarue, F., Georgacopoulou, S., Laurens, P., Taisne, A.-M. (edd.) (1996). *Epicedion: hommage à P. Papinius Statius 96–1996*. Poitiers

Dougherty, C. (1994). 'Pindar's second Paean: civic identity on parade' *CP* 89.205–18

Fairbanks, A. (1900). *A Study of the Greek Paean*. Cornell Studies in Classical Philology 12

Feeney, D. (1993). 'Horace and the Greek lyric poets' in Rudd (ed.) (1993) 41–63

— (1998). *Literature and Religion at Rome: Cultures, Contexts, and Beliefs.* Cambridge

Fraenkel, E. (1957). *Horace*. Oxford

Gagé, J. (1955). *Apollon romain*. Paris

Galinsky, K. (ed.) (1991). *The Interpretation of Roman Poetry: Empiricism or Hermeneutics?* Studien zur klassischen Philologie 67

Gruen, E.S. (1990). *Studies in Greek Culture and Roman Policy*. Berkeley, Los Angeles and London

Hardie, A. (1977). 'Horace *Odes* 1,37 and Pindar, *Dithyrambs* 2' *PLLS* 1.113–40

— (1996). 'Pindar, Castalia and the Muses of Delphi (the Sixth Paean)' *PLLS* 9.219–57

— (1996a). 'Statius and the *Carmen Saeculare* of 88' in Delarue, Georgacopoulou, Laurens, Taisne (edd.) (1996) 261–82

Harrison, S.J. (ed.) (1995). *Homage to Horace: a Bimillenary Celebration.* Oxford

Harvey, A.E. (1955). 'The classification of Greek lyric poetry' *CQ* n.s. 5.157–75

Heath, M. and Lefkowitz, M.R. (1991) 'Epinician performance' *CP* 86.173–91

Hülsen, Ch. (1932). 'Neue Fragmente der Acta Ludorum Saecularium von 204 nach Chr.' *Rh.M.* 81.366–94

Käppel, L. (1992). *Paian: Studien zur Geschichte einer Gattung, Untersuchungun zur antiken Literatur und Geschichte* 37. Berlin and New York

Lane Fox, R. (1986). *Pagans and Christians*. Harmondsworth

Lefkowitz, M.R. (1963). 'The first person in Pindar' *HSCP* 67.177–253

— (1991). *First-person Fictions: Pindar's Poetic 'I'*. Oxford

— (1995). 'The first person in Pindar reconsidered — again' *BICS* 40.139–50

Lonsdale, S.H. (1993). *Dance and Ritual Play in Greek Religion*. Baltimore and London

MacBain, B. (1982). *Prodigy and Expiation: a Study in Religion and Politics in Republican Rome*. Brussels

Maltby, R. (1991). *A Lexicon of Ancient Latin Etymologies* (ARCA 25). Leeds

Mommsen, T. (1905). 'Die Akten zu dem Säkulargedicht des Horaz' reprinted in *Reden und Aufsätze* (Berlin) 351–9

Mullen, W. (1982). *Choreia: Pindar and Dance*. Princeton

Nagy, G. (1979). *The Best of the Achaeans: Concepts of the Hero in Archaic Greek Poetry*. Baltimore

Parker, R. (1983). *Miasma*. Oxford

Pasquali, G. (1920). *Orazio lirico*. Florence

Pighi, G.B. (1941). *De ludis saecularibus populi romani Quiritium libri sex*. Milan

Putnam, M.J.C. (1986). *Artifices of Eternity*. Cornell

Race, W.H. (1990). *Style and Rhetoric in Pindar's Odes*. Atlanta

Radt, S.L. (1958). *Pindars zweiter und sechster Paian: Text, Scholien und Kommentar*. Amsterdam

Rudd, N. (ed.) (1993). *Horace 2000: a Celebration*. London

Rutherford, I.C. (1988). 'Pindar on the birth of Apollo' *CQ* 38.65–75

— (1991). 'Neoptolemos and the paean-cry: an echo of a sacred aetiology in Pindar' *ZPE* 88.1–7

— (1993). 'Paeanic ambiguity: a study of the representation of the παιάν in Greek literature' *QUCC* n.s. 44.77–92

— (1995).'*Et hominum et deorum ... laudes* (?): a hypothesis about the organisation of Pindar's *Paean*-book' *ZPE* 107.44–52

— (1997). '*For the Aeginetans to Aiakos a Prosodion*: an unnoticed title at Pindar, Paean 6,123, and its significance for the poem' *ZPE* 118.1–21

Schmidt, P.L. (1985). 'Horaz' Säkulargedicht — ein Prozessionslied?' *AU* 18.4.42–53

Slater, W.J. (1969). 'Futures in Pindar' *CQ* n.s. 19.86–94

Syndikus, H.P. (1973). *Die Lyrik des Horaz* Vol. II. Darmstadt

Wilamowitz-Moellendorff, U. von (1922). *Pindaros*. Berlin

Wimmel, W. (1987). 'Zum Problem doppelsinniger Formulierung beim späten Horaz' *Glotta* 65.241–50

Wissowa, G. (1912). *Religion und Kultus der Römer*[2] (repr. Munich, 1971)

Woodman, T. and West, D. (edd.) (1986). *Poetry and Politics in the Age of Augustus*. Cambridge

Zanker, P. (1988). *The Power of Images in the Age of Augustus*, tr. A. Shapiro. Ann Arbor

PAPERS OF THE LEEDS INTERNATIONAL LATIN SEMINAR   TENTH VOLUME (1998) 295–312
Published by Francis Cairns (Publications) Ltd (Leeds 1998). ARCA 38. ISBN 0 905205 95 2

MERETRIX OR MATRONA?
Stereotypes in Ovid *Ars Amatoria* 3

R.K. GIBSON
University of Manchester

The social status of the women of Ovid's *Ars Amatoria* is a notorious issue. This paper will argue that the standard views of it need revision. Usually the debate has been conducted with and around the binary opposition of *meretrix* and *matrona*. I hope to show that this simple opposition cannot deal with the complexities of the text of *Ars* 3.

Ovid, as is well known, insists that the recipients of his erotic instruction in *Ars* 3 are unmarried freedwomen.[1] For, according to the *lex Iulia de adulteriis*, married women (whether freeborn or of freed status), concubines, widows, divorcees and freeborn virgins, if found guilty of illicit sexual relations, could be punished with exile, confiscation of property and, in certain circumstances, death.[2] There appear to have been no comparable restrictions, however, on the sexual relations of unmarried freedwomen.[3] Nevertheless, a good proportion of the subject-matter of *Ars* 3 would be of use to any woman — whether aristocratic matron or former slave — for example the advice on sending secret love letters (485–98) and the passage on how to give a *custos* the slip (619–58).[4] Furthermore, Ovid does appear to hint that his lessons in seduction in fact apply to all Roman women. At 483–4

---

[1] Most explicitly at *Ars* 3.611–16. Cf. also 3.57–8, 483; 1.31–4; 2.599–600; *Rem.* 361–90.

[2] On the *lex Iulia*, see most recently Treggiari (1991) 275–98, Edwards (1993) 37–42.

[3] See Veyne (1988) 69–70 with 216 n.8, 77–80 with 221 n.51 and Stroh (1979) 325–6, *contra* Little (1982) 319, 330. Relations between men and low-class dancers and actresses, bar-maids, waitresses and innkeepers, although these women may have been of freeborn or freed status, were also not necessarily subject to the law on adultery; see Evans (1991) 133–6.

[4] For similar passages in the earlier books of the *Ars*, see Sharrock (1994) on the myth of Mars and Venus (2.535–603).

Ovid prefaces his instructions on sending secret messages to a lover
with the words *sed quoniam, quamvis vittae careatis honore,/ est vobis
vestros fallere cura viros* (But since, although you are without the
honour of the fillet, it is your care to deceive your *viri*). In a recent
article, J.F. Miller writes of this couplet, "it is clearly implied that
married women and meretricious freedwomen share a desire to cheat
their male keepers, and thus, that Ovid's instructions to the courtesans
are valid also for Roman matrons".[5] Later Miller widens this inter-
pretation of the couplet into a general principle for reading *Ars* 3, "...
the female mannequins that Ovid has assembled for the course ... are
wearing masks no less than is Ovid himself. At certain points the de-
signed slippage in [Ovid's] own persona, the revelation of a playful
smile behind the mask of morally scrupulous *praeceptor*, amounts to an
unmasking of his avowed addressees, to the application of the lessons
in seduction to all Roman women".[6]

Miller's reading of *Ars* 3 is no doubt representative of the views of
many,[7] and it appears inherently plausible. Ovid, it could be argued,
would hardly have added his disclaimers had he not been conscious of
passages, such as those on the *custos* and secret communication above,
which were valid in some sense for both *meretrix* and *matrona*. And
the disclaimers, so it might be said, far from resolving the issue of in-
tended audience, only serve to draw attention to it. Hence, any reader
familiar with the spirit of Ovid's earlier poems, the *Amores*, must con-
tinually be suspecting that *matronae* are Ovid's 'real' audience. But
(and it is the purpose of this paper to draw attention to this fact) power-
ful complications lie in wait for those prepared to read in such a
straightforward manner. In a good many passages the stereotypes
implicit in Ovid's advice make difficulties for those ready to see the
matrona behind the *meretrix*.

Ars 3.749–68

In lines 749–68 the *praeceptor* tackles the subject of dinner-parties.
Here the ignorance of Ovid's addressees on how to behave is said to
make them quite dependent on his guidance (749–50). This is a signi-
ficant point to which we shall return later. The first piece of advice
given to them is that they should arrive late, because "delay is a great
procuress" (751–2), and because by then it will be dark and the men

---

[5]   Miller (1993) 235.
[6]   Miller (1993) 235–6.
[7]   See e.g. Otis (1970) 20; Rudd (1976) 3–4; Little (1982) 330–1.

will be drunk. This will be of decided advantage to the ugly among Ovid's pupils, *etsi turpis eris, formosa videbere potis,/ et latebras vitiis nox dabit ipsa tuis* (753–4). Following their arrival, Ovid moves on to the subject of food. He emphasises that his addressees are to use the tips of their fingers to lift food, rather than their whole hands, for fear of besmearing their faces with grease, *carpe cibos digitis (est quiddam gestus edendi),/ ora nec immunda tota perungue manu* (755–6). If, in order to avoid the appearance of an appetite at dinner, Ovid's addressees are tempted to eat at home beforehand, they should not do so, but rather exercise self-restraint at the dinner itself and stop before they are sated, *neve domi praesume dapes, sed desine citra/ quam capis: es paulo, quam potes esse, minus* (757–8). Presumably it would be an insult to the hospitality of the host to eat beforehand and have nothing at dinner. It is important, so Ovid says, to have a sparing appetite, as greed repels men (759–60). After food, Ovid moves on to drink (and sex). Again his addressees must exercise control over their appetites:

> hoc quoque, qua patiens caput est animusque pedesque
> constant nec, quae sunt singula, bina vides.
> turpe iacens mulier multo madefacta Lyaeo:
> digna est concubitus quoslibet illa pati.
> nec somnis posita tutum succumbere mensa:
> per somnos fieri multa pudenda solent.   (763–8)

A drunken woman is a repulsive sight, and, according to Ovid, if men use her sexually in any way they wish, that is only what she deserves.

Ovid's advice about behaviour at dinner parties has some quite specific social resonances. The subject of instruction, the *cena*, is frequently the focus of concern about 'taste' and social status in Roman literature.[8] More specifically, bad table manners are a standard part of the stereotype of low-status women.[9] In, for example, a memorable Eubulan fragment (41 K–A = Athenaeus 13.571f), the speaker describes the behaviour of the heroine of the play at a banquet. Here her superior social graces mark her out from her fellow ἑταῖραι.[10] Thus behind Ovid's advice on how to eat properly lies the concern that his pupils should not appear vulgar. As for drink, common prostitutes are

---

[8] See (e.g.) Shero (1923), Hudson (1989).
[9] Cf. e.g. Ter. *Eun.* 935–40 (of *meretrices*); Lucian *Dial. Meretr.*6.3 (of ἑταῖραι), also (of low-born men) *Merc. Cond.* 15.
[10] ὡς δ᾽ ἐδείπνει κοσμίως,/ οὐχ ὥσπερ ἄλλαι τῶν πράσων ποιούμεναι/ τολύπας ἔσαττον τὰς γνάθους καὶ τῶν κρεῶν/ ἀπέβρυκον αἰσχρῶς, ἀλλ᾽ ἑκάστου μικρὸν ἄν/ ἀπεγεύεθ᾽ ὥσπερ παρθένος Μιλησία.

frequently stereotyped as drunken.[11] Of special significance here is the
hint at 765–6 that, if a woman does become inebriated, then she de-
serves whatever sexual treatment she gets. Such treatment may be con-
doned or justified by the elite where low-status women are involved,[12]
or even, by a circular reasoning, taken as proof that the female victim is
a prostitute. The speaker at [Demosthenes] 59.33 alleges it as evidence
of Neaera's status as an ἑταίρα rather than a citizen that, while she was
drunk at a party and her lover was asleep, a succession of men in-
cluding the host's slaves had sex with her.[13] Thus Ovid is threatening
his addressees with the consequences of behaving in a manner con-
ventionally associated with low-status women such as prostitutes.

Who are we to envisage as Ovid's addressees in this passage? Be-
fore this question can be answered, some general characteristics of
ancient didactic must be reviewed. First, although didactic in fact often
tells readers what they already know (e.g. Epicureans reading Lu-
cretius' *De Rerum Natura*), in the present context Ovid's female ad-
dressees are represented as ignorant readers — explicitly and pro-
minently so at the beginning of the passage, *sollicite expectas, dum te
in convivia ducam,/ et quaeris monitus hac quoque parte meos* (749–
50). The *Ars* of course is not alone among didactic texts in this ploy of
constructing for itself an audience which is ignorant and in urgent need
of enlightenment;[14] and the particular implication of the pupils'
ignorance here is that they need to be taught how not to act in a vulgar
manner. Cicero's *De Officiis* (a text which has been convincingly
shown to be of some significance for understanding the *Ars*) deals with
vulgar behaviour in a notably contrasting way.[15] Cicero never implies
that his readers need to be taught how to avoid acting in such a manner.

---

[11] Cf. e.g. Men. *Sam.* 390ff.; Plaut. *Truc.* 854–5; Prop. 4.8.29–32; Lucian *Dial. Meretr.*
6.3; also the alcoholic *lenae* of *Am.*1.8 and Prop.4.5. Conversely hard-drinking women
of respectable status are depicted as behaving like prostitutes; cf. e.g. Hor. *Carm.*
3.6.25–32; Tib. 1.9.59–64; Sen. *Epist.* 95.21; Juv. 6.300–305.

[12] Cf. e.g. Cicero's defence of his client's alleged involvement in a gang-rape of a mime
actress in a provincial town on the grounds that it was *factum a iuventute vetere
quodam in scaenicos iure maximeque oppidano* (*Planc.* 30).

[13] καὶ ἐκεῖ ἄλλοι τε πολλοὶ συνεγίγνοντο αὐτῇ μεθυούσῃ καθεύδοντος τοῦ
Φρυνίωνος, καὶ οἱ διάκονοι οἱ Χαβρίου. Cf. also Prop. 4.8.32 (of the prostitute Teia)
candida, sed potae non satis unus erit; 3.11.30 (of Cleopatra, the *meretrix regina*)
famulos inter femina trita suos.

[14] Cf. e.g. Lucr. 1.112–16; 2.14–19; Verg. *Georg.* 1.40–2; Ov. *Ars* 1.1 (with Hollis'
note); 2.9–12, 161–6; 3.41–52, 251–60; *Rem.* 41–4. On the varying treatments of the
addressee in didactic poetry, see the articles in Schiesaro, Mitsis and Strauss Clay
(1993). In Greek didactic, Hesiod and Empedocles are conspicuous for the intensity
and consistency with which they portray their pupils' need of their advice.

[15] See Labate (1984) 121–74.

Nor does he declare or assume his readers to be ignorant and in urgent need of enlightenment. Rather Cicero deals with the question of vulgar versus sophisticated behaviour as a matter of values shared between author and reader, which Cicero is conveniently restating and re-affirming. Whereas Ovid addresses his instructions squarely at his female audience through the use of the imperative, Cicero avoids directly addressing his readers by using passive directive expressions such as the gerundive. Cf. e.g. *De Officiis* 1.130 (on personal appearance):

> formae autem dignitas coloris bonitate *tuenda est*, color exercitationibus corporis. *Adhibenda* praeterea munditia est non odiosa neque exquisita nimis, tantum quae fugiat agrestem et inhumanam neglegentiam. Eadem ratio est *habenda* vestitus, in quo, sicut in plerisque rebus, mediocritas optima est.

The gerundives here are used to express the necessity or desirability of an action in a particular way, i.e. there is no *tibi* or *vobis* to make it clear that it is the readers who are required to act in a certain way or conform to a certain standard. The gerundives simply express the fact that, under certain circumstances, certain behaviour is desirable or strongly preferable.[16] In English we might translate the gerundives as 'one should'. Cicero's gerundives thus allow his readers to conclude that such values are simply being restated. By contrast the imperative form characteristic of the *Ars* and of other didactic verse texts allows little space or choice to their readers. Readers are under relative pressure here to identify themselves as the target of the directive. And being the target of a directive which directly states 'do XYZ' rather than 'one should ...', carries the implication that the target is in need of being taught what it is being told.

Further evidence that Ovid is targeting his readers in a highly directive manner in the *Ars* comes from a further contrast between his preferred imperatival expressions and those found in the closely related genre of didactic or technical literature in prose. These prose texts are often characterised by their liking for passive and other forms of directive expression which avoid the direct address of the reader.[17] The

---

[16] See further Gibson (forthcoming), where I survey all the major types of directive expression found in Latin didactic verse and prose.

[17] See Gibson (forthcoming), where it is argued that in general didactic prose displays a preference for passive, impersonal and other forms which avoid the direct address of the reader, such as the gerundive, and impersonal and third person indicative verbs. By contrast didactic verse texts prefer active forms (such as the imperative and third person subjunctive active) which allow the reader to be addressed more directly.

third person passive indicative, again characteristically used without an accompanying *tibi* or *vobis*, is frequently found. If the passage from *Ars* 3 under discussion were written in this idiom characteristic of didactic prose, the imperative phrases would be rendered as follows:

Ars 3	'Prose'
carpe cibos	*cibi carpuntur*
ora nec ... perungue	*ora nec perunguntur*
neve praesume dapes	*nec praesumuntur dapes*

The passive forms give the impression of listing a simple catalogue of vulgar faults which are normally avoided on social occasions. The reader remains relatively uninvolved and unimplicated. By contrast the active and direct imperative mode appears to imply that the addressee needs to be informed of what they are being told. Ovid's female addressees might, then, act in a vulgar manner unless taught otherwise. What does this tell us about these addressees? And how does what it tells us cohere with the theory that we should read *Ars* 3 with the suspicion that when Ovid says '*meretrix*' he really means '*matrona*'? On such a reading we shall expect to find our pleasure as readers in the discrepancy between appearance and reality. We would collude, apparently with Ovid, in the knowledge that while on the surface *meretrices* are being addressed, in reality the pupils are *matronae*. However a passage such as the one above on the *cena* must challenge such expectations. Here Ovid implies that his addressees need to be taught how to avoid vulgar behaviour. Can he mean *matronae* here? Of course, the idea that well-brought-up young ladies never need advice on, for example, bad table manners would surprise their mothers through the ages.[18] Such vulgarity is part of the social comedy of many novels. But the *Ars Amatoria* is not a novel laying before its readers a comic scene in which a character, someone other than the reader, must learn to eschew vulgar behaviour. Rather Ovid addresses his female readers frankly and directly, and through this direct address he tells his female readers that they are capable of acting in a vulgar manner. If we are ready with the assumption that *matronae* are Ovid's 'real' addressees, then we find something unexpected happening, i.e. the text is creating humour at the expense of the 'real' addressees. This finding conflicts with a consequence of that assumption; namely that the text is supposed to give readers the more straightforward pleasure of being

---

[18] *Matrona* technically refers to any woman who is married, whether freeborn or not. But the stereotype covers only those of freeborn status, as only the latter were 'really' *matronae*. See Veyne (1988) 74–5.

party to the knowledge who the 'real' audience is. Now the text appears to be turning on its supposed 'real' audience. The difficulties created by taking the 'real' audience as *matronae* inevitably raises the opposite possibility. Should we take Ovid at his word and believe him when he says that his addressees are freedwomen? After all, the dominant stereotype of the low-born woman suggests it was she rather than the elite woman who needed to be told how to avoid acting in vulgar ways. The correlative stereotype held that refined manners and ways were innate in the high-born. From this latter stereotype derives the common plot of the well-born young, deserted in youth and sold into slavery, only to be rediscovered years later — a moment often foreshadowed by their uncommon refinement and beauty.[19] The result is that Ovid's *Ars* is a piece of social comedy directed now at the low-born rather than at the daughters of the elite. Furthermore, readers sensitive to the literary ancestry of Ovid's advice on how to behave at a dinner-party might in fact find themselves encouraged to take this alternative of envisaging his addressees as 'really' freedwomen. For Ovid's source probably featured the instruction of a low-status woman on how to behave elegantly in the company of the well-to-do. The sixth of Lucian's *Dialogi Meretricii* depicts an impoverished mother, forced to turn her daughter over to prostitution, telling the daughter how to become a successful courtesan. The daughter, Corinna, is not to act at a dinner party in the manner which comes naturally to her, but is rather to conduct herself as if she were the social equal of her wealthy lovers (6.3). The close parallels with Ovid's advice on bad table manners in *Ars* 3 have been often taken to suggest a common source in New Comedy.[20] In addition it is noteworthy that Ovid's advice in *Ars* 3 finds no parallel in the first two books of the *Ars*. There the *praeceptor* concentrates on wine (1.229–

---

[19] The excellent table manners of the girl in Eubulus fr. 41 K–A (see above) probably foreshadow her discovery as a freeborn citizen. See Hunter's commentary *ad loc.* (= Hunter fr. 42).

[20] [Mother] ἢν δέ ποτε καὶ ἀπέλθῃ ἐπὶ δεῖπνον λαβοῦσα μίσθωμα, οὔτε μεθύσκεται — καταγέλαστον γὰρ καὶ μισοῦσιν οἱ ἄνδρες τὰς τοιαύτας — οὔτε ὑπερεμφορεῖται τοῦ ὄψου ἀπειροκάλως, ἀλλὰ προσάπτεται μὲν ἄκροις τοῖς δακτύλοις, σιωπῇ δὲ τὰς ἐνθέσεις οὐκ ἐπ' ἀμφοτέρας παραβύεται τὰς γνάθους, πίνει δὲ ἠρέμα, οὐ χανδόν, ἀλλ' ἀναπαυομένη ... καὶ ἐπειδὰν κοιμᾶσθαι δέῃ, ἀσελγὲς <οὐδὲν> οὐδὲ ἀμελὲς ἐκείνη ἄν τι ἐργάσαιτο. For the closeness of the parallel, and the likely common source in New Comedy, see Day (1938) 94. More exotic sources, such as the 'pornographer' Philaenis, have been suggested; see Cataudella (1974).

52, 565–602) — not on table manners.[21] This concentration is in accordance with the general practice of elegy which, like lyric, seems to have found the mention of food, but not wine, inappropriate to the genre.[22] This may be significant. For while no developed picture of the *iuvenes* emerges from the first two books of the *Ars*, the addressees are consistently treated in accordance with the stereotype of the young and penniless sons of the elite.[23] Can the factor which 'forces' the *praeceptor* to ignore the proprieties of the genre in *Ars* 3 be his 'awareness' that his low-born pupils need to be taught how to eat in company?

It is, then, possible for the reader to take Ovid at his word and envisage his addressees as low-status women such as former slaves. But such a route might perhaps seem naive, especially in view of the spirit of the earlier *Amores* and the way that Ovid's disclaimers serve to draw attention to issues of status rather than to resolve them. However it is at least a little unexpected in *Ars* 3 to find the text supposedly creating humour at the expense of the assumed 'real' addressees (the *matronae*) when we have been encouraged to look forward to the more straightforward pleasure of being party to the knowledge who the 'real' audience was. *Matronae* may be imagined by readers to enjoy the collusive knowledge that the instructions on how to give a *custos* the slip at 619–58 are equally valid for them. But few modern readers will have expected to watch them being taught, as the 'real' addressees, the lessons of a passage such as *Ars* 3.749–68, where their ignorance of how to behave at dinner-parties is advertised to the world; where the ugly among them are told to arrive late in order to take advantage of the failing light and the drunkenness of the men; where they are given firm

---

[21] For men criticised for their table manners by their social 'superiors', cf. Lucian *Merc. Cond.* 15.

[22] See Griffin (1985) 82–3, Gowers (1993) 22–3. Mention of food is associated with genres such as comedy and satire.

[23] The *praeceptor* (e.g.) flatteringly recommends at 1.459–68 that his pupils should learn oratory not solely in order to defend clients in court or to address the senate, but also to impress their beloveds. Cf. also the flattering use of *ingenuus* at 2.121, 216, 530, where the meaning is not just 'freeborn' but 'gentleman(ly)'. Note in this connection the differences between the passages on drink in *Ars* 3 (see above) and 1.589–602. In the former, as noted, Ovid warns against heavy drinking by threatening his pupils with the consequences of being seen to behave in a manner stereotypically associated with common prostitutes. But in *Ars* 1 the advice to men against heavy drinking suggests the standards of the aristocratic symposium, and the tradition of sympotic literature on the pleasures of a moderate intake and the danger of violence generated by excessive drinking (for which see Hunter on Eubulus fr. 94). It was socially acceptable for men to be drunk in the right context, and the warning against violence suggests (perhaps again flatteringly) the stereotype of the hot-headed young sons of the elite. Such flattery is conspicuously absent from the *Ars* 3 passage.

advice on how not and where not to eat; and where they are frankly told to drink in moderation or to face the inebriated prostitute's lot of drunken rape and worse.

Ars 3.469–84

Before speculating any further on what is going on in *Ars* 3, we ought first perhaps to broaden our view and look at some more passages. At 469–78, Ovid gives the *puellae* advice on receiving and replying to a lover's letter. Readers may view themselves as enjoying 'collusion' with Ovid in these lines. Advice not to reply immediately to a lover's letter and not to give the lover a definite 'yes' or 'no', although ostensibly intended for freedwomen alone, may be thought useful advice for any female reader of the *Ars*. The following lines, in which the *praeceptor* prescribes the appropriate style for a love letter, call this interpretation into question:

> munda sed e medio consuetaque verba, puellae,
>   scribite: sermonis publica forma placet.
> a, quotiens dubius scriptis exarsit amator
>   et nocuit formae barbara lingua bonae! (479–82)

For whom is the advice on *barbara lingua* (482) intended? Any female reader? The reference is to what the grammarians called '*barbarismus*'. Quintilian gives a list of examples which includes the use of foreign words, the omission, addition and transposition of letters and syllables, and mistakes in number and gender.[24] Such errors are, according to the stereotype, typical of the poorly educated and low-born.[25] Are we as readers to imagine *matronae* as the 'real' addressees here, in the same way that we may have been happy to imagine them as the 'real' addressees in the immediately preceding lines on receiving and replying to a love letter (469–78)? According to another stereotype elite women are conventionally thought to favour 'correct' forms, and are often praised as guardians of the 'purity' of the Latin language.[26] But here we appear to find Ovid covertly warning them about turning potential lovers away with their 'bad' Latin. Is the text again making fun of the 'real' addressees? Is it covertly mocking them for their

---

[24] For the term *barbarismus*, cf. e.g. *Rhet. Her.* 4.12.17 and see *TLL* 2.1734.3ff. Quintilian gives us his list at *Inst.* 1.5.5–17. Ovid returns to the subject at *Rem.* 335 *barbara sermone est, fac tecum multa loquatur.*

[25] For the speech of the freedmen and freedwomen in Petronius, see most recently Boyce (1991). For a real-life example of 'bad Latin' from the wax writing tablets, found near Pompeii, of the businessman C. Novius Eunus, a former slave, see Adams (1990).

[26] See Gilleland (1980) 180–1, Adams (1984) 43, 44.

similarity to their low-status counterparts — when we expected the
covertness merely to consist in a collusion by the readers in the know-
ledge of who the real audience is?

It could be objected here that Ovid is not so much saying "you write
bad Latin; stop it", as "do not write bad Latin". But a contrast with a
parallel passage in the first book of the *Ars* is revealing. At 1.459–62
the *praeceptor* tells his pupils to learn rhetoric not only to defend *trepi-
dos ... reos* (460). For a girl will be won over by the lover's rhetoric
quite as much as *populus iudexque gravis lectusque senatus* (461). This
flatters the pretensions of the male addressees by way of prefacing
some advice on the appropriate style of a love-letter:

> sed lateant vires, nec sis in fronte disertus;
>   effugiant voces verba molesta tuae.
> quis nisi mentis inops tenerae declamat amicae?
>   saepe valens odii littera causa fuit.
> sit tibi credibilis sermo consuetaque verba,
>   blanda tamen, praesens ut videare loqui.   (1.463–8)

Here young men are warned about the error to which their background
and education are assumed to make them prone, namely cultivation of
an overwrought style. They must aim for the plain style (*lateant vires,
credibilis sermo, consuetaque verba*). The implication of this passage
for *Ars* 3's advice on letter writing is that the female addressees too are
being warned about an error to which they are assumed to be prone.
They too must aim for the plain style (*munda sed e medio consuetaque
verba*). But the typical error against which the *puellae* must guard is
not a bombastic style learned in the schools of rhetoric, but simply
'bad' Latin typified by *barbarismus*. Are we as readers being invited to
imagine *matronae* as the recipients of this advice? Or are we again to
take Ovid at his word and imagine that he is addressing *meretrices*?
Ovid could be interpreted as going out of his way to include *matronae*,
since the very next couplet is the one in which Miller and others have
detected the inclusion of both married women and meretricious freed-
women, *sed quoniam, quamvis vittae careatis honore,/ est vobis vestros
fallere cura viros* (483–4).[27] In context, however, this couplet now
looks not so much a license to read *Ars* 3 as covertly addressed to *ma-
tronae*, but rather the explicit formulation of a problem for the reader.
According to the available stereotypes, Ovid's advice is appropriate to
the lowborn (such as the freedmen and women of Petronius' *Cena*),
rather than to *matronae*. If it is the case that the *praeceptor* is signalling

---

[27] Miller (1993) 235.

covertly that his instructions are appropriate (also) to *matronae*, we are then forced to ask whether this includes the advice on bad Latin (in which case the passage becomes a piece of social comedy for readers at the expense of *matronae*). Or are we to imagine *matronae* listening to the advice on corresponding with a lover but suddenly ignoring that on bad Latin? It may be suggested that these powerful complications ought to create a serious unease about the straightforward acceptance of *matronae* as Ovid's real addressees.

Ars 3.529–76

Further complications are thrown up by Ovid's attempt to persuade his pupils to adopt the protocols of *amicitia* rather than to ask for money and presents:

> vos quoque, de nobis quem quisque erit aptus ad usum,
>   inspicite et certo ponite quemque loco.
> munera det dives; ius qui profitebitur, adsit;
>   facundus causam nempe clientis agat.
> carmina qui facimus, mittamus carmina tantum:
>   hic chorus ante alios aptus amare sumus.
> nos facimus placitae late praeconia formae:
>   nomen habet Nemesis, Cynthia nomen habet,
> Vesper et Eoae novere Lycorida terrae,
>   et multi, quae sit nostra Corinna, rogant.   (3.529–38)

In this passage Ovid is telling women how to benefit materially from their lovers. They should accept the services which each lover is best suited to offer. These are given, it is understood, in return for the favours of the *puellae*. Here Ovid is alluding to a set of protocols which would have been instantly recognisable to his audience — namely those of *amicitia* and of the reciprocal exchange of 'services' which they involve.[28] But by the end of the passage Ovid has given up trying to persuade his pupils to adopt these protocols, and he advises only that they be circumspect in their rapacity for fear of scaring off their lovers, *dissimulate tamen, nec prima fronte rapaces/ este: novus viso casse resistet amans* (553–4). The reason is that Ovid is 'forced' to face the fact that all his pupils really want is money, *a doctis pretium scelus est sperare poetis;/ me miserum! scelus hoc nulla puella timet* (551–2). Such rapacity is the stereotypical trait of the greedy *meretrix*.[29] Ovid by implication demands that his readers should see that this is what his

---

[28] See Gibson (1995) 64–6.
[29] For this stereotype, see Nisbet–Hubbard on Hor. *Od.* 2.4.19.

female pupils are — *meretrices*.[30] Underneath the mask of the *meretrix* lies, that is, the *meretrix*. It could be argued that, in context, the implication has less to do with actual social status than with the poet's attempt to bully his addressees by allusion to the stereotype, as elegists often accuse their mistresses of being *meretrices* in order to gain rhetorical advantage over them. That is to say, the implication that Ovid's pupils are *meretrices* is designed to encourage them to accept poetry instead of asking for presents and money. However it is notable that Ovid continues at 553–4 (quoted above) with the assumption that his pupils are '*meretrices*'. But this is not so obviously part of his bullying rhetoric: rather he appears to have accepted that this is what his pupils are. The stereotype of the *meretrix* then shapes the advice which Ovid subsequently gives on how to attract various types of lover without scaring them off (555–76). But the stereotype itself is not the centre of attention.

What are the implications of all this for the addressees of 529–76? Whether we assume the addressees to be freedwomen or women of the elite, a sharp social humour is the result. The categories of 'freedwoman' and 'prostitute' were often implied to overlap; the social origins of the former slave, so the elite liked to think, made the freedwoman a stranger to morals.[31] If we take Ovid at his word, that his pupils are freedwomen, then he is implying his female addressees to be *meretrices* in order to bully them. If his pupils in 529–54 want money instead of poetry, then that is all that can be expected of freedwomen. They are, so Ovid lets us know, all really *meretrices* anyway. The poet then moves to his passage on attracting various kinds of lover (555–76) with this assumption firmly in mind. In this case, the passage becomes a piece of social comedy at the expense of Ovid's freedwomen pupils. Elite readers can find their prejudices about those of low status with regard to money and morals comfortably confirmed. Social 'comedy' is equally the result if we assume Ovid's real addressees to be *matronae*. The implication of the poet's advice in 529–76 is that *matronae*, like real prostitutes at the bottom of the social scale, are characterised by their eagerness for material gain from sexual liaisons. In this case, the question for readers is whether they are prepared to accommodate the stereotypical traits of the *meretrix* within their own stereotype of the *matrona*. Here we are not concerned with a Clodia Metelli whose

---

[30] The demand is quite explicit at 1.435–6 *non mihi, sacrilegas meretricum ut persequar artes,/ cum totidem linguis sint satis ora decem.*

[31] See Veyne (1988) 75–80.

widely-rumoured flouting of conventional values might make her vulnerable to the rhetorical ploy of being charged with acting like a *meretrix*. Those who take *matronae* to be Ovid's real addressees usually understand them to be *matronae* as a class. If the implied *meretrix* stereotype is taken to apply also to *matronae*, then once again we discover the poem making fun of the very women it was supposed to entertain as its covert addressees.

The main point to take away from the above discussion is that, whichever way *Ars* 3.529–76 is understood, an uncomplicated reading of the passage in the way that Miller and others have perhaps encouraged us to expect is hardly possible.

Ars 3.251–80

The final passage for analysis is one which is representative of much of the material of *Ars* 3.[32] At 251–62 the *praeceptor* acknowledges that truly beautiful women, such as the legendary heroines Europa and Helen, would have no need of his *praecepta*, and asserts that his addressees consist instead of a *turba* composed of both the *pulchrae* and the *turpes*, where the *turpes* ('ugly') predominate. He then proceeds to tell them how to conceal their bodily blemishes (263–80):

> si brevis es, sedeas, ne stans videare sedere,
>   inque tuo iaceas quantulacumque toro;
> hic quoque, ne possit fieri mensura cubantis,   265
>   iniecta lateant fac tibi veste pedes.
> quae nimium gracilis, pleno velamina filo
>   sumat, et ex umeris laxus amictus eat.
> pallida purpureis tangat sua corpora virgis,
>   nigrior ad Pharii confuge piscis opem.   270
> pes malus in nivea semper celetur aluta,
>   arida nec vinclis crura resolve suis.
> conveniunt tenues scapulis analemptrides altis,
>   angustum circa fascia pectus eat.
> exiguo signet gestu, quodcumque loquetur,   275
>   cui digiti pingues et scaber unguis erit.
> cui gravis oris odor, numquam ieiuna loquatur,
>   et semper spatio distet ab ore viri.
> si niger aut ingens aut non erit ordine natus
>   dens tibi, ridendo maxima damna feres.   280

In principle Ovid's instructions could apply to any woman and not just freedwomen. But it is hard to imagine the wicked delight of the

---

[32] For other passages which contain physically based humour, cf. e.g. 101–6, 163–8, 193–8, 207–18, 769–88, 807–8.

daughters of the elite in picking up these *praecepta* behind the con-
venient smokescreen of freedwomen. For Ovid speaks frankly and with
little softening of the blows about female imperfections. Of course
momentary identification with the problems addressed is possible and
no doubt likely. What person who thought themselves short would not
at least consider taking the advice given in 263–4? But the advice is
given in such a way as to preclude the simple assumption that under-
neath the mask of the *meretrix* lies the *matrona* smiling with delight at
Ovid's clever concealment of his purpose of telling them how to com-
mit adultery. For there is a price to be paid for identifying with the
addressees of this passage. First there is the *praeceptor*'s declaration
that the majority of his pupils are 'ugly' and it is this majority which is
in need of the advice which is to follow (251–62). Secondly the advice
on concealing imperfections is broadcast to readers in an unvarnished
manner. The presentation is not noticeably shaped by the respect for
female 'sensitivities' about physical appearance which Ovid recom-
mends to his young male addressees in the first two books of the *Ars*.[33]
As with the advice on dinner parties, identifying with the addressees of
the advice is not without its penalties. But unlike the *cena* precepts (and
the others above) there are no exclusive links between Ovid's advice
and stereotypes of low-status women. Women of low status are often
stereotyped as ugly,[34] while those born in the higher ranks are often by
convention beautiful. But *matronae* may be ugly too — at least in
satire, as Horace's warnings on the horrors possibly lurking beneath the
matron's full length dress remind us.[35] But for all that, readers sensitive
to the literary ancestry of Ovid's advice may well be inclined to think
of women of low status as the *praeceptor*'s intended audience. For
there is little sustained tradition of the idea of physically imperfect
married women as there is for women of low status. Particularly rele-
vant is a passage from the Greek comic poet Alexis (fr. 103 K–A =
Athenaeus 13.568a–d) which appears to be the ultimate source for
Ovid's advice in *Ars* 3.263–80. In it the speaker warns of the rapacity
of ἑταῖραι (103.1–6) and then elaborates on the devices which they use
to conceal their bodily blemishes (103.7–21[36]). There are substantial

---

[33] For Ovid's conception of female 'sensitivities', cf. especially *Ars* 2.641–68.
[34] Cf. e.g. Gell. 12.1.17 (a mother should act as her own wet nurse) *praesertim si ista
quam ad praebendum lactem adhibetis, aut serva aut servilis est et, ut plerumque
solet, externae et barbarae nationis est, si inproba, si informis, si inpudica, si
temulenta est.*
[35] Hor. *Sat.* 1.2.77–95.
[36] τυγχάνει μικρά τις οὖσα· φελλὸς ἐν ταῖς βαυκίσιν/ ἐγκεκάττυται. μακρά τις·
διάβαθρον λεπτὸν φορεῖ/ τήν τε κεφαλὴν ἐπὶ τὸν ὦμον καταβαλοῦσ' ἐξέρχεται·/

similarities between the passages in terms of subject matter, in both cases a catalogue format is used, and Ovid and Alexis alike move from a list of 'devices' to the subject of laughing and smiling.[37] This strongly suggests the existence of an intermediary between the Greek comic poet and Ovid, perhaps a Roman comedian. Readers who know of the link might be tempted to think of ἑταῖραι as Ovid's intended audience. At any rate the purposes of the speakers in both cases might not be very different. In the Alexis passage the speaker intends to expose to a male audience the physical imperfections which women try to conceal from men. In the *Ars* the ostensible purpose of the speaker is to become complicit with his female addressees and advise them on how to conceal their imperfections from men. But given that men too read *Ars* 3, Ovid's real purpose was perhaps not so far removed from that of Alexis.

Conclusions

The passages discussed above suggest that it is difficult to sustain the belief across the whole of *Ars* 3 that beneath the mask of the ostensible audience of *meretrices* lies the real audience of *matronae*. This is perhaps what we ought to have expected from Ovid all along. The comic tension provided for the reader by such a belief is, arguably, not particularly complex. Reading the poem in this manner inevitably has a reductive effect, and serves to create a one-dimensional text. That Ovid expected the reader to be sustained across the 812 lines of *Ars* 3 by such a collusive suspicion without further complication must in principle be open to question. So, if the poem is not straightforwardly about telling *matronae* how to commit adultery under the guise of telling *meretrices* how to conduct affairs, what is really going on? It seems to me that, very broadly speaking, there are four ways of trying to make sense of what is happening in *Ars* 3.

(1) Since a proportion (although not all) of the poem's advice is particularly appropriate to the stereotype of women of low status, the

---

τοῦτο τοῦ μήκους ἀφεῖλεν. οὐχ ἔχει τις ἰσχία·/ ὑπενέδυσ' ἐρραμμέν' αὐτήν, ὥστε τὴν εὐπυγίαν/ ἀναβοᾶν τοὺς εἰσιδόντας. κοιλίαν ἁδρὰν ἔχει·/ στηθί' ἔστ' αὐταῖσι τούτων ὧν ἔχουσ' οἱ κωμικοί·/ ὀρθὰ προσθεῖσαι τοιαῦτα τοὔνδυτον τῆς κοιλίας/ ὡσπερεὶ κοντοῖσι τεύτοις εἰς τὸ πρόσθ' ἀπήγαγον./ τὰς ὀφρῦς πυρρὰς ἔχει τις· ζωγραφοῦσιν ἀσβόλωι./ συμβέβηκ' εἶναι μέλαιναν· κατέπλασεν ψιμυθίωι./ λευκόχρως λίαν τίς ἐστιν· παιδέρωτ' ἐντρίβεται./ καλὸν ἔχει τοῦ σώματός τι· τοῦτο γυμνὸν δείκνυται./ εὐφυεῖς ὀδόντας ἔσχεν· ἐξ ἀνάγκης δεῖ γελᾶν,/ ἵνα θεωρῶσ' οἱ παρόντες τὸ στόμ' ὡς κομψὸν φορεῖ. For further information on the fragment, see Arnott's commentary *ad loc*. (= fr. 103, Ἰσοστάσιον).

[37] *Ars* 3.281–90 = Alexis frg. 103.20–21 K–A (quoted above).

reader could conclude that the addressee is sometimes the *meretrix* and sometimes the *matrona*. This instability of the addressee might be seen as involving in one passage the *matrona* as addressee wearing the mask of the *meretrix*, in another the *meretrix* addressed directly with no need of a mask. Such confusion might be thought to have been useful to Ovid, helping to give some plausibility to his claim to be writing only for freedwomen and creating a convincing smokescreen — except that it was not very convincing, as Augustus would later make clear to Ovid.

(2) The reader might simply take Ovid at his word. The passages examined above suggest an audience conforming to the stereotype of low-status women. So, when Ovid says his addressees are freedwomen, perhaps we should believe him. But the belief is perhaps difficult to sustain through *Ars* 3 in the face of passages such as that on how to get rid of your male chaperone and meet your man (619–58) which are equally 'valid' and 'useful' for both *meretrix* and *matrona*.

(3) The reader might reflect that, if the text turns on the *matrona* and makes fun of her, or if the *matrona* is uncertain whether or not she is the real addressee, then perhaps it is not, after all, women who are the 'real addressees' of the text. Perhaps the real audience is men, and the text has a male perspective and creates male based humour for men at the expense of women. A male audience seems virtually to be written into the scenario of women receiving erotodidactic instruction. A male audience is brought along to hear Socrates instruct the courtesan Theodote (Xenophon *Memorabilia* 3.11); and male eavesdroppers are central to the scenes in New Comedy and elegy in which women receive lessons in love from other women (Plautus *Mostellaria* 157–312; *Poenulus* 210–332; Propertius 4.5; Ovid *Amores* 1.8).[38] Ovid aligns himself with this tradition in the opening lines of *Ars* 3. After briefly introducing the subject (1–6), he turns straightaway to men and spends over 30 lines answering male objections to the idea of women being instructed in love (7–40). Thus at the very start of *Ars* 3 our attention is drawn both to the existence and to the importance of a male audience for it. These men 'overhear' Ovid's instruction to his *puellae* in much the same way and in the same tradition as the eavesdroppers of earlier comedy and elegy.[39] Men are invited to hear and enjoy Ovid giving advice which creates humour at the expense of the *puellae* and

---

[38] Cf. also Herodas 1.47–8; Apul. *Met.* 9.15,

[39] The existence of a male audience is drawn to the reader's attention again explicitly at 585–6 when the *praeceptor* turns, with revealing casualness, to address married men (their wives ought to mistreat them in the same fashion as *puellae*).

female readers of the poem (as e.g. in 251–80 above).

(4) A final option for the reader is to consider whether Ovid might be deliberately 'spiking' his text for his readers. Traditional stereotypes of the *matrona* were undoubtedly rather unattractive for less conventional women. What young fashionable *matrona* would want to model herself on the dutiful Cornelia of Propertius 4.11, when she might be the more passionate Arethusa of 4.3 or particularly the Cynthia of 4.7? Given the limitations of the traditional stereotype, the prospect for *matronae* of behaving like *meretrices* might seem quite alluring. But Ovid appears not to want to allow his female readers quite so easy an outcome. Some of the advice which he gives makes it clear that those who wish to identify themselves as his (covert) addressees must be prepared to 'slum it'. Readers would have to ask themselves how alluring taking on the role of the *meretrix* might be. The type of the aristocratic *meretrix* might appear (despite the best efforts of Cicero and Sallust) quite alluring in the guise of a cultured Sempronia or a daring Clodia Metelli. But some of Ovid's advice suggests a different world and the poet seems to ask his readers to what extent they consider themselves his addressees. Other passages challenge traditional stereotypes. Is the advice on 'bad Latin' valid for all types of women, or just the stereotypically badly-educated woman of low-status? The passage on money and presents raises questions of what a *meretrix* is. Are women really all alike, united by their greed for money? Readers are led to question such conventional sentiments as that expressed by Horace, *ut matrona meretrici dispar erit atque/ discolor, infido scurrae distabit amicus* (*Epistulae* 1.18.3–4).

All the options outlined above have their problems. The last two, however, move far beyond the simple opposition of *meretrix* versus *matrona*.[40]

Bibliography

Adams, J.N. (1984). 'Female speech in Latin Comedy' *Antichthon* 18.43–77
—, (1990). 'The latinity of C. Novius Eunus' *ZPE* 82.227–47
Arnott, W.G. (1996). *Alexis, the Fragments: a Commentary*. Cambridge

---

[40] This paper was given at the ICS in London. Many thanks to the participants for their helpful comments, especially Susanna Morton Braund and Maria Wyke. Special thanks are owed to the following for their help and advice over the course of the many versions which this paper has seen: David Bain, Francis Cairns, Ian DuQuesnay, Richard Hunter, Ted Kenney and Jim McKeown. Of course, none of the above should be presumed to agree with the argument of the paper.

Boyce, B. (1991). *The Language of the Freedmen in Petronius' Cena Trimalchionis*. Leiden

Cataudella, Q. (1974). '*Initiamenta amoris*' *Latomus* 33.847–57

Day, A.A. (1938). *The Origins of Latin Love Elegy*. Oxford

Evans, J.K. (1991). *War, Women and Children in ancient Rome*. London and New York

Edwards, C. (1993). *The Politics of Immorality in ancient Rome*. Cambridge

Gibson, R.K. (1995). 'How to win girlfriends and influence them: *amicitia* in Roman love elegy' *PCPS* 41.62–82

—, (forthcoming). 'Didactic poetry as 'popular' form: a study of imperatival expressions in Latin didactic verse and prose' in C. Atherton (ed.) *Form and Content in Didactic Poetry* (Nottingham Classical Literature Seminar 5) Bari

Gilleland, M.E. (1980). 'Female speech in Greek and Latin' *AJP* 101.180–3

Gowers, E. (1993). *The Loaded Table. Representations of Food in Roman Literature*. Oxford

Griffin, J. (1985). *Latin Poets and Roman Life*. London

Hollis, A.S. (1977). *Ovid: Ars Amatoria Book I*. Oxford

Hudson, N.A. (1989). 'Food in Roman satire' in S.Braund (ed.) *Satire and Society in ancient Rome* (Exeter) 69–87

Hunter, R.L. (1983). *Eubulus: the Fragments*. Cambridge

Labate, M. (1984). *L' arte di farsi amare: modelli culturali e progetto didascalico nell' elegia ovidiana*. (Biblioteca di MD 2) Pisa

Little, D. (1982). 'Politics in Augustan poetry' *ANRW* 2.30.1.254–370

Miller, J.F. (1993). 'Apostrophe, aside and the didactic addressee: poetic strategies in *Ars Amatoria* III' in Schiesaro, Mitsis, Strauss Clay (1993) 231–41

Nisbet, R.G.M. and Hubbard, M. (1978). *A Commentary on Horace: Odes Book II*. Oxford

Otis, B. (1970). *Ovid as an Epic Poet*, 2nd ed. Cambridge

Rudd, N. (1976). *Lines of enquiry: studies in Latin poetry*. Cambridge

Schiesaro, A., Mitsis, Ph. and Strauss Clay, J. (1993) (edd.) *Mega Nepios: il destinatorio nell' epos didascalico* (MD 31) Pisa

Sharrock, A.R. (1994). 'Ovid and the Politics of Reading' *MD* 33.97–122

Shero, L.R. (1923). 'The *cena* in Roman satire' *CP* 18.126–43

Stroh, W. (1979). 'Ovids Liebeskunst und die Ehegesetze des Augustus' *Gymnasium* 86.323–52

Treggiari, S. (1991). *Roman Marriage: Iusti Coniuges from the time of Cicero to the time of Ulpian*. Oxford

Veyne, P. (1988). *Roman Erotic Elegy: Love, Poetry and the West*. Chicago

PAPERS OF THE LEEDS INTERNATIONAL LATIN SEMINAR   TENTH VOLUME (1998) 313–36
Published by Francis Cairns (Publications) Ltd (Leeds 1998). ARCA 38. ISBN 0 905205 95 2

THE SPEECH OF PYTHAGORAS AT OVID *METAMORPHOSES* 15.75–478

KARL GALINSKY
University of Texas at Austin

1. Introduction

As befits Ovid's *carmen perpetuum*, interest in the exact function of Pythagoras' speech in *Metamorphoses* 15 continues to be unceasing. Recent discussions have provided some valuable new perspectives,[1] but it seems useful at this point to take another comprehensive look at this important part of Ovid's chef d'oeuvre. 'Comprehensive' does not mean detailing previous interpretations *prima ab origine mundi*. Rather, my concern will be the totality of the various aspects of the passage. I begin with a brief survey of some of the obvious givens and shall then explore some of the ramifications.

First, with over four hundred lines, this is one of the longest episodes in the *Metamorphoses*. As it comes in the final book, some kind of programmatic purpose or, as is always the case with Ovid, several purposes, can be assumed. In terms of literary traditions alone, Ovid has regaled us in the preceding fourteen books with a vast array of styles and genres; and it is clear that this variety provides the pointer to the real significance of the role of genre in the *Metamorphoses*.[2] Absent, until the last book, have been a long philosophical disquisition and a speech yet longer than that of Ulysses in Book 13. One of the reasons, therefore, for Ovid's inclusion of this philosophical

---

[1]   Esp. Myers (1994) and Hardie (1995).
[2]   For the combination and interaction of genres in the *Metamorphoses* see the useful articles by Horsfall (1979) and Farrell (1992); cf. Solodow (1988) 18–25. W.S. Anderson's review of S. Hinds *The Metamorphosis of Persephone* (Cambridge 1987) in *Gnomon* 61 (1989) 356–8 puts the issue of genre into perspective relative to other jissues with which Ovidian scholars should be concerned.

rodomontade is simply to round out his whole bravura collection with yet another bravura piece.

Secondly, the choice of Pythagoras was congenial for that purpose and several others. By Ovid's time, 'Pythagoreanism' stood for a syncretistic collection of the teachings of various philosophical schools, mysticism, pseudo-scientific speculation, and religious and spiritual dispensations.[3] Accordingly, Ovid's Pythagoras offers an eclectic farrago indebted to all kinds of philosophical teachings: his own, Heracleitus', Empedocles', and the Stoics', along with frequent allusions, mostly for the sake of counterargument, to Lucretius and the Epicureans. The procedure finds its fitting analogue in Ovid's choice of material for the *Metamorphoses*, which is similarly varied, not doctrinaire, and not consistent. Ovid's poem is, "among other things, an anthology of genres" and styles;[4] Pythagoras' speech is an anthology of philosophies.

It is more: Philip Hardie, with typical learning and astuteness, has recently argued that through the speech of Pythagoras, in conjunction with the cosmogony in Book 1 and the historical passages in the second part of Book 15, Ovid is claiming his place in the Roman epic tradition, exemplified by Ennius and Vergil.[5] According to Hardie, Ovid does so by linking philosophy and history in an Empoclean key. This argument will be reconsidered later. For the moment, an obvious fact, acknowledged by Hardie in a footnote,[6] can be stated: Empoclean colouring is absent from fully half of Pythagoras' speech, the catalogue of θαυμαστά and παράδοξα (15.259–452). Not surprisingly, we have here a typically Ovidian invitation, in this case facilitated by the very nature of Pythagoreanism, to reader response.[7] Some highbrow readers may concentrate on the philosophical evocations and pursue them beyond the text. For differently oriented readers, what is memorable is the vignettes from Pythagoras' version of Ripley's 'Believe It or Not', such as the birth of green frogs from mud (15.375–7), dead people's spine marrow mutating into snakes (15.389–90), and putrefying war horses generating hornets (15.368).

---

[3] See Burkert (1961) 236–46 for a concise and substantive summary; more detail in Ferrero (1955) and, with an excellent collection of the ancient sources, Garbarino (1973).
[4] Kenney (1986) xviii.
[5] Hardie (1995).
[6] Hardie (1995) 205 n.7.
[7] A study of the *Metamorphoses* from this aspect is still a desideratum; for such approaches and their application to Roman literature, cf. Woodman (1992) 208 with n.17.

Then, thirdly, there is the relationship between the philosophical and scientific mode on the one hand, and the mythological and poetic on the other, as indicated especially in Ovid's cabinet of *mirabilia*, proffered by the same philosopher Pythagoras. Are these modes of explanation merely juxtaposed or is one privileged over the other? A similar issue is raised by the cosmogony of Book 1 — is Ovid there indebted to philosophy rather than poetry? These dichotomies, which have often been used to frame the discussion, may in fact have to be modified in view of the low content of science and philosophy in Roman Pythagoreanism. Fourthly, given the fact that the *Metamorphoses* was in many ways meant to be an alternative to the *Aeneid*, how does Ovid's treatment of philosophy contrast with Vergil's? Vergil's most sustained use of philosophical models, including Pythagoreanism, comes of course in *Aeneid* 6 or, to put it with Ovidian insouciance, in hell from where Ovid studiously omits it.[8] Moreover, Vergil studied philosophy with Philodemus and that fact is relevant to some of his characterisations in the *Aeneid*.[9] Vergil's integration of myth and philosophy was in many ways a response to Lucretius, whom we must also consider in this context. Finally, and without going into all the details of narratology, Pythagoras' presentation of his subject and of his exempla of change clearly calls for a comparison with Ovid's own narrative presentation in the rest of the *Metamophoses*. Is the philosopher a foil for the poet or a complement?

2. Why Pythagoras?

For the Roman audience Ovid's choice of Pythagoras as the archetypal philosopher made excellent sense. Since the time of Aristotle, Pythagoras was credited with being the εὑρετής of the very word φιλόσοφος.[10] Modern scholarship is sceptical about the claim, but it found huge resonance in antiquity and became a staple in handbooks up to the time of Isidore of Seville; Cicero furnishes one of the lengthier attestions in *Tusculans* 5.8–9. Secondly, Pythagoras had a Roman affiliation which was particularly suitable for one of the main themes of the last book of the *Metamorphoses*, the transfer from Greece to Rome. The theme is continued with the story of Asclepius' arrival in Rome and, for that matter, with Julius Caesar's catasterism; a further link is

---

[8]   *Met.* 4.432–80; see Bernbeck (1967) 4–30 and Galinsky (1989) 82–6.
[9]   Cairns (1989) Chh.1–3.
[10] By Heracleides of Pontus; the various sources are listed and discussed by Burkert (1960).

that one of the appellations (coined at Croton) of Pythagoras was "Hyperborean Apollo"[11] — Apollo was, of course, the father of Asclepius and the patron god of Augustus. The Roman component of Pythagoras needs some further comment. One aspect is the development of Pythagoreanism in Italy and Rome. The other is the association of Pythagoras and Numa. My aim, in both instances, is to work towards defining the horizon of expectations of Ovid's contemporaries.

Pythagoras, *ortu Samius* (15.60), migrated to Croton; and in Magna Graecia he was reputed to have taught the Romans along with Lucanians, Messapians, and Peucetians.[12] Testimonia of continuing Roman interest in him include, besides the link with Numa, the Romans' selection of Pythagoras, sometime in the fourth century BC,[13] as "the wisest Greek" to be honored with a statue in the Comitium, and the gens Aemilia's deriving its name from one of Pythagoras' sons.[14] As for Pythagoreanism, Aristotle called it simply "the Italian philosophy."[15] But what was it? The ancient sources acknowledge that the old, authentic Pythagoreanism became extinct. That, however, did not mean the end of a thriving production, especially in Hellenistic times, of pseudo-Pythagorica that obviously responded to considerable demand. There was, in Walter Burkert's words, a flood of Pythagorean writings, but there were no Pythagoreans.[16] By the late Republic that had changed: Varro wanted to be buried *Pythagorio modo* (Pliny *Naturalis Historia* 35.160), Nigidius Figulus was exiled; and Sextius was credited with establishing a Pythagorean sect that, however shortlived, was *roboris Romani* (Seneca *Naturales Quaestiones* 7.32.2).[17]

The character of this new and Roman Pythagoreanism was, however, quite different from the old. It shared, as noted, a trend toward syncretistic convergence as, due to the influence of Posidonios in

---

[11] Aelian *Var. Hist.* 2.26 (citing Aristotle); cf. Iambl. *Vita Pythag.* 140. Another connection would be Pythagoras' claim to be the reincarnated Euphorbus (*Met.* 15.261), who was prominently associated with Apollo in the *Iliad*. According to Diogenes Laertius 8.21, Pythagoras received his teachings from the Delphic priestess; hence *Delphos ... meos ... recludam ... et augustae reserabo oracula mentis* (*Met.* 15.144–5). On *augustae*, see Bömer *ad loc.*

[12] Aristoxenos fr. 17 (Wehrli) = Porph. *Vita Pythag.* 22; Iambl. *Vita Pythag.* 241; Diog. Laert. 8.14.

[13] Pliny, *NH* 34.26; Plut. *Numa* 8.10; cf. Coarelli (1985) 119–23.

[14] Plut. *Aem.* 2.2; Festus p. 23 L.; cf. Burkert (1961) 237 n.5 and Maltby (1991) *s.v. Aemilius* 12–13.

[15] οἱ Ἰταλικοί: *Met.* 987a10, 31; 988a26.

[16] Burkert (1961) 234.

[17] On the Sextii, see Ferrero (1955) 360–78; cf. von Arnim in *RE* II.4.2040–41.

particular,[18] it incorporated aspects of Platonism and Stoicism. The phenomenon is part of a wider panorama. On one hand, it relates to the kind of poetic and intellectual eclecticism that informs, for instance, Horace's thought in the first Roman Ode,[19] i.e. a sort of philosophical *Allgemeinbildung*.[20] On the other, and on a more popular level — in contrast to Horace, Ovid never proclaimed *odi profanum vulgus et arceo* — hard science had no appeal in Rome and serious philosophy had a limited audience. What was in demand was the "popular, the watered down, and the coarsened ... A Roman, who inquired about the cosmos, and the forces and laws that ruled it, did not come upon Plato's *Timaeus*, nor upon Archimedes and Eratosthenes, but upon an extract from Platonic, Aristotelian, and Stoic cosmology which, in combination with some isolated and half-understood insights into science, had been melded into a pseudoscientific whole and been put under the name of Pythagoras."[21] In so many words, Ovid's audience would not look to 'Pythagoras' for hard science or philosophy, and we should not either. This does not mean that (Neo)Pythagoreanism and its titular founder were held in low, derisive regard. Rather, the gibes of Horace and Laberius, like those directed by Aristophanes at Socrates, further confirm that Pythagoras and his supposed teachings were a matter of topical fascination among a large public. If Ovid wanted to mix some 'philosophy' into the *Metamorphoses*, he could not have made a better choice. Further confirmation of its suitability comes from the mythological decorations, twenty-eight in all, of the Pythagorean underground 'basilica' at the Porta Maggiore: "La singulière architecture et la proliférante richesse du décor semblent avoir été conçues pour défier à jamais toute tentative d'exégèse systématique"[22] — an apt characterisation of the *Metamorphoses* too.

3. Pythagoras and Numa

The association of Pythagoras and Numa was an equally fascinating topic. The earliest testimonium is that of Aristoxenos,[23] which should not lead us to believe that Aristoxenos' writings reached Rome in the

---

[18] Ferrero (1955) 268–80; Segl (1970) 103–4 (with reference to Lafaye); Bömer (1986) 269–70.

[19] Cairns (1995) 122.

[20] Cf. Bömer (1986) 270–71; Due (1974) 30; Segl (1970) 94–6.

[21] Burkert (1961) 245; cf. Hirzel (1891) 1308–11.

[22] Sauron (1994) 630.

[23] See n.12, above. Garbarino (1973) 63–72 has conveniently assembled the ancient sources (20 in all). For extensive discussions see Ferrero (1955) 142–7; Garbarino (1973) 230–38; Gruen (1990) 158–70; Humm (1996) 340–45.

fourth century and led forthwith to the acceptance of the story there.
Rather it accords well with the Hellenistic fascination for things
Pythagorean. There can be little doubt, however, that the tale gained
further currency and was well established in Rome by the early second
century. It was hard to dislodge; as has been observed correctly, the
vehement attacks on it by Cicero, Dionysius, Livy, and others are
indicative of the legend's strength. There was no need for these writers
to pound away at its chronological absurdity if only a few misguided
souls believed that Numa had been taught by Pythagoras. Plutarch's
account is a good example of the stubborn longevity of the story. He
confronts the problem in the very first chapter of his *Life of Numa*,
offers various explanations and justifications, and then proceeds, in
Ch.8, with a recital of Numa's relation to Pythagoras, including a list of
his Roman institutions that were due to the philosopher's precepts.
Much as he likes the traditional story, Plutarch is forced to restate, in
the concluding sentence, that there is a great deal of dispute
(ἀμφισβητήσεις) about "these matters" and that it would be contentious
to pursue them further.

One of the most clamorous incidents in the tradition of the tale
occurred in 181 BC. According to the earliest account, that of Cassius
Hemina,[24] the stone *arca* of Numa turned up on the Janiculum in the
course of excavation. It also contained several books, and *in his libris
scripta erant philosophiae Pythagoricae — eosque combustos a Q.
Petilio praetore, quia philosophiae scripta essent*. In the subsequent
annalistic tradition, the usual accretions appear: the books, varying in
number, are now said to consist equally of Numa's pontifical laws and
philosophical (*Graecos* or *Pythagoricos*) writings. In Livy's account
(40.29.2–14), there are two *arcae* and both sets of books are burned,
whereas Valerius Maximus (1.1.12) has it that only the Greek books
were burned *quia aliqua ex parte ad solvendam religionem pertinere
existimabantur*, a version followed by Lactantius (*Divinae Institutiones*
1.22.1, 5–6). Plutarch (*Numa* 22.2–3) does not miss the opportunity to
point out that Numa followed Pythagorean practice in commanding that
the (pontifical) books he wrote should be buried with him while their
precepts should be memorised and passed on by the living.
Accordingly, when the books were found in conjunction with "twelve
others of Greek philosophy," the praetor has them burned because it

---

[24] Fr. 37 Peter = Pliny *NH* 13.84–6. The testimonia (12 altogether) again in Garbarino
(1973) 64–9. The most recent discussion, which proceeds along different lines from
mine, is Gruen (1990) 163–70; cf. Gruen (1992) 259.

was not *ius* or *fas* that they should be made public (*Numa* 22.8).

As can be expected, the episode has received different, and sometimes elaborate, interpretations. My own inclination would be to rely mostly on Hemina's report, which is closest in time to the event and free from embroidery. He speaks only of the Pythagorean books found with Numa. Subsequent authors added the pontifical books because they were *de rigueur* for Numa, and this could lead to the absurdity of both sets of books having to be burned. Hemina's version, and the action taken by the Roman magistrate, makes sense in the context of the quackery that produced pseudo-Pythagorica en masse. What is important for our purposes is that the tradition linking Pythagoras and Numa was widespread, lively, and disputatious. Ovid wrote his own version against this backdrop and could expect his readers to be familiar with much of it. Therefore he did not have to subject the legend to the same overt, rationalist, and chronological critique as other late Republican and Augustan writers; his readers could do so for themselves. The conclusion that Ovid disregards the problem or even accepted the legend ignores the implied reader and the more nuanced nature of poetry. As so often, Ovid's own hints are unobtrusive but plentiful.

Ovid disassociates himself from most versions of the legend by not speaking of Numa as actually meeting Pythagoras. In his quest for *rerum natura* (15.6), Numa journeys to Magna Graecia. One of the indigenous *seniores* (15.10) — a favourite Ovidian narrator, especially when distance from a tale is sought[25] — tells him about the foundation of Croton. The events belong to *veteris aevi* (15.11); Numa and Pythagoras are not contemporaries. The addressee, therefore, of Pythagoras' speech is not Numa, but *coetus silentum* (15.66); the shift from Numa to them is emphasised by the repetition of *rerum causas* (15.68), now a theme in Pythagoras' discourse to that group. But what group is it? Elsewhere in Ovid and Latin poetry, *silentes* are the dead.[26] The reader again has the choice to understand the phrase in that sense or as referring to the proverbial silence preached by the Pythagoreans. In addition to not being the original listener, Numa qualifies on both counts. From the temporal perspective of Ovid's readers, Numa was, of

---

[25] Cf. *Met.* 8.721-2, with my comments in Galinsky (1996) 232-3.

[26] *Met.* 13.25; cf. Hor. *Epod.* 5.51; Lucan 6.513; Sen. *Med.* 740; Verg. *Aen.* 6.432; Prop. 3.12.33. I follow Barchiesi (1989) 76-7 rather than Bömer *ad loc.* There may be more to it yet: Plato (*Phaedo* 64 a and b) mentions a (comic?) tradition according to which philosophers were endemically enamoured of death; cf. Middle Comedies entitled 'Pythagorists' (Diels–Kranz 58E).

course, long dead and, as for his silence, we do not hear a word from or
about him for the duration of his informant's recital of Pythagoras'
disquisition. He reappears at the very end as the purported recipient of
Pythagoras' instructions (15.479–84):

> talibus atque aliis instructum pectora dictis
> in patriam remeasse ferunt ultroque petitum
> accepisse Numam populi Latiaris habenas;
> coniuge qui felix nympha ducibusque Camenis
> sacrificos docuit ritus gentemque feroci
> adsuetam bello pacis traduxit ad artes.

Not only do these few compact lines deliberately contrast with the
verbosity of Pythagoras, but they do nothing to establish Numa as his
follower. The Romans' main interest in philosophy was in ethics and
there was plenty of relevant Pythagorean material in circulation. Ovid
systematically ignores all of it, relegating it, at best, to the unarticulated
aliis dictis. He reduces Pythagorean ethics to vegetarianism — this is
the subject of the *peroratio* in lines 459–78 to which *talibus dictis*
refers — and, yet more important, "presents it in a position more ex-
treme than that usually ascribed to Pythagoras."[27] This does not make
Pythagoras' speech a parody — such labels are too facile because the
speech is more than one-dimensional — but it reduces Pythagoras'
credibility *qua* philosopher. Furthermore, strident vegetarianism, of
course, was not one of Numa's teachings nor is it likely to have figured
in the writings of Castor of Rhodes, a pro-Roman chronographer (first
century BC), who "accepted that early Roman institutions had been
influenced by Pythagoreanism."[28] Once more, Ovid deliberately passes
over a connection that could have been made: Plutarch (*Numa* 8.8)
relates that Numa's sacrifices "had great similitude to the ceremonials
of Pythagoras, for they were not celebrated with effusion of blood, but
consisted of flour, wine, and the least costly offerings." Ovid rejects
this tradition in two ways. In the first instance he credits Egeria and the
Camenae, not Pythagoras, with helping Numa establish *sacrificos ritus*
for the ferocious Romans.[29] Secondly, he says nothing about their
bloodlessness, nor, in the parallel version in the *Fasti* (1.337), does he
attribute the origin of bloodless sacrifices to Pythagoras. In fact, later in
the *Fasti,* in connection with the incubation oracle of Faunus, Numa is
shown to be sacrificing sheep and a pregnant cow (4.652, 671).

---

[27] Rawson (1985) 294.
[28] Rawson (1985) 293 on the basis of Plutarch *Quaest. Rom.* 10.
[29] Cf. Barchiesi (1989) 79.

Ferunt, as has been noted,[30] serves both for distancing and for giving the story the patina of antiquity. In this instance, the former effect appears to be predominant: in his catalogue of teacher and disciple pairs in *Ex Ponto* 3.3.41-4, Ovid uses the same qualifying expression only for Numa and Pythagoras. At the same time, and as throughout the *Metamorphoses*, Ovid leaves enough latitude even for the true believer.[31] While he does not make Pythagoras and Numa coevals, he refrains from pointing out, as Dionysius had done at some length (*Antiquitates Romanae* 2.59.3-4), that Croton was founded four years after Numa's accession. In addition, the range of *aliis dictis* is left entirely to the reader. It is elastic enough to allow for the inclusion of the philosophical-scientific topics which Pythagoras outlines initially (*Metamorphoses* 15.66-72), but completely fails to develop.[32]

4. 'Philosophy' in Pythagoras' speech

Ovid does not take long to disabuse the reader of any expectations of serious philosophical discourse. The primary theme, concisely rendered in lines 177-8 (*nihil est toto, quod perstet, in orbe. cuncta fluunt*) is, of course, Heraclitean, though it belonged to popular philosophy, if not simply the realm of proverbial expression, by Ovid's time.[33] Moreover, at the first opportunity (15.186-236) Ovid ignores the actual cosmic tenets of the Pythagoreans and others and instead has Pythagoras present some routine, if not banal, examples of change: i.e. night, day, the seasons, and the ages of man. The issue is not a complex philosophical doctrine, but an everyday insight into the obvious. The equation of the ages with the seasons may go back to Pythagoras,[34] but it was clearly one of his least challenging intellectual properties. The narrator happens to be a philosopher; we are dealing, to use Quintilian's phrase for the impressionistic unity of the *Metamophoses* (*Institutiones Oratoriae* 4.1.77), with a *species*, with the appearance of philosophy rather than anything of substance.

Similarly, the subsequent discussion of the elements (237-51) had become the common property of virtually any philosophical school. This is reflected by the variety of sources modern scholars have identified, such as "peripatetic eclecticism", "jungepikureisch," and Stoic,

---

[30] By Bömer *ad loc.*
[31] The story of Philemon and Baucis is another paradigm; see Galinsky (1975) 202.
[32] Cf. Myers (1994) 141-2.
[33] Detailed documentation in Segl (1970) 43-4 and Bömer *ad loc.*
[34] Diog. Laert. *Vita Pythag.* 8.10; full discussion in Segl (1970) 51 and Bömer *ad loc.*

especially Posidonian.[35] Empedocles too figures in the mix, but hardly in a privileged position.[36] We are dealing with an 'eclecticism' — a very Augustan characteristic — that implies the convergence of different philosophical schools. In Horace's first Roman Ode, they could be summoned in support of the *mos maiorum*; in Pythagoras' speech, they illustrate that change is a topic common to all philosophical schools. In both cases, the effort is to produce some philosophical colouring and not a sectarian attempt to deal thoroughly with the specific tenets of one philosophy or the other. It has been well noted that Ovid, in this passage, "uses (philosophical) terms without being concerned about the meaning they had in previous literature."[37] The lack of concern about terminology, however, is only a result of the more fundamental lack of concern about the subject itself: no sooner has Pythagoras proclaimed that *haec quoque non perstant* (15.237), echoing the theme of *cuncta fluunt* (15.178), than he promptly speaks of the *aether* as *aeternus* (15.239), which may be a witticism. Fittingly, he had used *aether* in line 195 devoid of the numerous connotations the term had acquired in previous philosophy and science.[38]

The remainder of Pythagoras' 'philosophy' consists of his injunctions, with which he brackets his speech, against animal sacrifices and the consumption of animal meat. It appears that, in the teachings of the Sextii, the reason for emphasis on vegetarianism was not metempsychosis, but hygiene and the avoidance of cruelty to animals.[39] Ovid follows that emphasis: his depiction of the sacrificial victim (15.130–40) is rendered with unusual sympathy, as is Pythagoras' concluding appeal (462–9).[40] But we are not dealing with 'philosophy' here. Spirituality and metaphysics are eschewed and while Ovid strikes a humanitarian note, this extreme vegetarianism was, as we saw earlier, not part of the Roman mainstream or of Numa's legacy.

Ovid's refusal to develop Pythagorean philosophy proper had been prepared for in the preceding books; and it belongs in the general context of his endeavour to distance himself from philosophical creeds. For instance, in contrast to Lucretius' rationalist critique that denied the existence of mythical *portenta* such as Scylla and Centaurs, Ovid

---

[35] See Haupt/Ehwald/von Albrecht (1966) and Bömer *ad loc.*
[36] Segl (1970) 136 n.223; cf. Bömer *ad* 252–3.
[37] Segl (1970) 47 (with reference, e.g., to *quattuor genitalia* in line 239).
[38] Segl (1970) 45–7.
[39] Sen. *Epist.* 108.18; see Haussleiter (1935) 296–9 and Ferrero (1955) 374–5.
[40] Galinsky (1975) 141–3.

makes them the centerpieces of some of his own stories.[41] Similarly, Lucretius (2.700–703, 707) had rejected the possibility of meta- morphoses of humans into trees; in the *Metamorphoses*, the trans- formations of Daphne and of Phaethon's sisters figure prominently near the beginning of the poem. Ovid deliberately chose these *exempla* to achieve contrast because they showed Lucretius at his most doctrinaire; he knew that this attitude does not consistently inform the Epicurean poet's treatment of myth.[42] We should keep in mind, of course, that Ovid is uncanonical in all areas and not just vis-à-vis philosophers and philosopher-poets: whereas the depiction, for instance, of dolphins in trees and boars in the waters is the hallmark of the bad artist in Horace's *Ars Poetica* (29–30), it does not take long for these vignettes to materialise in Ovid's description of the deluge (*Metamorphoses* 1.302–3, 305).

5. Poetry and philosophy: the paradoxa and the cosmogony

As most commentators have noted, almost half of Pythagoras' dis- course, the catalogue of *mirabilia* and paradoxa (15.259–452), has almost no basis in Pythagoreanism, whether old or new. The closest connection that can be made is to (pseudo-)Sotion's treatise on the paradoxa of rivers, springs, and pools.[43] But the more important point is that Ovid's preceding treatment of Pythagoreanism has set the tone: we should not now expect an exploration of these phenomena in terms of probing science and philosophy. The relationship of paradoxography to Greek science corresponds to that of the pantomime to Greek tragedy: anything serious and substantive is eliminated in favour of small, easily digestible snippets concentrating on the fascinating and the sen- sational.[44] Both developments are the result of the taste of a large public, and Ovid knew his audience. By his day, pseudoscience and science were intermingled in Hellenistic Greece and Rome: the elder Pliny's massive collection provides continuing attestation.[45] Even if the distinction between the two may be clearer to us than to Ovid's

---

[41] Lucr. 2.700–29; 4.732–45; 5.878–924; see Myers (1994) 145–7.

[42] Gale (1994); cf. below, Section 6.

[43] Segl (1970) 57 with n.265; Crahay and Hubaux (1958) 286.

[44] See the collections of the Greek paradoxographers by Westermann (Amsterdam 1963) and Giannini (Milan 1965). Cf. Galinsky (1996) 265–6 on the affinities of pantomime and *Metamorphoses*; from there the road leads to the 'Ovide bouffon' of the 17th century (Moog-Grünewald [1979] 124–56).

[45] Cf. Myers (1994) 150–52 with n.79.

contemporaries, Lucretius' *De Rerum Natura* had shown that rational, scientific thought was not incompatible with poetry. The presentation of an elaborate contrast, then, between philosophical and poetic modes is not one of the objectives of Pythagoras' speech. In its first part, Ovid flattens out philosophy to the point where it is indistinguishable from generalised, popular ideas, while in the second part he simply juxtaposes, rather than opposes, scientific-philosophical and poetical-mythical explanations in his large catalogue of miraculous happenings.

Franz Bömer and Sara Myers have thoroughly documented this procedure with example after example.[46] So a few additional comments only are required. One involves Ovid's mention of the spring of wondrous waters near the town of Clitor in Arcadia (15.324–8). Whoever drank from them would abstain from drinking wine in perpetuity. Ovid compresses the scientific explanation into one line; in fact, it is not an explanation as much as it is a matter-of-fact observation: *seu vis est in aqua calido contraria vino* (324). He then goes on to summarise the mythological tale (325–8):

> sive, quod indigenae memorant, Amythaone natus,
> Proetidas attonitas postquam per carmen et herbas
> eripuit furiis, purgamina mentis in illas
> misit aquas odiumque meri permansit in undis.

The mythological explanation is four times the length of the scientific one. But before this is construed as Ovid's privileging poetry over natural philosophy, Vitruvius should be called into play. Vitruvius treats such phenomena in the first part of Book 8, which deals with hydrology. In many cases, including that of the wine-blocking springs of Clitor, he does not even trouble to suggest a scientific cause. Instead, he simply tells the tale, expanding it, in the case of Clitor, to cite in full the ten-line epigram inscribed at the site (8.3.21). If a prosaic, practical writer like Vitruvius, who stressed that an architect should diligently study philosophy (1.1.3), could realise that natural philosophy would not go far in such instances, so would Ovid.

Moreover, the mention of alternative explanations for wondrous phenomena has ample precedent in *Metamorphoses* 1–14, even if those alternatives are not explicitly correlated.[47] Ovid reminds the attentive reader of his practice in his very introduction of Pythagoras. The sage's

---

[46] Bömer (1986), esp. *ad* 15.324; Myers (1994) 152–9.
[47] Cf. Little (1970) 349–55. A kindred procedure is Ovid's frequent use of "the language of physics to describe myths of the most fabulous nature" (Myers [1994] 49, with a discussion of several examples on pp. 47–9; cf. Section 6 below).

subjects include *quae fulminis esset origo, / Iuppiter an venti discussa nube tonarent* (15.69–70). Ovid had already offered a naturalistic cause for lightning at 1.56 (*cum fulminibus facientes fulgora ventos*) only to depict it subsequently as the traditional mythological accoutrement of Jupiter (1.197, 253) — the thunderbolts there are *tela ... manibus fabricata Cyclopum* (1.259). Small wonder, then, that Pythagoras has nothing more to say about the subject. Similar dual explanations were given for the creation of man (1.78–83, cf. 1.363–4), the support of the aether and air above the earth (1.26–31, 2.293–7), and the cause of the rainbow (6.61–4, 11.589–90). One explanation, Ovid implies, is no better than the other. Nor is their credibility distinguishable — and this reveals further common ground between poetry and philosophy. Just before the philosopher starts speaking, Ovid comments that his teachings may be learned, but not altogether believed: *primus quoque talibus ora / docta quidem solvit, sed non et credita, verbis* (15.73–4).[48] In their position, these lines refer to the entire speech, and not just to Pythagoras' injunctions about vegetarianism or metempsychosis. Ovid, in turn, in his apologia to Augustus, explicitly characterises the titular subject of the *Metamorphoses* as not to be believed (*Tristia* 2.63–4):

> inspice maius opus, quod adhuc sine fine tenetur,
> in non credendos corpora versa modos.

> (Look at my major work, which is still unfinished, look at the bodies who were transformed unbelievably).

This assertion is reinforced by the enumeration of *mirabilia* as *adynata* in *Tristia* 4.7.11–20: the majority are myths which occur in the *Metamorphoses*.[49] To be sure, there is a distinction between natural wonders, such as the spring of Clitor, and transformations of human bodies, since the former verifiably exist and call for an explanation, whether scientific or mythological. But Ovid deliberately blurs the line by sprinkling, throughout Pythagoras' speech, references to myths which he had told earlier and by failing altogether, in the case of the Symplegades (15.337–9), to give a "scientific" reason. Similarly included without explanation are transformations from inanimate to animate (375–7), and decomposing to live matter (368, 389–90). Several assertions of

---

[48] *Primus* may be a reference to the tradition that Pythagoras was the εὑρετής of the word 'philosopher'; see n.10, above. Also relevant may be Callimachus *Iamb.* 1 (fr. 191) lines 62–3: οἱ δ' ἄρ' οὐχ ὑπήκουσαν, οὐ πάντες with the astute emendation by H. Lloyd-Jones: οἱ Ἰταλοὶ δ' ὑπήκουσαν, οὐ πάντες, and with the further remarks by M.L. West in *CR* 21 (1971) 330–1.

[49] Cf. Little (1970) 347–8.

disbelief, therefore, are a constituent part of Pythagoras' speech (282–3, 359, 389–90). It is not possible to place credence either in the *fides poetica* or the *fides philosophica*. As a result, Ovid's poetic immortality, a topic which will recur, is not based on the traditional claim of the *vates* to have revealed the truth, but on the truthful prediction of the *vates* — and that is the only truth they may possess — that Ovid and his fame will be immortal (15.878–9):

> perque omnia saecula fama,
> siquid habent veri vatum praesagia, vivam.

To turn from the end of the poem to its beginning: since it is Ovid's overture to the *Metamorphoses*, the cosmogony (1.5–75) is poetic rather than philosophical. This introductory passage and the speech of Pythagoras have rightly been considered as balanced thematic landmarks[50] — although it is also important to be alert to the differences between them. Like the discourse of Pythagoras, the cosmogony does not fit the simple matrix of (mythological) poetry vs. (natural) philosophy. But its suggestive model is far more emphatically poetic, i.e. Homer's description of Achilles' shield, *imago mundi*, as Stephen Wheeler has recently argued.[51] Two brief observations may be added to his cumulative argument. First, reading Ovid's cosmogony to some extent as poetology, he identifies *deus et melior natura* (1.21) with "a figure for the poet" (117); I would argue that this notion is picked up by Ovid's phrase in the sphragis (15.875) that *melior pars mei*, exactly his *esprit créateur* and the works produced by it,[52] will escape oblivion and live on forever. Secondly, as Wheeler points out, by Ovid's time there had been a joining of poetry and philosophy in the interpretation of Hephaestus' shield, which had come to be considered as an allegory of the creation of the universe by a demiurge. The primacy, of course, belonged to Homer, just in purely chronological terms. "As a result of this type of exegesis, Roman poets came to regard the shield as a primary model for describing the origin and structure of the universe."[53] I would add that Ovid's choice of the Homeric shield as a model suggestively enhances his placement of the *Metamorphoses*

---

[50] Cf. Pythagoras' reference to *magni primordia mundi* at *Met.* 15.67.

[51] Wheeler (1995), with extensive references to previous scholarship. As always in Augustan poetry, several inspirations coexist; see Helzle (1993) for the Callimachean aspect of the cosmogony. The cosmogony then becomes an immediate illustration of the poetic program announced in lines 1–4: the combination of *carmen perpetuum* with *carmen deductum*.

[52] See Bömer *ad loc.*

[53] Wheeler (1995) 98, summarizing Hardie (1986) 66–70, 346–58.

directly in the Homeric, rather than the Empedoclean, tradition. The ancient view was that all the literary forms took their origin with Homer. He was the 'Ocean' — a description curiously relevant to the shield of Achilles — from which all literary streams flowed.[54] Over time, they had been disjoined, but the *Metamorphoses* was Ovid's grand attempt to bring them back together. In this light, Ovid's procedure of presenting "not merely one cosmogony, but a series" and "suggesting that the cosmogonic process is one that will continue throughout the poem: *ad mea tempora*"[55] takes on its true dimension. It is his poetic program of recreating and reuniting the various literary forms which originated with Homer.

Philosophy is assimilated and subordinated to this purpose. As with the discourse of Pythagoras, numerous attempts have been made to identify philosophical sources in Ovid's cosmogony. Once again, Ovid includes enough allusions to lend philosophical colouring to the piece. At the same time, and as befits the poet of metamorphosis who changed many poetic traditions, he makes some changes in the received philosophical tenets. Significantly, these changes apply to Empedocles and his doctrine of Love and Strife.[56] In the first instance, and in contrast also to Orpheus' song in Apollonius' *Argonautica* 1.497–511, Ovid presents Strife not as triggering the evolution of the cosmos, but as perpetuating chaos. What creates order is not an abstract philosophical principle, but a benevolent creator who is easily assimilable, as we have seen, to the ποιητής: *deus et melior natura* (1.21). Similarly, despite the importance of love as a theme in the *Metamorphoses*, Ovid excludes it as a natural-philosophical agent from his cosmogony. The avoidance of emphasis on serious philosophy is the same here as in Pythagoras' discourse.

6. Ovid, Vergil, and Lucretius

As can be expected, the speech of Pythagoras is relevant to another major aspect of the *Metamorphoses*, i.e. the constant comparison which Ovid asks the reader to make between his poem and Vergil's *Aeneid*. One dimension of this, which has been illustrated, is that the *Metamorphoses* is an even more comprehensive heir to Homer than is the *Aeneid* because Ovid was able to incorporate into it genres such as

---

[54] Documentation in Williams (1978) 87–9, 98–9; cf. Galinsky (1996) 262. Cf., with reference to the *Aeneid*, Cairns (1989) 150 and Hardie (1986) 22–4 .

[55] Myers (1994) 27.

[56] Wheeler (1995) 95–7.

comedy, pantomime, and burlesque that were not suitable for the Roman national epic. Another dimension involves Ovid's usual technique of inversion. In *Aeneid* 6, Vergil had to compensate for the incredibility of myth by infusing it with a heavy dose of serious philosophy. We know from Cicero, Propertius, and others that credence in the actual mythology of the underworld, such as the ferryman, the frogs, and the swamps, was at a low ebb among the Roman intelligentsia.[57] Hence Vergil drew heavily on various philosophical traditions to make Hades meaningful while providing another hint at the very end, through the conundrum of the Gate of False Dreams, that not all of his account, and especially the less spiritual θαυμαστά, was to be taken literally.[58] Ovid, by contrast, completely humanises the underworld in Book 4;[59] he has Pythagoras engage in a lengthy recitation of θαυμαστά; and he absolutely minimises the weight and significance of philosophy in the discourse of Pythagoras. Pythagoras' pointed dismissal (15.154–5) of the underworld as an "empty name" (*nomina vana*) and "stuff for poets" (*materiem vatum*) — all this while he is addressing *coetus silentum*, which was bound to recall the underworld — is a comment both on Vergil's brave remythologizing of Hades and on Ovid's repeated choice of it as a subject (besides Book 4, it appears in Books 5, 10, and 14).[60] Furthermore, as has been observed, Ovid blithely concedes Pythagoras' point by stating that the myths he tells "are not to be believed";[61] but naturally he tells them anyway and announces that he will be immortal for doing so.

By raising issues central to his work, Ovid appeals to the reader to reflect on the nature of mythological poetry and to compare him, in this important respect, with his two major Roman predecessors, Vergil and Lucretius. Virgil has already been commented upon in this respect; as regards Lucretius, it has traditionally been argued that, because of his ostensible attacks on myths, he demythologised myth, while Vergil and Ovid subsequently remythologised it. In actuality Lucretius' attitude is

---

[57] Cic., *Tusc.* 1.48; Prop. 2.34.53–4, only a few lines before Propertius' famous reference to the *Aeneid* (61–6).

[58] Cf. Wlosok (1990) 386–7.

[59] See the insightful and delightful discussion by Bernbeck (1967) 10–26.

[60] Book 5: Ceres and Proserpina (341ff.); 10.40–48 (Orpheus); 14.101–53: Aeneas and the Sibyl. Only 20 lines after his dismissive remarks, Pythagoras lays claim to being *vates* (15.174: *vaticinor*); his topic, vegetarianism, is consigned to *materies vatum*.

[61] *Trist.* 2.63–4, cited above, p.325. The phrase cannot be restricted to mean "bodies transformed in amazing ways"; cf. Luck *ad loc.* and Little (1970) 347–8. Ovid was taking no great risk as there was a strong tradition that 'veracity' was not to be expected of poets; for documentation and discussion see Feeney (1991) 5–56 and Myers (1994) 49–51. Cf., from a different perspective, Asmis (1995) 31.

more complex.[62] He wanted to be both an Epicurean and a poet, and being a poet meant that he had to use myth, which seems to have been precisely one of the reasons Epicurus had rejected poetry. Lucretius proceeded to combine the two hitherto irreconcilables by devising his own, Epicurean 'theory' of myth on the basis of several differentiations. Parallel to the Epicurean theory that sensations bear some relation to (external) reality, he posited that myths have a *hyponoia*, an underlying phenomenon that needed to be explained. In both cases, the problem is not one of reality or of the phenomenon itself, but one of faulty inferences and interpretations — in this case, the traditional myths. Myth, therefore, can be retained for its power to attract and charm readers, provided the *vera ratio* is pointed out at the same time. "The mythological passages in the *DRN*," therefore, "act as a powerful polemical and didactic tool: at one and the same time, Lucretius is able to dispose of rival theories of myth satisfactorily by substituting his own account of its origins and nature; and to use myth didactically to illustrate and enhance his own argumentation."[63] Lucretius, then, appropriates myth, which was formerly deceptive, for his own philosophical purposes; hence his use of the 'myths' of Venus and the plague to bracket his poem — just as Ovid does with the ostensibly 'philosophical' episodes of the cosmogony and Pythagoras.

This is only part of Ovid's response to Lucretius. Another involves the juxtapositions already observed of mythical-poetical and natural-philosophical explanations. Such juxtapositions are frequent in Lucretius, and they have a deeper reason: the demonstration of *vera ratio*. The theme is sounded in his apologia for poetry (1.921–50, repeated at 4.1–25): *id quoque enim non ab nulla ratione videtur* (1.935). It re-appears in the pivotal *exempla* of the Magna Mater (2.596–645) and Phaethon (5.396–415). In both the traditional mythological version is ascribed to *veteres Graium poetae* (2.600, 5.405); and in both Lucretius emphasises that *longe sunt tamen a vera ratione repulsa* (2.645) and *procul a vera nimis est ratione repulsum* (5.405–6). The difference from Ovid is clear: for Ovid, there is no *vera ratio* of myth and serious philosophy is next to non-existent in Pythagoras' discourse. In Ovid's catalogue of θαυμαστά the juxtapositions, therefore, become a mere literary device without any profound significance.[64] And just as Lucretius had appropriated the language and evocativeness of mythology

---

[62] See the sensible study by Gale (1994) on which my following remarks are based. Cf. Myers (1994) 53–9.

[63] Gale (1994) 230.

[64] Aristotle's comment τὸ δὲ θαυμαστὸν ἡδύ (*Poet.* 1460a17) is apropos.

for his philosophical tenets, so Ovid uses the Lucretian language of natural philosophy for some of his most fantastic transformations.[65] The inversion is complete: these *portenta* now are dressed up as if they were phenomena that can be explained in terms of rationalist science. A paradigm is the transformation of Lichas (9.216–25):

> dicentem genibusque manus adhibere parantem
> corripit Alcides et terque quaterque rotatum
> mittit in Euboicas tormento fortius undas.
> ille per aerias pendens induruit auras,
> utque ferunt imbres gelidis concrescere ventis,
> inde nives fieri, nivibus quoque molle rotatis
> adstringi et spissa glomerari grandine corpus,
> sic illum validis iactum per inane lacertis
> exsanguemque metu nec quicquam umoris habentem
> in rigidos versum silices prior edidit aetas.

This passage contains multiple appropriations from and inversions of Lucretius. The slingshot in line 218 recalls a piece of "pseudo-science taken on trust by Lucretius (*DRN* 6.177–9, 306–7),"[66] with a venerable pedigree that included Leucippus, Democritus, and, possibly, Anaxagoras.[67] Ovid treats this "scientific fact" by turning it inside out: he has the slingshot freeze and harden rather than heat up.[68] Ovid proceeds to explain the actual petrifaction of Lichas as a meteorological phenomenon; the model is Lucretius 6.495–523 and 527–34. Moreover, he mimics and inverts Lucretius by distancing himself from this event, now garbed in natural philosophy: cf. *ferunt* (220), which also hints at the borrowing of the explanation from Lucretius, and *prior edidit aetas* (225), which also corresponds to Lucretius' distancing himself from the mythological stories of the *Graeci vates*. This process also provides the larger context for Ovid's use of *ferunt* to disavow Pythagoras' influence on Numa (15.480).

7. Conclusions

Ovid's treatment of the discourse of Pythagoras is viewed best not as a unifying philosophical pivot of the *Metamorphoses*, but as a contribution to an ongoing discussion about the roles of myth and philosophy in the grand poetic tradition. One of Ovid's uses of this extended

---

[65] See Myers (1994) 47–9.
[66] Kenney in Melville (1986) 390.
[67] See Leonard and Smith (1961) *ad loc*. As Bömer points out (*ad Met.* 9.218), there is also an element of anachronism.
[68] See Bömer *ad Met.* 9.220 with reference to *Met.* 2.727–9.

passage is to call attention to his poetic aims and to his place in the poetic tradition.[69] He does not limit himself to writing Empedoclean epic; if anything, he places his poem in the tradition originating with Homer, a tradition that he 'metamorphoses' throughout his poem by numerous innovations. The speech of Pythagoras and related passages in the *Metamorphoses* highlight the nature of Ovid's contribution and his differences both from Lucretius' insistence on *vera ratio* and Vergil's reinvestment of myth with great spiritual, moral, and historical meaning. Ovid downplays the historical component, i.e. the connection of Pythagoras and Numa, and he banalises philosophy. The didacticism of Lucretius and philosophy in general are deflated by the jarring disjunction of the 'hyperdidactic' mode of the speech,[70] which is marked by a profusion of protreptic injunctions and didactic pronouncements,[71] and the minimalism of both philosophical content and a substantial addressee — the latter, as we have seen, is not Numa, who receives Pythagoras' ramblings only second- or third-hand, but the shadowy *coetus silentum* (15.66). Pythagoras' discourse would, therefore, be an intrinsically dubious vehicle for the poet if he were really laying serious claim to Empedoclean epic. At the same time, Ovid uses the speech of Pythagoras as a means of calling attention, once more by way of contrast, to his distinctive contribution to mythological poetry on a grand scale. It lies, to restate stubbornly what I said more than a score of years ago, in the realm of narrative.[72]

In terms of narrative, Pythagoras' presentation of change is designed to invite comparison with Ovid's in the previous books of the poem. To be sure, Pythagoras' speech is not a deliberately bad piece of poetry; Dryden and others singled it out for praise, and E.J. Kenney has observed that "the speed and fluency of the writing match the theme."[73]

---

[69] I cannot emphasise strongly enough that this is only one aspect of the passage. It is legitimate for academics to be attentive to aspects of poetology, genre, and the like in the *Metamorphoses*, provided we realise that these are not the immediate reasons for the popularity and appeal of the poem through the ages. The increasing interest in this aspect of the *Metamorphoses* is gratifying; see the recent the collections of Martindale (1988), Anderson (1995), and Walter and Horn (1995). As I stated initially, the entertainment value of the *mirabilia* and the topicality of "Pythagoras" would assure Ovid a broad public.

[70] Barchiesi (1989) 77, 80–82.

[71] E.g., *animos advertite* (140); *animos adhibete* (238); *mihi credite* (254); *tollite ... nec fallite ... nec includite ... nec celate ... perdite ... perdite* (473–8); *nonne vides* (361, 382); *magna... canam* (146–7); *doceo* (172); *vaticinor* (174); *docebo* (238).

[72] Galinsky (1975) 104–7. Cf. Kenney (1982) 435: "If the *Metamorphoses* is in some sense significant ... it can only be on the strength of Ovid's treatment of his material, the myths themselves."

[73] Kenney (1986) 460.

The reason is simple and does not have to be over-determined by narratologists "carried away by [their] hyperfunctionalist enthusiasm."[74] As always, Ovid has it both ways (although, as we could see from Lucretius' utilisation of myth, Ovid was not alone in this). The up-front narrator is Pythagoras. Ovid is the narrator *al fondo* who demonstrates, through his handling of Pythagoras' discourse, that he can assimilate 'philosophy' to his mythological poem just as easily as any other subject, genre, style, or tradition. The basic point is that Ovid, by presenting the subject through Pythagoras in this particular manner, alerts us to the fact that the material could be presented in other ways. This is true, as has been shown, of his failure to develop the multiple connections, discussed by other writers, between Pythagoras and early Rome, and it is implicit in his refusal to develop a significant philosophical discourse. Ovid makes no more than a bow to both traditions: he also knew that, as Cicero had pointed out,[75] philosophy and oratory were thought of as being united; hence the length of Pythagoras' speech is a running *contrapposto* to the thinness of its philosophical content proper. But, as has already been seen on several occasions, the speech looks back to the first fourteen books as well. There is reference after reference to stories that Ovid had told earlier: the Cyclops, Lucifer, Hercules, Scylla, Salmacis, the Centaurs, Phoebus, Myrrha, Phaethon, Aurora, the underworld. They are a constant reminder of how differently stories such as these could be told. Or, to take a subject like sex change, Pythagoras baldly mentions the hyena (15.408–10) while Ovid tells the stories of Iphis and Caeneus at length and with gusto. Ovidian polyphony is replaced by the monotone of Pythagorean taxonomy.

Simultaneously, Ovid uses Pythagoras' discourse as a reminder of the challenge which he himself faced in stringing together a mass of often heterogeneous material. Ovid's solution was to create imaginative, and sometimes deliberately outrageous, transitions, whereas those of Pythagoras lack such brio and can be artless and mechanical, an aspect that has been repeatedly commented upon. For instance, the connective *et quoniam* is used twice here (15.143, 176) and does not occur elsewhere in the *Metamorphoses*. Along the same lines, I remain convinced that Pythagoras, or Ovid through Pythagoras, articulates the realisation that the listener's attention may be flagging

---

[74] Genette (1988) 48. For a plain exposition of levels of narration and embedded narrative texts see Bal (1985) 134–48.
[75] *Or.* 11–19, cf. 113–19.

due to Pythagoras' narrative mode. At least this is the strong implication of lines 418–20: "The day will wane, the Sun beneath the waves will plunge his panting steeds before my tale recounts the sum of things that take new forms" (tr. A.D. Melville):

> desinet ante dies, et in alto Phoebus anhelos
> aequore tinguet equos, quam consequar omnia verbis
> in species translata novas.

Taking issue with my observation, Bömer in his commentary (*ad* 418) avers that it is not boredom that is suggested here. Rather, and borrowing a phrase from the Italian scholar Cupaiuolo, he writes that we are dealing, in the Ovidian trope, with "accorgimenti tecnici e . stilistici consueti nella prosa retorica." That is an even better way of making my point.

One of the main differences between 'Pythagoras' and Ovid is, of course, that Pythagoras' speech deals single-mindedly with change whereas most of the stories in the *Metamorphoses* do not. Kenney's observation that love (or, as I would put it, love in all its variations — or metamorphoses in that sense), rather than metamorphosis pure and simple, is the principal theme of the poem is still on the mark. Just as important, while the philosopher, represented by Pythagoras, proclaims change to be the controlling principle of the world, Ovid ends Book 15 and the *Metamorphoses* by emphasizing that he and his poetry will be impervious to it. *Nihil est toto, quod perstet, in orbe: cuncta fluunt*, says Pythagoras (177–8). Ovid, by contrast, will transcend the *orbis terrarum*:

> super alta perennis
> astra ferar, nomenque erit indelebile nostrum (875–6).[76]

---

[76] Paratore (1959) 193 has briefly adverted to the echo of Hor. *Od.* 2.20.1–4 (*ferar/ ... per liquidum aethera/ ... neque in terris morabor*), but the associations between the ode and the sphragis of the *Metamorphoses* are more extensive. In addition to dealing with the topos of poetic immortality (cf. the reference to *Od.* 3.30.1 in *Met.* 15.871), the ode was congenial because of its graphic description of metamorphosis, which anticipates several of the Ovidian depictions. There is also the usual alteration of the model: Horace, who is being transformed into a bird, becomes *biformis vates*, pretending to immortality, whereas Ovid, the poet of metamorphosis, concedes to the *vates* the power of predicting his immortality. Another connection is Horace's claim that he will be known among the barbarians at the fringes of the Roman Empire — precisely the kind of place where Ovid completed the *Metamorphoses*. Similarly, there is yet another point to Ovid's ascent *super astra*: his deification will be even greater than Julius Caesar's, whom Venus simply *caelestibus intulit astris* (15.846); cf. Feeney (1991) 249. Fittingly, Ovid ends the *Metamorphoses* with a blaze of allusions that add perspective to his achievement; the topic of Ovidian closures bears revisiting.

The contrast is played out yet further in the phrase which Pythagoras had used to introduce his maxim. He employed a well-known metaphor for poetry: *magno feror aequore* followed by *plenaque ventis vela dedi*, but his poetic pretensions are subverted from the start by yet another *et quoniam*, his second such use of that connective within less than thirty-five lines. It is a formula that is at home, e.g., in Cicero's *De Officiis*,[77] but not in poetry.

The speech of Pythagoras, then, has several purposes. Pythagoras personifies the confluence of Greece and Rome, a theme that shapes Book 15 and, in a larger sense, the entire *Metamorphoses* and the culture of the Augustan age. Pythagoras and his discourse also stand for the synthesis of various philosophies; Pythagoreanism, in fact, had evolved into such a synthesis, especially in Rome, by the first century BC. In that sense, Pythagoras is the 'compleat philosopher'; after all, he was credited with inventing the term. Further, Pythagoras' speech is a *tour de force*, just like Ovid's poem, but it is a very different *tour de force*. It is a demonstration of what Ovid could have done throughout the *Metamorphoses*, but did not. It also suggests what Pythagoras could have done and did not, both in terms of treating philosophy and narrative. The passage is also part of Ovid's ongoing dialogue with his Roman predecessors: with Ennius by recall of the earlier poet's Pythagorean colouring of the beginning of the *Annales*,[78] and especially with Lucretius and Vergil. Overall, the passage is a final demonstration of Ovid's inversion of Lucretius by Lucretian means. Lucretius had assimilated myth to his philosophical poem by stripping it of its traditional perspectives. Ovid reciprocates by assimilating philosophy to his mythological poem by divesting it of its real content. As in the case of any Augustan creation — and the *Metamorphoses* is very Augustan, unless one accepts the usual dichotomies — the main task for the interpreter of Pythagoras' discourse is to be attentive to the multiplicity of its aspects and to consider each individual aspect, such as the philosophical colouring, within this totality.[79]

---

[77] *Off.* 122, 132, 138; see Haupt/Ehwald/von Albrecht (1966) *ad* 15.75 and 143.

[78] It should be clear from Ovid's treatment of "Pythagoras" and Pythagoreanism that the passage in the *Metamorphoses* provides no basis for any inferences about Ennius' Pythagoreanism, whatever its nature. Ennius' principal point was that he was Homer's reincarnation. By recalling Ennius, Ovid, therefore, also recalls Homer, an aspect that is central to the *Metamorphoses*.

[79] A very preliminary version of this paper was delivered at the Leeds International Latin Seminar in February 1996. A more extensive version was presented at the Universities of Budapest and Szeged later that year. I am grateful to these audiences and, in

Bibliography

Anderson, W.S. (1995) (ed.). *Ovid. The Classical Heritage*. New York and London

Asmis, E. (1995). 'Epicurean poetics' in D. Obbink (ed.) *Philodemus and Poetry* (Oxford) 15–34

Bal, M. (1985). *Narratology. Introduction to the Theory of Narrative*. Toronto

Barchiesi, A. (1989). 'Voci e istanze narrative nelle *Metamorfosi* di Ovidio,' *Materiali e Discussioni* 23.55–97

Bernbeck, H.J. (1967). *Beobachtungen zur Darstellungsart in Ovids Metamorphosen*. Munich

Bömer, F. (1986). *P. Ovidius Naso. Die Metamorphosen. Buch XIV–XV*. Heidelberg

Burkert, W. (1960). 'Platon oder Pythagoras? Zum Ursprung des Wortes "Philosophie" ' *Hermes* 88.159–77

— (1961). 'Hellenistische Pseudopythagorica' *Philologus* 105.16–43, 226–46

Cairns, F. (1989). *Virgil's Augustan Epic*. Cambridge

— (1995). 'Horace's First Roman Ode (3.1)' *PLLS* 8.91–142

Coarelli, F. (1985). *Il Foro Romano* II. Rome

Crahay, R., and Hubaux, J. (1958). 'Sous le masque de Pythagore' in N.I. Herescu (ed.) *Ovidiana* (Paris) 283–300

Due, O.S. (1974). *Changing Forms. Studies in the Metamorphoses of Ovid*. Copenhagen

Farrell, J. (1992). 'Dialogue of Genres in Ovid's "Lovesong of Polyphemus" (*Metamorphoses* 13.719–897)' *AJPh* 113.235–68

Feeney, D. (1991). *The Gods in Epic. Poets and Critics of the Classical Tradition*. Oxford

Ferrero, L. (1955). *Storia del Pitagorismo nel mondo romano*. Turin

Gale, M. (1994). *Myth and Poetry in Lucretius*. Cambridge

Galinsky, K. (1975). *Ovid's Metamorphoses*. Oxford

— (1989). 'Was Ovid a Silver Latin Poet?' *Illinois Classical Studies* 14.69–89

— (1996). *Augustan Culture*. Princeton

Garbarino, G. (1973). *Roma e la filosofia greca dalle origini alla fine del II secolo A.C.* Turin

Genette, G. (1988). *Narrative Discourse Revisited*. Ithaca

Gruen, E. (1990). *Studies in Greek Culture and Roman Society*. Leiden

— (1992). *Culture and National Identity in Republican Rome*. Ithaca

Hardie, P. (1986). *Virgil's Aeneid: Cosmos and Imperium*. Oxford

— (1995). 'The Speech of Pythagoras in Ovid's *Metamorphoses* 15: Empedoclean Epos' *CQ* 45.204–14

Haussleiter, J. (1935). *Der Vegetarismus in der Antike*. Berlin

particular, to Alessandro Barchiesi and my colleague Stephen A. White, for some helpful suggestions.

Helzle, M. (1993). 'Ovid's Cosmogony. *Metamorphoses* 1.5–88 and the traditions of ancient poetry' *PLLS* 7.123–34

Hirzel, R. (1891). 'Philosophie im Zeitalter des Augustus' in V. Gardthausen *Augustus und seine Zeit* (Leipzig) 1296–1317

Horsfall, N. (1979). 'Epic Burlesque in Ovid's *Metamorphoses* 8.260ff.' *CJ* 74.319–32

Humm, M. (1996, 1997). 'Les origines du pythagorisme romain' *LEC* 64.339–53 and 65.25–42

Kenney, E.J. (1982). 'Ovid' in E.J. Kenney and W.V. Clausen (edd.) *The Cambridge History of Classical Literature* II (Cambridge) 420–57

— (1986). Introduction and Notes to *Ovid. Metamorphoses*, transl. by A.D. Melville. Oxford

Leonard, W.E. and Smith, S.B. (1961) (edd.). *T. Lucreti Cari De Rerum Natura Libri Sex*. Madison

Little, D. (1970). 'The Speech of Pythagoras in *Metamorphoses* 15 and the Structure of the *Metamorphoses*' *Hermes* 98.340–60

Maltby, R. (1991). *A lexicon of ancient Latin etymologies* (ARCA 25). Leeds

Martindale, C. (1988) (ed.). *Ovid Renewed*. Cambridge

Moog-Grünewald, M. (1979). *Metamorphosen der Metamorphosen. Rezeptionsarten der ovidischen Verwandlungsgeschichten in Italien und Frankreich im XVI. und XVII. Jahrhundert*. Heidelberg

Myers, K.S. (1994). *Ovid's Causes. Cosmology and Aetiology in the Metamorphoses*. Ann Arbor

Paratore, E. (1959). 'L'evoluzione della "sphragis" dalle prime alle ultime opere di Ovidio' *Atti del Convegno Internazionale Ovidiano. Sulmona 1958* (Rome) 173–203

Rawson, E. (1985). *Intellectual Life in the Late Roman Republic*. Baltimore

Sauron, G. (1994). *Quis deum? : l'expression plastique des idéologies politiques et religieuses à Rome à la fin de la République et au début du principat* (Bibliothèque des Écoles françaises d'Athènes et de Rome 285). Rome

Segl, A. (1970). *Die Pythagorasrede im 15. Buch von Ovids Metamorphosen*. Diss. Salzburg

Solodow, J. (1988). *The World of Ovid's Metamorphoses*. Chapel Hill

Walter, H. and Horn, H.-J. (1995) (edd.). *Die Rezeption der "Metamorphosen" des Ovid in der Neuzeit: Der antike Mythos in Text und Bild*. Berlin

Wheeler, S. (1995). '*Imago Mundi*: Another View of the Creation in Ovid's *Metamorphoses*' *AJPh* 116.95–121

Williams, F. (1978). *Callimachus' Hymn to Apollo: A Commentary*. Oxford

Wlosok, A. (1990). 'Et poeticae figmentum et philosophiae veritatem. Bemerkungen zum 6. Aeneisbuch' in E. Heck and E.A. Schmidt (edd.) *Res humanae — res divinae. Kleine Schriften* (Heidelberg) 384–91

Woodman, T. (1992). 'Epilogue' in T. Woodman and J. Powell (edd.) *Author and Audience in Latin Literature* (Cambridge) 204–15

PAPERS OF THE LEEDS INTERNATIONAL LATIN SEMINAR   TENTH VOLUME (1998) 337–57
Published by Francis Cairns (Publications) Ltd (Leeds 1998). ARCA 38. ISBN 0 905205 95 2

MARTIAL BOOK 8 AND THE POLITICS OF AD 93[*]

K.M. COLEMAN
Harvard University

Martial's extant *oeuvre* spans the reigns of four emperors, from Titus to Trajan. Of the four, Domitian is both chronologically and ideologically dominant; during his reign nine of Martial's twelve numbered books were published in the form in which they have come down to us. There is a clear 'political' purpose to a collection of epigrams devoted exclusively to the achievements of an emperor, such as what survives of Martial's *Liber Spectaculorum*, celebrating the dedication of the Colosseum by Titus in AD 80. But when epigrams about affairs of state (in effect, the affairs of the emperor) are all mixed up with poems on other themes which are proportionately much more numerous than the imperial poems, the effect is different.[1] Those who reject panegyric on principle might say that the intention of this apparent jumble should be construed as a subtle insult to the head of state;[2] but the ideology pervading the *Epigrams* is so alien to our modern way of thinking that we have to be particularly careful about importing our own ethical standards into an interpretation of what Martial was doing.[3]

---

[*] This paper was originally delivered at a seminar on 'politics and epigram' in Leeds in November 1995. In turning ideas into argument I have benefitted greatly from acute suggestions by Professor R.G.M. Nisbet.

[1] As recognised by Citroni (1988) 26.

[2] Cf. the attempts of Garthwaite (1990) and (1993) to demonstrate that when Martial flatters the emperor for a practice that he condemns in somebody else within the same book he must be covertly criticising the emperor; this assumption, born of a desire to impute 'sincerity' to Martial, aims to impose consistency of attitude within a genre that by its own admission depends upon startling juxtaposition of content and approach.

[3] Nauta (1995) 358–70 demonstrates that the anachronistic views broadly subsumed under the term 'Herrscherkritik' rely upon (i) a distortion of rhetorical techniques such

In trying to evaluate the 'political' role of the *Epigrams* it is useful to take account of the following points, obvious as they may be. (i) In an age of autocracy and informers the authorities would be constantly on the *qui vive* for coded insults. (ii) Martial intends the book to make a positive impression on his readership, i.e. emperor plus all his other actual and potential patrons, fans, purchasers; subversion would taint all the individuals associated with the book. (iii) Martial makes a notable effort to gain Nerva's confidence under the next regime; he does not say that of course when he flattered Domitian everybody knew he meant the opposite. (iv) Epigram pushes issues to extremities; its traditional features — brevity, antitheses, pointed conceits, hyperbole, bathos, paradox, and all the rest — exclude qualifications and compromise. (v) In the context of formal exercises in panegyric, imaginative compliments to the emperor advertise the versatility of the author in registering the equilibrium of the official ideology; 'naked flattery'[4] is a value-judgement as unproductive as the attempt to portray Martial in the guise of a revolutionary, 'sincerity' is an anachronistic concept imported from the aesthetics of Romanticism, and we are well reminded by Michael Dewar that "the extravagance of the medium, with the high value it placed on sheer extravagance of idea and expression alike, will always be alien in some measure to the modern reader".[5]

Whatever its original scope, the *Liber Spectaculorum* may represent the imperial commission that shot Martial to fame. Thereafter he cultivated a wider public, and put together full-scale *libri* that required a wider thematic spectrum in which the imperial theme played a proportionate role but not a dominant one; even in *Xenia* and *Apophoreta*,[6] composed before the sequence of numbered books, Domitian is part of the frame of reference within which the epigrams are composed. Leaving aside these two books, which adopt the form of 'dedicated' collections of mottoes to accompany presents,[7] during the reign of Domitian Martial published ten heterogeneous collections of epigrams, of which nine survive intact. The tenth we possess only in the politically correct form in which Martial re-issued it under Nerva, with

---

as σχῆμα as set out by Quintilian and (ii) transgression of the limits of applicability in similes and comparisons, especially those from mythology.

[4] E.g. Hofmann (1983) 246: "Im 8. und 9. Buch der Jahre 92 und 93 tritt die Kaiserhuldigung quantitativ und inhaltlich als offene Heuchelei hervor."

[5] Dewar (1994) 209.

[6] See Leary (1996) index *s.v.* Domitian.

[7] For a succinct assessment of the literary undertaking represented by these collections see Leary (1996) 21-3.

suitably adverse comment about Domitian in tandem with compliments to the new regime.[8] In the nine surviving Domitianic collections, there is a marked increase in 'imperial' poems from Book 4 onwards.[9] From Book 5, published in AD 90, the proportion of imperial poems in each rises steeply, peaking in Books 8 and 9, where the proportion of imperial poems amounts to a little over 25%. The following table sets out statistics for the distribution of 'imperial' epigrams in the books of Martial numbered 1 to 9 (issued under Domitian) and 10 to 12 (issued under Nerva and Trajan); those with a preface are denoted by an asterisk. This exercise is to some extent subjective, depending on how one defines an 'imperial' poem;[10] but I have included epigrams addressed to court-functionaries and excluded those in which an imperial reference seems to be entirely incidental:[11]

Book	Total	'Imperial'	Date
1*	117	9	86 (early)
2*	93	3	?
3	100	0	87 (Sept./Oct.)
4	89	6	88 (Dec.)
5	84	9	89 (Dec.)
6	94	9	?
7	99	12	92 (Dec.)
8*	82	23	?Dec. 92–Dec. 95
9*	103	27	?Dec. 92–Dec. 95
	861	98	
10	104	5	ed.[2] Apr.–Oct. 98 (ed.[1] ?Dec. 95)
11	108	6	Dec. 96
12*	98	5	Dec. ?101

Book 8 is one of the five books of the *Epigrams* to have a preface. In it Martial does not actually explain why the book contains such a high proportion of imperial poems; he merely describes this as an *occasio pietatis*, with a bow to the inspiration furnished by the emperor (8 *praefatio* 3–6): *omnes quidem libelli mei, domine, quibus tu famam, id est vitam, dedisti, tibi supplicant; et, puto, propter hoc legentur. hic tamen, qui operis nostri octavus inscribitur, occasione pietatis*

---

[8] The evidence is set out by Friedländer (1886) 62–5.

[9] Stressed by Merli (1993) 241ff.

[10] Cf. the discrepancies between the list of 'imperial' poems in Book 9 compiled by Barwick (1958) 287 and Garthwaite (1993) 100 n.14.

[11] By my (elastic) definition the following epigrams in Books 1–7 and 9–12 qualify as 'imperial': 1.4–6, 14, 22, 48, 51, 60, 104; 2.2, 91–2; 4.1, 3, 11, 27, 45, 74; 5.1–3, 5–6, 8, 15, 19, 65; 6.1–4, 10, 80, 83, 87, 91; 7.1–2, 5–8, 12, 40, 56, 60–61, 99; 9.1, 3, 5, 7, 11–13, 16–18, 20, 23–4, 28, 31, 34, 36, 39, 42, 49, 64–5, 79, 83, 91, 93, 101; 10.6–7, 28, 34, 72; 11.1–5, 7; 12.4–5, 8–9, 15.

frequentius fruitur. What he does explain, however, is the presence of non-imperial themes in the book, which he defends by appealing to the principle of *variatio* (8 *praefatio* 7–10): *quam [materiam] quidem subinde aliqua iocorum mixtura variare temptavimus, ne caelesti vere-cundiae tuae laudes suas, quae facilius te fatigare possint quam nos satiare, omnis versus ingereret.* And out of respect for Domitian's strict tenure of the office of censor he exercises self-denial by excluding obscene epigrams (8 *praefatio* 13–17): *illis [epigrammatis] non permisi tam lasciue loqui quam solent. cum pars libri et maior et melior ad maiestatem sacri nominis tui alligata sit, meminerit non nisi religiosa purificatione lustratos accedere ad templa debere.*

Sullivan, adopting White's theory that smaller collections circulated prior to the publication of 'omnibus' editions,[12] thought that this book comprised "the original *libellus* sent to the court [and] later augmented for the public".[13] But when Martial says *pars libri et maior et melior ad maiestatem sacri nominis tui alligata [est]* (8 *praefatio* 14–16) he is claiming that the most important element in the book comprises poems to do with the emperor; it is not necessary to postulate a pre-existing collection of court poetry. Some of the epigrams addressed to named individuals (Domitian included) may already have been presented to them, but others may have made their first appearance in the published collection. Fowler, in reaction against White, recommends starting from the premise that Martial crafted each book for publication as an organic whole; he concentrates upon epigrams concerned with books and reading, and argues that what were previously regarded as 'in-consistencies' revealing the 'gap' between genesis and publication are in fact deliberate instances marking the tension between the fiction of oral presentation in Roman literature and the actuality of circulation in literate form.[14] This may be over-subtle; in a heterogeneous genre like epigram, internal consistency within a published collection is not merely unimportant but would actively subvert the impression of spontaneity and immediacy that is the hallmark of this sort of poetry; and, as White has subsequently demonstrated with analogies from modern poetry,[15] we may be tempted to ascribe to programmatic state-ments within a collection a consistency and status to which the poet himself did not accord any importance.

The issue of immediacy is of course fundamental to any assessment

---

[12] White (1974) 44–5.
[13] Sullivan (1991) 40.
[14] Fowler (1995).
[15] White (1996).

of Martial's poetry, and requires a basic familiarity with the chronology of his published work. For a century after Friedländer no significant contributions were made to the chronology of Martial's books. But recently Mario Citroni has established that in addition to Books 13 and 14, Books 4, 5, 7, 11 and probably the first edition of Book 10 were all published in December, perhaps with a view to a potential market as gifts for the Saturnalia.[16] The outline of a pattern emerges in which Martial published a book annually at the end of the year; in the table above I have included rough estimates for the date of publication. Martial's frequent complaints about plagiarism strongly suggest that his epigrams circulated orally (probably piecemeal) before the definitive written text appeared with the *editio* of the book as a whole. The compilation of the collection then may have approximated to 'highlights of the year's output'.

In the context of the *Silvae* topicality is not all that important, at least not where private commissions are concerned: Statius still includes in Book 1 the *soteria* he composed for the distinguished consular Rutilius Gallicus on the occasion of his recovery from illness, even though in the meantime the old man has suffered a relapse and died (1.4). But that is a rather special case, in that under the circumstances the publication of this encomiastic poem serves as a type of *laudatio funebris*. When it comes to topical epigrams commemorating aspects of Domitian's policy or events of national importance such as the emperor's return from a foreign campaign, it would seem politic for Martial to sustain his programme of annual publication and include in the 'book of the year' highlights that had occurred during the course of it. But it was more than politic: topical subjects also advertised the epigrammatist's versatility in reflecting contemporary affairs; aside from their satiric slant, we may see an analogy in the modern custom of re-publishing in collections selected political cartoons that originally appeared in our daily papers. The artistic qualities of Martial's topical poems as individual examples of epigrammatic brilliance, and the cumulative effect of the *variatio* and scope within the book, would engage the attention of posterity.

Book 7 appeared at the end of 92. A prominent group of epigrams near the beginning (5–8) looks forward to the emperor's imminent return from the Danube; this 'prospective' view creates the expectation of a 'sequel', which is then fulfilled in the following book by the variations on the theme of the emperor's grand return. The pattern of

---

[16] Citroni (1989).

annual publication, with its concentration upon 'highlights of the year', makes it likely that Book 8 appeared in 93. But an apparent anomaly is introduced by poem 66, in which Martial expresses the hope that, now that Silius Italicus' older son has added a second consulship to his father's office (in AD 68), the younger son will add a third. The *Fasti Ostienses* for the year 94 give L. Silius Decianus a suffect consulship in September: *k. Sept. L. Silius Decianus, T. Pom[ponius Bassus]*.[17] Hence it has been supposed (most recently by Sullivan)[18] that Book 8 cannot have appeared before the last quarter of 94. But this seems very late to be publishing a collection that contains poems which celebrate the advent of peace at the beginning of the previous year. Under Domitian it is not known for certain at what stage of the year suffect consuls were appointed. *Ordinarii* were appointed in the autumn for office the following year, and under the Julio-Claudian emperors there are some instances of *suffecti* being appointed at the same time;[19] the inconsistency of procedure observable under the Julio-Claudians may have persisted into the Flavian era. On the evidence of Pliny's *Panegyric*, however, it is clear that by AD 100 suffect appointments were announced early in the tenure of the *consules ordinarii* for the year, and it has been suggested that this procedure was introduced under the Flavians.[20] Hence Citroni concludes that Book 8 was published early in 94.[21] It is, however, possible that Martial composed this compliment to Silius Italicus towards the end of 93, if by then it was already known that his son would be consul a year hence (8.66.3–4): *bis senos iubet en redire fasces,/ nato consule*. At all events, the datable references in Book 8 all belong to 93 and create the atmosphere of a year characterised by rejoicing at the emperor's return to Rome.

The epigrams on 'imperial' themes in Book 8 can be baldly summarised and listed as follows (those in round brackets are addressed to members of Domitian's court; in those in square brackets celebration of the emperor is approached obliquely by means of compliments to private patrons):

1	Invocation to Minerva
2	Janus' prayer for longevity for Domitian
4	Vows discharged for the emperor's safety (3 January)
8	Domitian *redux* in Janus' month

[17]   Cf. Degrassi (1947) 222.
[18]   Sullivan (1991) 40.
[19]   Talbert (1984) 202.
[20]   Talbert (1984) 207.
[21]   Citroni (1989) 224 n.40.

11	Domitian *redux* acclaimed in the Circus
15	Rome celebrates as though in triumph
21	*Adventus* of Domitian
24	Request for Domitian at least to accept petitions
26	Domitian's display of tigers
(28	To Parthenius about a toga)
30	Performance of 'Mucius Scaevola'
[32	Recall of Aretulla's brother from exile]
36	Domitian's palace reaches to the stars
39	Banquet in Domitian's palace
49	Domitian's *cena recta*
53	Lion displayed in the arena
56	Domitian's *congiarium*
65	Temple of Fortuna Redux and triumphal arch
[66	Consulships for the Silii]
(68	To Entellus about his greenhouse)
[78	Stella's races in the circus]
80	Domitian's restoration of unarmed combat in the arena
82	Request for imperial acknowledgement

The inclusion of epigrams on 'political' themes (in the broadest sense of the word) invests the book with celebratory status: what they sacrifice in topicality they gain in commemorative value. By including poems on imperial themes Martial is at the very least acknowledging the emperor's impact on contemporary affairs. But it would be wrong to interpret this as a response (reluctant or not) to intense pressure from a megalomaniac ruler. Martial was vitally interested in sales-figures. He boasts that he is read world-wide, and he takes great care in directing prospective purchasers to available stocks. His credit with the emperor is played up, not down; under an established regime admiration of the ruler is part of the generally accepted value-system. Books 4 to 9 of the *Epigrams* span more or less the last six years of Domitian's reign. Each begins with a poem to or about him (indirectly, in the case of Book 6) and, furthermore, in each case the introductory poem forms a cluster with other Domitianic material.[22] Two instances, Books 7 and 8, also end with a poem to the emperor. After the initial cluster of Domitianic material the rest of it is scattered throughout each book, interspersed with poems about mean patrons, impotent lovers, bad poets, plagiarists, doctors, handicapped people, charioteers, birthday presents, the Saturnalia — the whole panoply of urban life. In other words, the emperor is woven inextricably into the fabric of Roman society. He is part of normality, albeit a normality that is distorted and

---

[22] For a detailed analysis see Merli (1993) 237–51.

exaggerated by the conventions that Martial has established in composing epigram.

It follows that Domitian's 'presence' in the *Epigrams* should correspond to his actual presence in Rome; or, to put it another way, his return to Rome after an absence should register in the *Epigrams*. At the end of 85 he returned after several months' absence engaged in the *prima expeditio Dacica*; Book 1, containing eight 'imperial' poems, was published early in 86. In August 89, having defeated the Chatti, he returned from seven months' absence on the Rhine and the Danube that had been precipitated by Saturninus' revolt; Book 5, containing nine 'imperial' poems, appeared in December of that year. In January 93 he returned from the expedition against the Sarmatae; Book 7, containing eleven 'imperial' poems, was published in December 92 when Domitian was already known to be on his way back.[23] He remained based in Rome for the rest of his reign; Books 8 and 9, containing the greatest proportion of 'imperial' poems in Martial's entire output, reflect his renewed presence in the capital.

An emperor's return to Rome from abroad was an occasion of great significance and corresponding ceremonial. The importance of the *adventus* ceremony in late Antiquity has its roots much earlier. The theme of *dux redux* is the Leitmotif of the opening series of epigrams in Book 8,[24] in which Martial lays the same stress upon *consensus* that is characteristic of the welcome accorded the emperor in late Antiquity (8.15.1–4):[25]

> Dum nova Pannonici numeratur gloria belli
> omnis et ad reducem dum litat ara Iovem,
> dat populus, dat gratus eques, dat tura senatus,
> et ditant Latias tertia dona tribus.

The mounting anticipation as the crowds assemble before dawn on the day of his arrival is conveyed in an epigram addressed first to *Phosphorus* and then to the emperor himself (8.21). If (as is increasingly shown to have been the case)[26] Martial arranged the order of his published poems himself, why does he flout chronology to the extent that several epigrams describing the reception Domitian got on his return from the frontier actually precede the poem celebrating his re-entry into

---

[23] On the chronology of Domitian's absences abroad see Strobel (1989) 116–21.

[24] Normally a safe return from campaign would be attributed to *Fortuna Redux*; hence the phrase *ad Reducem ... Iovem* implies that Domitian has divinely engineered his return himself: Wistrand (1955) 10.

[25] MacCormack (1981) 18.

[26] E.g. by Barwick (1958); Citroni (1988); Merli (1993); Fowler (1995).

the city? Admittedly, poem 21 is nicely offset by two short poems on either side.[27] But this still does not explain why this trio of epigrams was not placed earlier in the book. It is, however, noteworthy that a similar disruption of chronological sequence is a feature of the *Eclogues*, and of the *Odes* and *Epodes*. Whatever their circumstances of composition, once poems are integrated into a general book that does not purport to be a narrative of a chain of events, chronological order becomes irrelevant and is superseded by aesthetic considerations. A disrupted order defies predictability, and for a reader starting Book 8 at the beginning the epigram describing Domitian's *adventus* claims attention because of its unexpected position in the sequence and in the book as a whole.

There must be a reason why Book 8 has proportionately more poems to do with the emperor than any other book. To what extent was Martial reacting to contemporary political circumstances? AD 93 has been represented as a year of crisis for Domitian in three respects. One was the continuing threat in the region of the Danube, which had been troublesome throughout his reign. If, in the words of Sir Ronald Syme, the conclusion of the Danubian campaign at the end of 92 meant that "[a] period of ease and security for the government might now seem vouchsafed",[28] this impression, reflected by Martial, was not sustained by the military position. The Sarmatae represented a formidable menace:[29] one of their constituent groups, the Roxolani, are illustrated on Trajan's column, clad from head to toe in chain-mail and employing cataphract cavalry like the Parthians; to the West were the Iazyges, who crossed the Danube into Pannonia in 92 and wiped out a whole legion, XXI Rapax (Suetonius *Domitian* 6.1), thereby precipitating Domitian's departure for the frontier to prosecute the Second Pannonian War, probably in May.[30] By the end of the year the Romans had won a victory over the Sarmatian Iazyges which probably enforced their status as Roman *foederati*[31] but did not eliminate the threat posed by the Marcomanni and Quadi further west: Domitian deposited the laurels of victory in Jupiter's lap on the Capitol at Rome without celebrating a triumph, and Nerva's successful prosecution of the Third Pannnonian

---

[27] Barwick (1958) 286 interprets 11, 15 and 21 as a triptych in which the theme of rejoicing supplies the frame (11.4 *laetitia*, 21.1 *gaudia*).

[28] Syme (1983) 123.

[29] Abundantly illustrated by Wilkes (1983).

[30] Domitian was absent from Rome for eight months (Mart. 9.31), returning early in January 93 (Mart. 8.2 8): see Strobel (1989) 101.

[31] Mart. 7.6, Strobel (1989) 102.

War at the outset of his reign in AD 97 must presuppose extensive preparations by Domitian before his assassination.[32]

This unresolved threat brought another in its train: financial problems. The wars on the Danube destabilised Domitian's external policies; they cost lives; and they cost money.[33] The financial burden imposed by the campaigns on the Danube was at its most severe by the early nineties, precisely the point at which Domitian introduced new measures to generate income by accepting inheritances, increasing revenue from the *fiscus Iudaicus*, and confiscating senatorial property.[34] It was indeed senatorial resistance that constituted the third major threat that Domitian faced in 93: a consolidation of senatorial resistance at home. This is to be inferred from the rash of charges that were brought in the latter half of the year:[35] seven cases (Pliny *Epistles* 3.11.3), resulting in three executions and four sentences of exile (with attendant confiscation of property); the victims can be tabulated as follows:

Helvidius Priscus (younger), cos. suff. (pre-86 or 93[36])	executed[37]
Herennius Senecio, quaestor	executed[38]
Q. Iunius Arulenus Rusticus, cos. suff. (92)	executed[39]
Fannia, d. of Paetus, widow of Helvidius Priscus (elder)	exiled
Arria (younger), widow of Paetus	exiled[40]
Iunius Mauricus, brother of Arulenus	exiled
Gratilla, wife(?) of Arulenus	exiled[41]

[32] Including the transfer of Legio XIV Gemina from Moguntiacum (Mainz) to Pannonia in the spring of 97: Strobel (1989) 105ff. For the possibility that Domitian was already engaged in a full-scale campaign in this region before his assassination see the discussion of the epigraphic evidence by Jones (1992) 153–5. Even if this was indeed the case, it was still Nerva who brought the affair to a conclusion.

[33] Strobel (1989) 114–15.

[34] Rogers (1984) 75.

[35] Bauman (1974) 160–2, Jones (1992) 122, Rogers (1960), Salles (1986) 762–4, Syme (1983) 123–6.

[36] Syme (1983) 124.

[37] For mocking Domitian's divorce in a mime about Paris and Oenone: Suet. *Dom.* 10.4.

[38] For praising the elder Helvidius Priscus (Tac. *Agr.* 2.1) and composing his biography (Plin. *Epist.* 7.19.5, Dio 67.13.2). Dio quotes the additional charge that Herennius stood for no further office after the quaestorship.

[39] For praising Thrasea Paetus (in a biography?) and calling him *sanctissimus*: Tac. *Agr.* 2.1, Suet. *Dom.* 10.3, Dio 67.13.2. Suetonius apparently muddles Arulenus with Herennius in attributing to him a biography of Helvidius also.

[40] Fannia was charged with supplying Herennius Senecio with documentary material for his biography of her late husband, and Arria was charged with complicity with Fannia, who denied that her mother was involved (Plin. *Epist.* 7.19.5); but both were exiled (Plin. *Epist.* 9.13.5).

[41] Tac. *Agr.* 45 records the exile of both Mauricus and Gratilla without specifying the charge, which was perhaps defamation: Bauman (1974) 162 n.177.

The exact circumstances are hard to recover; but the penalties, at least
for the victims who were executed, cohere with charges of *maiestas*.
Two of the accused included former consuls, one appointed by
Domitian only a year before; to warrant such drastic action, the
situation must have been perceived by the emperor as a sudden and
serious crisis. After dealing with these individuals, he banished philo-
sophers from Rome *en bloc*.[42]

The coincidence of internal and external threats to the stability of
Domitian's regime is accorded considerable significance by Karl
Strobel.[43] When Martial and Statius in 93 give especial prominence to
the emperor's leadership and magnificence, are they responding to
instructions from Domitian for the court-poets to rally round and
counter sudden panic among the public at large? Syme warned that the
carnage and disgrace that Agricola was spared from witnessing might
be a Tacitean exaggeration (... *eadem strage tot consularium caedes,
tot nobilissimarum feminarum exilia et fugas*: *Agricola* 45.1). But even
if Domitian did indeed have to tackle severe problems simultaneously
on the frontiers, with the treasury, and in the Senate, the question is
whether these problems, and Domitian's response to them, were such
as to shake public confidence in him. Who was aware of the political
threats to the stability of the Flavian regime in AD 93?

The first consideration is the context of Domitian's return in January
93. He had waged a campaign against the Germans and the Sarmatae,
culminating in the defeat of the Sarmatian Iazyges. To mark his success
he deposited the laurels of victory in the Temple of Capitoline Jupiter.
The reasons for his self-restraint in foregoing a triumph are much
debated: refusal of honours was uncharacteristic of an emperor who
had already celebrated four triumphs (the first over the Chatti in 83, the
second over the Dacians in 86, and a double triumph over the Dacians
and the Germans in 89) and would hold his seventeenth consulship two
years later in AD 95. He may have wanted to put the Sarmatian
problem 'on hold' until he could strengthen the Danube frontier and
score a decisive victory; the absence of a triumph might be intended to
convey this message to the Senate. Or he may have been advised to
return because of mounting opposition at home in his absence; in that
case his refusal of a triumph might be interpreted as an attempt to
impress upon the Senate his modesty and self-restraint. These

---

[42] None of the three offenders executed was condemned for a philosophical work *per se*
(see Salles [1986] 763); all of them were senatorial, i.e. representing 'educated
opinion', a tradition of liberty, and Stoic teaching (Syme [1983] 123).

[43] Strobel (1989) 114.

suggestions[44] are not mutually exclusive, and a combination is possible. If the laurel-laying ceremony was interpreted as a second-class festivity, the poets may be regarded as glamourising it so as to make it appear equivalent to an actual triumph.[45] But it was actually a ceremony of great pomp and cultic significance in its own right, and since Domitian chose to substitute it for a triumph he presumably did not anticipate a disappointed and dissatisfied reaction; the excitement and anticipation evoked by Martial may be an accurate reflection of the contemporary atmosphere.

Martial's contemporaries also had to negotiate Domitian's choice, each according to his genre. When Venus in the *Punica* is in despair at the sight of Hannibal poised to invade Italy, Jupiter adapts Anchises' precedent and reassures her with a prophetic speech, concentrating (of course) on the Flavian dynasty. Bacchus will be eclipsed by Domitian's triumphs in the East; the Danube where the Sarmatae live will be brought under control (Silius *Punica* 3.614–17):[46] *hic et ab Arctoo currus aget axe per urbem,/ ducet et Eoos Baccho cedente triumphos./ idem indignantem tramittere Dardana signa/ Sarmaticis uictor compescet sedibus Histrum.* The scope of the *Silvae* means that Statius is able to weave into a broad thematic canvas allusions to the emperor's gesture in foregoing a triumph over the Sarmatae. He explains it on the grounds that Domitian's *clementia* prevented him from granting these nomadic tribes the status of being an enemy over whom the Romans would indeed celebrate a triumph: a sort of magnanimous snub (*Silvae* 3.3.167–71):

> haud mirum, ductor placidissime, quando
> haec est quae victis parcentia foedera Cattis
> quaeque suum Dacis donat clementia montem,
> quae modo Marcomanos post horrida bella vagosque
> Sauromatas Latio non est dignata triumpho.

Later he takes the opportunity to urge Domitian to compromise these principles and let Rome honour him with further triumphs after all

---

[44] Jones (1992) 153.

[45] In modern scholarship Domitian's ceremony is sometimes called an *ovatio* (e.g. *RE* XII.2575 s.v. Flavius 77 [Weynand], Jones [1992] 152–4), although this term is nowhere used in the ancient sources. The *ovatio* (*minor triumphus*: Plin. *NH* 15.19, Serv. *Aen.* 4.543; cf. Dion. Hal. 8.67.10) was a Republican ceremony which is attested sporadically under the early Principate: see *RE* XVIII.1.1890.50–1903.36 s.v. Ovatio (G. Rohde). It took the form of a procession, like the triumph, but the privileges specific to a triumphant general were omitted (e.g. the general's wreath was of myrtle instead of laurel): see Versnel (1970) 166.

[46] For the dating of this passage after the campaign of 92 see Strobel (1989) 102.

(*Silvae* 4.1.39): *mille tropaea feres; tantum permitte triumphos.*

The brief compass of epigram, however, entails a direct approach; the conclusion to poem 15 is a *tour de force* and crucial for assessing the 'political' direction Martial was taking in Book 8 of the *Epigrams* (8.15. 5–8):

> hos quoque secretos memorabit Roma triumphos,
> nec minor ista tuae laurea pacis erit.
> quod tibi de sancta credis pietate tuorum,
> principis est virtus maxima nosse suos.

> 5 memorabit β: memorauit γ   6 erit β: erat γ   6–7 *post* 6 *plenius distinxit Shackleton Bailey, post* 7 *vulg.*

A brilliant oxymoron expresses the paradox of Domitian's low-key victory, *memorabit* (5) in pointed juxtaposition with *secretos*; the matching pentameter simultaneously stresses that the *depositio* of the laurels is no less than a triumph (although of course technically they were not equivalents) and lays emphasis on the advent of peace; the concluding couplet reassures the emperor that a triumph is not necessary to convince his subjects of his victory.[47] Was that indeed the case?

If less of the *Epigrams* and the *Silvae* had survived, or more of the rest of contemporary literature, their atmosphere might seem less exaggerated and their compliments more conventionally representative of current ideology. An important programmatic comparison is available in the iconography of the Cancellaria reliefs. Erika Simon has shown that the friezes known as A and B illustrate respectively *pietas principis* in the person of the emperor as Pontifex Maximus and *virtus principis* in his role as Imperator: frieze A, symbolic of the victorious conclusion to the Imperator's campaign, depicts the dedication of the laurels of victory to Jupiter; the figure of the emperor, which must originally have represented Domitian dedicating the laurels in AD 93, was re-worked in Antiquity to portray Nerva, whose ceremony dedicating the laurel from Pannonia on 27 October 97 coincided with the date of his adoption of Trajan.[48] For the association of *virtus* and *pietas*

---

[47] Wistrand (1955) 19–23 followed the text of γ, adopted the conventional punctuation, and interpreted line 6 as a parenthesis; he objected that the ceremony Domitian celebrated was too public to be described as *secretos ... triumphos* and concluded that this phrase referred to Domitian's reputation in his own palace as opposed to his public honours. By adopting the text of β and punctuating 5–8 as a pair of regular end-stopped couplets Shackleton Bailey (1978) 281 has restored cohesion: *suos* (8) refers to the emperor's subjects as a whole rather than to the restricted circle of his court.

[48] Simon (1985) 554.

as a Domitianic ideal Professor Simon adduces the evidence of Quintilian (*Institutiones Oratoriae* 3.7.9): *laudandum in quibusdam, quod geniti inmortales, quibusdam, quod inmortalitatem virtute sint consecuti: quod pietas principis nostri praesentium quoque temporum decus fecit*; this corresponds exactly to the combination attested in the final couplet of Martial 8.15 (quoted above). Hence the poets and the artists of the Cancellaria reliefs exhibit the same confidence in Domitian's rule.

One might object that poems may be composed hastily and reliefs carved at the double to convey a political message at a moment of crisis. But an architectural structure, necessarily the fruits of a long-term project, cannot plausibly be interpreted as a panic-reaction. The group of epigrams about Domitian's return from the Danube are followed by a cluster of poems about Domitian's palace and his munificence in entertaining the populace. His magnificent edifice on the Palatine was really a complex of separate buildings to which traditional (if misleading) names have been assigned: on the north side the Domus Tiberiana, remodelled by Domitian, and a building of uncertain function that he started and which has recently been designated by the neutral term 'Forum Building';[49] to the south on one level the Domus Flavia and the upper storey of the Domus Augustana, and on the level beneath them the lower storey of the Domus Augustana and the so-called 'Hippodrome'.[50] Enough of this complex of structures survives today for it to be obvious that its site at the edge of the Palatine overlooking the Circus Maximus gave it a dominating aspect overlooking the Tiber and the grand estates on the far bank. The greater part of the complex was completed by AD 92. Martial had already complimented Rabirius, the architect, in a poem in the seventh book (7.56), which elegantly combines the equation of Domitian with Jupiter: if Olympia wanted to build a new home for Phidias' statue of Zeus it would borrow Rabirius from Domitian to design it.

Both Statius and Martial express the idea that the palace provides a heaven on earth for Domitian. While it is essential to appreciate that they are both saturated with the same ideological stream of ideas as the architect Rabirius and the army of interior decorators, mosaicists, stuccoists and fresco artists who decorated the palace, MacDonald may go too far in extrapolating architectural details from the celestial atmo-

---

[49] Following Darwall-Smith (1996) 180.
[50] Darwall-Smith (1996) 182–3.

sphere evoked by the poets.[51] Nevertheless, the heavenly analogies impart divine status to the emperor, holding sway in the centre of his domain and radiating an aura (Statius *Silvae* 4.2.40–44):

> ipsum, ipsum cupido tantum spectare vacavit
> tranquillum vultus et maiestate serena
> mulcentem radios summittentemque modeste
> fortunae vexilla suae; tamen ore nitebat
> dissimulatus honos.

The towering structure of the palace, already elevated on the prominent face of the Palatine, seems to touch the stars (Martial 8.36.11): *quae vertice sidera pulsat,/ par domus est caelo*. The central banqueting-hall, its ceiling studded with the constellations, replicates heaven within its walls (Statius *Silvae* 4.2.30–31): *longa supra species: fessis vix culmina prendas/ visibus auratique putes laquearia caeli*. The analogy with heaven naturally accommodates a series of equations: Domitian is equated with Jupiter;[52] a state banquet is equated with a feast on Olympus; the wine served is equated with nectar (Martial 8.39.3, Statius *Silvae* 4.2.11, 54); the servant administering the wine is equated with Ganymede (Martial 8.39.4, Statius *Silvae* 4.2.10–11). The vast palace is only cramped in one respect: it is too small for its divine occupant; Martial and Statius express the same concept in strikingly similar terms: *par domus est caelo, sed minor est domino* (Martial 8.36.12), *effusaeque impetus aulae ... tantum domino minor* (*Silvae* 4.2.23–5).[53]

The last mention of the palace in the *Epigrams* occurs in Book 12, published under Trajan (12.15). It illustrates precisely the political opportunism that was demanded of an epigrammatist giving expression to current fads and trends: all the sumptuous treasures in the palace, the *deliciae gravesque luxus* of a *rex superbus*, have at last been put to a properly democratic purpose; they have been transferred (either by Nerva or by Trajan himself) to public view in temples, chiefly (apparently) that of Capitoline Jupiter (12.15.1–5):

---

[51] E.g. MacDonald (1982) 73: 'the vaulted imitations of the heavenly arc invited the celestial analogies of the poets'; Darwall-Smith (1996) 193–9 warns against making technical deductions from non-technical vocabulary. The debate on the roofing of the state halls of the Domus Flavia is summarised by Gibson *et al.* (1994) 77–80; they conclude that in each case a timber truss and tile roof is the only possibility.

[52] This hall was reputedly known as *cenatio Iovis* (*SHA, Pertinax* 11.6).

[53] For an architectural reconstruction that endorses the remarkable size and height of the banqueting-hall see Gibson *et al.* (1994); on the atmosphere that the literary sources evoke (i.e. an earthly home for a divine occupant) see in general Darwall-Smith (1996) 203–5.

> quidquid Parrhasia nitebat aula
> donatum est oculis deisque nostris.
> miratur Scythicas virentis auri
> flammas Iuppiter et stupet superbi
> regis delicias gravesque luxus.

The temporal 'then and now' contrast, typical of epigram, is a moral contrast too:[54] by entering the public domain these 'whims and oppressive luxuries of a haughty monarch' have acquired political respectability. There is a striking match with Pliny's sentiments in the *Panegyricus*, where Domitian is constantly portrayed as a foil to the beneficent and fair-minded Trajan.

The munificence of Martial's sponsors, actual and potential, private and imperial, is a constant preoccupation throughout the numbered books of the *Epigrams*. Just as he loosely grouped together near the beginning of Book 8 the epigrams about Domitian's return from the Danube, so towards the middle he has grouped the epigrams concerned with the palace and the feasting hosted by the emperor, thus giving imperial munificence central prominence in the book. Poem 39, the banquet in the state apartments, is balanced by 49, a *cena recta* held for all the social orders combined. The opening parallel from mythology (the banquet celebrating the victory of the gods over the giants) implies that the occasion Martial is commemorating was associated with a real triumph (8.49.1, 5): *quanta Gigantei memoratur mensa triumphi ... tanta tuas, Caesar, celebrant convivia laurus.* Towards the end of the book he will claim that the games held by Arruntius Stella in honour of Domitian's victory would have enhanced the gods' victory over the giants or Bacchus' triumph over the Indians (8.78.1–3): *quos cuperet Phlegraea suos victoria ludos,/ Indica quos cuperet pompa, Lyaee, tuos,/ fecit Hyperborei celebrator Stella triumphi.* To patrons thus complimented would the mythological references seem hackneyed?

We may be tempted to interpret these mythological equivalencies cynically as absurdities parroted by a sycophant to massage the ego of a tyrant and his associates and to disguise the mediocrity of his achievements. But mythology is the natural recourse of panegyrists; precisely because a mythological analogy cannot literally be true, it affords scope for imaginative inflation in expressing compliments that would be heavy-handed without the mythological flourish. A whole repertoire of

---

[54] Such a contrast, natural in epitaph, is adopted with enthusiasm in declamatory contexts as the *locus communis de fortuna*; it is much favoured in Hellenistic epigram, where it provides a neat antithetical framework for a short poem. Examples abound in the *Greek Anthology*, usually of a decline but sometimes (as here) of an improvement.

instant equations is at hand: Janus to welcome the emperor in January, whether back from the Danube in 93 (as in Martial Book 8) or assuming the consulship two years later (as in *Silvae* 4.1); or Bacchus' triumph in India, found wanting by comparison with Domitian's celebrations on his return from the north (the point of comparison being the tigers at Domitian's celebratory games, more numerous than the pair drawing Bacchus' triumphal chariot: 8.26); or, to take an example from the private sphere, Calliope predicting Lucan's greatness (*Silvae* 2.7). An early modern example may help to show how panegyric can exploit mythology as a literary resource without implying anything about the contemporary belief-system: among the Restoration panegyrists celebrating the return of Charles II from exile in Holland Dryden imagines him sacrificing to the deities of the sea (*Astraea Redux* 119–24):

> With alga who the sacred altar strows?
> To all the sea-gods Charles an offering owes:
> A bull to thee, Portunus, shall be slain,
> A lamb to you, the tempests of the main:
> For those loud storms that did against him roar
> Have cast his shipwracked vessel on the shore.

Such conceits embellish the expression of loyalist sentiments with a mantle of fantasy culled from the literary repertoire; and the fantasy in itself permits sentiments that are by rational standards excessive.

Martial, like Statius, seizes the opportunity to mention the loyalty demonstrated by his aristocratic patrons towards the imperial regime. Arruntius Stella is an old friend of both of them, first encountered in Book 1 of Martial's *Epigrams*.[55] The games he held to honour Domitian's victory (which is elevated by Martial to the status of a 'Hyperborean triumph', *Hyperborei ... triumphi*) are given a prominent position towards the close of Book 8 (Martial 8.78). They lasted several days and included thirty chariot-races (8.78.7, 13), so they must have been put on in the circus.[56] There was also a distribution of *missilia* by means of tokens instead of gifts in kind; the spectators could cash in the tokens afterwards for birds, and for the animals they had been watching (8.78.9–12). The emphasis on generosity is marked; Stella's thirty prizes in the chariot races surpassed the usual total for both consuls combined (8.78.13–14): *quid numerem currus ter denaque praemia palmae,/ quae dare non semper consul uterque solet?* Since the

---

[55] *PIR²* A 1151, White (1975) 267–72.

[56] Presumably Stella had special permission to do this, since it was the prerogative of the consuls to put on games there, whereas in 93 he appears only to have been praetor; he became suffect consul in 101, or possibly 102: Mart. 12.3.10, White (1975) 270 n.11.

occasion is held in the emperor's honour, the association is clear:
loyalty inspires munificence.

Public benefaction was a prominent feature of Domitian's reign,
well attested by Suetonius: one of the means by which Domitian cele-
brated his victory was the distribution of a third *congiarium* to the
people of Rome; poem 56 claims that the people love his largesse
because of Domitian, not vice versa. The emperor's achievements in
the moral sphere too do not go unremarked: just as Statius is to com-
pliment him on his vine-edict and his prohibition on castration (*Silvae*
4.3.11–15), so in Book 8 Martial praises his ban prohibiting gladiators
fighting with weapons (80), an excellent example of the contemporary
preoccupations of a society at peace, engaged in the normal activities of
urban life. Part of the expression of this normality is Martial's charac-
teristic self-presentation as a loyal client expecting patronage.
Reminders to this effect are evenly spaced in the course of the book. In
poem 24 he begs Domitian to allow him to file a petition, even if he
will not grant it; drawing an analogy between sculpture and panegyric
he claims that real divinity is bestowed not by iconography but by
petitionary prayer. And the last poem in the book reminds the emperor
that Martial has fulfilled his side of the contract: where others file
petitions he has composed honorific poetry (8.82.1–2): *dante tibi turba
querulos, Auguste, libellos/ nos quoque quod domino carmina parva
damus.*

The Flavian regime and its value-system had been established for
more than a quarter of a century. It seems unlikely that the broad
spectrum of the population at Rome would have regarded Domitian's
campaign against the Sarmatae as anything short of an unqualified
success; or that they would have perceived incipient financial strain; or
that they would have been unsettled by the removal of a group of
aristocratic dissidents associated with a tradition of perversity. When
the mutiny led by Saturninus had precipitated Domitian's departure for
the Rhine at the beginning of 89, the traitor was duly rebuked in
Martial's collection of epigrams published at the end of the year (4.11);
but the *maiestas* cases of 93 register no audible echo in Book 8. Martial
does not belong to the senatorial circle; he is not actively engaged in
politics. What he is self-confessedly anxious about is imperial patron-
age, and the most obvious way to court it is to give glittering and
memorable expression to the emperor's centrality in contemporary
affairs. As Ovid had amply demonstrated in his poems from exile, this
is easier to do in the emperor's presence than in his absence. There is
also another route available, via the emperor's closest associates. Four

years previously Martial had already noted that access to Domitian was controlled by his *a cubiculo*, Parthenius[57] (5.6.7–8): *admittas timidam brevemque chartam/ intra limina sanctioris aulae*. By 93 Martial seems to be making some progress along this route: in a comparatively long epigram involving an elaborate pun on Parthenius' name he thanks him for the gift of a toga 'as white as its donor' (8.28.16); another epigram compliments Entellus,[58] Domitian's *a libellis*, on his greenhouse, interpreted by Martial as a triumph of human ingenuity over the rhythms of nature (8.68).

In the first edition of Book 10 Martial must have equalled or even surpassed the scope of his compliments to Domitian and his entourage in Books 8 and 9, hence the corrected edition under Trajan. But he drastically overestimated the stability of the Flavian regime, though Domitian, constantly fearful of assassination, did not (Suetonius *Domitian* 14). In seeking access to the emperor through his freedmen, Martial seriously misread the situation at court: it was not the Stoic opposition that assassinated Domitian in AD 96 but palace freedmen, including precisely Parthenius and Entellus (Dio 67.15.1–6). Juvenal underlines the irony (4.153–4): *sed periit, postquam cerdonibus esse timendus/ coeperat: hoc nocuit Lamiarum caede madenti*. Martial must have been glad that he had already addressed two epigrams to Nerva (8.70, 9.26). His former relations with Parthenius, potentially a source of embarrassment, he adroitly exploited by continuing to flatter the tyrannicide and requesting of him a recommendation to the new emperor (11.1, 12.11). Once again, he had miscalculated: six months after Nerva's accession Parthenius was murdered by the Praetorian Guard. Not long afterwards, Nerva died. Some of Martial's early sponsors, like Arruntius Stella, were destined to make good under Trajan's rule, but the fundamental discontinuity between the Flavian regime and its successors rendered obsolete Martial's attempts to reflect the political atmosphere of Domitian's Rome. If he soon became disenchanted with the boredom and provincialism of the rustic idyll with which he had taunted Juvenal (12 *praefatio* 18), at least Bilbilis was sufficiently far away to excuse him from engaging with the treacherous world of politics that had proved more protean than even an epigrammatist's wit.

---

[57] *PIR* P 101.
[58] *PIR*² E 66.

Bibliography

Quotations and citations of Martial follow the text and numeration in the Teubner edition by D.R. Shackleton Bailey (Stuttgart, 1990).

Barwick, K. (1958). 'Zyklen bei Martial und in den kleinen Gedichten des Catull' *Philologus* 102.284–318

Bauman, R.A. (1974). *Impietas in Principem*. Munich

Carradice, I.A. (1978). 'A denarius of AD 92' *ZPE* 28.159–60

Citroni, M. (1988). 'Pubblicazione e dediche dei libri in Marziale' *Maia* 40.3–39

—. (1989). 'Marziale e la Letteratura per i Saturnali (poetica dell'intrattenimento e cronologia della pubblicazione dei libri)' *ICS* 14.201–26

Darwall-Smith, R.H. (1996). *Emperors and Architecture: A Study of Flavian Rome*. (Collection Latomus Vol. 231) Brussels

Degrassi, A. (1947). *Inscriptiones Italiae* XIII 1. Rome

Dewar, M. (1994). 'Laying it on with a trowel: the proem to Lucan and related texts' *CQ* n.s. 44.199–211

Fowler, D.P. (1995). 'Martial and the book' *Ramus* 24.31–58

Friedländer, L. (1886). *M. Valerii Martialis epigrammaton libri* I. Leipzig

Garthwaite, J. (1990). 'Martial, Book 6, on Domitian's moral censorship' *Prudentia* 22.13–22

—. (1993). 'The panegyrics of Domitian in Martial Book 9' *Ramus* 22.78–102

Gibson, S., DeLaine, J. & Claridge, A. (1994). 'The Triclinium of the Domus Flavia: a new reconstruction' *PBSR* 62.67–97

Hartley, B. & Wacher, J. (1983) (edd.) *Rome and her Northern Provinces*. Gloucester

Hofmann, W. (1983). 'Martial und Domitian' *Philologus* 127.238–46

Jones, B.W. (1992). *The Emperor Domitian*. London–New York

Leary, T.J. (1996). *Martial Book XIV: The Apophoreta*. London

MacCormack, S.G. (1981). *Art and Ceremony in Late Antiquity*. Berkeley

MacDonald, W.L. (1982). *The Architecture of the Roman Empire* I. (rev. ed.) New Haven

Merli, E. (1993). 'Ordinamento degli epigrammi e strategie cortegiane negli esordi dei libri I–XII di Marziale' *Maia* 45.229–56

Nauta, R.R. (1995). *Poetry for Patrons: Literary Communication in the Age of Domitian*. Diss. Leiden

Rogers, P.M. (1984). 'Domitian and the finances of state' *Historia* 33.60–78

Rogers, R.S. (1960). 'A group of Domitianic treason-trials' *CP* 55.19–23

Salles, C. (1986). 'L'écrivain romain face au pouvoir impérial: la censure littéraire au 1er siècle de notre ère' *Latomus* 45.751–67

Shackleton Bailey, D.R. (1978). 'Corrections and explanations of Martial' *CP* 73.273–96

Simon, E. (1985). 'Virtus und pietas. Zu den Friesen A und B von der Cancellaria' *JDAI(R)* 100.543–55

Strobel, K. (1989). *Die Donaukriege Domitians*. (Antiquitas 1 Vol. 38) Bonn

Sullivan, J.P. (1991). *Martial: the Unexpected Classic*. Cambridge

Syme, R. (1983). 'Domitian: the last years' *Chiron* 13.121–46 = *Roman Papers* IV. 252–77

Talbert, R.J.A. (1984). *The Senate of Imperial Rome*. Princeton

Versnel, H.S. (1970). *Triumphus*. Leiden

White, P. (1974). 'The presentation and dedication of the *Silvae* and the *Epigrams*' *JRS* 64.40–61

—. (1975). 'The friends of Martial, Statius, and Pliny, and the dispersal of patronage' *HSCP* 79.265–300

—. (1996). 'Martial and pre-publication texts' *ECM/CV* 40, n.s.15.397–412

Wilkes, J.J. (1983). 'Romans, Dacians and Sarmatians in the first and early second centuries' in Hartley & Wacher (1983) 255–89

Wistrand, E. (1955). *De Martialis Epigr. VIII 15 Commentatiuncula*. (Acta Universitatis Gotoburgensis LX) Göteborg

PAPERS OF THE LEEDS INTERNATIONAL LATIN SEMINAR   TENTH VOLUME (1998) 359–72
Published by Francis Cairns (Publications) Ltd (Leeds 1998). ARCA 38. ISBN 0 905205 95 2

MARTIAL 8.21, LITERARY *LUSUS*, AND IMPERIAL PANEGYRIC*

LINDSAY WATSON
University of Sydney

Phosphore, redde diem: quid gaudia nostra moraris?
  Caesare venturo, Phosphore, redde diem.
Roma rogat. placidi numquid te pigra Bootae
  plaustra vehunt, lento quod nimis axe venis?
Ledaeo poteras abducere Cyllaron astro: 5
  ipse suo cedet nunc tibi Castor equo.
quid cupidum Titana tenes? iam Xanthus et Aethon
  frena volunt, vigilat Memnonis alma parens.
tarda tamen nitidae non cedunt sidera luci,
  et cupit Ausonium luna videre ducem.   10
iam, Caesar, vel nocte veni: stent astra licebit,
  non derit populo te veniente dies.

"A highly poetical epigram, but spoiled by the grossness of the flattery." Thus Paley and Stone[1] on the twenty-first poem of Martial book eight, which depicts Martial and Rome awaiting with impatience the appearance of the Morning Star which will usher in the day when Domitian returns triumphant to the city from his successful Danubian campaign.[2] The epigram is one of a cycle of nineteen poems in Martial's eighth book dealing with Domitian, to whom the volume as a whole, published early in 94, is dedicated. Paley and Stone damn 8.21

---

* Thanks are due to my colleague Dexter Hoyos for reading and commenting constructively upon an earlier version of this article.
[1] F.A. Paley and W.H. Stone *M.Val. Martialis Epigrammata Selecta* (London 1881) *ad loc.*
[2] Domitian's return took place in January AD 93.

with a casually dismissive flick of their late Victorian pens. I would suggest that there is rather more to the poem than these critics have allowed.

8.21 is composed in the dramatic mode much beloved of epigrammatists from Hellenistic times onwards. The opening couplet apostrophises Phosphorus, the Morning Star, asking him to delay his appearance no longer (*Phosphore, redde diem: quid gaudia nostra moraris?*). Next (3–4), Martial speculates whimsically on the reason for that delay: can he have hitched a ride with the notoriously slow-moving constellation of Bootes? In a further piece of humorous whimsy, he complains that Phosphorus' arrival might have been expedited (5–6) by borrowing from the catasterised Dioscuri Castor's famously swift[3] steed Cyllarus. The Sun-god and his team are raring to go, Dawn is already awake, he urges Phosphorus: it is perhaps implied that these deities share the enthusiasm of the populace for the sight of Domitian. But they cannot mount the sky until he has banished night and stars (7–8). Now comes a further attempt to rationalise Phosphorus' tardiness: it seems that the Moon-goddess too is anxious to look upon the emperor. The concluding couplet is addressed to Domitian, and asks him to come, even by night: his radiant presence will provide sufficient illumination for his people to view him.

The poem is carefully structured so as to lead up to the final conceit, which exploits a familiar idea in a highly original context. The idea in question is the comparison of the emperor to the sun, or the conceptualisation of him as a new or second sun. This motif-complex, which has its roots in oriental and Egyptian solar-symbolism,[4] was applied to Alexander the Great by his new subjects, and subsequently inherited by the Diadochi: one thinks, for example, of the notorious hymn of the Athenians to Demetrius Poliorketes, which described him in the following terms:

> Σεμνόν τι φαίνεθ᾽, οἱ φίλοι πάντες κύκλῳ,
> ἐν μέσοισι δ᾽αὐτός,
> ὅμοιον ὥσπερ οἱ φίλοι μὲν ἀστέρες,
> ἥλιος δ᾽ἐκεῖνος,[5]

---

[3] According to the *Etymologicum Magnum* 544.54 Cyllarus' name is derived παρὰ τὸ κέλλειν, ὁ ταχύς.

[4] E.R. Goodenough 'The political philosophy of Hellenistic kingship' *YCS* 1 (1928) 55–102 at 78–83.

[5] Powell *Collectanea Alexandrina* p.174.9–12 = Duris *ap.* Ath. 253d.

or of Antigonus I, who was styled ἡλίου παῖς καὶ θεός.[6] The theme was appropriated in Antonian[7] and, importantly, Caesarian propaganda. Horace, for instance, envisaged the populace hailing Augustus as *o Sol/ pulcher, o laudande* (*Odes* 4.2.46–7), and, in a famous passage, remarked

> lucem redde tuae, dux bone, patriae.
> instar veris enim vultus ubi tuus
> adfulsit populo, gratior it dies
> et soles melius nitent. (*Odes* 4.5.5–8).[8]

Sun imagery was an important feature of early imperial propaganda, taken up by Tiberius, Caligula, and Nero, and in turn utilised by the Flavians, Domitian included.[9] In the present poem, as often, the image is applied in the context of an imperial *reditus* or *adventus* (cf. *venturo* 2 and *veni* 11).[10] The particular *color* imparted to the theme by Martial closely reflects the prescriptions of the rhetorical schools. Thus the language and thought of line 12 find a close parallel in two sections of Menander Rhetor's instructions for the composition of an ἐπιβατήριος λόγος or speech of welcome to an arriving dignitary. The first runs

> εἶτα ἐπάξεις ὅτι ὥσπερ νυκτὸς καὶ ζόφου τὰ πάντα κατειληφότος αὐτὸς καθάπερ ἥλιος ὀφθεὶς πάντα ἀθρόως τὰ δυσχερῆ διέλυσας (*Rhetores Graeci* 3.378.21–3 Spengel),

the second

---

[6] S. Weinstock *Divus Iulius* (Oxford, 1971) 381.

[7] The male member of the twins borne to Mark Antony by Cleopatra in 40 BC was called Alexander Helios (see Tarn *JRS* 22 (1932) 135–60). From an earlier period note the remark that with the death of the younger Scipio in 129 BC the second sun was extinguished (Cic. *ND* 2.14 with Pease *ad loc.*), and the description of Brutus as the sun of Asia (Hor. *Sat.* 1.7.23–5, Weinstock (n.6) 382).

[8] For the fuller picture on Augustus' exploitation of solar propaganda, see Weinstock (n.6) 370–84, and Woodman on Vell. Paterc. 2.59.6, pp. 119–21.

[9] See Weinstock (n.6) 384 and K.M. Coleman on Stat. *Silv.* 4.2.42, adding *Silv.* 1.1.76–7 and 3.4.53, F. Sauter *Der römische Kaiserkult bei Martial und Statius* (Stuttgart/Berlin 1934) 137–45 and K. Scott *The Imperial Cult Under the Flavians* (Stuttgart/Berlin 1936) 113–5.

[10] See H. Halfmann *Itinera Principum* (Wiesbaden 1986) 148–51, and for a comparable use in Horace *Odes* 4.5, I.M.LeM. DuQuesnay 'Horace *Odes* 4.5: *Pro Reditu Imperatoris Caesaris Divi Filii Augusti*' in S.J. Harrison ed. *Homage to Horace* (Oxford 1995) 128–87 at 157–8. B.W. Jones *The Emperor Domitian* (London/NY 1992) 150 notes that Domitian was the first emperor since Tiberius to spend long periods of time outside Rome.

ὦ μεγίστης ἀρχῆς, ἡδίστης δὲ ἡμέρας, καθ' ἣν ἐπέστης· νῦν ἡλίου
φῶς φαιδρότερον· νῦν ὥσπερ ἔκ τινος ζόφου προσβλέπειν
δοκοῦμεν λευκὴν ἡμέραν (*Rhetores Graeci* 3.381.15–18 Spengel).[11]

In every case the arrival of the honorand occasions the dispelling of
darkness: the only difference between the Menandrian passages and
Martial is that in the former case the darkness is metaphorical, in the
latter, literal.

The closing couplet of Martial's poem in short harnesses thoroughly
tralatician material. But the framework in which this material is incor-
porated is most unusual, an appeal to the Morning Star to hasten his
coming. The bulk of the poem is in fact devoted to the Star and his
unconscionable tarrying, rather than to Domitian.[12] The address to
Phosphorus, and the complaint that his hour of arrival is unseasonable
in fact conjures up a very different thematic, one which appears at first
sight to have little to do with imperial panegyric. This is the address of
the lover to the Morning Star or Dawn objecting that his (her) untimely
appearance has foreshortened the night of passion which the speaker is
enjoying in the arms of his inamorata. The best known Latin specimen
of this kind of composition, which in medieval times went under the
title of *alba* or *tageliet*, is the thirteenth poem of Ovid *Amores* Book I.
But Ovid had ample precedent in earlier Greek literature, and par-
ticularly in Hellenistic epigram.[13] If we compare surviving specimens
of such poems with Martial's epigram, the resemblances prove sur-
prisingly extensive.

Two such Greek poems, for example, are headed, like Martial 8.21,
by an address to Phosphorus. The first, by Meleager of Gadara, who

---

[11] For rhetorical influences on solar imagery in encomiastic or epideictic contexts, see E.
Doblhofer *Die Augustuspanegyrik des Horaz in formalhistorischer Sicht* (Heidelberg,
1966) 19–21 and 87–91.

[12] It is this focus on Phosphorus and his reluctance to speed his arrival which
distinguishes Martial 8.21 from a passage such as Ov. *Fast.* 4.673–6 *hanc quondam
Cytherea diem properantius ire/ iussit et admissos praecipitavit equos,/ ut titulum
imperii quam primum luce sequenti/ Augusto iuveni prospera bella darent*, which also
speaks of disrupting the natural rhythms of day and night in order to expedite
celebration of an imperial success (cf. *Fast.* 5. 545–8 for a comparable idea). I am
grateful to Geraldine Herbert-Brown for drawing these passages to my attention.

[13] In general on poems about lovers at dawn, which are found all over the world, see
A.T. Hatto ed. *Eos. An Enquiry into the Theme of Lovers' Meetings and Partings at
Dawn in Poetry* (The Hague 1965). The ancient Greek and classical, later, and
medieval Latin exemplars are treated by J. H. Mozley and J. Lockwood at 255–63 and
271–81 respectively. Mozley's list is incomplete: add *AP* 12.136 and 9.286. See
further J.C. McKeown *A Commentary on Ovid Amores Book I* (Leeds 1989) 337–9.

wrote four epigrams on this theme[14] runs Ἠοῦς ἄγγελε, χαῖρε, Φαεσ-φόρε, καὶ ταχὺς ἔλθοις/ Ἕσπερος, ἣν ἀπάγεις, λάθριος αὖθις ἄγων (*Anthologia Palatina* 12.114), the second, *Anthologia Palatina* 5.223, although late,[15] is altogether typical of the genre. I quote only the immediately pertinent lines: Φωσφόρε, μὴ τὸν Ἔρωτα βιάζεο (1) ... οὕτω μοι περὶ νύκτα, μόγις ποθέοντι φανεῖσαν,/ ἔρχεο δηθύνων, ὡς παρὰ Κιμμερίοις (5–6). The apostrophe to the Morning Star, or the Dawn, remonstrating with the deity for appearing so prematurely, is in fact the single most characteristic feature of the poems under discussion:[16] the lover engages in a futile tirade against the relentless approach of day. Under these circumstances, it is unsurprising that dawn-poems are structured about the thematic axis haste/delay. Thus the refrain in Ovid *Amores* 1.13 runs *quo properas <Aurora>?*, *Anthologia Palatina* 5.172 (Meleager) begins Ὄρθρε, τί μοι, δυσέραστε, ταχὺς περὶ κοῖτον ἐπέστης, while *Anthologia Palatina* 5.173, also by Meleager, complains that, when the poet was abed with Demo, the dawn came all too swiftly (ὠκύς), whereas now, when she lies in the arms of another, it is slow (βραδύς) to appear.[17] In an alternative formulation, slowness is enjoined upon the Dawn/the Morning Star in a pointless attempt to retard the deity's approach: cf. *Anthologia Palatina* 5.223.6 quoted above and Ovid *Amores* 1.13.39–40 *at si quem manibus Cephalum complexa teneres,/ clamares "lente currite, noctis equi"*;[18] the motif of slowness is equally to the fore in what may be described as the mirror-image of the *alba*, sc. the perception of lovers that the night which will reunite them, or bring them together for the first time in marriage, is tardy in coming: cf. Ovid *Metamorphoses* 4.91 (Pyramus and Thisbe) *et lux tarde discedere visa est*, or the interesting treatment of the topic in Nonnus *Dionysiaca* 7.280–307, where Zeus awaits with impatience the coming of the night on which he will commingle sexually with

---

[14] In addition to *AP* 12.114 quoted in the text, *AP* 5.172–3 and 12.137.

[15] *AP* 5.223, by Macedonius of Thessalonica (6th century AD).

[16] Cf. *AP* 5.172–3, which open with Ὄρθρε, and Ov. *Am.* 1.13 which, except for the opening and closing couplets, consists of an appeal to Aurora to delay her arrival. A variation on this format is the schetliastic address to the cockerel, complaining that he has roused the *amator* much too early from his bed of love: see *AP* 5.3, 9.286, 12.137, and cf. 12.136.

[17] For other matutine lovers' complaints against the too-swift appearance of the dawn, see *AP* 5.3.6 and Prop. 2.18A.11–12 (by Aurora herself!). Cf. also *AP* 5.172.3 and 12.114, which request that the Morning Star return swiftly in its other incarnation as the Star of Eve, thereby reuniting the lovers which it now precipitately separates.

[18] Cf. also Prop. 3.20.13–14, Ov. *Am.* 1.13.47–8 *iurgia finieram. scires audisse: rubebat,/ nec tamen adsueto tardius orta dies*, and *AP* 5.173, referred to in the text.

Semele, a passage studded with complaints against Night's dilatoriness in coming: see in particular 284–6 καὶ δολιχὴν Φαέθοντος ἐμέμφετο δείελον ὥρην ...Ἔννεπε, Νὺξ χρονίη, φθονερὴ πότε δύεται Ἠώς; and 291–2 Ἥλιε, κλονέεις με, καὶ εἰ μάθες οἶστρον Ἐρώτων·/ φειδομένη μάστιγι πόθεν βραδὺν ἵππον ἱμάσσεις;[19] Also of relevance here is Statius *Silvae* 1.2.217–8 *quam longa morantur/ sidera! quam segnis votis Aurora mariti* (Stella awaits with impatience the dawning of the day which will see him married to Violentilla). The motif of delay may be enshrined in the *Leitwörter mora/morari*, as in Propertius 3.20.13–14 *nox mihi prima venit! primae data tempora noctis!/ longius in primo, Luna, morare toro*, or Ovid *Heroides* 18.111–14 (Leander to Hero):

> iamque fugatura Tithoni coniuge noctem
> praevius Aurorae Lucifer ortus erat.
> oscula congerimus properata sine ordine raptim
> et querimur parvas noctibus esse moras.[20]

Central to the lover's apostrophe to the Dawn in the *alba* is his perception that she is a refractory and unsympathetic personage. This idea receives its fullest expression in Ovid *Amores* 1.13, which is as much a tirade against Aurora as a *suasoria* designed to persuade her.[21] Aurora is *ingrata viris, ingrata puellis* (9), unwelcome in fact to individuals engaged in a whole range of occupations (11–24). Her envious heart is as black as her son Memnon's skin (31–2), and her motive in rising so early is suspect — ennui with her aged husband Tithonus (33–42).[22] The same hostile perception of Aurora also surfaces in opprobrious epithets directed at her by the *alba*-poet, such as δυσέραστος (*Anthologia Palatina* 5.172.1, 173.1), ἐπιχαιρέκακος (*Anthologia Palatina* 5.173.4), φθονερνή/*invida* (*Anthologia Palatina* 5.3.2; Ovid *Amores* 1.13.31), or in the accusation that she has a νηλεὲς ἦτορ (*Anthologia*

---

[19] For the converse, the need to expedite matters, cf. 293 and 301–7.

[20] Cf. also Claud. *Epithal. de Nupt. Honor. Aug.* 14–15 *incusat spes aegra moras longique videntur/ stare dies segnemque rotam non flectere Phoebe* and Prop. 3.20.11–12 *tu quoque, qui aestivos spatiosius exigis ignes,/ Phoebe, moraturae contrahe lucis iter*, both instances of what has been described in the text as the mirror-image of the *alba*. Compare also Xen. Eph. 1.8.1.

[21] Cf. *iurgia* 47. For an analysis of the poem as a *suasoria*, cf. A. Elliot 'Amores I.13: Ovid's art' *CJ* 69 (1973) 127–32. This elegy is akin in spirit to *Am*. 3.6, the lover's abusive address to the river in flood which bars his passage to his mistress.

[22] Cf. especially 41–2 *cur ego plectar amans, si vir tibi marcet ab annis?/ num me nupsisti conciliante seni?* For the same dubious motive ascribed to the Dawn, cf. *AP* 5.3.5–6.

Palatina 5.223.2).[23]

The most fervent wish of the *alba*-poet is to retard the progress of Aurora's chariot. Consequently he may wish upon her a celestial traffic accident (*Amores* 1.13.29–30),[24] or a disruption of the normal sequence of night and day (*ibid.* 27–8 *optavi quotiens ne nox tibi cedere vellet,/ ne fugerent vultus sidera mota tuos!*).[25] To that end a mythological precedent may be enlisted, such as Jupiter's prolongation of the night in order to enjoy Alcmena's favours (Ovid *Amores* 1.13.45–6; *Anthologia Palatina* 5.172.5–6 ἤδη γὰρ καὶ πρόσθεν ἐπ᾽ Ἀλκμήνῃ Διὸς ἦλθες/ ἀντίος· οὐκ ἀδαής ἐσσι παλινδρομίης).[26]

The above will suffice to erect a generic profile of the Dawn-song. It remains to establish the relevance of this to Martial 8.21. As a first step, the formal resemblances between such poems, and the epigram, can be highlighted. The epigram commences, like the *alba*, with an address to Phosphorus, which is moreover couched in the anaphoric style much affected by Ovid in *Amores* 1.13.[27] Considerable prominence is given by Martial to the terminology of haste/delay which is so characteristic of dawn-poems: cf. *quid gaudia nostra* **moraris**? 1, *numquid te* **pigra** *Bootae/ plaustra vehunt,* **lento quod nimis** *axe venis?* 3–4, *quid cupidum Titana* **tenes**? 7, **tarda** *tamen nitidae non cedunt sidera luci* 9, **stent** *astra licebit* 11. As in the *alba*, Dawn is addressed in highly personal terms, and invested with a conspicuous reluctance to conform to the poet's wishes — in the present case, anomalously, that she should expedite her arrival. Also as in the *alba*, celestial ἀδύνατα are canvassed. Has the Morning Star become Bootes' passenger? Can she not hasten her arrival by appropriating Cyllarus from the astral Twins? There is mention of the stars yielding (*cedere* 9) — in the present case, not yielding — to the daylight.[28] The speaker in Martial 8.21, which

---

[23] A comparable malignity is imputed to the cockerel, or the chattering birds, which arouse the lovers from their bed (*AP* 5.3, 237; 9.286; 12.137; cf. also *AP* 12.136 and *Anacreontea* 10 West).

[24] The felicitous phrase is that of Elliot (n.21) 129.

[25] Compare *AP* 5.172.3 εἴθε πάλιν στρέψας ταχινὸν δρόμον Ἕσπερος εἴης and Sappho fr.197 = Liban. *Orat.* 12.99. Cf. also *AP* 5.223.5–6 and 283.5–6, and Nonn. *Dionysiaca* 7.293–301.

[26] Cf. also *AP* 5.283.3–4 (Dawn once before delayed in deference to the Sun, who was abed with Clymene). Nonn. *Dionysiaca* 7.300–1 makes a similar point.

[27] See Ovid lines 3, 9, and 31; 5–7; 27–30; 11–24 (anaphora of *tu*). The anaphora is in part a function of the poem's status as an inverted form of κλητικὸς ὕμνος, in which the goddess is enjoined not to come, but to stay away: see McKeown (n.13) 339.

[28] Cf. Ov. *Am.* 1.13.27–8 *optavi quotiens ne nox tibi cedere vellet,/ ne fugerent vultus sidera mota tuos!*

shares with dawn-poems a dramatic framework, is, like the speaker of
the latter, characterised by impatience — in conventional instances of
the form, impatience of Dawn's arrival, but in an inverted[29] instance
such as the present, impatience of her delay.[30]

It will be apparent from the above that, if I am justified in affiliating
Martial 8.21 to the genus dawn-song, it constitutes an instance of a
highly deviant kind. In particular, where in the epigram can one dis-
cover the amatory component that provides all such poems with their
motivation? A clue, I suggest, is to be found in the *impatience* with
which the speaker awaits the Morning Star (instead of, as is normal,
bemoaning its approach). A further clue resides in the phrase *quid
gaudia nostra moraris?* (line 1). In the context of the *alba*, as of love
poetry in general,[31] *gaudia* would normally refer to the carnal pleasures
shared by the nocturnal lovers, and truncated by the dawn: cf. Ovid
Heroides 18.107–12 *non magis illius numerari gaudia noctis/ Helles-
pontiaci quam maris alga potest ... iamque fugatura Tithoni coniuge
noctem/ praevius Aurorae Lucifer ortus erat ...* (Hero and Leander).
Here, by contrast, the *gaudia* are those of Martial, and of the citizenry
as a whole, which are frustrated by Phosphorus' tardy appearance, and
the delay that this entails for Domitian's approach.[32] In short, I would
suggest, Martial is using the conventions of the dawn-song, and the
related notion that lovers await with eagerness the return of the day
which will reunite them with the beloved,[33] to represent the populace,
in Periclean terms, as ἐρασταὶ τῆς πόλεως,[34] or, to be more precise, as
ἐρασταὶ τοῦ αὐτοκράτορος. It was by no means unusual in the Greek
world to characterise civic loyalty or patriotism by means of erotic

---

[29] It has become conventional in such cases to speak, with Giangrande, of an
"Umkehrung", or with Francis Cairns (*Generic Composition in Greek and Roman
Poetry*, Edinburgh 1972) of generic "inversion".

[30] Though see also above on the 'mirror image' of the *alba*. A further point of
resemblance between Martial 8.21 and the main Latin exemplar of the *alba*, Ov. *Am.*
1.13, is the mention in both poems of Dawn as Memnon's parent (Mart. 8, Ov. 31–2).

[31] Cf. Pichon *Index Verborum Amatoriorum s.v. gaudere*.

[32] *Caesare venturo 2, iam, Caesar, vel nocte veni* 11.

[33] Cf. Longus 2.8.2 ἐπιθυμοῦσιν <οἱ ἐρῶντες> ἀλλήλους ὁρᾶν· διὰ τοῦτο θᾶττον
εὐχόμεθα γενέσθαι τὴν ἡμέραν, *ibid.* 2.24.4 εὐχόμενος δὲ τὴν ἡμέραν γενέσθαι
ταχέως. See also Catull. 50.11–13 *sed toto indomitus furore lecto/ versarer cupiens
videre lucem,/ ut tecum loquerer simulque ut essem* with C. Macleod *Collected Essays*
(Oxford 1983) 171–2; Stat. *Silv.* 1.2.217–18 quoted in the text *supra*.

[34] The famous and somewhat extravagant phrase from Pericles' funeral oration (Thuc.
2.43.1) is widely assumed to have originated with Pericles himself (see Gomme and
Hornblower *ad loc.*) — hence perhaps the extensive comic play which Aristophanes
made with it: see Neil and Blaydes on *Eq.* 1340–4 and Blaydes on *Ach.* 143–4.

metaphors. The language used by Aristophanes in mocking public speakers who deploy such metaphors, and Δῆμος' receptivity to their insincere protestations, is most revealing: πρῶτον μέν, ὁπότ' εἴποι τις ἐν τῆκκλησία,/ ὦ Δῆμ' ἐραστής τ' εἰμὶ σὸς φιλῶ τέ σε/ καὶ κήδομαί σου καὶ προβουλεύω μόνος ... (*Equites* 1340–2). But such terminology was also employed in more serious contexts, for example at Aeschylus *Eumenides* 851–2 ὑμεῖς δ' ἐς ἀλλόφυλον ἐλθοῦσαι χθόνα/ γῆς τῆσδ' ἐρασθήσεσθε,[35] or Plato *Gorgias* 481D ἐρῶντε δύο ὄντε δυοῖν ἑκάτερος, ἐγὼ μὲν Ἀλκιβιάδου τε τοῦ Κλεινίου καὶ φιλοσοφίας, σὺ δὲ δυοῖν, τοῦ τε Ἀθηναίων δήμου καὶ τοῦ Πυριλάμπους.[36] The terminology of love was equally applied by the Romans to the sentiment of patriotism. A trawl through *TLL* volume I under *amare* and its cognates will turn up in literary and epigraphic sources a host of phrases like *fidaei patrieq. semper amator* (*Carmina Latina Epigraphica* 714.1), *quaedam tui nominis caritas amorque in te singularis omnium civium* (Cicero *Ad Familiares* 11.8.1, addressed to Brutus), *quo amore ... inflammati esse debemus in eiusmodi patriam* (Cicero *De Oratore* 1.196), *a tota civitate amatur, defenditur, colitur* (Seneca *De Clementia* 1.13.4, a protreptic for the youthful Nero), or *patriae amantissimae* ('most beloved', *CIL* 3.6998),[37] while Horace, in his ode on the Ship of State (*Odes* 1.14), memorably borrowed the language of erotic discourse in order to express his feelings of love and solicitude for the beleaguered commonwealth: cf. lines 17–8 *nuper sollicitum quae mihi taedium,/ nunc desiderium curaque non levis.*[38]

In this connexion it will bear emphasis that Domitian, like Augustus before him,[39] liked to emphasise his universal popularity, and the love and affection in which he was supposedly held by his subjects.[40] This is

---

[35] "You will long for this land like lovers" (Sommerstein *ad loc.*). This passage perhaps gave the first impetus to the phrase ἐραστὴς τῆς πόλεως.

[36] Cf. Plat. *Alcib.* 132A, Isocr. 183D and 262A, and Σ to Ar. *Plut.* 550, further J. Taillardat *Les Images d'Aristophane* (Paris 1965) 401 and W.R. Connor *The New Politicians of Fifth Century Athens* (Princeton 1971) 97–8 with n.14.

[37] See further *TLL* 1.1828.64–1829.14, 1954.51–4, 1958.74–9, 1969.17–56.

[38] I take it as beyond question that this ode is addressed to the Roman ship of state. For a convenient summary of alternative readings, see H.D. Jocelyn 'Boats, Women and Horace' *CPh* 77 (1982) 330–5. Jocelyn is unfortunately misled by his (entirely convincing) demonstration that the poem has nothing to do with an ageing *inamorata* into a denial that *taedium, desiderium*, and *cura* are lovers' words (333). See rather the commentary of Nisbet and Hubbard *ad loc.*

[39] See *Res Gestae* 9.2, 10.2, 12.1, 21.3, 25.2–3, 34.1, 35.1.

[40] See J.P.Sullivan *Martial. The Unexpected Classic* (Cambridge 1991) 135–6 and A. Hardie *Statius and the Silvae. Poets, Patrons and Epideixis in the Graeco-Roman World* (Liverpool 1983) 46.

a topic to which Martial often lends his voice, in language that bears closely upon the interpretation of the present poem. Of particular note are 8.11.7–8 *nullum Roma ducem, nec te sic, Caesar, amavit:/ te quoque iam non plus, ut velit ipsa, potest*, 8.56.3–4 *diligeris populo non propter praemia, Caesar,/ te propter populus praemia, Caesar, amat*, 9.7.9–10 *dilexere prius pueri iuvenesque senesque,/ at nunc infantes te quoque, Caesar, amant*, and 7.5.1–4:

> Si desiderium, Caesar, populique patrumque
>   respicis et Latiae gaudia vera togae,
> redde deum votis poscentibus. invidet hosti
>   Roma suo, veniat laurea multa licet,

which comes from a poem that, like 8.21, looks forward with anticipation to Domitian's triumphant return to Rome.[41]

If the above analysis is correct, Martial has in 8.21 exploited the conventions of the dawn-song in an oblique, sophisticated, and above all witty fashion to represent the Roman citizenry as ἐρασταί of Domitian: in the present poem, the 'lovers' desire daylight so as to enjoy what the state/Domitian have to offer — an amusing inversion of how private lovers normally feel about daytime. That wit is a feature of 8.21 has already been suggested (see above on the humorous whimsy of lines 3–6). It is equally present in the surprise turn of the final couplet where, after futile appeals to Phosphorus to expedite her arrival — and appeals in the *alba* are always futile[42] — Domitian is exhorted to come anyway: his presence will illuminate the darkness.

It remains to ask two questions: would Domitian have been alert to the polished literary play of 8.21, and would he have relished the treatment of his august personage in a less than serious fashion? To the first question a provisional 'yes' can be offered. Domitian was a notable patron of literature,[43] felt a special attachment to Minerva, who presided over the arts,[44] and was himself an active poet, who composed

---

[41] For the *amor populi erga Domitianum*, see also 7.6–8, 8.4, 8.16 and 8.49. Sullivan (n.40) 135 suggests that the prominence of poems in book 8 proclaiming the people's love for Domitian reflects the tensions of the times and the need which the emperor felt for reassurance concerning his popularity.

[42] The illogic of an appeal to retard the course of nature humorously underscores the monomania of the lover.

[43] See G. Williams *Change and Decline. Roman Literature in the Early Empire* (Berkeley 1978) 141–2, Hardie (n.40) 45, and especially Mart. 8.82.5–6 *fer vates, Auguste, tuos; nos gloria dulcis,/ nos tua cura prior deliciaeque sumus*.

[44] Dio 67.1.2, Suet. *Dom*. 15.3, Sullivan (n.40) 138 and 144, J.-L. Girard 'Domitien et Minerve: une prédilection impériale' *ANRW* 2.17.1 (1981) 233–45.

and recited epics on the wars of 69 AD, on the wars in Judaea, and perhaps on his own campaigns against the Chatti in 83 and 88.[45] As to the second question, no definite answer is possible, although it is suggestive that Domitian was not averse to penning a literary joke at his own expense: he is known to have composed a *libellus de cura capillorum*, apparently in ironic allusion to his premature baldness (Suetonius *Domitian* 18.2).[46] What can be said with certainty is that Martial did not regard imperial panegyric, and the exercise of wit, as in any way irreconcilable. This is not just a function of the epigrammatic *lex operis*. Literary precedent and, no doubt, temperament, also have a part to play. Hellenistic poetic panegyric had already proved extremely receptive to the incorporation of humour. One need look no further than Callimachus' *Coma Berenices*, in which, among many other delicious touches, the catasterised *coma* wishes to be reunited with her mistress's regal locks, even if this precipitates an astral cataclysm.[47] Other poets too blended encomium of princes with humour. It is striking that Theocritus sets his poem on Queen Arsinoe's celebration of the Adonia in the framework of a conversation between two prattling females at whose banality, querulousness, and perfervid enthusiasms the reader is invited patronisingly to smile (*Idyll* 15), striking too that the preceding Idyll, a mocking and ironic portrait of a dejected lover, concludes with a resounding panegyric of Ptolemy's φιλανθρωπία and the benefits of service in the Ptolemaic army. A drunken and disingenuous old procuress is likewise an amusingly improbable mouthpiece for a rehearsal of the glories of Egypt under Ptolemaic rule (Herodas *Mime* 1.21–36). But perhaps the most startling instance of the blending of humour with encomium is Callimachus' linking of royal praise, the *Victoria Berenices*, to a ludicrous myth about the invention of the mousetrap by

---

[45] Williams (n.43) 141, Mart. 5.5.7–8. It may be noted that there has been considerable disagreement over the degree of Domitian's personal commitment to literature. Suetonius *Dom.* 20 damned him as a philistine. Jones (n.10) 13 and, apparently, F. Millar *JRS* 57 (1969) 19 accept Suetonius' judgement (though Jones modifies his position in his summing up of D., 198). K.M. Coleman 'The Emperor Domitian and Literature' *ANRW* 32.5 (1986) 3087–3115 offers a balanced study of the question, and concludes that Domitian was genuinely interested in the subject.

[46] For humorous compositions on such trivia, see A.S. Pease 'Things without honour' *CPh* 21 (1926) 27–43. For another instance of witty self-ironising by Domitian, see his remark, reported by Suet. *Dom.* 20 *vellem ... tam formosus esse quam Maecius sibi videtur.* This is quoted by Suetonius *loc. cit.* as one instance of Domitian's *dictorum interdum etiam notabilium.*

[47] Catullus 66.89–94 (with Fordyce *ad loc.*), in his Latin translation of the *Coma* (=*Aetia* fr. 110 Pf.): the Greek original is unfortunately missing at this point.

Molorchus (*Supplementum Hellenisticum* 254–69, from the beginning of *Aetia* book 3)![48]

There is, then, ample literary warrant for the wedding of imperial panegyric to humour. This is in fact a key element in Martial's literary programme, which he justifies by appealing to the example of the triumph, in which glorification of the triumphator is commingled with levity and obscene humour (cf. 1.4 and 7.8). In the preface to book 8, dedicated to Domitian, he remarked *quam materiam* (sc. praise of Domitian) *quidem subinde aliqua iocorum mixtura variare temptavimus, ne caelesti verecundiae tuae laudes suas, quae facilius te fatigare possint quam nos satiare, omnis versus ingereret.* Martial is there referring to the judicious blending of encomium and humorous epigrams within a single volume. But he equally conjoins wit and panegyric within the compass of a single poem. It is for example a favourite device of his to tie praise of a Domitianic initiative — e.g. the emperor's reaffirmation, in his capacity as censor, of the Julian law against adultery — to satiric attacks upon those who flout such provisions, or who observe the letter, but not the spirit, of the law. A case in point is 6.7:

> Iulia lex populis ex quo, Faustine, renata est
> atque intrare domos iussa Pudicitia est,
> aut minus aut certe non plus tricesima lux est,
> et nubit decimo iam Telesilla viro.
> quae nubit totiens, non nubit: adultera lege est.
> offendor moecha simpliciore minus.

Martial returns in this epigram to a topic which he had treated in more serious vein three poems earlier, the renewal of Augustus' law against adultery (*Lex Iulia de adulteriis coercendis*). That poem had enumerated the various benefactions and achievements for which Rome was indebted to Domitian — triumphs, new or rebuilt temples, spectacles and so on, concluding with the sentiment *plus debet tibi Roma quod pudica est.* Now, in a striking instance of variation, the same subject is given a conspicuously humorous twist. In the thirty or so days which have elapsed since the revival of the Julian law, Telesilla has married ten times. The breathtaking rate at which the lady chalks up husbands, her sexual Charybdism, and her barefaced disregard for the spirit of the law are quite risible, but the joke in 6.7 depends primarily upon a verbal play in *nubo*, which, like γαμεῖν, can mean

---

[48] See P. Bing *The Well-Read Muse* (Göttingen 1988) 82 with n.54.

'have intercourse with' as well as 'marry'.[49] Legally speaking Telesilla
nubit in the second sense, but in practical terms she does so in the first,
a situation captured in the witty paradox *adultera lege est*. Praise of
Domitian's marital legislation thus becomes the springboard for witty
dispraise of an individual who responds both farcically and evasively to
the new order of things by engaging in a highly dubious form of serial
monogamy.[50]

If 6.7 depended for its effect upon a combination of pun and para-
dox, another epigram exemplifies how straightforward encomium of the
emperor can be leavened by a dash of wit, as in the following example,
with its neatly deflationary close:

> Hiberna quamvis Arctos et rudis Peuce
> et ungularum pulsibus calens Hister
> fractusque cornu iam ter improbo Rhenus
> teneat domantem regna perfidae gentis
> te, summe mundi rector et parens orbis:
> abesse nostris non tamen potes votis.
> illic et oculis et animis sumus, Caesar,
> adeoque mentes omnium tenes unus
> ut ipsa magni turba nesciat Circi
> utrumne currat Passerinus an Tigris. (7.7)

This poem, like several at the beginning of book 7, deals with
Domitian's Danubian campaign of 92 AD, his successful return from
which inspired the epigram which is the subject of this paper. Its
message is straightforward enough: "although absent in body,
Domitian, you are never absent from our hearts and minds, the constant
subject of our prayers. And this monomania (so to speak) has expressed
itself in a fashion at once unheard of and patriotic. The citizens of the
metropolis, notorious for their devotion to the pleasures of the amphi-
theatre (a devotion which you have fostered and indulged), have so

---

[49] For the ironic use of *nubo*, cf. Plaut. *Cist.* 40–5 and *Cas.* 486. The argument of J.
Garthwaite 'Martial, Book 6, on Domitian's moral censorship' *Prudentia* 20.1 (1990)
13–22 that 6.7 and related poems (see following note) ironically mock the
ineffectiveness of Domitian's marital legislation ignores the fact that Martial sees his
primary role, *qua* epigrammatist, as that of a critic of society, which is represented by
the individuals whom he attacks: cf. 10.4.

[50] For other satiric pieces turning on Domitian's revival of the *Lex Iulia*, see 5.75, 6.22,
6.45, 6.91, also 6.2. Another favourite target is those who try to circumvent the
emperor's reaffirmation of the *lex Othonis*: see 5.8, 5.14, 5.23, 5.35, 5.38 and 6.9.
Further pieces dealing in humorous/satiric vein with Domitianic enactments or grants:
2.92, 8.31, 9.66, 7.61, 9.40.

focussed their thoughts upon the welfare of the absent *princeps* — that they cannot even tell which star horse is running in the Circus!"[51]

I suggest that we have in poem 8.21 a comparable admixture of humour and panegyric.

---

[51] The joke is repeated at 8.11.5–6. Other poems of Martial in which flattery of Domitian is blended with wit: 5.49, 6.87, 9.3, 9.70 and especially 5.19.

PAPERS OF THE LEEDS INTERNATIONAL LATIN SEMINAR   TENTH VOLUME (1998) 373–90
Published by Francis Cairns (Publications) Ltd (Leeds 1998). ARCA 38. ISBN 0 905205 95 2

GREEK ADVICE
FOR A ROMAN SENATOR:
Cassius Dio and the Dialogue between
Philiscus and Cicero (38.18–29)[*]

ALAIN M. GOWING
University of Washington

Tullus Laurea, one of Cicero's freedmen according to the Elder Pliny, made a generous claim for his patron: *totum legitur sine fine per orbem* (*Natural History* 31.3.8). While we can believe this of most educated Romans, does the statement apply equally to Greeks? A preliminary answer might reasonably be sought in the two standard studies of Cicero's *Nachleben*, by Zielinski and Weil.[1] To judge from the former, the only Greeks to exhibit any familiarity with Cicero are Plutarch, Appian and Cassius Dio. Zielinski's interest lies not so much in the fact that they are Greeks as historians (who, in his view, distorted the historical tradition about Cicero), and a single paragraph suffices for his observations about them.[2] Weil is only slightly more expansive. In his survey of the influence of Cicero in the imperial period, the sole Greek author to receive substantial mention (an entire chapter) is Plutarch. He does, however, find some significance in the fact that Plutarch was a Greek: in Weil's view that sets him apart from the other

---

[*]   An earlier version of this paper was read at the Leeds International Latin Seminar colloquium held on 7 May 1993. I would like to extend my thanks to the various seminar participants for their many valuable observations, especially Jo-Marie Claassen and Nicholas Petrochilos.
[1]   Th. Zielinski *Cicero im Wandel der Jahrhunderte* (Leipzig 1912); B. Weil *2000 Jahre Cicero* (Zurich 1962).
[2]   Zielinski (n.1) 15.

writers influenced by or interested in Cicero.[3]

Zielinski and Weil understandably sought direct evidence for the influence of Cicero — passages, that is, where he is explicitly cited or discussed. If we adhere to that standard, we must exclude writers like Dio Chrysostom, Lucian, Arrian, Aelius Aristides, or Athenaeus, in whose works one seeks in vain for even the name of Cicero. In contrast to Plutarch, Appian and Cassius Dio Roman history was not their central concern, so the relevance of Cicero to their work is less immediately apparent. It is possible, perhaps even likely, that these writers had read some Cicero (there can be little doubt that they knew who he was), but any impact that reading might have had is difficult if not impossible to gauge. Something is possibly to be surmised from their silence: when Greeks looked to Cicero — if and when they looked at all — it was not in order to be educated about philosophy or politics. They had their Plato, and thus no need for what must have been largely regarded as a Roman rehash of Greek philosophy. Indeed, Cicero himself anticipated that there would be many even among his own countrymen who would continue to prefer the Greek philosophers to his productions (*De Finibus* 1.1), and his vigorous insistence that his philosophical works possessed an intrinsic political value of their own (e.g. *De Divinatione* 2.4–5, *De Officiis* 1.6) would scarcely suffice to attract the attention of Greeks.[4]

Only when the topic is rhetoric do we find an explicit reference to Cicero in a Greek writer outside of the historians, and only one at that: 'Longinus' compares the speaking styles of Demosthenes and Cicero (*De Sublimitate* 12.4–5).[5] The situation does not appear to be

---

[3]   Weil (n.1) 67.

[4]   A possible exception to this is a work ascribed by Ammianus (22.16.16) to Didymus Chalcenterus, a Greek polymath of the late Republican/early Augustan period, in which he allegedly attacked Cicero and more specifically, perhaps, the *De Re Publica*. The slim evidence for the latter supposition is a statement in the *Suda* that Suetonius responded to Didymus' attack with a work entitled περὶ τῆς Κικέρωνος πολιτείας (*s.v.* Τράγκυλλος, T895). Whether or not the work should be assigned to Didymus Chalcenterus (as Ammianus would have it), to Arius Didymus (the Augustan philosopher) or to Didymus Claudius (first century AD) is less important than the evidence it provides that at least one Greek who was not a historian had read some Cicero. One would like to know, however, the precise nature of Didymus' attack, i.e. whether he took issue with Cicero on philosophical or historical grounds. On Didymus and the authorship of this work see E. Rawson 'Roman rulers and the philosophic adviser' in M. Griffin and J. Barnes (eds.) *Philosophia Togata* (Oxford 1989) 233–57, 244. (I would like to express my gratitude to H.B. Gottschalk for his instructive correspondence on this point.)

[5]   Despite appearances, this cannot be taken as firm proof that 'Longinus' had read any

significantly different for Latin writers. Although, unsurprisingly, they refer to Cicero far more often than their Greek counterparts, there is not much evidence that many Romans gave Cicero's philosophical works serious study;[6] they most often cite the speeches and rhetorical works, a clear indication of their respect for Cicero's unparalleled skill as an orator. In contrast to 'Longinus', however, the Roman admiration for Cicero's oratorical skill is capable of going beyond mere academic curiosity. There is nothing in Greek, for example, to approximate Tacitus' *Dialogus*, a text which, in its evocation of the Ciceronian form and ethos, testifies to the symbolism Latin authors could attach to Cicero and the freedom of speech his work represented.[7]

The political dimension of the nostalgia for Cicero (if it may be called that) seems largely absent in Greek writers. So despite the fact that most of the Greek authors cited above can be shown to have had an interest in Roman culture (an interest enhanced by their own contact with or involvement in affairs in Rome), for the most part they appear to have felt Cicero the author or philosopher eminently worth ignoring.[8] Plutarch strengthens the impression, and that from a Greek

---

Cicero. The contrast drawn here between Cicero's and Demosthenes' oratorical style is a commonplace (e.g. Quint. *Inst.* 10.1.105–8; Plu. *Dem.* 3), and may be traced to the synkrisis of Demosthenes and Cicero composed by Caecilius of Calacte, whose περὶ ὕψους inspired 'Longinus'' own treatise ('Longin.' 1.1). The synkrisis, probably written shortly after Cicero's death, is cited by Plutarch (*Dem.* 3); the author is doubtless the same Κεκίλιος cited often by 'Longinus'. See G. Kennedy *The Art of Rhetoric in the Roman World* (Princeton 1972) 368–9; Zielinski (n.1) 289–90.

6   To be sure, they are occasionally cited, but when, for instance, Seneca advises *lege Ciceronem* (*Ep.* 100.7) — in one of the very few letters in which he refers to the philosophical works (*ibid.* 9) — he is in fact advising the study of Cicero's *compositio*, not his philosophy. In Seneca's view, Cicero was not a *sapiens* because he was unable to put up with his misfortunes (*Dial.* 10.5), a common opinion that doubtless reduced the value placed on his philosophical works (see refs. in n.16). Cf. Quint. *Inst.* 10.1.112: *apud posteros vero id consecutus ut Cicero iam non hominis nomen sed eloquentiae habeatur*. The paucity of Quintilian's references to Cicero's philosophical works in comparison with those to his speeches and rhetorical works corroborates this general impression. See further on Cicero's reputation among imperial Latin authors M. Winterbottom 'Cicero and the silver age' in *Éloquence et rhétorique chez Cicéron* (Entretiens sur l'antiquité classique 28, Geneva 1982) 237–66.

7   See esp. A. Michel *Le 'Dialogus des Orateurs' de Tacite et la philosophie de Cicéron* (Paris 1962); R. Koestermann 'Der taciteische *Dialogus* und Ciceros Schrift *De re publica*' *Hermes* 65 (1930) 396–421; and D.E. Koutroubas 'Ο Κικερων στο Διαλογο περι ρητορων του Τακιτου' in *3. Panellenio Symposio Latinikon Spoudon* (Thessalonika 1987) 125–47.

8   Elizabeth Fisher has demonstrated that the knowledge of Latin literature among Greeks was greater than generally supposed, noting that Greek translations of Cicero were readily available ('Greek translations of Latin literature in the fourth century

who clearly had read some Cicero.[9]

In the early third century, however, at least one Greek writer —
Cassius Dio — took a keen interest in Cicero, an interest that tran-
scends his involvement in the historical events Dio narrates and is
distinctly political. It surfaces, moreover, less in the narration of
Cicero's actions than in the two lengthy and carefully composed
speeches Dio places in his mouth.[10] Yet Dio's attention to Cicero
appears not to be a wholly isolated instance. His coeval Philostratus,
the writer whose name looms largest in the history of the Second
Sophistic, makes an apparently deliberate and pointed allusion to the
orator (*Life of Apollonius* 7.11), a rare departure from the silence on
Cicero that characterises most previous Greek writers. There are
grounds for believing that this is not mere coincidence. It is the purpose
of this paper to investigate the nature of one unique episode in Dio's
account of Cicero and to suggest that in addition to confirming his
unusual preoccupation with his Roman predecessor, this episode, taken
together with Philostratus' allusion to Cicero, may reflect a shared and
largely unprecedented interest in Cicero on the part of two imperial
Greeks.

Cicero and Philiscus

The episode in question occurs in Book 38 of Dio's *History*.[11] Cicero,
in exile in Macedonia in 58 BC, encounters a man named Philiscus

---

A.D.' *YCS* 27 [1982] 173–215, 183–5). But what was available were translations of
his speeches, suggesting again that Greek interest was confined to Cicero's skill as an
orator (and, coincidentally, his instructiveness as an example of good Latin) rather
than a thinker. On Greek familiarity with Latin literature in general and Cicero in
particular see now B. Rochette *Le latin dans le monde grec* (Brussels 1997), esp.
279–86. Rochette's inquiries substantiate the claim I make here, that Greeks were not
interested in Cicero's philosophy.

[9] Plutarch seldom mentions the philosophical works and implies that their chief
accomplishment was the rendering of Greek terms into Latin (*Cic.* 40.2; cf. 24.5, and
Comp. Cic. et Dem. 1.3): no hint, that is, that Plutarch's Greek readers might find
Cicero's treatises instructive. On his familiarity with Cicero's writings see J.L. Moles
(ed.) *Plutarch: the Life of Cicero* (Aris & Phillips 1988) 28–31.

[10] 44.23–33 (Cicero's plea for amnesty for the assassins) and 45.18–47 (Dio's version
of a Ciceronian *Philippic*).

[11] For the text of the *Roman History* I cite the edition of U.Ph. Boissevain *Cassii Dionis
Cocceiani Historiarum Romanarum quae supersunt* 5 vols. (Berlin 1895–1931;
photoreprint of 1–4, Berlin 1955). Books 61–80 are cited in accordance with
Boissevain's divisions, with the traditional numberings provided in parentheses, e.g.
77[76].2.1. Translations of Dio are those of E. Cary *Dio's Roman History* 9 vols.
(Loeb Classical Library 1914–1927).

whom he had allegedly met earlier in Athens. After reproaching Cicero
for his incessant caterwauling (38.18.1), Philiscus engages the orator in
philosophical dialectic (his term, 38.18.4) to bring him back to his
senses. The subsequent eleven chapters are given over to the conver-
sation between the two, the bulk of which consists of Philiscus' advice
to Cicero. At the conclusion of this exchange Dio comments on the
soothing effect Philiscus has had on the Roman orator, who never-
theless presently returns to Rome, contrary to his friend's advice
(38.30.1).

This scene is manifestly fictitious. No other source mentions the en-
counter, and apart from that, there is the evidence of Cicero himself. He
often speaks of his exile and his reaction to it, but his own corre-
spondence on the subject, much of which was composed during his
residence in Thessalonica from May to November of 58, contains no
allusion to anyone who remotely resembles Philiscus or to any such
meeting.[12] The exchange between Cicero and Philiscus therefore
appears to derive entirely from Dio's own imagination.[13] It has been
plausibly maintained, however, that Dio's Philiscus is a thinly dis-
guised version of a rhetor by the same name known to us through
Philostratus' *Lives of the Sophists*. This Philiscus held the chair of
rhetoric in Athens in Dio's time and was, like Philostratus and perhaps
Dio, a member of the circle of the empress Julia Domna (*Lives of the
Sophists* 2.30).[14] Quite possibly the dialogue was composed

---

[12]   He in fact laments the lack of anyone with whom he could converse (*Att.* 3.12.1 = SB
       57). Atticus, whose loyalty to Cicero during the time of his exile was well known (cf.
       Nep. *Att.* 4.4), is the one historical character who comes close to fulfilling the
       function served by Dio's Philiscus. In the correspondence Cicero himself casts
       Atticus as a sort of philosophic advisor, whose amicable yet frank and occasionally
       severe advice Cicero values highly: see esp. *Att.* 3.1 = SB 46; 3.10.2 = SB 55; 3.11.2
       = SB 56; 3.13.2 = SB 59; 3.15 = SB 60. On Cicero's letters from exile see J.-M.
       Claassen 'Dio's Cicero and the consolatory tradition' *PLLS* 9 (1996) 29–45, 35.

[13]   This is the view shared by all who have studied the speech: see esp. J.R. Berrigan
       '*Consolatio philosophiae* in Dio Cassius' *CJ* 42 (1966) 59–61; F. Millar 'Some
       speeches in Cassius Dio' *MH* 18 (1961) 11–22, 17.

[14]   F. Millar *A Study of Cassius Dio* (Oxford 1964) 19–20, 50 (hereafter Millar *Study*);
       cf. D. Fechner *Untersuchungen zu Cassius Dios Sicht der Römischen Republik*
       (Hildesheim 1986) 49–50, summarising various theories about the identity of
       Philiscus. Both argue that Dio's Philiscus was indeed modelled on Philostratus'
       acquaintance. G. Bowersock, on the other hand, offers evidence that the inspiration
       for Dio's Philiscus may be a relative of the historian by the same name (review of F.
       Millar *A Study of Cassius Dio*, Gnomon 37 [1965] 469–74, 472). For further details
       on Philostratus' summation of Philiscus' career see S. Rothe *Kommentar zu
       ausgewählten Sophistenviten des Philostratos* (Heidelberg 1989) 252–61; G.
       Anderson *The Second Sophistic: a Cultural Phenomenon in the Roman Empire*

independently of the *History* as both a tribute to Philiscus and entertainment for the circle of the empress who, according to Philostratus, took great delight in all sorts of rhetorical exercises (καὶ γὰρ τοὺς ῥητορικοὺς πάντας λόγους ἐπῄνει καὶ ἠσπάζετο, *Life of Apollonius* 1.3). But whatever the identity of or model for Philiscus, this episode in Dio's *History* merits attention principally for what it reveals about his views on and use of Cicero.

What Philiscus says

A product of the Greco-Roman declamatory tradition,[15] the speech of Philiscus is a hodgepodge of philosophical commonplaces. I wish to focus first, however, on his analysis of Cicero's character and behaviour, and secondly on the advice he imparts toward the end of the speech.

Philiscus' respect for Cicero is apparent throughout. He commends Cicero's wide and varied education (38.22.1); calls Cicero the wisest of men (*ibid.*), the most just (38.22.2), the bravest (38.22.4); and claims that he has attained the pinnacle of σωφροσύνη (38.22.3), has acquired distinction, and also possesses, Philiscus interestingly adds, the talent necessary to writing history (38.28.3). Clearly, then, Cicero possesses certain qualities that would appear to merit emulation.

Nevertheless, the orator's current distress has exposed a weakness in his character: he is not self-sufficient (αὐτάρκης, 38.18.5).[16] As

---

(Routledge 1993) 33–4. Dio's own membership in the circle of Julia Domna is inferred rather than proven: see the discussion of Bowersock *Greek Sophists in the Roman Empire* (Oxford 1969) 102–4, 108 (hereafter Bowersock *Greek Sophists*). Dio, however, has some knowledge of the circle, noting that it consisted of the empress, who was conversant in both Latin and Greek, and "the most prominent men" (τοὺς πρώτους), with whom she increasingly devoted herself to the study of philosophy (78[77].18.3; cf. 76[75].15.7). This information is trotted out in order to contrast the learned mother with her vile son Caracalla, for whom Dio has little use and who had not heeded his mother's "excellent advice". While Dio does not explicitly name himself as a member of this circle (which fact alone, as Bowersock observes [*Greek Sophists* 108], argues against his participation), it is likely, given his position, that he knew and knew well the "prominent men" who *were* members of Julia's circle, including Philiscus.

15 Apart from its obvious roots in the *consolatio ad exulem* (see n.32), the speech shows affinities in terms of theme with the Cicero-based *suasoriae* (cf. e.g. Sen. *Suas.* 6 and 7) as well as with the sophistic *meletai* in terms of language and thought. On the similarity between *suasoriae* and *meletai* see Anderson (n.14) 18–19; see further G. Kennedy 'The sophists as declaimers' in G.W. Bowersock (ed.) *Approaches to the Second Sophistic* (University Park PA 1974) 15–22, 19–20.

16 Evidently a common complaint about Cicero (cf. Sen. *Dial.* 10.5; Plu. *Cic.* 32.5; Sen.

Philiscus asserts, Cicero alone is responsible for his plight and must bear the responsibility for extricating himself. Beginning in chapter 26 Philiscus discusses how Cicero should now conduct himself. Among other courses of action he recommends that Cicero not return to Rome, but instead find some pleasant spot to live out his life. He advises that having no choice in the matter, we must bend to the dictates of τὸ δαιμόνιον (38.26.4).[17] In chapter 28 he provides specifics: Cicero should retire to a remote seaside villa (a significant detail to which I shall presently return) and write history after the fashion of two famous and very Greek exiles, Xenophon and Thucydides.[18] This activity, Philiscus alleges, is the most lasting (διαρκέστατον) and most fitting (ἁρμοδιώτατον) for every man *and for every state* (πάσῃ δὲ πολιτείᾳ, 38.28.2: see n.45). In other words, removing oneself from the Roman political scene is not necessarily equated, as it often was by Cicero himself, with withdrawal from public life.[19]

At 38.28.5 Philiscus elaborates his call to the Epicurean life of leisure. As Cicero should know, there are various lifestyles from which to choose but a life devoted to σχολή or *otium* is best. Consider, Philiscus asks, "how much better quiet is than turmoil, tranquillity than

---

Suas. 6.22), though in this instance Dio may be thinking specifically of Plato *Rep.* 387d, a passage which seems to have inspired Philiscus' opening remarks at 38.18.1 (see below).

[17] A detail that points to Dio's hand in the speech: on Dio's understanding and use of τὸ δαιμόνιον, see my *The Triumviral Narratives of Appian and Cassius Dio* (Ann Arbor 1992) 29; see also J. Puiggali 'Les démons dans l'Histoire romaine de Dion Cassius' *Latomus* 43 (1984) 876–83.

[18] Cited also by Plutarch in his essay on exile (*Mor.* 605b). Philiscus' advice is therefore not new but, considering the author, clearly of heightened importance.

[19] In the 50's, at least, Cicero steadfastly opposed the Epicurean idealisation of *otium* commended here by Philiscus (see next paragraph). Cf. his praise of Cato for rejecting a life devoted to *otium* at *Rep.* 1.1 (cf. 3.6) with the comment *ad loc.* of J.E.G. Zetzel (ed.) *Cicero: De Re Publica* (Cambridge 1995); see also *id.* 'Looking backward: past and present in the late Roman Republic' *Pegasus* 37 (1994) 20–32, 24. As J.-M. André has shown (*L'otium dans la vie morale et intellectuelle romaine* [Paris 1966] 284), Cicero significantly altered his views of *otium* over the course of his career, and thus in the 40's he could argue that the *otium* imposed on him by political circumstances was in fact conducive to civic action in the form of philosophical writing (*Off.* 3.1–4). It is the *imposition* of *otium* that matters: even in 44 Cicero cannot condone the man who voluntarily seeks refuge in *otium*. On the contrary, he ironically imputes to such a person the ambitions of a king (*Off.* 1.69–70). See further on Cicero and *otium* J.P.V.D. Balsdon 'Auctoritas, dignitas, otium' *CQ* 10 (1960) 43–50, esp. 46–50; J. D'Arms *Romans on the Bay of Naples* (Cambridge MA 1970) 70–72, who notes the Ciceronian association of *otium* and retirement to a country villa (cf. Cic. *Off.* 1.69); and L. Perelli *Il pensiero politico di Cicerone* (Florence 1990) 3–15.

tumults, freedom than slavery, and safety than dangers" (σκέψαι δὲ ὅσον ἥ τε ἡσυχία τῆς ταραχῆς καὶ ἡ εὔροια τῶν θορύβων ἥ τε ἐλευθερία τῆς δουλείας καὶ ἡ ἀσφάλεια τῶν κινδύνων διαφέρει, 38.28.6).[20] By following the course urged by Philiscus, Cicero will assure a great name for himself; but if he resumes his political life in Rome, he will ruin his reputation. Naturally, Cicero will reject this advice, thereby, in Dio's view at least, ruining his reputation as well as sealing his own fate. This is anticipated by Philiscus' prophetic remarks in the next chapter: "... is it not a dreadful and disgraceful thing to have one's head cut off and set up in the Forum, for any man or woman ... to insult?" (καίτοι πῶς μὲν οὐ δεινόν, πῶς δ' οὐκ αἰσχρὸν ἀποτμηθῆναί τέ τινος τὴν κεφαλὴν καὶ ἐς τὴν ἀγορὰν τεθῆναι, κἂν οὕτω τύχῃ, καὶ ἄνδρα τινὰ αὐτῇ καὶ γυναῖκα ἐνυβρίσαι; 38.29.2). This of course alludes to precisely what will befall Cicero in 43, an event Dio describes in gruesome detail (47.8).

Philiscus alleges that Cicero cannot return to Rome because he is powerless to combat the forces arrayed against him. Among those forces are people he once called friends and from whom he cannot expect help, because "those who have a passion for power regard everything else as nothing in comparison with obtaining what they desire" (οἱ ... δυναστείας ἐρῶντες παρ' οὐδὲν πάντα τἆλλα, πρὸς τὸ τυχεῖν ὧν βούλονται, τίθενται, ἀλλὰ καὶ τοὺς φιλτάτους καὶ τοὺς συγγενεστάτους πολλάκις ἀντὶ τῶν ἐχθίστων ἀντικαταλλάσσονται, 38.29.4). In Dio's usage "power" (δυναστεία) generally means tyranny,[21] and in fact Dio envisions the Rome of the first triumvirate as being under a virtual tyranny. Thus, to cite but one example, shortly before the dialogue begins Dio describes Caesar as "proposing, advising and arranging everything *as though he were sole ruler*" (μόνος ἄρχων, 38.8.2). Philiscus shows Cicero a way to avoid the wrath of this 'tyranny' while still remaining an effective political force.

---

[20] Philiscus' advice to Cicero ironically resembles that which Caesar himself gave to Cicero in April of 49: *postremo quid viro bono et quieto et bono civi magis convenit quam abesse a civilibus controversiis? ... neque tutius neque honestius reperies quicquam quam ab omni contentione abesse* (*Att.* 10.8B.2 = SB 199B); on this occasion Cicero seemed to welcome the advice (*Att.* 10.9.1 = SB 200). But by the same token, the notion that exile provides a haven from political strife is a commonplace of the *consolatio ad exulem* (cf. Plu. *Mor.* 604b).

[21] See Fechner (n.14) 104–5, 154–63.

The 'imperial' and Dionian nature of Philiscus' advice

Despite these reassurances, Philiscus' invitation to the life of leisure is of course directly antithetical to the Ciceronian and Republican ideal, which valued *negotium* over *otium*. The archetypal Republican senator Cicero would have been appalled at Philiscus' advice, at least in 58,[22] but not the imperial senator Cassius Dio. In fact, Dio's Philiscus adduces a distinctly imperial view of the senator's function, according to which *otium* and *quies* (σχολή and ἡσυχία, to use Dio's terms)[23] could indeed serve a politically useful purpose.[24] What Dio argues for, then, is not renunciation of public life but rather a course of action whereby the senator can survive and best serve the state: write history and stay out of the way. In short, Dio pictures Cicero in a dilemma analogous to that frequently faced by the imperial senator, and it is therefore likely that Philiscus' arguments, though anachronistic in 58 BC, would seem familiar and sound to Dio's imperial readers.

The connections between Philiscus' logic and Dio's own senatorial philosophy emerge with clarity if we consider the way he depicts senators and the Senate in his contemporary books. The cases of three characters are particularly relevant, though perhaps the most telling involves Julius Solon, whose adlection into the senatorial order (*ca* AD 186) Dio ironically describes in terms of exile. His property is seen as being "confiscated", his admittance to the senate as "banishment": καὶ ἤδη τινὲς πάντα τὰ ὑπάρχοντά σφισιν ἀναλώσαντες βουλευταὶ ἐγένοντο, ὥστε καὶ λεχθῆναι ἐπὶ Ἰουλίου Σόλωνος ἀνδρὸς ἀφανεστάτου ὅτι ἐς τὸ συνέδριον τῆς οὐσίας στερηθεὶς ἐξωρίσθη

---

[22] In the mid 40's Cicero himself was capable of producing Dio's own argument (see n.19) and even of delivering his own *consolatio* of sorts to the (voluntarily) exiled Marcellus (cf. e.g. *Fam.* 4.7 = SB 230; 4.8 = SB 229; 4.9 = SB 231). See Claassen (n.14) 38–9.

[23] The collocation is common and often associated with the practice of philosophy (cf. Cic. *De Orat.* 3.56) or counted among the advantages of exile (e.g. Plu. *Mor.* 603e–604a).

[24] The whole notion of *otium*, of course, undergoes a transformation in the imperial period, becoming linked with the peace and prosperity supposedly afforded by the new order: Seneca's fragmentary *De Otio* (*Dial.* 8) is the best witness to this transformation (cf. *Ep.* 73.9–11). In a world, that is, where the Ciceronian paradigm had become obsolete, so too had the standard objections to *otium* lost their force; praising *otium* came instead to serve the rationalisation of the curtailed political role most senators were now forced to play. See above all the incisive discussion of this point by A.J. Woodman (ed.) *Velleius Paterculus: The Caesarian and Augustan Narrative (2.41–93)* (Cambridge 1983) 240–44; see also André (n.19) 531–41, and M. Griffin 'Philosophy, politics, and politicians' in M. Griffin and J. Barnes (eds.) *Philosophia Togata* (Oxford 1989) 1–37, 20.

(73[72].12.3). Dio uses much the same vocabulary to describe Cicero's exile: καὶ ἡ ... οὐσία αὐτοῦ ἐδημεύθη ... τρισχιλίους τε γὰρ καὶ ἑπτακοσίους καὶ πεντήκοντα σταδίους ὑπὲρ τὴν Ῥώμην ὑπερωρίσθη (38.17.6–7). That Dio should equate the acquisition of senatorial status in the early third century with a state of exile points to the fundamental powerlessness experienced by men such as Dio and Solon who more often than not felt like outcasts from rather than participants in the process of rule. But, to continue the analogy, the rank of senator could offer one of the same advantages as exile, the opportunity to write, preferably history.[25] If a senator had any power at all, it lay in his pen. The rest was all a matter of rank and privilege. Writing history therefore afforded an outlet; a narrative of the past was a less risky vehicle for contemporary political comment than a philosophical treatise aimed at the present. Not surprisingly, therefore, in dealing with the emperor Dio favors acquiescence rather than defiance, a notion captured in a word that Dio often uses throughout the *History* with reference to successful senators: μεσεύειν, to take the middle course or remain neutral.[26]

The senators whom Dio openly admires are indeed men who take the 'middle course', who live their lives quietly and unobtrusively, almost, one might say, in virtual exile. He singles out for praise Quin-tillus Plautianus, a "man of the noblest birth and long counted among the foremost members of the Senate" (εὐγενέστατός τε ὢν καὶ ἐπὶ πλεῖστον ἐν τοῖς πρώτοις τῆς βουλῆς ἀριθμηθείς), who lived in the country "interfering with no one's business and doing nothing wrong" (οὔτε πολυπραγμονῶν τι οὔτε παραπράσσων, 77[76].7.4). One of the more highly regarded senators in Dio's contemporary books is a certain Aemilianus, who "surpassed all the senators of that day in under-standing and in experience of affairs" (πάντων τῶν τότε βουλευόντων καὶ συνέσει καὶ ἐμπειρίᾳ προφέρειν ἐδόκει) by "remaining neutral" (μεσεύων) and "watching events" (ἐφεδρεύων τοῖς πράγμασι, 75[74].6.2). The best paradigm for this attitude is Dio himself, who was particularly adept at self-preservation. He had maintained a villa at Capua to which he regularly retreated from the fray of politics in Rome, and it was here over a 22 year period that he wrote his *History* (77[76].2.1). As Millar and Letta have noticed, this sounds rather like

---

[25]   Plu. *Mor.* 605b. Plutarch also maintains that exile affords "free speech" (παρρησία, *ibid.* 606b).
[26]   On this concept see Gowing (n.17) 24.

what Dio has Philiscus advise Cicero to do: retire to a country villa and write history.[27] Thus while the notion that exile can be conducive to literary productivity is a commonplace (cf. Plu. *Mor.* 605a–d), the detail in Dio is too pointed to be merely that.

Philiscus' speech therefore need not be read as Dio's banal and irrelevant *consolatio ad exulem* — although it is firmly rooted in that genre (see n.32) — but rather as a novel and entertaining twist on the *consolatio* which spoke to his readers' situations as 'senatorial exiles'. Still other aspects deserve consideration, not least of which is the possible connection to the aforementioned allusion in Philostratus.

The 'Greekness' of the speech: Plato and Philostratus

The juxtaposition of Greek and Roman — not unprecedented in the literature of the Second Sophistic[28] — is one of the most striking aspects of this episode, and it would be tempting to imagine that Dio intends the Greek Philiscus to 'show up' the Roman Cicero.[29] I believe, however, that this is not at all the case. It must be borne in mind that Dio writes as a member of the Roman senate; whatever criticisms he may have of Cicero (he views him chiefly as a meddling, irritating man who thoughtlessly impeded Rome's conversion to monarchy)[30] are not those of an outsider looking in, but of a full participant in and supporter of the Roman political system. If the praise Philiscus metes out to Cicero seems inconsistent with Dio's view,[31] we should recall that Dio himself observes that Cicero aroused both contempt and respect among his peers (38.12.7). Moreover, while it is likely that Dio has the Platonic model uppermost in his mind (see below), the form and even some of the contents of the exchange are reminiscent of a Ciceronian dialogue, leading one to suspect that Dio seeks in a general sense to

---

[27] C. Letta 'La composizione dell'opera di Cassio Dione: cronologia e sfondo storico-politico' *Ricerche di storiografia antica* 1 (Pisa 1979) 117–89, 159–60; Millar *Study* 51.

[28] Plutarch's *Lives* is of course the most obvious example. It is interesting to note that in Plutarch's view the Greek Demosthenes on balance proved himself superior to Cicero who, among other flaws, bore his exile badly (*Comp. Cic. et Dem.* 4; *Cic.* 32.5–7).

[29] And all the more tempting in light of Cicero's attempts to assert the superiority of Roman practice over Greek philosophy (cf. e.g. *Tusc.* 1.1–3; see Griffin [n.24] 13). Dio responds, however, not to Cicero's philosophy *per se* but rather to the facts of his life.

[30] See Millar *Study* 46–55; Gowing (n.17) 143–5; A.W. Lintott 'Cassius Dio and the history of the late Roman republic' *ANRW* II.34.3 (1997) 2497–523, 2514–17.

[31] This has been the standard opinion, but Fechner (n.14, 48–58) persuasively contends that Dio's and Philiscus' views on Cicero are not overly much at odds.

confront Cicero on his own ground.[32] It might be noted as well that in
support of his arguments Philiscus pointedly adduces several Roman
exempla (Camillus, Scipio, Drusus, the Gracchi, Capitolinus, Corvinus,
M. Valerius Corvus)[33] in addition to five well-known Greeks
(Aristides, Themistocles, Xenophon, Thucydides, Solon). Finally,
Philiscus presents himself as someone well-informed about the
intentions of Cicero's enemies (38.27.4). In short, Philiscus himself is
made to adopt the stance of an insider, well-versed in and well-
connected to the situation in Rome.

It should not be imagined, in other words, that Dio intends to pit a
superior Greek against a weaker Roman. And yet apart from language,
Philiscus' speech announces its Greekness in some obvious ways: it is
set in Greece; the speaker is a Greek; and he draws heavily on disparate
but stock elements of Greek philosophy, including some apparent
allusions to Plato (to be discussed below). Dio's readers would have
found the clever interplay of Greek and Roman entertaining as well as
informative.

For this and other reasons Fergus Millar concluded that Dio wrote
the dialogue to amuse the circle of the empress Julia Domna, a circle to
which, as we have seen, Dio may have belonged and whose members
included the Athenian rhetor named Philiscus. It is therefore of some
interest to observe that not only do we know of this Philiscus through
Philostratus, but that one of the very few direct references to Cicero in
a Greek writer apart from the historians is found in Philostratus' *Life of
Apollonius*. That passage shows some affinity with the Cicero/Philiscus
exchange in Dio and, if not a direct precedent for Dio's piece, at least
testifies to a shared interest in Cicero and the problem of exile.[34]

---

[32] There are, in fact, several points of contact with Cicero's own philosophical works,
especially the *Tusculan Disputations* (in which exile is a prominent theme),
suggesting not so much direct influence as adherence to the conventions of
consolation literature: see Millar (n.13) 16 with n.60; *id. Study* 50–51 with n.5. J.-M.
Claassen has proposed that Dio may have in mind *Att.* 3.15 = SB 60 ('Cicero's
banishment: tempora et mores' *AC* 35 [1992] 19–47, 30), though I remain skeptical
that Dio ever read Cicero's letters. On the extent to which Philiscus' speech
resembles a standard *consolatio* see Claassen (n.14); and A.V. van Stekelenburg *De
redevoeringen bij Cassius Dio* (Diss. Leiden 1971) 21–8.

[33] Far more than Plutarch who, in his essay on exile (*Mor.* 599–607), includes only three
Romans (Camillus, the emperor Tiberius and Cicero), preferring instead to focus on
Greek exempla.

[34] While I think it likely that the *Life* appeared prior to the composition of Dio's Book
38, I am not arguing for the influence of one text on the other and therefore leave
aside the question of chronology and composition except for the following
observations. The consensus is that Philostratus' *Life* appeared after 217, after the

In Book 7 of the *Life*, Apollonius is summoned to Italy to appear before the emperor Domitian and answer a charge of sedition. He lands at Dicaearchia, just north of Naples, where he is met by a resident philosopher named Demetrius. Demetrius leads Apollonius to a villa explicitly identified as having once belonged to Cicero (*Vita Apollonii* 7.11). This is most likely the orator's villa at Cumae, his *Cumanum*, a seaside complex purchased after his return from exile in 57 and the site of Book I of the *De Finibus* as well as the spot where he composed the *De Re Publica* (cf. *Ad Quintum Fratrem* 2.12.1 = SB 17).[35] But Philostratus adds a detail: the conversation between Apollonius and Demetrius takes place not merely at Cicero's villa, but beneath a plane tree at Cicero's villa to the accompaniment of a chorus of noisy cicadas. The unmistakable allusion to the *locus amoenus* of Plato's *Phaedrus*[36] is apt and establishes a link not only with Plato but Cicero as well. Cicero himself had named this part of the villa the "Academia", modelling it on Plato's Academy in Athens,[37] and a reader

---

death of Julia Domna (Bowersock *Greek Sophists* 5). Dio's *History*, on the other hand, was composed during a 12-year period from, according to one view, 207–219 (Millar *Study* 28–32) or, according to another, from 222–234 (Letta, and T.D. Barnes 'The composition of Cassius Dio's *Roman History*' *Phoenix* 38 [1984] 240–55; see Barnes 240–41 for summary of the various arguments). It is entirely possible, in any case, that the Philiscus/Cicero exchange was composed independently of and later inserted into the *History*; and regardless of their precise date, both Philostratus' *Life* and Dio's *History* are indisputably the product of the same intellectual milieu if not the same literary circle. It should be noted that Dio is fully aware of the court's interest in Apollonius and knows something about him (78[77].18.4), which may well imply that Philostratus' *Life* was available to him. There may be more concrete evidence. Dio shares with Philostratus the opinion that Calypso lived in Campania, near Cumae, and that it was here that Odysseus lived with her (48.50.4). This information appears in Philostratus at 7.10 — precisely in the midst of the Demetrius/Apollonius episode discussed here. That, combined with the fact (previously, as far as I am aware, unnoticed) that Dio and Philostratus are the only two sources for this view of Calypso's home (which argues against the notion of a shared 'tradition'), at the very least improves the likelihood that Dio knew Philostratus' *Life*.

35   On the identification of this particular villa see D'Arms (n.19) 146 n.143.

36   *Phdr.* 230b–c, 258e, noted by G. Anderson *Philostratus: Biography and Belles Lettres in the Third Century A.D.* (London 1986) 164 with n.77; cf. *id.* (n.14) 235. On the considerable popularity and influence of the *Phaedrus* in the Second Sophistic see Anderson (n.14) 77–8 and esp. M.B. Trapp 'Plato's *Phaedrus* in second-century Greek literature' in D.A. Russell (ed.) *Antonine Literature* (Oxford 1990) 141–73. See also P. De Lacy 'Plato and the intellectual life of the second century A.D.' in G.W. Bowersock (ed.) *Approaches to the Second Sophistic* (University Park PA 1974) 4–10, 6–7.

37   Plin. *NH* 31.6–7; Cicero also maintained an 'Academy' at his villa in Tusculum (*Div.* 1.8; cf. *Tusc.* 2.3).

familiar with the *De Oratore* would know that that dialogue was like-
wise set beneath a plane tree in an equally deliberate reminiscence of
the *Phaedrus* (*De Oratore* 1.28–9).[38] In short, the setting for
Philostratus' dialogue both adduces and connects Cicero and Plato in
much the same way as Cicero had done in virtually all of his philo-
sophical works. Dio likewise evokes Plato at the outset of Philiscus'
speech: Philiscus' criticism of Cicero's "womanish" weeping and
wailing (38.18.1) resembles, verbally and otherwise, Plato's own criti-
cisms of Homer's Achilles in Book 3 of the *Republic*;[39] and Cicero's
request that Philiscus remove the mist from his eyes (38.19.1) recalls
almost verbatim a passage in the conclusion of the *Alcibiades II* (150d–
e), a dialogue considered in Dio's day to be by Plato,[40] just as his
request in that same sentence to be led back up to the light (38.19.1)
conjures the image of the cave in the *Republic*.[41] And then, too, the
very form of the Cicero/Philiscus exchange is clearly inspired by the
Platonic dialogue, quite in keeping with the spirit of the Second
Sophistic.[42]

More important than their shared Platonic veneer, however, is the
fact that the two texts share a common topic, the proper response to
tyranny or near tyranny. The exchange between Philiscus and Cicero
deals with Cicero's reaction to his exile (and coincidentally with the
issue of whether he should return to Rome or remain in exile); the
dialogue between Apollonius and Demetrius focuses on how Apol-
lonius is to react to the imperial summons: should he proceed to Rome
and confront the tyrannical Domitian? Or should he withdraw? Citing
the example of the exiled Neronian consular Telesinus, Demetrius
urges the latter course, "… for the hand of tyranny", he claims, "is less
heavy upon distinguished men, if it perceives that they only desire to
live quietly and not put themselves forward" (αἱ γὰρ τυραννίδες ἧττον
χαλεπαὶ τοῖς φανεροῖς τῶν ἀνδρῶν, ἢν ἐπαινοῦντας αἴσθωνται τὸ μὴ
ἐν φανερῷ ζῆν, *Life of Apollonius* 7.12).

These similarities — the explicit conjoining of Cicero and Plato, the
topographical setting of the meeting in Philostratus and the allusion to

---

[38] On Cicero's evocation of the *Phaedrus* in this and other works see Trapp (n.36) 146,
      165–6.
[39] *Rep.* 387e–388b; cf. 605c–e. Cf. Cic. *Tusc.* 2.48–49.
[40] Cf. D.L. 3.59. See W.K.C. Guthrie *A History of Greek Philosophy* (Cambridge 1978)
      V 387.
[41] *Rep.* 515a–516a; cf. *Phdr.* 261e. Cicero himself envisions his exile as an "escape
      from light" (*Att.* 3.19.1 = SB 64, *Att.* 3.7.1 = SB 52; cf. *Brut.* 12).
[42] See Anderson (n.14) 67.

the seaside villa in Philiscus' speech in Dio, the chronological setting
(in the past rather than the present), and the very topic of the two
passages (the proper response to tyranny or near tyranny) — do not
appear coincidental, particularly if Philostratus and Dio did indeed
belong to the same literary circle. If correct, this interpretation suggests
among other things that in articulating responses to their political
situation, both Philostratus and Dio looked not simply to a Greek
tradition but to a Roman tradition as well, as exemplified by Cicero.

Conclusion

If both texts thus demonstrate, as Anderson has neatly put it in dis-
cussing the episode in Philostratus, a "convergence of Greek and
Roman declamatory tradition" (n.14, 235), neither of course indicates a
profound knowledge of Cicero's writings on the part of either author.
Rather, their importance lies in the way these texts use Cicero. In
Philostratus' case the allusion is surprising not merely because it is so
rare in a Greek writer, but because of the effect it achieves. In support
of political quietism, it evokes the memory of a famous Roman who
had experienced exile. Yet while it evokes him in a philosophical
context,[43] the reference does not evoke Ciceronian philosophy: that is,
it neither presumes nor urges a familiarity with Ciceronian ideas,
though Philostratus is doubtless aware that Cicero was himself a philo-
sopher of sorts; hence the appropriateness of locating the meeting at his
villa. More germane to Philostratus' purposes is a familiarity with the
historical Cicero; his allusion would mean little to a reader who knew
nothing of Cicero's own exile, but to judge from Plutarch's essay on
the subject, such knowledge could easily be presumed.

The exchange between Philiscus and Cicero in Dio is still more un-
usual: not only does it surface in the context of a historical narrative,
but it constitutes an unusual example of the use of speech in a history,
the articulation of a philosophical response to an individual's private
circumstance.[44] It should be noted that Cicero virtually disappears from

---

[43]   Anderson instead maintains that "Cicero's defiance of Antony" is evoked (n.14, 235),
       but I see no reason for a reader to make such an association: Cicero was overtaken by
       Antony's henchmen at Caieta, where he also owned some property (Plu. *Cic.* 47.7;
       App. *BC* 4.19), not Cumae, the site of the meeting of Apollonius and Demetrius (see
       n.35).

[44]   As Millar notes (n.13, 17), the only analogy to this in the *History* is the advice
       imparted by Livia to Augustus (55.14–21); but there the theme is clemency, certainly
       not in the tradition of the *consolatio*, and thus not an exact parallel.

Dio's narrative after this episode; the details of the orator's career between his return from exile in 57 and his emergence following the Ides of March in 44 are of scant interest to the historian. To be sure, Dio is hardly interested in providing biographical details about a character who is not central to his larger concern, the struggle between Pompey and Caesar. Nor, apparently, was he interested in investigating the nuances of Cicero's thinking as it evolved over the years between his exile and death. Had he done so, he might well have noticed that Cicero's response to Caesar was not unlike what Dio advocated for the imperial senator.[45] In short, Cicero functions in the Cicero/Philiscus exchange in much the same way as he does in the Philostratus passage, as an historical exemplum.

It is certain, I think, that Dio did not regard Cicero as a political theorist worthy of serious attention. He clearly respected Cicero's skill as an orator, as his imitation of a Ciceronian *Philippic* at 45.18–47 attests: in order to produce that particular *tour de force*, he must have studied the originals in some detail.[46] But the facts of Cicero's life suggested a man whose political beliefs appeared diametrically opposed to Dio's; Dio found it difficult to get past Cicero's misguided opposition to Caesar's monarchy and persistent defense of the Republic. If we may fault Dio for failing to appreciate the nuances of Cicero's thinking as it developed in the turbulent years before his death, it should be borne in mind that Dio is less concerned with the historical accuracy of his portrait than with the opportunity Cicero's exile presents — the opportunity to address a relevant contemporary issue: how should an imperial senator handle the 'exile' imposed by his circumstances?[47] In Dio's view, Cicero's response to his own exile had

---

[45]   That is, Cicero did eventually come to the realisation that the only recourse available lay in his writing — not history, of course, but philosophy. He views his philosophising both as 'protection' (*Fam.* 9.18.2 = SB 88) and a form of political activity (see n.19). In this, too, Dio may have found fault: he himself had chosen history as a more efficacious (if not more honorable and safer) means of expressing dissent, hence the importance of Philiscus' insistence that a retirement spent writing history could be beneficial to the state, and it has often been observed that Dio seems possessed of a general bias against philosophers (cf. e.g. Maecenas at 52.36.4; see Millar *Study* 13, 156). The fact that Philiscus parades his philosophical learning should therefore not be taken as a recommendation on the part of Dio to engage in the subject, but rather as additional evidence that the piece was composed to satisfy the philosophical tastes of Julia's circle (on which see T. Mantero *Ricerche sull'Heroikos di Filostrato* [Genoa 1966] 26–9).

[46]   See Gowing (n.17) 96 n.3, 237–9.

[47]   Letta's view (n.27, 157–63), that the impetus behind the Cicero/Philiscus exchange is the fact that Dio himself had been forced to spend his second consulship in 229 in

clearly been the wrong one; he should have retired to write history.

While we obviously cannot revise our conclusions about the extent to which Greeks may have read Cicero, both of these texts testify to a heightened interest in him in imperial salons of the Severan period. What of course distinguishes this from the earlier Antonine era — when Fronto (a Ciceronian devotee par excellence) could readily admonish the emperor Antoninus Pius to read a speech by Cicero if he wanted to learn something about managing the army and the provinces (*De Bello Parthico* 10 = Haines 2.30) — is the increasingly Eastern character of the court. If, however, Julia Domna is any indication, to whose ability in both Latin and Greek Dio attests (78[77].18.2), the intellectual interests of this court may have extended to Latin as well as Greek literature, Roman as well as Hellenic history.[48] Dio typifies precisely the sort of imperial courtier who, through his writing, catered to the interests of such a court. In him we encounter an Easterner for whom Cicero was not a mere historical curiosity, a relic of a Roman past to which Dio wished to deny any links. This was not an historian who spent his time reviving the faded glories of a Hellenic past, but one who took it upon himself to interpret Roman history for the Easterners who were coming to serve in the Roman senate in increasing numbers. The central issue here is therefore not Cicero's Romanness but his status and conduct as a Roman senator, a position he shares with Dio, a man who, having spent the better part of his life in Italy and 22 years writing a *Roman History*, could lay fair claim to being Roman himself. By the same token, this is not at all meant to suggest that Dio discarded his cultural heritage. On the contrary, he comes from Bithynia; his language is Greek; his cultural frame of reference is certainly in large part Greek. He is, in short, neither fully Greek nor fully Roman — he is both, and by the late second and early third centuries, his is not a unique perspective. Dio envisions himself as an heir to and mediator of both cultures, as the dialogue between Cicero and Philiscus reflects. It

---

virtual 'exile' (Letta's term) from Rome, deserves consideration. The strength of the assertion depends, however, on the date of the composition of Book 38 (after 229, according to Letta); regardless of that, Dio's own view of senatorial life as virtual exile links the episode to a broader context.

[48] Despite our slim knowledge of Latin letters in the early third century, there is evidence that Cicero continued to be read and imitated among Latin authors as well, in the form of the *Octavius* of Minucius Felix (fl. AD 200–240), a dialogue Ciceronian in design and even content (see P. MacKendrick *The Philosophical Books of Cicero* [New York 1989] 258). In other words, it would seem certain that Cicero remained a standard among Latin-speaking members of the court.

would be wrong, moreover, to dismiss this episode as a trite rhetorical exercise. In rewriting history in this curious and subtle way, Dio aimed at and achieved something no previous historian, Greek or Roman, had accomplished. He has brought to the fore the Greek philosophic advisor, a character whose importance in late Republican intellectual life we now know to have been profound.[49] While Philiscus and his encounter with Cicero may be fictitious, it is certainly not in the least inaccurate to stress the extent to which Romans — none more so than Cicero — looked to Greeks for their philosophical education. Appropriately, then, in Dio's unique reconstruction of Cicero's exile, it is a Greek, in Greece, who gives the exiled Roman the most important piece of advice he had ever gotten — and ignored. Regardless of the extent to which they could claim familiarity with Cicero's writings, the profound irony of this was surely not lost on Dio's readers.

[49]   On this subject see above all Rawson (n.4).

POSTSCRIPT

The 'Leeds International Latin Seminar' (LILS) resumed in 1988 the work of its predecessor, the Liverpool Latin Seminar, which had operated from 1975 to 1985 (see *PLLS* 5.491–502). The activities of LILS — in particular its concentration on Latin (and Greek) literature, especially poetry — have resembled those of its predecessor, although the title LILS also recognizes that what began as a British institution had by the early 1980s developed a strongly international character.

LILS has evolved over the eleven years of its existence towards its present formula of one thematic meeting per term, the first two involving four speakers, and the third being a Colloquium. Over the years, a conscious effort has been made, both in LILS meetings and in its publications, to integrate papers on ancient Greek topics to the fullest extent possible.

Like its predecessor, LILS has generated five volumes of papers, i.e. *PLLS* 6–10, the acronym having been preserved and the numeration continued from the Liverpool seminar.

PLLS 10 consists, as did earlier volumes in the series, in part of revised and usually expanded versions of papers presented at seminar meetings and in part of further papers contributed at the invitation of the editors. Editorial input has been similar to that of *PLLS* 6–9, and *PLLS* 10 like them has benefited from the expert proof-reading of Professor Neil Adkin.

When LILS' predecessor was set up in 1975, there were few forums where British Latinists and Hellenists could collaborate at the highest scholarly level towards publication, and also work with scholars from abroad. Over the intervening years this situation has changed dramatically: there is now, if anything, an oversupply in Britain of conferences and colloquia (many international in character), along with departmental and interdepartmental seminars, while attendance by British classicists at international meetings and collaboration with foreign colleagues are now much easier and more frequent.

The organizers of LILS continue to believe that high-level collaborative work towards publication is essential for the academic health of the classical community. But they are also convinced that a radical rethinking of objectives and activities is essential to meet the new needs of the new millennium. For this reason LILS will take a sabbatical during the academic year 1998–99, so that its future can be reviewed.

FC, MH   *August 6, 1998*

The Leeds International Latin Seminar 1988 – 1998

7th October 1988: NEW COMEDY AND ROMAN COMEDY
Prof. W. Geoffrey Arnott (University of Leeds).Why the *Dyscolos* fails
Dr Walter Stockert (University of Vienna). Wood and wax: hendiadys in Plautus
Prof. Sander M. Goldberg (University of California, Los Angeles). Roman Menander
Chairman: Dr Robert Maltby (University of Leeds)

2 December 1988: JUVENAL AND ROMAN SATIRE
Prof. Rita Cuccioli (Università di Bologna). The *Cena* in Juvenal
Mr T.E.S. Flintoff (University of Leeds). Juvenal 4 – something fishy in the state
Dr Yvan Nadeau (University of Edinburgh). *Canis satiricus* – Juvenal 5
Chairman: Dr William Barr (University of Leeds)

3 February 1989: CATULLUS AND CATULLAN STUDIES
Prof. Freddy Decreus (University of Gent). Catullus 8: changing interpretations
Prof. H.D. Jocelyn (University of Manchester). Catullus – the poetry of insult
Dr Lindsay Watson (University of Sydney). Catullus 22 – rustic Suffenus
Chairman: Dr D.P. Fowler (Jesus College, Oxford)

29 April 1989: *COLLOQUIUM*: THE REAL AND THE UNREAL IN GREEK AND ROMAN LITERATURE
First Session. Chairman: Mr J.G. Randall (University of Leeds)
Dr Elizabeth Craik (University of St Andrews). The staging of Sophocles *Philoctetes*
Dr Judith Mossman (Christ Church, Oxford). The prologue of Euripides *Hecuba*
Dr Malcolm Heath (University of Leeds). Some deceptions in Aristophanes
Prof. Graham Zanker (University of Canterbury, New Zealand). Hellenic myth in
    Theocritus
Dr Alessandro Schiesaro (Università di Pisa). Unreal monsters in Lucretius Book 5
Second Session. Chairman: Prof. Heinz Hofmann (Rijksuniversiteit Groningen)
Mr I.M. LeM. DuQuesnay (Jesus College, Cambridge). Credibility in the first book of
    Propertius
Prof. John Ferguson (Wooster College, Ohio). Did Horace's young ladies exist?
Dr Stratis Kyriakides (University of Thessaloniki). Night in the *Aeneid*: the time of
    reality
Dr Jo-Marie Claassen (University of Stellenbosch). Ovid's poetic Pontus
Dr Victor Schmidt ((Rijksuniversiteit Groningen). Ovid in Tomi: reality or fiction?

13 October 1989: PROPERTIUS AND PROPERTIAN STUDIES
Prof. Hans-Peter Stahl (University of Pittsburgh). On interpreting Propertius
Prof. Paulo Fedeli (Università di Bari). Propertius 3.23, Catullus 42 and lost writing-
    tablets
Dr Stephen Heyworth (Wadham College, Oxford). Textual questions about Propertius
    3.16 and 3.17
Chairman: Prof. Francis Cairns (University of Leeds)

1 December 1989: ROMAN RHETORIC AND HISTORIOGRAPHY
Prof. Elizabeth Keitel (University of Massachussets at Amherst). Speeches and
    generalities in Livy

Prof. Charles Brink (Gonville and Caius, Cambridge). The *Dialogus de Oratoribus* and Tacitus the historian
Dr Jef Kemper (Rijksuniversiteit Groningen). Curtius Rufus - rhetor?
Chairman: Mr Stephen Ryle (University of Leeds)

2 February 1990: ETYMOLOGY AND POETRY IN FIRST CENTURY BC ROME
Dr Robert Maltby (University of Leeds). Varro's attitude to Greek etymologies
Dr Wilhelm Pfaffel (Bayerisches Staatsministerium für Unterricht und Kultus, München). Literary and linguistic reconstruction in Varro
Prof. Louise Deschamps (Université de Bordeaux III). Varro and the poets
Chairman: Prof. David West (University of Newcastle)

27 April 1990: *COLLOQUIUM*: CALLIMACHUS AND HIS INFLUENCE
Colloquium Director: Prof. Richard Thomas (Harvard University)
Dr Alison Sharrock (University of Keele). "Callimacheanism" and the long and short of art
Ms Virginia Knight (Corpus Christi, Cambridge). Potnia polyptoli: Artemis and the cities in the Hymn to Artemis
Dr Marco Fantuzzi (Università degli Studi di Trento). Callimachus' Hymns 5 and 6: the prehistory of the literary genre
Dr Annette Harder (Rijksuniversiteit Groningen). Substantial voices (Callimachus *Aetia*)
Prof. Peter Parsons (Christ Church, Oxford). Callimachus and *koine*
Dr Brian Arkins (University College, Galway). Callimachus and Catullus
Prof. William W. Batstone (Ohio State University). Catullus 7 and the tomb of Battus
Prof. F. Decreus (Rijksuniversiteit Gent). Language in the *Hymn to Apollo* and Catullus 64
Dr Maria Grazia Bajoni (Università Cattolica del Sacro Cuore, Milan). *Ales equos*: Catullus 66.54 and Callimachus
Mrs Anne Gosling (University of Natal). Political Apollo: from Callimachus to the Augustans
Prof. Peter E. Knox (Columbia University, New York). Ovid's Phyllis: a Callimachean heroine?
Prof. A. Ramírez de Verger (Universidad de Sevilla). Ovid *Amores* 3.6.1-22
Dr Martin Pulbrook (St Patrick's College, Maynooth). The influence on Ovid of the *Aetia* of Callimachus

26 October 1990: ANCIENT POETS AND THEIR ANCIENT COMMENTATORS
Prof. Franco Montanari (Università di Genova). Ancient and modern Homeric scholarship: general remarks from the scholia
Dr Malcolm Heath (University of Leeds). The Pindar scholia: *Nemean* 7
Prof. Peter L. Schmidt (Universität Konstanz). *Pereant qui ante nos nostra dixerunt*: Traditions of literary interpretation in the *Commentum Terenti* of Aelius Donatus
Prof. Charles Murgia (University of California, Berkeley). The truth about Virgil and his commentators
Chairman: Dr Stephen Harrison (Corpus Christi College, Oxford)

[8 February 1991: CICERO: MULTIPLEX INGENIUM
Prof. R.G.M. Nisbet (Corpus Christi College, Oxford). Indecorum in Cicero's speeches
Prof. N. Horsfall. 'Cicerone e la poesia': from Accius to Horace
Dr Jonathan Powell (University of Newcastle upon Tyne). The cosmic viewpoint in Cicero's *De Republica*
Prof. John Glucker (Tel Aviv University). How Cicero translates Greek technical terms
Chairman: Dr W.Barr (University of Leeds). *Meeting cancelled because of snow*]

3 May 1991 *COLLOQUIUM*: ENMITY, ENVY AND INSULT IN ANCIENT POETRY
Colloquium Director: Prof. Matthew Dickie (University of Illinois)
Dr Douglas L. Cairns (University of Otago). Affronts and quarrels in the *Iliad*
Dr Judith Maitland (University of Western Australia). Permissible insults in the Homeric poems
Prof. A.J. Podlecki (University of British Columbia). *Archilochum proprio rabies armavit iambo*: another look at Archilochean invective
Prof. R. Alden Smith (Rutgers University). The battle of the sexes in Catullus 10
Prof. W. Jeffrey Tatum (Florida State University). Catullus 79: personal invective or political discourse?
Dr S.J. Heyworth (Wadham College, Oxford). Horace's *Ibis*
Prof. Connie Rodriguez (Loyola University). Palatine Apollo and *recusatio*
Prof. Allan Kershaw (Penn State University). The enmity between Martial and Statius
Dr Vincent Hunink (Katholieke Universiteit, Nijmegen). Lucan and Nero
Dr Susan Braund (Exeter University). Naevolus in Juvenal *Satire* 9

25 October 1991: IMAGES OF THE STATE IN HORACE
Prof. Matthew Santirocco (University of Pennsylvania). Horace and Augustan ideology
Dr D.P. Fowler (Jesus College, Oxford). Horace and the aesthetics of politics
Prof. Zsigmond Ritoók (Eötvös Loránd Tudományegyetem, Budapest). *Quid leges sine moribus...?*
Prof. Ernst-Gunther Schmidt (Friedrich-Schiller Universität, Jena). Transformations of popular philosophical themes in Horace
Chair: Dr John Moles (Durham University)

7 February 1992: GREEK IMPULSES IN THE ROMAN WORLD
Prof. A. Grilli (Università degli Studi di Milano). Cicero and the Greeks
Prof. Egil Kraggerud (Universitetet i Oslo). Polyphonic Vergil: the poet's voice and those of his models
Dr A. Hardie (FCO). Greek cults and Roman poetry
Dr A.J.S. Spawforth (University of Newcastle upon Tyne). The Greek world in the early Roman empire: culture and politics
Chair: Prof. Andrew Wallace-Hadrill (Reading University)

8 May 1992: *COLLOQUIUM*: RELIGION AND POETRY IN THE ANCIENT WORLD
Colloquium Director: Professor Karl Galinsky (University of Texas at Austin).
Mrs Elizabeth Craik (University of St Andrews). Epithets and epiklesis
Dr Marília P. Futre Pinheiro (Universidade de Lisboa). Prayer and poetry in Euripides' *Hippolytus*
Professor David Kovacs (University of Virginia). The gods in Euripides' *Troades*
Dr Richard Seaford (University of Exeter). Religion and the textual criticism of tragic poetry
Professor Ian Rutherford (Harvard University). Tourism and the sacred: aspects of *theoria* in ancient literature
Miss Anne Wilson (University of Leeds). Dionysian ritual objects in Hellenistic epic
Dr Stephen Instone (University College, London). Catullus and Attis
Professor Joseph C. P. Cotter (Penn State University). *Tellus Mater*, Catullus' dead brother, and the crux at 68.157
Professor Karl Galinsky (University of Texas at Austin). *Key-Note Address*: The 'Golden Age' in Augustan religion, literature and art

Professor Hans-Peter Stahl (University of Pittsburgh). Vergil's use of religion in
    supporting the rule of Augustus
Professor John F. Miller (University of Virginia). The poetics of the Roman triumph
Professor Kathryn Argetsinger (University of Rochester). Religious ritual in Latin
    birthday poetry
Professor Martin Helzle (Case Western Reserve University). Religion in Lucan

30 October 1992: ARCHAIC GREECE AND AUGUSTAN POETRY
Dr T.J. Cornell (University College, London). The archaic age through Augustan eyes
Prof. Richard F. Thomas (Harvard University). Virgil and epinician
Mr J.G. Howie (Edinburgh University). *Pindarum quisquis*: a study of emulation in
    Horace's *Odes*
Prof. F. Cairns (University of Leeds). Intimations of the archaic in Roman elegy?
Chair: Mr James R.G. Wright (University of Newcastle)

12 February 1993: OVID
Prof. John Barsby (University of Otago). Ovid's *Amores* and Roman comedy
Prof. J.C. McKeown (University of Wisconsin-Madison). The dating of Ovid's *Heroides*
Prof. Paola Pinotti (Università degli Studi di Bologna). Old age in Ovid
Mr A.S. Hollis (Keble College, Oxford). Ancient and modern commentators on the
    Metamorphoses
Chair: Mr Ian M. LeM. DuQuesnay (Jesus College, Cambridge)

May 7 1993: *COLLOQUIUM*: GREEK VIEWS OF THE ROMANS, ROMAN VIEWS OF THE GREEKS
Colloquium Director: Prof. Nikos Petrochilos (University of Thessaloniki)
Dr Andrew Erskine (University College, Dublin). Money-loving Romans
Prof. Jo-Marie Claassen (University of Stellenbosch). Dio's Cicero and the consolatory
    tradition
Prof. Alain M. Gowing (University of Washington, Seattle). Greek advice for a Roman
    senator (Cassius Dio 38.18-29)
Prof. Jürgen Werner (Universität Leipzig). Latin as a Gerek dialect
Prof. William M. Owens (Ohio University). Honest Romans and dishonest Greeks in
    Bacchides
Prof. Luciano Cicu (Università di Sassari). *Graeci, natio comoeda*
Mr M.B. van Moerik Broekman (Edinburgh Academy). *Pallium*: dress and xenophobia in
    Rome
Dr Kathryn Lomas (University College, London). Constructing 'the Greek': ethnic
    identity in Magna Graecia
Prof. Stephen Hinds (University of Washington, Seattle). Constructions of Neotericism
Prof. Jeri B. DeBrohun (Florida State University). How Greek is the Roman
    Callimachus?
Prof. Alessandro Barchiesi (Università di Verona). Passages to Italy: plots of
    Hellenisation in Roman epic

29 October 1993: POEMS IN BOOKS
Prof. Nita Krevans (University of Minnesota). Structure and genre in the *Aetia*
Dr Béla Németh (Debreceni Kossuth Lajos Tudom nyegyetem). Once again, *Catulli
    Veronensis Liber*
Prof. James L. Butrica (Memorial University). The art and architecture of Propertius
Mr Alan Griffiths (University College, London). Horace's *Odes*: just where do you draw
    the line?
Chair: Prof. Peter Parsons (Christ Church, Oxford)

19 February 1994: POST-BIMILLENARY VIRGIL

Prof. Mario Geymonat (Università degli studi di Venezia). Returning to the text
Dr P.R. Hardie (New Hall, Cambridge). Paradoxology in Virgil
Professor Antonie Wlosok (Johannes Gutenberg-Universität Mainz). Illustrated Virgil manuscripts, Rezeption and exegesis
Dr Damien Nelis (University of Durham). Virgil's Homer from Propertius to Knauer
Dr Carina Malan (University of Stellenbosch). The interdependence of the theoretical and the personal in interpreting Virgil
Dr Lorenz Rumpf (Universität Frankfurt). Eclogue 10.14, '*sola sub rupe iacentem*': some changes in a bucolic image
Dr Monica Gale (Royal Holloway College, London). Lucretius and the Georgics: influence, allusion or intertextuality?
Dr Matthew Leigh (University of Exeter). Virgil's *senex Corycius* and Parthenius
Dr S.J. Harrison (Corpus Christi College, Oxford). Caesar or Augustus: *Aeneid* 1.286
Chair: Mr J.G. Randall (University of Leeds)

6 May 1994: *COLLOQUIUM*: TRUTH, LIES AND HYPOCRISY IN GREEK AND ROMAN ANTIQUITY

Colloquium Director: Prof. J. Tatum (Florida State University)
Prof. Archibald Allen (Pennsylvania State University). On lying to enemies: *Agamemnon* 1372ff.
Dr A.G. Keen (University of Manchester). *Nil nisi bonum*: lies about Lysander
Prof. John M. Marincola (Union College, New York). Were ancient historians hypocrites?
Mr Robin Seager (University of Liverpool). *Ut dux cunctator et tutus*: Ammianus and Valentinian
Prof. Allan Kershaw (Pennsylvania State University). Propertian Acanthis
Dr Robert Hannah (University of Otago). The astrology of P. Nigidius Figulus (Lucan 1.649-65) revisited
Dr Hugh Lindsay (University of Newcastle, New South Wales). Tiberian hypocrisy and family funerals
Dr Janet Huskinson (Open University). Truth, lies and indifference: a warning from Roman funerary art
Dr Siegrid Weber (Leipzig). Truth, lies and hypocrisy in jurisdiction
Dr Graham Anderson (University of Kent). Tall story-telling in antiquity
Dr Costas Panayotakis (University of Glasgow). *Mimicae fallaciae* in Petronius' *Satyrica*
Mr Stelios Panayotakis (University of Crete). Lucian's *On Slander* and Apuleius' tale of Cupid and Psyche
Prof. Carl P.E. Springer (Illinois State University). Scriptural truth and poetic imagination in the Biblical epics of late antiquity

28 October 1994: LANGUAGE, STYLE AND CHARACTER IN LATIN LITERATURE

Professor Hubert Petersmann (Universität Heidelberg). Plautus
Mr Ian Du Quesnay (Jesus College, Cambridge). Virgil's *Eclogues*
Professor Gregson Davis (Cornell University). Ovid's *Heroides*
Professor Wade Richardson (McGill University). *Utique propter mascarpionem*? (Petronius *Satyricon* 134.5)
Chair: Dr J.N. Adams (University of Manchester)

17 February 1995: SILVER AND GOLD: AUGUSTAN AND POST-AUGUSTAN RECONSIDERED

Professor Elaine Fantham (Princeton University). Golden threads amongst the silver

Professor Anthony J. Boyle (University of Southern California). Recuperating Senecan
    tragedy
Dr Lars Nyberg (University of Lund). Valerius Flaccus
Mr Donald Hill (University of Newcastle). Statius *Thebaid* 1 revisited
Chair: Professor H.M. Hine (University of St Andrews)

**5 May 1995: *COLLOQUIUM*: DE VINO VERITAS: WINE IN GRECO-ROMAN
RELIGION, LITERATURE AND CULTURE**
Colloquium director: Dr. R.W. Brock (University of Leeds)
Mr. A. Greaves (University of Leeds). The importance of wine in the Greek and
    barbarian societies of the Black Sea
Mr Tim Santon (Royal Holloway College, London). Columella's attitude to wine
    production
Dr Hanneke Wirtjes (Wadham College, Oxford). Galen on wine
Dr Matthew Leigh (University of Exeter). Vergil *Georgics* 1.302
Professor T.S. Johnson (Baylor University). Wine and the *potens vates*: Horace's
    sympotic persona
Mr Konstantinos Niafas (University of Exeter). Dionysiac imagery in Horace *Odes* 1.18
Professor Barbara Pavlock (Lehigh University). Pia testa: the function of wine in Horace
    Odes 3.21
Dr H.W. Bird (University of Windsor). Emperors, wine and fiction
Dr Lucette M. Oostenbroek (Mare Vini Consultancy for wine history). The betraying
    kiss: women and wine in greco-roman times
Dr Simone Beta (Università di Milano). Women and wine in Greek comedy
Mr J.J. Paterson (University of Newcastle upon Tyne). The rhetoric of drunkenness

3 November 1995: POLITICS AND THE EPIGRAM
Dr Gregor Weber (Katholische Universität Eichstätt). Hellenistic rulers and their poets:
    silencing the critics
Professor W. Jeffrey Tatum (Florida State University). Politics in Catullan epigram
Professor K.M. Coleman (Trinity College, Dublin). Martial Book 8 and the crises of AD
    93
Mr E.L. Bowie (Corpus Christi College, Oxford). Greek epigram and Roman power in
    the second century AD
Chair: Dr David Bain (University of Manchester)

16 February 1996: ROMAN POETRY AND THE PHILOSOPHY OF ITS TIME
Dr H.B. Gottschalk (University of Leeds). Philosophical innovation in Lucretius?
Professor Guido Milanese (Università Cattolica di Milano). Virgil's ethical vocabulary
Dr J.L. Moles (University of Durham). Horace in the *Epistles*
Professor G. Karl Galinsky (University of Texas at Austin). Ovid's Pythagoras: arch-
    philosopher and arch poet
Chair: Professor Jonathan Powell (University of Newcastle upon Tyne)

**3 May 1996: *COLLOQUIUM*: THE TROJAN WAR IN ANCIENT LITERATURE
AND ART**
Colloquium director: Dr Oliver Taplin (Magdalen College, Oxford)
Professor Richard Whitaker (University of Cape Town). Images of the Trojan War in the
    Odyssey
Dr Jonathan Burgess (University of Toronto). The non-Homeric nature of the Trojan War
    in early Greek art
Professor Mary L. Hart (University of Texas at Arlington). The *Iliupersis* in archaic and
    classical Athens

Dr Susan Woodford (British Museum). Recognising Telephos: an engraving by
    Tischbein and some sherds from HMS Colossus
Professor Eleonora Cavallini (Università degli studi di Bologna). The Trojan War in the
    poetry of Ibycus
Professor José B. Torres-Guerra (Universidad de Navarra). The Trojan War in Ibycus
Mr Gordon Howie (University of Edinburgh). Pindar and Bacchylides on the Trojan War
Professor David Kovacs (University of Virginia). Aulis and Thrace: the sacrifices of
    Iphigenia and Polyxena compared
Dr Andrew Erskine (University College, Dublin). Homeric heroes in South Italy
Professor Lisa B. Hughes (The Colorado College). Virgil's Andromache
Dr Susanna Phillippo (Oriel College, Oxford). Astyanax and the story of Troy that might
    have been
Mr Peter Heslin (Trinity College, Dublin). Achilles' heel: venerable or vulnerable?

1 November 1996: WORD-PLAY IN ROMAN POETRY
Professor David West (University of Newcastle-upon-Tyne). Etymology, atomology in
    Lucretius?
Professor James O'Hara (Wesleyan University). Callimachus and Virgilian etymologies
Professor Hans-Christian Günther (Universität Freiburg). Word-play in Latin elegy
Professor Stephen Hinds (University of Washington). Propertius, Ovid and the limits of
    etymologising interpretation
Chair: Dr Robert Maltby (University of Leeds)

14 February 1997: ROMAN HISTORY AND ROMAN POETRY
Dr R.J. Clare (University of Leeds). Octavian in the *Georgics*
Professor M. Citroni (Università degli Studi di Firenze). The memory of Philippi in
    Horace and the interpretation of *Epistle* 1.20.23
Professor T.P. Wiseman (University of Exeter). Ovid and Servius Tullius (*Fasti* 6.569-
    636).
Professor W.J. Dominik (University of Natal). History in Silius Italicus' *Punica*
Chair: Professor Francis Cairns (University of Leeds)

**2 May 1997 *COLLOQUIUM*: MYTHOLOGY, POLITICS & POWER IN GREEK
& ROMAN LIFE & LITERATURE**
Colloquium director: Profesor T.J. Cornell (University of Manchester).
Dr Susan Deacy (University of Keele). Political enmity and mythic tradition
Dr Martin Steinrück (Université de Lausanne). King and tyrant in the archaic Greek
    imaginaire
Professor Philip Holt (University of Wyoming). Hippias' Oedipal dream (Herodotus
    6.107).
Professor Graham Anderson (University of Kent). Hellenising mythology in the second
    sophistic
Professor Rory B. Egan (University of Manitoba). Athenian *pietas* in Augustan Carthage:
    Aeneid 1 and *Oedipus Coloneus*
Dr Llewelyn Morgan (University College, Dublin). Autobiography in the *Aeneid*
Dr Fer van Campen (Utrecht). Augustus in the *Metamorphoses*
Dr Michael Hendry (University of Alabama). Propertius 2.1-2 as declaration of poetic
    suicide
Professor Chad Turner (Loyola University). Patroclus and Domitius Ahenobarbus in
    Lucan *Pharsalia* 7
Professor Harry Bird (University of Windsor). Making and mocking a myth in the Late
    Roman Empire

Dr Gráinne McLaughlin (University of Birmingham). The use of myth in Greek and Latin panegyric

Mr Roger Rees (University of St Andrews). Maximian Herculius: the power of myth

31 October 1997: VARRO AND INTELLECTUAL CULTURE IN THE FIRST CENTURY B.C.

Dr Ray Astbury (University College, Dublin). At the grave of Menippus

Professor Pierre Flobert (Université de Paris-Sorbonne). Varronian etymology in Book 7 of *De Lingua Latina*

Dr Thomas Baier (Albert-Ludwigs-Universität Freiburg). Myth and politics in Varro's historical writings

Mr Thomas H. Tarver (Magdalen College, Oxford). Theatres of memory? Varro and the Roman past

Chair: Professor H.D. Jocelyn

13 February 1998: RITUAL AND ROMAN POETRY

Dr Denis Feeney (New College, Oxford). Interpreting ritual: a problem of models

Professor Peter Knox (University of Colorado). Religion and politics in Ovid

Professor Giancarlo Mazzoli (Università degli Studi di Pavia). The religion of the evil in Seneca's tragedies

Dr Harm-Jan van Dam (Leiden). Ritual and Statius' *Silvae*

Chair: Professor John North (University College, London).

1 May 1998: *COLLOQUIUM*: HELLENISTIC INTO ROMAN: CULTURAL, HISTORICAL & LITERARY CONTINUITIES

Colloquium director: Mr Peter G. McC. Brown (Trinity College, Oxford).

Professor Richard Thomas (Harvard University). Look who's talking! Callimachus and Virgil

Dr S. Hatzikosta (University of Athens). How did Virgil read Theocritus?

Dr Eleni Kyriakidou-Peraki (University of Thessaloniki). Virgil's *bugonia*

Dr Stratis Kyriakidis (University of Thessaloniki). Virgil *Aeneid* 5.822-6: the catalogue as proem

Dr Andrew Dalby (Goodenough Trust, London). Cato's readership

Ms Sara Rubinelli (University of Leeds). Cicero's *De Inventione* and the use of Greek philosophical sources

Dr Maria Broggiato (University College, London). Crates of Mallos and the *polymatheia* of the poet

Dr Amiel D. Vardi (Hebrew University of Jerusalem). Hellenistic poetry collections and a muddle in the Roman generic system

Dr H. Karamalengou (University of Athens). Hellenistic influences on Ennius' conception of *rex*

Mr Boris Dunsch (University of St Andrews). Dream reports in Greek and Roman comedy

Professor Alden Smith (Baylor University). Paper or plastic? Gaze and the Hellenistic heroine in Propertius 1.3

Dr Martin Pulbrook (National University of Ireland, Maynooth). Hellenisms in Ovid's *Heroides*

PLLS: Contents of volumes 1 – 10

All volumes of PLLS are included in the series ARCA (Classical and Medieval Texts, Papers and Monographs, ISSN 0309-5541). Volumes 1 to 5 (edited by Francis Cairns) were published as *Papers of the Liverpool Latin Seminar* (ISSN 0261-0698). Volumes 6 to 10 (various editors) are *Papers of the Leeds International Latin Seminar* (ISSN 1362-3818).

Papers of the Liverpool Latin Seminar 1976
ARCA 2. ISBN 0-905205-00-6. vi+310pp. Paper. 1977.
Classical Latin Poetry

C. Tuplin: *Cantores Euphorionis* (1-23)
I.M. LeM. DuQuesnay: Vergil's fourth *Eclogue* (25-99)
E.L. Harrison: Structure and meaning in Vergil's *Aeneid* (101-12)
A. Hardie: Horace *Odes* 1,37 and Pindar *Dithyramb* 2 (113-40)
C.W. Macleod: Propertius 4.1 (141-53)
R. Seager: Horace and the Parthians (summary) (155-56)

Medieval Latin Poetry

P.G. Walsh: *Pastor* and pastoral in medieval Latin poetry (157-69)
S.F. Ryle: The Sequence: reflections on literature and liturgy (171-82)
M. Davie: Dante's Latin *Eclogues* (183-98)
A.B.E. Hood: The Cambridge Songs (summary) (199-200)
M. Levy: *Persona* in twelfth-century Latin poetry (summary) (201-2)
K. Maguire: The revision of the Breviary Hymnal under Urban VIII (summary) (203-5)

Greek Poetry

J.G. Howie: Sappho *Fr.* 16 (LP): self-consolation and encomium (207-35)
G.J. Giesekam: The portrayal of Minos in Bacchylides 17 (237-52)
G. Giangrande: Three Alexandrian epigrams: *APl* 167; Callimachus *Epigram* 5 (Pf.); *AP* 12,91 (253-70)
G. Giangrande: Aspects of Apollonius Rhodius' language (271-91)
F. Cairns: The Distaff of Theugenis – Theocritus *Idyll* 28 (293-305)

Papers of the Liverpool Latin Seminar, Second Volume, 1979
ARCA 3. ISBN 0-905205-03-0. viii+360pp. Paper. 1979.
Vergil and Roman Elegy

E.L. Harrison: The Noric Plague in Vergil's third *Georgic* (1-65)
H.D. Jocelyn: *Vergilius cacozelus* (Donatus *Vita Vergilii* 44) (67-142)
T. Krischer: UnHomeric scene-patterns in Vergil (143-54)
J.C. Yardley: The door and the lover: Propertius 1,16 (155-62)
J.C. McKeown: Ovid *Amores* 3,12 (163-77)

Medieval Latin Poetry and Prose

W. Barr: Claudian's *In Rufinum*: an invective? (179-90)
J.E. Cross: Popes of Rome in the *Old English Martyrology* (191-211)
R. Wright: The first poem on the Cid: the *Carmen Campi Doctoris* (213-48)
K. Bate: Twelfth-century Latin comedies and the theatre (249-62)
J. Margetts: *Christus vitis, praedicator 'quasi vitis'*: some observations on Meister Eckhart's Latin sermon style (263-76)
J. Foster: Petrarch's *Africa*: Ennian and Vergilian influences (277-98)7

Greek Lyric and Drama

J.G. Howie: Sappho *Fr.* 94 (LP): farewell, consolation and help in a new life (299-342)
W.G. Arnott: Time, plot and character in Menander (343-60)

Papers of the Liverpool Latin Seminar, Third Volume, 1981
ARCA 7. ISBN 0-905205-08-1. vi+423pp. 1981.

E. Fantham: Plautus in miniature: compression and distortion in the *Epidicus* (1-28)

I.M. LeM. DuQuesnay: Vergil's first *Eclogue* (29-182)

M.W. Dickie: The disavowal of *invidia* in Roman iamb and satire (183-208)

E.L. Harrison: Vergil and the Homeric tradition (209-25)

P. Fedeli: Elegy and literary polemic in Propertius' *Monobiblos* (227-42)

R. Maltby: Love and marriage in Propertius 4,3 (243-47)

F. Williams: Augustus and Daphne: Ovid *Metamorphoses* 1,560-64 and Phylarchus *FGrH* 81 F 32 (b) (249-57)

H. Hine: The structure of Seneca's *Thyestes* (259-75)

H.D. Jocelyn: Difficulties in Martial, Book 1 (277-84)

K.-D. Fischer: Pelagonius on horse medicine (285-303)

J. McClure: The biblical epic and its audience in late antiquity (305-21)

C. Codoñer: The poetry of Eugenius of Toledo (323-42)

R. Wright: Late latin and early romance: Alcuin's *De Orthographia* and the Council of Tours (AD 813) (343-61)

P.G. Schmidt: Elias of Thriplow – a thirteenth-century Anglo-Latin poet (363-70)

B. Bergh: A saint in the making: St Bridget's life in Sweden (1303-1349) (371-84)

J.W. Binns: Biblical latin poetry in renaissance England (385-416)

Brief notes:

K.-D. Fischer: Lucretius 4,1201ff. and Ovid *Ars Amatoria* 2,484 (417-18)

W.A. Camps: Horace *Epistles* 2,1,156ff. (418-19)

F. Cairns: *Lesbia mentoreo* (Propertius 1,14,2) (419-22)

W. Barr: *Res* = 'a thing'? Persius 4,1 (422-23)

Papers of the Liverpool Latin Seminar, Fourth Volume, 1983
ARCA 11. ISBN 0-905205-17-0. viii+369pp. 1984.

H.D. Jocelyn: Anti-Greek elements in Plautus' *Menaechmi* (1-25)

R. Maltby: The last act of Terence's *Heautontimorumenos* (27-41)

S. Hinds: *Carmina Digna*: Gallus *P Qaṣr Ibrîm* 6-7 metamorphosed (43-54)

R. Whitaker: Gallus and the 'classical' Augustans (55-60)

F. Cairns: Propertius 1,4 and 1,5 and the 'Gallus' of the Monobiblos (61-103)

R.G.M. Nisbet: Some problems of text and interpretation in Horace *Odes* 3,14 (*Herculis Ritu*) (105-19)

F. Williams: *Vox clamantis in theatro* (Juvenal 3,153) (121-27)

R. Seager: Some imperial virtues in the Latin prose panegyrics (129-65)

Averil Cameron: Corippus' *Iohannis*: epic of Byzantine Africa (167-80)

R. Collins: Poetry in ninth-century Spain

M. Collins: *Mercator pessimus*? the medieval Judas (197-213)

M.S. Haywood: Word-play between θέω/θοός and θεός in Homer (215-18)

N.J. Richardson: Recognition scenes in the *Odyssey* and ancient literary criticism (219-35)

M. Dickie: Phaeacian athletes (237-76)

J.G. Howie: The revision of myth in Pindar *Olympian* 1. The death and revival of Pelops (25-27; 36-66) (277-313)

J. Fairweather: Traditional narrative, inference and truth in the *Lives* of Greek poets (315-69)

Papers of the Liverpool Latin Seminar, Fifth Volume, 1985
ARCA 19. ISBN 0-905205-28-6. viii+502pp. 1986.

W. G. Arnott: Terence's prologues (1-7)

G.M. Paul: Sallust's Sempronia: the Portrait of a Lady (9-22)
G. Lieberg: *Poeta creator*: some 'religious' aspects (23-32)
J. Moles: Cynicism in Horace *Epistles* 1 (33-60)
R.F. Thomas: From *recusatio* to commitment: the evolution of the Vergilian programme (61-73)
A. Wlosok: *Gemina doctrina*: on allegorical interpretation (75-84)
P.R. Hardie: Cosmological patterns in the *Aeneid* (85-97)
S. Harrison: Vergilian similes: some connections (99-107)
M. Paschalis: Atlas and the mission of Mercury (*Aeneid* 4,238-258) (109-29)
E.L. Harrison: Foundation prodigies in the *Aeneid* (131-64)
M. Dickie: The speech of Numanus Remulus (*Aeneid* 9,598-620) (165-221)
H. Hofmann: Ovid's *Metamorphoses*: carmen perpetuum, carmen deductum (223-41)
R.E. Fantham: Ovid, Germanicus and the composition of the *Fasti* (243-81)
A.M. Wilson: The prologue to Manilius 1 (283-98)
H.D. Jocelyn: The new chapters of the ninth book of Celsus' *Artes* (299-336)
S. Harrison: *Fronde verecunda*: Statius *Silvae* 1,5,14 (337-40)
M. Billerbeck: Aspects of Stoicism in Flavian epic (341-56)
H. Funke: The universe of Claudian: its Greek sources (357-66)
J.M. Bremer: Four similes in *Iliad* 22 (367-72)
G. Burzacchini: Some further observations on Alcaeus *Fr.* 130b Voigt (373-81)
N.J. Richardson: Pindar and later literary criticism in antiquity (383-401)
T.C.W. Stinton: Heracles' homecoming and related topics: the second stasimon of Sophocles' *Trachiniae* (403-32)
Composite indexes to PLLS I–V (1976-1985) compiled by Neil Adkin (437-83)
Corrigenda to volumes 1 to 4 (N. Adkin) (484-87)
List of Meetings of the Liverpool Latin Seminar, 1975-1985

Papers of the Leeds International Latin Seminar, Sixth Volume 1990

Edited by Francis Cairns and Malcolm Heath
ARCA 29. ISBN 0-905205-81-2. viii+375pp.1990.

Roman Poetry and Drama
W. Stockert: Wood and wax: 'hendiadys' in Plautus (1-11)
L. Watson: Rustic Suffenus (Catullus 22) and literary rusticity (13-33)
R. Mayer: The epic of Lucretius (35-43)
S.J. Harrison: Dictamnum and moly: Vergil *Aeneid* 12.411-19 (45-47)
N. Horsfall: Virgil and the illusory footnote (49-63)
J.-M. Claassen: Ovid's poetic Pontus (65-94)
R.G.M. Nisbet: The dating of Seneca's tragedies, with special reference to the *Thyestes* (95-114)
P. Cutolo: The genre of the *Copa* (115-119)
T.E.S. Flintoff: Juvenal's Fourth *Satire* (121-37)
R. Cuccioli: The 'banquet' in Juvenal *Satire* 5 (139-143)
A. Hardie: Juvenal and the condition of letters: the Seventh Satire (145-209)
Greek Epic, Comedy, Rhetoric
G. Zanker: Loyalty in the *Iliad* (211-27)
M. Heath: Some deceptions in Aristophanes (229-40)
P.G. McC. Brown: Plots and prostitutes in Greek New Comedy (241-66)
M. Dickie: Talos bewitched: magic, atomic theory and paradoxography in Apollonius *Argonautica* 4.1638-88 (267-96)
J. Moles: The Kingship Orations of Dio Chrysostom (297-375)

Papers of the Leeds International Latin Seminar, Seventh Volume 1993
Edited by Francis Cairns and Malcolm Heath
ARCA 32. ISBN 0-905205-87-1. viii+219pp.1993.
Roman Poetry and Prose
N. Horsfall: Cicero and poetry: the place of prejudice in literary history (1-7)
M. Dickie: Malice, envy and inquisitiveness in Catullus 5 and 7 (9-26)
A. Kershaw: *A!* at Catullus 68.85 (27-29) [*correction: for* 68.85 *read* 66.85]
W. J. Tatum: Catullus 79: personal invective or political discourse? (31-45)
R. Maltby: Varro's attitude to Latin derivations from Greek (47-60)
P.E. Knox: Philetas and Roman poetry (61-83)
S.J. Heyworth: Horace's *Ibis*: on the titles, unity and contents of the *Epodes* (85-96)
S. Kyriakidis: *Aeneid* 6.268: *Ibant obscuri sola sub nocte per umbram* (97-100)
F. Cairns: Imitation and originality in Ovid *Amores* 1.3 (101-22)
M. Helzle: Ovid's Cosmogony: *Metamorphoses* 1.5-88 and the traditions of ancient
    poetry (123-34)
V. Hunink: Lucan's praise of Nero (135-40)
Greek Rhetoric and Poetry
G.M. Paul: Josephus *Bellum Judaicum* 4.559-63: invective as history (141-54)
D.L. Cairns: Affronts and quarrels in the *Iliad* (155-67)
M. Heath: Ancient interpretations of Pindar's *Nemean* 7 (169-99)
V. Knight: Landscape and the gods in Callimachus' *Hymns* (201-11)
C.A. Wilson: Dionysian ritual objects in Euphorion and Nonnus (213-19)

Papers of the Leeds International Latin Seminar, Eighth Volume
1995. Roman Comedy, Augustan Poetry, Historiography
Edited by R. Brock and A.J. Woodman. *For Ronald Martin at 80*
ARCA 33. ISBN 0-905205-89-8. x+307pp. 1995.

W.G. Arnott: Amorous scenes in Plautus (1-17)
M. Willcock: Plautus and the *Epidicus* (19-29)
R. Maltby: The distribution of Greek loan-words in Plautus (31-69)
P.G.McC. Brown: Aeschinus at the door: Terence, *Adelphoe* 632-43 and the traditions of
    Greco-Roman comedy (71-89)
F. Cairns: Horace's first Roman Ode (3.1) (91-142)
E.L. Harrison: The metamorphosis of the ships (*Aeneid* 9.77-122) (143-64)
S.J. Heyworth: Propertius: division, transmission, and the editor's task (165-85)
E.J. Kenney: 'Dear Helen ...': the *pithanotate prophasis*? (187-207)
R. Brock: Versions, "inversions" and evasions: classical historiography and the
    "published" speech (209-24)
T.J. Luce: Livy and Dionysius (225-39)
B. Dickinson & B. Hartley: Roman military activity in first-century Britain: the evidence
    of Tacitus and archaeology (241-55)
A.J. Woodman: A death in the first act: Tacitus, *Annals* 1.6 (257-73)
E. Keitel: Plutarch's tragedy tyrants: Galba and Otho (275-88)
R.G. Mayer: *Graecia capta*: the Roman reception of Greek literature (289-307)

Papers of the Leeds International Latin Seminar, Ninth Volume
1996. Roman poetry and prose, Greek poetry, Etymology, Historiography
Edited by Francis Cairns and Malcolm Heath
ARCA 34. ISBN 0-905205-90-1. viii+350pp.1996.

A. Erskine: Money-loving Romans (1-11)
J.G.F. Powell: Second thoughts on the Dream of Scipio (13-27)

J.-M. Claassen: Dio's Cicero and the consolatory tradition (29-45)

D.H. Berry: The value of prose rhythm in questions of authenticity: the case of *De optimo genere oratorum* attributed to Cicero (47-74)

A. Michalopoulos: Some etymologies of proper names in Catullus (75-81)

J.L. Butrica: Two two-part poems in Propertius Book 1 (1.8; 1.11 and 12) (83-91)

R. Maltby: Sense and structure in Tibullus (2.2.21-2, 1.1.78, 2.1.83-90, 1.5.1-8, 1.6.5-8) (93-102)

P.R. Hardie: Virgil: a paradoxical poet? (103-21)

M. Leigh: Vergil, *Georgics* 1.302 (123-25)

S.J. Harrison: *Aeneid* 1.286: Julius Caesar or Augustus? (127-33)

J.A. Barsby: Ovid's *Amores* and Roman comedy (135-57)

A.S. Hollis: Traces of ancient commentaries on Ovid's *Metamorphoses* (159-74)

R. Hannah: Lucan *Bellum civile* 1.649-65: the astrology of P. Nigidius Figulus revisited (175-90)

R. Seager: *Ut dux cunctator et tutus*: the caution of Valentinian (Ammianus 27.10) (191-96)

J.G. Howie: The major aristeia in Homer and Xenophon (197-217)

A. Hardie: Pindar, Castalia and the Muses of Delphi (the sixth *Paean*) (219-57)

J. Moles: Herodotus warns the Athenians (259-84)

A.G. Keen: Lies about Lysander (285-96)

J.L. Butrica: Hellenistic erotic elegy: the evidence of the papyri (297-322)

F. Cairns: Asclepiades *AP* 5.85 = Gow-Page 2 again (323-26)

M. Dickie: An ethnic slur in a new epigram of Poseidippus (327-36)

D. Bain: The magic of names: some etymologies in the *Cyranides* (337-50)

Papers of the Leeds International Latin Seminar, Tenth Volume, 1998. Greek Poetry, Drama, Prose, Roman Poetry

Edited by Francis Cairns and Malcolm Heath

ARCA 38. ISBN 0-905205-95-2. x+390 pp. Cloth.

M. Reichel: How oral is Homer's narrative? (1-22)

M. Heath: Was Homer a Roman? (23-56)

D.L. Cairns: "Αωτος, "Ανθος, and the death of Archemorus in Bacchylides' ninth Ode (57-73)

J.G. Howie: Thucydides and Pindar: the *Archaeology* and *Nemean* 7 (75-130)

I. Rutherford: Theoria as theatre: pilgrimage in Greek drama (131-56)

C.A. Wilson: Wine rituals, Maenads and Dionysian fire (157-68)

A.S. Hollis: Nicander and Lucretius (169-84)

E.A. Schmidt: Freedom and ownership: a contribution to the discussion of Vergil's First *Eclogue* (185-201)

F. Cairns: Tibullus 2.2 (203-34)

A. Michalopoulos: Some cases of Propertian etymologising (235-50)

A. Hardie: Horace, the Paean and Roman Choreia (*Odes* 4.6) (251-93)

R.K Gibson: Meretrix or matrona? Stereotypes in *Ars Amatoria* 3 (295-312)

G.K. Galinsky: The speech of Pythagoras at Ovid *Metamorphoses* 15.75–478 (313-36)

K.M. Coleman: Martial Book 8 and the politics of AD 93 (337-57)

L. Watson: Martial 8.21, literary *lusus*, and imperial panegyric (359-72)

A.M. Gowing: Greek advice for a Roman senator: Cassius Dio and the Dialogue between Philiscus and Cicero (38.18-29) (373-90)

PLLS: Author-index of volumes 1 – 10

Adkin, N.: Composite indexes to PLLS I-V (1976-1985). 5.437-83

—: Corrigenda to PLLS volumes 1 to 4. 5.484-87

Arnott, W. G.: Terence's prologues. 5.1-7

—: Time, plot and character in Menander. 2.343-60

—: Amorous scenes in Plautus. 8.1-17

Bain, D.: The magic of names: some etymologies in the *Cyranides*. 9.337-50

Barr, W.: Claudian's *In Rufinum*: an invective? 2.179-90

—: *Res* = 'a thing'? Persius 4,1. 3.422-23

Barsby, J.A.: Ovid's *Amores* and Roman comedy. 9.135-57

Bate, K.: Twelfth-century Latin comedies and the theatre. 2.249-62

Bergh, B.: A saint in the making: St Bridget's life in Sweden (1303-1349). 3.371-84

Berry, D.H.: The value of prose rhythm in questions of authenticity: the case of *De optimo genere oratorum* attributed to Cicero. 9.47-74

Billerbeck, M.: Aspects of Stoicism in Flavian epic. 5.341-56

Binns, J.W.: Biblical latin poetry in renaissance England. 3.385-416

Bremer, J.M.: Four similes in *Iliad* 22. 5.367-72

Brock, R.: Versions, "inversions" and evasions: classical historiography and the "published" speech. 8.209-24

Brown, P.G. McC.: Plots and prostitutes in Greek New Comedy. 6.241-66

—: Aeschinus at the door: Terence, *Adelphoe* 632-43 and the traditions of Greco-Roman comedy. 8.71-89

Burzacchini, G.: Some further observations on Alcaeus *Fr.* 130b Voigt. 5.373-81

Butrica, J.L.: Two two-part poems in Propertius Book 1 (1.8; 1.11 and 12). 9.83-91

—: Hellenistic erotic elegy: the evidence of the papyri. 9.297-322

Cairns, D.L.: Affronts and quarrels in the *Iliad*. 7.155-67

—: ῍Αωτος, ῍Ανθος, and the death of Archemorus in Bacchylides' ninth Ode. 10.57-73

Cairns, F.: The Distaff of Theugenis – Theocritus *Idyll* 28. 1.293-305

—: *Lesbia mentoreo* (Propertius 1,14,2). 3.419-22

—: Propertius 1,4 and 1,5 and the 'Gallus' of the Monobiblos. 4.61-103

—: Imitation and originality in Ovid *Amores* 1.3. 7.101-22

—: Horace's first Roman Ode (3.1). 8.91-142

—: Asclepiades *AP* 5.85 = Gow-Page 2 again. 9.323-26

—: Tibullus 2.2. 10.203-34

Cameron, Averil: Corippus' *Iohannis*: epic of Byzantine Africa. 4.167-80

Camps, W.A.: Horace *Epistles* 2,1,156ff.. 3.418-19

Claassen, J.-M.: Ovid's poetic Pontus. 6.65-94

—: Dio's Cicero and the consolatory tradition. 9.29-45

Codoñer, C.: The poetry of Eugenius of Toledo. 3.323-42

Coleman, K.M.: Martial Book 8 and the politics of AD 93. 10.337-57

Collins, M.: *Mercator pessimus*? the medieval Judas. 4.197-213

Collins, R.: Poetry in ninth-century Spain. 4.181-95

Cross, J.E.: Popes of Rome in the *Old English Martyrology*. 2.191-211

Cuccioli, R.: The 'banquet' in Juvenal *Satire* 5. 6.139-143

Cutolo, P.: The genre of the *Copa*. 6.115-119

Davie, M.: Dante's Latin *Eclogues*. 1.183-98

Dickie, M.: The disavowal of *invidia* in Roman iamb and satire. 3.183-208

—: Phaeacian athletes. 4.237-76

—: The speech of Numanus Remulus (*Aeneid* 9,598-620). 5.165-221

—: Talos bewitched: magic, atomic theory and paradoxography in Apollonius *Argonautica* 4.1638-88. 6.267-96

—: Malice, envy and inquisitiveness in Catullus 5 and 7. 7.9-26

—: An ethnic slur in a new epigram of Poseidippus. 9.327-36

Dickinson, B.: (with B. Hartley) Roman military activity in first-century Britain: the evidence of Tacitus and archaeology. 8.241-55

DuQuesnay, I.M. LeM.: Vergil's fourth *Eclogue*. 1.25-99

—: Vergil's first *Eclogue*. 3.29-182

Erskine, A.: Money-loving Romans. 9.1-11

Fairweather, J.: Traditional narrative, inference and truth in the *Lives* of Greek poets. 4.315-69

Fantham, R.E.: Plautus in miniature: compression and distortion in the *Epidicus*. 3.1-28

—: Ovid, Germanicus and the composition of the *Fasti*. 5.243-81

Fedeli, P.: Elegy and literary polemic in Propertius' *Monobiblos*. 3.227-42

Fischer, K.-D.: Pelagonius on horse medicine. 3.285-303

—: Lucretius 4,1201ff. and Ovid *Ars Amatoria* 2,484. 3.417-18

Flintoff, T.E.S.: Juvenal's Fourth *Satire*. 6.121-37

Foster, J.: Petrarch's *Africa*: Ennian and Vergilian influences. 2.277-98

Funke, H.: The universe of Claudian: its Greek sources. 5.357-66

Galinsky, G.K.: The speech of Pythagoras at Ovid *Metamorphoses* 15.75–478. 10.313-36

Giangrande, G.: Three Alexandrian epigrams: *API* 167; Callimachus *Epigram* 5 (Pf.); *AP* 12,91. 1.253-70

—: Aspects of Apollonius Rhodius' language. 1.271-91

Gibson, R.K: Meretrix or matrona? Stereotypes in *Ars Amatoria* 3. 10.295-312

Giesekam, G.J.: The portrayal of Minos in Bacchylides 17. 1.237-52

Gowing, A.M.: Greek advice for a Roman senator: Cassius Dio and the Dialogue between Philiscus and Cicero (38.18-29). 10.373-90

Hannah, R.: Lucan *Bellum civile* 1.649-65: the astrology of P. Nigidius Figulus revisited. 9.175-90

Hardie, A.: Horace *Odes* 1,37 and Pindar *Dithyramb* 2. 1.113-40

—: Juvenal and the condition of letters: the Seventh Satire. 6.145-209

—: Pindar, Castalia and the Muses of Delphi (the sixth *Paean*). 9.219-57

—: Horace, the Paean and Roman Choreia (*Odes* 4.6). 10.251-93

Hardie, P.R.: Cosmological patterns in the *Aeneid*. 5.85-97

—: Virgil: a paradoxical poet? 9.103-21

Harrison, E.L.: Structure and meaning in Vergil's *Aeneid*. 1.101-12

—: The Noric Plague in Vergil's third *Georgic*. 2.1-65

—: Vergil and the Homeric tradition. 3.209-25

—: Foundation prodigies in the *Aeneid*. 5.131-64

—: The metamorphosis of the ships (*Aeneid* 9.77-122). 8.143-64

Harrison, S.: Vergilian similes: some connections. 5.99-107

—: *Fronde verecunda*: Statius *Silvae* 1,5,14. 5.337-40

—: Dictamnum and moly: Vergil *Aeneid* 12.411-19. 6.45-47

—: *Aeneid* 1.286: Julius Caesar or Augustus? 9.127-33

Hartley,B.: (with B. Dickinson) Roman military activity in first-century Britain: the evidence of Tacitus and Archaeology. 8.241-55

Haywood, M.S.: Word-play between θέω/θοός and θεός in Homer. 4.215-18

Heath, M.: Some deceptions in Aristophanes. 6.229-40

—: Ancient interpretations of Pindar's *Nemean* 7. 7.169-99

—: Was Homer a Roman? 10.23-56

Helzle, M.: Ovid's Cosmogony: *Metamorphoses* 1.5-88 and the traditions of ancient poetry. 7.123-34

Heyworth, S.J.: Horace's *Ibis*: on the titles, unity and contents of the *Epodes*. 7.85-96

—: Propertius: division, transmission, and the editor's task. 8.165-85

Hinds, S.: *Carmina Digna*: Gallus *P Qaṣr Ibrîm* 6-7 metamorphosed. 4.43-54

Hine, H.: The structure of Seneca's *Thyestes*. 3.259-75

Hofmann, H.: Ovid's *Metamorphoses: carmen perpetuum, carmen deductum.* 5.223-41
Hollis, A.S.: Traces of ancient commentaries on Ovid's *Metamorphoses.* 9.159-74
—: Nicander and Lucretius. 10.169-84
Hood, A.B.E.: The Cambridge Songs (summary). 1.199-200
Horsfall, N.: Virgil and the illusory footnote. 6.49-63
—: Cicero and poetry: the place of prejudice in literary history. 7.1-7
Howie, J.G.: Sappho *Fr.* 16 (LP): self-consolation and encomium. 1.207-35
—: Sappho *Fr.* 94 (LP): farewell, consolation and help in a new life. 2.299-342
—: The revision of myth in Pindar *Olympian* 1. The death and revival of Pelops (25-27; 36-66). 4.277-313
—: The major aristeia in Homer and Xenophon. 9.197-217
—: Thucydides and Pindar: the *Archaeology* and *Nemean* 7. 10.75-130
Hunink, V.: Lucan's praise of Nero. 7.135-40
Jocelyn, H.D.: *Vergilius cacozelus* (Donatus *Vita Vergilii* 44). 2.67-142
—: Difficulties in Martial, Book 1. 3.277-84
—: Anti-Greek elements in Plautus' *Menaechmi.* 4.1-25
—: The new chapters of the ninth book of Celsus' *Artes.* 5.299-336
Keen, A.G.: Lies about Lysander. 9.285-96
Keitel, E.: Plutarch's tragedy tyrants: Galba and Otho. 8.275-88
Kenney, E.J.: 'Dear Helen ...': the *pithanotate prophasis*? 8.187-207
Kershaw, A.: *A!* at Catullus 68.85. 7.27-29. [*for* 68.85 *read* 66.85]
Knight, V.: Landscape and the gods in Callimachus' *Hymns.* 7.201-11
Knox, P.E.: Philetas and Roman poetry. 7.61-83
Krischer, T.: UnHomeric scene-patterns in Vergil. 2.143-54
Kyriakidis, S.: *Aeneid* 6.268: *Ibant obscuri sola sub nocte per umbram.* 7.97-100
Leigh, M.: Vergil, *Georgics* 1.302. 9.123-25
Levy, M.: *Persona* in twelfth-century Latin poetry (summary). 1.201-2
Lieberg, G.: *Poeta creator*: some 'religious' aspects. 5.23-32
Luce, T.J.: Livy and Dionysius. 8.225-39
Macleod, C.W.: Propertius 4.1. 1.141-53
Maguire, K.: The revision of the Breviary Hymnal under Urban VIII (summary). 1.203-5
Maltby, R.: Love and marriage in Propertius 4,3. 3.243-47
—: The last act of Terence's *Heautontimorumenos.* 4.27-41
—: Varro's attitude to Latin derivations from Greek. 7.47-60
—: The distribution of Greek loan-words in Plautus. 8.31-69
—: Sense and structure in Tibullus (2.2.21-2, 1.1.78, 2.1.83-90, 1.5.1-8, 1.6.5-8). 9.93-102
Margetts, J.: *Christus vitis, praedicator 'quasi vitis'*: some observations on Meister Eckhart's Latin sermon style. 2.263-76
Mayer, R.G.: The epic of Lucretius. 6.35-43
—: *Graecia capta*: the Roman reception of Greek literature. 8.289-307
McClure, J.: The biblical epic and its audience in late antiquity. 3.305-21
McKeown, J.C.: Ovid *Amores* 3,12. 2.163-77
Michalopoulos, A.: Some etymologies of proper names in Catullus. 9.75-81
—: Some cases of Propertian etymologising. 10.235-50
Moles, J.: Cynicism in Horace *Epistles* 1. 5.33-60
—: The Kingship Orations of Dio Chrysostom. 6.297-375
—: Herodotus warns the Athenians. 9.259-84
Nisbet, R.G.M.: Some problems of text and interpretation in Horace *Odes* 3,14 (*Herculis Ritu*). 4.105-19
—: The dating of Seneca's tragedies, with special reference to the *Thyestes.* 6.95-114
Paschalis, M.: Atlas and the mission of Mercury (*Aeneid* 4,238-258). 5.109-29
Paul, G.M.: Sallust's Sempronia: the Portrait of a Lady. 5.9-22
—: Josephus *Bellum Judaicum* 4.559-63: invective as history. 7.141-54

Powell, J.G.F.: Second thoughts on the Dream of Scipio. 9.13-27
Reichel, M.: How oral is Homer's narrative? 10.1-22
Richardson, N.J.: Recognition scenes in the *Odyssey* and ancient literary criticism. 4.219-35
—: Pindar and later literary criticism in antiquity. 5.383-401
Rutherford, I.: Theoria as theatre: pilgrimage in Greek drama. 10.131-56
Ryle, S.F.: The Sequence: reflections on literature and liturgy. 1.171-82
Schmidt, E.A.: Freedom and ownership: a contribution to the discussion of Vergil's First *Eclogue*. 10.185-201
Schmidt, P.G.: Elias of Thriplow – a thirteenth-century Anglo-Latin poet. 3.363-70
Seager, R.: Horace and the Parthians (summary). 1.155-56
—: Some imperial virtues in the Latin prose panegyrics. 4.129-65
—: *Ut dux cunctator et tutus*: the caution of Valentinian (Ammianus 27.10). 9.191-96
Stinton, T.C.W.: Heracles' homecoming and related topics: the second stasimon of Sophocles' *Trachiniae*. 5.403-32
Stockert, W.: Wood and wax: 'hendiadys' in Plautus. 6.1-11
Tatum, W.J.: Catullus 79: personal invective or political discourse? 7.31-45
Thomas, R.F.: From *recusatio* to commitment: the evolution of the Vergilian programme. 5.61-73
Tuplin, C.: Cantores Euphorionis. 1.1-23
Walsh, P.G.: *Pastor* and pastoral in medieval Latin poetry. 1.157-69
Watson, L.: Rustic Suffenus (Catullus 22) and literary rusticity. 6.13-33
—: Martial 8.21, literary *lusus*, and imperial panegyric. 10.359-72
Whitaker, R.: Gallus and the 'classical' Augustans. 4.55-60
Willcock, M.: Plautus and the *Epidicus*. 8.19-29
Williams, F.: Augustus and Daphne: Ovid *Metamorphoses* 1,560-64 and Phylarchus *FGrH* 81 F 32 (b). 3.249-57
—: *Vox clamantis in theatro* (Juvenal 3,153). 4.121-27
Wilson, A.M.: The prologue to Manilius 1. 5.283-98
Wilson, C.A.: Dionysian ritual objects in Euphorion and Nonnus. 7.213-19
—: Wine rituals, Maenads and Dionysian fire. 10.157-68
Wlosok, A.: *Gemina doctrina*: on allegorical interpretation. 5.75-84
Woodman, A.J.: A death in the first act: Tacitus, *Annals* 1.6. 8.257-73
Wright, R.: The first poem on the Cid: the *Carmen Campi Doctoris*. 2.213-48
—: Late latin and early romance: Alcuin's *De Orthographia* and the Council of Tours (AD 813). 3.343-61
Yardley, J.C.: The door and the lover: Propertius 1,16. 2.155-62
Zanker, G.: Loyalty in the *Iliad*. 6.211-27